A COLD WAR EXODUS

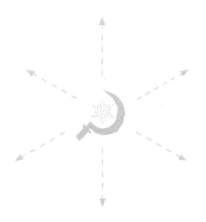

A COLD WAR EXODUS

HOW AMERICAN ACTIVISTS
MOBILIZED TO FREE
SOVIET JEWS

SHAUL KELNER

NEW YORK UNIVERSITY PRESS

NEW YORK

NEW YORK UNIVERSITY PRESS
New York
www.nyupress.org

© 2024 by New York University
All rights reserved

Please contact the Library of Congress for Cataloging-in-Publication data.

ISBN: 978-1-4798-7939-7 (hardback)
ISBN: 978-1-4798-7280-0 (library ebook)
ISBN: 978-1-4798-5910-8 (consumer ebook)

This book is printed on acid-free paper, and its binding materials are chosen for strength and durability. We strive to use environmentally responsible suppliers and materials to the greatest extent possible in publishing our books.

Manufactured in the United States of America

10 9 8 7 6 5 4 3 2 1

Also available as an ebook

Parts of chapter 1 are adapted from "Commentary on William Korey's 'The "Right to Leave" for Soviet Jews: Legal and Moral Aspects.'" *East European Jewish Affairs* 50, no. 3 (2020): 284–86. Parts of chapter 2 are adapted from "Ritualized Protest and Redemptive Politics: Cultural Consequences of the American Mobilization to Free Soviet Jewry." *Jewish Social Studies* 14, no. 3 (2008): 1–37, and "The Bureaucratization of Ritual Innovation: The Festive Cycle of the American Soviet Jewry Movement." In *Revisioning Ritual: Jewish Traditions in Transition*, edited by Simon J. Bronner, 360–91. Jewish Cultural Studies 3. Oxford: Littman Library of Jewish Civilization, 2011.

Excerpts from *The Jews of Silence* by Elie Wiesel. Copyright © 1966 by Elie Wiesel. Reprinted by permission of Georges Borchardt, Inc., on behalf of the author's estate.

The research presented here was conducted in accordance with Vanderbilt University Institutional Review Board approval no. 171069.

This book has been made possible in part by the National Endowment for the Humanities: Democracy demands wisdom (award no. FT-229663-15). Any views, findings, conclusions, or recommendations expressed in this book do not necessarily represent those of the National Endowment for the Humanities.

Additional support for this research has been provided by the following:

Lippman Kanfer Foundation for Living Torah
College of Arts and Science, Vanderbilt University
Frankel Institute for Advanced Judaic Studies, University of Michigan
Robert Penn Warren Center for the Humanities, Vanderbilt University
Brandeis-Genesis Institute for Russian Jewry
Hadassah-Brandeis Institute
Centre for European Research at the University of Gothenburg, Sweden (CERGU)
Jewish Historical Society of the Upper Midwest

THE ACADEMIC COMMITTEE ON SOVIET JEWRY

Chairman
HANS J. MORGENTHAU
University of Chicago
City University of New York

Secretary
HARRIS SCHOENBERG

SPONSORS

DANIEL AARON
Smith College
DANIEL BELL
Harvard University
SAUL BELLOW
University of Chicago
BRUNO BETTELHEIM
University of Chicago
MAX BLACK
Cornell University
JUSTUS BUCHLER
Columbia University
LEWIS A. COSER
SUNY, Stony Brook
HERBERT S. DINERSTEIN
Johns Hopkins University
RICHARD ELLMANN
Northwestern University
VICTOR ERLICH
Yale University
HERBERT FEIS
Historian
LEWIS S. FEUER
University of Toronto
MILTON FRIEDMAN
University of Chicago
WALTER GALENSON
Cornell University
ELI GINZBERG
Columbia University
NATHAN GLAZER
Harvard University
LOUIS GOTTSCHALK
University of Chicago
HENRY F. GRAFF
Columbia University
LOUIS M. HACKER
Columbia University
OSCAR HANDLIN
Harvard University
PHILIP M. HAUSER
University of Chicago
CARL G. HEMPEL
Princeton University
ABRAHAM J. HESCHEL
Jewish Theological Seminary
BERT F. HOSELITZ
University of Chicago

IRVING HOWE
Hunter College
IRVING L. HOROWITZ
Rutgers University
ABRAHAM KAPLAN
The University of Michigan
ALFRED KAZIN
SUNY, Stony Brook
PETER B. KENEN
Columbia University
MILTON R. KONVITZ
Cornell University
ROBERT LEKACHMAN
SUNY, Stony Brook
ABBA LERNER
University of California, Berkeley
DANIEL LERNER
M.I.T.
MAX LERNER
Brandeis University
SEYMOUR M. LIPSET
Harvard University
SEYMOUR MELMAN
Columbia University
ROBERT MERTON
Columbia University
SIDNEY MORGENBESSER
Columbia University
ERNEST NAGEL
Columbia University
ALBERT B. SABIN
Weizmann Institute
ITHIEL DE SOLA POOL
M.I.T.
MEYER SCHAPIRO
Columbia University
BENJAMIN I. SCHWARTZ
Harvard University
MELFORD E. SPIRO
University of California, San Diego
LIONEL TRILLING
Columbia University
MELVIN TUMIN
Princeton University
GEORGE WALD
Harvard University

JACOB WOLFOWITZ
University of Illinois

Academic Committee to Free Soviet Jewry sponsors list. 1971. American Jewish Historical Society, RG I-540, box 10, folder 10.

For Boaz and Shoshana

The emigration of Jews from the Soviet Union is not an objective of American foreign policy. And if they put Jews into gas chambers in the Soviet Union, it is not an American concern.

—Secretary of State Henry Kissinger
to President Richard M. Nixon, March 1, 1973

CONTENTS

List of Figures and Tables xv

List of Acronyms xvii

Introduction: Let Them Live as Jews or Let Them Leave 1

1 Illuminate the Past and Present 27

2 This Is the Matzoh of Hope 42

3 How to Find and Meet Russian Jews 86

4 From Russia, with Angst 134

5 We've Said No to PepsiCo 177

6 Natasha's Dream 223

7 My Soviet Twin 257

Conclusion: Voices of the Vigil 297

Acknowledgments 311

Appendix: Soviet Jewish Emigration Statistics 317

Notes 319

List of Interviews 379

Bibliography 381

Index 425

About the Author 437

FIGURES AND TABLES

FIGURE 2.1:	"L'Shanah Tovah Tikatavu!" Rosh Hashanah greeting card text	73
FIGURE 2.2:	"The Prayer"	75
FIGURE 3.1:	Travelers represented in the AJHS Archives, 1970–91	89
FIGURE 3.2:	*How to Find and Meet Russian Jews*	115
FIGURE 3.3:	Insiders Club *Guidebook for Contacting Jews in the Soviet Union*	123
FIGURE 3.4:	Page from the Insiders Club Questionnaire	129
FIGURE 4.1:	Page from Banana Republic's spring 1986 catalog, "Soviet Safari"	158
FIGURE 4.2:	Hand-drawn map of tourist hotels and Jewish sites in Baku	164
FIGURE 4.3:	Hand-drawn maps with directions to apartments of refuseniks	165
FIGURE 4.4:	Page from refusenik database	167
FIGURE 4.5:	"Refusenik Profile" sheet on Daniel Fradkin	168
FIGURE 5.1:	"Say No Pepsi" poster	181
FIGURE 5.2:	"Some UNrefreshing Facts about Pepsi" flyer	184
FIGURE 5.3:	Student marchers in prison stripe costumes	188
FIGURE 5.4:	Anatoly Altman Prisoner of Conscience medallion kit	190
FIGURE 5.5:	Anatoly Goldfeld Prisoner of Conscience medallion, obverse and reverse	191
FIGURE 5.6:	Ingrid Bergman and Sylva Zalmanson wearing Prisoner of Conscience medallions	196

FIGURE 5.7:	"Anatoly Sharansky" Prisoner of Conscience bracelet	200
FIGURE 5.8:	Jane Fonda at Annual 10K Run for Soviet Jewry	206
FIGURE 5.9:	"Freedom Run and Rally for Soviet Jewry" brochure	207
FIGURE 5.10:	Detroit Freedom Run for Soviet Jewry	209
FIGURE 5.11:	"Save a Soviet Jew Today," postcard distributed at Philadelphia Flyers / Soviet team hockey game	213
FIGURE 5.12:	"Olympics Da, Moscow Nyet," logo of the International Committee to Monitor the 1980 Olympics	216
FIGURE 6.1:	*Natasha's Dream*, cover graphic	226
FIGURE 6.2:	UCSJ president Morey Schapira with daughters at protest	229
FIGURE 6.3:	*Teaching Soviet Jewry* curriculum planning grid	241
FIGURE 6.4:	Play rubles from *Exodus: The Russian Jewry Simulation Game*	248
FIGURE 6.5:	Rebus from *Soviet Jewry Purim Puzzler*	250
FIGURE 6.6:	Detail from the board game *Route to Freedom*	251
FIGURE 6.7:	Winning entry, 1980 "Competing for Freedom" poster contest	255
FIGURE 7.1:	Sharon Sobel, "Let My People Go," Bat Mitzvah service prayer booklet	270
FIGURE 7.2:	Mark Podwal, *Let My People Go: A Haggadah*	271
FIGURE 7.3:	Washington Committee for Soviet Jewry *Bar and Bat Mitzvah Twinning with Soviet Jews* cover page	279
FIGURE 7.4:	Action for Soviet Jewry *Bar and Bat Mitzvah Twinning with Soviet Jews* cover page	280
TABLE A.1:	Jewish emigration from the USSR and former Soviet Union, 1954–2018	317
FIGURE A.1:	Jewish emigration from the USSR and former Soviet Union, 1954–2018	318

ACRONYMS

AAU	Amateur Athletic Union
ADL	Anti-Defamation League
AJC	American Jewish Committee
AJCONGRESS	American Jewish Congress
AJCSJ	American Jewish Conference on Soviet Jewry (precursor to NCSJ)
AJHS	American Jewish Historical Society
ASJ	Action for Soviet Jewry (Boston)
BACSJ	Bay Area Council on Soviet Jewry (later "for Soviet Jews")
BJE	Board/Bureau of Jewish Education
CAJE	Coalition for Alternatives in Jewish Education
CCSA	Cleveland Committee on Soviet Anti-Semitism (later "Cleveland Council")
CSSJ	California Students for Soviet Jews
GNYCSJ	Greater New York Conference on Soviet Jewry
IMC80	International Monitoring Committee for the 1980 Olympics
IOC	International Olympic Committee
JCCGW	Jewish Community Council of Greater Washington
JCRC	Jewish Community Relations Council
JDL	Jewish Defense League
JEC	Jewish Education Committee (New York)
KGB	Komitet Gosudarstvennoy Bezopasnosti (Committee for State Security)
LICSJ	Long Island Committee for Soviet Jewry

MACSJ	Minnesota (later Minnesota-Dakotas) Action Committee for Soviet Jewry
MOHIR	Mifal Hatzolas Yehudei Rusiah (Enterprise for the Rescue of the Jews of Russia)
MUSE	Museum Utilization for Student Education
NCSJ	National Conference on Soviet Jewry (successor to AJCSJ)
NJCRAC	National Jewish Community Relations Advisory Council (formerly National Community Relations Advisory Council, NCRAC)
NYCCSJ	New York Coordinating Committee for Soviet Jewry
NYYCSJ	New York Youth Conference for Soviet Jewry
ORT	Organization for Rehabilitation through Training (originally Obshestvo Remeslennogo i Zemledelcheskogo Truda, Artisan and Agricultural Labor Society)
OVIR	Otdel Viz i Registratsii (Office of Visas and Registration)
POC	Prisoner of Conscience
RCA	Rabbinical Council of America
SAC	Student Action Committee for Soviet Jewry (University of Minnesota)
SCCSJ	Southern California Council for Soviet Jews
SFCSJ	South Florida Conference on Soviet Jewry
SJC	Soviet Jewry Council of the JCRC of Greater Philadelphia
SJLAC	Soviet Jewry Legal Advocacy Center
SSSJ	Student Struggle for Soviet Jewry
UCSJ	Union of Councils for Soviet Jews
USY	United Synagogue Youth
VIVA	Victory in Vietnam Association (later Voices in Vital America)
WCSJ	Washington Committee for Soviet Jewry

INTRODUCTION

LET THEM LIVE AS JEWS OR LET THEM LEAVE

Activists in the worldwide campaign to free Soviet Jewry did not think they could force changes in Kremlin policy. The Union of Soviet Socialist Republics paid scant heed to its own citizens; why should the Politburo fold before a bunch of American or British or Canadian protesters? "Nothing more than students and housewives," scoffed the KGB.[1] Yet the problem remained. Contemplating the Soviet government's suppression of Judaism, Martin Luther King Jr.—an ally of the struggle for Soviet Jewish rights—called the situation "a kind of spiritual and cultural genocide."[2] For the Soviet Union's three million Jews, there was no exit. The same government that had murdered their poets, imprisoned their rabbis, shuttered their schools, confiscated their books, set quotas on their university acceptances, and restricted their job opportunities also barred their emigration. "Let them live as Jews, or let them leave," Western activists demanded.[3] Was this chutzpah? Naïveté? Why would protesters imagine that demonstrations in New York, London, and Montreal could move Moscow—imperial capital, leader of the communist world, hegemon over half the globe, with nuclear-tipped ICBMs pointed at the city blocks where marchers waved their cardboard placards?

In October 1963, members of a synagogue book club in Cleveland, Ohio, established a "Committee on Soviet Anti-Semitism," the first American organization dedicated to aiding Soviet Jews.[4] No headline-grabbing event prompted NASA engineer Louis Rosenblum, psychologist Herbert Caron, and Rabbi Daniel Litt to organize. Details about anti-Jewish policies and practices in the USSR had been filtering out for years, often with Israeli help. The latest, a January 1963 overview of the status of Jews in the USSR published in *Foreign Affairs* magazine, made it onto the book club's list. The group read it and decided to act. They hoped to lobby President Kennedy, but November brought his fateful trip to Dallas.

As awareness of the problem grew, so did pressure on Jewish American leaders to do something about it. In April 1964, six months after the Clevelanders had organized, representatives from twenty-four of America's venerable Jewish mass membership groups, congregational assemblies, fundraising bodies, policy agencies, and nonprofit organizations gathered in Washington to take up the Soviet Jewish issue at a cautiously calibrated conference. With prodding from the Cleveland Committee on Soviet Anti-Semitism's (CCSA's) Rosenblum and Caron, both in attendance, the delegates created an umbrella agency to coordinate national efforts. They gave their American Jewish Conference on Soviet Jewry (AJCSJ) neither a fixed budget nor a permanent staff. The Cleveland faction left feeling only a partial sense of accomplishment.[5]

They were not alone in their dissatisfaction. Jewish American youth, in the spirit of 1960s generational conflict, expressed skepticism that the men in suits would follow through. A few weeks after the AJCSJ's founding, two hundred students gathered at Columbia University to plan their own response: "We don't need a conference . . . but a struggle."[6] They quickly took to the streets. On May Day, seven hundred marched outside the Soviet Mission to the United Nations. They called themselves "Student Struggle for Soviet Jewry" (SSSJ). Their rally inaugurated a quarter century of sustained Jewish American public protest.[7]

From the outset, activists in the CCSA and SSSJ understood their situation: They had no power to compel the Soviet Union to do anything. But others with more leverage might be positioned to influence the Soviets' decision-making calculus. And no one held more enticing carrots and more threatening sticks than Uncle Sam. The groups' leaders therefore aimed to enlist their own government to take up the Soviet Jewish cause. They had allies. Senators Jacob Javits (R-NY), Abraham Ribicoff (D-CT), and Supreme Court Justice Arthur Goldberg had actually been out ahead of the Jewish groups, bringing the issue to Congress and the White House and urging Jewish organizations to get on board.[8] But theirs were solitary voices. Moving Washington would be no easy task. The US-USSR bilateral agenda was packed with other issues—avoiding nuclear Armageddon, for one. The State Department showed little interest in stoking confrontation over a matter of Soviet domestic affairs. Nor was it eager to give the Russians an opening to respond in kind—not when images of police dogs tearing the flesh of Black Americans were being televised around the globe.[9]

Leaders in the campaign to free Soviet Jewry expected that without sustained pressure, the Russia hands in Foggy Bottom would offer lip service, nothing more.[10] Perhaps, as Jews, the activists were projecting their own post-Holocaust trauma—the type that, fairly or unfairly, recalled the Roosevelt administration's response to the Nazi genocide as a chronicle of apathy and abandonment.[11] Perhaps they were making a clearheaded assessment of the predilections of the State Department's Ivy League clique—its father-knows-best disdain for a citizenry with the gall to interfere in foreign policy making. Its tweed-jacketed condescension that labeled Jewish politics "special pleading." And if there were voices in 1964 that said this was not a parochial Jewish issue but a matter of the American values at stake in the Cold War and a human rights issue of universal significance, the foreign policy realists knew where they stood on such noble irrelevancies. Activists had no illusions about any of this, and so their objective was clear: bring enough political pressure to ensure that their elected government would represent their interests in deed as well as word. The ballot box alone would not suffice. They would need to protest in the streets and lobby in the halls of power.

This was a tall order. What lobbying pressure could a synagogue book club from Cleveland or seven hundred college students bring to bear? The Jewish community's leading institutions could use their clout. But so far, they had chosen not to. Jewish Americans were a well-organized ethno-religious community, with thousands of organizations, umbrella groups connecting them together, and even umbrella groups of the umbrella groups—national coordinating agencies like the Conference of Presidents of Major American Jewish Organizations, the United Jewish Appeal, and the Council of Jewish Federations and Welfare Funds. Surely, the fundraising behemoths and other groups—the Union of American Hebrew Congregations, the American Jewish Committee, and the Anti-Defamation League of B'nai B'rith, for instance—held some political sway. But before April 1964, they had not cared to test the extent of their influence. Not on the Russian issue. Their constituents, about 5.6 million

Jewish Americans, were only vaguely aware of what was happening to their cousins in Russia. They were not pressing their communal agencies to act. And without pressure, the organizations contented themselves with a committee here, a fact-finding mission there.[12] Rabbi Abraham Joshua Heschel, a theologian and voice of conscience, was so dismayed by the lack of urgency that he threatened to launch a campaign on his own.[13]

Jewish Americans' half measures contrasted with Israel's approach. In 1952, five years after gaining independence, the Jewish state established a semiclandestine office dedicated to aiding Soviet Jews and prodding activism in the West.[14] Created by the founders of Israel's intelligence services and utilizing personnel stationed in the USSR, Western Europe, and the United States, the agency—officially called Nativ (Heb., route, pathway) but colloquially referred to as the Liaison Bureau (Lishkat Hakesher) or even just "the Bureau" (Lishkah)—reported directly to David Ben-Gurion, the new country's first prime minister. A decade after Nativ's creation, the American Jewish communal apparatus had still not stirred to action. When it finally started to rouse in 1964, it did so only hesitantly.[15]

Against this backdrop of an uninformed Jewish population, a reluctant Jewish communal establishment, and a noncommittal American government, the American Soviet Jewry movement's earliest activists—people like Rosenblum and Caron of the CCSA and the Student Struggle's Jacob (Yaakov) Birnbaum—arrived at the same conclusion: aiding Soviet Jews required a mass mobilization of American Jews. Only if the people demanded action would their organizations press the fight in the halls of government. And only a combination of public protest and quiet lobbying would bring Washington on board. And only Washington had the leverage to influence Soviet policy. This was the model of change that guided the campaign for three decades: (1) mobilize the American Jewish populace to (2) pressure major Jewish organizations to (3) pressure the US government to (4) pressure the Kremlin to let Jews emigrate.[16]

Other layers were added as time went on. In the 1970s, movement leaders in the US linked up with Jewish activists in the USSR and jointly exerted pressure on the American and Soviet governments from within and without. They built relationships with movement groups in other countries that were pursuing similar strategies with their own

INTRODUCTION

governments. Sometimes American activists worked in concert with the Israelis; sometimes they went their own way. Sometimes the mobilized masses circumvented Jewish organizations to take the cause directly to their elected officials; sometimes the Jewish organizations galvanized mass action to create more political pressure. Sometimes activists let allies in Congress take the lead and backed their efforts by stirring up a political groundswell.[17] Throughout, however, the four-step causal chain remained constant.

The strategy worked. Not all at once. Not without setbacks. (Activists spent years chasing legislation that tried to use economic pressure to extract concessions. After the Jackson-Vanik Amendment to the Trade Act of 1974 became law, the Soviets curtailed emigration for a time.)[18] And not in its entirety. (Even as the Kremlin began allowing some Jews to leave, it still refused to grant full religious and cultural rights to those who remained.)[19] Nevertheless, at each stage of the four-step plan, activists achieved what they had set out to do. When Soviet premier Mikhail Gorbachev arrived at the White House in December 1987 to sign a nuclear arms reduction pact with President Ronald Reagan, he was greeted by a quarter million demonstrators. Jewish Americans had descended on the National Mall in Washington, DC, from all corners of the country. Gone were the days when they were unaware of the predicament of Soviet Jewry and unmoved to speak out. A quarter century of mass mobilization had raised their consciousness and taught them to raise their voices. Jewish Americans had been gathering in the hundreds of thousands each spring in New York since 1973. Now they donned their winter coats and took their demonstration to the nation's capital.

The major Jewish organizations that had been so reticent in 1964 had come around by the early 1970s and had transformed the underresourced AJCSJ into an independent, permanently staffed National Conference on Soviet Jewry (NCSJ). When Reagan announced the summit, this NCSJ sprang into action and organized the Freedom Rally for Soviet Jews in just five weeks.

By 1987, decades of sustained pressure on the US government had united allies across party lines. George H. W. Bush shared the podium with John Lewis. "Mr. Gorbachev, let these people go!" the Republican vice president demanded, echoing the call from the book of Exodus that Jewish Americans had adopted as their rallying cry. Lewis, the civil rights movement icon turned Georgia Democratic representative, proclaimed, "Until all Jews in the Soviet Union are free, we are all Jews in the Soviet Union." A who's who of congressional leadership joined them on the dais: Speaker of the House Jim Wright (D-TX); Senate minority leader Bob Dole (R-KA); Dole's future 1996 vice presidential running mate, Representative Jack Kemp (R-NY), Senate Democratic caucus secretary Daniel Inouye (D-HI), and others. There were governors and mayors, labor leaders and celebrities. Pearl Bailey sang. Christian clergy stood as allies.[20] Nobel Peace Prize laureate Elie Wiesel—the voice of Holocaust memory and author of the Soviet Jewry movement's galvanizing 1966 book *The Jews of Silence*—contrasted the efficacy of activism for Soviet Jewry with the failure to save European Jewry a generation earlier. "Had there been such a demonstration of Jewish and human solidarity and concern in 1942, 1943," he lamented. And with them were heroes of the day, recently emancipated Soviet Jewish political prisoners, newly immigrated to Israel. Anatoly Shcharansky (Heb., Natan Sharansky), Vladimir and Maria Slepak, Ida Nudel, Yosef Mendelevich.[21] To millions of Jewish Americans whose lives had been touched by the Soviet Jewry movement, they were household names. They were present because Soviet leaders had responded to Western entreaties, releasing some as gestures of goodwill, trading others to secure the return of Soviet spies.[22]

Not only famous activists got out. The American campaign for Soviet Jewry's multistage strategy—sparking a grassroots campaign to enlist Jewish American organizations in a total Jewish communal mobilization to press the US government to take up the issue with the Soviet government—resulted in mass emigration by the 1970s. Between 1971 and 1979, the USSR allowed 25,000 Jews on average to leave each year. When the movement had launched a decade earlier, that annual figure had been hovering at around only 500. The more emigration permits the Russian visa office, OVIR (Otdel Viz i Registratsii), granted, the more new applications Soviet Jews filed. Many of these were refused, leaving the applicants—known in the West as "refuseniks"—in a precarious position. Nevertheless, unprecedented numbers of exit visas were being approved. In 1979, 51,400 Jews emigrated—almost 100 times the 537 who left in 1964.[23]

Each step in the strategy had proven itself. Jewish Americans were taking to the streets in the hundreds of thousands. Jewish American organizations were partnering with congressional allies. By building bipartisan support in the early 1970s for the Jackson-Vanik trade bill amendment that tied US-Soviet economic relations to Soviet respect for free emigration, the movement had threatened détente and thereby forced a reluctant Nixon administration to place the Soviet Jewish issue on the bilateral negotiating agenda.[24] (Reluctant may be an understatement, if Kissinger's remarks, quoted in the epigraph, are any indication.) Once on the agenda, it stayed on. Jimmy Carter's emphasis on human rights and Reagan's renewed Cold War stance (along with Secretary of State George Schultz's personal embrace of the issue) kept the matter alive.[25]

But there was a catch. American pressure on the Kremlin risked provoking Soviet responses that harmed, rather than helped, Soviet Jews. Because the strategy hinged on US government leverage, it only extracted concessions when Moscow saw an interest in conciliation. The movement succeeded in partially opening the gates of the Soviet Union in the 1970s by turning Jewish emigration into a symbol that Moscow could use to signal its desire for warmer relations with the West. When Moscow was not interested, it used emigration to signal that too. Hoping to forestall passage of the trade bill amendment, the Kremlin rolled back a restrictive emigration tax and allowed more Jews to leave. When Jackson-Vanik moved forward anyway, the Soviets curtailed emigration (but still kept the numbers in the tens of thousands).[26] The Soviet Union allowed more Jews to leave during the lead-up to the SALT II arms limitation talks, resulting in the 1979 peak of over fifty thousand emigrants. When the Cold War chilled again in the early 1980s, the Soviet government closed the gates almost entirely. Then came the 1987 thaw, and numbers crept back up. In 1988, after the summit and rally, almost twenty thousand Jews departed. In 1989, almost eighty thousand.[27] Then about two hundred thousand each year in 1990 and 1991, the last two years of the USSR's existence.

When the Soviet Union crumbled, most of its citizens did not pack their bags for other countries.[28] Most of its Jews did. Over half the Jewish population had left by 1994.[29] Between 1992 and the end of the millennium, eight hundred thousand fled the political and economic turmoil of the immediate post-Soviet years. Emigration continued in the twenty-first century, with four hundred thousand departing between 2000 and

2018 and tens of thousands more leaving Russia and Ukraine when the former invaded the latter in 2022.[30]

All told, since 1970, almost two million Jews and members of Jewish families have emigrated from the Soviet Union and its successor states. The emigration is among the largest in Jewish history. It has created a vibrant new Jewish diaspora whose members—from the poorest babushkas to the wealthiest billionaires—maintain connections across continents. The exodus has revolutionized global Jewish demography, helping make Israel—for the first time since antiquity—the largest Jewish population center in the world. With one out of every six Israelis a native Russian speaker, the emigrants and their children have reshaped the country's politics, culture, and economy—pushing its foreign policy in a more conservative direction, bolstering the secularist camp in the culture wars over religion and state, and filling the ranks of Israel's hypercharged tech sector.[31]

The exodus was not by chance. The nationalisms that helped shatter the Soviet empire gave Jews an extra push. Slavic nationalisms bore a long and violent anti-Jewish streak, and even though the late Soviet period fostered some measure of rapprochement and mutual sympathy, it also opened a space for expressly antisemitic political movements.[32] Moreover, by 1989, Soviet Jews had already seen hundreds of thousands of their coethnics leave for the US, Israel, Canada, West Germany, and other countries outside the communist bloc. For Jews, emigration was imaginable. From the 1970s onward, it was also feasible—almost uniquely feasible.[33]

The worldwide movement to free Soviet Jewry paved the way for this mass exodus. It placed Jewish emigration—not emigration generally, but *Jewish* emigration specifically—on the Cold War agenda, turning it into a symbol that the Soviet government could use in its own geopolitical interest to signal good relations with the West. The movement laid the legal, logistic, and administrative groundwork that translated Soviet exit permits into Western entry visas. And it ensured that resettlement support—housing, financial aid, job placement, language training, and so forth—awaited the newcomers in the Americas, Western Europe, Australia, and Israel. As the Soviet Union broke apart and the vast majority of Soviet citizens had no ability to secure refuge elsewhere, Soviet Jews found themselves with escape routes and support networks waiting for them in the places they landed. The emigrants of 1989–91 were generally not the refusenik activists whom Westerners imagined when they thought of "Soviet Jewry."[34] Mostly, they were the beneficiaries of activism, owing their freedom of movement to the exit routes and entry portals that refuseniks and their allies had paved in the preceding decades.[35] All told, the worldwide movement for Soviet Jewry—operating on both sides of the Iron Curtain, combining state-based and nongovernmental activism, and motivated by a desire to fight state-sponsored, institutionalized, systemic antisemitism—enabled more than a million human beings to exercise their long-denied right to emigrate for other shores.[36] It numbers among the most effective transnational human rights mobilizations of the twentieth century.[37]

MASS MOBILIZATION TACTICS: TURNING A POLITICAL STRUGGLE INTO A CULTURAL MOVEMENT

The campaign to free Soviet Jewry was centered in three countries: the USSR, where Jewish activist cadres mobilized for themselves and to the benefit of millions of other fellow Jews; Israel, where a government agency worked in semisecrecy; and the United States—leader of the "Free World," home to the then-largest Jewish population on earth—where the campaign drew hundreds of thousands to the streets, filtered into almost every synagogue in the country, and refashioned American Judaism for the Cold War era.[38]

This book focuses on the mass mobilization in America. It is not a sweeping history of the global movement from start to finish. Readers interested in the high politics and human drama can look to Gal Beckerman's award-winning account of the "epic struggle."[39] Nor is it about American activists' lobbying efforts or policy work. Readers interested in that can peruse the scholarship by political scientists and historians who have covered that well.[40] Instead, here, we explore in all its richness that crucial first step in activists' multistage strategy to free Soviet Jews: mobilizing Jewish Americans to take up the cause.[41] The entire effort, activists reasoned, depended on getting this right. Without sustained pressure on the US government by American citizens, there would be little hope of enlisting American power to pry open Soviet gates. But how were activists to create and sustain a mass mobilization of Jewish

Americans? What would it look like? What would people actually do? (Behavior was key, after all.) And for how long would it have to go on? A decade? A century? No one knew the answers to these questions. There was no blueprint. If activists wanted to create a movement to save Soviet Jewry, they would have to invent it as they went along. They did, and their success had profound unintended consequences. Although the movement was ostensibly about aiding Soviet Jews, the mobilization ended up reshaping the private lives and public culture of American Jews throughout the 1960s, '70s, and '80s. In so doing, it also created a distinctively Jewish American experience of the Cold War.

A Cold War Exodus asks how activists made this happen. First, how did activists mobilize the Jewish American populace for a campaign of unknown duration to secure the human rights of millions of oppressed Jews, just a few decades after the Holocaust, on the opposite side of the Iron Curtain, in the midst of a global Cold War? In other words, how did the Soviet Jewry movement invent its mass mobilization tactics?[42] To answer this, each chapter examines a particular set of tactics: mobilizations of holiday rituals (chapter 2); mass tourism (chapter 3); travel writing (chapter 4); consumer and leisure culture (chapter 5); education and schoolchildren (chapter 6); and the tactic that drew much of this together, bar and bat mitzvah "twinning," which transformed the traditional coming-of-age ceremony into a symbolic pairing of American and Soviet Jewish youth (chapter 7). But the processes of tactical innovation are not our only concern. For each set of mobilization tactics, we also ask, How did they shape the late twentieth-century Jewish American experience? These questions are both historical and sociological. Answering them will reveal how the Soviet Jewry movement—as a mass phenomenon in Jewish American life—emerged, developed, and worked. Answering them will also help us see beyond this individual case to better understand how social movements in general manage to have cultural consequences, regardless of their policy outcomes, just by virtue of mobilizing people (or as sociologists would phrase it, how social movements function as engines of "cultural production").[43]

Among the core findings is a lesson for other aspiring social movements: activists who want to build a sustainable mass mobilization would do well to build their campaign not as a narrowly defined political effort but as a cultural movement in the broadest sense. The Soviet

Jewry movement succeeded in rallying massive Jewish American support for over a quarter century because it did precisely this. The particular policy issues around which activists organized at any given moment were never the be-all and end-all of the campaign. They were simply moments in a larger cultural mobilization. On the conceptual level, the movement synthesized the timeless meanings of Jewish religious core narratives with the timeliest meanings of American Cold War liberalism and consumer culture. On the practical level—*tachlis*, brass tacks—mass mobilization meant creating new forms of behavior and spreading these behaviors into as many spheres of Jewish American life as activists could think of. And activists could think of a lot. They left few areas untouched. They mobilized religion—creating new rituals for synagogues and homes, for holidays and life cycle events. They mobilized leisure time and consumer culture—using mass tourism, the fitness craze, jewelry, and the Cola Wars. They mobilized adults at work—tapping the professional identities of doctors and lawyers, scientists and clergy. They mobilized children at school and at play—writing curricula, staging escape-from-Russia simulations at summer camps, and designing board games and puzzle books. They mobilized arts and culture—music, photography, graphic design, museum exhibitions. As we trace all these in the pages ahead, even James Bond spy movies and Banana Republic safari clothing will make cameo appearances.

Although the name "Soviet Jewry movement" suggests that the mobilization was about Soviet Jews, in actuality, it was also very much about American Jews—their identities, their politics, their religious faith, their version of being Jewish in a Cold War America that knew both a civil rights movement and a Reagan Revolution, their version of being American in a Jewish world traumatized by the Holocaust and awestruck by the Six-Day War. The specific policy issues that Soviet Jewry movement activists tried to get Jewish Americans engaged with changed over the years. In the 1960s, they marched to overturn restrictions on matzoh baking. In the 1970s, they lobbied for Jackson-Vanik's linkage of economic policy with human rights. In the 1980s, they pressed for the release of political prisoners. They experienced victories and losses. Their mobilization sustained it all because this was never just a policy movement; from the outset and for its duration, activists built the American campaign for Soviet Jewry as a cultural movement—as timeless as it was timely, ubiquitous in communal institutions, and woven into the fabric of Jewish Americans' lives—at home, on the streets, at prayer, at work, and at play.

SOVIET PLIGHT, AMERICAN RESPONSE

Westerners called it "the plight of Soviet Jewry." In his opening address to the AJCSJ's April 1964 inaugural meeting, held at the Willard Hotel in Washington, DC, B'nai B'rith president Label Katz read the litany:

> In 1920 . . . there were 98 Yiddish or Hebrew newspapers and periodicals. Today not a single Jewish daily newspaper. . . .
> In the mid-30s, there were 17 permanent Jewish theatres in the USSR. Today there is none.
> As late as 1938, there were 800 Jewish primary and secondary schools in White Russia and the Ukraine alone. Today there is no such school anywhere in the USSR.[44]

Katz did not mention the Nazis' part in this institutional devastation. They and their collaborators murdered 2.7 million Jewish citizens of the USSR—journalists and readers of the Yiddish and Hebrew newspapers, actors and audiences of the Jewish theaters, teachers and pupils in the Jewish schools.[45] Rather, Katz focused on the continuities between prewar Soviet policies that had already been hollowing out Jewish communal infrastructure and postwar policies that prevented Jews from rebuilding any semblance of communal life. The postwar assault—during the last years of Stalin's rule, between 1948 and March 1953—targeted more than institutions. "Soviet Jews still speak of that era as the '*shvartze yohrin*—the black years,'" Katz noted.[46] That they could attach such a bleak label to the years immediately *after* a genocide says a lot.

Developments on the international scene affected Soviet domestic policy toward its Jewish citizens. With the start of the Cold War and the creation of the State of Israel, Jews increasingly came to be seen as "a potentially disloyal nationality."[47] (In the USSR, Jews were considered a national group; their official identification documents listed them as *Evrei*—Hebrew—just as Ukrainians' internal passports were marked *Ukrainets* and Russians' *Russkii*.) Kinship ties to Jews in the US—most of whose ancestors had left czarist Russia—and religious and nationalist affinities for the Western-aligned Jewish state—democratic socialist though it was—made all Jews in the USSR suspect.[48] Russian nativism as much as Soviet ideology inspired the Judeophobia. Jews who embraced a Jewish identity—especially in its Hebraic religious or Zionist forms, but even in its secularized communist form—were regarded as disloyal. Even mourning the Holocaust was deemed nationalist and anti-Soviet. The Nazi invasion had claimed over twenty million Soviet lives; why privilege the Jewish dead?[49] Jews who ignored their Jewish connections to become successful Russified Soviets were deemed insidious—ready to subvert the country from within. As the chronicler of the twentieth-century Russian Jewish experience, Yuri Slezkine, has written, "Being Jewish became a crime: those who claimed a separate Yiddish culture were 'bourgeois nationalists'; those who identified with Russian culture were 'rootless cosmopolitans.'"[50] Convenience trumped consistency; anti-Jewish campaigns accused Jews simultaneously of both.[51]

The "Black Years" of which Katz spoke saw Jewish culturalists purged. Rabbis and Zionist activists were sent to the gulag.[52] "Yiddish-in-form, socialist-in-content" intelligentsia were put to death.[53] When the government decided to disband the same Jewish Anti-Fascist Committee that it had created to raise foreign support during the war, it did not simply eliminate the budget line; it murdered the committee members. These were the country's most renowned Yiddish writers and artists. In 1948, secret police threw Solomon Mikhoels under a truck. In 1952, Lubyanka prison guards executed Itzik Fefer, Dovid Bergelson, and Peretz Markish along with ten others. The death sentences had been decreed before the trial even began. They were all shot on the same day. Decades later, American activists would commemorate the anniversary as the "Night of the Murdered Poets."[54]

Stalin also moved against Jews who had no personal or professional associations with Jewish culture. The campaign against assimilated Russified Jews gathered steam in 1952 with the arrest of physicians (most of them Jewish) on trumped-up charges of conspiring to poison party officials. The anti-Jewish press campaign associated with the so-called Doctors' Plot—a misnomer, since it was Stalin, not the doctors, who plotted—suggested that this was a prelude to a larger purge. Rumors circulated of mass deportations akin to those that had displaced the Crimean Tatars and Volga Germans.[55]

The campaign ended abruptly. In March 1953, Stalin died. The state freed the doctors and dropped the charges. The Khrushchev years also saw the release of prisoners from the gulag and the posthumous rehabilitation of some of the murdered Yiddishists. Nevertheless, anti-Jewish campaigns did not entirely abate.[56] Among fifty-nine death sentences handed down in economic show trials between July 1961 and November 1963 in the Ukrainian Soviet Socialist Republic, fifty went to Jews; in the Byelorussian SSR, six out of seven; in the Moldavian SSR, six out of eight. Russia lagged behind the Soviet Union's other republics with only twenty-two out of thirty-nine (56 percent) in the Russian Soviet Federated Socialist Republic.[57] Soviet press coverage often highlighted the Jewishness of the accused.

In this environment, educational and occupational discrimination was common. Early on, the revolution had realized some of its promise of social uplift—turning Jews into a well-educated, urbanized, Russian-speaking professional class.[58] However, Jews' Cold War–era treatment as a suspect minority brought downward mobility. Opportunities closed. With school placements and job allocations controlled by state committees, younger generations faced university prospects incommensurate with their academic performance and job prospects incommensurate with their college educations. Whether they identified with their Jewishness or not, the fact of their Jewishness—stamped on their passports and coded in their patronymics—closed doors and created glass ceilings.[59] In the words of Yaacov Ro'i, the primary chronicler of Jewish activism in the Soviet Union itself, Jews became an "oppressed elite."[60]

All the while, the government continued shuttering Jewish institutions. By the 1950s, only the synagogue remained in any substantial number, but even this was under assault. There were 450 state-authorized synagogues across the USSR in 1956. Katz reported to his audience in 1964 that the number had dwindled to 97. The trend continued. In 1972, only 58 remained. Over those sixteen years, the government had closed nine out of ten synagogues. This left one house of worship per 62,500 Jews, compared to one church for every 2,000 Russian Orthodox Christians. No new rabbis were being trained.[61]

American activists agreed on the nature of the Soviet Jewish "plight." As Katz called it in his AJCSJ-inaugurating address, it was "a senseless, neither-nor world for the Soviet Jew, which says to him: 'You are a Jew—but you can't be Jewish.'"[62] Activists agreed on the linchpin of the strategy to address the problem. "The road to Moscow went through Washington," wrote Myrna Shinbaum, the NCSJ's longest-serving professional and one-time director.[63] But activists disagreed on the details of policy and process. Should they emphasize free emigration or equal rights within the USSR (a key policy question in the 1960s)? Should they fight to pass the Jackson-Vanik Amendment and thereby challenge Nixon's efforts to foster a US-Soviet détente (the major policy question between 1972 and 1974)? Should they bow to Nativ's pressure to steer the emigrants to Israel even though most wanted to come to the United States (the major policy question from 1975 to 1979)?[64]

Like many social movements, the American campaign to free Soviet Jews had factions. Internal movement-speak distinguished the "grassroots" from the "establishment." Movement leaders considered the distinction important. They built organizational identities around the rivalry.[65] Some of the differences were real, some imagined. It is important not to overstate the divide. Much of this book will describe a shared movement culture created by mass mobilization tactics that flowed back and forth across the factions. Individuals with feet in both camps passed ideas between them. Competition and common challenges furthered the convergence into a single movement-wide culture. Organizations learned from and copied each other, sometimes to one-up the competition, sometimes to avoid being left behind.[66]

Factionalization began with the movement's birth. If we date the start of the American campaign to the creation of its first dedicated organizations—the CCSA, the AJCSJ, and SSSJ—we can say that the social movement got underway between fall 1963 and spring 1964.[67] The CCSA and SSSJ were activist-driven single-issue organizations dedicated to Soviet Jewry and nothing else. The AJCSJ was an umbrella agency serving a coalition of twenty-four national Jewish organizations—most of them mass membership bodies—each with a different mission, each answerable to different constituencies, each taking on the Soviet Jewish issue as one item among many on their agendas. These structural differences were at the heart of the grassroots/establishment conflict.[68] Small, operationally nimble, and governed from the top down, the CCSA and SSSJ took decisive stances and pressed for more action, more quickly, more aggressively. In contrast, the AJCSJ proceeded more deliberately—consulting, coordinating, and compromising to maintain consensus. Different relationships with the Israeli government reinforced these diverging tendencies. Grassroots groups rejected Nativ's presumptions to dictate movement-wide policy; establishment organizations showed themselves more willing to defer to Israeli wishes, though never entirely so.[69]

Grassroots leaders pioneered the strategy of mobilizing Jewish Americans to force their organizations to take up the issue.[70] Louis Rosenblum, the Battle of Okinawa veteran and NASA engineer who headed the CCSA, and Jacob (Yaakov) Birnbaum, the thirty-eight-year-old British immigrant who founded Student Struggle for Soviet Jewry, assessed the situation similarly. They recognized that if the national Jewish agencies were to make Soviet Jewry a priority, these organizations would wield influence in Washington beyond what their own small groups could muster (or so they thought at first). Throughout the 1960s, they pressed the AJCSJ's members to give the Conference permanent funding, permanent staff, and operational independence. At the same time, they broadened the effort to appeal directly to Jewish Americans, supporting the creation of more single-issue Soviet Jewry groups, including local SSSJ chapters as well as the Bay Area Council on Soviet Jewry (1967), the Southern California Council for Soviet Jews (1968), California Students for Soviet Jews (1968), and the Washington Committee for Soviet Jewry (1968). These "councils" (their names followed the CCSA, which had changed its name from Cleveland Committee to Cleveland Council in 1965) were mainly led by suburbanites—teachers and doctors, homemakers and businesspeople, women and men, most of them married, some with young children in the house. Frustration at the national agencies' refusal to give the AJCSJ sufficient resources eventually prompted council leaders to fill the vacuum themselves. In April 1970, the grassroots groups established a national coordinating body of their own, the Union of Councils for Soviet Jews (UCSJ). The creation of an organization to rival the AJCSJ helped force the issue. In June 1971, the national agencies reconstituted the American Jewish Conference on Soviet Jewry as the independent National Conference on Soviet Jewry, hiring former American Jewish Committee professionals Jerry Goodman and Myrna Shinbaum as the NCSJ's permanent staff.[71]

From then on, the factional rivalry played out mainly at the national level between the "grassroots" Union of Councils and the "establishment" National Conference. Internationally, the UCSJ partnered with the Women's Campaign for Soviet Jewry in the UK and Canada (also known as "The 35s"), with the Comité des Quinze in France, and with the Action Committee of Newcomers from the Soviet Union based in Israel; the NCSJ worked more closely with Nativ.[72] Despite the factional rivalries, the grassroots and establishment groups all shared a commitment to nonviolent public protest. Other groups emerging out of Orthodox Jewish communities did not define themselves in either camp. For a few years, a radical flank group briefly captured headlines by rejecting the commitment to nonviolence. Between 1969 and 1972, Meir Kahane's Jewish Defense League (JDL) repeatedly attacked Soviet interests in the United States, ostensibly to threaten détente and thereby force the US and Soviet governments to address the Soviet Jewish issue.[73] On the opposite end, Orthodox groups like Chabad-Lubavitch's Shamir and Lishkas Ezras Achim, Agudath Israel's Vaad Hahatzolah, and Rabbi Pinchas Teitz's Mifal Hatzolas Yehudei Rusiah (MOHIR; Enterprise for the Rescue of the Jews of Russia) rejected public protest. For two decades or so, they provided direct support to Jews in the Soviet Union, all the while contending that open criticism of the Soviet government could jeopardize those efforts and endanger the people they were trying to help.[74]

As the grassroots and establishment camps set to mobilize Jewish Americans, they both faced the predicament of having chosen to take on a problem that was largely unknown, oceans away, hidden by a police state, and impossible to televise. To have any chance of success, their mobilization tactics would have to make a distant problem close, an invisible problem visible, and an absent problem present. Their earliest mass mobilization tactics centered on raising Jewish Americans' awareness of the general contours of the problem. Mobilization tactics in the 1960s framed Soviet Jewry in the abstract, as a large and undifferentiated mass. They did not present Jewish Soviets as actual people with names and biographies.[75] By the 1970s, this changed. Led by the Union of Councils, activists shifted to emphasize "People-to-People" efforts—personalized advocacy for individual Soviet Jews with names, stories, and lives:

political prisoners, refuseniks waiting in limbo after requests for exit visas were denied, teenagers taken from their parents, babies needing medical care, and other causes célèbres. Later chapters will explain the causes of this shift. (There were many.) As for its effects, it sparked a flurry of tactical innovation, quickly expanding the ways people could get involved. Movement organizations created programs for sending greeting cards, writing letters, placing phone calls, mailing care packages, "adopting" families, "twinning" bar and bat mitzvahs, and even traveling to the USSR to visit Jews in their apartments.[76] None of this was inevitable. Activists built this movement from scratch. They could have chosen to build it differently. To understand what they did build, we have to examine how they constructed it, piece by piece. We also have to consider the contexts in which they were building.

CONTEXTS: AMERICAN, JEWISH, AND GLOBAL

How best to situate the American movement to free Soviet Jews? Cultural histories of Student Struggle for Soviet Jewry, Kahane's Jewish Defense League, and New Left groups like Jews for Urban Justice place the campaign in an American context of sixties-era social ferment and generational conflict. These studies, focusing on young urban activists working in New York, Washington, and Boston between 1964 and 1974, portray a movement of baby boomers embracing the discourses, aesthetics, and generational politics of the civil rights, Black Power, and antiwar movements, and adopting countercultural modes of protest to demand Soviet Jewish freedom and to press their too-cautious elders to do the same.[77]

These treatments emphasize the importance of Black liberation movements in inspiring and shaping Jewish American activism: "If injustice cannot be condoned in Selma, U.S.A., neither must it be overlooked in Kiev, U.S.S.R."[78] Whether the Soviet Jewry movement ends up looking like a struggle for Jewish civil rights overseas or a Black Power–style ethnic pride movement in America depends on whom researchers are studying: nonviolent student activists in the early 1960s or the sometimes violent radical flank in the 1970s. Researchers generally agree that young urban activists invented a uniquely Jewish American gloss on the era's culture of protest, influenced Soviet Jewry movement culture more widely, gave Orthodox Jews more prominence in communal affairs, and gave a rising generation of Jewish communal leaders their start. They debate whether their activism reinforced Jewish Americans' liberal commitments or reoriented their politics in a more tribalist direction.[79]

Other analyses situate the movement in global Jewish historical contexts. Some work presents the assistance to Soviet Jews as continuing more than a century of Jewish American foreign aid efforts on behalf of distressed Jewish communities overseas.[80] Other treatments speak to the importance of the newly established State of Israel in advancing Jewish American activism—concretely, by providing institutional support through Nativ; intellectually, by encouraging nationalist interpretations of Jewishness; and symbolically, by sparking an efflorescence of Jewish pride in the immediate aftermath of the 1967 Six-Day War.[81] Most prominently, however, research and memoirs emphasize post-Holocaust trauma as a driver of Jewish activism both in the USSR and around the world. In the US, where Jews contended with a sense of having failed their brothers and sisters in Europe, guilt, shame, and anger drove many to take up the Soviet Jewish banner.[82]

As for the larger global context, although the struggle between capitalism and communism figures in all studies of the movement, few cultural histories treat the Cold War as a central focus.[83] Research into the movement's policy efforts, by contrast, specifically concern themselves with the superpower standoff. Policy research has focused on the Soviet Jewry campaign's contribution to the rise of human rights discourses and monitoring frameworks in the 1970s and the challenges that these posed to détente's realpolitik approach to stabilizing US-Soviet relations. At the center of most studies in this vein is the Jackson-Vanik Amendment, which scuttled President Nixon's plan to improve economic ties with the USSR. Noteworthy for establishing a "linkage" between economic policy and human rights policy, this proviso to the 1974 Trade Act withheld trade benefits from communist countries that did not allow free emigration. Researchers have examined how the amendment was conceived, how Congress and Jewish American organizations interacted to secure its passage, and how the Nixon White House—and especially Henry Kissinger, the American architect of détente—failed to kill the amendment. They continue to argue over whether the amendment advanced or set back the goal of Soviet Jewish emigration.[84]

Because the movement focused on securing freedom of emigration for one particular oppressed group, not on overturning the structures that trampled on human rights generally in the USSR, scholars have debated whether the campaign to free Soviet Jews is better analyzed as a human rights campaign or a Jewish liberation movement.[85] Israeli scholarship, including work written by Soviet émigrés, has generally framed the campaign as an expression of Jewish nationalism. These interpretations derive from a research focus that does not emphasize American activism but rather highlights the work of refusenik leaders in the USSR and of the role played by Israel's Nativ.[86]

Scholarly debates over universalist versus particularist interpretations, human rights versus nationalism, and the relative weight of Soviet Jewish versus American Jewish versus Israeli leadership of the campaign are rooted in splits in the movement itself. In the 1970s, when the majority of Soviet Jewish émigrés (nonactivists) began choosing to go to America rather than Israel, a fight erupted among American Jews, Israel, and refusenik leaders over whether to pursue policies that steered emigrants to Israel.[87] After the movement's end, the factional disputes did not disappear. They simply migrated to the terrain of historiography.[88]

This is a broad set of influences: human rights, nationalism, the Cold War, Israel, Holocaust trauma, the generation gap, the counterculture, Black Power, the civil rights movement. It is no surprise, then, that researchers have not settled on a single representation of the movement's politics. Sometimes it appears as a movement of the left, a baby boomer revolt that used countercultural modes of protest to challenge an older, more cautious style of Jewish American politics.[89] Sometimes it appears as a movement of the right, a tribalist retrenchment that anticipated and advanced a Jewish neo-Conservatism.[90] And yet other times it appears as a movement that refused to be pigeonholed as left or right, mixing the two and destabilizing the conventional political categories altogether.[91]

The Soviet Jewry movement resists a single unifying narrative. As it should. All social movements take shape in the froth of converging historical streams. My approach to situating this movement will be eclectic. The many different global, American, and Jewish contexts gave activists numerous options when trying to engage people.[92] Mobilization tactics tapped them all, individually and in kaleidoscopic combinations.

Starting with the tactics and working from the bottom up, we shuttle across the contextualizing frames just as activists did.

Still, certain narrative threads emerge here more prominently than others. Like previous tellings, this one highlights a Jewish American population coming to terms with post-Holocaust trauma. Like others, it calls attention to the movement's origins in an era of widespread protest and social change. But it also presents the movement as a distinctly Jewish American fusion of Cold War liberalism and American consumer culture, and in doing so, it breaks with an emphasis in prior research. As noted, most studies of the Soviet Jewry campaign's political culture have focused on the connection to social movements of the 1960s and early '70s. And yet the countercultural youth-led factions and the violent Kahanists of the 1964–74 era were not the only actors shaping movement culture, nor were they necessarily the primary ones. Sociologically speaking, the preponderance of research into this corner of the movement to the neglect of others has skewed the sample.[93] The movement's staying power through the 1990s owed much to its diversity and breadth. Expanding the scope of analysis—in time, geography, and population—changes how we understand the Soviet Jewry movement's place in Jewish American culture. Pointing to Johnson-era youth who encircled the Soviet United Nations Mission blowing rams' horns to bring down the walls of oppression "Jericho style" offers one picture. Pointing to Reagan-era parents who jogged 10Ks for Soviet Jewry and transformed their children's bar and bat mitzvahs into Cold War rituals celebrating American freedom presents another. Juxtaposing the two helps us make sense of the continuities and discontinuities. If the teenage marchers of 1965 remained involved two decades later as the middle-aged joggers and parents of 1985, it was because the movement did not get stuck in the 1960s but changed with the people and with the times.

Even as this book extends the analysis of the countercultural dimensions of activism, it will quickly move in a different direction. By following the tactics, we will look further ahead, past the era of social movement ferment and into the "Me generation" years of the later 1970s and the Reagan Revolution of the 1980s; farther afield than New York City, into suburban living rooms where much of the nationwide activism took shape; beyond college clubs and radical collectives and over to the large bureaucracies that connected local Jewish communities across the nation and the offices where doctors, lawyers, scientists, educators, and business owners combined advocacy and professional work; beyond tousle-haired baby boomers in their college years to their salt-and-pepper coiffed middle-aged parenthood; and even beyond baby boomers entirely to the children of Generation X and especially to the older generations leading the UCSJ and NCSJ. Some of these movement leaders were World War II veterans. Others were Holocaust survivors. Most were American women and men born in the preboomer 1928–45 cohort—the so-called Silent Generation that turned out to be anything but.

This expansive view will reveal a key continuity in the movement's mass mobilization work. From beginning to end, activists framed the Soviet Jewish cause as both timeless and timely, enduring and immediate. They anchored the campaign in something eternal, weaving it into the spaces, stories, and rhythms of Jewish religious life to make it feel traditional, even normative. Movement leaders could have presented the plight of Soviet Jewry simply as a contemporary political issue. Instead, they reached for Judaism's foundational narrative, recited every year at the Passover seder: "We were slaves to Pharaoh in Egypt but the Lord our God took us out of there with a mighty hand and an outstretched arm." They roused American Jews to respond as if the Exodus paradigm itself were at stake, as if deliverance from slavery to freedom hinged on their choice to demand, "Let my people go!" They could have spoken of the movement only as a campaign to secure emigration rights; instead, they fought to "save" and "redeem" Soviet Jewry. They could have kept the movement in the streets; instead, they brought it into their synagogues, invoking Soviet Jewry when they worshipped their God, celebrated their holidays, and marked their life passages. They wove the campaign so thoroughly into children's religious education that a generation was raised knowing no other Judaism than one in which "Speak out for Soviet Jewry" was as much a commandment as "Remember the Sabbath day."

Yet even while touching the eternal, activists also created modes of engagement that let Jewish Americans feel themselves living at the cusp of their moment in history—repairing the breach of a Holocaust that had occurred in their lifetimes, marching for people's rights when the streets teemed with marchers for rights, wearing their ethnicity proudly when ethnic pride was the order of the day, and engaging as Jews and as Americans in the defining global conflict of the era, the Cold War—even if that meant personally boarding a Pan Am flight to take the battle to Moscow.

A COLD WAR SUBCULTURE

Leaders of the Soviet Jewry movement will likely push back against the suggestion that theirs was a Cold War campaign. Anatoly Shcharansky himself—the movement's most famous political prisoner—declared at his 1978 trial in Moscow, "Yes, in today's world . . . there is a struggle between two social systems. But not everything can be reduced to this dichotomy."[94] Mainstream organizations in the 1960s and '70s carefully avoided a rhetoric of anticommunism.[95] They made no claims for free markets over central planning or private property over state ownership. Activists insisted that they were not calling for political change or economic reform in the USSR—"only" for the government to let Jews emigrate for family reunification or national repatriation in Israel;[96] "only" to grant Jews the cultural rights guaranteed in the Soviet constitution.[97] UCSJ president Irene Manekofsky put it bluntly when she cautioned against aligning too closely with political dissidents in Russia: "Our business is Soviet Jewish emigration, not dissent or democratization of the Soviet Union."[98] Rhetorical distance from anticommunism was a key strategic frame. It served the movement well. For mobilizing at home, it made it easier to unite Cold War doves and hawks in common cause. For extracting concessions, it gave the Kremlin room to be flexible—allowing it to save face and to address Jewish demands without stirring up the more regime-destabilizing movements pressing for democracy or independence for the non-Russian republics. Jewish American activists kept their distance from proindependence nationalists in the Ukrainian American and Lithuanian American communities.[99] Nativ even initially resisted making a cause célèbre of Shcharansky because he was Andrei Sakharov's liaison with the Western press—linking the Jewish emigration rights movement with the dissident campaign for democratic reform.[100]

Activists' disclaimers of the Cold War label are part of the phenomenon to be explained, not a description of what actually was. Even a cursory glance at the artifacts of Soviet Jewry movement culture reveals a movement saturated in Cold War tropes. The pages ahead will bring bat mitzvah sermons that were paeans to life on the right side of the Iron Curtain; tourist travelogues that reached instinctively for spy novel clichés; and any number of posters, logos, letterheads, postage seals, and pendants emblazoned with hammers and sickles drawn on padlocks, and on chains, and as cages, and as weapons piercing human skulls.

The mass mobilization for Soviet Jews fashioned a uniquely Jewish American experience of the Cold War—one that drew from America's broader "Cold War culture" but also contributed something new and different to it. Social historians introduced the notion of Cold War culture in the late 1980s in an attempt to understand how foreign affairs influenced domestic developments in mid-twentieth-century America.[101] A main line of research has examined the Cold War's first decade, when a panic over missiles from abroad and subversives from within constrained the range of political possibilities by fostering a climate of mutual suspicion and self-repression. Cold War culture, in this vein, speaks of a time when Americans' sense of their own vulnerability led them to demand manly men and nurturing women—believers in God who would stay ever vigilant, rally all resources, and report all deviants to secure the common defense.[102] Other studies have offered different perspectives, showing, for instance, that the Cold War helped advance certain types of civil rights reforms (even if only so that the US could save face).[103] Critics have offered two main lines of dissent. One argues that the concept lends itself to being used too expansively: not all culture of the Cold War era should be called Cold War culture. Better to restrict the term to focus specifically on how people engaged the global conflict.[104] That is sound advice. We will follow it here. The second claims that "the Cold War was fought primarily at an elite level. It pervaded and shaped the experience of ordinary Americans far less than historians would have us believe."[105] To that, we can only respond, "Not in this case." We will see that precisely when détente encouraged many Americans to breathe a sigh of relief, Jewish Americans were briefing each other on how to smuggle technology to Russian Jewish refuseniks without getting caught by the KGB. This was no battle fought at the elite level. Thousands of average citizens made these trips. Millions fought in other ways from within the United States. For Jewish Americans in the era of the Soviet Jewry movement, Cold War culture was a grassroots phenomenon.

It was also a distinctive subcultural phenomenon. American Cold War culture of the 1970s and '80s was not that of the 1950s. It had changed overall and had also branched into diverse Cold War *cultures*, in the plural.[106] Whereas fear and vulnerability characterized the Cold War culture of the Eisenhower years, Jewish Americans' Nixon-, Carter-, and Reagan-era variants exuded confidence. Jewish Americans took for granted that the Soviet threat to Jewish existence endangered *Soviet* Jews, not themselves.[107] They considered the threat safely contained abroad, leaving them secure in the United States. And feeling powerful too. Precisely positioned to aid the less fortunate. This sense of their own invulnerability as Americans fanned their feelings of obligation to fight the Soviet superpower and filled them with the chutzpah to think they could win.

* * *

The Soviet Jewry movement was what it did. It was not a Jewish identity. It was not a set of rarefied notions about "Jewish peoplehood" or "American freedom." It was millions of people over three decades marching on Solidarity Sunday, wearing refusenik bracelets, smuggling blue jeans, twinning bat mitzvahs, raising the Matzoh of Hope, reading *The Jews of Silence*, singing "Leaving Mother Russia," playing escape-from-the-USSR simulations, and choosing Coke over Pepsi.[108] All these behaviors were the movement's mass mobilization tactics in action. All these behaviors brought new meanings into the world. The Soviet Jewry movement's mass mobilization tactics synthesized the Jewish and the American. These tactics refashioned ancient religion to engage a new era. They created distinctly Jewish American ways of participating personally in the epoch's defining global conflict and in the US's major social, political, and cultural trends. They offered a generation traumatized by memories of Jewish powerlessness an opportunity to try to heal by empowering themselves and aiding others.

Activists invented these tactics. They were intending to aid Jews in the Soviet Union. They ended up creating an entire Jewish culture in the United States.

1

ILLUMINATE THE PAST AND PRESENT

In 1971, the World Jewish Congress introduced an academic journal, *Soviet Jewish Affairs*, "to help illuminate the past and present of Jewish communities in the USSR." Its first issue opened with an article by Columbia-trained Sovietologist William Korey analyzing the gap between law and practice in Moscow's implementation of article 13 of the Universal Declaration of Human Rights: "Everyone has the right to leave any country, including his own, and to return to his country." As the lead item in a new journal, the piece and its placement would have been chosen with care. The editors aspired to create a publication "of interest and value to non-specialist readers" that would "combine academic integrity with practical vitality." Korey's writing struck the proper balance.[1]

It is no wonder, as Korey built a career blending scholarship, policy work, journalism, and activism. He left his position teaching Russian history at City College of New York in 1954 to take up civil rights work with the Anti-Defamation League of B'nai B'rith and then went on to head B'nai B'rith's United Nations office and later its International Policy Research department. With the National Conference on Soviet Jewry, he assisted in congressional monitoring of Soviet compliance with the Helsinki Accords' human rights provisions. His 1973 book analyzing antisemitism in the USSR, *The Soviet Cage*, became a standard text in Soviet Jewry movement curricula. As Korey continued teaching at universities around the New York area, he also became one of the Soviet Jewry movement's real-time chroniclers, penning *American Jewish Year Book* surveys of the fight over the Jackson-Vanik Amendment and the response to Anatoly Shcharansky's arrest.[2]

Research always mattered in the campaign to free Soviet Jews. Systemic antisemitism in the USSR was a distant and complex phenomenon—hard to see, hard to understand. Policy studies, statistical reports, case histories, and legal analyses could render it visible and help Westerners make sense of it. It also legitimized the campaign. Partisans, in their passion, would be tempted to overstate the problem; the Soviet government had an interest in denying it. Scholarship allowed the movement to ground its claims in verifiable facts and establish itself as a more reliable source of information than the Kremlin. At its most effective, Soviet Jewry movement research addressed three audiences at once—advancing scholarship for fellow academics, offering useful knowledge to activists, and communicating clearly to an educated public.

Soviet Jewry organizations recognized this early on. In the late 1950s, Nativ quietly established two research outfits: Moshe Decter's Jewish Minority Research bureau, housed at the American Jewish Committee in New York, and Emmanuel Litvinoff's periodical *Jews in Eastern Europe*, published out of London.[3] Decter wrote the 1963 *Foreign Affairs* article that prompted Louis Rosenblum and his fellow book club members to create the Cleveland Committee on Soviet Anti-Semitism.[4] Decter, a scholar-activist like Korey, then helped Nativ set up the Academic Committee for Soviet Jewry to organize academic support, convene symposia, and publish research. Political scientist Hans Morgenthau chaired the committee. Sociologists Bruno Bettelheim, Daniel Bell, Nathan Glazer, Seymour Martin Lipset, and Robert Merton added their names as sponsors, along with Milton Friedman, Lionel Trilling, and more than forty others from across the humanities, social sciences, and natural sciences.[5]

The Soviet Jewry movement is long over. The present book's examination of its tactics is far removed from the activist scholarship that Korey and Decter practiced. Nevertheless, the model of writing with academics, practitioners, and an interested general readership in mind remains valuable. The questions of how the Soviet Jewry movement invented its tactics and how this ended up shaping Jewish American life speak to many audiences. Jewish Americans who experienced the movement, children of Soviet émigrés, activists in present-day social movements, Cold War buffs, and others all have good—and very different—reasons for wanting to learn answers to these questions. For their part, scholars look to new research not just for what it teaches in itself but for how it contributes to the collective work of building academic fields. Before delving into the case itself, they want to know how the researcher is approaching the study. Why are the questions framed this way and not that? What method or plan of analysis guides the study? How will learning about this issue speak to larger matters beyond the particular case?

In this chapter, I will answer those questions. In the process, I will suggest to scholars in Jewish studies and social movement studies that some of their foundational ideas are showing cracks and that analyzing the Soviet Jewry movement's tactics and culture can help them reassess and rebuild. In the spirit of *Soviet Jewish Affairs*, I hope to make these conversations accessible and "of interest and value to non-specialist readers." Analysis of the tactics themselves will begin in chapter 2.

COLLECTIVE ACTION IN THE SOCIOLOGY OF AMERICAN JEWS

Activists in the Soviet Jewry movement invented mass mobilization tactics that sustained Jewish American communal engagement for thirty years. Their work altered the trajectory of Jewish American history. Their innovations shaped the texture of Jewish American life.

How does the sociology of American Jews account for this? It does not. Observers in the 1950s and 1960s did not foresee the Soviet Jewry movement's rise, nor did they imagine the new ways of being Jewish in America that it spurred.[6] Analysts in the 1970s and 1980s overlooked it, arguing instead that Jewish Americans were creating a "vicarious" Jewishness centered on Israel and the Holocaust—foreign shores and distant times. They failed to notice that the Jews around them were creating the largest sustained mass mobilization in their history and ignored that these Jews had built their campaign around the notion of *freedom*—America's supreme value and a term that bore heightened resonance during the Cold War. Jewish Americans' activism to "free" Soviet Jews certainly linked up with their efforts to memorialize the Holocaust and support the State of Israel. All three embodied what scholars of the era called the politics of "sacred survival." Jewish Americans responded to the traumatic memory of powerlessness by demanding—almost as a religious commandment—Jewish solidarity and political self-advocacy. But this was not a vicarious identity. The politics of sacred survival stood not on twin pillars of Israel advocacy and Holocaust commemoration but on a three-legged stool, with the third leg—the mobilization for Soviet Jewry—planted firmly and proudly in the American experience.[7]

Today, decades after the movement's end, common paradigms in the contemporary sociology of American Jews offer scant insight into how the Soviet Jewry movement came to shape Jewish American culture as much as it did. Researchers trying to explain changes in Jewish American communal life have most often grounded their claims either in large-scale surveys that examine demography and measure conformity to normative Jewish practices or in in-depth interviews that seek to discover how individuals define their own Jewish identities. Contrasting the two approaches, the scholar Bethamie Horowitz declares it the difference between asking "How Jewish are American Jews?" and "How are American Jews Jewish?" Practitioners debate the merits of the two approaches. Some try to combine them.[8] Neither approach, however, can account for what is detailed in the pages ahead. Demographic trends did not determine that the Soviet Jewry movement would become a defining feature of late Cold War–era Jewish American culture. Nor did the movement emerge through the spontaneous combustion of millions of individual Jews' aggregated identities.

This book locates the causal forces shaping the sociology of Jewish Americans not in demographic change writ large nor in personal Jewish identities writ small but in between, at the middle, or meso-, level where people engage in collective action to jointly construct a shared culture. How the Soviet Jewry movement emerged as a force in Jewish American life is indeed a question of "How are American Jews Jewish?" (or "How *were* they Jewish in their day?"). But to answer the question, we are not asking individual Jews what they thought and felt. Instead, we use the documentary record to examine how institutionalized collective action created historically situated practices that shaped an entire mode of Jewish life, one that came to define its era before passing from the scene.[9]

A GENERALIZABLE CASE:
THE IMPORTANCE OF MASS MOBILIZATION

The Soviet Jewry movement shaped Jewish life in America by getting large numbers of Jews actually to do things. To discover how, we have to look at the mass mobilization tactics involved—how they were invented, how they spread, and how they became part of people's lives.

There is a general principle here about social movements overall, not just the Soviet Jewry campaign: mass mobilization tactics are the main way social movements project their meanings into the world. Most people experience social movements by witnessing or participating in the behaviors that movements create to engage them. These behaviors perform meanings. They express understanding. And engaging in them can generate emotions and inculcate sensibilities.[10] Social movements give texture to their eras because they are continually churning out new practices to engage large numbers of people. For those interested in how social movements shape culture, studying mass mobilization tactics is a sine qua non. Sociology offers conceptual tools that can help. Not all these tools, however, work as well as one would hope. But that presents an opportunity. We can use the case study to improve sociology's conceptual toolkit.

BEYOND REPERTOIRE:
TACTICAL INVENTION VERSUS TACTICAL CHOICE

Some might be tempted to see the Soviet Jewry movement's tactical choices as foreordained—"naturally" emerging from its contexts. *Of course* Soviet Jewry activists would engage people by holding protest seders at Passover. Jews had "always" been mobilizing Passover seders to express their politics.[11] *Of course* they would stage those seders out in the streets. It was the 1960s—who wasn't taking guerrilla theater to the streets? Others might be tempted in the opposite direction, imagining tactical innovation to depend entirely on chance circumstances.

Both approaches render the question of tactical development moot. There is nothing to explain, so why bother trying? But what happened in the Soviet Jewry movement was neither completely predetermined nor totally idiosyncratic. The development of tactics was a social process—open-ended but structured. We can observe patterns and discover governing principles. For decades, sociologists have been studying the issue in other social movements. Thanks to their work, we begin our research on the Soviet Jewry campaign already knowing something.

First, movements arrive at their tactics by making *rational choices* shaped by the nature of the targets, the constraints of the "political opportunity structure," and a chess-like strategic maneuvering between activists and targets.[12] When analyzing the movement through this lens, we could point out, for instance, that Americans chose to protest at Bolshoi Ballet performances in the United States because it was easier to let Soviet targets come to them. Or that the US political system allowed American Jews to organize through government-recognized nonprofit agencies, whereas the Soviet system forced Jews to organize in underground networks.

Second, decisions about tactics can be an *expressive choice* meant to display collective identity, thereby uniting activists with one another.[13] Focusing on this, we could point out that when rabbis marched on the Soviet UN Mission wearing prayer shawls and blowing rams' horns, they were not only sending the Russians a message; they were affirming their own conviction that theirs was holy Jewish work. We might also note that American Jews regularly drew on the Passover meal as a symbol of protest but—no surprise here—never the Eucharist.[14]

Third, the choice of tactics can be *simultaneously rational and expressive*, resulting from access to certain resources or from jockeying among movement factions.[15] From this perspective, we could call attention to how bar and bat mitzvah twinning built on activists' access to synagogues as an operational base, just as the civil rights movement relied on Black churches.[16] Or we could highlight how the Jewish Defense League's use of violence was partly a way of positioning itself in opposition to the mainstream grassroots and establishment factions, both of which had embraced a philosophy of nonviolence.[17]

These findings from research into other movements are helpful, but there is a problem. They answer a different question. They speak to the issue of tactical *choice*, not to the creative process of tactical *innovation*. The tendency in social movement studies to ask not how activists *invent* their tactics but how they *choose* their tactics stems from the core metaphor that has guided research. Charles Tilly, one of the leading scholars in social movement studies, offered the language of tactical "repertoires" in the 1970s.[18] The notion of repertoire is lifted from theater and music, where it refers to a preexisting stock of pieces that actors or musicians can easily and regularly perform. Taken as a metaphor, it has also come to mean a stock of abilities and skills that a person can readily draw on.[19] In social movement studies, a "repertoire of contention" refers to the idea that in any given historical moment, protesters tend to rely on a stock of ready-made tactics (e.g., hold a rally, go on strike, create a hashtag). The metaphor captures something important, but like all metaphors, it is useful only to a point. Metaphors inhibit thinking as much as aid it.[20] By suggesting that tactics are ready and waiting to be drawn out of storage, the repertoire metaphor directs us to ask how activists choose among existing options.[21] It does not prime us to ask how they invent new ones, nor does it offer tools for investigating or modeling what happens inside the tactical creation process itself. That remains a black box.[22]

As we will see in the pages ahead, for instance, by the late 1970s, Soviet Jewry activists had settled into tried-and-true patterns in how they used tourism—precisely what Tilly meant by a repertoire. But how did they get there? There was no precedent for mobilizing international mass tourism in the early years of the Jet Age. There was no established tactical repertoire to adapt. Everything activists did to invent this new tactic was just that—an invention. And that is precisely what the notion of repertoire, with its assumption of choice among preexisting options, cannot explain. We bump up against the limits of the guiding metaphor, and little is gained by staying wedded to it. Better to use the opportunity to try a new approach.

For this, we have two advantages. First, we have access to expertise from outside social movement studies. The field of cultural sociology specializes in the dynamics of cultural production. All the knowledge it has amassed on that topic is available for analyzing the production of social movement tactics. Its conceptual frameworks and habits of mind are available too. Whereas political sociology encourages us to think of tactics as strategic action, cultural sociology enables us to examine tactics as cultural phenomena in a much broader sense.

Second, we have the advantage of an unexamined case. The Soviet Jewry movement was the largest mass mobilization in Jewish American history. It occupied presidents and premiers, forced itself onto the superpowers' negotiating agenda, spurred congressional human rights legislation, facilitated a mass emigration that moved 1.5 million people across the globe, and constituted part of the broader human rights campaigns that contributed to the collapse of the Soviet Union and the end of the Cold War.[23] No research in the sociological study of social movements has ever taken account of it. None of sociology's flagship social movement studies journals—*Mobilization*, *Social Movement Studies*, and *Research in Social Movements, Conflicts and Change*—have ever published an article on the Soviet Jewry movement. In fact, no article in *Mobilization*'s twenty-five-year history or *Social Movement Studies*' twenty-two years has ever mentioned the movement, even in passing.[24] Whatever the cause—benign neglect, implicit blind spots, or active erasure—the field's oversight presents an opportunity to use the case as a corrective. Sociological theories are built from case studies. Missing cases are problematic because they curtail the range of variation that theories are supposed to account for.[25] In this instance, we find an overlooked case—and not a minor one at that—whose model of tactical development cannot be well explained by theories of tactical repertoires. As such, even as we can draw on research from social movement studies to better understand the Soviet Jewry movement, we can use this long-ignored case to fill gaps in the understanding of how social movements work overall.

CULTURAL SOCIOLOGY AND SOCIAL MOVEMENT STUDIES

How does one undertake a cultural sociological analysis of the creation and consequences of mass mobilization tactics? First, we allow ourselves to recognize that tactical creation is a form of cultural production. Acknowledging this makes it possible to draw on conceptual and analytic tools offered by sociology's "production of culture" perspective. Codified by sociologist Richard Peterson, who studied the evolution of musical genres, this approach directs us to focus on how things like institutional logics and organizational structures channel the production process.[26] But we also want to understand the connection between the process of creating the tactics and the cultural consequences of deploying them. For all its analytic power, the "production of culture" perspective will take us only part of the way.²⁷ To push further, we will rely on and develop three basic ideas.

First is a *mobilizing gaze*. This refers to how activists view people and things in terms of their potential utility for advancing a cause. This way of looking at the world sparks tactical innovation, drives it forward, and is a key engine of social movements' larger cultural consequences. Second is *endogenous explanation*. The process of tactical innovation is driven not only by factors external to the tactics, such as strategic calculation, but also by internal logics—cognitive logics that channel how activists think and material and institutional logics that channel how cultural objects can be used. Third is *cultural coproduction*. Activists are not the sole producers of movement culture. The mobilized masses cocreate the mass mobilization tactics. Grassroots participation helps generate social movements' larger cultural consequences.

A MOBILIZING GAZE

What do the Fast of the Ninth of Av, travel writing, summer camps, Jermyn Street jewelry, poster contests, and the Olympics have in common? Nothing, save for the fact that Soviet Jewry activists looked at each of them as potentially useful and found ways to repurpose them to engage supporters.

Activists look at the world differently than others. They pay attention to how things they encounter relate to the causes they care about. They look at people differently too, seeing them in relation to the cause—as potential supporters, opponents, allies, spoilers, funders, and so on. The particular lenses might differ from movement to movement, but the orientation is the same. Activists scrutinize objects, practices, symbols, people—anything, really—to determine whether and how they can be enlisted. One might call this way of looking at the world a *mobilizing gaze*.

The word *mobilizing* carries a dual connotation. Take, for instance, Soviet Jewry activists' choice to use bar and bat mitzvah ceremonies as a way of engaging children. (Chapter 7 treats these "twinnings," which saw American youth recite bar and bat mitzvah blessings on behalf of Soviet Jewish youth, in absentia.) Activists made this life cycle ritual a *target* or *object* of mobilization, enlisting it and making it useful. The ritual's utility lay in its ability to serve as an *agent* of mobilization, bringing Jewish American youth into the movement. But this adds another layer—the idea that it would be a good thing to engage twelve- and thirteen-year-olds in the first place. Activists looked on these children as a population to be mobilized, another *target*. And although activists valued children's participation mainly as an end in itself, they also recognized that children could serve as a path to reach their parents—that is, they also saw children as potential *agents* of mobilization. In short, the mobilizing gaze looks at the world as full of people and things *to be mobilized* and *to help in mobilizing*. The objects and agents of mobilization are often one and the same.

In sociological parlance, the word *gaze* refers to a way of seeing that exerts power over what is looked at—defining it, categorizing it, bringing it under the gazer's control.[28] Bar and bat mitzvah twinning could not have been invented had activists not looked at teenagers as a target population to be mobilized and the sacred coming-of-age ritual as material to be repurposed for political action. The act of gazing also defines the gazers. The people who invented twinning had to think of themselves as responsible for mobilizing others, and they had to authorize themselves to rewrite the script of a time-honored synagogue ritual.

The mobilizing gaze is an orientation to action baked into how activists understand themselves and their work. It is part of their ingrained, habitual way of relating to the world, the one that reacts instinctively by thinking, "Let's see how we can use this for the movement."[29]

Always scrutinizing to determine utility and find more ways to aid the cause—and filled with chutzpah in claiming the right to enlist anything and everyone—the mobilizing gaze drives tactical innovation forward. It also drives it outward, spreading social movements into more and more domains of life and turning issue-focused political campaigns into totalizing cultural mobilizations.[30]

ENDOGENOUS EXPLANATION: INTERNAL LOGICS OF TACTICAL INNOVATION

Most research on social movements explains the evolution of tactical repertoires by pointing to "exogenous" factors—causes external to the tactics themselves. But if we stop thinking of tactics as repertoires that activists choose from and start recognizing them as cultural products that activists create, we discover that tactical innovation is not simply a matter of rational choices in pursuit of strategic ends or expressive choices to display collective identities. The invention of tactics is also channeled by things that emerge from within the innovative process itself. The most important of these "endogenous" factors are material affordances, institutional logics, path dependencies, and cognitive logics.[31] *Affordances* are the ways that materials we build with shape what can be done with them.[32] *Institutional logics* are deeply patterned behaviors that channel activity. Both open and encourage some possibilities while discouraging and foreclosing others. These concepts help explain, for example, how two-dollar brass medallions imprinted with Soviet Jewish prisoners' names evolved into limited-edition high-fashion gold necklaces designed by a jeweler to Queen Elizabeth. (If you are going to mobilize jewelry, then the rules of fashion start to apply.) *Path dependencies* are the economists' term for what the poet pondered as roads taken and not taken.[33] Soviet Jewry groups' Adopt-a-Prisoner programs evolved into Adopt-a-Family programs, which gave rise to bar and bat mitzvah twinning programs. *Cognitive logics* are like mental algorithms that push creative thinking down certain routes. Cognitive logics of categorical induction and deduction, for instance, led isolated Passover protests to evolve into systematic mobilizations of the entire Jewish holiday calendar.

Social movements often bring surprises as the ever-strategic mobilizing gaze collides with these hardly strategic internal logics. When activists develop a tactic, they enter into a relationship with it. They experiment. They learn. They encounter its limits. They discover its unforeseen potential. But the relationship is not a one-way street. Properties inherent to the tactic constrain and channel what activists do, leading them down paths whose logic is tied less to the strategy of the movement than to the internal logic of the tactic itself.[34] Activists who initially thought to use tourists as go-betweens to maintain contact with Soviet Jews ended up writing guidebooks for Jewish heritage travel in Russia. Consider it an irony of tactical innovation: unintended consequences feed back into the creative process of tactical innovation, setting activists down new and unlikely paths.

CULTURAL COPRODUCTION

Usually when thinking about the cultural consequences of a social movement, we focus on the aftereffects of achieving the explicit goals. For the Soviet Jewry movement, this might mean talking about how Russian-speaking immigrants and their children, now 15 percent of the Israeli population, are shaping that country's politics.[35] But a movement's cultural consequences result from more than just the policy outcomes; they start making themselves present in the very act of rallying people to the cause.[36] Social movements project meanings into the world. In successful mass mobilizations, these meanings shape how large numbers of people think, feel, and act. From this perspective, the Soviet Jewry movement's key cultural consequence was that it created a distinctive way of living Jewishly in America for the millions whose lives the movement touched—a way of living Jewishly that lasted for a quarter century and then disappeared once the movement stopped mobilizing.[37] We are interested in this second, less-explored aspect—not only to describe it but to understand how it was accomplished.

When political sociologists have taken up the questions of how social movements construct meaning and how tactics play a role in this, they have generally started from the premise that if activists are going to have any hope of succeeding, they need to convince people that some circumstance constitutes a problem, that the problem is of such-and-such a nature, that some course of action is therefore an appropriate solution, and that their participation can make a difference. Because there are always other ways to interpret what is going on, how best to respond, and who should be taking action, it is up to activists to strategically "frame" issues so that people will interpret the situation as they do and act accordingly. In other words, movements project meaning into the world by framing issues for the public. Roles are clearly delineated: the mobilizers produce meanings, and the mobilized receive them. This is rational, strategic action, explicitly discursive, aimed at achieving clearly defined goals. Tactics are important because they are part of this strategic framing work.[38]

Adopting this approach from political sociology would steer our analysis as follows: Since strategic framing is the main way activists project meaning into the world, those who want to understand how the Soviet Jewry movement wove itself into the fabric of Jewish American life should look at how activists rationally applied a means–end calculus to develop mass mobilization tactics whose meanings resonated with Jewish Americans and encouraged them to act. Such an approach would show how strategic choices had cultural consequences. I have already mentioned, for instance, that activists tried to distance themselves from overt anticommunism in order to build a bigger tent. This framing decision strengthened Jewish American solidarity.

The lenses of political sociology are precision-ground to discern these strategic dimensions of social movement tactics. The corollary is that they blur the nonstrategic dimensions. Switching to lenses from cultural sociology brings the latter into focus. The most ambitious cultural sociological analysis of how social movements construct meaning, and how tactics play a role in this, centers on the notion of *cognitive praxis*. This approach, developed by sociologists Ronald Eyerman and Andrew Jamison, does not conceive of movements as strategically oriented agents of policy change. Instead, it sees movements as brief moments when collective action brings new ways of thinking and behaving into the world. For a short period, new thinking inspires new behaviors, which shape new understandings. The two elements come together in a unique amalgam. That amalgam—or more precisely, the vibrant process of producing it—is the social movement.[39] Think of how movies about the civil rights and anti–Vietnam War movements look like 1960s period pieces, with their distinctive soundtracks and fashions. These are temporary moments. They don't last. But in their moment, they open a space for new types of knowledge-in-action to take shape and to be lived out in practice.

From this perspective, activists do not strategically "frame" tactics or graft meanings onto them in the hopes of making them resonate. Rather, the way they see the world inspires them to create tactics that are the necessary outcomes of their worldview. An example from the Soviet Jewry movement will clarify the difference. Activists in San Francisco staged Passover seders as protest rituals outside the Soviet Consulate. If we think of this as "framing," we could argue that movement leaders strategically chose to use the ritual to present their cause as religious. Soviet Jewry activism was not "really" religious, only framed as such. If we understand it as "praxis," we could argue that activists invented protest rituals because they knew themselves to be fighting a holy battle.

The struggle to redeem Soviet Jewry was a religious matter to them, and they acted accordingly. I find the latter approach applies better in this case and more accurately reflects how Soviet Jewry movement activists understood what they were doing.

Nevertheless, although thinking in terms of framing or praxis leads us to interpret activists' intentions differently, in both cases we are still focusing on activists as the main creators of movement tactics and treating their goals and interpretations as authoritative for a movement.[40] There is something to be said for this. We will analyze the Soviet Jewry movement this way when we focus on Jacob Birnbaum's experimentation with ritualized protests and Irene Manekofsky's work on a handbook to engage children, to name two. But focusing only on activists does not give the mobilized masses their due. Mobilization tactics are only recommendations until the mobilized enact them and make them real. Each target of a mobilization tactic, each "consumer," thereby becomes a "producer."[41] Every visitor who delivered medicine to refuseniks, every tourist who wrote a travelogue, every teenager who offered a bar or bat mitzvah twinning sermon, every child who submitted an entry to a poster contest created the tactic in their own way. Each enactment of a tactic reproduced parts of a common template, and each created something unique. Sometimes, the enactments realized activists' intentions. Other times they undercut them.

We will see that the mobilized masses helped produce the Soviet Jewry movement's mobilization tactics—and brought their meanings to life—in three main ways. First, through *embodied action*, millions of Jewish Americans translated activists' scripts into lived behaviors that performed meanings. Second, their behaviors themselves generated *emergent meanings*. Participating in the mass mobilization tactics—actually doing them—created a sense of knowing in the gut, not just in the head. It also generated new understandings, emotions, and ideas beyond those foreseen or planned by activists. Third, many of the mass mobilization tactics engaged people by asking them to produce their own works of *creative expression*. The Soviet Jewry movement inspired the creation of an enormous amount of homegrown literary, graphic, musical, and dramatic work. In their travelogues, bar and bat mitzvah sermons, school reports, poster contest entries, holiday greeting cards, clip-art prayer books, and the like, average Jewish Americans expressed their understandings of the Soviet Jewish plight in their own voices. They flooded the public square with grassroots messaging about Soviet Jewry and about American Jewry's fight on their behalf. Many of these local innovations also made their way back to large activist networks, which then circulated them nationwide.

Social movements are engines of cultural production. The struggle to free Soviet Jewry certainly was. Its activists spent a quarter century inventing tactics to engage millions of Jewish Americans in an ongoing fight to free Soviet Jews. The success of these tactics in mobilizing the masses profoundly shaped the texture of Jewish American life in the last decades of the Cold War. To understand how they accomplished this, we follow the tactics themselves, starting with the mobilization of sacred Jewish rituals.

2

THIS IS THE MATZOH OF HOPE

Urged to the streets by Student Struggle for Soviet Jewry (SSSJ), a thousand teenagers and young adults mustered under cloudy skies at Carnegie Hall on the last Sunday of March 1969. Dusk approached. Crowd members lit torches and began parading through Midtown Manhattan to the Soviet United Nations Mission at Sixty-Seventh and Lexington. With Passover days away, the marchers carried haggadahs, the script for the seder ritual, specially inscribed with holiday greetings in Russian, Yiddish, and English. Protesters intended to present the booklets to Soviet diplomats with a request to send them on to synagogues in the USSR. They did not expect the officials to open the doors or receive the haggadahs, but activists would send a message through their attempt. Outside the mission, marchers arrived to sidewalks lined with linen-covered tables heaped "high with matzos, bitter herbs and a giant 'cup of salvation,'" symbols from the traditional Passover meal. SSSJ chairman Rabbi Steven (Shlomo) Riskin, spiritual leader of the Modern Orthodox Lincoln Square Synagogue, took the unleavened bread and led the assembly in "the ancient ritual of the retelling of the redemption from slavery." This was the second year in a row that New Yorkers were bringing the Pesach ritual to the Soviet Mission. It was no traditional seder. Moved out of the home and onto the streets, conducted before the official start of the holiday, and staged before *New York Times* and Jewish Telegraphic Agency reporters, this version of the paschal rite adapted the ancient tradition to make "particular reference to the critical plight of the three million Jews of the USSR." It was ritual reconfigured as protest, protest reimagined as ritual—all pegged to the most important holiday in the Jewish calendar.[1]

SSSJ's first "Symbolic Seder of Redemption" was also its largest. The organization continued staging the protest rituals, later renamed Freedom Seders, almost every year between 1974 and 1990.[2] Other groups across North America and Western Europe took them up too. SSSJ was especially devoted to the practice. After moving its Passover protest from the Soviets' Midtown Manhattan UN mission to the gates of the ambassadors' residence in the Bronx (conveniently located a few blocks from SSSJ's new Riverdale offices but a schlep for protesters from Brooklyn and Queens), the group saw attendance dwindle to only a few dozen stalwarts.[3] The smaller numbers were no deterrent. The Student Struggle stuck with its strategy: demonstrate continually to keep the Soviet Jewish issue in the public eye.[4] The insistence on staying the course might explain why SSSJ's leaders continued protesting regardless of turnout. It does not explain why they continued organizing those protests as Pesach seders.

We might be tempted to explain away SSSJ's commitment to the tactic as just a function of repertoire and routine. Social movement organizations are most efficient when doing what they already know how to do. SSSJ had invested years honing the Passover protest. But when a mass mobilization tactic ceases to mobilize masses (at least for SSSJ in the Bronx; the tactic was still going strong in other cities[5]) we need to look beyond the economics of efficiency to weigh organizational and movement culture.[6] Here, this means examining religion.

To SSSJ's leaders, there was no mystery why Freedom Seders needed to be held regardless of low attendance. Speaking at the group's 1988 seder, SSSJ national chairman Rabbi Avraham (Avi) Weiss said, "[To] those who say to us, 'why do you keep coming out to protest over and over? My response is, how can you not come? How can you experience Passover and not speak out for those in the Egypt of today?"[7] If activism to free Soviet Jews was a religious obligation—a *mitzvah*—then protest had to be expressed through religious action, and religious Jews had to accept the responsibility to protest. That understanding was intuitive to Rabbi Weiss by the time SSSJ marked its twenty-fourth anniversary, but it was not intuitive when the group first formed.[8] SSSJ's holiday protests started as sporadic affairs. Activists experienced many Jewish holidays in the 1960s without speaking out for Soviet Jews. And when they did start rallying around Jewish festivals, they did not necessarily use the holidays' symbols or rituals in their protests. SSSJ's first Passover-time demonstration featured rams' horns, not matzohs. Its "break down the walls" theme invoked Joshua and the Battle of Jericho, not Moses and the Exodus from Egypt.[9]

By the mid-1970s, activists in SSSJ and movement-wide had transformed this occasional holiday-time Judaic mishmash into systematically planned protest rituals for almost every festival and fast day in the Jewish year. They themed each protest to its holiday. No more Battle of Jericho non sequiturs on Passover. Instead, there would be greeting cards for Rosh Hashanah, dances for Simchat Torah, tree plantings for Tu BiShvat, and all-night study sessions for Shavuot.[10] Each in its holiday's tradition. This systematic, near-total mobilization of the Jewish holiday calendar—ritualizing holiday protests in synagogues, schools, and homes and on the streets—meant that for the better part of two decades, American Jews' experience of the Soviet Jewry movement and their experience of their religion were regularly intertwined.

How did Soviet Jewry activists arrive at such a thorough mobilization of Jewish ritual and sacred time? What consequences did the use of ritualized holiday protest as a mass mobilization tactic have for the movement and for American Jewish politics and religion more broadly? In this chapter, we trace and analyze the process of tactical innovation, starting from the moment in spring 1964 when activists first began looking at rituals and holidays as potentially useful resources for mass mobilization.

CONTEXTS AND CAUSES

When thinking about how to rally Jewish Americans to the Soviet Jewish cause, activists had options. They could have asked them to travel to Washington to lobby elected officials. (They did.) They could have urged them to picket performances of visiting Soviet circus acts. (They did.) They could have encouraged them to fly to Moscow to pass messages to Soviet Jewish activists. (They did that too.) But in gathering them outside Soviet diplomatic offices to chant "This is the bread of affliction, *Ha lachma anya*," activists were not just asking demonstrators to speak out for Jews in Russia; they were urging them to say something about their own religious sensibilities as Jews in the United States.

What made this approach to mobilization seem imaginable, reasonable, and even intuitive in Soviet Jewry activist circles? Several contexts contributed. Like any mobilization in a religious community, the Soviet Jewry movement had access to all the assets that religion offers for activism. These, as detailed by sociologist Christian Smith, can include transcendent motivation and legitimation, symbolic and ritual resources, organizational resources and networks, shared identities and solidarities, geographic breadth, and more.[11] Soviet Jewry activists used them all.

But just because religious resources were available did not mean that Soviet Jewry activists were aware of them or obliged to use them (at all or in the ways that they did). Not all Jewish political movements invite Jews to perform sacred rites as guerrilla theater. Before the 1960s, the approach was rare. Outside the United States, it still is. Other factors were also at play—activists' biographies, for instance. Those who first brought Jewish rituals to the streets were religiously observant Orthodox and Conservative Jews, mostly men, often with rabbinic ordination.[12] They represented that corner of the American Jewish population accustomed to thinking in religious categories and adept in Judaic ritual practice. Still, their religious traditionalism might have militated against using religious sancta in such unconventional ways. At the time, many Orthodox Jews rejected any public protest for Soviet Jewry whatsoever, let alone Passover protest seders and Tisha B'Av protest fasts.[13] The activist rabbis' religious virtuosity was therefore only a necessary condition, not a sufficient one. In actuality, they were only a subset of the religious traditionalist camp—the one attuned to currents in American political culture and interested in synthesizing these with their Judaism.[14]

What were these sociopolitical currents, and how did they make it easier for Soviet Jewry activists circa 1964–66 to start parading Jewish holidays and rituals as vehicles of protest? Earlier generations of Jewish Americans would have worried that asserting themselves in all their unleavened Aramaic particularity could call their Americanness into question. By the 1960s, such concerns had receded, thanks in no small measure to the Cold War. The 1950s saw Jewish organizations navigate the Rosenberg trial and the Red Scare by purging communists and marginalizing what remained of a once vigorous Yiddish immigrant socialism.[15] Upwardly mobile families seeking the American dream in postwar Levittowns anchored their suburban Jewish communities in more than a thousand newly constructed synagogues—their contribution to the American religious revival that Eisenhower and other leaders were touting as a bulwark against the threat of Marxist-Leninist materialism.[16] Positioning themselves as equal partners in an America they were rechristening as "*Judeo*-Christian," Jews could bring their rituals into the public square to affirm America's religious freedoms and their own fundamental Americanness. After all, what could be more patriotic than to enlist God in a struggle against Soviet oppression?[17]

Whereas the Cold War culture born of the 1950s encouraged Jews to parade their religion as an American virtue, the civil rights movement culture of the 1960s encouraged them to bring their politics to the streets—especially through nonviolent direct action with strong visuals for the new television age.[18] From 1964 to 1966, when SSSJ and the American Jewish Conference on Soviet Jewry (AJCSJ) were starting to develop ritualized protest, a burgeoning antiwar movement was also adopting civil rights movement–inspired strategies of theatricalized, camera-ready protest. Later, as the 1960s gave way to the 1970s, identity-based social movements pressed their claims by emphasizing difference rather than downplaying it: "Black is beautiful!" "I am woman, hear me roar!" "We're here. We're queer. Get used to it!" The Jewish Americans singing "Am Yisroel Chai" (The Jewish people lives) while marching with haggadah in hand were part of the broader rise of a politics of multiculturalism. Their participation in these politics cannot be explained simply as derivative. Jewish Americans' intergenerational fights, steeped in post-Holocaust trauma, contributed to Soviet Jewry activists' decisions to perform Jewishness in the streets. "This time we will not be silent," read a favorite SSSJ placard. *This time*. This was no general countercultural "Don't trust anyone over thirty." It was a specifically post-Shoah "J'Accuse" leveled by young Jews against their Jewish parents for allegedly dithering while a third of all Jews on earth were being murdered. By performing Jewish difference in the streets, they critiqued what they saw as an older Jewish politics of fear and quiescence and demonstrated that they would take a more vocal, oppositional approach to the defense of Jewish rights and Jewish lives.[19] That they did this in the first half of the 1960s positions them in the early wave of multicultural politics, helping to shape the American environment, not merely reflect it.

These enabling contexts created possibility but determined nothing. To understand how holiday-centered ritual mobilizations became a centerpiece of the Soviet Jewry movement's mass mobilization efforts, it is not enough to invoke a zeitgeist. We have to trace the actual process of tactical innovation itself. When we do this, we see that two paths converged to produce the systematic mobilization of holiday rituals. One took holiday symbols out of the home and synagogue and placed them in the streets. The other moved in the opposite direction, bringing politics off the streets and into home and synagogue holiday observances.

TAKING RITUAL TO THE STREETS

Student Struggle for Soviet Jewry introduced and popularized the movement's holiday-themed street protests. Its leaders developed their approach by fusing two lines of mobilization that at first were only loosely coupled: (1) the use of holidays as scheduling anchors and (2) the use of pageantry to engage demonstrators and draw news cameras.

SSSJ looked on holidays as useful scheduling resources from the outset. Jacob (Yaakov) Birnbaum launched the Student Struggle at Columbia University on Monday, April 27, 1964. Four days later, the group assembled seven hundred demonstrators (some say one thousand) outside the Soviet Mission to the United Nations. They could have given themselves more time to plan, but Friday was May 1—May Day, International Workers' Solidarity Day—and they found something delicious in protesting the USSR on its national holiday. They also saw something useful. By marching on May Day, SSSJ dangled a timely hook before the news media.[20] The *New York Times* bit: "For the most part, Soviet officials and employees ignored the demonstration. A young boy walking past with his father asked in Russian, 'What is it all about?' The father replied, also in Russian, 'It's a First of May celebration.'"[21]

Nothing the Russian-speaking boy had seen would have indicated a May Day protest. The demonstrators made no use of the holiday's symbols or themes. Had he returned in 1971, the next time Jewish Americans gathered at the Soviet Mission on May 1, he would have heard allusions to the day: "Anti-Semitism is counter-revolutionary! . . . [The Soviets should] give genuine expression to the Socialism whose victory they are celebrating."[22] But at that first demonstration, activists did not think—or did not choose—to co-opt holiday themes for the holiday protest. Birnbaum did recognize the power of ceremony and symbolism, especially with news cameras present. He choreographed the demonstration as a solemn procession. Marchers, paired two by two (civil rights movement style) and dressed sharply in jackets and ties or long skirts (also civil rights movement style), circled back and forth in silence.[23] SSSJ national coordinator Glenn Richter explained the thinking: "We decided that . . . we'd have a silent demonstration because if the Jews in Russia were silent, so would we. That was the last time we ever made that mistake."[24]

But the marchers were not entirely silent. As in the civil rights demonstrations on which the May Day protest was modeled, the marchers intermittently broke into song. No "Internationale." No anthems of worker's solidarity. Only Hebrew chants with religious overtones, songs meaningful to the Jewish American students who marched. "Ani Ma'amin": "I believe with perfect faith in the coming of the Messiah, even though he may tarry." *Times* coverage explained that this hymn of Jewish spiritual resistance had been "sung by Jews being marched to Nazi concentration camps and gas chambers."[25] (Later, Birnbaum would encourage songwriters to compose original protest songs, one of which, Rabbi Shlomo Carlebach's 1965 "Am Yisroel Chai" [The Jewish people lives], became the movement's anthem.)[26]

The May Day rally displayed embryonic features of the dramatic, theatricalized, protest-as-religious-ceremony style of demonstrating that SSSJ would make its hallmark. In its solemn mode, the approach owed mainly to Birnbaum, a religiously observant Jew who believed with his own perfect faith that the fight for Soviet Jewry bore religious significance and who expressed this faith in grandiloquent language redolent with Judaic meaning. (Whereas other partners planning an April 1966 march referred blandly to a "Passover Youth Protest," Birnbaum only ever called it a "great *Geulah* March," invoking the Hebrew term for messianic redemption.) Richter was the main architect of SSSJ's second mode of ceremonialized protest—the decidedly nonsolemn playful mode that included birthday parties for Soviet leaders and black-robed Halloween exorcisms. "A lot of the stuff was not terribly thought through, except Yaakov in the beginning who insisted on the use of Jewish symbols," Richter said decades later. "We basically just blundered through and found [whether] things worked.... You did all this on the fly, you know. There wasn't a ritual committee."[27]

As Birnbaum planned SSSJ's second and third demonstrations, he turned the mobilizing gaze more deliberately onto religious ceremony and symbolism. In June 1964, he co-opted religious self-mortification by organizing an interfaith "fast-in" at the Soviet UN Mission. In August, to press the Democratic National Convention to mention Soviet Jewry in its platform, he staged a prayer-service-cum-protest-rally on the boardwalk outside the Atlantic City Convention Center.[28] Soviet Jewry activists got their plank: "We deplore Communist oppression of Jews and other minorities."[29] Meanwhile, the convention refused to seat the Mississippi Freedom Democratic Party's racially integrated delegation.

The Atlantic City prayer rally was the Soviet Jewry movement's first fully scripted Judaic protest ceremony. It cobbled together a hodgepodge of traditional rituals. Demonstrators recited psalms. They listened to a cantor chant a version of the El Moleh "God Full of Mercy" memorial prayer—reworked to reference "the fine flower of Russian Jewry who perished under communism."[30] Most significant to the future course of ritualization, SSSJ debuted the ram's horn as an instrument of public protest.[31] The shofar is a symbol with many meanings. In the Bible, the sound of the ram's horn accompanies the revelation at Sinai. Its blast rallies the Israelites to battle. It helps bring down the walls of Jericho. In Jewish eschatology, the shofar's sound will herald the End of Days. It also appears in the annual holiday cycle. At the Jewish New Year, Rosh Hashanah, worshippers sound the ram's horn as a wake-up call to the insufficiently penitent soul, as a wordless plea to God for salvation, and more. SSSJ used the shofar to evoke many of these traditional meanings—wake-up call, battle cry, prayer for redemption, and so on. When the group first deployed it at the Atlantic City rally, Rosh Hashanah was just two weeks away. Its proximity informed Birnbaum's thinking. His script introduced the shofar by mentioning the upcoming holiday: "The Jewish New Year is drawing near. During those days the ancient ram's horn, the 'shofar,' is sounded. It is the 4000-year old symbol of the call to conscience and the hope for redemption and freedom." Birnbaum structured the shofar blasts per a formula familiar from the Rosh Hashanah service—a long *tekiah* note followed by three medium-length *shevarim* notes, then nine short *teruah* bursts, concluding with a single extra-long *tekiah gedolah* blast.[32] He could have chosen other rhythms, but the holiday channeled his thinking.[33]

Even though Birnbaum recognized that he could incorporate seasonal rituals into protest ceremonies, SSSJ was not yet strategically building demonstrations around Jewish holidays. The Student Struggle's Atlantic City demonstration was not a Rosh Hashanah rally. That the Democrats scheduled their convention two weeks before the Jewish New Year was a coincidence. SSSJ capitalized on it. Throwing shofar blowing into the mix alongside all-season rituals like psalm recitations and the El Moleh memorial prayer was just part of the eclectic approach Birnbaum was taking as he explored ways to craft protest as religiously inflected guerrilla theater. A shofar here, a psalm there.[34] The main thing was to communicate through drama and symbolism.[35] Birnbaum stated his intentions explicitly. Instead of letting the performance speak for itself, the prayer service script directed protesters and journalists to pay attention to the stagecraft: "These two themes, the CALL TO CONSCIENCE and HOPE FOR REDEMPTION, are the themes of our service this evening and *they will now be dramatically symbolized* by the sounding of the shofar."[36]

In April 1965, SSSJ brought the shofars back to the streets for its next ritualized protest and largest demonstration yet—the "Jericho March." Behind seven prayer-shawled rabbis bearing seven Torah scrolls, seven students lifted seven shofars to their lips. Their seven blasts set three thousand marchers parading a two-block radius around the Soviet UN Mission. "Break down the walls," the placards declared. SSSJ reprised the Jericho March a month later at the Soviet embassy in Washington, DC, and again in New York the following April.[37]

The Jericho Marches are notable not only for what they did—reworking Judaic motifs into a pageant of ritualized protest was quickly becoming SSSJ's signature style—but also for what they did not do. They did not ground the protest ritual in the proximate holiday. The April 1965 Jericho March took place two weeks before Passover. The May 1965 march took place on the minor festival of Lag Ba`Omer. SSSJ drew no themes or rituals from those holidays. Instead they drew from a biblical story that had no connection to either. When SSSJ restaged the "Jericho style" encircling during the 1966 Passover rally, the abrupt shift from the book of Exodus to the book of Joshua was a religious non sequitur.[38]

No Jewish holiday commemorates the Battle of Jericho. Perhaps if one did, Jericho's symbolism might have been confined to it. But because the Joshua story was not associated with any particular time of year, it was equally available for use at any time. This free-floating availability was true of another symbol, the eternal light, or *ner tamid*—a lamp that hangs perpetually lit in the synagogue, symbolizing God's eternal presence, God's everlasting faithfulness to the Jewish people, and the Jewish people's enduring faith in God. Taking up the aesthetic of ritualized protest that SSSJ had pioneered, the American Jewish Conference on Soviet Jewry co-opted the *ner tamid*, moving it out of the synagogue and into Washington's Lafayette Park for the AJCSJ's first ritualized protest. The September 1965 "Eternal Light Vigil" drew ten thousand participants. It included shofar blasts and the lighting of a giant torch, the eponymous eternal light. Inscribed "The House of Israel Shall Endure," the torch remained lit for one week. In vigils across the United States, Jewish communities reprised the ceremonial lighting in subsequent years.[39]

Ritualized protest was spreading in 1965. The AJCSJ was not the only group to take up the practice. Two weeks after the Jericho March, New York chapters of Conservative Judaism's United Synagogue Youth staged a prayer rally at the United Nations, held during Passover at the United Nations Plaza. The program invoked the holiday in its title, "Festival of Freedom March," and included a seder song, "Adir Hu," near the end. Beyond this, however, the prayer service drew no language or symbols from Passover.[40]

As for SSSJ, between August and December 1965, it started refining its ritualization of protest to integrate calendar and content more tightly. In August, it staged a Tisha B'Av vigil in Rockaway Park.[41] In December, it paraded a twelve-foot-tall, eight-foot-wide, two-hundred-pound Hanukkah menorah through Central Park. The Hanukkah rally marked the first time that SSSJ specifically built a holiday-themed protest—scheduled on the holiday, named for the holiday, and drawing its symbols from the holiday. Staged on the first night of Hanukkah, the "Menorah March and Rally" drew one thousand participants. It was not entirely beholden to a Festival of Lights theme, however. Marchers carried signs demanding, "Let Our People Bake Matzos"—a Passover reference. They also sang a verse from Isaiah, "Nation shall not lift up sword against nation"—an odd choice considering Hanukkah's celebration of the sword-bearing Judah Maccabee.[42] Still, even as it continued SSSJ's symbolic eclecticism, the Menorah March marked a significant step in the development of ritualized holiday protest as a mass mobilization tactic. After the Hanukkah rally, SSSJ and other movement organizations increasingly anchored ritualized protests in the Jewish holiday calendar. In April 1966, SSSJ co-organized New York's first community-wide Passover-themed protest. In December, it reprised the Hanukkah-themed demonstration. In August 1967, it conducted its second Tisha B'Av protest fast. In October, it helped stage the American movement's first Simchat Torah dance rally. Ritualized protests on these holidays spread in the following years.

EXODUS MARCHES AND PROTEST SEDERS

For the earliest holiday-themed protests between 1965 and 1967, activists enlisted some festivals more than others. No single logic or grand strategy governed their preference for Hanukkah in the winter, Passover in the spring, Tisha B'Av in the summer, and Simchat Torah in the fall. If their criterion had been importance in the traditional schema, then why not mobilize Passover's companions, the other two biblical pilgrimage festivals—Shavuot and Sukkot?[43] If the criterion had been popularity, then why center fast-day protests on Tisha B'Av rather than the more widely observed Yom Kippur?[44] (The Day of Atonement's work restrictions were not an issue: Passover was work restricted, yet activists found ways to navigate around that constraint.) Maybe the one-holiday-per-season approach suggests limited capacity, but Soviet Jewry groups were organizing many nonholiday demonstrations at the same time, and in any case, they could have chosen different holidays for each season had they wanted to. We could argue that activists found it easiest to draw thematic connections between these four holidays and the situation of Soviet Jews. But why underestimate their intelligence and creativity? This was a movement that even found ways to enlist Hallmark holidays into the cause: in 1975, when the Soviets granted exit visas to parents but not to their children, SSSJ protested with an "Unhappy Father's Day" rally.[45]

Of the first four Jewish holidays in the Soviet Jewry campaign's calendar, Passover emerged as primus inter pares when it became the focus for community-wide rallies in New York two years in a row. In early 1966, a coalition of New York–area Jewish youth groups, including SSSJ, started planning a joint action.[46] They considered Sabbath-related programs and a protest fast on the Fast of Esther but decided instead to stage a rally and vigil for Passover.[47] Their 1966 Passover Youth Protest could have been a blip in movement culture, but coalition members regrouped as the New York Coordinating Committee for Soviet Jewry (NYCCSJ) for another Passover demonstration in 1967.[48] Along with the AJCSJ's 1966 launch of an annual "Matzoh of Hope" ritual for home seders, discussed below, the New York Jewish community's decision to make Passover the anchor of the primary Soviet Jewry demonstrations in the largest Jewish population center in the world helped elevate the themes, language, and symbols of the Pesach holiday as a master frame or leitmotif in Soviet Jewry movement culture.

Birnbaum volunteered to coordinate the twelve-thousand-person 1966 Passover Youth Protest (which SSSJ called the *Geulah* [Redemption] March). He took SSSJ's template—dramatically choreographed protest ceremonies built from a potpourri of Jewish symbols and generic signifiers of ritual solemnity—and added overt references to Passover. He recycled the "Jericho style" encirclings and "eternal flame" lightings from earlier demonstrations. But apropos of Pesach, he had columns of marchers pass through a parting crowd, a "symbolic re-enactment of the Crossing of the Red Sea."[49] The following year, Jewish groups staged Passover marches in eighteen cities across the United States. SSSJ provided advice and support, including the recommendation that organizers open their rallies with "blasts on the shofar"—a ritual object not associated with Passover observances.[50]

The NYCCSJ's 1967 Passover rally—a twenty-four-hour vigil outside the United Nations organized in partnership with the American Jewish Conference on Soviet Jewry—incorporated less Passover symbolism than in the previous year, mostly just words. "During the Festival of Freedom, Demand Free Expression for Jewish Life in Russia," the publicity poster declared. Organizers avoided any reference to the biblical Exodus, since the AJCSJ was not yet demanding free emigration. (On this, more below.) For ritualization, the vigil drew mainly from sources other than Passover—an end-of-Sabbath (*havdalah*) service, a "dramatic program [with] music composed for Soviet Jewry," and once more, an eternal flame. In a show of interfaith support, the program concluded with the ringing of church bells.[51] Not all was high ritual. Politicians made speeches. Comedian Henny Youngman, king of the one-liners, gave a "dramatic reading."[52]

In 1968, the NYCCSJ focused the ritualization more precisely on Passover itself. Instead of giving protesters whiplash by careening from one Jewish symbol to another—shofar, eternal light, Battle of Jericho, crossing of the Red Sea—it tethered the protest to Pesach's canonical rite, the seder. Sidelining SSSJ, the Coordinating Committee engaged Hollywood screenwriter Alvin Boretz (who would go on to write episodes of the television police drama *Kojak*) to design the program. For the 1968 protest outside the Soviet UN Mission, he wrote a script that drew from the Passover liturgy. Forty presidents from the Coordinating Committee's member agencies recited blessings over candles and wine; lifted the matzoh; asked the traditional question, "Why is this night different from all other nights?"; and chanted *"V'hee she'omdoh,"* a paragraph in the haggadah liturgy affirming faith in the Almighty's promise to liberate Israel from oppression. Mostly, however, they recited pledges of resistance; quoted long passages from Elie Wiesel's Soviet travelogue, *The Jews of Silence*; and declaimed tedious monologues about Jewish life under the Bolsheviks: "Let us take special note that the [ethnic] Germans in the Soviet Union, [in contrast to Jews,] have within the last ten years built up, with Government help, a vast network of radio and television broadcasts."[53]

Using a seder for political expression was not exactly a new idea. Early twentieth-century Bundists in Poland and Labor Zionist kibbutzniks in Palestine had written secular haggadahs to celebrate socialist ideals.[54] Before the Soviet government dismantled the Communist Party's Jewish Section and exiled or executed its leaders, the Jews of the Yevsektsia held "Red Seders" that called for enemies of the people—rabbis, Bundists, and Zionists—to be burned just as leaven (*khometz*) is consigned to the flames in the pre-Pesach purging.[55] In the US, Jews translated and illustrated haggadahs to celebrate allegiances to their American home.[56]

Likewise, after Soviet Jewry groups had introduced political seders as a mode of political expression, other Jewish movements followed suit. In 1969, a year after the first Soviet Jewry protest seder, Rabbi Arthur Waskow marked the anniversary of Martin Luther King Jr.'s assassination by leading a New Left "Freedom Seder" before news cameras in a Black church in Washington, DC.[57] Jewish women's groups introduced feminist seders in 1971, publishing the first feminist haggadah in 1974.[58] Cross-pollination between the movements fed back into the later evolution of Soviet Jewry movement seders.[59] SSSJ and other groups adopted Waskow's term "Freedom Seder," for instance.[60] But this was a phenomenon of the 1970s. The New Left and feminist seders of 1969, 1971, and onward did not retroactively influence Soviet Jewry activists' invention of the tactic in 1968. At that moment, they were operating on their own, with no examples of political seders from contemporaneous movements to draw from.

Emerging neither out of a deep Jewish political tradition nor out of an American Jewish countercultural zeitgeist but out of a specific line of tactical innovation that SSSJ had brought to the field, Boretz's Soviet Jewry seder created something radically new. It did not just use the Passover ritual as a medium of political expression as did the other movements. It transformed the seder into a vehicle of nonviolent direct action, moving it into political opponents' space, and staging it there as a guerrilla theater protest rally. This was without precedent. It was also without imitation. Feminists set their seders in homes and community organizations. Waskow ensconced his New Left Freedom Seder in a friendly church basement. Soviet Jewry groups, in contrast, took the paschal rite straight to the target's doorposts.[61]

The Student Struggle returned to ritualized Passover protest in 1969, taking up Boretz's approach and staging its own "symbolic Seder of Redemption" at the Soviet UN Mission. (Like Boretz's seder, SSSJ's also predated Waskow's New Left version.) As described in this chapter's opening, Birnbaum's first protest seder swapped the Hollywood screenwriter's speechifying for action-heavy symbol play in line with SSSJ's theatrical approach to ritualizing protest. But the Student Struggle also broke with its earlier practice by not inventing a wholly new ceremony like the Jericho encircling. Instead, it worked within the seder's existing template.[62] Hewing close to the traditional rite, the SSSJ seder added commentary about Soviet Jews as participants raised the ancient symbols and recited the traditional verses. This approach spread through the movement, becoming the standard model for Soviet Jewry protest seders through the 1990s.

SOVIET JEWRY SEDERS: MEDIUM AND MESSAGE

The story of the Israelites' redemption from slavery to freedom has been paradigmatic for modern liberation movements throughout the West.[63] For Jews, the Exodus is not just one Bible tale among many. It is their origin story, the canonical account of their birth as a people in relationship with their God.[64] Whereas Christians mainly engage the Exodus narrative by reading the Bible, Jews engage it primarily by performing an annual ritual of reenactment and reexperience. Before a table set with symbolic foods, each Jewish household symbolically passes from slavery to freedom not by reading the Bible but by reciting the haggadah. This thousand-year-old script for the Passover meal mediates Jewish encounters with the Exodus story. In the United States, seder attendance is one of the most popular Jewish holiday observances. In the early 1970s, more than four out of five American Jews could be found each April around a seder table.[65] The ritual is conducted in homes, no rabbi required. Jews read the text themselves and therefore know it well, or at least well enough. The haggadah's words, stories, symbols, and songs give them a shared language for speaking about the Exodus in a distinctly Jewish, rather than "Judeo-Christian," register. As a result, when Soviet Jewry activists began using the haggadah to craft Passover protests, they found it a rich, malleable, and well-known resource.

Protest seders generally unfolded like this: Outside Soviet diplomatic offices (or elsewhere, in cities that had no Soviet representation), and with news media present, organizers would set up tables with seder plates, traditional symbolic foods, and photographs of refuseniks or other visual references to Soviet Jewry. The crowd would stand (not recline as is customary in the traditional seder), and the leaders would conduct an abridged version of the haggadah's ceremony interspersed with musical selections. The seders were conducted mostly in translation, with their symbols explicitly linked to Soviet Jewry and their traditional words adapted to express new meanings. In North America and the UK, activists confined their adaptations to English, seldom revising the Hebrew or Aramaic. Alterations played on the source text, which was sometimes recited to anchor the wordplay and sometimes left implicit on the assumption that participants would catch the references. For a kingdom-wide Freedom Seder campaign in 1981, British activists took a passage praising God for delivering the ancient Israelites and revised it to affirm their religious obligation to work toward a modern-day deliverance of Soviet Jews. First, they recited the original text:

> Therefore it is our duty to thank, praise, laud, glorify, exalt, honour, bless, extol, and adore Him, who made all these miracles for our fathers and for us; He brought us from slavery to freedom, from sorrow to rejoicing, from mourning into feasting, from darkness to light, and from slavery to redemption.

Later in the seder, they recited this alteration:

> Therefore it is our duty to protest, to speak out, to bear witness, to demonstrate, to intercede on their behalf, that they may be brought from slavery to freedom, from sorrow to rejoicing, from mourning to feasting, from darkness to light, from slavery to redemption.[66]

Other juxtapositions used echoing and contrast to ironic effect. SSSJ's 1982 seder recited the traditional story of Rabbi Eliezer to set up a distorted funhouse mirror version:

> A tale is told of Rabbi Eliezer, Rabbi Joshua, Rabbi Elazar ben Azaryah, Rabbi Akiba, and Rabbi Tarphon. They were reclining in Bnei Brak and discussing the exodus from Egypt throughout the night, until their pupils came to them and said, "Masters, the time has come to recite the morning Shema [prayer]."
>
> And a tale is told of our Soviet brothers. They will be reclining and discussing the exodus from Egypt and the hope of another exodus, an exodus in our time, from Russia, throughout the night. But they will discuss the Passover in fear, not of their pupils coming, but of the KGB.[67]

Adaptations of the seder's traditional "Four Questions," on the other hand, diverged further from the source text.[68] As this central moment in the haggadah liturgy is structured to raise and answer questions, it lent itself to didactic pronouncements about whatever aspects of the Soviet Jewish situation activists wanted to highlight. Consider how different these adaptations of the third question are from each other as well as from the traditional text, "On all other nights we do not dip our food even once, so why on this night are we dipping our food twice?"

> Why is it that the Jews of Russia are made afraid to celebrate the festival of Passover?
> —New York Coordinating Committee for Soviet Jewry, 1968[69]

> Why can we not hear our language—or see it written—as others do?
> —Queens Council for Soviet Jewry, 1975[70]

> At all other sedarim we drink wine, here we drink water. [Why?]
> —National Council for Soviet Jewry of the United Kingdom and Ireland, 1981[71]

> Is this a propitious time for saving Soviet Jews?
> —Bay Area Council for Soviet Jews, 1985[72]

Here, only the 1981 British seder alluded to the traditional formulation "on all other nights." None used the notion of dipping or the poetic structure of "not once . . . why twice" as linguistic hooks.

The traditional seder uses foods as symbols to anchor the retelling of the Exodus.[73] Freedom Seders spun new commentaries around the symbolic foods, connecting current events with core religious narrative:

> The injunction is to remember the themes of oppression and liberation in Passover, but to Anatoly Sharansky, now in the solitary confinement cells of the Perm labor camp, it's real indeed. As we taste the bitter herbs, his entire life is bitterness.
> —SSSJ, 1981[74]

> Reminiscent of mortar and bricks, the charosis [chopped apples, nuts, and wine] suggests the oppressive slave labor that was forced on our ancestors.
>   Soviet Jewry application: The forced labor which is associated with the charosis, reminds us of the individuals currently in labor camps, on trumped up charges, for the "crime" of teaching Hebrew.
> —Bay Area Council for Soviet Jews, 1985[75]

If Soviet diplomats saw or heard any of these proceedings—the venetian blinds at their UN mission were usually shut[76]—the details would have been lost on them. In the seder's content, the protesters were speaking to themselves, glossing minutiae that carried emotional weight for them as Jews versed in the seder ritual. But these meanings were not meant for the Russians. To communicate to them, the low-resolution message sufficed: the seder was a stand-in for Jewish religion and culture generally. Russian diplomats should see American Jews performing Jewish rituals as an act of defiance. At the conclusion of the seders, however, protesters sometimes offered a more pointed message. Shifting the signifying power of the ritual items away from their metaphoric meanings toward their concrete materiality, the protesters used the seder objects to physically invade Soviet space. Children slid the matzoh and bitter herbs through the gates of Soviet compounds. Demonstrators dropped haggadahs on the doorsteps. They placed seder plates at the entryways.[77] The protesters knew that diplomatic offices were their government's sovereign territory. Violating that space was deliberately provocative. In its final symbolism, the Freedom Seder matzoh lay on Soviet ground as an accusation and as a reminder of the protesters' readiness to fight.

In this combativeness, we see the conceptual innovation that distinguished Soviet Jewry movement Freedom Seders from most other modern Jewish political seders. The wordplay and reinterpretation of symbols were commonplace. But the idea to reposition the seder as nonviolent direct action was new.[78] Of course, staging seders as guerrilla theater in front of Soviet consulates did not preclude also conducting Soviet Jewry–themed seders inside American Jewish communal spaces. This happened too. In this mode, activists operated in a more well-established Jewish political tradition. Bringing Soviet Jewry seders into the synagogue blunted their function as vehicles of protest, but they retained their potency as agents of consciousness-raising and as rituals of recommitment. This was how the first Soviet Jewry–themed seder functioned. In 1966, two years before activists came up with the idea of staging a Soviet Jewry seder as a protest, a school assembly at the Hebrew Academy of Cleveland used a model seder to teach children about the Passover rituals and about Soviet antisemitism at the same time. The script, paternalistic in the extreme, portrayed American Jewish children welcoming Russian Jewish children as guests for Pesach. Assuming the imaginary Russian Jews to be ignorant of the holiday, it positioned the American children as experts who could teach the Russians how to conduct a seder:

> NARR. 1: Here, sit next to me and I will help you follow in the *haggadah*. First, we make *kiddush*, and even a kindergarten child can do that.
> KINDERGARTEN: *Kiddush* [blessing over wine]. . . .
> RUSSIAN: We don't have any Jewish schools and our children know only what their parents teach them secretly. And if we want wine for Pesach we have to make it ourselves.[79]

American Jewish activists in the 1960s realized that if they wanted protests for Pesach, they, too, would have to make it themselves. They did not create the Freedom Seder in one fell swoop, nor did they create it by lifting a ready-made template from earlier generations, nor by channeling the zeitgeist. They found their way to Freedom Seders after having spent several years applying a mobilizing gaze to Soviet and Jewish holidays and to Jewish sacred symbols and rituals. As activists learned to work with Jewish sancta, explored their possibilities and potentialities as resources for protest, and honed their own aesthetic preferences for working with them in particular ways, they pushed tactical innovation down paths that channeled their work later. What began as SSSJ's ritual hodgepodge protests, not pegged to any particular holidays, evolved into the Freedom Seder first by adding Passover-themed symbolism to springtime protests, then by stripping out symbolism not associated with Passover and anchoring the protest in the Pesach haggadah's template for ritual action. As the originators gained press coverage for their seders and circulated their haggadahs to other groups, the mobilization tactic spread movement-wide.[80]

TAKING ACTIVISM TO THE HOME: "THE MATZOH OF HOPE"

In 1965, as the Student Struggle was making Jewish ritual a medium of protest out in the streets, the American Jewish Conference on Soviet Jewry started looking to family seders to bring activism into people's homes. It was not the first time Jewish groups had inserted the Soviet Jewish issue into religious observances. Synagogues around the world prayed for the welfare of Soviet Jews at Yom Kippur services in 1964.[81] Nor was the AJCSJ the first activist organization to cast a mobilizing gaze on the seder ritual. In 1964, an Israeli grassroots group, Ma'oz, encouraged people to set an empty chair at the seder table to symbolize the absence of Soviet Jews. New York's Park Avenue Synagogue took up the recommendation for its 1965 congregational seder.[82] Whether the AJCSJ knew of or was influenced by the Ma'oz initiative is hard to say. The following year, the AJCSJ introduced a new Passover ritual—the "Matzoh of Oppression," later renamed the "Matzoh of Hope." It became one of the movement's most widely adopted and longest-lasting ceremonial practices. Along with the Freedom Seders, the Matzoh of Hope elevated Passover as the central rallying moment in the Soviet Jewry campaign's holiday calendar.

The AJCSJ's choice to take on ritual creation is surprising. The twenty-four Jewish organizations that created the Conference established it to coordinate, support, and publicize their work, not to launch initiatives of its own. Moreover, while its religious constituents, like Orthodox Judaism's Rabbinical Council of America (RCA), typically worked in the ritual sphere, its secular members, like the socialist Labor Zionist Movement, typically did not. On the other hand, because the AJCSJ brought congregational unions together with the leading Jewish American mass membership organizations and umbrella agencies, it could activate networks reaching into every local Jewish community in the country. So when the AJCSJ, under the leadership of RCA president Rabbi Israel Miller, recommended in December 1965 "that every Seder should set aside a matzoh to symbolize the injustices imposed on Soviet Jewry and that an appropriate interpretive statement from the American Jewish Conference on Soviet Jewry be read during the Seder service," it could reasonably assume that millions of American Jews would at least hear—if not heed—the call.[83]

The AJCSJ launched the "Matzoh of Oppression" campaign in 1966, selling "most attractive" printed copies of the statement to Jewish organizations at $6.00 for every thousand.[84] The organizations circulated these to their members. In 1967, the AJCSJ rebranded the ritual under the more inspirational title "Matzoh of Hope." Here is the 1967 version of the text, written by Albert Chernin of the National Community Relations Advisory Council (NCRAC):

That the Jews of the Soviet Union may know that they have not been forgotten...

The American Jewish Conference on Soviet Jewry... urges that the following statement be read at the Seder of every American Jewish household.

THIS IS THE MATZOH OF HOPE...

This matzoh, which we set aside as a symbol of hope for the 3 million Jews of the Soviet Union, reminds us of the indestructible link that exists between us.

As we observe this festival of freedom, we know that Soviet Jews are not free to learn of their Jewish past, to hand it down to their children. They cannot learn the languages of their fathers. They cannot teach their children to be the teachers, the rabbis of future generations.

They can only sit in silence and become invisible. We shall be their voice, and our voices shall be joined by thousands of men of conscience aroused by the wrongs suffered by Soviet Jews. Then shall they know that they have not been forgotten, and they that sit in darkness shall yet see a great light.[85]

As the seder ritual traditionally sets aside three pieces of matzoh, the AJCSJ innovation was colloquially known as "the fourth matzoh." Out of respect for Orthodox religious law, however, the AJCSJ was careful not to suggest the addition of an extra matzoh and never specified whether the matzoh to be set aside for Soviet Jews was one of the obligatory three or a halachically dubious fourth. Nonetheless, the designation of a particular piece of matzoh as distinctly symbolic was the key innovation—or one half of the key innovation. The other half was the attempt to enshrine the practice nationwide as an annual tradition with a relatively fixed text.[86]

There is no way of knowing how many households performed the new ritual. Estimates from movement sources ranged from "tens of thousands"[87] (probably a conservative estimate) to "all American Jewish seders" (definitely an overcount).[88] Whatever the true number, the AJCSJ considered its campaign a success. Reviewing the 1966 debut, the AJCSJ estimated that "nearly one million copies of the statement were reprinted in various forms." The Conference alone had sold 175,000 copies to organizations like Hadassah (31,000), the Reform movement's Union of American Hebrew Congregations (15,000), and the San Francisco Jewish Community Relations Council (15,000). The new ritual took root and lasted into the 1990s. In 1978, the Greater New York Conference on Soviet Jewry (GNYCSJ) circulated more than one million copies. Synagogues and Jewish community centers posted the text in their buildings, reprinted it in their bulletins, and mailed it to their members. Commercially published haggadahs of the 1970s and '80s—including a 1972 Soviet Jewry–themed art book haggadah—contained the AJCSJ text or original variants. Advertisements promoted the statement in newspapers. Many of those papers—including the *Atlanta Constitution*, *Boston Globe*, *New York Times*, and *Washington Post*—also covered it or editorialized about it. Supermarket chains provided free copies in the Passover food aisle. After all this, if there were still any Jewish Americans who had managed to avoid hearing about the Matzoh of Hope, activists found a way to place the statement on their seder tables too. They convinced Horowitz Margareten, a leading commercial matzoh producer, to print it on its Passover matzoh boxes.[89]

Activists continually revised the Matzoh of Hope text to keep up with changes in the Soviet Jewish situation and in the American movement. Restrictions on matzoh baking featured prominently in the original 1966 version: "Most [Soviet Jews] cannot have matzoh on their Seder tables tonight. Conceive of Passover without matzoh—without that visible reminder of our flight from slavery."[90] One year later, the AJCSJ dropped this language due to the "increased availability of matzoh in the Soviet Union."[91] More substantial revisions came in 1970, reflecting changes not only in Russia but also in the AJCSJ's policy goals. As Soviet Jews began agitating for emigration to Israel and word of this filtered out to the US, the Conference replaced the paternalistic "They can only sit in silence and become invisible. We shall be their voice" with a more collaborative statement: "As their voices rise in Jewish affirmation and protest, we add our voices to theirs." Only then did the AJCSJ revise the Matzoh of Hope text to state outright that Soviet Jews were "not free to leave," reversing its earlier position that calling for emigration rights was unrealistic and impolitic.[92] Versions in Yiddish and Hebrew appeared in 1970.[93] In 1972, the AJCSJ responded to a Kremlin crackdown on emigration activists by adding a paragraph "remember[ing] with bitterness the scores of Jewish prisoners of conscience who sought to live as Jews and struggled to leave for Israel—the land of our fathers—but now languish in bondage in Soviet labor camps."[94]

After the AJCSJ popularized the use of a matzoh ritual to mobilize American Jews through their Passover seders, tactical development continued more democratically. Others began altering the Matzoh of Hope ceremony or creating new versions of their own. The real power to define the ritual rested with the seders' hosts. Each household could perform the Matzoh of Hope rite as it saw fit. Few norms governed the new practice. Beyond the call to set aside a piece of matzoh and read the text, the AJCSJ never specified precisely when and how in the course of the seder to perform the ritual.

Those seeking guidance could find it in the era's commercially published haggadahs. Some offered variants on the new ritual. (As with Horowitz Margareten, the private sector played a role here, too, in developing and diffusing Soviet Jewry movement tactics.) Alfred Kolatch's 1972 *The Family Seder: A Traditional Passover Haggadah for the Modern Home* gave instructions for including the decidedly nontraditional Matzoh of Hope alongside the equally novel empty chair: "As a tangible expression of our concern for the plight of Soviet Jewry . . . we now place one more chair at our Seder table. Before this Seat of Honor, we place a full table setting, and on the plate we place one whole *matzo* which we call the Matzo of Hope."[95]

Kolatch did not credit the AJCSJ or Ma'oz—a masking of origins that made the rituals seem like naturally emerging folk customs. He also instructed celebrants to recite a different text from the AJCSJ's: "This Seat of Honor and this Matzo of Hope . . . are here to remind us that although 35 centuries have passed since the Pharaohs conspired to destroy the Jewish people, enlightened and scientifically sophisticated nations like the Union of Soviet Socialist Republics have not yet learned the lesson of history."[96] The text appeared under a graphically indistinct header on a page of its own, sandwiched between the instructions for eating the last piece of matzoh (*tzafun*, the *afikoman*) and those for reciting the concluding grace (*barech*). This was a liminal placement, after the main action but before the formal conclusion of the liturgy. The formatting and placement not only indicated the nontraditional status of the Soviet Jewry ritual but also made the page appear to be an insert that had no predetermined place in the haggadah's precisely ordered text. Seder leaders could turn to it whenever they chose.

THIS IS THE MATZOH OF HOPE

On Wings of Freedom, published in 1989 by the Jewish college student organization Hillel, inserted its adaptation of the ritual after the point in the seder when the matzoh is first presented as "the bread of affliction." Hillel's approach pulled in opposite directions. On one hand, it presented the section as optional and thus made clear that the ritual was not traditional. On the other, it wrote in a traditionalizing style that moved the ritual closer to the realm of the timeless. It spoke in poetry, not prose; exchanged the litany of policy critiques for metaphors and allusions; expanded the scope of concern beyond the Soviet Union alone; dropped the concretizing plural, *Jews*, in favor of the definite singular, *The Jew* (an old anthropology trick for transforming real human beings into imaginary symbols); and steeped the poem in the language of messianic redemption.

> OPTIONAL DIRECTIONS: A person sitting near an empty chair holds up a piece of matzah and reads the following:
>
> > This is the bread for the person who is not here:
> > The Jew in the Soviet Union, learning Torah behind closed curtains,
> > Savoring hidden freedom like matzah covered by the cloth,
> > Waiting, like the afikomon, to be redeemed;
> > The Jew in hostile Arab lands, in impoverished Ethiopia. . . .
> > Let us look not only at the empty chair
> > But at the full plate of matzot,
> > The plate full of hope that freedom is not a fairytale,
> > But a tale as real as it is old.[97]

AD HOC EXPANSION

By fall 1967, activists had taken Passover, Hanukkah, and Tisha B'Av out to the streets and had brought the Soviet Jewry movement into Passover observances in the home. Having recognized holidays as resources and having gained some practical experience mobilizing them, movement organizations were positioned to expand the tactic if they chose. Most of the Jewish holiday calendar remained untapped. In 1967 and 1968, activists added holiday mobilizations for Simchat Torah and Rosh Hashanah. No grand strategy governed the choice of these two holidays over others in the Jewish calendar. New information filtering out about Jewish activism in Russia inspired some of the thinking, however. Unlike the uses of Passover's, Hanukkah's, and Tisha B'Av's themes to frame the troubles of Soviet Jewry in the context of Jewish sacred history and its cosmic cycle of oppression and redemption, the mobilizations of Simchat Torah and Rosh Hashanah ignored theology to focus on a sense of shared community. Emulating Soviet Jews' embrace of Simchat Torah as a rallying moment, Western activists staged Simchat Torah rallies to demonstrate that they were part of a single worldwide movement united across Cold War borders. Rosh Hashanah campaigns to send New Year's greetings to Soviet Jews represented similar expressions of solidarity across the Iron Curtain. Both holiday mobilizations became movement mainstays through the 1980s.

SIMCHAT TORAH

Unlike Passover, whose thematic links to a freedom struggle are apparent, nothing in Simchat Torah's traditional observance would lead one to predict that this "Festival of the Rejoicing of the Torah" would become a focal point for movement activity. The holiday falls in September or October. It marks the end and immediate restarting of the annual cycle of publicly chanting the Five Books of Moses in synagogues, chapter by chapter, week by week. Rabbinic in origin, the holiday is of lesser significance than biblical-era festivals. It is grafted onto the biblically mandated Eighth Day of Assembly, Shemini Atzeret, however, and is therefore work restricted. Simchat Torah is traditionally celebrated by carrying Torah scrolls around the synagogue sanctuary seven times. Each procession, or *hakafah*, is accompanied by singing and dancing with the scrolls—*horah*-style in circles or pressed together in snaking lines. At the end of each procession, the Torah scrolls are brought back together and liturgy is recited to begin the next round. In American synagogues, it is customary to honor different categories of congregants by calling them up to carry the scrolls for each *hakafah*. Off to the sides, drinkers toast *l'chayim*. An atmosphere of festivity reigns. Neither the themes nor the observance of Simchat Torah suggests matters of oppression and salvation, although the circlings and the immediate return to chapter 1 of Genesis after reading the last word of Deuteronomy do

THIS IS THE MATZOH OF HOPE

evoke the notion that cosmic time always recurs on itself in a never-ending cycle.[98]

Soviet Jewry groups in the US first decided to mobilize Simchat Torah in 1967. They were emulating celebrations of the holiday in Moscow. By doing so, activists sought to express solidarity and demonstrate the movement's transnational character. Simchat Torah first became a time of Jewish self-assertion in Soviet synagogues and in the gulag after Stalin's death in 1953. In the mid-1960s, the holiday had become a rallying point for the rising Jewish national movement there—its annual coming-out party, drawing crowds who sang and danced in the synagogues and in the streets outside. Young people dominated the festivities. Western journalists, tourists, and travel writers pointed to this as evidence of the vitality of Jewish religious and ethnic consciousness despite efforts to smother it.[99] Jews in the West had been largely unaware of the holiday's significance to Soviet Jews until Elie Wiesel devoted two chapters to it in *The Jews of Silence*. He wrote, "They came in droves. From near and far. . . . How many were there? Ten thousand? Twenty thousand? More. . . . They filled the whole street, spilled over into courtyards, dancing and singing, dancing and singing. They seemed to hover in mid air, Chagall-like, floating above the mass of shadows and colors below, above time, climbing a Jacob's ladder that reached to the heavens, if not higher."[100]

Following the book's publication, the notion of "the one night a year when thousands of Jews admit they are Jews and dance outside Moscow's synagogue despite the watchful eye of Soviet police" became a trope in Western discourse. News correspondents reported it through the early 1970s with little variation on the theme. After the coverage subsided, it continued to figure in activists' speeches at North American Simchat Torah rallies, even into the 1990s.[101] So formative was Wiesel's imagery that it shaped American Jewish tourists' expectations and accounts of their own trips to Russia, as seen in this excerpt from a travelogue by a rabbinic spouse, Ginger Jacobs, coleading a twenty-person San Fernando Valley congregational trip in 1976:

> It is Simchat Torah. The place is Moscow. In a short time, I will be dancing with the Soviet Jews in Moscow. Is this really happening to me? For years I have danced in the streets of America in support of the Soviet Jews,

this year I am here with them. Haven't I always been here? Won't I always be here in the future?

We get out of the cab and start walking up the street to the synagogue. It is dark and I don't see anyone, where are all the people? Was Eli[e] Wiesel mistaken, was it all another dream of his? No, there they are by the thousands. . . .

I am here in Moscow. I am dancing on the street in front of the synagogue in Moscow on Simchat Torah. I will always be here, I have always been here. And I will be back here. The words that I heard in America, "dance with your brothers and sisters in Russia" never had the impact that they do now. These people are my brothers and sisters, they are me. We *are* one. Please God, we will meet next year in Jerusalem.[102]

Western activists staged their first Simchat Torah rally in October 1967, the first occurrence of the holiday after the publication of Wiesel's *The Jews of Silence*. Carrying placards that read "Justice for Jews," three thousand people danced outside Manhattan's Park East Synagogue opposite the Soviet UN Mission. The NYCCSJ, SSSJ, and the New York Board of Rabbis initiated the event. The next year, promotional efforts by the AJCSJ helped spread Simchat Torah rallies to thirty-five communities nationwide. In 1969, there were fifty-six. By 1975, over one hundred Jewish communities on every continent staged the rallies.[103]

Simchat Torah rallies were ritualized celebrations of hope—festive, youth led (at least in outward appearance), held in public spaces, short on speeches, and long on singing and dancing. Much of this drew from the holiday's traditions, but movement groups staged the programs carefully. Activists sought to "mirror" the Simchat Torah celebrations in Moscow and create a sense that this was a single mass movement spanning both sides of the Iron Curtain. The AJCSJ's chairman, Rabbi Israel Miller, spelled out the theory of practice as the Conference planned its first nationwide Simchat Torah campaign in 1968:

Tens of thousands of young Jews gather on Simchat Torah to sing and dance all night in front of the Moscow and Leningrad synagogues. To cement the bond between Jewish youth of the world and that of the Soviet Union, we are urging that simultaneous outpourings take place in front of synagogues and squares throughout our country. . . .

You have natural programmatic tools to work with: The drama of the holiday itself—October 13 is Hoshana Rabbah, with its concept of salvation . . . and, of course, Simchat Torah, with the possibilities of building programs around

(a) Hakafot—processions of faith and solidarity
(b) speakers on the *plight* of Soviet Jewry
(c) dancing and singing, with youth & community participation
(d) utilizing open areas in front of synagogues, community centers, *public* squares and parks

Programs and rallies to mirror this Moscow event will undoubtedly encourage Soviet youth to continue to express their will to be Jews in spite of religious and cultural starvation by the Soviet government.[104]

A month later, the AJCSJ circulated even more detailed recommendations at a three-day retreat for Jewish youth groups. First on the twelve-bullet-point list was a call for "youth participation . . . in the forefront of all community committee pre-planning." Other items detailed the organization of dancing:

- Plant people in the key locations . . . to keep up spirit.
- Aside from the basic Hora, choose fairly simple-step dances for *large groups* . . . such as "Mayim" and "Hine Ma'tov." Avoid complicated "Dapka"-like step dances.[105]

Another bullet point emphasized the importance of constructing the rally as a ritual, keeping the profane at bay while sacralizing behavior through ritualization, including a ritual reading of Wiesel's text:

- Include *some* speeches, but try to keep them fairly short. And couple speeches with *ceremony*—possibly with appropriate readings, i.e., excerpts from Eli[e] Wiesel's book "Jews of Silence" describing the Simchat Torah celebration in the Soviet Union.[106]

In Simchat Torah, activists found a relatively unclaimed moment in the Jewish calendar. For American Jews, this was a minor holiday. It wrapped up a fall festival season dominated by Rosh Hashanah, Yom Kippur, and Sukkot. Inspired by the example of Soviet Jews, activists seized the holiday for their movement, raising it to a prominence in the American Jewish folk calendar that it had not attained before and has not since. In the 1970s and '80s, Simchat Torah stood alongside Passover as the holiday most associated with the Soviet Jewry movement. But activists utilized the two holidays differently. They used Passover's traditional themes to situate Soviet Jewish hardship and American Jewish activism in a deeper Jewish past and in their religion's eternally recurring cosmic cycle of Jewish oppression and redemption. In Simchat Torah mobilizations, traditional themes, canonical narratives, and rabbinic cosmologies were irrelevant. Instead, the dance rallies drew attention to contemporary practices in the Soviet Union—folk customs firmly situated in the historical present. They tapped sociology, not theology, emphasizing connections across space with other twentieth-century Jews rather than connections with ancestors and mythic forebears across time.

ROSH HASHANAH

"On Rosh Hashanah it is written, and on Yom Kippur it is sealed." Jews recite these words and ponder their fates every autumn when reading the High Holy Day liturgy. Ten days apart, the Jewish New Year and Day of Atonement are part of a larger whole—a season of introspection, repentance, and renewal. The Soviet Jewry movement devoted more attention to the first half of the holiday pair. Rosh Hashanah ritual is generally confined to the synagogue, not the home. Its signature element involves sounding the shofar during worship. Considering that activists brought the ram's horn out of the synagogue and into the street as one of the first ways they deployed ritualized protest, one might expect them to have easily moved in the opposite direction, adding Soviet Jewry–related themes into the Rosh Hashanah service's shofar ritual. They did not, and it is not clear why. A failure of imagination? Resistance from rabbis? Whatever the reason, beyond the addition of special prayers, they did not ritualize the Soviet Jewish cause in the Rosh Hashanah synagogue service. Instead, led by the grassroots Soviet Jewry councils, activists mobilized the folk custom of sending New Year's greeting cards.[107]

In June 1968, the Washington Committee for Soviet Jewry (WCSJ) circulated a proposal to activists in other cities, suggesting that "concerned people" send "a multitude of Rosh Hashanah greeting cards to Soviet synagogues" in order to "help raise the morale of Soviet Jews and to make it clear that we care about their fate."[108] They also suggested including a Jewish calendar—something that state-run Soviet presses would not print and whose scarcity made it harder to live according to the rhythms of Jewish sacred time. Taking up the idea the following March, the Minnesota Rabbinical Association sent a letter with Passover greetings to sixty-two Russian synagogues.[109] Then over the summer, the year-old Bay Area Council on Soviet Jewry (BACSJ) began promoting an international greeting card campaign for that September's Rosh Hashanah holiday.[110] Figuring that the American Jewish Conference on Soviet Jewry was better positioned to mobilize synagogues across the US, Bay Area Council founder Harold (Hal) Light asked the Conference to encourage American Jews to send cards to Russian synagogues as well as to the Soviet leaders, Leonid Brezhnev and Alexei Kosygin. AJCSJ chairman Lewis Weinstein demurred, warning that it might "be interpreted in the eyes of Soviet authorities as a conspiracy and a propaganda effort, that could ultimately be harmful to Soviet Jewry." Light proceeded independently. He circulated the addresses of eight Soviet synagogues and secured press coverage from the Jewish Telegraphic Agency, which was syndicated in newspapers across the United States and Europe. After the campaign's end, the BACSJ estimated that more than fifty thousand cards had been sent from around the world.[111]

When the Washington Committee and Bay Area Council joined with the Cleveland Council on Soviet Anti-Semitism and three other groups in 1970 to form the Union of Councils for Soviet Jews (UCSJ), the new coordinating body for the movement's "grassroots" faction took over the greeting card campaigns, expanded them, and ran them annually for Passover in the spring and Rosh Hashanah in the fall. Internal organizational needs channeled the tactic's subsequent development. Cleveland's Louis Rosenblum, the UCSJ's first president and orchestrator of the confederation, reoriented the greeting card program to help the UCSJ establish its footing. First, to put UCSJ supporters and Soviet Jews in direct contact—part of a "People-to-People" strategy that included travel to Russia and "adoption" of Soviet Jewish families—he gathered the names and addresses of Soviet Jews who had signed petitions appealing for exit visas. Rosenblum directed greeting cards to these activists, not to synagogues whose state-appointed rabbis he did not trust.[112] "Your card will afford them some measure of protection," a UCSJ advertisement explained, "since the Soviets hesitate to persecute those widely known to people in the Western world."[113] (By contrast, when the AJCSJ reversed its stance against greeting cards in 1970, it insisted that cards should go only to synagogues, not to individuals.)[114] Second, to solidify the UCSJ's financial position, Rosenblum reorganized the greeting card campaign as a fundraiser. Instead of asking people to add Soviet addresses to their greeting card lists as the Washington and San Francisco councils had done, Rosenblum enlisted the Cleveland-based American Greetings Corporation to design, produce, and donate specially made greeting cards. The UCSJ sold these at a dollar per pack: "Kit of 5 cards with message of solidarity in Russian & English. Includes names and addresses of 5 Soviet Jews." Covers featured color drawings of prayer books, the Western Wall, Babi Yar, the Arch of Titus, doves, and great Jewish men like Einstein, Spinoza, Disraeli, and Herzl. Inside, some had preprinted texts in Russian, Hebrew, and English. Others remained blank. An insert suggested messages and showed how to write them in the foreign scripts: "Greetings from the Jews of the U.S.A. and Canada to the Jews of the U.S.S.R., we have not forgotten you." Some inside flaps and back covers displayed Jewish holiday calendars or the Hebrew alphabet with a pronunciation guide in Cyrillic.[115]

Other groups in the US and UK picked up the idea, generating a small burst of activity around greeting card design. There were calendar wheels and circling *horah* dancers, men worshipping and families feasting. One card reproduced Gustave Doré's nineteenth-century engraving of Moses holding the tablets of the Ten Commandments. Others featured new works by contemporary Jewish artists from the US, Europe, and Israel—some commissioned specifically for the movement—as well as underground art by refuseniks still in the USSR.[116]

In the 1980s, the UK's National Council for Soviet Jewry (NCSJ-UK) turned card creation into an art contest to engage youth. Hundreds of British schoolchildren submitted entries to each year's design competition. Entries also arrived from France, Spain, Canada, and in one

Figure 2.1. "L'Shanah Tovah Tikatavu! Happy New Year! From the Jews of the USA to the Jews of the USSR. We have not forgotten you. And we will not forget you!" Rosh Hashanah greeting card text, Jewish Community Council of Greater Washington, 1970. American Jewish Historical Society, RG I-181A, box 1, folder 6.

instance, Russia (from a young refusenik). All the entries were displayed in public exhibitions. Winners were announced with fanfare and celebrity endorsements. "The prizes were presented by Vanessa Smart, the youthful lead in the West End musical, 'Annie.' Being only fourteen, Vanessa could have officially qualified as an entrant were her artistic talents of a different nature," the National Council announced in 1981.[117] Winners saw their drawings mass-produced as National Council Rosh Hashanah cards. The children's submissions often had an expressly political cast—locking the map of the Soviet Union in chains or drawing the country as a closed box filled with trapped people.

Professional artists exercised more restraint.[118] When the Washington Committee for Soviet Jewry asked Avrum (Avy) Ashery to design a card in the mid-1970s, it sought to avoid provoking Soviet mail censors, telling the DC-based graphic design artist that, in his words, "[we] need something that states Jewishness right out to the Jewish refusenik but we don't want it to say much to the KGB."[119] Ashery contributed a drawing he had created when pursuing his fine arts degree years earlier. His Christian professor had failed to recognize the man praying in prayer shawl and tefillin as a Jewish symbol. ("Avy, isn't that hat a little bit too small for his head?" he asked, misidentifying the phylactery.)[120]

All told, movement organizations annually sold or distributed hundreds of thousands of cards filled with holiday wishes, declarations of solidarity, Hebrew primers, and Jewish calendars.[121] Greeting card campaigns were well publicized. Amid puppet shows and challah baking workshops, Jewish holiday fairs featured booths where families could sign and send the cards.[122] Jewish newspapers announced each year's campaign. General-circulation newspapers wrote about the new practice as if it were an established Rosh Hashanah custom. ("Hartford area Jews this year, as in other years, have mailed thousands of cards carrying holiday greetings in Russian to Jews in the Soviet Union," wrote the *Hartford Courant* in 1976.[123]) Ex-refuseniks on American speaking tours attested to the campaign's efficacy in offering protection. ("'They may have saved my life,' Mrs. Lyuba Bershadskaya told a Sinai Temple audience last month," the *Los Angeles Times* reported in 1971. "Receipt of the cards was one of the main reasons she was allowed to leave the Soviet Union last July, she said."[124]) Americans visiting the USSR to meet with refuseniks found evidence that the cards indeed helped boost morale. Travelers reported that they saw the greeting cards decorating refuseniks' apartments, including Ashery's image of the man at prayer. Apparently, Soviet authorities also noticed it. Despite the WCSJ's efforts to find a design that censors would ignore, Ashery's drawing, according to a traveler's report in 1978, had been forbidden further entry into the country. The *Washington Jewish Week* reprinted the image to celebrate its dubious "honor of being banned by the USSR."[125]

Figure 2.2. "The Prayer," serigraph, ca. 1970s. Illustration by Avrum I. Ashery. Courtesy of the artist.

RATIONALIZED EXPANSION

The development of ritualized holiday protest as a mass mobilization tactic proceeded slowly at first, demonstration by demonstration, holiday by holiday. Activists used red-letter days in the Jewish calendar as scheduling anchors but did not use the holidays' symbolic resources to theme the demonstrations. They staged elaborately ritualized protest pageants drawing on Jewish symbols willy-nilly without regard for seasonal timeliness. Only after refining their practice over several years did they draw together the separate insights about the utility of holidays as scheduling hooks and the power of ritual to stir emotions and gain publicity, creating holiday protests themed to the holidays themselves. But even after setting a pattern with Menorah marches, Freedom Seders, Matzohs of Hope, and Tisha B'Av fasts, they still took a case-by-case approach when expanding the tactic to other holidays. The AJCSJ added Simchat Torah dance rallies. The UCSJ pursued Rosh Hashanah greeting card campaigns. But consider all the Jewish holidays this still left untapped: Tu BiShvat, Purim, Shavuot, Sukkot, Yom Kippur, the minor fasts, the modern Israeli holidays like Yom Ha`atzmaut and Yom Hashoah, and so forth.

Tactical innovation took a systematic turn in 1968. Meeting in April in New York City for its biennial conference, the AJCSJ adopted an eighty-seven-point action plan that opened, "Special efforts should be made to *project a long-range calendar for community action to be concerted* as part of overall national demonstrations." The first four recommendations built the projected calendar around the Jewish holiday cycle, suggesting "massive" demonstrations for Simchat Torah, a "massive automobile caravan" for Passover, "a special prayer" for the High Holidays, and a "week of activity" geared to Hanukkah.[126] The planning document's use of the term *calendar* and its grouping of the holidays together indicates a shift in activists' thinking. Before, they had been planning around each holiday separately. Suddenly, they were starting to think about holidays as a group and about the Jewish calendar as a whole. This type of thinking could let them work top down to identify other holidays and systematically plan to use them. But the conceptual shift was not yet fully crystallized. Despite its call to project a long-range calendar, the AJCSJ did not actually present a calendar structured by date. Nor when listing the four holidays did it present them in chronological order. Nor did it acknowledge the rationale for grouping the holidays together. Nor did it expand the list of holidays beyond those already used. Within three years, national and local Soviet Jewry groups would be doing all this, explicitly articulating a calendar-based approach to planning holiday protests.

In 1971, SSSJ, the National Jewish Community Relations Advisory Council (NJCRAC), and Philadelphia Jewish Community Relations

Council (JCRC) all published guides to activism that called for calendar-based planning around Jewish holidays, Soviet holidays, and significant dates in Soviet Jewish history. SSSJ's handbook advised activists to "Make a calendar of Soviet Jewry events through the year (as Simchat Torah, Hanukkah, Passover, November 7th anniversary of the Russian Revolution, etc.)."[127] NJCRAC's action plan systematized even more. Recommending "that each Jewish community develop a calendar," it itemized—in September-through-August chronological order, per the Jewish reckoning—six Jewish holidays and three significant movement-related anniversaries, including the August 12, 1952, executions of Soviet Jewish writers. It suggested programs and ritualized protests for each.[128] The Philadelphia JCRC did the same. "Holidays throughout the year provide opportunities for meaningful expressions on behalf of Soviet Jewry," it declared. Then it listed ten Jewish holidays in chronological order, suggesting synagogue programs for each.[129]

Some of the most famous sociological analyses of twentieth-century life argued that what makes modernity modern is the inexorable drive toward ever more systematic, rationalized planning. Once the dynamic is set in motion, it becomes self-sustaining.[130] In the 1960s, Soviet Jewry activists began with an improvised approach to mobilizing holidays. In the 1970s, they looked at what they had done and rationalized their efforts, introducing calendar-based planning that allowed them to expand to other holidays. This dynamic continued, becoming even more systematic in the 1980s. In 1984, the AJCSJ's successor, the National Conference on Soviet Jewry (NCSJ), published a "guide for year-round program planning" based on the 1971 Philadelphia calendar. The NCSJ's 1984 document fully realized the 1968 vision of projecting a long-range calendar to coordinate activism. With a cover graphic of a zodiac wheel marking the Hebrew months, the NCSJ guide bore the straightforward title "Calendar." It offered point-by-point programming suggestions for twelve Jewish holidays and general ideas for mobilizing around thirteen Soviet holidays, the trial dates and birthdays of seventy-one refuseniks and prisoners of conscience, and eighteen significant anniversaries in Soviet history, Soviet Jewish history, and US-Soviet relations. The document opened by naming and discussing each of the overarching categories (Jewish holidays, Soviet holidays, etc.) before listing the individual dates across the next twelve pages, month by month per the

January–December Gregorian reckoning.[131] What began in the 1960s with ad hoc mobilizations of a few Jewish holidays had evolved and expanded into the systematic mobilization of the entire Jewish holiday cycle and beyond.

For American Jews involved in synagogues, schools, and other communal organizations, this affected the experience of Jewish religious life. Messages about Soviet Jewry wove through the rhythms of religious time. On Tu BiShvat, the Jewish Arbor Day, schoolchildren repurposed the twentieth-century Zionist tradition of purchasing trees in Israel, dedicating saplings in honor of Soviet Jewish prisoners. For Shavuot, which commemorates the revelation at Sinai, activists turned the tradition of staying up all night to study Torah into dusk-to-dawn demonstrations and all-night study sessions about Soviet Jewry.[132] On the carnivalesque Purim, which celebrates the Book (Megillah) of Esther's tale of genocide averted, educators staged the traditional satires or parodies, *purimshpiels*, to "link the theme of Soviet Jewry to the plight of the Jews in the days of Haman."[133]

Mobilizing the entire Jewish calendar let activists communicate multiple meanings simultaneously. The consistent association with sacred Jewish time established the main theme—that the fight for Soviet Jewry was a sacred battle. The particulars of each holiday provided variations on the theme. Tisha B'Av fasts established the movement's religious character and highlighted the theme of loss and mourning. Dedicating Hanukkah candles in honor of underground Hebrew teachers established the movement's religious character and highlighted the theme of resistance to religious oppression. Pretending to welcome refuseniks as symbolic guests (*ushpizin*) in the sukkah established the movement's religious character and highlighted the theme of taking responsibility for the welfare of other Jews. All this deepened American Jews' knowledge of the Soviet Jewish problem's many facets. It also deepened the motivation to fight for Soviet Jewry by invoking a diverse array of Jewish religious values, each of which demanded action for different reasons.

By the movement's end, there were few Jewish holidays left untouched. Activists even mobilized the Fast of the Tenth of Tevet, which most Jews themselves have probably never heard of.[134]

THIS IS THE MATZOH OF HOPE

THINKING WITH CATEGORIES

The structure of the 1984 calendar offers clues to the spread of holiday mobilizations throughout the entire Jewish year. Here, the invention and expansion of tactics were not prompted by exogenous factors like the strategic chess match against the Soviet target or by cultural factors like the desire to express the movements' identity and values. Rather, tactical innovation was driven by an iterative logic of categorical induction and deduction based on scrutiny of prior tactical choices.[135] Activists first began by mobilizing Passover, Hanukkah, and Tisha B'Av. Then they recognized these as elements in a broader category, JEWISH HOLIDAYS. At first, this recognition was only implicit, but soon they articulated it explicitly. This shifted attention upward to the category itself, allowing activists to deduce the full set of elements belonging to the class: Tu BiShvat, Purim, Shavuot, Sukkot, and the like. Focusing on the category also helped them think inductively, allowing them to recognize JEWISH HOLIDAYS as but one element in even larger supersets: HOLIDAYS, SPECIAL CALENDAR DATES, and JEWISH SACRED TIME. Having named these, they could again work deductively to identify other elements. If HOLIDAYS, then why not SOVIET HOLIDAYS or AMERICAN HOLIDAYS?[136] If JEWISH SACRED TIME, then why not LIFE CYCLE CELEBRATIONS like bat mitzvahs, circumcisions, and weddings?

This articulates the process more explicitly than activists ever set in writing. Nevertheless, evidence that they had a working knowledge of tactical innovation via categorical induction and deduction is clear from the timeline: after they adopted a systematic calendrical approach, ritualized protest expanded to encompass previously unmobilized holidays. It is also clear from the structure of the 1984 NCSJ calendar, which proceeded from the general to the specific. It opened by explicitly identifying category headings (Jewish holidays, Soviet holidays, trial dates, and birthdays) and then discussed general principles for using each; only afterward did it enumerate the individual elements.

Categorical induction is a phenomenon of cognitive psychology, of processes occurring inside individual brains.[137] We cannot say anything about how activists had the initial flash of insight to recognize that they could think of Freedom Seders and Simchat Torah rallies as elements in a class. That remains a black box. However, we can identify how that insight became codified in organizational writings and practices. The documentary record even provides graphical evidence that once activists made their categorical thinking explicit, the rationalized, bureaucratic nature of organizational planning propelled the induction and deduction along. A 1979 curriculum for teaching about Soviet Jewry in religious schools built out holiday mobilizations by using the quintessential technology of systematized thought—the planning grid. Listing holidays in the rows and curricular areas in the columns, the grid laid out ways of using each holiday to relate Soviet Jewry to the teaching of subjects such as history, Bible, prayer, Hebrew, and Israel. In the last column, entitled "laws / customs / ceremonies," the authors placed ideas for new Soviet Jewry movement holiday rituals.[138]

Thinking about Jewish holidays not in isolation but as part of a whole calendar served the movement well. Categorical induction and deduction enabled activists to expand programming into holidays that had initially escaped notice. The calendar's cyclical nature helped them plan ahead rather than just react to events. The calendar's collective nature—a common time frame shared by all Jewish communities—helped them coordinate across cities so that the local holiday protests added up to a show of national strength greater than the sum of its parts.[139]

DESECRATION AND ZEALOTRY

Despite its advantages, mobilizing the religious calendar had risks. Activists scrutinized sacred holidays for their utility. Movement calendars on agency letterhead itemized the conclusions in passive-voice bureaucratese: Tisha B'Av "can be *used* to commemorate destruction of synagogues in the Soviet Union." Hanukkah "*offers many opportunities* to relate to the problem of Soviet Jewry."[140] Soviet Jewry activists applied a means–end calculus to something usually treated only as an end in itself. This risked being seen as bad faith or, worse, desecration.

The danger was less that opponents would level the accusation than that supporters would experience it as such. Religion was an asset to the movement precisely because it enlisted the transcendent motivating force of sacred beliefs, symbols, and practices.[141] Turning rituals into political instruments could denude them of the aura of sanctity that made them useful in the first place. All religious protests run this risk.

The Soviet Jewry movement navigated it successfully. Consensus support for the cause helped.[142] So did activists' choice to avoid suggesting innovations that violated Jewish law. Most important, activists neither construed nor presented ritual protest as a politicization of the sacred but as an elevation of the political—not a "desecration of the ritual" but a "sanctification of the ritual."[143] By experiencing their protest rituals as a realization of their religious values, activists behaved sincerely, and this personal sincerity communicated Jewish authenticity.[144]

And yet when considering the dangers of casting a mobilizing gaze on religious ritual, desecration is only one side of the coin. On the flip side, success might be self-defeating. Religious fervor could overtake a movement in a way that narrows the movement's appeal or substitutes doctrinal rigidity for strategic flexibility.[145] Disagreement over whether to allow religious logics to govern strategic thinking was at the heart of the few factional differences in the Soviet Jewry movement's approach to ritualized protest.

The Student Struggle allowed itself to be led further by a religious logic than the AJCSJ did. SSSJ's commitment to the Freedom Seders without regard for their worldly effectiveness is an example. If it indeed was a sacred imperative to say at Passover time, "Let my people go," it did not matter whether the Soviets were listening or not. One still had to say it. It was easy for SSSJ to take this approach because its leaders believed that religious authenticity and strategic necessity demanded the same thing—ceaseless, uncompromising, nonviolent action in defense of Jewish freedom—and because its core support came from the religiously engaged. The AJCSJ and its local affiliates, on the other hand, brought together diverse religious and secular mass membership groups. Their constituents also included organizations that represented Jewish American interests to the US government. More focused on coalition building and more networked into public policy circles, these groups tried to keep religion in check even as they invoked it, as if religion were like fire: useful when controlled, dangerous when unleashed.[146] Such were the two poles. Other movement organizations fell somewhere in between.[147]

The Matzoh of Hope best exemplifies the AJCSJ's calibrated approach to utilizing religion. "As we observe this festival of freedom," it wrote in its 1967 text, "we know that Soviet Jews are not free to learn of their

Jewish past, to hand it down to their children. They cannot learn the languages of their fathers. They cannot teach their children to be the teachers, the rabbis of future generations." The litany is striking for what it does not say. Nowhere does the text state that Soviet Jews were not free to leave. How could a ceremony analogizing Jews under Kremlin rule to Israelites enslaved to Pharaoh, a ritual prepared for the festival of Exodus itself, manage to avoid even whispering, "Let my people go"? At the time, the AJCSJ (and the Israeli government, whose positions the Conference often deferred to) viewed the call as impolitic. Free emigration would threaten the foundations of the Soviets' closed society. Demanding it would likely be a nonstarter. Better, therefore, to focus on securing cultural rights guaranteed by the Soviet constitution, something the AJCSJ believed might be achievable.[148] And so the Matzoh of Hope called for everything but exodus. The religious logic demanded more, but the AJCSJ was in the business of politics, not religion. Only when the political situation changed—when Soviet Jews began sending letters to the United Nations in 1969 demanding the right to leave, forcing the AJCSJ's hand—did it alter the text: "As we observe this festival of freedom, we know that Soviet Jews are not free—not free to leave." The 1970 revision did not merely mention Passover's theme of exodus; it put it at the top of the list, where the religious logic would have insisted it belonged all along.[149]

Tensions over ritualization surfaced when the factions collaborated. During the planning of the 1966 "Passover Youth Protest," the New York Youth Conference for Soviet Jewry tried to rein in SSSJ's plans for a ritual-heavy rally. Birnbaum scaled back, but he was adamant that a religious cause be expressed as such. The SSSJ leader insisted on calling the event the "*Geulah* [Redemption] March" and still managed to incorporate "Jericho style" encirclings, an "eternal flame," and a "symbolic re-enactment of the Crossing of the Red Sea."[150]

In the following years, the NYYCSJ's successor organizations sidelined Birnbaum's group in New York's community-wide rally planning. With SSSJ no longer leading the work, ritualization took a back seat, as did scheduling to coincide with Passover. The twenty-thousand-person 1970 "Exodus March" to the Soviet UN Mission was the movement's last major demonstration anchored to Pesach.[151] The next massive springtime demonstration was the 1972 "Solidarity Day for Soviet Jews," organized by the Greater New York Conference on Soviet Jewry, the National Conference, and NJCRAC.[152] Rallies on April 30 drew over one hundred thousand marchers in over ninety cities and towns across the US.[153] The GNYCSJ and its partners pegged the date not to the timeless, recurring themes of the Jewish holiday cycle but to the unique and timely events of that year. Richard Nixon was heading to Moscow to meet with Soviet premier Brezhnev in May. A rally during Passover in late March would have expressed religious sentiment well but would not have served immediate political needs. Nixon was no ally of the movement; he saw it as a threat to détente. The NCSJ wanted mass rallies shortly before the summit to pressure the president to place Soviet Jewish rights on the agenda.

"Solidarity Sunday" became a centerpiece of the movement's annual calendar, turning out one hundred thousand to two hundred thousand marchers each year through 1987. It had no "Jericho style" encirclings, no crowds parting like the Red Sea. The GNYCSJ maintained cordial relations with SSSJ but no longer involved it in rally planning. Instead, Solidarity Sundays applied a more conventional template. Ritualization was out. Jacob Birnbaum and Glenn Richter were off the dais; Tony Randall and Gregory Peck were on. Paul Simon sang. Dignitaries marched: Mayor David Dinkins and Senator Alfonse D'Amato, Ambassador Jeanne Kirkpatrick and Archbishop John J. O'Connor. And Mayor Ed Koch—a perennial fixture. They delivered addresses, their faces projected on Diamond Vision screens in one of the first uses of that technology for political rallies. Movement icons like Elie Wiesel and Avital Shcharansky appeared. And after the political prisoners Eduard Kuznetsov, Mark Dymshits, and Anatoly Shcharansky were freed, they spoke too. The *New York Times* called the Solidarity Sundays a "regular New York spring ritual." But it was a ritual that made sure to hold religion in check.[154]

RELIGIOUS IDENTITY POLITICS

In the 1970s and '80s, communally engaged American Jews would have had to have gone out of their way to avoid encountering the Soviet Jewry movement at holiday time. The holiday mobilizations were ubiquitous. Present from the most major of feasts to minor of fasts, the incessant ritualization of protest created a politically engaged Judaism that sanctified activism and proclaimed the responsibility to stand up for Soviet Jewish rights to be a religious obligation—a mitzvah.

Observers at the time said that if secularized American Jews had a religious passion for anything, it was their ethnic politics. Sociologist Jonathan Woocher labeled it "Civil Judaism"—*civil* in that the sacred focus was not God but the Jewish people, and veneration was expressed not through worship but through political activity. He and others were talking about Jewish American efforts around Holocaust commemoration and Israel, largely ignoring Soviet Jewry activism. But in all three instances, Jewish Americans oriented themselves globally and organized politically against Jewish vulnerability and in support of Jewish empowerment.[155] And core tenets of Woocher's Civil Judaism—"the unity of the Jewish people," "mutual responsibility" among Jews, and the imperative of "Jewish survival in a threatening world"—found clear expression in Soviet Jewry movement rallying cries: "We Are One!" "I Am My Brother's Keeper!" "Am Yisroel Chai! [The Jewish People Lives!]" "Never Again!"[156]

Maybe because Woocher and his fellow analysts did not look at the Soviet Jewry movement, they ended up arguing that the sanctification of Jewish identity politics expressed passions originating deep in Jewish American kishkes. In their accounts, leaders co-opted, channeled, or gave voice to these feelings, but at the root, they were an emergent phenomenon bubbling up from *amcha*, the Jewish street. Some analysts were so convinced that popular sentiment was leading the way, they even critiqued rabbis for acquiescing to the folk religion's displacement of normative Judaism.[157]

But this chapter has told a different story. Yes, the Soviet Jewry movement expressed a religious politics. It did this in about as religious a way as one can imagine—by creating new holiday rituals. But these protest rituals did not emerge naturally as an inevitable reflection of Jews' religious passion for the Soviet Jewish cause. Activists invented the tactic of ritualized holiday protest. They developed it not in one fell swoop but slowly over the course of many years. At first, they used holidays to schedule demonstrations, but they did not think to draw holiday content into their protests. Later, they connected timing and content, but only on a case-by-case basis, confining the politics to just a few holidays. Almost a decade passed before activists had the revolutionary idea to list all the Jewish holidays and propose Soviet Jewry movement programming for each. No groundswell of grassroots passion inspired that totalizing thrust. Credit that to categorical logics and rational planning. Activists working in movement organizations reflected on what they had been doing; figured out that they were working with a category, JEWISH HOLIDAYS, many of whose elements had been left untapped; and then circulated memos and planning grids to expand Soviet Jewry activism into the unclaimed territories of the holiday calendar. Through organizational networks connecting them with synagogues, schools, and community agencies nationwide, they introduced these new practices into the rhythms of Jewish religious life. They continued promulgating these practices season after season, year after year, for the better part of twenty years.

Many of these rituals reinforced rabbinic religion. This is ironic, as critics of Civil Judaism claimed that the laity had substituted contemporary politics for traditional faith. But every time American Jews turned out for a Freedom Seder or raised the Matzoh of Hope, they declared that in the oppression of Soviet Jews, they saw the endless cycle of slavery to redemption playing itself out once again.[158] "Declared" is actually too weak a word. They did not just speak. They acted. By performing the meanings as rituals, they created a religious reality out there in the world.[159] This generation of supposedly secular and assimilating American Jews affirmed—before themselves and others—that the Exodus paradigm was recurring in their generation and that the primal Jewish story was still, for them, a cosmological truth. In such ways did ritualized protest function in the moment as religious Jewish action.

There were many such moments. Passover was but one. By systematically mobilizing the Jewish calendar, activists transformed ritualized protest for Soviet Jewry from a series of one-offs to a leitmotif weaving through the entire holiday cycle. This bound the Soviet Jewry movement to the religious system more tightly than any occasional use of ritualized protest could ever have done. The movement succeeded in making Jewish politics religious and making Jewish religion political not by operating piecemeal—a menorah here, a matzoh there—but by embracing a totalizing whole.

3

HOW TO FIND AND MEET RUSSIAN JEWS

Fourteen tourists joined the lawsuit as individual plaintiffs. These American citizens had been detained, strip-searched, arbitrarily fined, or otherwise harassed. The organizational plaintiffs included thirty-eight of forty-four member agencies of the National Conference on Soviet Jewry (NCSJ). It was not clear whether the court had jurisdiction. The Conference argued that since Intourist operated in New York, it was subject to state consumer protection laws. In June 1986, they filed suit, charging the Soviet government's travel bureau with fraudulent advertising. Intourist's promotional activities created "a false and misleading impression that so long as tourists to the USSR obey Soviet law, they will not be subjected to various forms of government harassment. . . . This is absolutely not true for those tourists who . . . visit with Soviet Jewish families."[1]

Harassment of Westerners visiting Soviet Jewish refuseniks was nothing new. Soviet officials knew that movement organizations were using tourists as couriers to exchange information with the refuseniks and provide them with material support. They let it go on because their first priority was keeping Western tourist dollars flowing in.[2] Therefore, no broad crackdown—just modulated intimidation, sometimes random, sometimes targeting leaders of the American campaign, sometimes responding in the moment to tourists who were especially brazen. Most intimidation occurred at border crossings. Since the 1970s, movement organizations had been receiving reports about hostile customs agents, long detentions, strip searches, and confiscations of Judaica. When harassment followed tourists into the cities, it usually came in the form of 3 a.m. phone calls to hotel rooms with only static on the other end of the line, close and visible tails on the streets, and suitcases obviously rummaged through while tourists were out.[3] A small number of tourists, no more than a few score among the thousands who traveled, had more harrowing experiences: arrest, interrogation, expulsion—sometimes followed by denunciations in the Soviet press.[4]

Harassment worsened, in both frequency and severity, after détente's collapse. Assault joined the list of hazards. One American woman was thrown against a wall in the alcove of a refusenik's apartment building, slapped across the face to send her eyeglasses flying, punched—more to frighten than to hurt—and robbed. The three assailants fled by car. Lest she mistake this for a random mugging, the same car ostentatiously followed her over the next several days as she continued visiting Soviet Jews.[5] The Soviets' public messaging managed to be just as heavy-handed. When February and March 1984 saw three expulsions over three weeks, TASS, the government news agency, gilded the lily: "The incident with the American tourists is bound to serve as a lesson to those who, on coming to the U.S.S.R. as guests, intend to carry out assignments for foreign Zionist centers." The US State Department responded with a travel advisory for Leningrad.[6]

The activities that raised Soviet ire had become standard repertoire by 1986. Tourists who wanted to help Soviet Jews were briefed by activists before their trips and given refuseniks' names, addresses, and phone numbers, as well as instructions for coding the information into address books or checkbooks. They received maps to synagogues and apartment complexes and explanations for dialing from Soviet public telephones. Instructed on how to navigate airport customs inspections, they packed their suitcases with prayer shawls, yarmulkes, Jewish calendars, Passover haggadahs, Star of David charm necklaces, Israeli postage stamps, and paperback copies of Leon Uris's *Exodus*—gifts to aid Jewish observance, affirm Jewish solidarity, and inspire pride in Israel. Crammed alongside the Judaica were rock albums, art books, pantyhose, Wrangler jeans, Seiko watches, and Sony Walkmen—gifts for out-of-work refuseniks who could sell them on the black market to generate income.[7] For special delivery to leaders Ida Nudel and Dina Beilina, who coordinated support for political prisoners, tourists brought Flintstones-style children's vitamins, white chocolate, and lenticular 3D postcards of bikinied bathing beauties—nutrition for the prisoners, bribes for their guards.[8] Tourists deemed especially trustworthy were given specific missions: deliver a two-hundred-day supply of Enalapril to recently released prisoner Alik Z.

for his hypertension;[9] bring a two-volume commentary by Menachem Meiri, a thirteenth-century sage, to Eliyahu (Ilya) Essas, leader of Soviet Jewry's Orthodox revival;[10] deliver the letter from Congressman Hamilton Fish (R-NY) to Yuli Kosharovsky and the letter from the recently emigrated Vladimir Oliker to his wife, Yelena, still awaiting her exit visa.[11]

After settling into their hotels, travelers phoned refuseniks to arrange visits, pleaded headaches to stay back as the tour bus left without them, and then used the elementary Cyrillic reading skills covered in their briefings to navigate public transportation on their own. In refuseniks' homes, they spoke freely or guardedly, following their hosts' lead. They snapped photographs, recorded lists of items for the next round of tourists to bring, collected updates on the status of emigration applications, and gathered names, addresses, and phone numbers of new refuseniks. Those with specialized skills used them: Doctors performed checkups.[12] Lawyers consulted on legal affairs.[13] Rabbis taught Torah.[14] Scientists lectured at seminars run by refusenik academicians who had been fired from their university posts.[15] All that they did and learned, all the materials they collected, they passed along to movement organizations back home.

Jewish Americans in the 1970s and '80s referred to the trips colloquially as "delivering blue jeans to refuseniks." That it was hush-hush was an open secret. Most synagogues boasted congregants among the travelers. Synagogue Soviet Jewry committees connected potential tourists with briefers from local branches of the NCSJ and the Union of Councils for Soviet Jews (UCSJ). Even before *glasnost* prompted a surge in tourism to Russia, so many people were going that the NCSJ kept a travel agency on call. ("If you wish to use our travel agent, you can contact him directly: Mr. Mendy Goldberg, Perfect Travel, 26 Canal St., New York.")[16]

Upwards of ten thousand Westerners traveled for the movement, most at their own expense. The American Jewish Historical Society (AJHS) Archive of the American Soviet Jewry Movement holds itineraries, debriefing forms, travelogues, and other materials from more than 4,200 North Americans and 550 others who traveled between 1970 and 1991. Of the combined total, about 300 made at least one repeat visit.[17] Nativ's archives remain classified, but an in-house history of the Israeli agency's tourism effort cites 6,000 travelers over a similar time frame.[18] Travel from Europe was even more convenient than from the US, and groups like the 35s in Britain and the Comité des Quinze in France ran programs of their own. So did Orthodox groups, including Agudath Israel's Vaad L'Hatzolas Nidchei Yisroel (Organization to Rescue Dispersed Jews) and Chabad-Lubavitch's Lishkas Ezras Achim and Shamir, as well as a private UK-based initiative known as "Russian Religious Jews," led by Ernie (Yeshayahu) Hirsch. These sent perhaps a thousand people altogether, mostly rabbis and rebbetzins.[19]

Travelogues in American Jewish Historical Society files—most of them written for the National Conference, Union of Councils, and their local affiliates—show a cross section of America's affluent and well-educated Jewish population. People of all ages traveled, from children age ten to grandparents age eighty-five. The average age was forty-five to forty-six, with the middle half ranging from thirty-three to fifty-seven. Approximately 57 percent were men, 43 percent women. Work-wise, they were an assortment of business people, nonprofit workers, schoolteachers, scientists, students, doctors, psychologists, homemakers, academicians, artists, and attorneys. Women and men alike traveled in professional capacities and as leaders of Soviet Jewry movement organizations.[20] As might be expected, there was a heavy representation of rabbis and Jewish communal professionals. Lawmakers, congressional

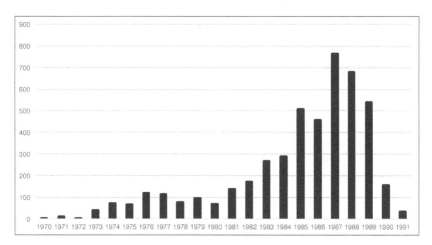

Figure 3.1. Travelers represented in the AJHS Archives, 1970–91. This chart underestimates the scale of the tourism enterprise. It includes only those travelers who shared trip reports and travel materials with movement organizations whose records are housed at the American Jewish Historical Society's Archive of the American Soviet Jewry Movement.

aides, and other government workers traveled too. Movement leaders especially sought their involvement. Many of the Jewish travelers went with family. At least 40 percent were married couples. On at least thirty-six occasions, parents had children or teenagers in tow. Non-Jewish travelers were more likely to be political and civic leaders, clergy, scientists, and attorneys—recruited because of their professional and public roles.[21]

In the USSR, these thousands of travelers mainly visited refuseniks in the three cities with the largest Jewish populations. Over 90 percent of tourists paid visits in Moscow, around 85 percent in Leningrad, and about a quarter in Kiev. Almost half (approximately 45 percent) also met refuseniks elsewhere. Smaller Jewish centers in the Baltics (Riga, Vilnius, Tallinn), Ukraine (Odessa), Byelorussia (Minsk), Georgia (Tbilisi), Uzbekistan (Tashkent, Samarkand), and Armenia (Yerevan) each received only between 4 percent and 8 percent of the tourists.[22] Statistics compiled by the UCSJ illustrate the scope of the travel: during the first four months of 1986, its tourists paid 842 visits to 309 refusenik households in Moscow and Leningrad. This does not include visits sponsored by other groups or UCSJ visits elsewhere in the USSR.[23]

Considering the scale of the enterprise, not all thought the NCSJ's lawsuit against Intourist wise. The Soviet Jewry Legal Advocacy Center (SJLAC), an arm of the rival grassroots Union of Councils, warned that jurisdictional questions would likely result in an "embarrassing early dismissal."[24] They were not far off: the court dismissed the suit not because it did not have jurisdiction but because the NCSJ and the organizational plaintiffs did not have standing. But this outcome was probably for the best, as the Legal Advocacy Center warned that the alternatives—losing or winning the case—would be worse. Activists had succeeded in creating a steady channel to refuseniks by helping tourists remain on the right side of Soviet law. Both the actual legality of the work and the rhetorical claim to legality were crucial. Losing the case, SJLAC legal director Donna Arzt cautioned, would place activists on the defensive, lending credence to Soviet claims of illegality. Winning could be counterproductive were it to lead Intourist to compile "an explicit list . . . of exactly what the Soviets consider to be prohibited activity by foreign tourists," Arzt wrote. "At the moment, that 'list' is an ambiguous and unpublished one. I'm not sure it's in the interest of the Soviet Jewry movement to have it otherwise."[25]

Criticism from within the National Conference's own ranks was more scathing. "Mortified," Bernard (Bernie) Dishler howled in a letter to NCSJ executive director Jerry Goodman. Dishler was chair of the NCSJ's travel committee but had found out about the lawsuit through an article in Philadelphia's *Jewish Exponent*. He claimed the NCSJ should be "doing all that [it] can to encourage travel," not stoking fears that would make it harder to recruit. "As you know," he reminded Goodman, "we base much of our Soviet Jewry program on our travel program." The April 1986 nuclear accident in Chernobyl had already "diminished the ranks of potential travelers and now this article must also take its toll."[26]

Dishler accurately assessed the travel program's importance. Tourism had become fundamental to the operations and culture of Soviet Jewry activism in the United States. By the mid-1980s, tourists had become the primary conduit linking activists in the US and USSR. Almost all the campaigns on behalf of particular refuseniks and consciousness-raising programs like Adopt-a-Family, Adopt-a-Prisoner, and bar/bat mitzvah twinning (see chapter 7) relied on information gathered by tourists. Beyond any assistance it brought to refuseniks, tourism also helped energize and sustain the campaign in the West. It was a key source of activist recruitment and leadership development, as travelers returned home inspired to do more.[27]

Tourism was also important by virtue of the time and resources it commanded. Soviet Jewry groups designated volunteers and hired professional staff to take on the tourism portfolio. They published travel guides, codified briefing procedures, and kept both continually up to date. They recruited tourists, coordinated travel, matched visitors with refuseniks, and provided materials for delivery. They met for hours upon end with tourists, orienting them beforehand and debriefing them afterward. They culled details from interviews, questionnaires, and travelogues and maintained card files and computer databases to systematize the information gleaned. They shared all this information and know-how through a network that linked local tourism committees worldwide.

How did this come to be? None of it was foreordained. None of it was ready-made. It had to be invented from scratch. Initially, activists only saw possibilities in travel by elites. There was precedent for that, and it required no special leap of imagination to send rabbinic delegations on fact-finding missions. Far from intuitive, however, was the notion that to help Soviet Jews, thousands of Westerners—including casual tourists of no particular expertise or official status—should flood in to deliver prayer books, Levi's jeans, bikini postcards, and purple children's Flintstone vitamins shaped like Barney Rubble. Nor was it intuitive that activists should invest resources to build an infrastructure to make that happen. And yet, somehow, the campaign to free Soviet Jewry made a shift from small-scale trips by a few traveling elite to a systematic mobilization of international mass tourism. Each step in the process of tactical innovation involved small acts of creativity—a guidebook here, a briefing kit there. These accumulated into a major act of social movement–driven cultural production, the result of which was a distinctly novel form of Jewish American Cold War travel—part aid mission, part quest, part roots tour, part adventure tourism.

CASTING THE MOBILIZING GAZE: INITIAL DISCOVERIES
FIRST FORAYS: TRAVEL BY RABBINIC ELITES

To use tourism to aid Soviet Jews, activists needed to be able to send tourists to Russia in the first place. Over 110,000 Americans visited the USSR in 1975, during the heyday of détente, when Aeroflot and Pan Am were flying jet airliners direct between Moscow and New York. Back in 1964, only 14,000 Americans made the trip, always with stopovers and still on propeller planes for some legs of the flight.[28] Further back, in the last years of Stalin's rule, tourism was close to impossible. In 1953, the year of the dictator's death, 42 Western tourists privately visited the USSR. (That was the high estimate.)[29] Stalin's successor, the reformist premier Nikita Khrushchev, reopened the country to international tourism in a public diplomacy effort that Americans billed as a "ruthlessly friendly" approach to waging Cold War.[30] In July 1955, Intourist authorized New York–based Cosmos Travel to serve as its representative. The State Department reciprocated by declaring US passports valid for travel to the Soviet Union.[31] Between 2,500 and 3,000 Americans traveled to Russia the next year.[32] Most went via official delegations and academic and cultural exchange programs.[33]

Rabbinic groups immediately recognized the opportunity. Days after Intourist and Cosmos inked their deal, the Rabbinical Council of America (RCA), representing seven hundred Orthodox rabbis, applied to the

Soviet embassy for permission to send a delegation. Rabbis David B. Hollander, Gilbert Klaperman, Samuel Adelman, Emmanuel Rackman, and Herschel Schacter were approved the following May, "the first rabbinical group officially permitted to enter Russia since the revolution and rise of communism in 1917."[34] Their six-week, twelve-city tour through Soviet Russia, Georgia, Abkhazia, Ukraine, and Lithuania was billed as "the most extensive... ever undertaken by any religious group."[35] This was a point of no small significance in Eisenhower's America, which looked to religion as a defense against "atheistic communism." (Around the time of the rabbis' visit, the president signed legislation establishing "In God We Trust" as the national motto.)[36] At the end of June 1956, the rabbis took off from Idlewild Airport. Stopping over in Amsterdam, they were briefed by Nativ staff member Nehemiah Levanon, who would later become head of the Israeli agency. A second delegation, representing the multidenominational New York Board of Rabbis, departed soon after.[37]

The RCA visit, the first use of travel to aid Soviet Jews in the Cold War era, took place seven years before the creation of dedicated Soviet Jewry movement organizations in the US.[38] Hollander, the delegation's head, told the press that they hoped to gather information, establish contact with local Jewish communities, and deliver religious assistance, including materials used in Jewish observances, if needed.[39] All these goals would remain present in the uses of tourism that followed in the decades ahead. In contrast to later tourist mobilizations, however, the RCA trip was notable for its public, quasi-official character. The rabbis understood themselves to be representing the American Jewish community. Soviet and American officials did too, viewing them as a formal delegation of American religious leaders. The Soviets appointed Moscow's chief rabbi, Solomon Schlieffer, to be their host and minder as they sat for meetings with government officials and ascended pulpits to deliver Yiddish-language sermons. The American embassy invited the rabbis to its Fourth of July cocktail reception, where they briefly engaged Khrushchev and Premier Nikolai Bulganin. The Soviet leaders deflected their questions about why the country had so few synagogues. American press coverage, which was ample, portrayed the rabbis as representatives of God-fearing Americans of all faiths.[40] Returning home, the rabbis reported back. For official Jewish communal use, they circulated a travelogue to leaders of Jewish organizations.[41] For the public, they contributed a ten-part, front-page series to a major New York daily. "The Uncensored Story of Russia's 'Lost' People" was featured as an exclusive by the *New York Journal-American*, a paper whose staunch anti-communism took its cue from the devout Christianity of its founder, William Randolph Hearst.[42]

The RCA was not alone in realizing that travel could be used to create links and deliver religious assistance. In April 1956, two months before Hollander's RCA embarked with great fanfare, Rabbi Menachem Mendel Schneerson, leader of the Brooklyn-based Chabad-Lubavitch Hasidic community, discreetly asked that an Italian business traveler heading to Russia take copies of the Tanya and other sacred texts and "leave/abandon them [*veya'azvam*] there at the synagogue for the benefit of the congregation." (This anonymous gifting differs from the movement's approach in the 1970s, when travelers delivered specific materials to specific individuals.) Chabad continued to send trusted emissaries during the 1960s, often drawing from Schneerson's personal staff and always eschewing publicity.[43] In contrast to the RCA delegation's trip—a public one-time affair—Chabad's steady trickle of travelers proceeded from the calculation that repeated "unofficial" visits held the potential to establish an ongoing connection with a network of contacts in the Soviet Union.[44]

Outside of Chabad, other Orthodox rabbis and rebbetzins independently made the same calculation and began traveling back and forth themselves. Rabbi Harry (Herschel Tzvi) Bronstein, a Polish-born Brooklyn-based member of the executive council of World Agudath Israel, traveled nine times to the Soviet Union and/or its satellite states between 1958 and 1967. Similarly, Rabbi Mordechai Pinchas Teitz of Elizabeth, New Jersey, made over twenty trips from 1964 through the end of the Cold War. The rabbis acted as unofficial itinerant religious functionaries. They ensured the kosher status of secret ritual baths, set up religious courts to provide for Jewish divorces, and performed circumcisions while also training others in the procedure. They, along with Rebbetzin Basya (Bess) Teitz, delivered items necessary for ritual observance, such as Jewish books, circumcision knives, kosher cured meats, and *esrogim* (citrons) for Sukkot. They eventually institutionalized their private efforts. Bronstein created Al Tidom ("Dare Not Remain Silent"). Teitz created Mifal Hatzolas Yehudei Russia (Enterprise for the Rescue of the Jews of Russia; MOHIR). Both agencies published Jewish religious materials in Russian and provided them to other travelers to distribute in the USSR. Despite the similarities, their paths quickly diverged. Teitz managed to secure limited cooperation from Soviet authorities, in part by maintaining distance from the public campaign in the West (a stance that subjected him to criticism from Western activists). In contrast, Bronstein described being arrested, tortured, and expelled in 1967 for smuggling in false Polish birth certificates. (Soviet Jews could use the documents to emigrate to Poland and from there to Israel.) Barred from reentering, Bronstein became an outspoken critic of Soviet policy, testifying alongside Jewish Defense League founder Meir Kahane before congressional hearings on Soviet antisemitism in 1968. Al Tidom focused on package deliveries to Soviet Jews via post and via tourists, activities that earned Bronstein denunciations in the Soviet press.[45]

DISCOVERING NEW UTILITY:
NATIV, ELIE WIESEL, AND TOURISM FOR THE SAKE OF TRAVEL WRITING

Some of the earliest deployments of tourism valued travel not only for what it allowed visitors to bring over but for what it allowed them to bring back: firsthand information to publicize in the West. Although Chabad and MOHIR avoided public reporting, considering it dangerous to their efforts to establish ongoing channels, others embraced it. The RCA delegation members all contributed to the front-page series in the *New York Journal-American*. Journalists like Chaim Shurer, Chaim Shoshkes, and Leon Crystal traveled in order to file columns in Israel's *Davar* and the New York Yiddish dailies, *Tog-Morgn Zhurnl* and *Forverts*.[46] Rabbi Baruch (Bernard) Poupko of Pittsburgh made reporting central to his efforts to aid Soviet Jews. A repeat traveler who visited three times between 1964 and 1967 (twice on family visits with his wife, Gilda, and once as head of an RCA delegation), Poupko used his visits to raise awareness by writing dozens of English and Yiddish articles syndicated in newspapers worldwide.[47]

These approaches all shared the idea that tourism presented experts an opportunity to gather information and fill gaps in knowledge. In the mid-1960s, Israel's Nativ introduced a variation on the theme. It enlisted Elie Wiesel to help.

Reviewers of Wiesel's 1966 travelogue *The Jews of Silence: A Personal Report on Soviet Jewry* agreed that its uniqueness rested not in what he wrote but in how he wrote it. "He tells us little that is new in terms of factual information or statistics," Max Hayward, the Oxford-based scholar of Russian literature, wrote in *Commentary*, "but he conveys more vividly than anyone else has yet been able to, the strange and contradictory nature of the problem."[48] This was precisely why Meir Rosenne and Ephraim Tari had recruited Wiesel to make the trip. The two Israeli diplomats, Nativ's officers in New York and Paris, were not looking for someone to discover unknown dimensions of Soviet oppression. They already had specialists disseminating hard facts—Moshe Decter at the Jewish Minority Research bureau in New York, and Emmanuel Litvinoff, publishing *Jews in Eastern Europe* in London.[49] Rosenne and Tari did not want another policy expert. They wanted a poet.

Their move was innovative twice over. First, whereas the 1956 RCA delegation thought of tourism as a vehicle to let fact finders see and learn, Wiesel's sponsors saw it as a way to help authors write. Text would not be a by-product of travel but its very purpose. Travel would be the means to produce a travelogue. Second, Tari and Rosenne recognized that because travelogues were first-person accounts, they could be used not just to inform but to engage. With a skilled pen, an account of a journey to meet Soviet Jews could bring readers along, draw them in, inspire them to feel, spur them to act.[50] Their invitation to Wiesel marked a new moment in the development of tactical thinking about how and why to enlist tourism—elevating travel writing over the act of travel itself and valuing that writing less for its ability to diagnose a problem and more for its ability to motivate people to do something about it.[51]

Hence the decision to send the thirty-seven-year-old memoirist-cum-journalist. The world already knew Wiesel, survivor of Auschwitz, for offering the commanding voice of first-person Holocaust testimony. Rosenne knew Elie from their days together at the Sorbonne. "You have been a witness before," he told the author of *Night*. "Now you must go and find out the Soviet Jews' true situation and testify for them."[52]

The Jews of Silence enjoys a reputation as the book that launched the Soviet Jewry movement, but that is incorrect. For one, it gets the dating wrong. For another, the notion that books launch social movements is a romantic myth.[53] Nevertheless, books can take on outsized roles in a movement's collective identity. This may explain why no other activist group tried to replicate Nativ's "produce-an-inspiring-travelogue" approach to mobilizing tourism. Wiesel's work sufficed. It served its purpose perfectly and stood the test of time. With chapters bearing titles like "Fear," "Solitude," "Celebration in Moscow," "The Dream of Israel," and "What They Expect of Us," *The Jews of Silence* traced a narrative arc that asserted the severity of the problem, testified against despair, and shamed the reader to act.

Written in French, the work originally appeared as an essay series in the Israeli daily *Yedioth Aharanoth*, with Hebrew courtesy of the poet and Eichmann trial journalist Haim Gouri. It was excerpted in Paris's *L'Express* and New York's *Saturday Evening Post* and then published in its entirety several months later by the Parisian publishing house Éditions du Seuil under the title, *Les juifs du silence: Témoignage* (testimony, or witnessing). Holt, Rinehart and Winston's editor in chief, Arthur Cohen, hired a translator and grabbed the full series for his press.[54] Wiesel's slim volume immediately became required reading for Westerners interested in the Soviet Jewish cause. Those not inclined to read it in English, Hebrew, or the original French could pick up translations in German, Spanish, Italian, Japanese, and Finnish. A theater company in Tel Aviv produced a stage version. For a quarter century, it was a mainstay of Soviet Jewry movement curricula and bibliographies. It remains in print to this day.[55]

Even the title became iconic. The phrase "Jews of silence" offered a single idiom to simultaneously frame the Soviet Jewish problem and shame Western Jews to action. "I returned from the Soviet Union disheartened and depressed," Wiesel wrote in the conclusion. "But what torments me most is not the Jews of silence I met in Russia, but the silence of the Jews I live among today." It was an arrow to an already wounded American Jewish heart, aimed there by the living embodiment of Holocaust testimony. In the years that followed, creators and chroniclers of the Soviet Jewry campaign would repeatedly allude to Wiesel's formulation, especially in titles proclaiming the awakening of Jewish resistance: *Silent No More, The Jews of Struggle, The Jews of Hope*.[56]

Nativ's role in recruiting Wiesel was not public knowledge when *The Jews of Silence* was published. Wiesel revealed the story in his 1995 memoir. Nativ, for its part, remained silent about its role in the most high-profile use of tourism that the organization ever undertook.[57] Nor did it seek to build on the lessons of this success. Nativ stepped up its uses of tourism, but not by sending more writers to bring back poetry. As Rosenne and Tari were briefing Wiesel, others in the organization were laying the groundwork for a strategic shift that would move Nativ's—and the entire Soviet Jewry movement's—use of tourism in a radically different direction.

NATIV'S PARADIGM SHIFT: FROM ELITE TO MASS TOURISM

From the moment travel to the USSR became feasible in the 1950s, Westerners interested in the situation of Soviet Jewry recognized tourism's potential to bring support over, build networks, gather information, and bring information back. Years passed, however, before they built systematically on this awareness. In an era when travel to the USSR was still novel, rare, elite, and newsworthy, Jewish groups looked to a handful of rabbis, academics, and writers to travel as surrogates for the masses who could hardly imagine flying to Moscow themselves.

In the late 1960s, Nativ shifted the paradigm from ad hoc uses of elite travel to systematic deployments of mass tourism. Established in 1952, the agency sought the emigration of Soviet Jews not just anywhere but specifically to Israel (i.e., *aliyah*). This long-term goal had no immediate prospects of success. Nativ therefore focused on countering assimilatory pressures so that when the gates did open, there would still be Jews with eyes fixed on Zion. The Kremlin sought to sever transnational Jewish connections. Nativ tried to break Soviet Jews' isolation, and it enlisted travelers to help. In the 1950s, Israel and the USSR maintained diplomatic relations. Nativ officers, stationed under diplomatic cover in Israel's Moscow embassy, smoothed the path for the occasional Israeli tourist to meet Jews in Russian synagogues. Sometimes, they recruited Israeli merchant mariners on shore leave in Odessa to contact Jews in the port city.[58] Sometimes, Nativ agents in the West provided guidance to travelers like the rabbis from the 1956 RCA delegation.[59] Sometimes they recruited an occasional traveler like Elie Wiesel.[60] In 1960, Nativ personnel in New York briefly installed a staff person at the Jewish American mass membership organization B'nai B'rith to brief American tourists, provide them books and symbolic gifts to deliver, and convey reports back to the Israeli consulate—all without revealing Israel's involvement to the tourists—but the effort lasted only a few months.[61] Before 1967, Nativ treated tourism as ancillary. For long-term relationship-building and intelligence gathering, the agency relied on its personnel stationed in Moscow.

That changed when the Soviet Union broke off diplomatic relations in response to the June 1967 Six-Day War. Israel closed its Moscow embassy, forcing Nativ to seek alternatives. Within a year, it was sending specially recruited "tourist-emissaries" (*tayarim-shliḥim*) to serve as conduits between the agency and *aliyah* activists in the USSR. The individual travelers always changed, but the constant back-and-forth established an unbroken stream of intelligence, funneling information from Jews across the Soviet Union into Nativ's headquarters in Tel Aviv. In the opposite direction, it provided a sustained mechanism for transferring information and materials to activists. A Londoner visiting in March would report back that such-and-such refusenik needed such-and-such a prescription. A tourist from Denmark would deliver the medicine in April. Neither traveler knew the other. Regarding the behind-the-scenes coordination, a code of silence prevailed.[62]

The roots of this approach to mobilizing tourism predated the Six-Day War, but the initial conception bore only a slight resemblance to the system that eventually took hold. Among the reasons for the distance between idea and implementation was that Nativ did not initiate the tactical innovation. An enterprising outsider did: Aryeh Kroll. When the agency eventually brought Kroll and his tourism project in-house, Nativ's institutional culture and organizational structures channeled the subsequent paths of tactical development.

Kroll was a religious kibbutznik who visited his native USSR in January 1965 to reunite with sisters he had not seen in decades. According to his version of the origin story, during his trip, he gave away his prayer shawl to an old Jew whom he encountered in his hotel. Moved by the experience, he went to the Israeli embassy, requesting and receiving additional religious materials to distribute. Kroll returned home to Kibbutz Saad in the Negev desert with the idea that, rather than relying on chance tourists to present themselves at the embassy as he had, Israel should recruit young religious Israelis as unofficial "tourist-emissaries" to inspire and support Jewish identity in Russia. Acquainted with David

Ben-Gurion by virtue of his work in Negev regional affairs, Kroll took the plan to the former prime minister, who brought it to Nativ's director, Shaul Avigur. By September 1965, at the same time Wiesel was recording his impressions of Simchat Torah in Moscow at the instigation of Nativ's European operatives, Kroll was back in Russia, conducting initial reconnaissance with seed funding from Avigur.[63]

For two years, Kroll operated independently. He raised funds from Israel's Ministry of Religion and sent his first group of tourist-emissaries in September 1966: four men and one woman, all, like him, members of religious kibbutzim. Plans to send ten couples in September 1967 never came to fruition. The severing of diplomatic ties rendered travel to Russia on Israeli passports impossible. Adapting, Kroll looked instead to diaspora Jews and to Israelis with foreign passports. He flew to Paris, London, and Stockholm, where he mobilized connections in the B'nai Akiva religious Zionist youth movement to raise funds and recruit travelers. Between November 1967 and Passover 1968, the next three groups went out—one from Britain, one from Scandinavia, one from France, with four people in each. The travelers drafted reports, and Kroll passed them to Nativ. He recruited his first American group—nine men and two women—in New York in June 1968 and sent them over for Yom Kippur.[64]

Satisfied with what today would be called "proof of concept," Avigur informed Kroll prior to the New York trip that Nativ would adopt his initiative. Kroll was hired in fall 1968 and made responsible for "the sending of tourist-emissaries to the Soviet Union for the purpose of establishing contact with *aliyah* activists."[65] The move inside Nativ channeled the subsequent evolution of the tactic in five main ways.[66]

First, it provided the financial and administrative basis to *scale up*. Working independently in his spare time, Kroll had sent twenty-three travelers between November 1967 and October 1968.[67] Employed as the full-time director of a government operation and overseeing field officers across Europe and North America, he managed to send over ten times that number every year—a total of around six thousand visitors over the project's lifetime.[68]

Second, although tactical development still involved trial and error, managing it inside a bureaucratic organization led inexorably to its routinization in *standard operating procedures*: Former Nativ travelers and a handful of trusted local Jewish leaders—among them, faculty at Yeshiva University and the Jewish Theological Seminary in New York—recommended candidates for travel. The Nativ field officer, or sometimes Kroll himself, would then vet, recruit, brief, send, and debrief the travelers.[69] Field officers also oversaw travel arrangements, prepared lists of refuseniks to meet, and gathered materials to be delivered. Briefings included lists of "thou shalts" and "thou shalt nots." They prepared travelers to make contact with Soviet Jews (show this photograph of Kroll's daughter eating a watermelon, which will confirm your trustworthiness), to recognize surveillance (the phone in your room may be listening even when it is on the hook), to maintain discretion (write refuseniks' names and addresses in a code of your own devising; do not discuss sensitive information aloud; write on children's toy magic slates so that your writing disappears when the plastic film is peeled up), to develop cover stories (Q: "Who gave you these names?" A: "My rabbi"), and to conduct themselves appropriately if interrogated (no long answers; sign nothing).[70] After face-to-face debriefings, liaisons filed summaries with the home office. Travelers submitted detailed reports.[71] Back at headquarters, Kroll's team broke the reports and cables into separate data points, resynthesized the information, and analyzed it holistically. They entered information into card files (later a computerized database) containing records on thousands of Soviet Jews.[72] This systematic information-processing created a comprehensive picture broader than anything visible to the travelers themselves.

The cycle of briefing, material and information exchange, debriefing, report writing, database processing, and back to briefing would become standard procedure in American and European movement organizations by the mid-1970s. The convergence around a common practice stemmed partly from activists independently arriving at similar solutions to shared challenges. But it also reflected the diffusion of Nativ's tactical innovations as former Nativ travelers got involved in other groups' tourism work.[73] Nevertheless, tactical innovation around tourism would unfold differently when situated in loosely federated American volunteer groups as opposed to a hierarchical, semiclandestine government agency. Nativ was very much the latter, and this fact was crucial to the third way that the organizational context channeled its application of the mobilizing gaze: working from inside Nativ allowed

Kroll to take a *tailored and cumulative approach* to the mobilization of tourism.

Kroll had initially thought that tourism would be useful for bringing support and inspiration to Soviet Jews. The goal was broad and generic. Each visit could do much the same as any other and still be considered a success. Moving tactical development inside a government office with roots in the intelligence services encouraged more elaborate goal-setting. Rather than think of the trips as a series of one-offs, each could be strategized with larger ends in mind.

Nativ tailored its work by seeking out and recruiting travelers (as opposed to accepting walk-ins) and by assigning them specific missions. Active recruitment produced a distinctive demographic profile, different from the broader pool of tourists who ended up traveling for other movement organizations. Generally, Nativ's tourists were religiously engaged Jews, twenty-five to sixty years old, fluent in Hebrew, familiar with Israel, and Zionist in orientation. All this stemmed from Nativ's goal of directing emigrants to Israel, Kroll's roots in religious Zionism, and the use of network recruitment through B'nai Akiva, Yeshiva University, the Jewish Theological Seminary, and former Nativ tourists. In addition, many of the travelers were married couples—a by-product of Nativ's preference to send tourists in pairs for operational and security reasons.[74]

Missions varied: Deliver a particular medicine or eyeglasses of a certain prescription. Coordinate a handover of authority to a new contact person prior to the emigration of the current contact. Confirm that refuseniks had made preparations for an upcoming visit of British parliamentarians.[75] As Nativ gained experience sending tourists, its mission focus became more precise. Sometimes it was so single-minded that travelers received only one task to complete—for example, meet this or that *aliyah* activist and verbally deliver a short message. For the rest of the trip, they were simply to maintain cover as "regular tourists" participating fully in their Intourist group's activities.[76]

The recognition that one could tailor individual trips to accomplish unique missions was a sine qua non for a later iteration of tactical tourism: using a succession of tours to carry out extended missions too large for a single trip. For Israel's Independence Day in 1986, Nativ's field officer in Copenhagen, Avi Moshavi, sent an Israeli dance troupe from Sweden to perform in refuseniks' apartments. The performances were filmed. Assuming that Soviet authorities would learn of the performance, stop the dancers at customs, and confiscate their film, Moshavi had them leave the reel with Nativ's primary contact in Moscow, Yuli Kosharovsky. A week later, Kosharovsky passed it to a different group of tourists, one of whom managed to smuggle it out in his underwear.[77] Nativ was not the only organization to recognize the utility of a cumulative approach to travel. The Orthodox group Agudath Israel made it the organizing principle of the travel program it launched in 1981. Led by travel agents Mordechai Neustadt and Mendy Goldberg—both also rabbis—the Vaad L'Hatzolas Nidchei Yisroel sent teachers to lead Torah classes for refuseniks, maintaining continuity in the curriculum by having each new teacher pick up where the last left off.[78]

A fourth way that Nativ's organizational context channeled the mobilizing gaze was by enabling deliberate *experimentation to hone the tactic*. Nativ's realization that each trip could lay groundwork for future trips converged with a recognition of the depth of resources available. Because Nativ had the capacity to send a steady stream of tourists, if one group failed to accomplish a mission, it could send another to try again. Not viewing tourists as an especially scarce resource informed Nativ's willingness to send them on single-task trips. It also gave Nativ the flexibility to take risks. Not in the sense of endangering travelers or Soviet Jews: briefings emphasized that only the "thou shalt nots" were absolute and no "thou shalt" was binding, and tourists were to abort missions if they deemed circumstances unsafe.[79] But Nativ was willing to risk sending tourists on operations with small or unknown chances of success. It adopted the stance of a learning organization, experimenting with the tactic in order to hone it. Would it be easier to cross the border unmolested by air or by train? By ferry to the Baltics? Was the direct flight from Niigata, Japan, to Khabarovsk a viable route? Would customs officers be more lenient with tourists coming from neighboring communist countries? Did it make a difference if tourists had Jewish surnames or stereotypically Jewish looks?[80] Nativ also culled information from travelers' reports to build up an understanding of Soviet border control, surveillance, and interrogation practices. The cumulative learning orientation was such that Nativ even knew that a certain redheaded Leningrad customs agent was especially problematic.[81]

Finally, Nativ introduced *work routines and language from the clandestine services* into Soviet Jewry movement tourism. The agency inhabited this institutional world. It shrouded its work in secrecy. Only in the 1990s did Nativ allow its name to be revealed.[82] Before that, American Jewish activists knew of the agency only as Lishkat Hakesher, "the Liaison Bureau," or simply as "the Bureau" (Lishkah). Even today, when thousands of old tourist reports filed with activist groups in the US and Europe are freely available online, the reports in Nativ's archives remain classified.[83]

We might regard all the language of mission, cover, briefing, debriefing—*meśimah, kisui, tidrukh, tiḥkur*—and practices like using code, cover stories, and magic slates simply as organizational culture playing itself out.[84] But it was more. Secrecy may have been the default setting, but it was intentional. Kroll and his team insisted that tourists work with discretion and without explicit or full knowledge of Nativ's role. They believed this to be necessary for safeguarding tourists, who were vulnerable to the charge of carrying out anti-Soviet activities on behalf of a foreign government; for safeguarding Soviet Jews, whose contacts with foreigners were often used against them; for safeguarding the Jewish activist network in the USSR, which Soviet authorities were intent on disrupting; and for safeguarding the agency's low profile, which gave Nativ more freedom of action. Western activist groups shared concerns that indiscreet tourists could endanger themselves and Soviet Jews and acted similarly to Nativ.[85]

Drawing on the tradecraft and jargon of intelligence services had cultural consequences. We will treat these in the next chapter. Here, just note that, notwithstanding their practice, activists inside and outside Nativ vigorously resisted any attempt to frame their work as espionage or spy play—whether these came in the form of Soviet accusations, well-meaning but sensationalist press accounts, or tourists' imaginative flights of fancy. They insisted that tourists were acting within the bounds of Soviet law, and in fact, they managed to sustain the tourist operation for over a quarter century because the travelers generally were. Or at least the travelers were not straying too far or too frequently over the line.[86] Advising tourists how to behave if caught, a Comité des Quinze briefing guide reminded them, "You are not a spy and should not have done anything illegal in visiting the refuzniks." This is a remarkable sentence.

All at once it constitutes a reassurance, a warning, and a speech-act that attempts to create reality by declaring it to be so. It was true, and it was also a necessary fiction. Precisely because the Soviets could have chosen to prosecute the tourists on charges of anti-Soviet activity on behalf of foreign interests, Nativ and the other organizations stood firm in their position. Nativ recruiters rejected candidates who seemed too enthusiastic about the clandestine aspects of the trips.[87] Western activists discouraged their travelers from thinking of their travel as spy games, as when NCSJ associate director Myrna Shinbaum reprimanded a traveler for local press coverage of her trip: "We purposely do not use the word 'mission' and we try not to project a 'James Bond Spy Adventure' in a trip of this kind."[88] The Union of Councils' 1978 "Guidelines for Briefers"—stamped "Confidential"—opened by denying its own title: "The briefing of tourists should be considered a security matter and not the subject of newspaper or newsletter articles. There is no place for the sentence, 'We brief tourists to go to the Soviet Union' in any materials you produce. It is all right to say, 'we are in touch with people who go to the Soviet Union.' There is a difference."[89]

This battle was lost from the start. As we will see in chapter 4, in a Cold War context where American tourists in Russia were sneaking away from their Intourist guides to meet critics of the Soviet system, an espionage frame was all but guaranteed.

WESTERN VARIATIONS: DIFFUSION OF THE INNOVATION, INDEPENDENT INVENTION, AND NETWORKED LEARNING

American movement organizations made no systematic efforts to deploy tourism in the 1960s. They seized opportunities, however, to learn from and publicize reports by returning travelers. At the October 1963 Conference on the Status of Soviet Jews—the precursor to the April 1964 meeting that established the American Jewish Conference on Soviet Jewry (AJCSJ)—organizers gave the podium to Berkeley sociologist Lewis Feuer, freshly returned from a four-month academic exchange in Moscow. Feuer reported firsthand observations in his keynote address, "The Soviet Jews: Resistance to Planned Culturocide." In 1966, Louis Rosenblum's Cleveland Committee on Soviet Anti-Semitism (CCSA) circulated another Berkeley professor's travelogue in one of the movement's first handbooks for activism. The traveler, immunologist David Weiss, had initially planned to protest Soviet treatment of Jews by publicly rejecting an invitation to an academic conference on the Black Sea. At the urging of Rabbi Abraham Joshua Heschel, an architect of the October 1963 conference, Weiss instead used the trip as a fact-finding mission. Before departing, he was briefed by Nativ's Meir Rosenne.[90]

Tourism became more available to the movement in the 1970s with the general increase in Western travel to the USSR—spurred by the tourism industry's growth as well as by détente. (*Fodor's* introduced its first USSR travel guide in 1974. A year later, the Helsinki Accords demanded more tourism as a vehicle for "mutual understanding.")[91] By 1970, details about Nativ's new systematic approach to mobilizing mass tourism had begun filtering out to Western activist groups. Although Nativ aspired to secrecy, some of its travelers shared information about their trips with leaders of the establishment Conference, the grassroots Councils, and Student Struggle for Soviet Jewry (SSSJ). The earliest trip report in the AJCSJ's files came from a Chicago attorney who traveled to Russia in May 1970 as part of an American Civil Liberties Union delegation. One of Nativ's rare walk-ins, he showed up at the Israeli consulate in New York and was briefed by Moshe Decter and Yehoshua Pratt. In addition to filing his posttrip report with the Israelis, the attorney shared the eighty-nine-page document with AJCSJ leaders.[92] In July 1972, SSSJ's Jacob Birnbaum received a "Dear Yaakov" letter from a couple who had traveled for Nativ the previous month: "My husband and I would like to pass on to you some of our experience . . ." Four pages of day-by-day accounts followed, with names, addresses, and phone numbers of those they met. The letter mentioned pretrip meetings with the "Israeli Foreign Office" in a matter-of-fact tone, as if Israel's work was common knowledge. "Arie Kroll gave us materials to take in." The list of materials followed. Birnbaum passed a copy of the letter to the Union of Councils.[93] Similarly, at the National Conference in 1974, director Jerry Goodman and associate director Myrna Shinbaum marked up a copy of a thirty-four-page Nativ trip report shared by its authors, a husband and wife team who worked at Brandeis University. Across the top in all caps and double underlined were the words "NOT FOR PUBLICATION. DO NOT COPY. RETURN TO R. ISRAEL." The copy was never returned.[94]

Leaders of Soviet Jewry organizations could glean elements of Nativ's methodology from these reports. But what really spurred the movement-wide diffusion of Nativ's tactical innovations were Nativ tourists who helped North American and British Jewish groups build travel programs of their own. When the NCSJ decided to prepare orientation booklets for travelers to the USSR in 1974, it drew on the expertise of people who had firsthand knowledge of Nativ's recommendations for meeting with Soviet Jews as well as the modes of briefing and debriefing. Among these was the Jewish studies scholar Deborah Lipstadt, whose 1972 Nativ-sponsored trip ended prematurely when the Soviets expelled her.[95] A Brandeis University graduate student at the time (she would later become a US ambassador, as Special Envoy to Monitor and Combat Antisemitism), Lipstadt had already given Jewish Americans access to Nativ's approach by authoring a chapter on Soviet travel in the *Jewish Catalog*, a 1973 best-selling manual for countercultural Jewish living, modeled after the *Whole Earth Catalog*.[96]

In the Union of Councils, tourist briefings in the Miami region came under the direction of Nativ travelers Joel and Adele Sandberg. Whether Nativ knew of the Sandbergs' leadership in the UCSJ-affiliated South Florida Conference on Soviet Jewry when it sent them in May 1975 is unclear. The KGB may have known. The Sandbergs were interrogated, expelled, and then denounced in the Soviet press. In Russia, the Sandbergs used their Nativ-sponsored trip to carry out extra work for the UCSJ. Returning home, Joel Sandberg took up the chairmanship of the tourist briefing committee, drawing on his experience with Nativ. He went on to become the UCSJ's national vice president in the 1980s, where he served as a liaison for the group's tourist briefers nationwide.[97]

Former Nativ travelers also initiated tourist briefing operations that worked simultaneously with American groups and the Israeli agency. Haskell Lookstein, the rabbi of New York's Kehillath Jeshurun synagogue, had been briefed by Nativ's Yehoshua Pratt for a September 1972 trip. Upon his return, he organized New York–area Orthodox congregations to form a tourist briefing committee that coordinated with Nativ, the Greater New York Conference, and the NCSJ.[98]

Besides the diffusion of Israeli practices, other factors led to common movement-wide approaches to mobilizing tourism. Each group learned for itself. Each shared its learnings through a web of information exchange. By the mid-1970s, the UCSJ and NCSJ were each running independent North American tourism committees. Each saw committee members from different cities trading knowledge via telephone, mail chains, and in-person gatherings. Internationally, the Union of Councils coordinated with the 35s in London and the Comité des Quinze in Paris. There was even cross-pollination between the grassroots UCSJ and the establishment NCSJ in spite of their mutual suspicions. Local affiliates in Philadelphia, Miami, and Washington acted as conduits passing information between the two national agencies. In addition, all the organizations relied on the same refusenik leaders for guidance, receiving from them largely the same recommendations for using tourists to serve Soviet Jews' needs.[99]

As with Nativ, organizational imperatives impelled the Union of Councils' entry into the mobilization of tourism and channeled its approach to tactical development. This was less true of the National Conference, whose entry was spurred less by a compelling need to use the tactic than by constituent demands and by competitive pressures to not cede the field to the UCSJ. If for the grassroots Union, tourism represented a solution to problems, for the establishment Conference, it represented a problem that needed to be solved.

THE UNION OF COUNCILS' QUEST FOR MISSION CONTROL (1970–74)

In the UCSJ, the first call to approach tourism systematically came in 1970, around the time that six local Soviet Jewry councils united to form the Union itself. Cleveland's Louis Rosenblum, the architect of the national confederation, presented on the use of tourism at a conference in February. A few months later, he revised the Cleveland Council's handbook for activism to introduce a distinction between "mass participation projects" and "spearhead projects" that would be limited in scope but "capable of producing deep penetration and impact." First on the spearhead list was "Tourist Briefing":[100]

> Over 50,000 Americans visit the Soviet Union each year as tourists. . . . More than 7,500 of these visitors are Jews. . . . [It is] vitally important that those visiting the USSR are properly briefed. . . . Visitors should recognize the potential they represent—a) for maintaining contact . . .

b) for bolstering the morale of Soviet Jews, and c) of providing . . . information on the condition of Jews. . . . On their return, tourists should be interviewed. . . . Those who speak well should be encouraged to participate in radio and television interviews and also to join your speakers bureau.[101]

Such rationales did not tell the full story. Rosenblum also had organizational considerations in mind. He envisioned using tourism to help establish the brand-new Union of Councils on independent footing. Tourism could solve several problems at once. It could provide a direct line of information from the USSR, eliminating reliance on Nativ.[102] Information flowing in from UCSJ tourists would help secure operational independence, insulating the Union from Israeli attempts to use information as a lever of control, and enabling the Union to use its own control of information to shape the public conversation. (When the National Conference wavered in its support for the Jackson-Vanik Amendment, the Union of Councils used its direct line to refuseniks to pressure Conference leaders not to break ranks.)[103] At the same time, tourism helped solve the practical problem of making a strategic shift from consciousness-raising in the United States—the councils' main focus in the 1960s—to direct assistance for individual Soviet Jews. Tourism was of a piece with the UCSJ's move into package deliveries, adoptions, phone calling, and the like. Not only could tourists bring aid straight into people's apartments in Russia, but they could also return phone numbers, addresses, and updates on personal situations—all of which could support the UCSJ's other "People-to-People" efforts.[104]

Having articulated the call to mobilize tourism, Rosenblum spent the next four years experimenting with implementation. In 1971, he began corresponding with travelers from across the country, receiving trip reports from them. With Rabbi Daniel Litt, he debriefed travelers from the Cleveland area. He also collected cassette recordings of debriefing interviews conducted by other Soviet Jewry councils.[105] At the end of the year, he tried (unsuccessfully) to set up a UCSJ clearinghouse to coordinate local briefing efforts. He recruited a couple who had been active in the CCSA to travel on a US Department of Health, Education and Welfare tour in November. The pair traveled with Susan Somers, a Russian-speaking Oberlin student who had lived in Leningrad on a study abroad program. (Somers later served as a prosecutor in the United Nations war crimes tribunal for the former Yugoslavia.) The three left their tour group to visit Soviet Jewish activists. They delivered a telephone call recording machine, among other items, and took names, addresses, and documents back to the US. Upon returning to Cleveland, Carol and Morris Mandel went on the speaker's circuit and briefed other travelers. Rosenblum appointed them heads of the new national briefing committee, but beyond a few initial memos, the effort went nowhere.[106]

Rosenblum's choice to send the Mandels reflected his early awareness, akin to Kroll's, of the drawbacks of relying on whichever travelers happened to present themselves. Other UCSJ leaders voiced similar concerns in later years. Rosenblum tried several strategies to gain more control over the recruitment, sending, and debriefing of tourists. In the first half of 1972, he and Bay Area Council on Soviet Jewry head Harold (Hal) Light mobilized the UCSJ network in support of "Have Guts, Will Travel," a recent college graduate's plan to recruit students to visit Jews in Russia in three overlapping waves during the summer. Each set of returnees would brief the next outgoing group. As a promotional letter explained, well-intentioned visitors "have gone independently, been briefed independently, and have reported back independently. . . . This results in the typical traveler discovering in two weeks what has been known for two years." The initiative sought to address the "total vacuum of communication and coordination." Operating out of London, it managed to send only two travelers. Have Guts, Will Travel collapsed when the program's coordinator became embroiled with thugs who described themselves as members of "an intelligence network in England involved with Jewish and Israeli security." Rosenblum described them as "loonies."[107]

Two years later, in April 1974, Rosenblum himself signed on to an American Express tour, along with the heads of the Los Angeles council, Si Frumkin and Zev Yaroslavsky, and the South Florida council's Robert Wolf, whose work recruiting and briefing tourists was touted as a model for other councils to emulate. The four UCSJ leaders spent six days in strategy meetings with about sixty activists in Moscow and Leningrad. They smuggled out film reels of their meetings by passing them to other tourists in their group. (Customs agents exposed decoy reels in the UCSJ activists' suitcases.) Back in America, they urged the UCSJ to increase its use of tourism: "It is extremely important for us to concentrate on briefing tourists who are going to the USSR. This is rapidly becoming the only channel left open for communication since the Russians are busily cutting the phones of most activists. . . . Books should be sent in by RELIABLE tourists. . . . Some tourists got panicky and dumped the books, and were later too embarrassed to admit the truth."[108]

After his trip, Rosenblum continued searching for ways of finding "reliable" tourists. He recruited his daughter, Miriam, and future son-in-law, Sheldon Benjamin. They flew over in July and also reported back that the lack of a coordinated tourism effort was causing problems. They voiced criticisms of their own: "We returned, by arrangement, to [refusenik Vladimir] Slepak's place about 11 p.m. and had our first taste of the average performance of the average tourist: ignorance, small talk, and overstaying of welcome." They also passed along criticisms leveled by the refuseniks themselves: "It's very nice that they come, [Ilya Zoblonsky] said, but . . . most tourists wasted their own time, and that of the activists: they were ill-informed, or not informed at all, about the situation of Soviet Jews; and they did not, in general, bring items of use or value."[109]

The dilemma was not a shortage of tourists. Rather, what Rosenblum had envisioned as a "spearhead project" was functioning in practice as a "mass participation" project, without support systems to manage it effectively. It was a classic problem of cultural mobilization: the medium had constraining characteristics.[110] Rosenblum failed to take into account that mass leisure travel was just that—leisure for the masses. He doubled down on his original vision. Who could be more reliable travelers than himself, his fellow council leaders, and his own daughter? But this offered no systemic solution, and he also spent that summer working on a plan "to insure a reliable and constant flow of responsible and competent tourists." At Rosenblum's request, Yaroslavsky, of the Southern California Council for Soviet Jews, wrote up a proposal for a $100,000 "Project Lifeline" to subsidize travel by specially recruited "courier-tourists" who would "penetrate" the Soviet Union and be "beholden to the organization in completing their assignments."[111]

Had it succeeded, "Project Lifeline" might have restructured the UCSJ tourism effort along the lines of Nativ's model, but the initiative never got beyond the planning phase. Career developments soon pulled

Yaroslavsky and Rosenblum away from Soviet Jewry activism— Yaroslavsky to public office and Rosenblum to greater responsibilities at NASA. In later years, activists in Washington, Boston, Philadelphia, and other cities succeeded in raising modest funds to subsidize small numbers of travelers, but Rosenblum's vision of a tightly controlled tourism effort built around trained recruits was never realized.[112] The approach worked well for Nativ, a state agency, but it was ill-suited to the UCSJ, a loose confederation of volunteer groups committed to broad public engagement.

THE NCSJ'S CUSTOMER SERVICE ORIENTATION (1971–74)

Nativ and the Union of Councils pursued tourism to answer organizational challenges. The National Conference on Soviet Jewry had tourism thrust upon it. Its precursor, the AJCSJ (1964–71), had welcomed travelers as guest speakers but made no systematic effort to mobilize travel.[113] Instead, it went the opposite route. Urged on by Nativ during the Six-Day War, the AJCSJ set a policy, binding on members, that "no Jewish organizations should officially sponsor tours to the Soviet Union."[114] (Some member agencies, like B'nai B'rith, had been offering leisure tour packages that included the USSR.)[115] The NCSJ inherited this policy. Travel was not entirely out of bounds. Conservative Judaism's United Synagogue Youth (USY) started running trips to Russia for its teenage leaders in 1969 as a "specially structured intensive Jewish content experience for young people."[116] The NCSJ also quietly supported an effort to send attorneys to press Jewish political prisoners' cases before Soviet legal authorities.[117]

Jewish establishment organizations revisited their stance on tourism via another national coordinating agency, the National Jewish Community Relations Advisory Council (NJCRAC). The NCSJ shared office space with the group and was a member of its International Affairs Commission.[118] In November 1971, commission members met to discuss tourism. They knew that a growing number of travelers were meeting with Soviet Jewish activists. Some knew the Israelis were involved. Others probably suspected. They were also aware that the rival UCSJ was entering the tourism field.[119] Framing tourist visits as "important to the morale of Soviet Jews," the chairperson, Theodore Mann, encouraged the commission to join the fray. Rabbi Jonathan Porath, who led the USY trips, addressed the group to explain the benefits. He described how the teenagers visited Russian synagogues to worship, deliver prayer books, and talk with Soviet Jews. (They held no private meetings, only public encounters, mostly in and around the houses of worship.)[120]

Commission members took the bait. They urged the NCSJ to "prepare basic orientation materials for prospective travelers." They also said it would be good to have "an orderly process for gathering and making available information and impressions from returned travelers," but they did not mandate specific action. And so with no plan to make use of travelers and no specific need for information from them, the NCSJ accepted the call to prepare orientation materials. It delegated the task to the American Jewish Congress (AJCongress), which ran a travel agency and thus had personnel and expertise.[121]

In July 1972, the NCSJ and AJCongress released *How to Find and Meet Russian Jews: Briefing Kit for Travelers to the U.S.S.R.* Written by Phil Baum, the director of the Congress's Commission on International Affairs, and his deputy, Zev Furst, the thirty-two-page booklet drew on Furst's experience traveling with his wife to meet Soviet Jews in April 1971. It recommended pretrip readings, including Wiesel's *The Jews of Silence*. It suggested bringing religious items as gifts: "It may be difficult, for example, to explain your reasons for carrying a dozen talitot (prayer shawls).... Take with you one or two." Per the title—which framed the trips as if they were safaris to the mysterious East and Russian Jews as if they were elusive, exotic game—the guidebook recommended finding and meeting the objects of the search at synagogues (addresses, directions, and maps provided), cemeteries, and universities. It also advised that "by wearing a necklace with a Magen David [Star of David], or by displaying a Yiddish paper under your arm, or by carrying an El Al flight bag, you can let it be known that you are a Jew and are interested in meeting Jews." Tongue in cheek, it added, "Some say that the most effective device is simply to stand on a crowded street corner and give a deep sigh!"[122]

Emphasizing conversations with Soviet Jews, the booklet devoted pages to the content of potential discussions. Rule number one: "In conversations with Russian Jews, you must allow them to take the lead." Suggested questions followed: "Are they aware of expressions of support from abroad?" "Do they have an opportunity to study Hebrew or Yiddish?" "What obstacles are there in the way of those Jews who wish to leave?" None of the questions would elicit new or useful information for the movement, but the guidebook did not mention or hint at that. It suggested questions that would help tourists learn for themselves what activists already knew.

Education of tourists was a clear priority. Assuming that American Jewish travelers knew as little about their own community as they knew about Russian Jewry, the booklet devoted three pages to facts about Jews in the United States. It devoted six pages to facts about Israel. In case they ended up in conversations with "Soviet authorities or apologists," the briefing kit provided ready answers for "tough questions," such as "How can you presume to know what Russian Jews really want?" and "Isn't the 'Soviet Jewry question' essentially a creation of the militant Jewish Defense League?" The answers probably would not sway any "authorities and apologists," but they could firm up the convictions of the tourists themselves.[123]

Although the subtitle billed the booklet as a "briefing kit," *How to Find and Meet Russian Jews* was not a guide for briefers. Nor did the NCSJ or AJCongress produce companion materials to help activists brief and debrief tourists. The booklet was a stand-alone publication addressed to travelers who were assumed to be leisure tourists, not recruits on movement business. The organizations treated visits to Russia mainly as an opportunity for tourists to learn firsthand about the Soviet Jewish predicament and their booklet mainly as a service they were providing to assist. "If you know of anyone who is planning to go soon," the AJCongress wrote to its field offices, "we urge that you ask them to be in touch with this office so that we might offer our help."[124]

They were treading cautiously. As word of visits to aid Soviet Jewry spread, more American Jews wanted to take part. But as the NCSJ had no need or intention of recruiting tourists, the guidebook had to manage expectations. You are "in a unique position to help Soviet Jews," the booklet declared. How? The guidebook suggested the bare minimum. Simply "let our fellow Jews in the U.S.S.R. know of our sense of fellowship and continuing concern for their future."[125] It said nothing about meeting emigration activists, nothing about reporting information back. Nativ used tourism in concrete ways like this. The NCSJ was

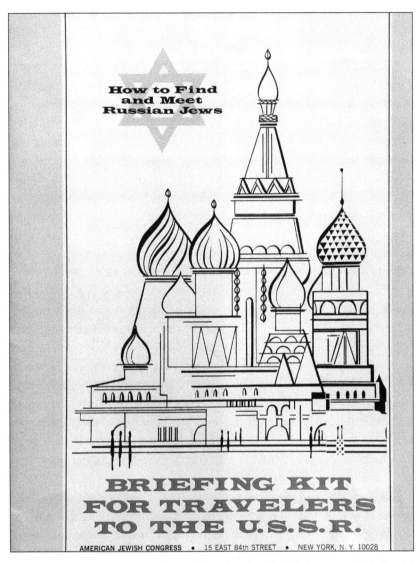

Figure 3.2. *How to Find and Meet Russian Jews*, American Jewish Congress, 1972. Special Collections Research Center, Temple University Libraries, Philadelphia, PA, SCRC 230, box 65, folder 13.

not inclined to duplicate, interfere, or compete with the Israeli bureau by creating its own parallel tourist-based information network. At least not in 1972.

Nor was the NCSJ eager to call attention to Nativ's clandestine work. It put nothing in writing that might lend credence to Soviet accusations of espionage or that might jeopardize travelers, Soviet Jews with whom they met, or the travel enterprise as a whole. The booklet opened with a disclaimer: "There is nothing in this Briefing Kit that recommends anything unlawful in the Soviet Union. . . . [Nevertheless], *to avoid any possible misunderstanding, we urge that this briefing packet itself not be taken into the Soviet Union.*"[126] (This did not stop the newspaper *Izvestia* from denouncing it as "anti-Soviet propaganda . . . [full of] anti-Soviet themes for verbal agitation and . . . recommendation[s] for making illegal contacts.")[127]

Nativ was undoubtedly aware of the Conference's move into tourism. A representative from the Israeli consulate, Yaacob Aviad, attended the November 1971 NJCRAC meeting. That no opposition was forthcoming suggests that Nativ saw an NCSJ tourism effort as unthreatening, perhaps even useful—whether by mobilizing more people to get involved in the movement, by heightening public pressure on the Soviets, by reaching a broader array of Soviet Jews beyond those visited by Nativ travelers, or by flooding the country with Jewish tourists to make it easier for Nativ's American travelers to blend in.[128] For any of these purposes, tourists only had to go in large numbers. Their value rested in their presence in Russia as concerned Jewish travelers. Which Soviet Jews they happened to meet was irrelevant.

Nativ and the Union of Councils saw tourism as useful for building networks with emigration activists in the USSR, delivering aid, and exchanging information. The National Conference saw tourism as useful for engaging more Jewish Americans in the movement, but not for using their involvement to any specific end. As a result, *How to Find and Meet Russian Jews* was deliberate in what it chose not to say. The NCSJ's first tourist guidebook drew no distinctions among Soviet Jews, treating any contact with the general population as valuable. It was full of practical advice for traveling in Russia but offered no suggestions for the return to America. It specified no posttrip expectations.[129] It was silent on debriefing. This was no failure of imagination but careful crafting. Intent on entering the tourism field but with no intention of enlisting travelers to serve specific needs, the NCSJ offered a guidebook that tried simultaneously to mobilize tourism and contain it.

Having wet its feet, however, the National Conference waded further in. External currents pulled it deeper. "Our agreement several months ago was not to go public in this fashion," NCSJ executive director Jerry Goodman admonished the AJCongress's Baum in December 1972, days after *Washington Post* coverage of the "travel brochure" had blindsided the Conference. But with the existence of the guidebook now public knowledge, he recommended expanding the tourism project, including "local or regional briefing procedures."[130] They had released the guidebook in July, too late to be useful during the 1972 vacation season. But if they planned in winter, they could promote the guidebook before people started making travel plans for summer 1973.[131]

The NCSJ's reluctant decision to position itself as a service provider in the tourism field soon generated consumer demand for the organization to do even more. With its name on the guidebook, the Conference found itself receiving requests for help from travelers and Soviet Jewry groups around the country. Responsive, the organization expanded its work, but without delineating any strategy to guide it. Trip reports started trickling in to the Manhattan headquarters in June 1973, mainly from New York and Philadelphia.[132] Soon, the office was receiving two or three a month from debriefers and from individual travelers across the United States. By 1974, NCSJ associate director Myrna Shinbaum was fielding inquiries from prospective travelers asking for names of refuseniks to visit—information that *How to Find and Meet Russian Jews* did not provide. She also began briefing and debriefing tourists, especially those from the New York area who wanted to supplement their local briefings with expertise straight from the national agency.[133] In August 1975, an overwhelmed Shinbaum dashed off a memo to Goodman: "I think is [sic] is essential we form a briefing committee of lay people staffed here with a volunteer working with me., [sic] at least one day per week.... It's getting too be [sic] to handle."[134]

SERVICE ORIENTATION, MISSION CREEP, AND HERITAGE TOURISM (1974)

As its tourism work grew, the NCSJ began preparing a new edition of the guidebook. Here, the agency's emphasis on service provision led the way, drawing the Conference into cultural production work that responded more to Jewish American travelers' yearnings than to Soviet Jews' needs. For a host of reasons rooted in Jewish, American, and Jewish American history, ranging from post-Holocaust trauma, to inspiration from the Black Power movement, to ambivalence over the price of success in attaining the American dream, many Jewish Americans in the 1970s were searching nostalgically for ethnic rootedness.[135] Heritage travel—to the Lower East Side, to Israel, and to the "Old Country" in the lands of the former czarist empire—afforded the opportunity to explore roots without being constrained by them.[136] In this context, Jewish American trips to the Soviet Union were more than leisure tourism and also more than a humanitarian aid mission. The NCSJ's leaders, having worked with Jewish American tourists to Russia, understood this. When they set out to revise the guidebook in 1974, they responded to Jewish Americans' complex motivations for travel. This responsiveness channeled the project in ways that lost sight of the immediate issue of aiding Soviet Jews.[137]

"Next to those in Israel, some of the world's oldest Jewish settlements are in the Soviet Union's Caucasian republics of Azerbaijan, Dagestan and Georgia.... Jews reached these regions during the sixth and seventh centuries B.C.E., first coming as traders from Palestine after Nebuchadnezzar's destruction of the first temple in Jerusalem in 586 B.C.E."[138] These opening lines of the NCSJ's unpublished *Travel to the U.S.S.R.: A Jewish Guide* set the tone for what was shaping up to be less a briefing kit for finding and meeting Soviet Jews than, as the title signaled, a general guidebook for Jewish heritage travel to the Soviet Union. The brochure displayed no expectation that travelers would spend their time skipping tours to sit with refuseniks. Actually, it assumed the opposite, directing tourists to sites of Jewish interest such as Moscow's Tolstoy Museum ("Includes a collection of Israeli-printed Hebrew translations of Leo Tolstoy's work") and the Sholom Aleichem House in Kiev. To further serve the Jewish tourist, the guide included general information about the country. ("Today the USSR covers more than eight million square miles. It is comprised of fifteen union republics.") It also offered helpful planning tips. ("Individual tourists may travel in the deluxe category, selecting any tour from a list of Intourist [itineraries], or may arrange a tour of their own.")[139]

It may be a misnomer to label the creation of the new guidebook an act of cultural "production." Little in it was actually authored by the NCSJ. The sections on Jewish history and heritage sites were retyped directly out of the only Jewish travel guide of the day, *The Landmarks of a People*. The general overview of travel to the USSR was lifted verbatim from *Fodor's Europe*. Much of the section on delivering support to Soviet Jews was copied from Lipstadt's chapter in the *Jewish Catalog*.[140] But although the words belonged to others, the idea of creating a resource to serve the Jewish American quest for roots even as Jewish Americans served the Soviet Jewry campaign was an innovation, one that the NCSJ could legitimately claim as its own. Whether it produced such a resource from scratch or from a patchwork of three existing texts was a technical matter. It might have been a legal matter had the project moved to completion. But for reasons unknown, and despite months of back-and-forth over revisions, the guidebook never saw the light of day.[141]

Although the guidebook never progressed beyond initial drafts, the attempt to produce it reveals just how much the initial deployments of tourism set Soviet Jewry groups down paths at once unanticipated but also recognizably part of tourism's universe. When first considering tourism's potential utility, no activists imagined producing a Jewish heritage travel guide to Russia. Neither Nativ nor the UCSJ ever entertained such an idea. They valued tourism primarily as a vehicle for collaborating with refusenik leaders.[142] The idea emerged in the NCSJ because it took a different approach to tourism, emphasizing simple human contact between large numbers of American and Soviet Jews. The Conference approached tourism in this way due to the peculiarities of its own organizational structure and history. Comfortably reliant on Nativ, it did not require an independent channel of information from Russia. Positioned as a hub in a nationwide network of hundreds of local Jewish community relations councils, it had the potential to reach millions of American Jews. Established by the major national Jewish organizations as a service organization to coordinate their activism, it was responsive to its constituents and to the Jewish communities they represented. The

NCSJ brought this service orientation to its tourism work. It saw its role as encouraging as much tourism as possible by providing help to the tourists: logistical help to make trip planning easier and practical help to enable tourists to satisfy their motivations for traveling. As these motivations involved interest in Jewish heritage travel, the NCSJ took up one of the tourism industry's ready models, the guidebook, and tried to produce one (or copy three) itself.

Perhaps this was mission creep. Or maybe it was a holistic approach to helping tourists serve the movement. Either way, guidebook production was not part of a preexisting tactical repertoire just waiting to be used. Rather, the NCSJ drew on its experience mobilizing tourism to follow this unanticipated path. It happened to be a dead end, but such dead ends show how much tactical innovation is truly an inventive process, full of trial and error.

ROUTINIZING THE TACTIC: GUIDEBOOKS, BRIEFING KITS, AND QUESTIONNAIRES

Around 1975, the NCSJ's and UCSJ's different paths into tourism converged. The Union moved closer to the Conference's service model; the Conference embraced the Union's transnational network-building approach. As we will see, the convergence largely began at the local level, in cities where activists were figuring out how to manage growing interest from tourists. Changes at the national offices also contributed. Louis Rosenblum's successors at the helm of the UCSJ were less preoccupied with finding a Nativ-style solution to control tourism. Inez Weissman (1974–75) and Irene Manekofsky (1977–78) brought a pragmatic approach gleaned from their experiences developing tourism programs at the Long Island Committee for Soviet Jewry and the Washington Committee for Soviet Jewry (WCSJ), respectively.[143]

As for the National Conference, after Jackson-Vanik passed in January 1975, the agency created a Soviet Jewry Research Bureau to assist congressional monitoring of Soviet emigration practices. With information-gathering from the USSR now part of the conference's mandate, and with a new department and staff dedicated to the work, tourism became useful to the NCSJ in ways it had not been before. As trip reports flowed in, the NCSJ culled data for the Research Bureau's use. It also began encouraging activists in its network to visit Russia in order to exchange information with refusenik leaders.[144]

Collaboration between local affiliates of the two national coordinating bodies also contributed to the convergence around a shared approach. Affiliates in Philadelphia and Miami—each of which operated robust tourism programs—maintained simultaneous membership in both the UCSJ and the NCSJ, sharing information with both parent agencies. But the local collaboration most responsible for creating a movement-wide set of work routines for mobilizing tourism came from the DC area. They called it "the Insiders Club."

In 1974, the Washington Committee for Soviet Jewry (a Union of Councils affiliate) and the Soviet Jewry Committee of the Jewish Community Council of Greater Washington (JCCGW, a National Conference affiliate), created the Insiders Club to coordinate their separate tourism efforts under a single umbrella. They hoped to eliminate duplication and reduce interorganizational conflict.[145] The by-product of their decision to coordinate was novel and consequential: a systematic articulation, in writing, of organizational practices for managing the tourism workflow.[146] The Insiders Club was the first American organization to publish a guidebook oriented toward prearranged meetings with Jewish activists in the USSR, to codify briefing and debriefing procedures, and to develop standardized paper work to compile information from returning tourists. Leaders of the Insiders Club assumed roles in nationwide tourism efforts, spreading their written materials and their expertise to the UCSJ, NCSJ, and local affiliates.[147]

THE INSIDERS CLUB GUIDEBOOK FOR TRAVELERS

The Insiders Club's 1974 *Guidebook for Contacting Jews in the Soviet Union* was written by two attorneys and a Jewish educator—the WCSJ's Herbert Beller, who first got involved in aiding Soviet Jews during a family vacation in Russia in October 1973; JCCGW volunteer Norman Goldstein; and the JCCGW's Soviet Jewry Committee staff person Samuel "Buddy" Sislen. Produced a year after travelers from Washington had reported back that Soviet Jews were disparaging the AJCongress's briefing kit as containing "meaningless instructions," the new guidebook took a different approach.[148] Not only would the Insiders Club serve tourists, but tourists would also serve the Insiders Club. The guidebook encouraged travelers specifically to visit Jews who had applied for emigration visas and urged coordination before and after:

> Information regarding applicants for emigration and their specific situations is received on an ongoing basis by the Insiders Club. Those tourists who wish to visit such persons are urged to contact us for more detailed information prior to departure.
>
> Perhaps the best "protection" that a Soviet Jew who has applied to emigrate can have is specific knowledge and monitoring of his or her situation by Westerners....
>
> We look forward to hearing from you when you return. Knowledge of your experiences is indispensable to perpetuating the goals of the Insiders Club.[149]

Like *How to Find and Meet Russian Jews*, the Insiders Club guidebook was deliberate in what it did not say. In contrast to the AJCongress guide, however, the silences sought not to keep tourists at bay but to protect the enterprise that was sending them. Comparisons of draft and final versions reveal initial cloak-and-dagger instincts held in check. Stricken from the final version was language informing readers that the Insiders Club could provide them with "specific information and photographs" of suspected KGB informants, advising them to "discreetly" hide materials from customs officers, and asking them to bring home information on "the identity of new applicants for emigration." The Insiders Club would communicate all this, but not in writing. They reserved it for in-person briefings that were not to be referred to as such in public. Where the draft said, "Contact us for a detailed briefing," the final text used the innocuous "Contact us for more detailed information."[150]

The "us" was prominently advertised. Unlike *How to Find and Meet Russian Jews*, which acknowledged AJCongress authorship at the bottom of its cover in a nondescript eight-point gothic sans serif and buried the NCSJ's name next to the $1.25 price on the back, the Insiders Club guidebook highlighted the group's name and logo in a large cover graphic. Dropping the veil of secrecy in favor of public-relations-minded branding added a new element to the movement's deployment of tourism—one that saw tourism's prestige as a usable asset.

Figure 3.3. *Guidebook for Contacting Jews in the Soviet Union*, cover graphic. Insiders Club, Washington Committee for Soviet Jewry and Jewish Community Council of Greater Washington, 1974. Graphic design by Avrum Ashery, uncredited. American Jewish Historical Society, RG I-181A, box 91, folder 2.

Branding the initiative served the practical function of pointing travelers to a single organization with an easily remembered name rather than forcing them to choose between confusing acronyms from the Jewish organizational alphabet soup. Internally, the shared brand smoothed the partnership, enabling the sometimes antagonistic WCSJ and JCCGW to come together as equal partners on neutral ground. As for the specific choice of brand identity, the name and logo reveal much about activists' thinking about their tactic. The creators of the Insiders Club understood that Soviet Jewry movement tourism could engage Jewish Americans by playing to their desires for adventure, prestige, and efficacy. Cold War culture and the leisure tourism industry overall both gave travel to the USSR cachet. Americans perceived the destination as exotic, impenetrable, and alluringly dangerous. In the idiom of the day, tourists might go *to* France, but they went *into* the Soviet Union. Even better for claiming prestige, few people actually went. The number of American tourists to the Soviet Union had risen to about eighty thousand in 1974, but this remained less than one-half of 1 percent of the US population. Russia was an elite destination. Returning tourists could brag about having been there. The "Insider" part of the brand name played on these connotations. As for the "Club," this not only spoke to the exclusive nature of the travel; it was also steeped in the prestige culture of American Jewish fundraising appeals, where donor categories bore names like Ruby Division, Prime Minister's Club, and Lion of Judah.

The Insiders Club logo was as powerful a representation of tourism's utility to the movement as activists could have hoped for. Created by Avrum Ashery, a graphic designer with the federal government who had created the tiger-stripe pattern for the Cincinnati Bengals' football helmets, the logo was a bold geometric rendering of a hammer and sickle, simple and striking. The stylized sickle—in the background, in light pink—was a perfect circle, almost entirely closed. Inside, it trapped a large, solid Star of David, which was foregrounded in dark pink. Also in the foreground was the hammer's handle, rendered as an arrow piercing the blade, reaching the six-pointed star in the center. Pulling triple duty, the star served as the hammer's head, as a representation of trapped Soviet Jews, and as a representation of the American Jewish tourists who had managed to break through and get "inside" to meet them.[151]

THE INSIDERS CLUB OUTLINE FOR BRIEFERS

In February 1975, four months after the guidebook's release, the Insiders Club met to establish standard operating procedures for briefing, debriefing, and sharing information. As with Nativ, here was another instance where organizational imperatives for bureaucratic routine channeled tactical innovation. The WCSJ and JCCGW needed codified policies and clear lines of authority to make the collaboration work. The follow-up memo outlined the procedure: All names, travel dates, and contact details of prospective travelers would be funneled to Jane and Herbert Beller (the guidebook author), who would coordinate the effort. They would assign briefers and debriefers, receive all travel reports, and act as a clearinghouse for all pre- and posttrip records, giving the Insiders Club a comprehensive view of the enterprise.[152]

Attached to the memo was a "Travellers Orientation Outline." Intended to guide face-to-face meetings with prospective travelers, this served as the briefers' companion to the tourists' guidebook. The outline covered information that required deeper explanation or that the Insiders Club preferred not to circulate in a public document: what types of surveillance to expect (telephone taps, bugs in the hotel room, Intourist reports to the KGB); how to take countersurveillance measures (magic slates, flushing notes in the toilet); how to legally transfer money to refuseniks, as cash gifts were against the law; how to bring materials for delivery; and how to return information to the US. It also gave an overview of the Soviet Jewry movement in the United States.[153]

Placed on its own at the top right of the page was a list containing four items, two of which were starred:

   A) Visiting family
   *B) Involved, visiting activists
   C) Uninvolved, poor background
   *D) Special Mission

Unassuming in appearance, the list was actually the conceptual advance that solved the problem of being pulled between the opposite poles of mission focus versus customer service orientation. The Insiders Club would divide tourists into categories and tailor different briefings to each. Only those in groups B and D would be told to flush notes in the toilet, taught to interpret the Soviet system for writing addresses, and instructed to deliver scientific journal articles and legal documents. Using a slightly different three-category division, the accompanying memo made it clear that the Insiders Club intended to keep walk-ins at arm's length, serving them only minimally. They would direct "casual tourists" only to public settings—"synagogues, [and] places of Jewish sightseeing interest"—similar to the NCSJ's approach in *How to Find and Meet Russian Jews*. At the other end of the spectrum, they would task "activists" in the American campaign with "special instructions," directing them to meet with "key activists" in the refusenik community. As for those in the middle—"travellers involved generally in [the] Soviet Jewry [campaign]"—they would be treated as casual tourists. If they asked to meet with refuseniks, the Insiders Club would give them addresses of "non-key activists."[154]

The decision to divide tourists into categories emerged out of a concern to not waste Soviet Jewish activists' time and also out of a growing sense that in the initial rush to send tourists, they had not "given serious thought to security." In January 1975, the Washington Committee's Irene Manekofsky had written UCSJ briefers across the country, warning of the "danger" in giving refuseniks' names and addresses "to people you are not entirely sure will be discreet." As she explained, "A tourist coming back from visiting refuseniks and speaking in a public place could say: 'I was sent to see so-and-so by the local Soviet Jewry organization' and the Soviets could slap a conspiracy charge on that Jew [i.e., the refusenik] for conspiring with foreign organizations."[155]

Concerns for the security of tourists, refuseniks, and the tourism operation were not misplaced—although the Soviets were more likely to respond aggressively to travel by movement leaders than by "casual" tourists. In February, even as the Insiders Club was codifying its plan to divide tourists into three groupings, UCSJ president Inez Weissman of the Long Island Council traveled to Moscow and Leningrad to discuss a similar tripartite categorization with refusenik leaders there. She reported this back to the Union of Councils confidentially. Soviet authorities, however, had surveilled the meeting, copied Weissman's notebooks, and decided to make a show of its omniscience.[156] An *Izvestia* "exposé" of the "Zionist emissaries [who] try like cockroaches, to crawl into the

Soviet Union through every crack" detailed the tourism plan category by category:

> They gathered in this apartment, as if it were a purely chance meeting, secretly, observing all the rules of conspiracy. . . . All these [tourists], as Inez Weissman explained to those present, would be sub-divided into three categories. Ordinary tourists . . . would be given the "simplest" tasks. . . . American employees of Zionist organizations would. . . . undertake agitation for the emigration of Jews to Israel, in particular people with scientific degrees. . . . And lastly . . . Leaders of American Zionists . . . would . . . meet only with so-called "leaders." . . .
>
> Those who came to the meeting with Madame President didn't know how to extricate themselves from this gathering and barely heard the Zionist recruitment speeches, which fall under a certain article of the Soviet Criminal Code.[157]

This show of surveillance power was a warning but not a setback.[158] The Insiders Club had been implementing the differentiated approach for over four months before the *Izvestia* article appeared. The practice spread through the UCSJ and NCSJ and became the standard operating procedure mainly because it reconciled the contradictions between using tourism to accomplish specific work in the USSR and using tourism to mobilize mass support in the US. Activists could rely on handpicked travelers for substantive tasks without turning away or dampening the enthusiasm of others who wanted to help.

This created a pecking order. Armed with contact lists and knowledge of the refusenik network's structure, the UCSJ and NCSJ substantially controlled Jewish tourists' access to Soviet Jews. The organizations were in a position to match high-status tourists with high-status refuseniks. Nevertheless, complaints about overburdening Soviet Jewish leaders with too many visitors persisted through the 1980s. Activists on both sides of the ocean repeatedly resurfaced the same proposed solution: send lower-status tourists to meet with lower-status refuseniks, especially out in the smaller republics. As one Soviet émigré told American activists in a 1976 meeting at NCSJ headquarters, "If everyone goes to Slepak because he lives in the right place, it is not only bad because others will not get tourists but it will make Slepak 'crazy.' His work is already difficult. He should be sent only those who are 'sophisticated' and have something to say." (Vladimir and Maria Slepak, among the most prominent refuseniks, lived a ten-minute walk from Red Square, on the main boulevard. Their apartment was the most visited of all refusenik domiciles.)[159]

The complaints were in vain, and the movement's organizational structure guaranteed this. The UCSJ and NCSJ were clearinghouses: they convened, they coordinated, but they did not command. Each city or state's Soviet Jewry movement organizations ran their own tourism programs. Each had the same incentive to send their own local community members. The inevitable result was a continual stream of tourists converging on the apartments of the same few refusenik leaders. Between January and April 1986, UCSJ tourists from the US and Britain paid 842 visits to 309 refusenik households in Moscow and Leningrad. The top 4 percent of these households received as many visits as the entire bottom 50 percent. Alexander and Rosa Ioffe were visited nineteen times by travelers from Baltimore, Boston, Chicago, San Francisco, London, and Manchester. Natasha and Gennady Khassin opened their doors to sixteen separate sets of visitors from Chicago, Cincinnati, Minneapolis, Philadelphia, Seattle, San Francisco, England, Israel, and Switzerland. The Ioffes, the Khassins, and the others in the top 4 percent, only twelve families, received a total of 157 visits—an average of thirteen each. Over the same four months, each of the 153 families who made up the bottom 50 percent were visited only once.[160]

THE INSIDERS CLUB DEBRIEFING QUESTIONNAIRE

The Insiders Club 1975 orientation memo ended by systematizing procedures for posttrip debriefings. Briefers were to give returning travelers a six-page "Insiders Club Questionnaire" and ask them to file a written report. Narrative reports buried the details. The questionnaire aimed for efficiency: isolate key facts and ready them for data processing. "Our goal is to insure the debriefing within 24–36 hours," wrote a tourism coordinator in Philadelphia who was using the Insiders Club Questionnaire. "It is often more practical to use forms rather than waiting for tourists to write a lengthy report."[161] Forms were standardized with checkboxes, multiple-choice questions, roman numeral outlines, and clearly labeled sections. First came questions about travel arrangements, then searches and confiscations at customs, then contact with Jews. An eighteen-point checklist asked about tour guides and hotel management, medications and transportation, surveillance and bugging: "Check if you had any adverse reactions."[162]

The longest battery of questions sought details on meetings with Soviet Jews: List their names, addresses, and working phone numbers

```
                                - 2 -

    III.  CONTACTS WITH JEWS

          A. Where did you meet them?
             [] synagogue?                  [] hotels?
             [] homes?                      [] other? _____

          B. How did you contact them?
             [] knock on their door?        [] telephone?
             [] prior letter or arrangement?

    IV.   DAILY ROUTINES (Check if you had any adverse reactions to the following:)
                         BE SURE TO INCLUDE WHEN AND WHERE

          Intourist guides _____   Service Bureau Personnel _____

          Hotel Management _____   Physical Conditions _____

          Matrons (key ladies) _____   Medications _____

          Visitors to your room _____   Airplanes _____

          Surveillance _____   Taxis _____

          Security _____   Metro _____

          Bugging _____   Buses _____

          Use of Phones _____   Locating an address _____

          Documents (i.e. visa, vouchers,    Other _____
          etc._____

    V.    SYNAGOGUE

          A. Which ones did you attend?
             _____
             _____

          B. Could you sit where you wished? _____
          C. Were certain seats assigned to you? _____
          D. Did you participate in Services? _____

             Explain: _____
                      _____

          E. Could you speak freely? _____
          F. With whom did you make contact?

             NAMES _____
                   _____

          G. Other relevant facts: _____
```

Figure 3.4. Page from the Insiders Club Questionnaire. Washington Committee for Soviet Jewry and Jewish Community Council of Greater Washington, 1975. American Jewish Historical Society, RG I-540, box 9, folder 10.

("working" because the government often cut refuseniks' lines). List the items you left and with whom you left them. List refuseniks' requests for future deliveries, person by person: "Did they give you specific items to take out with you? (i.e., letters, written articles, kopecs, etc.)." If they gave names of other potential emigrants, list those too, with "vital statistics, exact Russian spelling of names, birthdates, parents names." Ten more short-answer questions asked what Soviet Jews said about harassment at work, shortwave radio reception, prison conditions, and the like.[163] An eleventh question in a draft version asked if they conveyed "top secret information (i.e. military, political, etc.)"—a sign that activists themselves sometimes slipped into thinking of the trips as a form of espionage. A single stroke of a cautious pen crossed out that item, however. The final questionnaire asked nothing of the sort.[164]

With the information efficiently organized, it was ready for quick processing. Activists transferred questionnaire data into card files with folders for each refusenik. Master lists tracked who received what and what was needed for whom. In later years, the organizations migrated the whole system over to first-generation home computer databases. The record-keeping changed the movement. The campaign had begun with generalized expressions of support for Soviet Jewry as an anonymous mass. By the mid-1970s, activists were creating a known population of Soviet Jews from the steady compilation of data points on thousands of individuals, week after week, year after year.[165]

Activists shared what they learned. Memos and newsletters reported on changes in specific people's circumstances and gave general updates about refuseniks' and prisoners' conditions overall. Memos to other briefers shared information from past tourists to aid in sending future tourists. Activists used the questions about travel arrangements, customs searches, and the like to monitor and improve the tourism operation itself.[166]

The Insiders Club debriefing questionnaire also included one page that the tourists never saw. Printed with office routing checkboxes at the bottom, it asked debriefers to talent-spot: "Is this person open, responsible and receptive enough to be a speaker on Soviet Jewry?" "Can this person be helpful and therefore be invited to join the Insiders Club?"[167] Tourism could be made useful in many ways. Not only could it help bring support and information in and out of Russia; it could help bring supporters into the movement in the United States. Here, the tactic functioned at its most reflexive: Engaging travelers by involving them in the process of sending travelers.

The Insiders Club Questionnaire was circulated to NCSJ and UCSJ affiliates across the country. Philadelphia's Soviet Jewry Council removed the Insiders Club name and reset the layout but otherwise adopted the form verbatim. Washington and Philadelphia appear to have been the only communities providing standardized debriefing forms between 1975 and 1981. After that, other groups began creating their own, including the NCSJ and the UK's National Council for Soviet Jewry. Although never universally adopted, the use of standardized debriefing questionnaires to collect information from returning tourists nevertheless became widespread.[168]

CONVERGENCE ON A STANDARD SET OF WORK ROUTINES

For the UCSJ, the NCSJ, and their local affiliates, 1970 through 1975 was a time of trial and error. The groups experimented with different approaches to mobilizing mass tourism and learning about the tactic's potentials and pitfalls, opportunities and constraints. Although activists tried to lead the process, the process sometimes led them. After all, tourism contained an inner logic of its own. It also generated an enthusiastic response that activists struggled to handle. Although differences in organizational context initially led the UCSJ and NCSJ to approach the tactic from opposite angles—one seeking to render it serviceable, the other to hold it at bay—the organizations' structural similarities ended up outweighing their differences. Both were national umbrella agencies trying to coordinate a decentralized network of local affiliates. With limited budgets and small professional staffs, they depended on volunteers. Local groups holding dual affiliations with both national bodies helped the UCSJ and NCSJ converge on an approach that balanced a top-down mission focus with a bottom-up service orientation.

With the national circulation of the Insiders Club guidebook, briefers' outline, and debriefing questionnaire and with the networking of tourist briefing committee leaders across North America and Western Europe, the movement settled into standard work routines for mobilizing mass tourism. They continued tinkering at the perimeter—swapping out stapled briefing pamphlets for easy-to-update three-ring binders, adding instructions for photographing documents or choosing customs agents, and introducing role-playing scripts to prepare tourists for interrogation. ("'Why are you walking around at night with tang [orange drink powder]?' 'My doctor told me to take tang every few hours for my health.'")[169] But by 1975, the overall template for using tourism was set.

The template proved versatile, allowing activists to expand the deployment of tourism and tailor it to engage new populations and accomplish new tasks. It became especially helpful in mobilizing people via their professional identities, putting their specialized skills to use.[170] The movement's expertise in tourism enabled the UCSJ's Medical Mobilization for Soviet Jewry and the NCSJ's Medical Action Committee to send oncologists and obstetricians to run makeshift clinics in refuseniks' apartments.[171] It helped groups like the New York Legal Coalition for Soviet Jewry to send lawyers and judges to aid refuseniks contending with the Soviet criminal justice system.[172] It served the Committee of Concerned Scientists when it sent mathematicians and biochemists to lecture at underground seminars in the living rooms of defenestrated refusenik and dissident faculty.[173] And of course, it helped religious groups send more rabbis, hundreds more, to continue the work that David Hollander's RCA delegation started in 1956.[174]

CONCLUSION

In the 1970s and '80s, Soviet Jewry activists sent a continual flow of Jewish Americans to the USSR, tourist-emissaries who brought aid to refuseniks and information back to movement organizations. They developed tourism as a mass mobilization tactic not by choosing among existing tactical repertoires but by inventing something new. Activists began applying a mobilizing gaze to tourism in the 1950s, as soon as the political opportunity structure allowed. But these initial uses of travel were isolated, ad hoc, and limited to elites. Between 1968 and 1975, activists changed tack. They began systematically mobilizing mass leisure tourism. This strategic shift altered the Jewish American experience of the Cold War, creating a popular route through the Iron Curtain that let tens of thousands take the fight against Soviet human rights violations and systemic antisemitism directly to the USSR itself.

The travelers were, by and large, affiliated Jews embedded in communal networks—families, synagogues, federations, community centers. A shared experience around Soviet Jewry movement travel blossomed in Jewish American public culture. It even touched the lives of those who did not board the flights themselves. Synagogues mobilized congregants who were not traveling to assist those who were. Congregants set their laundry machines to heavy duty, washed and rewashed newly purchased blue jeans, and gave the now seemingly worn garments to travelers to deliver to refuseniks, who would sell them on the black market.[175] When the travelers returned—and there were travelers returning every few weeks for two decades—those who stayed home heard about the trips. Talk about visits with Soviet Jews filtered into American Jewish communal settings from the top down and the bottom up. Leaders of national agencies spoke about their travel at conventions and wrote about it in association magazines and newsletters.[176] Returning rabbis took the pulpit to preach.[177] Returning congregants ascended the pulpit, too, as did celebrities.[178] Soviet Jewry organizations sent returnees out to address local community groups.[179] Many travelers received their fifteen minutes of fame in Jewish newspapers and in the local press, where the notion of "Community member risks KGB to help oppressed Russian Jews" was irresistibly newsworthy.[180]

Activists were not intending to create a Jewish American culture around the trips. They thought they were using tourism to aid Soviet Jews and to gather information. The American cultural consequences were an unintended by-product. But such by-products are common when social movements create mass mobilization tactics that actually succeed in mobilizing masses. Activists created new behaviors that tens of thousands of Jewish Americans personally took up, and that indirectly engaged many times more. Jewish Americans found these behaviors meaningful. As we consider what Soviet Jewry movement tourism looked like from the travelers' perspectives, the theme of unintended consequences will become even more prominent. After all, if tourists understood things exactly as the activists did, then the briefers at Chicago Action for Soviet Jewry would never have had to admonish them, "DON'T make it sound like a James Bond movie."[181]

4

FROM RUSSIA, WITH ANGST

What follows is a description of an attempt to arrange a meeting with refuseniks Mark and Slava Shiffrin from the March 1984 trip report of Rabbi Howard Shapiro of Temple Israel, West Palm Beach, Florida, briefed by Hinda Cantor of the South Florida Conference on Soviet Jewry (SFCSJ). Note the style: straightforward, direct, dry. Just what one might expect, given the document's purpose: the SFCSJ requested the report in order to update its refusenik files, alert its advocacy network, and refine its tourist briefings:

> Wednesday Morning
> The day began kind of confusingly. We went downstairs and had breakfast and lo and behold there was no guide nor was there anybody waiting for us or looking for us to lead us around by the nose. So, we decided to go out on our own. We took a walk—walked two blocks from the hotel and behold there was another hotel—walked another two blocks more and finally found a telephone booth. We began with four different telephone calls. Finally connected with Mark Shiffrin. Mark was hard to understand on the phone with his directions but he told us to take the subway and to meet him at the Subway Station near the Pusshkin [sic] museum.[1]

"*We* went." "*We* decided." "*We* took a walk." Shapiro had a traveling companion, another Reform rabbi—Barry Tabachnikoff of Congregation Bet Breira in Miami. "RabTab," as his congregants affectionately called him. He also submitted an account of the same events. But whereas Shapiro delivered measured, just-the-facts prose, Tabachnikoff offered something very different. A rabbi from balmy Florida finds himself in snow-swept Moscow trying to arrange surreptitious meetings with people on KGB watchlists? Why not enjoy the absurd?

> Wednesday, March 21
> Up early and take a walk before breakfast to "get oriented." "Never use the phones nearest the hotel." TABACHNIKOFF's THEOREM states, "The further you travel from your hotel, the closer you are to the next hotel." We walk a few blocks to find an isolated phone. "No, let's not call from RED SQUARE. Perhaps not this phone, directly in front of a police station either. Nah, let's get out of the earshot of the nice crossing guard." ...
>
> As I dial for Mark and Slava Shifrin, I notice an elderly woman sweeping snow from the streets. She even cleans the inside of the phone booth adjoining ours. On the third ring, as I am about to make contact, the cleaning woman enters MY PHONE BOOTH—all I can think of is the film, "DR. STRANGELOVE" when he needs a coin to call the White House. "Shalom" "Shalom." Damn, I wish this lady would get out of here—how can I talk with "agents hanging onto my every word?"[2]

Playful from start to finish, Tabachnikoff reveled in the chance to write himself as an accidental spy in over his head. His travelogue opens with a wink:

> Departure on Monday, March 19. ...
> As expected, my departure gate was at the furthest possible point from the airport terminal. I arrived totally out of breath and was confronted with my first challenge. "Remember, once you reach the airport, you are an ordinary tourist, you are no longer a Rabbi." These words echoed in my mind as I stood toe to toe with a congregant's parents! "Going to New York, Rabbi[?]" they asked, in an off-hand manner. I looked both ways before admitting, with a casual shrug, "Perhaps." ...
> In flight I read Ken Follett: *The Man From St. Petersburg* [a spy novel], to get in the mood. Appropriately, the flight shows a James Bond flick.[3]

And it ends with a smile:

I feel reluctant about being relaxed until I have cleared Helsinki's Customs. Bought a few odds and ends while waiting and even smoked a Cuban cigar—to demonstrate my freedom!. . . .

WE ARE ALIVE AND WELL.

WE HAVE ENTERED AND LEFT.

MISSION ACCOMPLISHED WITHOUT MISHAP. . . .

P.S. WATCH FOR "THE FURTHER ADVENTURES IN NEW YORK" TO LEARN HOW THE AIRPORT WAS CLOSED AND TWELVE INCHES OF SNOW FELL UPON THE AMERICAN RABBIS.[4]

Like Tabachnikoff, Shapiro also wrote in a consistent style. Even when acknowledging emotions, he did so with sobriety. Consider his poignant concluding paragraph, so different from his companion's:

Our last day in Leningrad—had lunch with Mark Budnyatsky. He told us of his need for a mini tape recorder. We said good-bye—hard to do, and watch him walk away to the subway and continued slavery as we walked to our hotel and our return to the West and freedom. The image of his walking away from us and our turning our backs on him was very real and physical to me—I vowed it would not be symbolic—there would be a return to each other, hopefully, and with God's help in Israel, "speedily and in our day."[5]

Sometimes, the sense of living out a Cold War espionage thriller got the better of Shapiro too. He did not luxuriate in the genre like Tabachnikoff. He merely noted his anxieties—as in this description of a nighttime attempt to call a refusenik: "The line was busy and we wandered from telephone booth to telephone booth for half an hour waiting for the line to clear. It didn't. Of course our imagination ran wild; we figured our earlier phone call had been intercepted; the line was being kept busy by sinister forces, etc."[6]

Shapiro's and Tabachnikoff's reports contained all the standard information that Cantor and the SFCSJ would have found useful. They gave accounts of the customs inspection:

Items which were taken away from us included "Wanderings" by Chaim Potok, the little stickers that kids use with Israeli flags and menorahs on them, any identifiable religious article that they could find, and our watch pens. (Shapiro)[7]

They gave updates on refusenik's occupational and legal situations:

> We spoke with Mark and Frieda about Mark's situation vis a vis his job. He works as a stoker in one of the public baths in Leningrad and three of the other stokers are also Refuseniks. They work 24 hours and then they have three days off. . . . I get the impression that they are hopeful because they have to be, yet realistic as well. Mark is a fighter and will never stop fighting. A few weeks ago his Hebrew books were taken away from him by the authorities. (Shapiro)[8]

They documented health information:

> [Uri S.] is being treated for Lymphoma and has had Chemo and radiation, but the doctors are not certain of his illness. They will get us his medical test results for us to bring back for a consultation locally. . . . When they give me the papers, I fold them in my wallet along with my own EKG which makes it appear to be a part of my own medical "case history." (Tabachnikoff)[9]

They detailed items they distributed:

> We gave them all the things that we had brought, the two coats, the tape recorder, we gave Gregory his watch, and we had a camera for them as well. They told us about the problems they are having now with the cameras. The authorities have tightened up very greatly on the black market. (Shapiro)[10]

They conveyed requests for new materials to send:

> They requested that the next time someone comes to please bring jogging shoes, tee shirts, any kind. Natasha also only requested if it be possible to bring in a wig, even two, a long black one for nights and a short one for days. This is for the wife of a religious prisoner from Kiev. They would also like children's chewable vitamins. (Shapiro)[11]

Both reports also contained information that would probably *not* have been useful to the SFCSJ but that briefers were accustomed to seeing. This ranged from hotel restaurant reviews,

> At dinner, there was a band which changed clothes during the evening, but played the SAME MUSIC, constantly. Dinner we had delicious borscht, good caviar, beef stroganoff, chicken Kiev. Huge menu, but few items were actually available. (Tabachnikoff)[12]

to commentary on the tourist attractions,

> Our guide's name was Anya, a beautiful young lady who did her job well. On the way back from the Kremlin we stopped at the Memorial wall from World War II of the Unknown Soldier. It is very beautifully done. Brides and grooms were coming to the Memorial to have their picture taken. She explained to us that in Moscow a bride and groom will bring flowers to the grave of the Unknown Soldier. It is a sign that they remember; I said to myself: It is a different variation of [the Jewish wedding custom of] breaking the glass. Every society needs to have a symbol and a ceremony by which you remember the past. (Shapiro)[13]

to accounts of hospitality in refuseniks' apartments,

> We took a taxi to Lev's apartment and were greeted by him outside of his door. He is warm and he is caring. He fed us dinner and the traditional bottle of vodka which he was insistent that we finish. (Shapiro)[14]

> H.S. is hungry and cannot drink the Vodka so I must do double duty. Luckily, I am up to the task. (Tabachnikoff)[15]

to testimonials about the feelings elicited by the visits:

> Words fail to express the emotions, the depth of feelings, the humor, faith, warmth, goodness that flowed throughout the evening. (Tabachnikoff)[16]

What was the point of submitting rabbinic ruminations on the similarities between Russian and Jewish wedding memorial practices? Or turning in tales that fantasized babushka street cleaners as KGB agents? Surely, Shapiro and Tabachnikoff knew that this was not what the SFCSJ was looking for. And what are we to make of the different voices the two authors use, telling their stories in such different ways?

Activists had systematized a plan for using mass tourism to the movement's advantage. But there are adages about the hubris of planning. Whatever movement leaders imagined they were doing with tourism, the travelers had ideas of their own.

FROM TRAVEL TO TRAVEL WRITING

The Soviet Jewry movement's tactics of mass engagement ended up shaping the experience of being Jewish in late Cold War–era America. But precisely which mass mobilization tactics were being deployed here?

International tourism is only half the answer. As the Florida rabbis' accounts suggest, activists enlisted not only travel but also travel writing. The genre's conventions are familiar: "A non-fictional first-person prose narrative" whose "author, narrator and principal character [are taken to be] identical" and that describes the narrator's "travels and the spaces passed through or visited, and whose plot is determined by the order of the narrator's act of travelling."[17] Soviet Jewry trip report authors used the genre to translate experience into text—selectively describing the Soviet world and representing its people. They revealed their own self-understandings, intentionally and unintentionally, as they wrote about themselves interacting with the places and people they encountered.[18]

Of all the novel behaviors spread by the Soviet Jewry movement, tourism to aid refuseniks represents a special case because it included both immediate engagement in a movement activity and after-the-fact reflection on the meaning of that engagement. Activists helped shape a distinctive Jewish variant of American (or Western) Cold War culture twice over. First, they paved a unique route that brought fellow Philadelphians and Angelenos into refuseniks' apartments in Moscow and Leningrad and offered them a view of the USSR that few Americans ever got—and one that Intourist, the state tourism agency, certainly would not provide.[19] Second, they cemented an expectation that those who experienced this distinctive form of Cold War tourism would not let its memory fade but would write about it for others and for themselves.

"One of the objectives of every trip is transfer of information; both hard facts and feelings. You are the only one who experiences what you experience," declared a National Conference on Soviet Jewry (NCSJ) primer from the late 1980s. "We ask everyone to accept the responsibility of preparing a debriefing report." This was to cover the same information gathered by debriefing questionnaires—refuseniks met, materials delivered, and so on. But in addition, the NCSJ also allowed that "many people also like to include in their report . . . their own feelings about the entire situation" and sometimes even "a narrative of the entire trip."[20]

Never did the NCSJ suggest that the more all-encompassing the chronicle, the more useful it would be to the organization. Writers, however, had their own ideas. Soviet Jewry groups set tourists to writing, and once pen was put to paper, far more poured forth than activists needed, asked for, or anticipated. Thousands of travelogues flooded in, some over a hundred pages long, with photographs, hand-drawn maps, appendixes, and titles—smirking and sincere—inspired by Ian Fleming, by Soviet Jews, and by a sense of the absurdity of being thrust into stranger-than-fiction situations: "Mission to Moscow," "Our Russian Adventure," "Dr. M. Goes to the USSR," "From Russia with Angst," "They Are Surely Heroes," "We Can All Be Heroes," "How We Spent Our Christmas Vacation."[21] The organizations got their data, but they also got descriptions of Red Square, restaurant reviews, analyses of the Soviet economic system and its effects on national character, and reams of commentary on Russia's cultural quirks.

They also got reflections on the personal meaning of the trips—thousands of pages worth.[22] As the excerpts from Tabachnikoff's and Shapiro's reports suggest, travelers were writing not only for debriefers but also for themselves. Travel writing was a mode of self-expression. Travelers wrote for catharsis, to process emotionally laden experiences so out-of-the-ordinary that they prompted the question, "Is this really happening to me?" They wrote to validate their choice to risk travel; having potentially endangered themselves, they presented evidence to reassure themselves that the Soviet Jewish problem was real but not entirely hopeless and that their presence made a difference. They wrote to articulate their new self-understandings, to give voice to their sense of having returned home a different person from the one who set out.[23]

They wrote for posterity. Briefers had told them that their trips were not only "for Soviet Jews, for the advocacy effort," but also "for themselves. To be a part of history."[24] Many travelers agreed.

In asking tourists to report back, activists were not trying to spark an efflorescence of Jewish American travel writing. That was a by-product. Along with the creation of a distinctively Jewish form of Cold War tourism, the proliferation of self-revelatory Jewish American travel writing was another unintended cultural consequence of the movement.[25] The Soviet Jewry movement led thousands of people to use travel writing as a mode of Jewish meaning making. This is significant in itself as a phenomenon of Jewish life in the 1970s and '80s. It is also significant for the legacy it produced—a library unique to its era, the largest corpus of Jewish travel writing in history.[26] The travelogues, diaries, speeches, sermons, op-eds, and other writings of more than 4,200 tourists now reside in the archives of American Soviet Jewry movement organizations, most of which are available online. Several thousand more trip reports in Nativ's files remain classified, although their resemblance to the other reports can be gleaned from excerpts of the one hundred or so quoted in an in-house history of the Israeli agency's tourism effort.[27] In an archival record dominated by leaders' perspectives, these travelogues present diverse voices from the rank and file speaking in their own words about Soviet Jews, the Soviet Jewry campaign, and their own involvement. Ostensibly written to provide debriefers with information about Soviet Jews, they now offer later generations a window onto the sensibilities of their authors—post-Holocaust, Cold War–era Jewish Americans who encountered themselves anew via their engagements with coethnics in the USSR.[28]

By their nature, foreign encounters force people to "negotiate a complex and sometimes unsettling interplay between . . . difference *and* similarity."[29] The interplay here was especially complex. Meetings between American and Soviet Jews brought together members of a transnational community whose connections had been severed for over half a century—first by mass migration, then by genocide, then by Cold War. For the most part, the parents and grandparents of those meeting had all been Jews in czarist Russia. Some had emigrated. Some remained. This meant that the reunion of a fractured Russian Jewish diaspora was also a first encounter between American and Soviet strangers.[30] Or, viewed from the opposite direction, the meetings were a rare form of Cold War encounter in which hosts and guests were, as one traveler put it, bound by "the strong feeling, that one was a long lost relative."[31] Or as another visitor wrote, "Our similarities to the Russian Jews we met [were] greater than our differences. Though our daily languages are different, 'shalom' is 'shalom.'"[32]

Writers saw these bonds as consequential. "By virtue of an accident of birth," wrote Lois Neiter, a teacher and art collector who was traveling in 1976 with her San Fernando Valley synagogue, "I was born an *American* Jewess, not a Soviet Jewess. How lucky that makes me and how responsible that makes me for my brother."[33] Neiter's seamless move from accident to responsibility, fate to choice, history to morality, is characteristic of the corpus. As travelers used their writing to work through the broader meanings of their presence in Soviet Jewish apartments and synagogues, they brought the vagaries of history to the fore. What did it mean to travel as Jewish Americans to aid Soviet Jews just decades after the Holocaust, in the midst of the Cold War? Soviet Jewry movement travel provided Jewish Americans a means of experiencing themselves as living on the cusp of these histories. Travel writing provided both an opportunity and a means to interrogate the complexities of this experience.

HISTORICAL AGENTS, COLD WAR ACTORS

> Your trip was not an "adventure"; It was a mission.
> DON'T make it sound like a James Bond movie.
> —Chicago Action for Soviet Jewry[34]

> In the air, we transposed all of our assignments into secret code, intelligible only to us (e.g. Alec Ioffe became "Dr. Nice," Felix Aronovitch became "The Cat")
> —Trip report of Rabbi Albert Axelrad and Gerald Showstack, September 1978[35]

> You are not a spy.
> —Comité des Quinze[36]

> Both of us were wearing socks in which we had sewn in the addresses and names of people we were going to visit.
> —Trip report of Sharon Weintraub and Vicki Yudenfriend, August 1979[37]

> We try not to project a "James Bond Spy Adventure" in a trip of this kind.
> —National Conference on Soviet Jewry[38]

> As soon as [Rudy] left the lobby of the Hotel the doorman made a pre-arranged sign to one of the KGB goons. . . . [It] took him about an hour and a half to lose his "tail," and then only after stepping into apartment houses, going through the back doors, through backyards and into other apartment houses.
> —Trip report of Carole Abramson, Rudy Appel, and Sharyn Schneider, September 1978[39]

> Please urge tourist not to make his experience sound like a spy mystery.
> —Union of Councils for Soviet Jews[40]

> On the way to jail, which was only five blocks away, Allan Margolis switched the tape in the machine with a blank tape and placed the Slepak interview tape in his left pants pocket.
> —Trip report of Dean Goodman and Allan Margolis, May 1978[41]

One of the Cold War's defining elements was "the replacement of direct military confrontation with surrogate and covert warfare."[42] Indeed, this is what kept the war cold. It is also what made the espionage thriller the Cold War's quintessential genre.[43] Most people engaged spy stories as an audience—reading a John le Carré novel, seeing a James Bond film, watching television's *I Spy*. But by traveling to meet refuseniks, thousands of American and Western European Jews experienced themselves in a form of immersive role-play, personally confronting, evading, thwarting, and being thwarted by Soviet authorities in the USSR itself. Afterward, when writing about their experiences, they used espionage thriller tropes to tell their stories.[44] Scattered across the travelogues are tales of smuggled documents, messages penned in invisible ink, and rolls of film confiscated by Soviet officials (when not stashed for safekeeping in other tourists' luggage). There are secret meetings in the dead of night, brush passes to exchange packages on empty streets, and whispered warnings from strangers who suddenly vanish. Populating the stories are Russian Jews who shut their blinds tight before speaking freely and KGB agents who train telephoto lenses on these windows from cars parked on streets below.[45]

Movement leaders bristled at the notion of their tourists playing James Bond. Both the *play* and the *James Bond* irked. The proper emotion was concern for human beings in distress. The proper strategic frame was to maintain rhetorical distance from the Cold War. But leaders' protestations amounted to little. The Cold War was inescapably relevant to Soviet Jewry movement travel, and the spy thriller genre was simply too familiar, too alluring, and too useful to writers trying to make sense of their trips.[46] The genre shaped expectations prior to travel, filtered perceptions and suggested ways of behaving during it, and provided a template afterward for transforming experience into prose.[47] Some authors presented the spy tropes as a source of exhilaration; others, exasperation. Either way, the genre was salient. By invoking spy thriller genre conventions, travelers were able to write themselves not as secret agents but as historical agents—Cold War–era Americans empowered to challenge the Soviet Union and aid its oppressed citizens and prepared to brave personal risks behind the Iron Curtain in order to do so.

CHOICE AND CIRCUMSTANCE

Some authors embraced the Cold War adventure theme with gusto. Barry Tabachnikoff luxuriated in the storytelling, crafting his narrative as the misadventures of an accidental spy, in over his head. Most, however, wrote like Howard Shapiro—narrative voice dutifully dispassionate, cloak-and-dagger language sparingly used. Travelogues differed in how intentionally they used spy genre conventions. Some of the difference depended on whether authors were treating their writing overall as an opportunity for creative expression. Tabachnikoff represents one extreme, winking at the reader so frequently that one cannot help but notice that Tabachnikoff the author has invented a character, Tabachnikoff the unlikely agent. In contrast, Shapiro's plain style, devoid of artifice and literary pretension, invites readers to view the report as a direct representation rather than stylized storytelling.[48] But spy novel conventions even seeped into these seemingly straightforward reports, revealing how hard it was for travelers to escape thinking in terms set by the genre. Subtle cloak-and-dagger phrasings insinuated themselves throughout the corpus. Authors who could have said that they phoned or met refuseniks wrote instead that they "made contact." Those who could have written that they delivered gifts opted for language like "made the exchange" or "made the drop."[49]

The question of intentionality versus slippage refers to travel writers as *authors* and their literary crafting of travelogues as spy stories. We can point to an equivalent distinction when speaking of travel writers as *travelers* and their experience of control or lack thereof during the trips themselves. Sometimes travelers intentionally chose to role-play in accordance with genre expectations. Other times, it seemed to them that the spy genre imposed itself whether they wanted it to or not. In cases of the first type, posttrip write-ups tended to portray travelers as capable actors prepared to overcome obstacles as they took on sensitive work. Tabachnikoff was an exception. He positioned his enthusiastic embrace of the role-play as the catalyst for a series of misadventures. Al Rose, a family vacationer who visited Soviet Jews when his cruise ship docked in Leningrad, took a similar approach: "I couldn't help play 'spy and escape' with several suspicious people, only to find out no one really had bothered to follow us, but it was fun believing for a while!"[50]

More typical, though, was the account offered by Victor Borden, an obstetrician-gynecologist from New Jersey who made his first of several trips to Russia in July 1985.[51] At the beginning of his narrative, he describes steps he and his wife, Frani, took to prevent Soviet officials from discovering which refuseniks they were planning to meet:

> We realize that we are taking a great risk. . . . In spite of this apprehension and fear, we are determined to carry out this mission. . . . We have

taken some precautions in the way that we are carrying names and telephone numbers of Refusniks. We have devised three systems.... The first, suggested by Ann Bernstein [their NCSJ briefer], is a false checkbook with items and amounts entered that correspond to names and phone numbers. Additionally, in my wallet, I utilize pictures of my daughters by entering numbers as if they were dates, on the back of their snapshots. Last, Frani has entered messages and numbers with small pieces of tape attached to the adhesive part of her sanitary napkins and covered by the adhesive strip.[52]

Not all travelers described their methods for concealing information. Borden's decision to do so was an authorial choice. Placing it at the opening conformed to the chronological structure common to travelogues, but it also followed the genre convention familiar from James Bond films, in which, as a prelude to the main action, the hero equips himself for the challenges ahead. In this instance, no high-tech gadgets were used—only menstrual pads repurposed as concealing devices. Bernstein, the back-office expert who introduced the false checkbook, functioned in the role of Q. The literary effect is to situate the Bordens in something akin to a spy drama and to establish the protagonists' ingenuity, determination, and capability.

Other writers presented spy thriller tropes not as a frame that they had freely chosen but as something they were forced to reckon with as travelers and therefore compelled to document as authors. They suggested that either the spy frame was thrust upon them without their consent—as when government agents actually treated them as targets of surveillance—or it reflected anxieties that plagued them in spite of themselves. Such was the case on the rare occasions when Shapiro lapsed into an espionage frame. Note his use of the phrase "of course" when describing the nighttime attempt to call a refusenik from a public phone: "The line was busy and we wandered from telephone booth to telephone booth for half an hour waiting for the line to clear. It didn't. *Of course* our imagination ran wild; we figured our earlier phone call had been intercepted; the line was being kept busy by sinister forces, etc."[53]

Even in these instances, allusions to the spy thriller genre served to affirm that the travelers' presence in the USSR really did matter. Murray Kuhr, a New York pediatrician attending a genetics conference in

Moscow in 1978, described how threats from a Soviet agent provided external validation for his decision to travel. Seeing that the Soviet government took him seriously enough to harass him reinforced Kuhr's conviction that the problem he had come to address, his own power to do something about it, and the risks in trying were all real:

> I was crossing the courtyard to the tourist buses when a man called out my name and proceeded to say, "We are aware that you have been engaged in hostile acts against the internal security of the Soviet Union. You must cease these acts. We are prepared to take whatever extreme measures [are] necessary to assure that you do." When I protested that I didn't know what he was talking about, he retorted he was sure I did know, repeated the threat, and added "and your wife too" and walked away. First, I hypothesized I had done something illegal and felt guilty; then quickly discarded that hypothesis. Then I hypothesized I had done something stupid to put them on my trail, and got angry at myself, then quickly discarded that hypothesis. Then I realized that *I must be doing something right to have provoked them and felt some pride along with a modicum of fear.*[54]

Feelings of fear and self-efficacy were frequently interlaced when writers invoked the espionage genre. Trepidation fed the sense of empowerment. Fear reminded travelers that they were choosing to jump into potentially dangerous situations rather than try to avoid them. Tourists' tales of playing cat and mouse with Soviet agents gave voice to this. The stories juxtaposed gnawing anxiety and outright terror with righteous anger, the thrill of adventure, dark humor, cathartic release, and bewilderment at the absurd. They told of tourists' wins and losses alike, but whether they revealed travelers' capabilities or their limitations, they highlighted the fact that tourists were not passive observers. They were active participants trying to take direct action in face-to-face confrontations with Soviet authorities:

> We left for the [Aragvi] Restaurant. Again, at the restaurant we were pretty much isolated from others except for the "friendly fraternity" [of Soviet agents] that followed us wherever we went. . . . Some members of the group left to make a last "contact" in Moscow and the rest remained

to act as a decoy for the KGB. We left the restaurant and were followed by 3 "friends." As usual they were quite obvious and we began to treat the experience as a game. Richard doubled back to confront one agent as he rounded a corner. We laughed and made fun of them and Don took a picture of one of them as we left the street car. It struck me that the experience of being followed by the secret police is so alien to our experiences that it was unreal to us. We could only see it in the light of a fictional T.V. or movie episode. At times our behavior was too open, too taunting of authority. Our behavior created its own excitement and provided a release for our anxiety.
—Trip report of Lois Neiter, teacher and art collector, Los Angeles, October 1976[55]

B-GRADE: DISAVOWING THE GENRE THEY INVOKE

During the trips, travelers recognized that they were living in and living out genre moments, but when they acknowledged this in their writing, they usually disparaged it as cliché:

It was obvious—we were being followed. I stopped to buy something to drink and a young man began flirting with me. For a moment I thought—go with him, maybe he'll be a sort of protection—but then I knew I wouldn't. I am not the type. But I began to understand intrigue. *Those stupid movies I never cared for—I was living one.*
—Trip report of Rosalie Gerut, singer/songwriter, Boston, May 1985[56]

It's like a Grade B spy movie sometimes. The one time I was stopped by military police and asked for my passport, I was wearing my raincoat, dark glasses, and a scarf. I guess that's what spies really look like.
—Trip report of Judy Wellins, psychologist, Albany, spring 1986[57]

As pre-arranged, a bearded, heavily clothed young man walked along the waterfront opposite the hotel. . . . We headed in the same direction as the young man, on opposite sides of the street. As we all reached a construction site, the street curved, and we swung around the corner, out

of view of the hotel windows, blocked by construction walls. We walked a few hundred feet, made rapid contact, exchanged our package for his letter, and quickly parted. . . . In retrospect, *we really were reenacting a Grade B spy thriller. But it was for real, not for entertainment.*
—Trip report of Nat Kameny, advertising executive, New Jersey, March 1974[58]

We meet the next morning in a park. *A la Hollywood spy movie, she walks ahead to a far-off park bench and I follow.* I slip her the silk scarf I had brought and she quickly stuffs it into her pocket so that no one will see that I have handed her something and use it as a pretext for accusing her of passing and receiving state secrets. . . . Just before leaving Tashkent for our next city, we are called in again by some officials (KGB) and told that this is our second warning; if we continue to disobey Soviet law by visiting with Soviet citizens and "exchanging secrets," we will be expelled. *Something about these interrogations reminds me of a grade B Hollywood spy movie.*
—Trip report of Barbara Pfeffer, photographer, New York, September 1985[59]

I knocked and walked into a rather large office with a desk at the far end behind which was seated a large woman. On one side of the room was a couch with two young, mid twenties, men dressed with black overcoats and thin ties. *They looked exactly like you would expect two character actors in a grade B movie.* The woman asked me to sit on the couch opposite them and introduced them as gentlemen from the KGB. She said they wanted to question me.
—Trip report of Jeffrey Breslow, toy company executive, Chicago, November 1983[60]

No one ever compared their experiences to Oscar-winning espionage thrillers—only to B-grade spy movies, as if authors felt compelled to dissociate themselves from the genre even as they invoked it. How much of the ambivalence stemmed from discomfort as *authors* using the genre in ways they suspected were cliché versus discomfort as *travelers* experiencing themselves immersed in it? It is impossible to disentangle the two. No doubt, some of the disparagement of their own experiences as "B-grade" reflected the inevitable disappointment that comes from imagining that real life should have the characteristics of a well-crafted story—with narrative structure, depth, and closure. The actual experience of Soviet Jewry movement travel only alluded to the spy novel genre, offering episodic participation in fragmentary, genre-themed moments. Nor did travelers have access to the minds of others, as they would when reading characters in a novel. Did their KGB tails and interrogators have inner lives? Back stories? Motivations? Travelers rarely knew their names. They encountered them as stock villains and therefore recounted them as such—"blue scarf" distinguishable from "red scarf" in one travelogue, all of them lumped together as "the plaid scarves" in another.[61] Measured against the richness of a great novel or film, it is understandable that real life could feel B-grade.[62]

But the critique was more precise. Writers specifically panned their experiences as B-grade *spy movies*. Beyond generally failing as art, lived experience failed to realize the espionage thriller genre itself. Perhaps because there was no mystery to solve. Perhaps because the episodic genre moments did not build to a larger resolution. Run-ins with customs agents and other low-level functionaries never led up the hierarchy to some Soviet Jewry movement equivalent of a Dr. No in an Ian Fleming story or Karla in a John le Carré novel—an orchestrating authority whose existence would make sense of the broader problem of Soviet antisemitism. And even if travelers managed to "defeat" their local adversaries by sneaking items through customs or temporarily evading surveillance, these small wins did nothing to resolve the larger issues. At the end of these journeys, the world remained just as opaque as when the travelers set out, and the refuseniks just as trapped.[63]

As with the experience, so with the retelling. Although authors invoked spy genre tropes, they did not activate the genre's structural forms. These were travelogues, not novels or films. They had no character development, no plot twists, no mystery to solve—only sporadic allusions to spy thriller tropes. This heightened the sense of cliché.[64] We might suppose that authors labeled their espionage references as B-grade in order to protect their self-image as reasonably adequate writers, as if they were saying to the reader, "I know this is hackneyed. Don't blame me. Had this been fiction, I could have written it better." But this explanation does not work. The remainder of the travelogues are no different in literary quality, so why reserve caveats and disavowals only for sections that invoked the espionage genre?

Authors understood that the briefers who had asked them to write would be reading their travelogues as reports conveying information to be used, not as literature to be appreciated. Boston's Action for Soviet Jewry even directed briefers to tell tourists to "write their reports without using 'I' or 'we.'"[65] And yet, by framing their narratives as spy stories, authors were activating genre conventions inappropriate to the agreed-upon reading context and violating the implicit contract with the readers. Labeling the stories "B-grade" denied them aesthetic value, positioned them as facts, and thereby salvaged the text's status as a "report."

But the rhetorical move accomplished something more significant than this. Travelers understood why their briefers kept insisting, "Your trip was not an 'adventure'; It was a mission. DON'T make it sound like a James Bond movie." Yet so much of their experience elicited the sensation that the genre had come to life for them. If they were only writing for their briefers, they could have chosen to keep silent, but they were also writing for themselves, and they had much to work through. To compare their experiences to a grade-B spy movie was still to compare it to a spy movie. But by adding the caveat, they could make the comparison without suggesting that they had turned a serious aid mission into a game for their own enjoyment. "Grade B" communicated emotional distance, and this allowed travelers to retain their dignity while asserting what briefers warned them against saying aloud—that they felt themselves living out the quintessential genre of the Cold War.

TRAVELING AS POST-HOLOCAUST AMERICAN JEWS

All the ellipses in the following passage belong to the author, Elaine Siris, the national chair of the United Jewish Appeal. The text is complete. Nothing has been excised:

> I knew that I had to meet them in Russia. I had greeted the Chopin Express in Vienna . . . joined the deeply moving reception at Schonau . . . and welcomed them home at Lydda Airport.[66] I had been witness to their first steps on Jewish soil . . . in freedom. Yet, I knew that unless I met with

them there in Leningrad . . . in Moscow . . . in Georgia . . . in the land of my own father's birth . . . I would know only part of the story.

So we set out one July day . . . four determined women: Ruth Gruber Michaels, her daughter, Celia (age 20), my daughter, Penny Goldsmith (age 25) and myself. We carried a list of activists whom we had hoped to see, baggage loaded with Hebrew books and Mogen Davids and a great deal of bravado to hide the fact that we were scared stiff.

We began our fateful descent over Leningrad . . . half-asleep after a grueling eighteen-hour flight. A fine mist sprayed from the air jets over our seats . . . momentary horror . . . visions of the chambers of death from another time. Another nightmare shared.

—Trip report of Elaine Siris, New York, July 1973[67]

The three paragraphs opening Siris's account draw together common themes in Soviet Jewry movement travelogues, distilling them to their essence. In elliptical phrases, in single words, she writes of her sense of shared ancestry with Russian Jews, feelings of obligation, fear of the USSR. She invokes "freedom." She celebrates Israel. She positions herself as a witness to history, "deeply moved" by it, "determined" to be an actor in it—her travel to the USSR "fateful." (For herself? For others?) Bursting into the narrative are the "horror" and "nightmare" of "chambers of death from another time."

Was this a non sequitur? What did the Nazi genocide of the 1940s have to do with visiting refuseniks in Russia in the 1970s? And what was it about the context of travel that so primed thoughts of the Holocaust that a spray of fine mist from a jetliner air vent could jolt a traveler out of the present and into the trauma of the past?

Siris was right to call this a "nightmare shared." Holocaust references intruded into many other authors' travelogues too. The intrusions operated on two levels: narrators described horrific imagery invading their own thoughts unbidden, and these accounts burst suddenly into narratives without preparing readers for the abrupt shift:

> We leave Moscow that afternoon, at 2:00 p.m. for Leningrad by train (a nine hour ride). The train ride provides opportunity to reflect on the conflict in our minds over whether to proceed with our contacts [after intimidation by Soviet authorities]. We decide to proceed, after many

hours of white bleakness and an icy sunset combined with the images conjure[d] up so easily of "Nazi death trains" by the monotony and sight/sounds of the train ride.
—Trip report of Nancy and Greg Leisch, market researcher (Greg), Washington, March 1976[68]

For her part, Siris did not merely write of a "nightmare shared." She called it "*another* nightmare shared." There was more than one. Siris was drawing connections. Some might wonder at this. In fact, movement organizations took care with Holocaust analogies, aware that they would misrepresent both the Soviet Jewish situation and the uniqueness of the Nazi annihilation—exaggerating the one, minimizing the other, and undermining the credibility of activists' claims overall.[69] Elie Wiesel voiced the concern in his own travelogue, *The Jews of Silence*: "I was mindful, too, of the danger of drawing facile analogies between Communist Russia and Europe under the Nazis. Even with regard to the Jewish problem, one is forbidden to make such comparisons. An abyss of blood separates Moscow from Berlin. The distance between them is not only one of geography and ideology; it is the distance between life and death."[70] But when the author of *Night* is the one bearing witness, this itself establishes the analogy. Movement slogans functioned similarly. The incommensurability of the situations could be detailed ad nauseam yet undone with a single placard: "This time we shall not be silent!"[71]

Many references to the Holocaust had objective roots in travelers' experiences. They heard refuseniks tell of parents murdered by the Nazis and dutifully recorded this. And because much of the genocide unfolded in the Baltics, Ukraine, and other Western republics occupied by the Germans, tourists' visits there to Soviet Jews also enabled pilgrimage to Holocaust sites. Travelers to Kiev, Vilnius, and Minsk described visiting the killing fields at Babi Yar and Ponary and walking the streets over the remains of liquidated ghettos.[72]

Subjectively, the overlapping geographies collapsed past and present persecutions into a single frame. Authors describing Holocaust sites wrote more about the present than the past: refuseniks' efforts to build memorials, government resistance to acknowledging the Jewishness of the victims, official silence about local complicity, guides hindering travelers' attempts to bear witness. Visits to Holocaust sites were read for and written as evidence of contemporary Soviet minimization, distortion, and denial of the Nazi genocide—part and parcel of the anti-Jewish climate that tourists had come to see:[73]

> BABI-YAR: While this was listed on our Finnair tour itinerary, the Intourist guide had no intention of taking us there. . . . Some of us insisted. After protesting that this was not on her tour list, there must be an extra charge, she would have to check with her superiors, etc., the guide finally took us there the next morning. Recognizing that we had a Jewish interest in the place, she did tell us that Jews were killed there, although the Soviets seem clearly to be making it a memorial for Ukrainians slaughtered by the Nazis—I strongly suspect that non-Jews taken there are not told about the Jews.
>
> —Trip report of Nisson Finkelstein, President, International Latex Corporation, Wilmington, Delaware, July 1976[74]

Even when tourists discovered that sites were marked or that guides were helpful, expectations of Soviet bad faith still framed the accounts:

> At the request of our group we were taken by bus to Babi Yar—or at least to a place which they told us was Babi Yar. No resistance was offered to our request. Indeed, we were told in Moscow that we would go to Babi Yar, although it is highly unusual to have any information confirmed before actual arrival in a city. I thus gather it is Intourists' policy now to tell groups in advance that they can visit Babi Yar.
>
> The spot we were taken to, about a 1/2 hour ride from the main street, has a stone marker, about 5 feet wide and 3 feet high, and I have clear photographs of it so we can have the inscription translated. The guide did clearly state that about 100,000 people, 80% of them Jewish, had been killed here by the Nazis AND THAT THE MARKER HAD BEEN THERE A LONG TIME. No mention, of course, was made of the participation of the Ukrainians in these crimes. The area behind the monument is filled in, overgrown with bushes and plants. On this sunny spring day birds were singing and people were picknicking, and it did appear very pleasant.
>
> —Trip report of Joel Sprayregen, attorney, Chicago, May 1970[75]

More was at stake than simply presenting evidence of official antagonism to Jewish memory. American Jews were using their travelogues not only to report their perceptions of Soviet realities but also to make sense of themselves. After all, their trips were not just aid missions. They were heritage tours. Allusions to the Holocaust were bound up in ruminations on the gap between travelers' American present and the Russian Jewish past from which they had sprung and that was no more.[76] Borden, the New Jersey obstetrician quoted earlier, described stumbling upon an old chapel—an *alte shul*, in his grandfathers' Yiddish. It was July 1985, and Borden was attending Sabbath services at Leningrad's synagogue. He stepped out of the brightly lit main sanctuary:

> I walk through a side exit and around a corner and then past two doors into a dimly lit small "*Alte Shul.*" Everything here is old and dusty. The [prayer] books (*siddurim*) are tattered or torn, the blue velour covering of the prayer table is worn away in spots. In a corner of the room is a desk with a phone and bread crumbs on its top. A fly is eating away with relish. The eternal light is lit, but the Ark [for Torah scrolls] is locked. I envision the years of praying that the walls have absorbed. I sense that in just such an "*Alte Shul*" my grandfathers must have prayed. It is deathly silent here—symbolic of the death of European Jewry during the Holocaust and of the approaching extinction of Judaism in the U.S.S.R.[77]

Borden did more than paint the scene; he stated outright that the still life was "symbolic."[78] He presented the *alte shul*'s derelict state as representative of the Nazis' and Soviets' twofold assault on Jewish life in Europe—destroying it first in body, then in soul. Such talk pointed beyond the tribulations of Cold War–era refuseniks to a very real American Jewish sense of loss. This was not a foreign space. Staring around the old chapel, Borden turned the tourist gaze inward. Two generations, transatlantic migration, and rapid socioeconomic advancement had distanced professional, suburban American Jews from the world of old Russian *shuls*. Nevertheless, Borden imagined his grandfathers praying there and thereby wrote himself into the scene. Contemplating the chapel, Borden thought of the Holocaust and the Soviet persecutions and saw them both as part of something even larger: a cataclysmic

Jewish twentieth century that had rendered his grandparents' Old Country—his inheritance—a lost world.[79]

As heritage tourism, Soviet Jewry movement travel enabled American Jews to indulge this sense of loss, but from a safe remove, with gratitude for distance from the past and no desire to return to it.[80] This was certainly the case for Borden, a child of Holocaust survivors. It was also true of those whose parents and grandparents had come to the United States during the mass migration of 1881 to 1924. Visits to meet Jews in the USSR fostered awareness of the vicissitudes of twentieth-century Jewish history and the autobiographical consequences for travelers. Travel writing offered an opportunity to articulate and refine this awareness. Because their ancestors had chosen to emigrate, American Jews had avoided the calamities and tribulations endured by those whose families had remained in Russia. Not that the Americans were unscarred. Horrific imagery of gas chambers and trains to death camps still intruded on their thoughts and invaded their writings. But they were conscious that historical accidents positioned them as visitors rather than hosts, deliverers of aid rather than recipients. They recognized this as their good fortune, imagined how easily things might have been otherwise, and—seeing their Americanness as accidental but their Jewishness as essential—drew moral lessons about their obligations to Jews whom chance had favored differently.[81] Recall Lois Neiter, who traveled on her San Fernando Valley synagogue trip in 1976: "By virtue of an accident of birth, I was born an *American* Jewess, not a Soviet Jewess. How lucky that makes me and how responsible that makes me for my brother."[82] Or consider self-described "housewife" Patsy Gilbert, who was asked by one of her hosts about her "interest in Soviet Jewry." She gave a distinctively American Jewish response: "I felt our parents' generation had abdicated responsibility in the 30's and so 6 million perished—I intend to help those I can in my generation."[83] Shared history as Jews created the bond. Divergent history as Americans, removed from the brutalities of Europe, imposed the responsibility.

Although activists never intended it, the route they paved to the Soviet Union created a form of American Jewish heritage travel that partially echoed the Holocaust pilgrimages to Poland that became popular in the late 1980s. Scholarship on "March of the Living" trips has traced the voyage from America or Israel to Poland as a metaphorical descent from "lifeworld" to "deathworld" and back again—a journey in which "Eastern Europe is the past, America is the present, Israel is the future."[84] In Soviet Jewry movement travelogues, the linkage of Nazi annihilation and Soviet suffocation of Jewish life mapped a similar symbolic geography—similar, but not identical. American writers only sometimes affirmed Israel as the future, and even then only for Soviet Jews, not for themselves. They saw America as their Jewish "lifeworld" and themselves as having inherited a continuity with the Jewish past that had been severed in Europe. With this self-understanding, they took it upon themselves to bring Jewish books and calendars, teach Torah and Jewish history, and deliver information about Jewish life outside the USSR that would help refuseniks survive as Jews in the "deathworld" until they could leave to join the Jewish communities living, thriving, in Israel, the US, and elsewhere in the West. This was a form of post-Holocaust travel in which pilgrimages of remembrance took second place to missions of recovery, rescue, and resurrection.

EXPLORATION AND RECONSTRUCTION

Banana Republic touted what other Soviet Jewry movement travelogues left implicit. "Soviet Safari with Mel and Patricia Ziegler." The title of the spring 1986 catalog was probably inevitable. Before Gap rebranded the outfit, Banana Republic under the Zieglers billed itself as a "Travel & Safari Clothing Company." Jeeps and mosquito netting decorated its storefronts. Hand-illustrated catalogs with imperial-kitsch product narratives advertised 100 percent cotton twill Serengeti skirts in khaki and ivory: "Like the fine gentlewomen of the British empire . . . stylish yet nearly indestructible." Running in a sidebar down twelve of Catalogue No. 27's sixty-four pages, a stylized first-person narration told of the "peripatetic founders'" recent journey. They had "slipped into Russia . . . to experience life under the Soviet regime." Alongside descriptions of $25 Gurkha shorts and Authentic Bombay pith helmets "from Her Majesty's former burden," customers could read of the Zieglers' meeting with a refusenik, identified only by his first name, Sasha: "The refusal was especially cruel because his 8-year-old son lives [in Israel] with Sasha's ex-wife. He hasn't seen his father in six years." Accompanying the text—said to be "excerpts from Mel's journals"—was

Patricia's watercolor sketch of a forlorn Sasha, his two hands holding a small photograph of his little boy.[85]

The uniqueness of the Zieglers' travelogue did not rest in its use of safari literature tropes to frame the Soviet Jewish encounter. The American Jewish Congress had also embraced the exoticizing genre when titling its 1972 guidebook *How to Find and Meet Russian Jews*.[86] Readers of the trip reports may notice that many authors wrote of the trips as expeditions, portraying themselves as intrepid explorers and Soviet Jews as objects of the hunt to be spotted, photographed, met. Writers, however, displayed little self-awareness that they were invoking a literary tradition. Aside from the Zieglers, who were writing for a safari clothing catalog, none used the term *safari*.[87] (One professional author, in a piece for the *Saturday Review*, did refer to himself as a "journalist-turned-refusenik-hunter.")[88] None made self-referential comments about their uses of the genre, not even to disavow it as they did when invoking the espionage

Figure 4.1. Page from Banana Republic's spring 1986 catalog, "Soviet Safari," with sidebar account of meeting refuseniks. Author's personal collection.

FROM RUSSIA, WITH ANGST

genre. Nevertheless, the ease with which a Soviet Jewry movement travelogue could be written as a story of adventure and discovery hints at how this literary tradition structured Soviet Jewry movement travel and travel writing.

This is not an original claim. When the Soviet-born American scholar of Jewish literature Sasha Senderovich analyzed literary representations of Soviet Jews in Elie Wiesel's travel narrative *The Jews of Silence* and in comparable works by Bernard Malamud and Chaim Potok, he found them chock-full of Age of Exploration tropes.[89] Centuries ago, it was the European traveler (explorer, soldier, scientist, missionary) setting out from the metropole to map an undiscovered country, civilize the natives, and bring back new knowledge about the world that could serve as a foil to the home society, reaffirm its privileged status, and perhaps critique it. Along with a tale of adventure, the encounter with Otherness also purchased the traveler some new insight into the Self. In late twentieth-century Soviet Jewry movement travelogues, Jewish American (or French or British) authors wrote of themselves setting out to discover a lost community of downtrodden Jews in the East and using their advantaged position as empowered free Westerners to bring aid, Jewish education, and hope to this population in need.

The writers here were not Wiesels, Malamuds, or Potoks working at the pinnacle of their craft. They were amateurs. Their uses of the genre conventions emerged unselfconsciously. Their travelogues were awash in the classic tropes—not just the civilizing mission but the whole array: exploration, discovery, mapping, even scientific documentation. That these tropes proved so useful to them points to the deeper cultural project in which these accidental authors were participating.

Travel writers were undertaking a post-Holocaust, Cold War–era project that engaged them at the intersection of their Jewish and American identities. They were responding to a sense that the twentieth century's European calamities had shattered the Jewish world from which their parents and their grandparents had hailed. As travelers and as writers, they took on responsibility for reconstituting a Jewish whole out of the fragments. They would search for what was lost and recover it. Document it in word and image. Render it known and navigable. Bring its population back into the fold, person by person. Their own ignorance about Russian Jewry symbolized the brokenness of the Jewish world and the relative powerlessness of Jews that was a cause and consequence of this brokenness. Accumulating knowledge was a step toward empowerment. What was left unknown was left at the mercy of others. Knowledge was a prerequisite to control—at least a measure of it, at least a semblance of it. Just as Age of Exploration travel writing brought information from distant lands to concentrate knowledge-power in European capitals, Soviet Jewry movement travelogues explored, mapped, and documented, arrogating to American Jews the authority and responsibility for restoring a fractured Jewish world to wholeness. To American Jews. Not to the Israeli government. Not to the United States government. But to their own diaspora community. And yet, even though these expeditions of discovery and aid were premised on the notion of American Jewry's privileged position after the Holocaust and during the Cold War, they had an unintended consequence, shaking American Jewish self-confidence and prompting travelers to wonder whether their freedoms as Americans were exacting a price on them as Jews.

EXPLORATION AND DISCOVERY

The notion of the Soviet Union as terra incognita was one of the most hackneyed tropes in Western travel writing about the USSR.[90] Still, we should not brush it off merely as a projection of Western fantasies. The Soviet government was committed to concealment. It withheld accurate maps, deeming them state secrets. As for those maps it did provide, a 1988 *New York Times* article confirmed what tourist briefers had long assumed: "The Soviet Union's chief cartographer acknowledged today that for the last 50 years the Soviet Union had deliberately falsified virtually all public maps of the country, misplacing rivers and streets, distorting boundaries and omitting geographical features, on orders of the secret police."[91]

But even if official maps had been truthful, they would not have shown what Soviet Jewry movement tourists had come to see. No Intourist maps detailed the routes linking Samarkand's synagogues with its Jewish cemetery. None indicated the apartment of refuseniks Lev Ulanovsky or Alex Ioffe.[92] For travelers trying to "find and meet Russian Jews," the salient unknown was not the Soviet Union writ large but the world of Soviet Jewry. If this world had a coherent geography, the travelers did not grasp it. In this, they were not alone. Soviet Jews' own knowledge was also limited, having been so long denied the ability to create communal organizations that could enable them to think about their population in a holistic way. Western Soviet Jewry movement groups lacked knowledge as well. That was why they were sending tourists in the first place.

All this together—the foreign travel without hired guides, the Churchillian expectation that Russia would be "a riddle wrapped in a mystery inside an enigma," the official disinformation and concealment, the particular ignorance about Soviet Jewry, the incompleteness of the picture that even locals could draw—contributed to travelers' sense that they were entering uncharted territory on their own. Tasked with reporting back, they relied heavily on motifs that colonial travel writers had deployed in abundance—adventure, exploration, discovery, and taming the unknown through mapping and scientific documentation.

In the early years, before Western activists and refusenik leaders established partnerships that could direct tourists to specific people's apartments, travelers who wanted to speak with Soviet Jews had few options beyond approaching strangers at synagogues or signaling their Jewishness in public places in the hope that someone might approach them. Travel narratives highlighted the work that went into creating such encounters, recording even mere sightings of Jews as "success" and noting "unsuccessful" attempts as well.[93] This narrative emphasis on the search for encounters positioned tourists as explorers discovering their Soviet Jewish quarry in an unmapped terrain that would not readily surrender its secrets:

> SAMARKAND—May 18. . . . There was no address in [the Jewish heritage guidebook] "Landmarks of the People" but the taxi driver . . . asked many pedestrians for directions and finally delivered us to the synagogue in the squalid native quarter. . . . Incidentally, to find these synagogues the best direction I can say is that it involves proceeding from the main street on which the wretched Registan Hotel is located. . . . We took numerous photographs of the people and buildings. They steadfastly and repeatedly refused gifts of prayer books or shawls but allowed me to put money in the coin box. . . . The teenagers who showed up to gawk at the Americans were shooed away. However, the kids kept on coming back, and were very interested in my El Al bag.[94]

FROM RUSSIA, WITH ANGST

In later years, when tourists were being given refuseniks' names and contact information, the quest motif shifted. Tourists still positioned themselves as intrepid or unlikely explorers venturing into uncharted territory, but the nature of the expeditions changed. No longer scouting missions to find public spaces where Jews of all types might be encountered at random, instead, these were targeted efforts to arrange and keep appointments with the emigration activists on tourists' lists. After describing the challenges of trying to contact Mark and Slava Shiffrin by phone, Howard Shapiro went on to detail the complications of actually getting to their apartment:

> The subway is easy to use in Moscow and it is easier to use in Leningrad but it is imperative before anyone goes to the Soviet Union on this kind of trip that they learn the cyrillic alphabet. It is hard to get on a subway without being able to read in what direction the train is going. We were lucky—Barry [Tabachnikoff] was able to master the cyrillic alphabet very quickly and he was our guide and could basically figure out the names of the stations (I don't think we went the wrong way once—luckily). We arrived at the subway stop on time—2:00 o'clock. We went up stairs and waited for Mark to meet us. Unfortunately, we waited for forty-five minutes and Mark never showed up. We then decided that we would have to go find the apartment on our own, which we did. We found the street, eventually found the right street number, walked up the stairs knocked on the door with baited breath. Slava answered the door and said Shalom. She knew who we were. Mark meanwhile had been waiting for us at a different exit on the subway station. It is important to double check not only the name of the station, but also where on the subway station you are meeting, and does this subway station have more than one exit. We knew after this experience; we asked that question every time.[95]

Although the objects of the quest were now identifiable names from a distinctive subset of the Soviet Jewish population, the landscape nevertheless remained forbidding, or at least was recounted as an obstacle course of public phones, metros, and confusingly numbered apartment blocks.

TAMING THE UNKNOWN

Shapiro's comment about double-checking the metro station name and specifying where exactly in the station to meet was not a description but an instruction. Trip reports mostly focused on the past—what happened in Russia. But some parts pointed to the future. They advised briefers: the next time you orient tourists, tell them this so that they will not repeat our mistakes.

The sense of terra incognita that led travelers to write their quests for Soviet Jews as tales of intrepid exploration also motivated them to blaze paths for those who followed. Attorney Joel Sprayregen, who in his May 1970 trip carried a copy of the only English-language Eastern European Jewish heritage travel guide available at the time, took it upon himself to correct the guidebook when its information misled: "Incidentally, the Sephardic synagogue [in Tbilisi] is at 47 Lesildeze Street rather than no. 65 as is stated in 'Landmarks of the People.'"[96] More commonly, travelers tried to add new information by giving directions to places that Intourist maps and Jewish heritage guidebooks would never think of mentioning: "To get to [refusenik Lev Osvicher's] apartment. . . . Walk along Lenin Prospect (from downtown) toward the Philharmonia. You will pass a yellow church building. The church is set back from the street and has in front of it a lawn bounded by a head high stucco wall. Immediately past the church is an entryway to the courtyard of a large apartment building."[97] The author who wrote this also pasted in a clipping from an Intourist map of Minsk, drawing arrows to indicate the church and the apartment complex. Others sketched the maps that they wished they had had in hand.

On the surface, mapping was just a way of helping the movement create practical resources for the next round of tourists. At a deeper level, it was an act of repair. Cartography offered American Jews a way of searching out and recovering fragments that had been shattered by the Holocaust and the Cold War. By drawing maps, American Jews showed that they had some degree of control—that they could reconnect the pieces and thereby reconstitute the Jewish world as a coherent, knowable whole. As a collective enterprise, American Jews were also asserting their authority vis-à-vis the Soviet government: This is our population, not yours. Jews will take responsibility for mapping Jews, irrespective of national borders or claims to state sovereignty.

But even as the cartographic enterprise as a whole attempted to tame an unknown geography, each map individually served as a reminder of just how much the Soviet Jewish world remained fragmented and unknown in the minds of American Jews. Rare was the drawing that situated Soviet Jewish landmarks in relation to one another on the grid of a broader cityscape. (See figure 4.2.) Most centered on a single point of interest—a refusenik apartment, a synagogue, a cemetery—sketching only a short route linking it from a metro station, hotel, or easy-to-find tourist site. What was not on the path was not drawn, except for navigational landmarks and clarifications of where not to go. Each destination was drawn alone on its own map. (See figure 4.3.) Textual annotations sometimes accompanied the illustrations. The accumulated cartography presented a highly selective rendering of Soviet Jewish geography—showing it as an archipelago of movement-related sites,

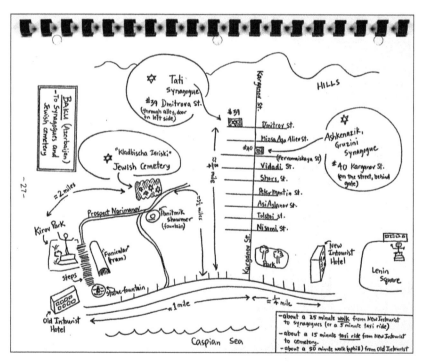

Figure 4.2. Hand-drawn map of tourist hotels and Jewish sites in Baku, with partial city grid. Trip report of Melodie and Sherman Rosenfeld, 28 September–20 October 1976. American Jewish Historical Society, RG I-505A, box 6, folder 18.

FROM RUSSIA, WITH ANGST

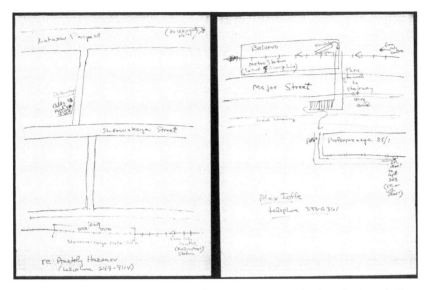

Figure 4.3. Hand-drawn maps with directions to apartments of refuseniks Anatoly Hazanov and Alex Ioffe. Trip report of William Michelson, 29 September–1 October 1984. American Jewish Historical Society, RG I-181A, box 85, folder 3.

each an identifiable haven in the midst of a vast unknown, no island connected to any other but all separately accessible to Westerners starting from launch points in the tourist districts.

As with mapping the landscape, so with documenting the population. Photography was enlisted first by travelers as a tool for recording the discovery of the unknown and later by organizations as a means of taming it. In the years before Soviet Jewry groups could provide names and addresses of refuseniks to visit, travelers used their cameras to capture images of strangers chanced upon in the streets, to return proof that the elusive Jews of the Soviet Union had indeed been sighted. "A Bukharan Jewish lady who operated a shoe repair booth just off the main street near the Registan Hotel allowed us to take her picture," a traveler in 1970 wrote.[98] As movement travel came to emphasize meetings with refuseniks, tourists instead delivered photographs of the people they met during home visits and whom they knew by name. As briefers had requested, these pictures adopted an evidentiary mode—posed portraits showing refusenik families sitting or standing together in their apartments, staring directly into the camera.[99] On the back, photos were labeled with the family's name. Photographers often took care not to mix family units. Sometimes they handed the camera to others and joined the pictures. More often, tourists remained invisible behind the lens.[100]

Taken with organizational processing in mind, the photographs added visual evidence to supplement an essentially text-based enterprise. Movement organizations tried to render Soviet Jewry knowable by cataloging the population, person by person. By the early 1970s, Western activists had shifted from a strategy centered on generic consciousness-raising to one emphasizing tailored efforts to support identifiable Soviet Jews through package deliveries, phone calls, adoptions, twinnings, and tourist visits. To support these efforts, movement organizations compiled lists of the Soviet Jews they were serving. These lists evolved into card files, and the card files became computer databases.[101] This data collection and processing effort amassed portfolios on thousands of refuseniks—duplicated many times over because the National Conference on Soviet Jewry, Union of Councils for Soviet Jews, and Nativ did not combine efforts.

As go-betweens linking refuseniks and movement organizations, tourists played a dual role. Briefed with information from the organizations' refusenik files, they brought over tailored aid packages. Then, when meeting refuseniks, they gathered new information, which they brought back to their briefers, who updated and expanded their data files. In practice, the tourists' work largely involved taking interest in the minutiae of strangers' lives and then setting this to paper, sometimes at length, sometimes in brief sketches:

> 10. Barski, Anatoly. Address: Chicherina St., No. 49, Apt. 31. Telephone: 257665. Physical defect: has to walk with aid of cane. Born 1950. Lives alone. Mother died 3 years ago. (? Father went to Rome?—USA?) Does watch repair at home. . . .
>
> 17. Spivack, Nadyezda. Not married. Refused 8/25/75 on basis that parents do not want to leave. Computer operator. Address: Bogdan Chmielnitsky St., No. 8, Apt. 3.
>
> —Trip report of Bernard Pomerantz, Philadelphia, August 1976[102]

Typically, they highlighted educational and occupational histories:

Moscow, USSR

VAGNER, VLADIMIR NUSINOVICH
Krasnoyarskaya 10, korp. 7, apt. 146
f. 3; r. 9/74, because mother-in-law
will not give permission.

VAITSBLIT, ILYA SHAYA-MENDELEVICH
(B-311) Vernadskogo 11/19, apt. 282.
b. 1918; radioelectronic eng., now pensioner; f. 1; a. 12/73; r. 2/74, because departure not in interest of govt.

VEKSLER, ARKADY MIKHAILOVICH
(107061) B. Cherkizovskaya 8, korp. 5, apt. 57.
b. 1948; auto mechanic (no higher education); f. 2; a. 6/73; r. 10/73, departure not in interest of govt. (served in army)

VIGDOROV, GRIGORI ALEKSANDROVICH
(129128) Malakhitovaya 10, korp. 2, apt. 165.
worker; f. 4; a. 3/73; r. 6/73, because served in Army.

VOLVOVSKY, LEONID ANANEVICH
Bulvar Slaviansky 43, apt. 252
b. 1942; Candidate Tech. Sci., mathematician, and radio-electronics, worked until 10/72; f. 1; a. 4/74; r. 9/74

YAKIR YEVGENY MORISOVICH
(B-488) Profsoyuznaya 100, korp. 5, apt. 35
Candidate Tech. Sci., eng. mechanical, presently not working; f. 3; a. 10/73; r. 1/74, because departure not in interest of govt.

YANKOLOVICH, ISAAK ZINOVEVICH
(125057) Leningradsky pr. 69, apt. 70.
b. 1921; economist eng.; son, aeromechanical eng.; daughter, nurse; f. 4; a. 8/72; r. 11/72 because of class. of wife's former job until 1967.

ZISMAN, LEONID ALEKSANDROVICH
(E-483) 1st Sovetakaya 12, apt. 8
b. 1949; librarian (prominent); f. 1; a. 9/73; r. 3/74, because parents refuse to give permission.

Leningrad, RSFSR

ABESGAUZ, EVGENY ZALMANOVICH
pr. Stachek 74, apt. 126
b. 1939; eng. until 12/70, now watchman; f. 4; r. 12/73, because former job class. 2nd form secret.

AKURA, ALEKSANDR LVOVICH
Moscovsky pr. 50, apt. 21
r. 6/75 because brother is army officer

ARONOVICH, FELIKS EFIMOVICH
Pestelya 13/15, apt. 16.
b. 1931; mechanical eng. until 12/60; f.1; r. 11/72, because former job classified 2nd form secret.

BARGMAN, MIKHAIL ISAEVICH
Bukharestskaya 33, k. 2, apt. 217.
b. 1946; theatre manager, now driver; f. 1; r. 2/74, because of army service (demob. 12/71).

BLIKH, IOSIF MENDELEVICH
per. Dzambula 19, apt. 5
b. 1939; mathematician until 1968; now computer programmer; f. 4; r. 9/72, because former job class. 2nd form secret.

BLUMENSTEIN, SOLOMON

BOGUSLAVSKAYA, IRINA VLADIMIROVNA
Bukharestskaya 86, k. 1, apt. 121
Marine eng., Candidate Tech. Sci. until 12/72, now elevator operator; husband, Alexander, marine eng. C.T.S.; f. 4; r. 2/74, because former job class. 2nd form secret.

BRAZ, NATALYA
Kazanskaya 7, apt. 14
b. 1938, economist/eng. until 7/70; f. 1; r. 7/72, because former job class. 2nd form secret.

BREGER, IGOR ANATOLEVICH
Vosstaniya 55, apt. 15
b. 1945; radio eng. until 1/72; f. 3; r. 3/74, because former job classified 2nd form secret.

CHERNYAK, IRMA NAUMOVICH
Perevozny per. 19, apt. 14.
b. 1929; electrical eng., Candidate Tech. Sci. until 1965, now elevator operator; f. 2; r. 5/73, because former job class. 2nd form secret.

- 8 -

Figure 4.4. Page from refusenik database. Union of Councils for Soviet Jews, 1975. Western Reserve Historical Society, MS 4011, box 8, folder 224.

```
NATIONAL CONFERENCE ON SOVIET JEWRY          SOVIET JEWRY RESEARCH BUREAU
10 East 40th St., N.Y., N.Y. 10016            (212) 679-6122
```

REFUSENIK PROFILE

NAME:	ADDRESS:
DANIEL FRADKIN	Shosse Revolyutsii 45/140 Leningrad K 248 RSFSR, USSR

no tel

FAMILY BACKGROUND:

Relationship	First Name	Date of Birth	Occupation/Profession
	Daniel	August 10, 1939	Mathematics teacher
Wife	Sarah	November 17, 1941	Music teacher
Son	Vladimir	April 24, 1968	
Daughter	Faina	January 5, 1971	

RELATIVES ABROAD: Avraam Fradkin (Daniel's father)
Shikun Habad 1/16
Lod, Israel

VISA APPLICATION HISTORY: Date of First Application: November, 1972

Reason for Refusal: State secrets   Date of First Refusal: March, 1973

Most Recent Refusal: Repeatedly   Permission:

CASE HISTORY/ADDITIONAL COMMENTS:

Until 1964, Daniel worked as a mathematician. In 1964, he changed jobs and began lecturing at the Leningrad Institute of Electronic Communications. Daniel was never exposed to any state secrets at either position. He was dismissed from his lecturing post in 1972 immediately after having submitted his application to emigrate to Israel -- an application that was later denied on the grounds of access to state secrets.

Since then, Daniel managed to support his family by working as an elevator operator, a mailman, a janitor and as a ticket inspector on public buses. In early 1980, he obtained a job selling insurance door-to-door on a commission basis.

The Fradkins are a religious family. Jewish traditions and festivals are marked and strictly observed. Daniel teaches Hebrew and Judaism to his children and to the children of other refuseniks. The family eats only kosher food. Daniel's father, Avraam Fradkin, a rabbi, emigrated to Israel in 1972. Daniel's mother died of starvation during the siege of Leningrad during World War II. Daniel suffers stomach disorders dating back to the years of hunger in Leningrad during the siege.

Daniel has been actively petitioning the Supreme Soviet to reinstate official policy allowing emigration on the basis of family reunification.

3/84

Figure 4.5. "Refusenik Profile" sheet on Daniel Fradkin. National Conference on Soviet Jewry, 1984. American Jewish Historical Society, RG I-181A, box 78, folder 6.

Eugene is a former scientist at the Institute for Shipbuilding where he specialized in medalurgy [sic]. He was employed there for 28 years in this capacity but, when he applied to leave the country, he was fired from his position as scientist and offered a position as a foreman for building repairs with the same Institute. He holds a P.H.D. in Physics of Solids. His wife, Sophia, is an economist with the Institute for Shipbuilding and she has not lost her job.
—Trip report of Nancy and Greg Leisch, Alexandria, Virginia, March 1976[103]

Family situations:

His second wife turned him into the state after their divorce, to get even. She testified against him and his studying companion, Pincus Polansky. His present wife (#3) is a giyoret (Convert) whose parents refuse to assent to her leaving the country; thus there is no possibility of their getting permission to leave for Israel since it would "divide a family."
—Trip report of Barry Tabachnikoff, Miami, March 1984[104]

Legal woes:

There are 2 cases which are presently under "investigation." One of them is the case against Lev involving his possession of narcotics, found on him during the transfer from one prison to the next.... It was an obvious frame up. Lev's fingerprints were not on the package. It was sewn into the shoulder and it appeared to be 25 grams of hashish.... They put Lev in a punishment cell for 2 weeks.
—Trip report of Harvey Barnett, attorney, Chicago, March 1980[105]

And health, medical conditions, and psychological well-being:

Has detached (L) retina operated on 5/87. Still has problems with eye. No gum problems but needs extraction of teeth # 13, 19, 20 and restorations in teeth # 1 & 17. Also should have lower partial denture.
—Trip report of Bruce Hochstadter, oral surgeon, Skokie, Illinois, November 1987[106]

Jews in North America did not typically relate to one another in this way. They reserved this mode of connection—brief, intense visits to interrogate and assiduously document the biographical details of strangers—for Soviet Jews. Barbara Stern, a Montrealer who chaired the Canadian Committee for Soviet Jewry, described the emotional effects of building a relationship on this basis: "These people were no longer just cases. They had become friends and family."[107] Other travelogue authors voiced similar sentiments:

> It is difficult to convey in words how emotional this visit was. We all had tears in our eyes the whole time, and we developed a very close bond in a very short time. It is hard to imagine that this could happen with strangers. But the whole point is that none of the people with whom we visited were strangers, they were all immediately like members of our family. It's hard to explain because we certainly don't feel this way about all Jews in Houston.
> —Trip Report of Ellen Trachtenberg, Jewish community leader, Houston, September 1985[108]

Many visitors strived for mutuality, sharing details about their own lives and families, but the relationships were not set up for parity. Travelogues show no evidence that visitors disclosed their medical histories or legal woes to Soviet Jews. Nor did refuseniks transcribe what they had learned about the tourists and transmit it for organizational processing.[109]

In documenting refuseniks' intimate lives for entry into the archive back in the United States, tourists incorporated representational modes associated with Age of Exploration scientific travel writing.[110] The Linnaean imperative was absent; this was not about structuring knowledge of distant flora and fauna into ordered categories. But in writing about Soviet Jews, they treated individuals as cases, selecting particular types of information as "data" to be recorded. And as with scientific travel writing, no Soviet Jewry movement travelogue was sufficient in itself. The information that each tourist returned was made useful by being added to an ever-accumulating fund of knowledge that movement organizations were amassing—depth knowledge about each particular case and breadth knowledge about the range of cases.

The compilation of the archive was a diaspora-building effort of the tallest order.[111] Typically, governments reserve to themselves the right to employ so-called biopolitical strategies to gain administrative knowledge and control over populations, such as using a census for the purpose of nation-building.[112] Here, however, the amassing of biographical and health information on thousands of individuals was undertaken by Jewish American voluntary groups in the name of global Jewish peoplehood, a concept of Jewish political community that transcends the confines of territorially bound nation-states.[113] By conjuring into existence a cumulative, systematic corpus of information that aspired to cover all refuseniks, American Jews attempted to replace their ignorance about Soviet Jewry with knowledge—knowledge that could be accessed to intervene on behalf of both individuals and the population overall; knowledge that could comfort, replacing feelings of helplessness with a sense of empowerment; knowledge that could stake a claim without seeking permission from any government, not Soviet, not Israeli, not American. American Jews authorized themselves to compile a register of a Jewish population in a foreign country. Jews would be responsible for biopower over Jews, and they would use this power to help move Jewish bodies across international borders.

Although the databases sat centralized in organizational offices and in activists' homes, data collection was participatory, involving thousands of Jewish tourists from across North America and Western Europe. If a global Jewish people is an "imagined community" in the Andersonian sense, akin to the nation, and if social identities are constructed by enacting them behaviorally (as gender is something that is "accomplished" or "done"), then the act of collecting refuseniks for the database became an important way that Jews of the West "did" Jewish peoplehood in the Cold War era.[114] In the relative dispassion of its data-oriented approach, the recording of biographical minutiae and health histories differed from other practices of peoplehood that the Soviet Jewry movement created or employed. It displayed none of the grandiosity of marching under "I am my brother's keeper" banners, none of the performativity of bar and bat mitzvah twinning speeches. It was less sweaty than the ten-kilometer Freedom Runs for Soviet Jewry. But its relative dispassion was only relative. The intimacy of the conversations and of the knowledge gained stirred travelers' emotions. They wrote this into their reports, burying the data in layers of personal testimony, commentary, and reflection.

REPRESENTING THE OTHER AND REFLECTING ON THE SELF

One year before Barry Tabachnikoff and Howard Shapiro traveled, a different pair of Florida rabbis undertook a similar excursion to meet refuseniks. In a Moscow apartment, Jeffrey Salkin and Richard Agler sat with Shelley and Oscar Mendeleev and their twin sons, Grigory and Valery. Refuseniks since age one, the boys were approaching their thirteenth birthday. Having listened to the twins prepare for their bar mitzvah ceremony, the rabbis used their travelogue to reflect on what they heard. In good rabbinic fashion, they drew out a moral lesson: "The boys read their Hebrew prayers for us. Some of the selections were revealing. They read the prayer that thanks God for teaching the rooster to distinguish between day and night. If only we Jews who live in the West could make the same distinction. How well we live . . . and how much of a spiritual price it is exacting from us."[115]

The rabbis' move, turning the observation of the Other into the basis for reflecting on the Self, is common in travel writing. When travelers encounter new places, the lenses they bring filter what they see. But as they try to assimilate new information into their preestablished conceptual frameworks, the otherness of the new makes for an imperfect fit. This forces travelers to revise and even redirects their gaze onto their interpretive lenses themselves. Foreign excursions thereby prompt inner journeys. Travel writing follows along this interior route.[116]

Salkin and Agler expressed their self-reflection as self-critique: "If only we Jews who live in the West could make the same distinction. How well we live . . . and how much of a spiritual price it is exacting from us." The lament is striking. It inverts the power relationship that motivated the movement's use of tourism in the first place. In the movement to "save" Soviet Jewry, American Jews understood themselves to be the fortunate ones doing the saving. Travelogues reflected this. In their Cold War and post-Holocaust modes, and in their uses of Age of Exploration tropes, the reports represented American Jews as empowered, free Westerners. They were heirs of a Jewish past that had been destroyed in Europe, discovering a lost community of downtrodden Jews in the East.

How fortunate they were to be able to use their advantaged position to bring aid, Jewish education, and hope to this population in need. It was not that the travelogues portrayed Soviet Jews as lacking agency. Refuseniks were named, individuated, spoken of as celebrities ("names we had only read about come to life"[117]). The reports portrayed refuseniks as acting on their own behalf politically and culturally, albeit under severe constraints. And although travelogues written by people less involved in the movement fell easily into Orientalizing depictions of Soviet Jews as simple, good-hearted people, pure of faith, grateful for Western beneficence, those written by leaders of the American campaign portrayed refuseniks as strategically minded colleagues to whom they looked for guidance on policy matters.[118] Nevertheless, throughout these travelogues, refuseniks remained positioned as beneficiaries of assistance that American Jews were able to provide by virtue of the privilege that life in the US had afforded them. For travelers, to be American meant to be empowered. Their trips to help Jews in the USSR helped them sense this in their bones, through immediate and intense feelings of self-efficacy.

Salkin and Agler's self-critique should be read against this context. Witnessing the Mendeleev twins' bar mitzvah prayers, the rabbis ventured a heresy. Perhaps the system on the Western side of the Iron Curtain also compromised Jews' ability to live full Jewish lives. And if so, perhaps the Jews of the United States of America were not as empowered and capable as they would have liked to think. Perhaps it was they who needed support. Perhaps it was the Jews of the Soviet Union who held the power to help them.

The rabbis, of course, were professionally committed to shepherding American Jews toward greater Jewish literacy and commitment. But they were far from alone in venturing the critique that abundance, security, and atomistic notions of freedom were taking a toll on Jewish life in the US.[119] Unlike Salkin and Agler, who made general reference to "we Jews who live in the West," Miami real estate agent Al Rose included himself among those he accused of a surfeit of Jewish apathy. Writing about his August 1973 cruise to Leningrad, when he and his wife and daughters distributed mezuzah necklaces to Soviet Jews, Rose suggested that complacent Jewish Americans might learn something about Jewish fortitude from their Soviet counterparts, as he had: "And to think that until recently we had rarely gone to Temple except for the minimum necessities. . . . Those in the USA who are smug and content about things should visit Russia for a rude awakening. Jews abroad wore *mezzuzahs* openly, and it was the first time for many. We were more proud to be Jews. We realized first hand what our forefathers had endured and fought to preserve against overwhelming suffering and bigotry. The *mezzuzahs* were a salute to them."[120]

Criticisms that American freedom was breeding Jewish apathy complicated but never overturned the power differentials inherent in the trips. Some even argued that learning from the refuseniks would help American Jews better fulfill their responsibilities as benefactors:

> There is much we can learn from the Jews of the USSR. During our visit they taught us how much we take for granted, and how so many opportunities for Jewish learning have passed us by simply because we don't place the value upon them that we should. In many ways, their determination to learn and to be Jews should serve as an example to us. We, too, need to be strong and learned if we are to have anything of enduring value to offer them in the years to come.
> —Trip Report of Jules Gutin, forty, United Synagogue Youth (USY) assistant director, New York, and Joshua Kanter, seventeen, USY vice president for social action, Syracuse, June 1990[121]

> They need us so much for both morale and (in some cases) financial support and we need them for their need of us. They reminded us of the beauty of Judaism, of the need to study it and learn more about it, of the basic truths it teaches us. And we need them also for the heroic Jewish struggle which they are undertaking for all Jews everywhere. They made us proud to be Jews and proud of our heritage, and they reminded us that in the land of freedom, it is easy to take too much for granted.
> —Trip Report of Ellen Trachtenberg, Jewish community leader, Houston, September 1985[122]

To build the critique of America's corroding influence on Jewish life, travelogue authors treated Soviet Jews as symbols, representing them as bearers of a pure and determined faith in the face of adversity. One might argue that the portrait smacks of romantic primitivism—the natives in their simplicity serving as foils to expose the corrupting effects of civilization.[123] But this oversimplifies—not only because travelogues depicted Soviet Jews as educated urbanites from the professional class but, more importantly, because tourists based these depictions on meetings with a highly unrepresentative subset of the Soviet Jewish population. These were activists. They were especially committed to living Jewishly, more than most Jews in Russia and more than most Jews in America. Travelers generalized incorrectly when writing of "Soviet Jewry" as a whole when they had "refuseniks" in mind. They were also making apples-to-oranges comparisons when evaluating the Jewish commitments of the general population of American Jews against those of Moscow's and Leningrad's activist core. Nevertheless, these were the comparisons that travelers chose to make. They had the effect of tempering any hubris the visitors might have arrived with regarding their Americanness as a purely privileged status.

Travel writing offers a window not only onto the places and people they purport to describe but also onto their authors' own self-understandings. Soviet Jewry movement travelogues reveal Jewish Americans experiencing a sense of their own empowerment. In their self-representations, tourists depicted themselves as capable of making a difference and taking action to do so. They understood their self-efficacy in its historical contexts. They wrote self-consciously as post-Holocaust American Jews trying to rebuild a Jewish world out of the remains of what the Nazis had destroyed. And they wrote—sometimes proudly, sometimes sheepishly—as Cold War–era Jewish Americans using all the tools they could muster from the pop-espionage tool kit to try to reunite a Jewish world that the Soviets had forcibly divided. The two historical contexts were linked in travelers' minds, Wiesel's caveats notwithstanding. They recognized two totalitarianisms, each arrayed in its own way against the Jews of the USSR. By fighting the Cold War on Soviet soil, they could feel themselves effecting post-Holocaust repair. By memorializing the Holocaust in places where the Kremlin preferred silence, they could feel themselves fighting the Cold War. In battling Nazis past and Soviets present, tourists understood themselves to be acting not only as Jews but also as Americans. Indeed, they saw their Americanness as the source of their efficacy, the circumstance that allowed them to be providers of aid rather than recipients.

And yet the tours chipped away at this unbridled self-confidence. It was not that the trips generated goodwill toward the USSR. These were not socialist friendship delegations.[124] Soviet Jewry movement travel thoroughly reinforced negative Cold War images of the Soviet system, endowing these notions with all the authority that came from discovering them off Intourist's beaten path.[125] Nevertheless, travelers' sense of America did not emerge unscathed. This was undoubtedly an unintended consequence of the Soviet Jewry movement's deployment of tourism. Encountering refuseniks in person in the USSR, American Jews began to see themselves not only as empowered agents of repair but also as weakened, compromised, and needing repair themselves. The brokenness of the Jewish world, they concluded, was not only contained on the other side of the Iron Curtain.

5

WE'VE SAID NO TO PEPSICO

Si Frumkin and Zev Yaroslavsky had been trying unsuccessfully to start a boycott since early 1971. Détente was progressing, and US-Soviet trade relations were making headlines. Like other skeptics of rapprochement, they took offense at the notion of business as usual, or better than usual, with the Russians. As they saw it, trade deals would make America complicit in the abuse of Soviet Jews. Rather than fill Kremlin coffers, they wanted a "total economic boycott of the Soviet Union."[1]

Frumkin, a Lithuanian-born Holocaust survivor who owned a successful wholesale drapery company, headed the Southern California Council for Soviet Jews (SCCSJ). Yaroslavsky, California-born and eighteen years his junior, had just finished undergraduate studies at UCLA, where he had founded California Students for Soviet Jews (CSSJ). The two worked closely together. As they considered détente's implications, they recognized that the push to improve economic ties gave activists leverage and created new pressure points.[2]

Few in the movement were thinking in these terms. In New York, Meir Kahane's Jewish Defense League (JDL) had issued a call in January 1971 to boycott American companies doing business with the Soviet Union and even succeeded in gaining an audience with the US commerce secretary. But as Frumkin and Yaroslavsky began planning their first boycott a month later, they were working with a tactic that was still untried in the American Soviet Jewry movement. Perhaps their Los Angeles perch positioned them better than others to see the potential for boycotts to raise awareness, engage supporters, and bring opponents to the table. Just two hours north, labor organizer Cesar Chavez had been leading a world-famous, five-year-long, ultimately successful boycott of California grapes. (The growers capitulated in July 1970.) This was local news. The

Los Angeles Times devoted more coverage to it than any other major daily in the United States. Frumkin and Yaroslavsky were among the millions who took part in the grape boycott. But whether this directly influenced their planning, merely set the context, or happened to be a coincidence of geography is impossible to know. Whatever the case, the Soviet Jewry movement's nationwide boycott of Pepsi-Cola, launched in 1972 and lasting more than a decade, traces its origins to Los Angeles and to the groundwork that Frumkin and Yaroslavsky had laid there.[3]

SCCSJ's and CSSJ's efforts to leverage consumer pressure first made headlines in March 1971. A travel industry trade journal reported that the organizations had been writing tour operators asking them to stop organizing trips to the Soviet Union. To add teeth to the request, Frumkin and Yaroslavsky said they would publicize a list of agencies that did and did not comply. "Ridiculous," responded a spokesperson for Intourist, the Soviet travel bureau. Word of the attempted tourism boycott reached the National Conference on Soviet Jewry (NCSJ), which rejected it out of hand.[4] In April, Frumkin and Yaroslavsky brought two hundred students to picket Los Angeles's largest department store, the May Company, "protesting its selling of Russian vodka, caviar and furs and its giving floor space to a travel agency selling tours to the Soviet Union."[5] In September, they redirected their campaign from travel to transportation. Mack Trucks, Inc. was seeking US government permission to build a factory in Russia. Protesting to the company and to the White House, Frumkin and Yaroslavsky threatened a boycott. Union of Councils (UCSJ) activists in San Francisco and Philadelphia also took up the issue. Ultimately, warnings that the trucks could end up in North Vietnamese hands made a more convincing argument than any appeals to human rights. Resistance from the military scuttled the deal. With no factory in the offing, the plan to boycott Mack Trucks was shelved.[6]

Soon enough, however, détente's economic rapprochement found "a poster child."[7] In November 1972, Donald M. Kendall—CEO of PepsiCo, chair of the business division of the Nixon campaign's Committee to Re-Elect the President, and head of the corporate sector's main lobby for closer US-Soviet economic ties, the Emergency Committee for American Trade—announced that his company had just signed a deal to provide Pepsi-Cola to thirsty Russians desperate for something other than the "Soviet near-beer called *kvas*."[8] It was not the first time that Kendall and Pepsi, with Nixon's help, had won over the Soviets. Thirteen years earlier, on the same day that then vice president Nixon and Soviet premier Nikita Khrushchev held their famous "kitchen debate," Kendall prevailed on Nixon to bring the Soviet leader to the Pepsi pavilion at the American National Exhibition in Moscow. Kendall, who at the time headed PepsiCo's European operations, gave Khrushchev two cups of the soft drink, one made locally and one brought over from the US. As Kendall tells the story, "I wanted . . . to show that we can make it as good in Moscow as we did in the United States. Khrushchev tasted both of them, then turned to the press—there were press all over the place—and said, 'Drink the Pepsi-Cola made in Moscow. It's much better than the one made in the United States.' Khrushchev then literally started handing them out."[9]

With no compelling visuals from the 1972 announcement, the *New York Times* ran a file photo from the 1959 scene to accompany its front-page coverage of the détente-era deal. In the picture, Khrushchev enjoyed his drink while behind him there stood younger versions of Nixon and Leonid Brezhnev, the political architects of détente, and Kendall, the businessman who would make détente's vision of economic rapprochement a reality. The deal was unprecedented. Pepsi-Cola would become the first American consumer good manufactured and distributed in the USSR. In return, PepsiCo, which imported Stolichnaya vodka to the US, would also sell Soviet brandies, wine, and champagne in the American market. The more Russian spirits PepsiCo could convince Americans to imbibe, the more bottles of Pepsi-Cola the Soviets would allow to roll off the production line. For Soviet Jewry activists, this added insult to injury. Not only was PepsiCo signing a contract with the USSR, but the company's profits hinged on American consumer dollars flowing to Moscow.[10]

PepsiCo announced the deal on a Friday. By Wednesday, the two California groups had delivered their response:

FOR IMMEDIATE RELEASE
November 22, 1972

SOVIET JEWRY ORGANIZATIONS TO BOYCOT[T] PEPSICOLA
"We are asking people to stop drinking Pepsi, to sell their stock in that company, and to inform the Pepsico Company that individual citizens

of our community cannot in good conscience support an outfit which directly or indirectly condones the ransoming of Soviet Jews," Frumkin said.[11]

The talk of "ransoming" was a timely reference. A few months earlier, the Kremlin had introduced an emigration tax that was widely seen as a ploy to extort money from Western Jewish groups.[12] "Pepsi has joined the slave trade generation," Yaroslavsky added, playing on the company's "Join the Pepsi Generation" advertising slogan.

Grassroots Soviet Jewry councils in other cities took up the call. On December 6, their umbrella organization, the UCSJ, declared a nationwide boycott of PepsiCo and its subsidiaries: Frito-Lay, Wilson Sporting Goods, Monsieur Henri Wines, and North American Van Lines.[13] The years 1973 to 1975 brought a flurry of activity. In the DC area, synagogues and Hillels wrote the Washington Committee for Soviet Jewry (WCSJ) to announce their intentions to cease serving Pepsi products. Under the slogan "We've said no to PepsiCo," activists in Cleveland inaugurated their boycott by picketing the local shopping mall. From Manhattan's Fifty-Ninth Street Bridge, Student Struggle for Soviet Jewry (SSSJ) staged a Boston Tea Party–style "Pepsi Party," dumping the soft drink into the East River. In Los Angeles, SCCSJ members plastered "Don't drink Pepsi. Pepsi sells to Russia. Russia sells Jews" bumper stickers on Pepsi delivery trucks. At PepsiCo's world headquarters in Purchase, New York, members of SSSJ's Westchester County chapter blocked the entrance to the shareholders' annual meeting and set a facsimile vending machine ablaze, shouting, "Burn, Pepsi, Burn!" In Massachusetts, supermarket owners wrote protest letters to Pepsi bottlers. At Columbia University, the Council of Jewish Organizations pressed the university to cancel its contract with Pepsi. The campus's JDL chapter threatened to smash soda machines in the dining halls. The university switched to Coke. At Super Bowl VII in Los Angeles, as the Miami Dolphins were cementing their victory over the Washington Redskins, a helicopter chartered by the California Students for Soviet Jews circled low over the Coliseum, banner in tow: "Help Soviet Jews—Don't Drink Pepsi." (Later, "irate Pepsi distributors" threatened to sue the charter company.)[14]

Grassroots pressure sparked by the UCSJ boycott forced Jewish institutions to take a stand. Synagogues, college Hillels, and other stand-alone

Figure 5.1. "Say No Pepsi" poster. Cleveland Council on Soviet Anti-Semitism, ca. 1973. Western Reserve Historical Society, MS 4011, box 9, folder 254.

organizations were more willing to sign on than community-wide umbrella agencies. In January 1973, the Washington Board of Rabbis "refused to endorse" the Pepsi boycott when prodded by the local UCSJ affiliate. Although it allowed that a "boycott may be indicated in due course," it considered the idea "counterproductive" to the larger strategy of pushing for the Jackson-Vanik Amendment, which would have a greater economic impact by denying most-favored-nation trade preferences to the USSR.[15] The National Conference on Soviet Jewry took the same position. Upon returning from the Christmas and New Year holidays, the NCSJ opened its 1973 agenda by convening a special executive committee meeting to set policy "in regard to the private sector." According to NCSJ executive director Jerry Goodman, "It was unanimously agreed that we should oppose boycotts aimed at U.S. firms who are trading with the U.S.S.R., holding open the option should conditions warrant such a step." An NCSJ plenum two weeks later instructed all member agencies, including Jewish federations and community councils, that they "were not to advocate for a boycott of Pepsi-Cola or any other company dealing with the U.S.S.R., at this time." They wanted to engage, not antagonize. They also thought the boycott was sure to fail and that pursuing a no-win strategy would be "a sign of weakness."[16]

Boycott supporters pushed back. A month after the policy announcement, a Washington-area synagogue urged Conservative Judaism's congregational union to break with the NCSJ and adopt the Pepsi boycott.[17] Critics charged that large Jewish organizations were kowtowing to major donors with business interests at stake. In 1977, when Baltimore's Jewish community gave the beverage contract for its annual Jewish cultural festival to a Pepsi distributor, opponents rallied a three-year nationwide campaign that included an eight-page advertorial, published in New York's main Jewish weekly, comparing festival sponsors to the Ku Klux Klan.[18] Against the straightforward message "Pepsi Sells to Russia, Russia Jails Jews ... The Choice is *Yours*. Happy Passover," opponents of the boycott never came up with more effective counterarguments than variants of "it's complicated."[19] Boycotters won the battle for command of the narrative in the Jewish American public square. Even Jews who did not join in heard the message: PepsiCo was not friendly to Jewish interests.

Despite their different stances, the National Conference and Union of Councils each used the boycott to arrange meetings with PepsiCo.

The agreement to meet was all that Pepsi was willing to concede. In March 1973, PepsiCo's vice president for corporate affairs, Cartha "Deke" DeLoach (formerly number three in J. Edgar Hoover's FBI) told a delegation of Chicago Jewish leaders that the Soviet Jewish issue was an "internal matter" for the USSR and that PepsiCo would not discuss it with the Soviet government. DeLoach took the same position with students burning the cardboard vending machine. Representatives from the NCSJ and American Jewish Committee (AJC) reported more sympathetic responses. PepsiCo officials "indicated that they would help wherever possible," but the company avoided specific commitments. Goodman came away doubtful that PepsiCo would follow through.[20] Kendall was not one to back down in the face of threats. In the early 1960s, when the Ku Klux Klan threatened a boycott after PepsiCo became the first Fortune 500 company to hire a Black senior executive, Kendall responded by hiring another. He also stood firm in his commitment to doing business with the Soviet Union, leading the corporate sector's unsuccessful fight to prevent and then to repeal the Jackson-Vanik Amendment. For the first type of principled stance, the AJC planned to honor Kendall with its Civic Leadership prize in 1975. Kendall's principled stance in support of free trade with the Soviet Union generated so much outrage in the Jewish community, however, that the AJC backtracked and abruptly canceled the award.[21]

The Pepsi boycott quickly grew beyond its origins in the Soviet Jewry campaign. When they first launched the boycott, advocates sometimes mentioned as a side note that PepsiCo did business in the Arab world but not in Israel.[22] (By contrast, in those years, T-shirts and bottles sporting the instantly recognizable Hebrew version of Coca-Cola's trademark script were popular souvenirs among tourists to the Jewish state.) PepsiCo consistently denied that it was honoring the decades-long Arab League boycott of Israel. Nevertheless, its presence in Soviet and Arab markets coupled with its absence from Israel, refusal to advocate for Soviet Jews, and leadership in the campaign against Jackson-Vanik all combined to reinforce a sense among Jewish Americans that the company was, at best, insensitive to their concerns. As time passed, the attacks on PepsiCo increasingly mentioned Soviet Jewry and the Arab boycott in tandem, especially after 1975, when Israel stepped up its campaign against the Arab boycott more broadly. Groups in the UCSJ network circulated a poster showing photographs of two Pepsi-Cola bottles, one bearing a Russian label, the other, Arabic. The text listed "Some UNrefreshing facts about Pepsi . . . difficult for Jews to swallow." Sandwiched between the bottles was the question, "Do YOU drink Pepsi?" In Denver, a rabbi asked his congregation to "join him in a 'Pepsi pledge' to abstain from the company's products 'until that time that Mr. Kendall will intervene in behalf of Soviet Jews and Pepsi will recognize the State of Israel.'" The Arab League boycott rationale even came to overshadow the Soviet Jewry issue in the Baltimore Jewish Cultural Festival fight, which was led not by Soviet Jewry activists but by an ad hoc group calling itself "Jews Against the Arab Boycott."[23]

At no point in the boycott campaign did UCSJ activists expect to force PepsiCo to cancel its Soviet contract. They understood that even if the Jewish community united fully behind the boycott, it would have no effect on PepsiCo's bottom line.[24] If judged by that standard, the boycott was a failure and foreordained to be. PepsiCo was the world's second-largest company in the $15 billion soft drink industry. Its global market share, 20 percent in 1972, expanded to 25 percent at the end of the

Figure 5.2. "Some UNrefreshing Facts about Pepsi" flyer. Student Struggle for Soviet Jewry, ca. 1976. Yeshiva University, Mendel Gottesman Library. Call No. 1993.099, box 371.

WE'VE SAID NO TO PEPSICO

decade. Sales, net income, and earnings per share each grew by more than 15 percent a year over that time and more than 20 percent a year from 1976 to 1980.[25] Whatever impact the boycott had, it was not on Pepsi. Activists understood that. They saw the boycott as a way of raising awareness about Soviet Jewry and giving supporters a way of bringing activism home through their daily food and shopping choices. As UCSJ founder Louis Rosenblum put it upon learning of Pepsi's Russian contract, "Few Americans buy Mack Trucks. Almost all buy soft drinks. Pepsi Cola is *traif* (unclean) as of this date. Spread the word."[26]

The advantage of picking an unwinnable fight was that activists could drag it on for as long as they wanted. Pepsi was popular and prominent and was not going to disappear. The call to boycott PepsiCo for placing "profits before human rights" could serve as a perpetual rallying cry.[27] Still, when they launched the boycott in 1972, Frumkin and Yaroslavsky could not realize how fortuitous their choice of targets was. They had hitched their campaign to a rising star. Pepsi was encroaching on Coca-Cola's market dominance, so much so that in 1980 a new term entered the American lexicon: the "Cola Wars" became a decade-defining pop culture phenomenon. Whitney Houston and Elton John enlisted for Coke. Michael Jackson soldiered for the other side, becoming the Cola Wars' most famous casualty. (He was rehearsing a Pepsi commercial when pyrotechnics set his hair ablaze.) And in September 1989, as the world readied itself to bid the decade farewell, Billy Joel traced the entirety of postwar history in song, from Harry Truman forward, culminating in "Rock and roller cola wars, I can't take it anymore!" The song shot to number one.[28] In the midst of all this, perhaps alone among American groups (aside from Atlantans), Jewish Americans had a way of choosing between Coke and Pepsi that hinged on something more meaningful than which drink was sugared better. Few were 100 percent committed to refusing Pepsi every time. But because more than a decade's worth of activism had drummed into them the notion that PepsiCo preferred the Kremlin to refuseniks and the Arab states to Israel, every time Jewish American shoppers and diners were faced with the decision between Coke and Pepsi, the boycott gave them a chance to turn their consumer choice into a Jewish choice.

MOBILIZING THE LEISURE SOCIETY

Consumerism and leisure culture are fundamental building blocks of modern life. It took a while for social theorists to take them seriously. For much of the nineteenth and twentieth centuries, a combination of snobberies deflected attention or sought to denigrate rather than understand.[29] Part of this was the legacy of Christian asceticism, which even in its secularized version could not shake the idea that idle hands are the devil's handiwork. Part of it was sexism, particularly the "separate spheres" binary that grouped men/earners/serious on one side and women/spenders/frivolous on the other. Part of it traced to sociology's Marxist tradition, whose founder understood social life as relations of production, not relations of consumption, and never issued the call, "Consumers of the world unite!"

By the time American human rights activists were battling Pepsi for selling cola to Marx's Soviet disciples, these orthodoxies were starting to crumble. Academics would soon discover what the advertising industry knew well: the free market economic system works by turning people not only into producers but also into consumers.[30] As production costs were falling to a point where it would be hard to lower them much more, profits increasingly depended on imbuing functionally equivalent products with symbolic value and selling that symbolism to consumers for a premium. In other words, every industry was a culture industry, producing and circulating symbols.[31] And as feminism connected the societal to the personal, it became possible for scholars to acknowledge that in an economy of symbols, consumption was a fundamental way that human beings constructed personal and group identities.[32]

Activists in the Soviet Jewry movement might have been hard pressed to articulate this principle explicitly, but they demonstrated a working understanding of the idea. Searching for ways to engage supporters, they cast a mobilizing gaze on as many facets of people's multiple identities as they could think of. Activists engaged Jewish religious identity through holiday and ritual mobilizations. They tapped whatever sense of a Cold War self Americans might have had, giving them opportunities to play spy in the USSR. The 35s–Women's Campaign for Soviet Jewry organized around gender identity. The Student Struggle organized around generational identity. Even in a consumer society, activists recognized that work identities mattered a lot, and they created ways for people to place their professional skills in the service of the cause.[33] Doctors joined the Medical Mobilization for Soviet Jewry. Lawyers wrote briefs for the Soviet Jewry Legal Advocacy Center. And amid all this, in the tenor of the times, activists developed protest tactics that spoke to people's consumer identities, mobilizing around leisure pursuits, body projects, media spectacles, and the culture industries that enabled these.

Earlier chapters treated the Soviet Jewry movement's use of that iconic form of leisure culture—international tourism. "Why go to the Soviet Union?" *Fodor's* asked at the opening of its inaugural travel guide to the country. "First and foremost, because it's the biggest adventure in the world." Activists in Washington played on the prestige associated with travel to the remote and forbidding Soviet Union by naming its tourism program the "Insiders Club."[34] In this chapter, we focus on other ways that activists applied the mobilizing gaze in a consumerist, leisure-driven, media-saturated society. Having begun with their effort to influence Jewish Americans' shopping decisions about what *not* to put *into* their bodies, we turn next to activists' move in the opposite direction—using fashion and fitness to place the movement *onto* their bodies. Then we examine how activists denied American consumers the luxury of imagining that culture was apolitical by taking protests into their places of leisure—the concert halls and sporting arenas where US-Soviet cultural exchange was taking place. Such protests built momentum toward the movement's effort to move the 1980 Olympics from Moscow, a campaign targeting the most popular sports-entertainment megaevent in the world.

BODY PROJECTS
WEARING THE CAUSE: CLOTHING, COSTUMES, AND SOVIET JEWELRY

Social movements commonly use dress to build solidarity, foster collective identity, and make presence visible.[35] The campaign to free Soviet Jewry was no exception. Although photographs of demonstrations mostly show protesters in regular daily wear—collared shirts and blouses in the early 1960s, sweat shirts and jeans in the 1980s—some people made a point of dressing for the occasion. Affluent members of the 35s–Women's Campaign for Soviet Jewry took to British streets in fashionable black sweaters, blouses, and slacks. This sartorial strategy, drawn from the South African antiapartheid movement, earned them the moniker "the ladies in black." Although they chose their look with the press in mind, the outfits were drawn from their wardrobes, expressing the gender and social class identities that they comfortably inhabited. Not so the prison outfits that they started donning after the elegant look stopped drawing news cameras. Demonstrating in costume became easier with repetition. Soon the 35s were swapping out black and white prison stripes for colorful clown outfits to picket a visiting Russian circus troupe and for ghostly sheets to confront the mayor of Odessa as he visited Karl Marx's London grave. Costuming became a signature of the 35s' protests and a valued part of the group's collective identity. In New York, something similar happened in Student Struggle for Soviet Jewry. Its telegenic, themed demonstrations featured rabbis in prayer shawls, Halloween exorcists in black robes, and cadres of marchers in striped prisoner pajamas.[36]

Costuming was not a day-to-day approach to mobilizing dress. It was episodic, used only when demonstrating. It was also mutable. When

Figure 5.3. Student marchers in prison stripe costumes, Brooklyn, New York. Student Struggle for Soviet Jewry, April 1, 1979. Yeshiva University, Mendel Gottesman Library. Call No. 1993.099, box 22, folder 2.

WE'VE SAID NO TO PEPSICO

members of the 35s marched for an ailing refusenik, they dressed as nurses. When protesting dead-of-night arrests that pulled Soviet activists from their beds, they wore pajamas.[37] Because organizers themed their costumes to the demonstrations, no single style of dress emerged as a standard symbol of the movement. Costumes were also consciously carnivalesque. Outfits were selected to attract attention from passersby and news cameras. They were aimed more at the viewer than the wearer. And in spite of the fact that this was a highly visible approach to wearing the movement, it never engaged large numbers. Even among members of the 35s and SSSJ, only a minority costumed up.

To use dress in a way that engaged not just a few hundred but hundreds of thousands, Soviet Jewry activists adopted a different strategy. They avoided pageantry in favor of intimacy and focused not on what people wore to rallies but on what they wore every day. In keeping with the consumer culture that shaped people's understandings of what it meant to get dressed in the morning, activists chose to fashion their movement-wear as fashion.

The Soviet Jewry movement's signature bodily adornment was not clothing but jewelry. Supporters kept the cause close to their skin and close in mind by symbolically shackling their own bodies with pendants and bracelets bearing the names of Soviet Jewish prisoners and refuseniks. When American Jews lowered the medallion chain over their necks or placed the nickel-plated cuff on their wrists, they could feel the cold metal, a reminder of Soviet Jewish bondage. Movement organizations from the grassroots and establishment factions alike commissioned and sold the jewelry. The necklaces were large and hard to miss when worn outside the shirt. Bracelets were more subtle. People unconnected with the movement might have struggled to make sense of them, but those who wore them understood their meaning and recognized the jewelry on others. The bracelets, especially, became a symbol of the Soviet Jewry campaign to those involved, and they have remained so even after the movement's end, featured in museum exhibitions and often mentioned by rank and file supporters in their reminiscences.[38]

The bracelets of the 1980s were a variation on medallions of the 1970s, which themselves were variations on the slogan-bearing lapel pins and buttons that activists had been wearing from the movement's first days. SSSJ founder Jacob Birnbaum presented President Lyndon Johnson with one of the group's buttons in 1965.³⁹ In 1966, the Cleveland Council on Soviet Anti-Semitism began selling one-inch-diameter lapel buttons featuring a ram's horn and the words "I Am My Brother's Keeper" in English or Hebrew at ten cents apiece, twenty for a dollar.⁴⁰ Buttons with other slogans proliferated: "Save Soviet Jewry," "Are We 'The Jews of Silence'?" and "Russia Is Not Healthy for Jews and Other Living Things" (playing on a 1960s antiwar slogan).⁴¹ The medallions changed the medium for the message. Buttons were simple promotional-wear. By contrast, as Zev Yaroslavsky explained when introducing the first pendants in July 1972, "The medallion is an attractive piece of jewelry."⁴²

Yaroslavsky's partner in activism, Si Frumkin, had come up with the idea for Prisoner of Conscience (POC) medallions. A wholesaler by trade, Frumkin reckoned that in addition to raising awareness, the medallions could also raise funds. As Yaroslavsky later recalled, "He knew wholesale prices versus retail prices. So he says, 'Well, at 15 cents apiece, we could sell these things for a dollar apiece and make an 85-cent per medallion profit and it would fund our organization.'" Frumkin envisioned most of

Figure 5.4. Anatoly Altman Prisoner of Conscience medallion kit. Union of Councils for Soviet Jews, ca. 1970s. Courtesy of Weitzman National Museum of American Jewish History, Philadelphia, 1991.51.8.2.

Figure 5.5. Anatoly Goldfeld Prisoner of Conscience medallion, obverse and reverse. Union of Councils for Soviet Jews, ca. 1970s. Author's personal collection.

the profits coming from bulk sales to synagogue gift shops, which could serve as a national distribution channel. The campaign grossed well over $100,000, dwarfing the revenues generated from membership dues.[43]

It remains unclear how Frumkin first seized on the idea of selling medallions. Yaroslavsky recollects that his partner was influenced by the Vietnam War POW-MIA bracelets that were adorning millions of American wrists at the time. Like the medallions, these too had originated in Southern California, introduced in May 1970 by the conservative Victory in Vietnam Association (VIVA). According to Yaroslavsky, Frumkin opted for a medallion necklace so as not to directly imitate or compete with the Vietnam War symbol.[44]

Frumkin and Yaroslavsky's Prisoner of Conscience (POC) medallions were innovative several times over. For one, they introduced and popularized jewelry as an element of Soviet Jewry movement material culture.[45] This gave people a new way to interact with the campaign. Although intended for display, the medallions were hung on necklaces that could be tucked in and worn privately, close to the heart. In this, they differed from the buttons and pins that preceded them. As for wearing them out over the shirt for others to see, this could be a fashion statement as well as a political statement. Yaroslavsky did, after all, advertise them as "attractive." Medallions introduced aesthetics as a meaningful dimension of engagement with the Soviet Jewish cause.

Moreover, the medallions could be (and were) treated in the customary way that consumer societies treat jewelry—as objects not just to purchase for oneself but also to give and cherish as gifts. Intangible commitments to the Soviet Jewish cause congealed in a tangible, transferable medium. When Jewish Americans gave the medallions as gifts, they were offering not just the physical object but the value commitments that the gift signified. They were also activating norms of reciprocity.[46] The expectation was not that the recipient would offer jewelry in return but that they would show respect for the values that motivated the giving of the medallion—that is, they should try to care a bit for Soviet Jewry. Announcing a new issue of five thousand medallions in December 1973, Yaroslavsky and Frumkin offered a timely pitch: "We might also suggest that the medallions make meaningful Hanukkah gifts for people of all ages."[47] Here, they addressed individuals. Other promotions targeted organizations, encouraging synagogues to buy the medallions in bulk for presentation as congregational gifts to bar mitzvah boys and bat mitzvah girls. By introducing gift giving as a form of involvement in the Soviet Jewry movement, the medallions loaded a political cause with sentimental meanings tied to personal relationships and special moments.[48]

Medallions also changed the nature of movement-wear by making it personalized and individualized. Buttons and lapel pins had borne only generic slogans. Medallions, in contrast, placed the names of Soviet Jews onto American Jews' bodies—with each wearer carrying a different name. The UCSJ medallions did contain generic elements, but only on one side. The obverse of each 1.75-inch-wide brass Star of David was stamped with the Southern California Council for Soviet Jews logo—an image of a smaller six-pointed star chained with a hammer-and-sickle padlock.[49] The words "Let My People Go" in English and Hebrew flanked the image. The reverse, however, varied. Above the words "U.S.S.R. Prisoner of Conscience," each medallion was individually stamped with the name of one of fifty different Soviet Jews imprisoned for their activism. (Volunteers at the SCCSJ office used a hand-press to stamp the names, running five hundred per hour at peak speed.)[50] In other words, the POC medallions were actually a *line* of jewelry. From afar, each necklace looked identical. Only on closer inspection could one know whether this was a Sylva Zalmanson or a Lassal Kaminsky. The wearer would know. The point was to create a sense of personal connection with the prisoner whose name one wore.

This approach was born of the Union of Councils "People-to-People" strategy, announced in 1970, which tried to deepen Americans' commitment to the cause by having them directly support specific, identifiable Soviet Jews.[51] Prisoner adoption was one of the earliest programs under the People-to-People rubric, and medallions were created in connection with this. Not every refusenik had a medallion bearing their name—only prisoners, and only a subset among them. Advertisements did not specify who among the "50 Jews held prisoner in Russia" the purchaser would receive for the $2.00 payment. One might hope for an Anatoly Goldberg but end up with an Anatoly Altman. It depended on the luck of the draw. Whoever one got, an accompanying card described their unhappy situation: "Crime: JEW. Punishment: Slow Death. . . . Anatoly Altman. Arrested in connection with the Leningrad 'hijacking' case on 6/15/70. Tried on 12/15/70 and sentenced to 15 years." The card also listed a prison address to encourage the medallion's owner to deepen the connection by writing to the person whose name they wore.[52]

There was an intimacy to this. The name one wore was ever-present and tangible—encountered in the routine of putting the necklace on, adjusting it during the day, fingering it mindlessly when fidgeting. Few of the medallion wearers ever met the prisoner whose name they chained around their necks, but the act of carrying the person's name day in and day out created a sense of identification, even possession. The name on your pendant was "your" prisoner; the name on your neighbor's was "theirs."

The idea caught on. In January 1973, five months after the medallions debuted, the Union of Councils announced customer number one hundred thousand, nine-year-old Lori Efron of San Antonio, Texas: "My Dad sent off for two P.O.C. necklaces (one for me and one for my sister). I really love the idea! It's Great!"[53] Other organizations took notice. Rejecting Frumkin and Yaroslavsky's calculus, Orthodox Judaism's National Conference of Synagogue Youth copied the POW-MIA bracelet design.[54] So did the University of Minnesota's Student Action Committee for Soviet Jewry (SAC). The Minnesota group's metal wrist cuff, which bore a prisoner's name in English and the words "Asir Zion" (Prisoner of Zion) in Hebrew, gained attention when SAC president Jeff Brochin presented the first bracelet to George McGovern during the Democratic presidential candidate's visit to campus in October 1972. Three weeks later, to "meet the numerous requests for Soviet Jewry bracelets," the SAC began selling them for $3.00 apiece at the local Judaica store, Brochin's Gift Shop.[55] Other groups created their own versions of the UCSJ medallions. In 1973, the Greater New York Conference on Soviet Jewry (GNYCSJ) created "Freedom Shields," which the National Conference and its affiliates sold around the country. One inch high and "bear[ing] the name of a Soviet Jewish prisoner engraved on a Star of David" along with the words "Free Them Now," the Freedom Shields were advertised as "made of jewelers metal." At $1.50, it was not a precious metal. Nevertheless, the designers' intent that it be worn as jewelry was evidenced in the order form's options. With a pin back as well as a top loophole, purchasers could choose to wear them "as a lapel pin, a brooch," or for twenty-five cents, "on a silver-finish chain."[56]

In London, the 35s–Women's Campaign for Soviet Jewry took a different approach, producing jewelry that would cost much more than the Americans' paltry $1.50. Frumkin and Yaroslavsky had been content to hand over the design of their brass medallion to group member Seymour "Sy" Lauretz, a certified public accountant from Beverly Hills. The leader of the 35s, Doreen Gainsford—a former public relations professional—marched into a Jermyn Street jewelry shop to enlist the man known as "the father of modern jewelry." Andrew Grima had received commissions from Queen Elizabeth and Princess Margaret. His work adorned the bodies of Princess Anne, Jaqueline Kennedy Onassis, any number of Vanderbilts and DuPonts, and movie stars like the first "Bond Girl," Ursula Andress. He was already at the pinnacle of his fame when he presented a medallion design as a gift to the 35s in early 1973.[57] Cast in eighteen-karat gold, Grima's large circular pendant featured six isosceles triangles cut out to form a Star of David in the negative space. Like the UCSJ medallion, it bore the words "U.S.S.R. Prisoner of Conscience" and a name. Most were inscribed "Sylva Zalmanson," who was then serving ten years of hard labor for her part in the "Operation Wedding" Leningrad hijacking affair.[58] The medallion was designed as women's jewelry and was priced accordingly, at £125 (equivalent to £1,265 or almost $1,600 in 2023 currency). For those disinclined to make such an investment, a silver version could be acquired for £25. For

WE'VE SAID NO TO PEPSICO

those strongly disinclined, gold- and silver-plated versions went for £4 apiece.[59] At any price point, they were a hit. Members of the 35s wore them. Elizabeth Taylor was said to wear one too (the eighteen-karat-gold version). Across the UK, 35s chapters gave the medallions as gifts to actresses and political wives who lent their support to the cause. The first celebrity recipient, Ingrid Bergman, modeled it for the press. In 1974, when Zalmanson—released early and granted an exit visa—visited England to meet with the 35s, Bergman presented the former prisoner with a medallion of her own, engraved with the names of her husband and brothers still languishing in the labor camps.[60]

The medallion campaigns marked a moment in the movement's unfolding history. Prominent for only a few years, they were quickly relegated to the realm of nostalgia. "Remember the Silva Zalmanson medallion pendants sold by the '35s Campaign for Soviet Jewry and worn by thousands of women throughout the country?" London's *Jewish Chronicle* asked in 1979. "When this refusenik was released from a Moscow prison the medallions were set aside and now lie forgotten in many a cupboard." But Zalmanson was returning to the UK to lobby on behalf of her still imprisoned husband, so the *Jewish Chronicle* urged, "Dig them out and wear them next Sunday."[61] In the US, too, the medallion campaigns quickly tapered off. Most of the prisoners whose names were stamped on the original issue had been sentenced to terms of five years or less and were out of prison and out of the USSR by 1975. Jewish newspapers continued to report new arrests and imprisonments, but this did not spark a surge in new jewelry production. In 1973, Philadelphia's Soviet Jewry Council had run large advertisements in the *Jewish Exponent* to sell both the UCSJ and NCSJ medallions. In 1977, it made no mention of jewelry whatsoever in its Adopt-a-Prisoner program manual. Likewise for the Greater New York Conference. In 1973, the GNYCSJ had been the driving force behind the NCSJ's Freedom Shields. In 1978, not a word about the shields appeared in the New York group's comprehensive guidebook for activism.[62]

But POC jewelry would soon make a comeback. To forestall the likelihood of protests before the international media at the 1980 Moscow Summer Olympics, the Soviet government began imprisoning and exiling political dissidents well in advance of the games. Hundreds, including Anatoly Shcharansky, were arrested between January 1977 and

Figure 5.6. Actress Ingrid Bergman, right, and former prisoner Sylva Zalmanson wearing POC medallions, designed by jeweler Andrew Grima for the 35s–Women's Campaign for Soviet Jewry, at the House of Commons in London at an August 1974 ceremony marking Zalmanson's emigration. Photo by Keystone Press / Alamy Stock Photo.

July 1980.⁶³ May and June 1978 brought a crackdown against the leadership of the Jewish emigration movement. On May 17, Iosif Begun was arrested outside the courtroom where Yuri Orlov, the founder of Moscow's human rights–monitoring Helsinki Watch Group, was being tried for "anti-Soviet agitation." On June 1, Vladimir and Maria Slepak were arrested for hanging a banner reading "Let Us Go to Our Son in Israel" outside their apartment window near Red Square. A day later, the refusenik community's liaison with prisoners, Ida Nudel, was arrested for protesting the Slepaks' arrest. By the end of the month, three of the four had been sentenced to exile in Siberia—Vladimir Slepak, five years; Nudel, four; Begun, three. (Maria Slepak received a three-year suspended sentence.) Two weeks after those verdicts were handed down, the highly publicized trial of Anatoly Shcharansky reached its conclusion. Shcharansky, who was prominent not only in the Jewish emigration movement but also in the dissident human rights campaign—he often served as Andrei Sakharov's spokesperson to the Western press—had been arrested shortly after Orlov in the wave of repression targeting the Moscow Helsinki Watch Group. Sitting in Lefortovo prison since March 1977 and facing trumped-up charges of spying for the CIA, Shcharansky potentially faced the death penalty. On July 14, 1978, he was sentenced to thirteen years of prison and forced labor. The next week, his sad eyes stared out from the cover of *Time* magazine on newsstands across America. Above his painted portrait, in letters of cement, the word *détente* crumbled down.⁶⁴

Considering the prominence of this new cohort of prisoners, it could have been an auspicious time to reinvigorate the medallion campaigns. But instead of issuing an updated series of pendants, the Union of Councils announced in August that it was launching an entirely new line of jewelry—Prisoner of Conscience bracelets. It is not clear why the UCSJ decided to shift from necks to wrists. Any number of reasons might plausibly have contributed. Organizational dynamics might have played a role. The Southern California Council had developed the medallion campaign and managed production and distribution. This time, the Washington Committee for Soviet Jewry took the lead. It might have been impractical or impolitic for the WCSJ to simply take over an SCCSJ operation. Perhaps fickle fashion tastes played a part. Having already sold hundreds of thousands of medallions whose designs had never been updated, it might have been hard to convince customers in a saturated market to buy another copy of something they already owned, especially something that looked so 1972. A new product line might revive interest.

Most likely, direct intervention by the father of the POW-MIA bracelets made the difference. As metal cuffs bearing the name of a prisoner and their date of arrest, the UCSJ Prisoner of Conscience bracelets were not at all new. Most Americans would have found them familiar. They were identical in every respect to the Vietnam War POW-MIA bracelets being worn by millions: the same nickel-plated metal, the same minimalist text in exactly the same format, the name stamped in all-caps sans serif letters painted black, the date written in month-day-year hyphenated numeric format. This was no coincidence. When it announced the new project, the UCSJ wrote that "Rep. Robert Dornan (R-CA) has been a driving force behind this idea." This was the same Dornan who had been the driving force behind the original POW-MIA bracelets back in 1969–70 when he was making a name for himself as a popular conservative Los Angeles television talk show host. A former air force pilot who had spent time in Vietnam as a reservist and news correspondent, he had, since 1965, been wearing a wristband given him by a Montagnard chieftain: "[He] asked me not to take it off until the Communists stop kidnapping his people." In late 1969, trying to help the wives of three missing pilots, Dornan linked up with the Victory in Vietnam Association (soon renamed Voices in Vital America). VIVA's student leaders—Carol Bates, Kay Hunter, and Steve Frank—decided to adapt Dornan's wristband to raise awareness about POW-MIAs. Abandoning their first plan to go to the Montagnards to bring back wristbands from Vietnam, they looked to their groups' adviser, Gloria Coppin, for help. Coppin contracted a Santa Monica metal shop to mock up ten prototypes. Dornan introduced VIVA's POW-MIA bracelets on his talk show. By the time VIVA disbanded in 1976, it had sold almost five million of them.[65]

Speaking with Avital Shcharansky during her visit to Congress a few days after her husband's sentencing, Dornan suggested a POW-MIA-style bracelet to raise awareness for Anatoly. The Washington Committee, which handled the UCSJ's congressional relations, immediately took up the idea and expanded it. Presumably with Dornan's assistance, they hired the California-based manufacturer of the POW-MIA bracelets to create a line of Prisoner of Conscience bracelets using the same template. The bracelets would bear not only Shcharansky's name but Begun's, Nudel's, Slepak's, and many others—twenty names in all, eighteen refusenik prisoners and two nonrefusenik Helsinki Watch dissidents (Yuri Orlov and Alexander Ginzburg). Having seen how quickly medallions were rendered obsolete by carrying names whose prison terms ended in 1973 and 1974, the Washington Committee drew a lesson: "Only prisoners with more than one year left on their sentence will be included." The WCSJ would not get stuck with expired inventory. But the logic of mass production did not mean that the group could not also be responsive to consumers: "Special orders can be taken for any name you submit." And unlike the medallions, the order form for bracelets let people choose which of the twenty names they wanted at $3.00 a piece with bulk discounts available.[66]

The first bracelets shipped in September 1978. Dornan gave one to every member of Congress. He also took to the House floor—and then to the airwaves—to promote them:

> I am going on the ABC "AM America" Show October 9, and I am going to discuss our missing [in action, in Vietnam]. I will also hold up this new bracelet that I am wearing for Anatoly Shcharansky. . . . Since I am the person who started the POW bracelet, I feel I am entitled to use it for a new tragic cause. . . . I am going to try to help this new bracelet to spread like wildfire. . . . Those freedom-loving fighters behind the Bamboo Curtain and behind the Iron Curtain will be heartened when they hear that thousands of Americans are wearing their names.[67]

When Shcharansky addressed Congress in 1986, three months after gaining his freedom, he and Dornan symbolically broke the bracelet that the congressman had been wearing for the past eight years. Actually, "It did not quite break," Dornan said. "It was bent into a 'V'—a 'V' for 'victory,' I said, but he said; 'No a V for visa.'"[68]

The bracelets caught on. The NCSJ again followed the UCSJ and created its own version. It also used the jewelry to advertise the organization, inscribing its name, "National Conference on Soviet Jewry," just underneath the prisoner's. These "Refusenik Identification Bracelets" also expanded beyond prisoners to feature the names of long-term refuseniks.

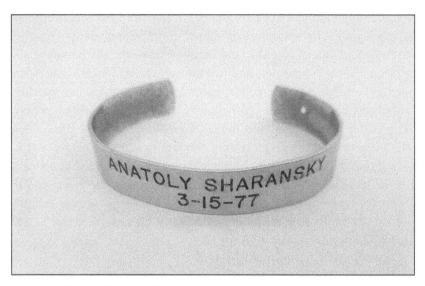

Figure 5.7. "Anatoly Sharansky" Prisoner of Conscience bracelet, showing his March 15, 1977, arrest date. Union of Councils for Soviet Jews, ca. 1978. Courtesy of Lorna Graff. Author's personal collection.

Throughout the 1980s, Soviet Jewry organizations cross-marketed the bracelets when promoting prisoner adoption, family adoption, and bar and bat mitzvah twinning programs. The bracelets became a familiar element in the Soviet Jewry movement's material culture. Synagogues gave them to their members. Newspapers mentioned them in human interest stories (far more than they ever mentioned medallions). After the movement ended, museums collected them, and reminiscences invoked bracelet-wearing alongside "delivering blue jeans to refuseniks" as a shorthand for Soviet Jewry activism itself.[69]

FITNESS: FREEDOM RUNS

Organizers billed San Francisco's October 1981 "Freedom Run for Soviet Jewry" as "the toughest 10K in the city." The steep opening climb from Pacific Avenue to Divisadero was a metaphor. Promotional flyers highlighted the case of Boris Kalendarov, a refusenik "running an up-hill race that he hopes will lead him away from Soviet oppression, to freedom." (The race route did not lead away from the Soviets but intentionally passed their consulate.) To draw the Jewish community, the race's sponsor, the American Jewish Congress (AJCongress), asked the Jewish Community Relations Council (JCRC) to fold its annual Simchat Torah rally into the event. To draw runners, the AJCongress enlisted the San Francisco Marathon Clinic as a cosponsor. The race was officially sanctioned by the Pacific region of the Amateur Athletic Union (AAU). The *San Francisco Examiner* listed it in the sports section, one of eleven races that weekend mentioned in the Runners' Calendar. San Francisco was not unique in organizing a 10K for Soviet Jewry. The previous year, two thousand runners raced in Los Angeles, and Arizona governor Bruce Babbitt inaugurated Tucson's first Freedom Run, an annual tradition that outlasted the Soviet Union. Pitching the idea to the JCRC, AJCongress director Joel Brooks pointed to the success of the Los Angeles and Tucson races "as a medium for educating both Jews and non-Jews about, and involving them in, the Soviet Jewry issue." He thought a San Francisco run would be just as successful, if not more, "in view of the popularity of running in the Bay Area."[70]

Running certainly was popular, and not only in the Bay Area. In 1979, after President Carter brought running into the headlines by almost collapsing during a 10K near Camp David, the *Washington Post* proclaimed the sport "The Phenomenon of the '70s." Interest in it had surged. Fifty-five entrants ran the first New York Marathon in 1970—four loops around Central Park. In 1980, 12,483 ran a course that passed through all five boroughs. By 1990, participation hit 23,729. Jim Fixx's 1977 *Complete Guide to Running* topped the *New York Times* bestseller list for eleven weeks and was at the time the most successful hardcover nonfiction book ever published.[71] Even as the sport gained adherents around the world, Americans understood it to be particularly American—part of the fitness "fad" that gave them aerobic workouts, Richard Simmons videotapes, Jane Fonda records, Adidas short shorts, and neon leg warmers. They brought this understanding with them when going abroad. "I went running through the streets of Leningrad," thirty-four-year-old psychologist Judy Wellins, from Albany, New York, wrote in a trip report describing her 1986 visit to refuseniks. "I heard people yell 'faster' in three different languages. I raced two boys on their bicycles headlong through the puddles. I felt like a walking advertisement for America and fitness—with my Mickey Mouse t-shirt, my nylon shorts and trendy sunglasses."[72]

In cities across the US, "Freedom Runs for Soviet Jewry" became annual events in the 1980s. They were one of the many ways activists tapped the zeitgeist to engage Americans as Americans. It was not that the idea of bringing people out to move their bodies through the streets was novel. Marches and demonstrations did that all the time. Nor was the notion of engaging in feats of physical endurance new. The Soviet Jewry movement had hunger strikers too, mainly in Soviet prisons but also in solidarity strikes in the US.[73] Nor was it innovative to combine bodily movement with feats of endurance. When the "sponsored walk fundraisers" popularized in Britain and Canada by Christian humanitarian groups came to America in 1969, Jewish groups quickly took up the idea.[74] The first Soviet Jewry "walkathons" included a Rochester, New York, synagogue youth group's 1970 event and a 1971 walk organized by activists in Orange County, California. There, 250 participants traversed an eighteen-mile round-trip route between Anaheim's Temple Beth Emet and Santa Ana's Temple Beth Shalom.[75] Student Struggle for Soviet Jewry encouraged activists to organize sponsored walks, explaining how to do so in its 1971 handbook: "Stage a 'walk-a-thon' for Soviet Jewry. A route is established; participants may march part or the whole of the way. Each participant secures 'sponsors' who pay for each mile walked, according to their means. For instance, a participant's little brother sponsors him at 50¢ a mile walked, his aunt at $3 a mile and the local drugstore at $5 a mile. The money is then donated to the Soviet Jewry protest movement."[76]

SSSJ often staged its walkathons around Passover and promoted them in terms that connected holiday- and motion-related themes. "Ancient Israelites' Passover Exodus reinterpreted as . . . 10-Mile Walkathon for Soviet Jews," read one promotional piece. "I cannot sit motionless while Soviet Jews are unable to share in the freedom of Passover," read another. Walking dramatized the idea that the social movement actually moved. Motion meant action.[77]

There were other types of "thons" too. In October 1976, two hundred bicyclists wearing "Save Soviet Jews" T-shirts tied up Manhattan city streets in the Student Struggle's first bike-a-thon—a twelve-mile, police-escorted ride that stopped for "minirallies" at Herald Square, the United Nations, and the Soviet UN Mission.[78]

Borrowing from the toolkit of foreign Christian charities, walkathons and bikeathons were not a product of America's burgeoning fitness culture. The Freedom Runs, however, were. The earliest were organized in Canton, Ohio, as ten-mile five-person-team torch relays, held annually from 1971 through 1975.[79] SSSJ recommended relays and torch runs in its 1971 handbook.[80] These were precursors, as was the torch relay that youth group members ran when lighting a nine-foot-tall menorah at Minneapolis's 1971 Hanukkah Vigil for Soviet Jewry.[81] As a movement-wide phenomenon, competitive running to raise awareness for Soviet Jewry came into vogue only after 1978, when two UCSJ leaders, avid runners, decided to bring the athletic and activist dimensions of their identities together, with the television cameras rolling.

Bernard Dishler, a general dentist from Elkins Park and chair of Philadelphia's Soviet Jewry Council (SJC), had taken up running after reading Kenneth Cooper's *Aerobics*, the 1968 bestseller that had coined the term and that had helped launch Americans into their fitness-filled future. As is still common among those who spend their early mornings on the tracks, trails, and streets, running became a part of Dishler's identity. When he traveled to meet refuseniks in the Soviet Union in March 1977, he made a special connection with Yuli Kosharovsky, an organizer of underground Hebrew language classes who was also an avid runner. Reporting back on their conversation, Dishler noted that when the police had taken Kosharovsky in for questioning the previous autumn, "he was arrested while jogging in a sweatsuit. He was not permitted to return home to change clothes." Others might have glossed over this detail, but not Dishler, who knew what it felt like to be in a sweatsuit after a run: "He was 8 hours at the Militia station and then took a six hour ride to prison before he could change. He was ill for several weeks after."[82]

Like Dishler, Joel Sandberg, a North Miami Beach ophthalmologist who chaired the South Florida Conference on Soviet Jewry, also loved to jog. When Sandberg briefed tourists, he tried to send joggers to his fellow runner, Kosharovsky. He also made sure that they delivered him "good running shoes . . . in addition to the usual Hebrew books and blue jeans."[83]

Early one morning in September 1978, before a full day of programming at the UCSJ's annual meeting in Washington, DC, Dishler and Sandberg stepped out of the Channel Inn hotel to go for a run. As they jogged, they talked about their shared interest in running. They also talked about their mutual friend. Dishler said he had entered a race under Kosharovsky's name and had managed to get television coverage. He encouraged Sandberg to do the same, offering to send him a T-shirt he had made for the occasion. In November, Sandberg entered Yuli Kosharovsky in the Miami Jewish Community Center's second annual 8-Mile Hanukkah Run. He informed the press that he would run in Kosharovsky's place if the refusenik could not get permission to fly to Florida for the December 17 race. Next to two photos of Sandberg in his special T-shirt (*front*, "Free Soviet Jews," with the UCSJ padlocked Star of David logo; *back*, "I am running for Yuli Kosharovsky Moscow USSR" in iron-on letters), a local paper described Kosharovsky's situation. Copying verbatim from the press release, it took up the thematic hook that Dishler and Sandberg used to create newsworthiness: "One arrest came as he finished jogging and was hauled off to prison in his sweat suit."[84]

As they would also do with bar and bat mitzvah twinning (see chapter 7), movement leaders transformed their personal activism into a mass mobilization tactic to engage others. In January 1979, Sandberg circulated a memo to Union of Councils groups nationwide: "Re: Project for Yuli Kosharovsky. . . . Easy to accomplish and fun (a rare combination in the Soviet Jewry movement)."[85] He recommended Dishler's idea, suggesting that activists enroll Kosharovsky in local races, recruit runners on his behalf, don the T-shirts, and alert the press. The idea of mobilizing runners for Kosharovsky circulated beyond the UCSJ. Soon, activists in Southern California were making it the centerpiece of a larger program.

When the Los Angeles Jewish Federation Council organized its first 10K Run for Soviet Jewry in 1979, it dedicated the race in Kosharovsky's honor: "You can join Yuli and symbolically run with him as he struggles to gain freedom."[86] With this move, the Los Angeles Jewish Federation took the UCSJ's new approach to capitalizing on feelings of solidarity in the community of running enthusiasts and combined it with a highly visible, greatly debated phenomenon in that community. The surge in charitable and corporate-sponsored races had "grown beyond anyone's ability to record," the *Los Angeles Times* reported in a feature published the same month that Sandberg circulated his memo. Competitive racers were lamenting "'junk runs' with poorly handled finishes and meaningless times." Traffic tie-ups had prompted the Los Angeles

Police Department to deny all new permit applications for races on city streets. On the plus side, the boom was creating a new market for professional race producers. It also brought an influx of corporate money: "Pepsi Cola will spend about $300,000 in the coming year for its series of 'Diet Pepsi' races around the country—races frequently cited by runners as examples of well-run events."[87] (Protesting the company at the 1981 Pepsi Challenge Run across New York's George Washington Bridge, SSSJ sent six runners who taped "Pepsi Fails the Human Rights Challenge—Save Soviet Jewry" signs to their Hebrew Coca-Cola T-shirts.)[88]

The Jewish Federation managed to get the LAPD to approve a permit for an AAU-sanctioned December 1979 Run for Soviet Jewry. They hired one of the professional race producers. There is no record of whether they sold Pepsi. The race drew 1,700 people in Los Angeles and one in Moscow. As reported in the *Los Angeles Times*, "It was pitch dark and a raw 30 degrees when Jewish dissident Yuli Kosharovsky set out on Sunday night on his daily jog along the railroad tracks through the quiet streets of his Moscow neighborhood." The *Jerusalem Post* explained that Kosharovsky "had changed his daily regime and ran in Moscow at night, in order to coincide exactly with the Los Angeles runners."[89]

The Los Angeles Run for Soviet Jewry became an annual event. Two thousand ran in 1980, including actor Martin Sheen, who ran in the name of Anatoly Shcharansky. Actor turned anti–Vietnam War activist turned exercise guru Jane Fonda joined in 1981, along with her husband, Port Huron Statement author Tom Hayden—then a candidate for State Assembly. The events spread: Tucson, San Francisco, Denver, Detroit, Chicago, Philadelphia, Tel Aviv, and other cities. The National Jewish Community Relations Advisory Council (NJCRAC, a partner of the NCSJ) circulated instructions to help communities plan the races.[90] The promotional materials spread too. To promote its 1981 Freedom Run, San Francisco copied the black-and-white photograph of a young male runner that advertised Los Angeles's 1979 race. Tucson also used the Los Angeles image for its first Freedom Run in 1980, but it rendered the runner in silhouette, wrapped him in chains, and superimposed him on a Star of David inside a circle. In 1986, Philadelphia copied the Tucson logo.[91]

Figure 5.8. Actor, activist, and fitness guru Jane Fonda at Los Angeles Jewish Federation Council's Third Annual 10K Run for Soviet Jewry. Rancho Park, California, November 8, 1981. Photo by Ralph Dominguez/MediaPunch/Shutterstock.

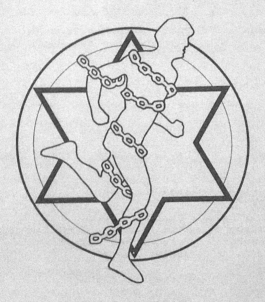

Figure 5.9. "Freedom Run and Rally for Soviet Jewry," program brochure cover. Soviet Jewry Council of the Greater Philadelphia Jewish Community Relations Council, 1986. Special Collections Research Center, Temple University Libraries, Philadelphia, PA, SCRC 403, box 1, folder 71.

Chain imagery notwithstanding, the Freedom Runs defied any claim that raising awareness about oppression had to be a somber affair. The events exuded American Jewish self-confidence as their community challenged the Soviet Union in the midst of the Cold War with the backing of a sympathetic Reagan administration. The runners demonstrated fortitude, pushing their bodies beyond normal limits. They ran in a mass, never alone, with allies by their side. And although there was talk about Soviet Jewish problems, they ran in an atmosphere that was festive, vibrant, and energetic. Music filled the air. Balloons too. Politicians pressed the flesh. Some even ran. (Colorado governor Richard Lamm, 5K, 1983, 175th place. His time: 25:48.)[92] Often, the Freedom Runs took place during Israel Independence Day festivals, Simchat Torah fairs, and other Jewish community-wide celebrations indicative of the Soviet Jewry movement's place in American Jewish political religion. As the serious runners raced competitively, families and children joined in "fun runs."[93] Organizers thanked corporate sponsors like 20th Century Fox (Los Angeles, 1981) and Caesar's Pocono Resorts (Philadelphia, 1986).[94] Like the "freedom" reference in the event name, corporate sponsorship further situated the races in their Cold War context. Promotional materials for Tucson's 1980 Freedom Run gave Golden Eagle Distributors top billing even over the city's Jewish Community Council.[95] Jewish organizations did try to guard against capitalism's excesses. NJCRAC cautioned event planners, "In one case, a sponsor supplied T-shirts bearing a Soviet Jewry motto and a logo advertising the sponsor's product—a degree of commercialization to be avoided if possible."[96] But NJCRAC looked askance only at the corporate branding on the T-shirts, not at the notion of using athletic wear to raise awareness for the cause. They took that for granted, just like the idea that there should be Soviet Jewry movement racing trophies. American fitness culture contained a logic of its own, and once activists enlisted it, it channeled their decisions, turning what otherwise might seem curious into something that came naturally.

Over time, activists expanded beyond Kosharovsky to dedicate races to other refuseniks. But Kosharovsky, the runner, remained an important symbol throughout. When he finally got permission to leave in 1989—"the last of the longterm refuseniks to be released by the Soviet Union, exactly 18 years after he first applied for an exit visa"—his emigration made it possible to stage a public ritual of closure akin to

Figure 5.10. High tube socks, Sony Walkmen, sweatbands, and Mickey Mouse make their appearance at a Freedom Run for Soviet Jewry held at the Jewish Community Center of Metropolitan Detroit, September 25, 1983. Photo courtesy of Jewish Historical Society of Michigan.

Dornan's and Shcharansky's bending of the bracelet into the V for "victory" and "visa." At Philadelphia's Freedom Run, held that year in May, Kosharovsky met up with the activist who had first donned a racing T-shirt in his honor. Dishler had altered his shirt for the occasion. No longer "I am running for Yuli Kosharovsky," it read, "I am running *with* Yuli Kosharovsky." Next to him, the former refusenik ran in a similar T-shirt, presented to him by Dishler as a gift. It proclaimed simply, "I *am* Yuli Kosharovsky."[97]

PROTESTING CULTURAL AND SPORTING EXCHANGE

As détente ushered in greater US-Soviet cultural exchange, Americans had more opportunities to spend leisure time and disposable income enjoying visits by the Bolshoi Ballet company, the Moiseyev folk dancers, and the Moscow Circus. When not jogging or doing aerobics, they could cheer on American basketball and hockey teams facing off against

Soviet opponents. Outside performance halls and arenas, and sometimes inside, they were met by Soviet Jewry activists who came to remind them that "Soviet cultural events, the moment they become purely cultural, also legitimize the political—so they must never be allowed to become purely cultural."[98]

Of course, it was commonly understood that the visits were part of a Cold War "struggle for cultural supremacy." One chronicler of this cultural Cold War noted what an anomaly this was in the annals of great power conflict: "There was no precedent: Christians and Muslims, Catholics and Protestants, revolutionary France and conservative Britain, had not dispatched their best ballerinas, violinists, poets, actors, playwrights, painters, composers, comedians and chess players into battle."[99] Americans and Soviets did. It was safer than sending nuclear missiles. Audiences could feel good about enjoying the performances and sporting matches, as they were draped in a rhetoric of peace and coexistence.[100] But to activists, such rhetoric threatened to cement an unacceptable status quo. So they descended on Carnegie Hall, leaflets at the ready: "Greetings, members of the Usipov Balalaika Orchestra and the Bolshoi Opera and Ballet. We welcome this opportunity for contacts between the American and Russian peoples. *But bridges cannot be built over the sea of human misery.*"[101]

The movement's radical flank opposed cultural exchanges outright. Members of Kahane's Jewish Defense League disrupted performances by calling in bomb threats, releasing mice and ammonia inside theaters, detonating canisters of tear gas, throwing bags of blood at musicians, and rolling marbles at ice skaters. JDL members were charged in January 1972 office bombings that targeted promoters of Soviet cultural visits, Sol Hurok and Columbia Artists Management, killing a Hurok employee, twenty-seven-year-old Jewish American Iris Kones.[102]

The mainstream movement organizations—the NCSJ, UCSJ, SSSJ, 35s, and their affiliates—were committed to nonviolence. They paid lip service to the value of cultural exchange and turned the visits to their advantage, using them to solve a basic mobilization problem. The USSR was thousands of miles away. Soviet Jews, the beneficiaries of Western activism, were not immediately visible. Soviet authorities, the targets, were not immediately accessible. What was a social movement to do? One option was to go to the Soviet Union. Another was to let the Soviet

Union come to it. When the Kirov Ballet visited, demonstrators could protest directly before Soviet eyes, confident that KGB minders would report everything back to Moscow. They could also use the performances to make the Soviet Jewish troubles visible to concertgoers, dance lovers, and sports fans. The more performances, the more opportunities to demonstrate. And since the cultural exchanges were newsworthy in their own right, activists could piggyback on them to publicize the Soviet Jewish cause.

Like the JDL, the nonviolent protesters also brought the demonstrations into the performance halls. At the precise moment when Bolshoi Ballet dancers took the stage in Montreal in June 1974, thirty-nine members of the Women's Campaign, dressed in black formal attire, stood and filed out of their seats. They left the fortieth member sitting there in prison stripes, a lonely figure amid the empty rows.[103] That same year in Manhattan, at the opening performance of the Georgian Dance Company and Choir, the International Committee for the Rescue of Georgian Jews (an ad hoc front group for SSSJ and the GNYCSJ) staged a louder protest, blowing a shofar, unfurling banners, and shouting slogans. Unlike the JDL, they took care not to interrupt the dancers. It took "split-second timing," the lead organizer wrote the next day: "[We waited] for the moment when all the audience was seated and quiet, the second before the lights went out (we needed the lights so that the banners would be seen; also we knew we would create hostility if we actually disrupted the dance itself), it had to be the second before the curtain opened.... And amazingly (we had expected the opposite), people from all over the hall began applauding us—not a few, but very many."[104]

Demonstrations at visiting Soviet performances and sporting events became a movement mainstay, especially for SSSJ in the US and the 35s in the UK and Canada.[105] Between 1970 and 1990, the Student Struggle staged over sixty such demonstrations, as many as seven in one year. When the Bolshoi Ballet came to New York in 1974, 1975, 1979, 1987, and 1990, SSSJ was there. They greeted the Moscow Circus in 1972, 1975, 1977, 1988, and 1990. They demonstrated at performances of the Moiseyev Dancers in 1970, 1974, 1986, and 1989. One could rewrite the punchline of the famous joke to accurately describe SSSJ's efforts: "How do you get to Carnegie Hall? Protest!" Their demonstrations got them not only to

WE'VE SAID NO TO PEPSICO

Carnegie Hall but also to Lincoln Center, Madison Square Garden, the Felt Forum, the Beacon Theater, and Radio City Music Hall.[106]

Repeated protests have a weakness, however. The more they happen, the less newsworthy they become. To prevent the press from losing interest, activists had to find a way to turn cultural exchange visits into a renewable resource for generating publicity. Their solution: theme the protests to the performances. Demonstrating outside the Bolshoi Ballet's 1974 performances at the London Coliseum, the 35s enlisted help from the minicab drivers who regularly drove them to demonstrations: "We dressed one of them—John—as a ballerina. He was such a sport. He stood night after night outside the theatre in a tutu and plimsolls (his feet were too large for ballet shoes.)"[107] When the Moscow Circus came to Winnipeg in 1977, the local 35s chapter organized a protest march led by members dressed in bear costumes.[108] The largest and probably most successful themed protest was organized by Philadelphia's Soviet Jewry Council in January 1976. Before a sellout crowd of 17,077, the defending Stanley Cup champion Philadelphia Flyers took on the Soviet Central Army team in the final match of the "Super Series" ice hockey tour that had seen the Central Army team defeat the New York Rangers and the Boston Bruins and tie the Montreal Canadiens. The *Philadelphia Daily News* called the game the "Third World War on Ice." It was "a chance to tell the Russians to go to hell with impunity. And the crowd loved it." Working with the management of the Spectrum, the Flyers' arena, SJC leaders secured permission to hang banners and sell promotional materials at the game. News of the banners and their message about Soviet Jewry spread nationwide when Associated Press coverage mentioned that the Russian team refused to take the ice until the signs were removed. In Philadelphia, the *Daily News* gave the SJC even more publicity: "The anti-Soviet feeling was a boon to the Soviet Jewry Council, which was mobbed by buyers of T-shirts that read: Free Soviet Jews. Spectators grabbed every copy of a Flyers souvenir book with a council insert card that read, 'You can take a Soviet Jew out of the penalty box today.'" The inserts included a preprinted postcard to Soviet leader Leonid Brezhnev. Between periods, volunteers from the SJC circulated in the aisles to collect the signed cards. Outside the Spectrum, the SJC erected a giant facsimile hockey puck bearing the slogan "The Puck Stops Here. Save Soviet Jews."[109]

Figure 5.11. "Save a Soviet Jew Today," postcard distributed at Philadelphia Flyers / Soviet team hockey game. Soviet Jewry Council of the Greater Philadelphia Jewish Community Relations Council, 1976. Special Collections Research Center, Temple University Libraries, Philadelphia, PA, SCRC 230, box 80, folder 14.

Themed protests captured audience and press attention by dressing the call for Soviet Jewish rights in language and imagery drawn from the immediate context. Audiences sometimes encountered these messages outside the performance venues as slogans on placards or as guerrilla theater. Near the entrance to the Metropolitan Opera House one night in June 1976, SSSJ members danced the hora and sang Hebrew songs as a counterperformance to the Russian Festival of Music and Dance. Other members of their group surrounded them with signs reading, "Russian Dances—Yes. Jewish Dances—No. Why?" "Why Were Jewish Dancers Beaten in Leningrad?" and "No 'Russian Festival' for Soviet Jews."[110] But those who did not want to be troubled by politics could easily look away, so just as often, protesters employed surreptitious means to place their message before theatergoers. SSSJ and the 35s regularly distributed fake program books designed to look like the real thing. Only upon opening them would audience members discover that alongside the "cast" were also listed the "outcasts," prisoners and refuseniks whose cases the brochure detailed. Event sponsors themselves were sometimes taken in. A 1979 London *Jewish Chronicle* article entitled "Red Faces at Exhibition" opened, "Some Soviet officials at the USSR National Exhibition at Earls Court are in trouble—for instead of giving out the official exhibition leaflet they spent two days giving out nearly identical ones prepared by the Women's Campaign for Soviet Jewry, the 35's."[111]

As long as the playbill cover appeared official enough to convince people to take one, there was no need to theme the inside copy to the specific performance. SSSJ almost always chose to do so, however, treating the brochures not just as PR pieces but as creative outlets. Each visiting art exhibition, symphony, and circus presented a puzzle to solve. How could activists connect the movement to the show? SSSJ was ever ready with an answer:

> The Knoedler Gallery is presenting art on loan from the Soviet government and the Hermitage Museum in Leningrad. . . . As you enjoy these masterpieces, remember these "masterpieces" of another Soviet "art"—the harassment and hate anti-semitism [sic].[112]
> —September 1975

> Tonight the MOSCOW STATE SYMPHONY ORCHESTRA is at Carnegie Hall. Their presence shows the possibilities of East-West contacts. . . . But true détente will never be achieved until the Kremlin ceases orchestrating its symphony of hate against Jews and Israel.[113]
> —November 1975

> Welcome to the Soviet circus! As you enjoy the acts, remember that there's another Soviet circus—one you can't get to see—inside Russian courtrooms. The Kremlin isn't clowning around when it . . . jails Jews as BORIS ZATURENSKY . . . kidnaps teenagers as MARINA TIEMKIN.[114]
> —December 1975

Perhaps the playfulness and punning hooked the unsuspecting readers. They certainly grabbed the writers.

"OLYMPICS DA, MOSCOW NYET!"

In their counterdemonstrations against cultural and sporting exchange visits, activists created a recognizable culture of Soviet Jewry movement protest. But the actions outside concerts, circuses, and hockey games could not fully prepare them to take on the Olympic Games—the epicenter of the collision between sports, entertainment, media, commerce, nationalism, and international politics. In April 1978, Soviet Jewry groups began preparing to mobilize around the 1980 Summer Olympics in Moscow. Activists developed slogans and logos, cultivated athletes and sports journalists, lobbied television networks and the United States Olympic Committee, circulated petitions, sold T-shirts, staged torch runs, and prepared to do more. In the UK, this culminated in a burst of activity as the games approached, but American efforts petered out, stymied by the US boycott of the games.

Activists had not sought the Olympic stage. When the USSR originally tendered the bid for Moscow to serve as host city, the NCSJ and UCSJ lobbied against it—especially after Soviet soldiers and police harassed Israeli athletes and their Russian Jewish fans at Moscow's 1973 World University Games.[115] After the International Olympic Committee (IOC) awarded Moscow the games in 1974, activists largely dropped the matter. In spring 1978, they took it up again and started planning in earnest.

In April, the Union of Councils began debating whether to call for a boycott, press for moving the games to another country, or mobilize around them. They discussed using the Olympics to spotlight human rights abuses, protest corporate sponsors, bring protest into the stadium, and the like.[116] Deciding not to call for a boycott just then, the UCSJ joined with the Student Struggle, the British and Canadian 35s, and France's Comité des Quinze to form the International Monitoring Committee for the 1980 Olympics (IMC80). Avrum Ashery, who handled the Washington Committee for Soviet Jewry's graphic design, created a logo: five Olympic rings with the bottom two drawn as a human head shattered by a sickle and hammer. ABC Television sportscaster Warner Wolf joined the honorary board. Representative Jack Kemp (R-NY) signed on as chair. Kemp, with Senator Wendell Anderson (D-MN), was sponsoring a congressional resolution calling for the games to be moved.[117] In July, the IMC80 launched a petition campaign demanding the same. They thought to deliver the petitions to IOC president Lord Michael Killanin in 1979 on the anniversary of Shcharansky's arrest. But the March 15 date passed with some forty thousand signatures sitting in Bay Area Council on Soviet Jewry offices and no clear plan for using them.[118] An opportunity presented itself in January 1980, when Jimmy Carter raised the possibility of an Olympic boycott in response to the Soviet invasion of Afghanistan. The UCSJ enlisted Congressman Robert Drinan (D-MA) to send Carter the petitions (now at sixty-five thousand signatures) as "an indication of the support for your current efforts."[119]

Meanwhile, the NCSJ and NJCRAC formed their own committees to coordinate Olympic-related activity. They pursued a line similar to that of the IMC80, with some minor differences: They, too, would issue no

Figure 5.12. Logo of the International Committee to Monitor the 1980 Olympics, with "Olympics Da, Moscow Nyet" slogan, detail from T-shirt order form. Student Struggle for Soviet Jewry, ca. 1978–79. Illustration by Avrum I. Ashery, uncredited. American Jewish Historical Society, RG I-487, box 125, folder 3.

WE'VE SAID NO TO PEPSICO

immediate call for a boycott but would keep the option open.[120] They would try to maintain calibrated pressure on the Kremlin—enough "to convince the Soviet Union of America's serious resolve" without "ringing down the Iron Curtain again."[121] At first, this meant encouraging support for the Kemp-Anderson resolution, mostly as an "expression of moral indignation," since they did not see any chance that the IOC would heed the call to move the games.[122] Within a few months, the futility of the effort, combined with opposition from the Nativ-led World Conference on Soviet Jewry, prompted them to "place [their] energies in other areas." (Israel wanted to see its athletes in Moscow.)[123] Rather than press for relocating the games, the NCSJ and NJCRAC would mobilize around them: "Strategically the Olympics, if held in Moscow, offer opportunities to gain leverage, to further our aims."[124]

All the groups quickly determined that they would need to keep pressure not only on the Soviets but also on NBC. The television network had won exclusive rights to broadcast the Olympics in the US and was paying the USSR and IOC $85 million in advance for the privilege. With ad sales averaging $75,000 per thirty-second spot, NBC was estimating gross revenues of $172 million. Activists were not the only ones worried that the combination of communist censorship and capitalist profit motive could prove fatal to impartial coverage of the USSR's human rights record. The *New York Times* put the question simply: "Will NBC become an unwilling vehicle of the Soviet propaganda apparatus by having invested upward of $100 million in the Moscow Olympics?" The Soviets had a track record of pulling the plug on foreign broadcasts that presented the country in a negative light, and NBC had an interest in keeping its transmission live.[125]

When pressuring NBC, Soviet Jewry groups mostly opted for engagement over confrontation. The Student Struggle, which earlier had recommended using two groups—one more restrained, one with a freer hand—played both sides.[126] It focused its own efforts through the IMC80 but simultaneously lent support to a small outfit that ran full-page advertisements in the *Washington Post* and *New York Jewish Week* under titles like "Moscow's TV Con Job" and "The Great Sellout." With comparisons to the "clever propaganda coup the Nazis put over in 1936," the ads called for boycotts of NBC ("just the tip of the iceberg") and its advertisers, like Coca-Cola, Burger King, and McDonald's:[127]

While Soviet dissidents rot in prison, more shocking is the fact that 50 American business giants—whose names are household words—are paying NBC $160,000 per minute for TV commercials to bring communist propaganda into your home—proving that Big Business in America doesn't give a damn about the plight of the Soviet dissidents or the cause of human rights. . . .

Make them understand that they will lose your patronage if they go through with this Russian Ripoff! . . .

Forward my name and address to the Kremlin and their American partners. I am not afraid! Tell them I will not watch their Olympic TV coverage. Tell them I will not buy their Olympic products.[128]

A group calling itself the 1980 Committee on Human Rights had purchased the ads. The organization was bankrolled by Leo Henzel, a businessman, impresario, and convicted felon who had orchestrated the $300 million contract to market 1980 Olympic commemorative coins in the West. After the Soviets awarded broadcast rights to NBC, they placated the rival ABC by cutting its representative in on the coin deal. To make room, the other partners froze Henzel out. Henzel was suing the partners when he funded the 1980 Committee's "Tell them I will not buy their Olympic products" ads. (He was also suing the Soviet Union for breach of contract on another deal.)[129] Henzel remained behind the scenes. A rabbi and a City University philosophy professor co-chaired the group and served as its public face. They managed to get the endorsement of New York governor Hugh Carey and Congressman Steven Solarz. The political leaders withdrew their support after they saw the ads. The NCSJ also repudiated the group. The UCSJ "terminated direct contact" with Henzel.[130]

The 1980 Committee grabbed attention for a few months, then disappeared. Meanwhile, the long-standing Soviet Jewry movement organizations continued pressuring NBC, but with less vitriol—"forceful but responsible."[131] SSSJ held a small protest outside NBC's Los Angeles studios, but otherwise the network was spared large-scale demonstrations. The NCSJ raised its concerns with company executives discreetly. Its leaders met privately with NBC-TV's president, Robert Mulholland. The UCSJ and NJCRAC mobilized their local chapters to send letters and arrange meetings with NBC, its local affiliates, and its advertisers to "voice [their] strong concern," "press for assurances," and ask them to add programming about Soviet Jews to balance out their broadcasts from Moscow. The Greater New York Conference on Soviet Jewry suggested that "public service time, during the broadcast of the games, should be made available for prerecorded messages featuring athletes." The UCSJ also considered approaching ABC and CBS, probably expecting that they would be receptive to programming that would shame NBC.[132] Activists lobbied the US Olympic Committee. They also met with owners and executives of professional sports teams like the Chicago Bears and Chicago White Sox to try to enlist their support.[133]

To bring visibility to the campaign, the Los Angeles 35s sold "Move Moscow Olympics" postage seals. SSSJ made buttons: "Berlin 1936, Moscow 1980, Olympics of Oppression." The Cincinnati Council for Soviet Jewry's chair, Sheldon Benjamin—son-in-law of UCSJ founder Louis Rosenblum—emblazoned the IMC80's pierced skull logo on a T-shirt with the slogan "Olympics Da, Moscow Nyet." The Cincinnati Council had already sold 1,200 in the US, England, Israel, and Sweden by the time Carter threatened an Olympic boycott. The *Cincinnati Enquirer* called Benjamin a man "ahead of his time." Benjamin told the paper, "Thanks to Afghanistan, I'll probably sell out."[134]

In line with its practice of theming cultural exchange protests, SSSJ circulated a template for staging a "Soviet Jewry Decathlon":

> Hurdles: Fastest time running over a hurdles course. Each hurdle is labelled with a different obstacle in the way of getting a visa.
> Run-in-Place Endurance Race: Who can run in place the longest, just as refuseniks have to, often for years, without job, money, support.
> Discus or Javelin Throw: Who can throw farthest a discus or javelin which has attached to it a letter to the West.
> Olympic Souvenir Making: How many Olympic souvenirs can a prisoner make in a set amount of time.[135]

Many ideas for mass engagement never made it to the planning phase. UCSJ activists had considered buying blocks of tickets and sending protesters to fill the stands in Moscow: "E.g., T-shirts to spell out a slogan in the stadium seats." Former refuseniks cautioned that this would be too dangerous for protesters and Soviet Jews alike. If this was not enough to scuttle the idea, activists soon learned that they would be hard pressed to buy any tickets, as they were being sold mostly to people in Olympic fan clubs.[136] General plans to use the wave of Olympic tourism to bring support to refuseniks also fell apart quickly. SSSJ's Glenn Richter proposed placing advertisements in *Sports Illustrated* headlined "Want to Make Your Stay in Moscow More Interesting?" By 1979, however, it had become clear that the Soviets were planning to restrict tourists' movements outside the Olympic zone, and even if tourists could slip away, there would be no one to meet, because the government was also taking steps to remove most of the Jewish activists from Moscow beforehand.[137] Likewise, plans to engage Olympic athletes faced hurdles. In October 1978, the GNYCSJ floated the idea of asking potential Olympians to adopt a Soviet Jewish refusenik, to "create a bond and a point of concern when the athletes travel to the USSR to compete." But by June 1979, IMC80 working chairman Morey Schapira was reporting to honorary chairman Jack Kemp's office that "since our athletes are chosen only weeks before the Games, not much can be done here. And since Lord Kilianan [sic] has 'threatened to strip the medals off the chests of athletes who dare....'"[138]

Launching the IMC80 in June 1978, Union of Councils president Irene Manekofsky expressed hope that the Olympics could serve as a "focus" for activism to carry the movement through the next two years.[139] The Red Army's invasion of Afghanistan on Christmas Eve 1979 cut those plans short. In the US, talk of boycotting the Moscow Olympics took center stage. It worked to the Soviet Jewry movement's disadvantage. The focus on Soviet military aggression sidelined the human rights issues that the UCSJ and NCSJ had been trying to highlight.[140] Then once the boycott was a fait accompli, it deprived the movement of a culminating rallying point. NBC canceled its contract to broadcast the games. Instead of tuning obsessively to scenes from Moscow, Americans spent July and August propelling reruns of *The Jeffersons* to the top of the Nielsen ratings.[141]

Isolated events took place here and there. In June 1980, one month before the Moscow Games, SSSJ staged a "Freedom Olympics" at a Brooklyn high school. This was a more traditional athletic competition than those who had read its decathlon planner might have expected. Competing in the name of Soviet Jewish prisoners, athletes took part

WE'VE SAID NO TO PEPSICO

in a day of track and field events, basketball, football, tennis, and swimming.[142] In July, four days before Russian basketballer Sergei Belov lit the Olympic cauldron, the vice president of the United States Olympic Committee, John B. Kelly Jr., ran in Philadelphia, torch in hand. He led seven men, including the Soviet Jewry Council's Bernie Dishler in his Kosharovsky T-shirt, on a six-minute "Freedom Run" from Liberty Bell Pavilion to city hall. The event was staged to mark the second anniversary of Shcharansky's sentencing.[143] The GNYCSJ organized a similar event on the day the Olympics began.[144]

Lingering reverberations of a campaign that had spent itself, the SSSJ Freedom Olympics and Philadelphia and New York Freedom Runs combined the movement's nascent embrace of the "fitness craze" with its established practice of framing cultural exchange protests in thematically relevant ways. Would the UCSJ and NCSJ have built this into something larger had America stayed in the Olympics? Who knows? The first 10K Freedom Run, held in Los Angeles in December 1979—three weeks before the Afghanistan invasion—made no reference to the Olympics. On the other hand, a coordinated push for Olympics-themed competitions was not hard to imagine, even at the time. In the United Kingdom, which did not boycott the Moscow Games and saw its team bring home twenty-one medals, British activists organized a monthslong nationwide campaign "using the Moscow Olympics to highlight the desperate situation facing Jewish students in Russia." Organized by the Student and Academic Campaign for Soviet Jewry, with supporting programs from the UK's National Council for Soviet Jewry (NCSJ-UK), "Competing for Freedom" opened in February 1980 with a two-mile jog through London to deliver a petition to Prime Minister Margaret Thatcher at her Downing Street residence. Runners wore T-shirts that bore a Competing for Freedom logo—Olympic rings, some with hands outstretched for help, others transformed into a key and keyhole. The athletic events continued through July. There were torch runs and "Jogs for Freedom" in Glasgow, Cardiff, Cambridge, Leeds, and Manchester; a "Freedom Games" day of races, football matches, and other competitions at Birmingham's Alexander Stadium; and a "Picnic for Freedom" in London's Regent's Park that featured "leapfrogging for freedom, wheelbarrow races for freedom, boating for freedom, etc." The "Disco for Freedom" may have been relaxing or yet one more way to work up a sweat.[145]

The campaign also included one contest that was not athletic but artistic. A few days before a field full of dancers in Misha the Bear costumes performed in the opening ceremonies at Moscow's Luzhniki Stadium, a London art gallery displayed a poster of a more sinister Misha. The Olympic mascot was still smiling as he led a sad little man behind him on a chain. The man, with an iron cuff around his neck, wore a Star of David on his shirt. This was the winning entry in the "'Competing for Freedom' paint-a-poster competition." Hundreds of children from Jewish schools across the United Kingdom competed to produce the "best design illustrating the situation of Jews in the Soviet Union in the light of the summer's Olympics."[146] The contest was only partly the result of the movement's push to make the Olympic Games a focus for activism. Another driving principle was also at work. In the UK as in North America, activists sought to mobilize the Jewish community. They defined community expansively, including children, whom they recognized to be political actors in their own right.

How did the movement come to cast a mobilizing gaze on society's youngest? A poem written by a ten-year-old refusenik points to some answers.

6

NATASHA'S DREAM

At Passover there is matzo
In every Jewish home.
There are in my Israel,
Fortresses and palaces.

There are schools, stadiums,
Automobiles, homes . . .
This is my beloved country.

Matzo is what our forefathers ate.
They were baked in the sun, in the hot desert.
They were going home, relieved from slavery.

And a miracle happened.
Moses went up the mountain.
And brought down the Ten Commandments
For the people of Israel.

He accomplished his mission,
He brought his people home.
But Moses did not live to see his native land.

Oh Israel! I promise you
That I shall come to you
But not now; we have to wait until
God will hear our prayers.[1]

When ten-year-old Natasha Korenfeld wrote her "Poem of My Land" in 1973, she and her family had already been living as refuseniks for two years. Her parents, Ilya, a mechanical engineer, and Lydia, a tour guide, had been fired from their jobs. Her older sister, Ludmilla, had been expelled from the Moscow Electronics Institute. The family endured arrests and police harassment. Western activists tried to help—writing, calling, and visiting. Congregation Har Zion, one of the early leaders in Philadelphia's campaign for Soviet Jews, "adopted" the family. Nevertheless, the stresses of life in refusal took their toll. A mental health crisis sent the youngest Korenfeld to the hospital. Natasha wrote the poem to heal. It helped, but it also brought new troubles.[2]

Natasha's mother shared the poem with British and American activists who published an English translation in local newspapers. It caught more attention than expected. In January 1974, Natasha received a letter bearing a London postmark, purportedly from the Palestinian Black September terrorist group: "Do you want to be killed in the Middle East or your parents? Stay in the Soviet Union it is your future and your only country . . . even Moscow is not to[o] far from us." Lydia and Ilya suspected that the KGB wrote the letter. The London postmark appeared false. As for the writing, the Queen's English it was not.[3]

The threats against Natasha breathed life into efforts to circulate the poem. In February, Rabbi Moshe Tutnauer, a Phoenix-based Soviet Jewry activist, published a column about it in Israel's English-language *Jerusalem Post Magazine*. The poem appeared in a sidebar. Later that year, Sister Ann Gillen's National Interreligious Task Force on Soviet Jewry included it in a flyer announcing "Operation Write-On," a pen pal program for American and refusenik youth. But the widest exposure came when movement leaders in Washington used Korenfeld's poem and the story behind it as the centerpiece for the Soviet Jewry campaign's first guide to children's activism.[4]

Natasha's Dream: Children's Handbook on Russian Jews and What We Can Do was published in August 1974 by the Washington Committee for Soviet Jewry (WCSJ), an affiliate of the Union of Councils for Soviet Jews (UCSJ). Written by Davida Manon and her mother-in-law, WCSJ president Irene Manekofsky—the pair would later become UCSJ executive director and president, respectively—the booklet appears to have been responding to the same call that led Gillen to create Operation

Write-On. Earlier that year, the UCSJ's founder, Louis Rosenblum, had circulated a memo urging activists to recruit American children to write to children of refuseniks.[5] Operation Write-On and *Natasha's Dream* both drew directly from the list of names and addresses that Rosenblum had compiled. But unlike Operation Write-On, which focused narrowly on the pen pals, *Natasha's Dream* dreamed bigger. In fifteen pages, it offered elementary schoolers something new: a comprehensive guide to becoming Soviet Jewry movement activists themselves.[6]

Illustrated in magic marker by the school-age niece and nephew of the booklet's art director, Avrum Ashery—who had created the Insider's Club logo and would later contribute the Olympics Monitoring Committee logo but who thought better of trying to draw like a child himself—*Natasha's Dream* explained Soviet Jewry's problem in simple language. To personify the plight, it recounted the travails of two girls—the titular Natasha Korenfeld, whose poem appeared twice in the booklet, and the fourteen-year-old Marina Tiemkin, whose story unfolded under the heading "Kidnapped!" The middle pages featured a photo collage of children's faces, numbered to match an address list: "Pick a name from the list. . . . That child will be your special penpal." Later editions explained what and how to write and reprinted letters received in reply. The booklet recommended other ways to get involved, such as writing to American and Soviet political leaders, wearing "a jeans patch with the name of a Soviet Jew on it," distributing *Natasha's Dream* to friends, and asking teachers to invite WCSJ speakers to class.[7]

Natasha's Dream was successful enough that it went through four editions and sixteen printings. When Manekofsky visited Moscow in 1975, she brought a copy of the booklet to the Korenfelds. Taken by the title, Natasha insisted that Manekofsky take a picture of her pretending to be dreaming in bed. The photo graced later editions. Even though Natasha realized her "dream" and immigrated to Israel with her family in 1976, the booklet bearing her name and poem remained in use. When it saw its last printing in 1990, Natasha had been living in Israel for fourteen years. During that time, the "Poem of My Land" had jumped from the handbook to religious school curricula, where it was sometimes juxtaposed with passages from Anne Frank's diary. It also found its way into synagogue sanctuaries as bat mitzvah girls recited it in their coming-of-age ceremonies.[8]

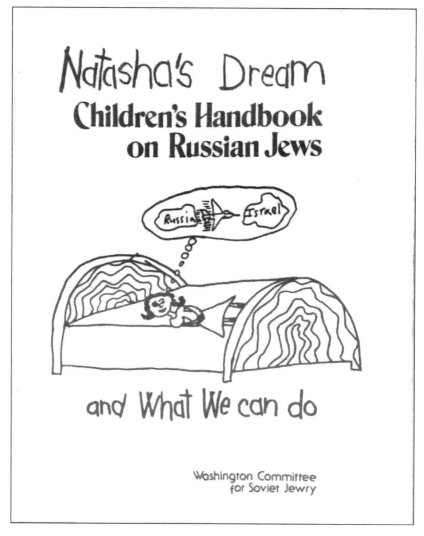

Figure 6.1. *Natasha's Dream*, cover graphic. Washington Committee for Soviet Jewry, 1974. American Jewish Historical Society, RG I-540, box 11, folder 7.

Americans who recall the refuseniks today usually mention the names of adults—people like Anatoly Shcharansky, Ida Nudel, Vladimir and Maria Slepak, Sylva Zalmanson, and Eduard Kuznetsov. Natasha Korenfeld does not typically make the list. But at the movement's height, she symbolized the suffering refusenik child. If she is not well remembered today, it is partly because few adults knew of *Natasha's Dream*, as activists targeted the handbook narrowly. This gap in awareness highlights something important about the mobilization for Soviet Jewry. At a certain point, activists came to think of children as a distinct group that they could and should mobilize. The publication of a book explicitly subtitled *Children's Handbook on Russian Jews* articulated this awareness to an unprecedented degree. Nevertheless, the awareness was present from the outset, expressed every time activists brought Soviet Jewry education into schools and rallied American Jewish youth groups to demonstrate in the streets.

The Soviet Jewry movement shaped the experience of being Jewish American in the late Cold War era. Children probably felt the movement's influence even more than adults. Per capita, they were more involved, not because children cared more, but because activists mobilized the Jewish educational system. They successfully inserted the movement into synagogues, schools, summer camps, youth groups, community centers, and boards of Jewish education. Adults engaged with these organizations by choice. Students, by necessity. They were subject to institutional authority in ways adults were not. Synagogues set requirements for bar and bat mitzvah training. Children were obliged to fulfill them. Educators determined Sunday school curricula and camp programs. Children dutifully took part. Still, young people had autonomy. Many embraced the opportunities to speak out for Soviet Jewry and did so in their own words. Nevertheless, when activists managed to recruit Jewish educational institutions, they engaged students and campers wholesale. What's more, since the children in the 1970s and '80s had no memory of a Judaism before the Soviet Jewry movement, the weaving of Soviet Jewry activism into their education made it, for them, as natural a part of Jewishness as God, Torah, and Israel. To be a student in most synagogues, schools, and summer camps during the last decades of the Cold War was to learn that the Jewish religion itself, in the name of the commanding voice at Sinai and at Auschwitz, made it a sacred duty to use American freedoms to "redeem" the Jews of the USSR.

CHILDREN IN SOCIAL MOVEMENT STUDIES

The passion of youth can fan the flames of activism. When it does not, veteran crusaders harrumph at the supposed apathy of the new generation. But when adults speak of youth activism, which youth do they envision? The protests of the 1960s planted images of young adults—college age, maybe older teenagers—in popular imagination. Elementary school children do not spring as quickly to mind. But they too are the youth of youth activism. Scholarly literature on social movements has suffered from this popular blind spot, saying much about teenagers' and young adults' activism (though not always with an explicit focus on "youth" as an analytic category), little about children as social movement participants, and even less about young children as targets of adult activists' mobilization efforts.[9]

In one of the only attempts to theorize the role of young children in social movements, sociologist Diane Rodgers distinguishes three modes of involvement. First, activists sometimes use children strategically as symbols, "presenting a living image of exploited innocence that is intended to evoke righteous indignation or sympathy"[10]—Natasha Korenfeld, for instance. In the 1970s, Soviet Jewry activists also organized campaigns around an infant, Jessica Katz, appealing for her exit on medical grounds. They also rallied for a time around the fourteen-year-old Marina Tiemkin, whose parents' custody battle ended with her father in Israel, her mother steadfastly remaining in Moscow, and Marina snatched by the KGB and flown against her will to a youth camp near the Black Sea.[11] In the 1980s, when activists matched American and Soviet children as bar and bat mitzvah "twins," they represented the children as symbols of things other than just innocent victimhood. Activists wanted the similarity in age to symbolize to the American twins that their Soviet pen pals were just like them. They positioned the American bar mitzvah boys and bat mitzvah girls as symbols, too, in order to inspire feelings of pride among American Jewish adults: Behold! You have raised your children well. See how they care for other Jews.[12]

Children can also engage in social movements as actual participants, whether voluntarily or "by default," as when activist parents bring their children to rallies.[13] These are the second and third modes of involvement. Rodgers teases them apart for analytic clarity, but they usually overlap.

Consider Sunday schooler Lisa Perlbinder's yellow-construction-paper-covered report "Sylva Zalmanson: A Russian-Jewish Heroine Near Death," about a well-known Prisoner of Conscience. It earned her the teacher's red-pen comment, "Because information is so hard to obtain, I'm giving you an A." On one hand, Lisa wrote the paper because her parents enrolled her in religious school and the teacher assigned the work. On the other hand, Lisa chose the topic, did the research, created the cut-and-paste cover art, and expressed her wishes in her own words: "So I hope next year we can see Sylva in Jerusalem." Because activists mobilized through the Jewish educational system, most American Jewish children encountered the movement as Lisa did—in involuntary contexts that created opportunities for voluntary participation.[14] But in Lisa's case, an added dimension makes it harder to tease out the voluntary from the involuntary. Her mother, Grayce Perlbinder, was vice president of the Long Island Committee for Soviet Jewry. Lisa grew up

Figure 6.2. UCSJ president Morey Schapira with his daughters, ages five and seven, at a protest event outside the Soviet consulate in San Francisco, ca. 1985–86. Photo courtesy of Morey Schapira.

NATASHA'S DREAM

with the movement in her home, an involuntary context that framed her voluntary activism in response to the involuntary school assignment. As we will see, there were other children like Lisa, anti–red diaper babies whose parents were taking on activist roles.

WHY ACTIVISTS THOUGHT CHILDREN SHOULD BE SEEN AND ALSO HEARD

What of those children who did not have activist parents? These were the majority, after all. Often, they helped bring the movement to their elders. Children served as a primary link connecting adults to Jewish community organizations. Parents might not attend the adult education program on Soviet Jewry, but they might learn something at the dinner table when asking their fourth graders, "What did you do in Hebrew school this afternoon?" Aunts and uncles donning their Saturday best to watch a niece called to the Torah might unexpectedly find themselves on the receiving end of a thirteen-year-old's sermon about why they must help a Soviet Jewish family in distress.[15]

Activists understood that children could be paths to adults, but this was not the main reason they tried to mobilize them. They valued children's participation for its own sake. Leaders sought a fully mobilized American Jewish community, and they included children in that conception. Rank and file participants also took the initiative to draw in children. Many rabbis and educators chose to raise awareness about Soviet Jewry when working with students. One might wonder at the Soviet Jewry campaign's seemingly intuitive recognition of the value of engaging children. After all, research on social movements in the US has had so little to say about children that one might assume that American activists generally ignore society's youngest. This is probably an erroneous assumption, but since it is a common one, it is worth probing why the Soviet Jewry movement pursued youth mobilizations with such gusto.

First, activists' biographies and social networks played a role. This unfolded in two ways: through activist parents' work-life integration and through educators' occupational activism.[16] Shcharansky's KGB interrogators famously taunted him, "What do you think, that your fate is in the hands of those people and not ours? They're nothing more than students and housewives!"[17] In fact, much of the American movement was run out of the kitchens of local activists who were also mothers (and fathers) of young children. These parents found ways to involve their own children—at home, on the streets, in their synagogues, and in their schools. When thinking in the abstract about mobilizing children, they could draw on personal experience. Bar and bat mitzvah twinning (see chapter 7) partly got its start when movement leaders, mostly mothers, paired their own children with those of refuseniks.[18] As for educators' occupational activism, mobilizing children was not only a top-down phenomenon led by movement organizations. Teachers and camp counselors took it upon themselves to bring the cause into their classrooms and bunks. Just like doctors who traveled to Russia to run pop-up medical clinics in refuseniks' apartments and lawyers who worked pro bono to advocate for Soviet Jewish prisoners' rights, educators placed their expertise at the service of the campaign and realized their activism through their profession.

Second, established institutional cultures structured new forms of activism. Among the main ways Jewish Americans organize communally is by creating educational institutions—religious schools, summer camps, youth movements, boards of Jewish education, teacher training colleges, and the like.[19] So important is education in Jewish American organizational life that it has even shaped the development of the American synagogue. By the time the Soviet Jewry movement emerged, synagogues had taken on so many educational functions that sociologists, rabbis, and religious revivalists were calling the houses of worship "child-oriented." It was not meant as a compliment. At first, the traditionally minded in the 1950s leveled the charge. In the 1970s, the Jewish counterculture did. These were baby boomers who had grown up as beneficiaries of a child-centered Judaism. Entering their twenties, they critiqued child-centeredness as an obstacle to creating a young-adult-centered Judaism for their own young adulthood.[20] As a criticism it was not entirely fair, but as a description it was not off base. Synagogues and other community organizations were in fact structured to serve young families with children. When the Soviet Jewry movement worked with these institutions, it did not press a new mission on them; it encouraged them to incorporate Soviet Jewry–related components into their existing activities. For the campaign, this reproduced in microcosm the American Jewish community's overall prioritization of youth work. In this, the movement was not exceptional. American Jewish mobilizations for Zionism, civil rights, women's equality, and the environment have also galvanized children through the community's educational system.[21]

To this child-oriented, education-heavy institutional context, add that many who took up the cause believed Judaism demanded it. Soviet Jewry activism embodied an encompassing religious praxis. This was a third factor pushing activists to engage children in the campaign. If this is what Judaism required, then this is what educators should be teaching. How else could they prepare children to be good American Jews? Playing on the haggadah's traditional story of four children—one wise, one wicked, one simple, and one too young to ask—a 1969 Soviet Jewry seder from Oakland, California's Jewish Educational Council expressed it succinctly:

> What says the wise son?
> He asks: Why do we dedicate today's seder to Soviet Jews? And how can we help them. . . .
> What says the wicked son?
> He asks: Why do you have to worry about the Russian Jews? Why do you have to make so much noise? By the word "you" it is clear that he does not include himself, and has withdrawn from the community. He should be scolded.[22]

In short, activists engaged children and schools not only out of rational calculations about how to help Jews in the USSR but also out of value commitments, largely taken as self-evident, about raising good Jewish children in the United States. This may be exceptional when contrasted with other American social movements, although I doubt it. In the American Jewish context, it is a well-trodden path.

THE CHANNELS OF YOUTH MOBILIZATION

As with other mass mobilization tactics in the Soviet Jewry movement, efforts to engage children grew more systematized as the years progressed. The WCSJ's 1974 *Natasha's Dream* was the movement's first document to identify "children" explicitly as a category unto itself. This was less a watershed than a moment of crystallization. From the movement's earliest days, activists recognized the value of engaging "youth," broadly conceived. In April 1964, Jacob Birnbaum founded College Student Struggle for Soviet Jewry. Within days, he dropped the age-restrictive first word.[23] This opened the way for an immediate push to mobilize in Jewish summer camps.[24] It also made possible stories like journalist Yossi Klein Halevi's. He tells of first encountering Student Struggle for Soviet Jewry (SSSJ) as an elementary schooler in 1965. The group's national coordinator, Glenn Richter, was leafleting in Brooklyn's heavily Orthodox Borough Park neighborhood. "When a woman passed him with a baby carriage, he dropped a leaflet under its canopy. 'Babies can help too,' he said." Little Yossi approached: "'I'm in sixth grade,' I said. 'Am I too young to join?'" Richter "piled boxes filled with sheets onto my arms: Soviet Jewry facts and figures . . . buttons and stickers. 'Congratulations,' said Glenn Richter, 'you are now the Borough Park elementary school chairman of SSSJ.'"[25]

Others also thought that children could and should be invited to take up the cause. As we saw in chapter 2, some of the earliest Passover rallies were youth oriented, as was the movement's first Soviet Jewry–themed Passover seder, conducted during a 1966 holiday assembly at Cleveland's Hebrew Academy elementary school:

AMERICAN: I am really very happy to have you as our guest for Pesach. . . . We have a choice of many different Matzoh. . . .
RUSSIAN: We have no Matzah. . . . We are afraid to invite any guests to our Seder. . . .
NARR 1: Here, sit next to me and I will help you follow in the *haggadah*.[26]

Two years later, at the 1968 biennial of the American Jewish Conference on Soviet Jewry (AJCSJ), delegates approved an action plan for mobilizing various constituencies. Section 2 of the plan focused on "Youth." Placed after "The Jewish Community" and before "Government," this section treated children in congregational schools, but it lumped them together with students in rabbinic seminaries. With the age range expansive to the point of incoherence, the term *youth* found its conceptual unity in the notion of students in school settings. The AJCSJ was applying a mobilizing gaze not to children as such but to the educational system, articulating ways of using it to engage students of all ages.[27]

These examples point to the four main approaches that channeled the Soviet Jewry movement's youth mobilizations. First, activist groups worked from the top down and from the outside in, reaching children by mobilizing the educational system. The 1968 AJCSJ biennial called for this approach.

Second, educators and students worked independently, from the inside, developing their own curricular materials and program activities. Teachers wrote lesson plans for and with their students. Cleveland's Hebrew Academy used this homegrown model for its 1966 seder. Teenage youth group members and summer camp counselors planned educational programs for their peers.[28]

Oakland's Jewish Educational Council took a third route for its 1969 seder (the one that mentioned the wise and wicked sons). Here, educational materials on Soviet Jewry were developed in a middle space—not by Soviet Jewry movement organizations and not by teachers and students directly but by the Jewish education field's professional service agencies. These included local Boards or Bureaus of Jewish Education (BJEs), professional associations like the Coalition for Alternatives in Jewish Education (CAJE), and the educational arms of national congregational unions.

Fourth, movement organizations and other groups independently produced educational materials, which they delivered directly to families and children or marketed to schools, synagogues, and summer camps. The WCSJ's *Natasha's Dream* is one example. SSSJ's 1964 program kit for summer camps is another.[29] So are children's books of the 1980s like *Alina: A Russian Girl Comes to Israel* and *Dmitry: A Young Soviet Immigrant*, black-and-white photograph books published by commercial presses and likely marketed to school libraries but also available for direct purchase.[30] One of the early large-scale efforts of this type was the 1971 "Freedom Caravan for Soviet Jews" from the Cleveland Council on Soviet Anti-Semitism (CCSA). With funding from the Canadian Jewish Congress, the CCSA packed four college students into a white Ford rental van plastered with "Save Soviet Jewry" bumper stickers and sent them touring forty Jewish summer camps across the American Northeast and Midwest and southern Ontario. With guitars and a mandolin, they spent three months teaching about Soviet Jewry "through song, story and drama," leading discussions and enlisting over nine thousand

NATASHA'S DREAM

campers in a postcard drive to write to Soviet Jewish families. Camps paid to host the caravan, $70 a visit.[31]

In practice, the various channels flowed into one another, as the professional service agencies, classroom educators, and activist groups collaborated and drew on one another's expertise.

TEACHING ABOUT SOVIET JEWRY

Soviet Jewry activism was an engine of Jewish American cultural production. In the educational sphere, the movement spurred the creation of three decades worth of learning activities, instruction plans, resource books, and other pedagogical materials. Full-fledged curricula began appearing in the late 1960s. A rabbinic student, Jonathan Porath, wrote the earliest, using it to teach Hebrew high school classes at a Long Island synagogue during the 1967–68 school year. Porath had specialized in Russian when studying abroad at the Hebrew University of Jerusalem. He made his first trip to the USSR in 1965. Later, as a rabbi, he would lead summer tours to Russia annually from 1969 to 1974 for Conservative Judaism's United Synagogue Youth. Temple Israel of Great Neck made Porath's curriculum—which focused on Russian and Soviet Jewish history and culture—available to educators and activists even before its completion. Conservative Judaism's denominational press later published it in 1973, selling about seven thousand copies.[32]

In 1968, as Porath was creating his curriculum, staff members of New York's central Jewish educational agency, the Jewish Education Committee (JEC), produced a "Resource Teaching Unit on Soviet Jewry." This aimed to "acquaint the pupils" with the "problems that Russian Jews face in living as Jews" as well as with the "efforts that are being made outside Russia to bring pressure."[33] Like Porath's curriculum, the JEC's circulated nationally. Miami's Bureau of Jewish Education received a copy and shared it with Jewish school directors. It also wrote its own three-session curriculum. The Miami BJE was a member of the South Florida Conference on Soviet Jewry (SFCSJ), which coordinated activism in the region. Under SFCSJ auspices, the bureau arranged for all the local Jewish religious schools to use these curricula to teach about Soviet Jewry during the same month in spring 1968. The effort culminated in a petition drive ("We, the students of Jewish schools . . . protest the denial to Soviet Jews . . .") and essay and art contests ("'What is happening to the Jews in Russia?' For students in grades 4 thru 7 in Public Schools . . . First Prize—$75, Scholarship to Camp Judea or $40, cash").[34] Via the South Florida Conference, a copy of New York's JEC curriculum also found its way to the Cleveland Council on Soviet Anti-Semitism. There, Louis Rosenblum edited and incorporated it into the 1970 edition of the CCSA's nationally circulated activist's handbook.[35] A year later, this revised version—attributed to the Cleveland group rather than the New York educators—formed the backbone of a Soviet Jewry curriculum prepared by the Jewish Community Council of Orange County, California.[36]

Tracing the JEC curriculum's path from New York to Miami to Cleveland to Southern California shows just how much American Jewish education in that era was a nationally networked field. With numerous local entry points connected to strong central agencies and umbrella groups that were in touch with one another, the system was set up to diffuse innovations. Soviet Jewry movement educators could prepare pedagogical materials for one community, insert them into the network, and watch them spread nationwide. (Actually, there were three networks: the educational field, the Jewish communal service field, and the Soviet Jewry activist field. The 1968 JEC curriculum traveled along all three of these lines, switching tracks where the paths intersected.) At each step along the way, new users could adapt what they had received and reenter their altered versions back into the exchange network to be picked up and changed again. The sum total was a set of educational materials that maintained family resemblances even as they continually evolved.

The following years brought more curricula. Activist groups authored some. In 1978, the Canadian Jewish Congress published the *Soviet Jewry School Kit: A Course in Five Lessons*, written by the Montreal Committee for Soviet Jewry's educational coordinator, Wendy Litwack Eisen, for a grade six class she was teaching at a Hebrew day school in Côte Saint-Luc. (Eisen also served as chairperson of the Montreal 35s.)[37] In 1984, Chicago Action for Soviet Jewry published the exhaustively titled *Let My People Go: A Curriculum for the Study of Jewish History in Russia and the Soviet Union with an Emphasis on the Modern Emigration Movement and the Plight of the Refuseniks*.[38]

Other curricula emerged from partnerships between activist groups and local educational agencies, often with the participation of teachers who had already taught about Soviet Jewry in their classrooms. In 1979, the Jewish Community Council of Greater Washington (JCCGW) published a *Teaching Soviet Jewry* curriculum, co-authored by the local Soviet Jewry committee and the local BJE. Their collaboration was made easier by the fact that the activist group and the educational agency both operated under the JCCGW's auspices.[39]

In other instances, Jewish educational agencies initiated the projects themselves. This was the case at the community level, such as in Cleveland (1970) and Baltimore (1976), where local boards of Jewish education produced curricula of their own.[40] It was also true more broadly. At the Reform movement's rabbinic seminary, Hebrew Union College (HUC), in 1983, the Museum Utilization for Student Education (MUSE) program commissioned a curriculum, *By Spirit Alone*, to accompany a traveling photographic exhibition on Soviet Jewish life.[41] When CAJE established its Task Force on Soviet Jewish Education in 1979, this North American network for the rising generation of professional Jewish educators gave the task force the following charge: prepare an annotated index of existing lesson plans on Soviet Jewry, establish a clearinghouse for the exchange of teaching resources, and develop curricular guidelines for teaching about Soviet Jewry in Jewish American and public schools. In 1984, with financing from the National Conference on Soviet Jewry, CAJE published a curriculum, *Making Gates: The New Soviet Jewish Crisis*.[42]

With so many curricula being developed across North America, children receiving Jewish education in those years would have found it difficult to avoid at least some exposure to lesson plans on the plight of Soviet Jewry.

CURRICULA AND THE SHAPING OF GEN-X AMERICAN JUDAISM

Because curricula are explicit about learning objectives, they provide insights into the cultures that create them.[43] Soviet Jewry movement curricula were written by educators for educators. Their authors identified learning goals, specified unit objectives, and named their intentional use of set induction techniques and trigger activities to help students connect to the material in a personal way. They gave teachers standard curricular templates with sections on background information, suggested reading material, motivation, presentation, and so forth. More than any other genre of writing that the Soviet Jewry movement produced, its curricula strove to articulate, step by step, what American Jews should know about the Soviet Jewish situation, how it fit into a bigger picture, why it was important, why they should care, how they should feel, and how they should act.[44] Implicit in all the curricula, and explicitly stated in some, was a governing principle: "Integrate teaching about Soviet Jewry into the total curriculum."[45] This was not simply a mobilizing tactic. It was an ethos being lived out in practice. To those who grounded their commitment to fighting the oppression of Soviet Jews in religious claims about Jewish history, Jewish ethics, and Jewish cosmology, there could be no rationale for cordoning off movement education as if it were disconnected from Judaism writ large.

For American Jews of Generation X, children in the 1970s and '80s, the integration of the Soviet Jewry movement into all aspects of their Jewish schooling had consequences. Even if to lesson planners it may have seemed a choice, to students, who were not privy to planning decisions and too young to know a Jewish education without a Soviet Jewry component, it appeared seamless, appropriate, and—most consequentially—normal. By contributing to what children took for granted about being Jewish, the Soviet Jewry movement in its day helped shape the experience of growing up Jewish in America, both in substance and in texture. What, then, were students learning, and how were they learning it?

WASHINGTON'S *TEACHING SOVIET JEWRY*

Consider the JCCGW's 1979 manual *Teaching Soviet Jewry*. Presenting itself as a resource book, it was the most expansive of the movement's educational guides. Its fifty pages brought together elements from other curricula. It referenced some of these, including Montreal's *Soviet Jewry School Kit* and, in the second edition, Chicago's *Let My People Go*. Although it is hard to know how or whether teachers implemented the book's lesson plans, we do know from the text itself that, at least in some instances, it drew on lesson plans that had already been taught.[46] Other evidence for the curriculum's connection to practice is circumstantial. Among its contributors were educators from DC-area Jewish schools.

Educators could be two-way conduits, bringing school practice into the curriculum and bringing the curriculum back into school practice. In 1984, the JCCGW updated *Teaching Soviet Jewry* for a second edition, something it would have been unlikely to do had teachers not been using it.[47]

Unlike other movement curricula that sequenced the lesson plans, *Teaching Soviet Jewry* used a modular format. It offered over three dozen stand-alone "enrichment projects" that could be inserted into the broader school curriculum. Seven of these came with detailed lesson plans. The others were summarized in a few words, a sentence, or a paragraph. A bit more than half of the resource book consisted of appendixes with supporting texts, graphics, scripts, and songs. *Teaching Soviet Jewry* used a hodgepodge of formats for presenting the material. Its opening pages were broken into sections that separately addressed teachers of holidays, of Hebrew language, and of Jewish history. To holiday teachers, the book suggested that for the Jewish New Year they "post a 'No Services Allowed' notice on the door and conduct an 'underground' service as if in Moscow or Leningrad." In the half page devoted to Hebrew instruction, it advised language teachers to have students "utilize letters from prisoners . . . as Hebrew language texts."[48]

Teaching Soviet Jewry presented these suggestions to holiday and Hebrew teachers with little commentary. When speaking to history teachers, however, the editors explained the pedagogical rationale. First, they offered the governing principle: "The contemporary struggle of Soviet Jewry . . . is an important and useful example of many historical events studied in our schools." Then they gave point-by-point analogies:

> Maccabees: The struggle of the Maccabees for religious and national freedom is directly parallel to the similar struggle of Soviet Jews today. . . .
>
> Persia, Spain, Etc.: Literary "golden ages" can be compared to the great Russian Yiddish literary period. The narrowly averted destruction of Jewry as the result of anti-Semitism and totalitarian powers can be compared to Soviet Jews' struggle today.[49]

The analogies continued across nine topics, from the biblical "Exodus" to modern-day "American Jewry." This represented the entire scope of a standard religious school curriculum in Jewish history—or more accurately, Jewish memory.[50] The JCCGW resource made Soviet Jewry education relevant at every point. It did this not because teaching about Soviet Jews was solely an end in itself but because teaching the topic was also a means to a larger end. Here again, a mobilizing gaze was at work. Note the instrumental bent of the governing assertion: Soviet Jewry education would provide a *useful* example." Why useful? Because the schools were socializing children into a grand narrative of Jewish historical memory. By showing that the present recapitulated key themes of the Jewish past, the plight of Soviet Jewry would testify to Jewish collective memory as a living truth.[51]

As for translating principle into practice, the curriculum guide left teachers to assemble the pieces themselves. The history section listed fifteen program recommendations and resources in no particular order and with no specific reference to which era or theme they might testify. The next section of *Teaching Soviet Jewry* partially rectified this. (Bear in mind that this was a committee project with different authors writing different sections.) The center of the booklet featured a twelve-by-six planning grid. Rows indicated the Jewish holidays, organized chronologically, with additional rows dedicated to Shabbat, Thanksgiving, and Jewish Book Month. Columns indicated the main topics in the standard religious school curriculum: History, Bible, Prayer, Hebrew Language and Literature, Israel, and Laws, Customs, and Ceremonies. Into the cells went recommendations for integrating Soviet Jewry movement education in both timely and thematic ways: one to three recommendations per row, two to ten per column (the ten were in the "History" column). There were twenty-six recommendations overall, seven of which were then detailed with full lesson plans. Here is a sampling:

Row: High Holidays
Column: Prayer
Title: Prayer Without Prayerbooks
Description: Lack of Religious Objects
Media/Format: Creative Prayers

Row: Israel Independence Day
Column: Israel
Title: Aliyah [Heb., immigration to Israel]

Description: Process of Obtaining Visas
Media/Format: Simulation

Row: Shavuot
Column: History
Title: Obeying the Law
Description: Arrests & Soviet Justice System
Media/Format: Mock Trial[52]

The topics and themes in *Teaching Soviet Jewry* were consistent with those of other Soviet Jewry movement curricula, the range of teaching modalities just as broad. The learning activities helped students contextualize the Soviet Jewish present in the sweep of Russian Jewish history; interrogate the Soviet Jewish plight policy by policy, persecution by persecution; and take their first steps into activism. To situate the particulars within the larger project of American Jewish moral and civic education, educators called on biblical and rabbinic texts—sometimes in Hebrew, sometimes in English—to provide the guiding language: "*Kol*

HOLIDAY/SEASON	HISTORY	BIBLE	PRAYER	HEBREW LANGUAGE AND LITERATURE	ISRAEL	LAWS, CUSTOMS & CEREMONIES
HANUKKAH						
Title:	Maccabees				Jewish Awakening	Covenant
Description:	Struggle for Religious & National Freedom				Development of Refusnik Movement	Reborn in Freedom
Media/Format:	Dramatic Presentation				Debate: Homeland or Motherland	A Creative Brit/Pidyon Service
PURIM						
Title:	Rescue	Special Purims				
Description:	Efforts to Free Soviet Jews	Documenting a Personal Rescue for Later Generations				
Media/Format:	Create a Jewish Rescue Organization	Write a Family Megillah				
PESACH						
Title:		Exodus	From Slavery to Freedom			Maot Hittim
Description:		Flight from the Gulag	Life as a Jew in Russia			Organizing Collection of Funds; Purchasing and Mailing Greeting Cards
Media/Format:		Compose New Dayenu	Soviet Jewry Seder			Tzadaka Project

Figure 6.3. Curriculum planning grid. In *Teaching Soviet Jewry*, Jewish Community Council of Greater Washington, 1979. American Jewish Historical Society, RG I-538, box 2, folder 8.

Yisrael Arevim Zeh Bazeh," all Jews are responsible for one another (Babylonian Talmud, Shevuot 39a);[53] "Don't stand idly by the blood of your neighbor" (Leviticus 19:16).[54] All this content, all these values, could be taught using the full array of pedagogical techniques and media in the Jewish educator's tool kit. The curricula offered texts to read and filmstrips to watch, board games to play and reports to research. They presented oratorios to recite and sociodramas to improvise, cartoons to interpret and mobiles to hang, stories to analyze and poems to compose. They proposed vigils to attend, relief packages to mail, and letters to Congress to write. Curriculum authors intended this not to be knowledge for knowledge's sake. This was education for empathy, responsibility, and action. *Teaching Soviet Jewry*'s seven fully developed lesson plans articulated these goals explicitly.

For instance, to incorporate education about Soviet Jewry into the teaching of prayer (column) during the Sukkot fall harvest festival (row), the curriculum recommended adapting a traditional custom known as Ushpizin. The holiday is celebrated by eating meals outdoors in a temporary hut (sukkah) for eight days. For the Ushpizin ritual, Jews symbolically welcome biblical personages like Abraham, Moses, and King David into the sukkah to dine, one character each day. *Teaching Soviet Jewry* included a lesson plan for symbolically hosting refuseniks in the sukkah. Students would conduct biographical research, create artwork about the refuseniks to display in the sukkah, and write and recite a prayer of welcome. Explaining the pedagogical rationale, the authors wrote the following objectives:

1. The students will understand the concept of "All of Israel are responsible for one another" in the illustration of remembering all Jews in our celebrations—emphasizing "We" instead of "I."
2. The student will recognize the Refuseniks as part of a long chain of Jewish heroes, standing up for freedom and justice.
3. Through researching the background of these Refuseniks, the students will come to recognize them as individuals, rather than an anonymous group, and in so doing, personalize their plight.[55]

For a "Prayers of Freedom" activity that had students compose liturgy and illustrate a Soviet Jewry–themed Passover haggadah–style booklet for the Thanksgiving meal (row: Thanksgiving; column: Prayer), educators specified the following learning goals:

1. All of our celebrations must be tempered with the remembrances of those who may not be able to share our joy.
2. The students should be able to contrast the policies of the U.S. and USSR governments re: religious and cultural freedom, and the subsequent effect on an ethnic group's development.[56]

And for an "If I Were a Refusenik Child" role-playing game that included discussion of Natasha Korenfeld's "Poem of My Land" and composition of "a poem like Natasha's describing how it feels to be a refusenik child" (row: Lag Ba`Omer; column: Laws, Customs, and Ceremonies), the curriculum explained that the goal was to "relate a contemporary situation to the situations we recall at Lag Ba`Omer and to create a sense of empathy with Refusenik children."[57]

Educators sought to engage students emotionally and cognitively at the same time, help Jewish children in America imagine themselves in Soviet Jewish shoes, cultivate feelings of identification and empathy, and inculcate a sense of responsibility to act—a sense grounded both in Judaism's communitarian norms and in America's ethos of individual liberty.[58]

EMPATHY AND IDENTIFICATION

Of the active learning projects that educators used to elicit empathy and identification, two were especially popular: family history research and simulations. *Teaching Soviet Jewry* mentioned both. Other curricula developed them more extensively.

As we have already seen, Jewish Americans who visited refuseniks often felt an acute sense of "There, but for the grace of God, go I." The 1880–1924 mass migration brought more than two million Jews from the Russian Empire to Ellis Island and other American portals. Most Jewish Americans traced their ancestry to this immigration wave. Many who were adults in the 1970s and '80s had grown up with Yiddish-speaking immigrant parents or grandparents. They understood how the choice to emigrate had spared their branch of the family from pogroms,

Einsatzgruppen, and gulags. But as the immigrant generations passed, the children of baby boomers grew up with fewer living links to the Old World. Family history assignments formalized the intergenerational transmission of immigrant memory. What the children of immigrants heard in their kitchens, the great-grandchildren researched for school projects.

Thanks in part to the television miniseries *Roots*, family heritage research became popular in American middle school curricula in the 1970s and '80s. Jewish education picked it up too. With a grant from the National Endowment for the Humanities, the Hebrew Union College's MUSE program created a family history workbook based on the Jewish experience but crafted for public school use. In 1984, when HUC's Skirball Museum presented *By Spirit Alone*, the photo exhibition on Soviet Jewish life, MUSE drew from the workbook to create a teacher's guide supporting the exhibition for use in Jewish schools.[59] Before introducing any material on Soviet Jews, the *By Spirit Alone* curriculum first had teachers send students home to ask about their own family histories. The questions emphasized migration: Where did ancestors come from? Why did they leave? Why did they come to the US? In class, the students brought their individual stories together on wall maps and timelines. Curriculum designers knew that this would draw attention not only to diversity but also to the commonality of the American Ashkenazi Jewish experience: "We are noticing a lot of [families coming] from country 'x' in the years ___." This set up the segue to Russian Jewry: "We are really beginning to piece together part of the contemporary history of the Jewish people. . . . In our next lesson we are going to focus specifically on the history of the Jewish population of Eastern Europe and Russia."[60]

The curriculum's author, Gail Dorph—at the time a rising leader in the Jewish educational field and later the director of the School of Education at American Jewish University—explains the pedagogical rationale:

> If you want kids to empathize, identify, understand something so far away, you start with themselves. And in this case . . . many of them will find that their grandparents or great-grandparents actually came to this country from Russia or Poland, or what have you. They may not know that. And that's a way in which they both connect to their families and bring their

families into this. But it also is a way for them to think, "Oh, this could be my family." You want them to think, "Oh, these are people—they are like me. I am like them."[61]

This approach collapsed the distinction between educating about Soviet Jewry and educating about Jewish American heritage. Learning one meant learning the other. The movement thus wove itself into the fabric of Jewish American children's self-understandings and conceptions of Jewishness.

Whereas family history assignments fostered identification with Soviet Jews by exploring similarities and shared histories, simulations elicited empathy by helping students imagine themselves into situations foreign to their own experience. In addition to the JCCGW's *Teaching Soviet Jewry*, curricula from the Baltimore BJE, Chicago Action for Soviet Jewry, and the Soviet Jewry Group of London's Edgeware and District Reform Synagogue included role-playing games that simulated the process of applying for an exit visa from the USSR. Chicago's version, from 1984, simply retyped with minor edits twenty-seven pages from Elissa Blaser's *Exodus: The Russian Jewry Simulation Game*, originally published by a commercial press in 1974. Blaser's was one of the earliest Soviet Jewry simulations, but it was not the first. At a two-week-long 1972 programming workshop for Reform Judaism's summer camps and youth groups, held at Kutz Camp in New York's Hudson Valley, campers and faculty jointly created *Underground: A Simulation of the Path of Soviet Jews from Oppression to Freedom*. This became a staple of Reform movement youth programming.[62]

All the simulations shared the same core structure. Students role-played Soviet Jews trying to emigrate. They moved around the classroom—or sometimes through the wing of a school building or across an entire campground—traveling to different stations representing OVIR (the Soviet exit visa office), the Dutch embassy (which gave Israeli entry visas), the workplace (which gave character references required for the exit visa), and the like.[63] Staff played "bureaucrats with whom the Jews must contend in order to obtain release from Russia."[64] In some simulations, small groups moved together sequentially through each station. Blaser's *Exodus*, however, gave each participant an identity to role-play (e.g., a forty-four-year-old psychiatrist with a daughter suffering from a kidney disease) and a unique path to travel.[65]

This skeletal description belies the emotional character of the simulation. The point of running from station to station was not to memorize steps in the emigration process but to discover Kafka's castle. What was the nature of Soviet oppression? In these tellings, a bureaucracy intentionally designed to wear people down. Generally impersonal, except when it was not. A hostility so systemic that functionaries had tacit permission to add their own anti-Jewish nastiness into the mix. How would students learn this? By feeling frustrated and powerless as they ran the bureaucratic gauntlet. Blaser's *Exodus* framed it as "actively experiencing the plight of those Jews who wish to exit from Russia."[66] Kutz Camp's *Underground* was more precise: "This program aims at giving participants a sense of the fear, frustration, humiliation and triumph of the Soviet Jew making his or her way to freedom."[67] Stations ("dimly lit," per Kutz) could be located far from each other, sometimes on opposite sides of a campground. Participants would run between offices, back and forth. After filling out forms in duplicate, children would wait five minutes in a bank line only to be told to go to the KGB station to get security clearance and then come back, whereupon they might discover that the teller was out on a *chai* break. Those playing the Russian officials with the power to grant or withhold *vyzovi, karakteristikii,* and *razrashenii* were instructed to make things difficult. "Participants endeavor to get the various documentation required in the face of bureaucracy and anti-semitism which should be as realistic & ruthless as possible," read the British group's instructions. "Include a few 'KGB' operatives further to harass the applicants." To allay any skepticism among participants, the instructions continued: "Try to get an ex-refusenik along & after the game discuss with the class their feelings along the tortuous route. Any feelings they might have that the 'officials' over-reacted will be proved wrong by the ex-refusenik."[68] Kutz's *Underground* offered scripts for hostile officials to recite: "Let me see if I can guess why you are here. You want to leave our paradise on earth, yes? Are we not good enough for you selfish Jews? . . . You foolish people are gluttons for punishment."[69] Blaser stacked the deck, predetermining the outcomes so that only 60 percent would get out. The others would get stuck in limbo—unless students cheated or convinced staff to go against their written instructions, which was permissible and may have been part of the lesson.[70]

Not all staff played hostile Soviet bureaucrats. Some played members of an underground Jewish support network, Israeli and American Jewish officials, and the helpful Dutch ambassador. At the end of the simulations, all participants would join those who "escaped." Kutz Camp suggested using a van to drive them "to 'Israel' for a celebration and party."[71] Washington's *Teaching Soviet Jewry* tiered the escape: "Those who reach [the transit station in] Vienna receive a book of Jewish Symbols or a Shabbat packet. Everyone comes together in Israel to eat falafel."[72] In addition to the party, there would be group discussions to process and reflect.

Ultimately, the point of the cognitive and emotional learning was to elicit "Empathy with the Situation of the Russian Jew," identified as "Conceptual Goal No. 1" in Blaser's *Exodus*: "In simulating the experience of the Russian Jew, the student will begin to understand what the Russian Jew must 'go through' to emigrate, how he must feel, and what it is like to be in that dilemma. He will empathize with the Russian Jew even if he does not agree with the Russian Jew's behavior response; even if the student feels he would act differently in that situation."[73]

Although educators sought to create a sense of frustration, the role-playing and gamification nevertheless made the simulation fun. The artifice was blatant. *Exodus* encouraged participants to speak in Russian accents. Its play rubles, given out at the bank station, bore Stalin's profile, American-dollar style, above the words "In Stalin We Trust," "Trusty Stalin."[74] Kutz's *Underground* suggested ominous staging and encouraged staff to costume up. Recognizing how strongly the context encouraged counselors to craft their Soviet characters as cartoon villains, it urged them to "play it straight to make the greatest impression. Don't make a joke of the program." But the necessity of such a plea speaks volumes.[75] The program created a play environment that could be fun, very fun.

FUN

We might wonder whether gamification, instead of fostering empathy, could work against it. It is easy to imagine the objections to making education about oppression fun. An ethical critique might argue against it on principle. A practical objection might warn that if the simulation

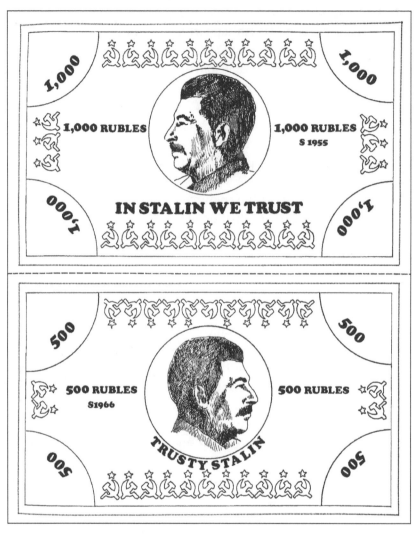

Figure 6.4. Play rubles from Elissa Blaser's *Exodus: The Russian Jewry Simulation Game*. Behrman House, 1974.

were enjoyable, students would misunderstand the Soviet Jewish situation and therefore be unable to truly empathize. Soviet Jewry movement activists and educators never embraced the first argument. As for the second, experience taught them otherwise. In practice, making simulations fun engaged people more thoroughly, made the frustration tolerable, and opened students to cognitive and emotional learning.[76] Still, the fact that the experience of persecution was simulated and not real and that the simulation was enjoyable, offers yet more evidence that Soviet Jewry movement education was as much or even more about American Jewishness as about the refuseniks themselves. The implicit curriculum taught that America was secure. One could learn about Jewish history as a recurring series of persecutions. One could learn that it was proper to identify with Jewish victims, past and present. But Jewish American children learned this from a vantage point safely outside history. Oppression of Jews? That is over there. That was back then. America is different. Here, now, Jews are safe, Jews are free. To experience antisemitism, one must re-create it in simulation. This could be turned into a game—a serious game, but still a fun one to play.[77]

Educators also used other types of games to make Soviet Jewry education fun. In advance of the carnivalesque Purim holiday in late winter 1983, the Greater New York Conference on Soviet Jewry (GNYCSJ) circulated a puzzle book with a smiling clown on the cover. "Purim is a time for fun," proclaimed the introduction. "Purim is also a time for learning—learning how Jews overcame their oppressors in the past, and how we must continue to do so in the present.... We hope you enjoy our Soviet Jewry Purim Puzzler and that you use what you learn to help Soviet Jews." The first puzzle had children unscramble six holiday-related words—*Megillah*, *Haman*, *Adar*, *Esther*, *Fast*, and *Mordechai*—to reveal the letters E, M, D, R, E, F, and O. These, in turn, were to be rearranged to answer the question, "What does every Soviet Jew want? (Hint: You have it.)" Ten more pages of Purim- and Soviet Jewry–themed word searches, rebuses, crossword puzzles, and cryptograms followed. Dead ends in the "Journey to Jerusalem" maze bore labels like "Your mother knows 'state secrets' from her job" and "It's 'inconvenient' to let you go now." The answer to a math puzzle, 52283, gave the date of May's upcoming Solidarity Sunday rally.[78]

While the "Purim Puzzler" was mainly for use in the New York area, the GNYCSJ joined with New York's Board of Jewish Education to produce a board game for national distribution. To play *Route to Freedom: A Game of Escape from the Soviet Union*, one rolled dice and moved a token along a convoluted pathway from a starting space marked "USSR" to a final square labeled "Israel." Covering the hand-drawn game board

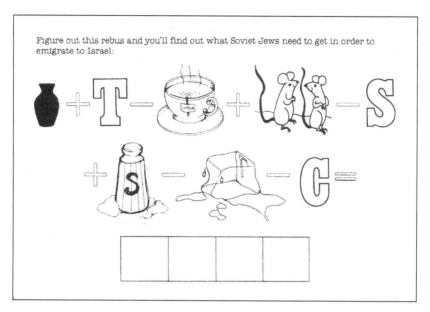

Figure 6.5. Rebus. *Soviet Jewry Purim Puzzler*, Greater New York Conference on Soviet Jewry, 1983. American Jewish Historical Society, RG I-362, box 1, folder 14.

were over thirty illustrations documenting moments in the emigration process. Obstacles sent players back or diverted them into detours: "Your employer refuses to give you a character reference" or "You are sentenced to 15 days to 15 years in prison for expressing publicly your wish to leave." Spaces indicating assistance offered solace but no movement forward: "You meet some American visitors" or "You get a letter from American friends." The archival record does not tell us whether American children ever played the game. Numerous curricula and BJEs listed it as a resource. It appears to have been valued less for its playability than for its symbolism. As the cover declared, "Route to Freedom" was created by Shoshana Ramm, "a young Soviet Jewish girl who played the game and won." Ramm, a daughter of refuseniks, drew the game with all its illustrations on four cardboard shirt inserts when she was fourteen years old. A leader of Philadelphia's Soviet Jewry Council, Connie Smukler, spirited the game out of the USSR when she visited Shoshana's family in Moscow in 1974. (Smukler taped the shirt boards around her torso, donned a large sweater, and walked through customs and onto the plane.) Ramm emigrated two years later. When the GNYCSJ published the game in 1976, it urged players to have fun but also to learn, empathize, and help: "We hope you enjoy this game but we also want you to 'live it'—try to imagine yourself as a Soviet Jew who faces these dangers and uncertainties every day. All of us can help open the route to freedom."[79]

In thinking about how to engage children in the Soviet Jewry campaign, activists and educators saw fun not as something to be avoided, as if it would make light of refuseniks' experience, but as something to be embraced and put to use. Whatever this reveals of their pedagogical philosophies, it reflects something deep in the movement's ethos. Activists had girded themselves for the long haul. They were waging a fight of unknown duration against a nuclear-armed superpower. To sustain motivation and morale, activists on both sides of the Iron Curtain insisted on maintaining a sense of enjoyment and a sense of humor. Tongue-in-cheek protest rallies included a public birthday party for the Soviet premier, complete with a kosher cake decorated in buttercream roses and piped letters: "Happy Birthday Mr. Brezhnev. Let My People Go."[80] After bar mitzvah twinnings inspired UCSJ president Morey Schapira to symbolically pair his newborn son's ritual circumcision, a fellow board member touted the idea to the entire UCSJ in a

Figure 6.6. Detail from the board game *Route to Freedom* by Shoshana Ramm. Board of Jewish Education of Greater New York in cooperation with the Greater New York Conference on Soviet Jewry, 1976. American Jewish Historical Society, RG I-362, box OS1F, folder 1.

NATASHA'S DREAM

memo that read, "Program suggestions... Brit Milah twinning (Morey Schapira will come to your city as Mohel and Caterer)."[81] This was a movement whose activists even published a book called *The Jokes of Oppression*—276 pages filled with the humor of Soviet Jews: "Rosenfeld emigrated to Israel in 1970. 'How old are you?' he was asked by an Israeli immigration official. 'Twenty-two,' was the man's reply. 'What? You must be at least seventy,' said the official. 'Maybe so,' replied Rosenfeld, 'but can you really call the last fifty years living?'"[82]

Thanks to Freud, modern Jews have taken to the idea that maintaining a sense of humor is one of their age-old strategies of hope and perseverance. True or not, the assertion has taken on a life of its own and become part of American Jewish talk about the meaning of Jewishness.[83] The movement mobilized this too, engaging adults and children with a smile, sometimes with a wink, and socializing youth not only into foundational narratives ("From Slavery to Freedom," one of *Teaching Soviet Jewry*'s "useful themes"),[84] into core tenets of faith ("Netzach Yisrael Lo Yishaker," God's promise to the Jewish people is irrevocable),[85] and into central value imperatives ("Don't stand idly by the blood of your neighbor")[86] but also into a culture that defined humor as an essential part of being Jewish.

EMPOWERING CHILDREN TO EMBRACE THE RESPONSIBILITY TO ACT

By mobilizing through Jewish educational institutions, activists brought children into the Soviet Jewry movement as involuntary participants. This was just a first step. They hoped to make their participation voluntary, to raise American Jewish children who wanted to stand up for Soviet Jews and who felt compelled to do so. Educators laid the groundwork by trying to inculcate values and instill proper emotions. But to raise young activists, they had to encourage children to recognize their own power to speak out. This they did in schools, synagogues, and the public square. Educators empowered and validated children as political actors who could contribute their own voices to the movement. Active learning projects in the classroom encouraged children and teenagers to express movement messages in their own words, to be producers of movement culture, not just consumers. One lesson plan in the JCCGW's *Teaching Soviet Jewry* instructed twelve- to seventeen-year-olds each to write a sentence about Soviet emigration in the style of the haggadah's *dayenu* poem, all of which would be combined into a Soviet Jewry–themed Passover liturgy to be read aloud in class.[87] At Beth El Hebrew Congregation in Alexandria, Virginia, the fifth grade class told one refusenik family's story by writing and performing a play with paint-stick puppets they had made:

> ITZAK KOGAN: Shalom. I am Itzak Kogan. This is my wife Sophia.
> SOPHIA: These are our daughters Anya, who is 13, and Simma, who is 6....
> ANYA: My classmates make fun of me because I am a Jew.
> SIMMA: That's not fair! Why can't we move?[88]

Contrast this with other movement scripts, such as the Student Struggle's 1970 guerrilla theater mock trial of Boris Kochubievsky and the symbolic Passover seder that television screenwriter Alvin Boretz created for the New York Coordinating Committee for Soviet Jewry two years earlier. Those were circulated nationally. The performers recited words that others had written.[89] But the fifth graders in Ms. Warshawsky's class decided themselves, "with a little help from their teacher," what to say and how to say it.[90]

Activists elevated children's voices outside the classroom too, using essay and art contests to encourage youngsters to craft public messages for the movement. The practice of staging essay contests dated back long before the Soviet Jewry movement to the 1870s, when governmental, business, and civil society organizations in England and America began using them to intervene in the educational system and influence curricula from the outside. They were an effective medium for inculcating values—or at least creating a public culture that celebrated certain values—because they encouraged entrants to express normative messages in their own words.[91] Essay contests had featured as a standard part of the twentieth-century American Jewish educational tool kit and came easily to mind when Soviet Jewry movement educator-activists began thinking of ways to organize community-wide youth mobilizations. When the New York area youth groups met to start planning the 1966 Passover Youth Protest, they first considered sponsoring an essay contest.[92] In 1968, the AJCSJ put out a call for essay and poster contests, the Miami BJE sponsored the essay and art contest mentioned earlier, and the Bay Area Council on Soviet Jewry sponsored an "oratorical contest," sending the two teenage winners to Washington, DC, to speak with Soviet officials. At the embassy, "They were received courteously, they 'debated' the Soviet attaché Ikar Zavrazhnov, [and] presented him with 5,000 petitions."[93]

In the 1980s, art contests replaced essay contests as the main medium for elevating children as creators of movement messages and public materials.[94] The United Kingdom's National Council for Soviet Jewry (NCSJ-UK) began fielding an annual Rosh Hashanah greeting card design contest in 1981 (see chapter 2). This intervention into Jewish school systems across Western Europe gave children the hope of seeing their Soviet Jewry movement art printed and sold as holiday cards.[95] The competition offers an example of how tactics can evolve through a logic of combinations: it blended the adult mobilization tactic of producing greeting cards with the youth mobilization tactic of engagement through art contests. A year before it introduced the greeting card design competition, the NCSJ-UK had organized its first art contest, timed to coincide with the 1980 Moscow Summer Olympics (see chapter 5). Hundreds of children ages fifteen and under submitted entries to the "Competing for Freedom" poster competition. A London art gallery displayed the posters. Eleven-year-old Jackie Rubin from Hendon won the first-prize trip to Israel for her pen-and-ink drawing of a smiling Misha the Bear (the Soviet Olympic mascot) leading a small, sad-looking man with a Star of David on his shirt, tethered and chained by the neck. The links of the chain led almost, but not quite, to the chainlike Olympic rings on Misha's belt. Jackie's mother did not even know her daughter had entered the contest.[96]

Two years prior, in Montreal, the Women's Campaign for Soviet Jewry ("the 35s") had sponsored a poster contest for sixth graders around the theme "Soviet Jewry Freedom," also displaying the entries at a public exhibition. Alain Lancry's winning drawing of two prisoners dreaming of Jerusalem was circulated across North America as the cover graphic for the 35s' *Soviet Jewry School Kit*—a curriculum that self-referentially included a recommendation to run poster contests.[97] When Chicago Action for Soviet Jewry picked up the idea in 1983, it explained to religious school directors that the goal of its citywide "I Want to Be Free" poster contest was "to directly involve young people through their creative

NATASHA'S DREAM

Figure 6.7. Winning entry, UK National Council for Soviet Jewry 1980 "Competing for Freedom" poster contest. Illustration by Jackie Rubin. Image courtesy of Board of Deputies of British Jews. London Metropolitan Archives ACC 3087, folder 317.

efforts." The youngest winner was in second grade. The oldest, seventh grader Annie Fishbeyn, had emigrated from the Soviet Union in 1981.[98] The Chicago branch of Israel's Bank Leumi underwrote the project and displayed the winning entries in the lobby of its building on LaSalle Street in the Downtown Loop.

NATASHA'S DREAM

By sponsoring art contests, the Soviet Jewry movement distributed the work of social movement cultural production. This contributed to the flourishing of grassroots creative expression around movement themes. But the competitions were important not only for giving children a chance to create. They were also important for giving children a chance to be recognized. Both aspects helped transform children from involuntary to voluntary participants. Contest participants not only learned about Soviet Jews; they also learned that their own voices mattered. They could contribute their ideas and creativity to the movement and see this taken seriously by adults who circulated their artistic creations as greeting cards, displayed them in art galleries, and featured them in lobbies of international banks in the heart of city financial districts.

All these efforts to mobilize the Jewish educational system, to rally children to the Soviet Jewish cause, to inculcate a sense of responsibility toward fellow Jews, to cultivate feelings of empowerment and efficacy, and to encourage young people to speak out with confidence converged in one of the Soviet Jewry movement's most audacious and most successful tactics for mass mobilization. In bar and bat mitzvah "twinning," activists co-opted American Jewry's favorite life-cycle ritual. A fixture of 1980s Sabbath synagogue services, and engaging tens of thousands of children and hundreds of thousands of worshippers or more, twinning shaped what it meant to come of age as an American Jew in the last decade of the Cold War.

7

MY SOVIET TWIN

In December 1987, days after the 250,000-person rally for Soviet Jews on the National Mall, newspapers in New York and Florida reported human interest stories with identical themes. Thirteen-year-olds Jill Goldsmith and Dawn Dorn had celebrated their bat mitzvahs—Jill in her Conservative synagogue in Westchester County, New York; Dawn in her Reform temple 1,300 miles to the south near Fort Lauderdale, Florida. Each covering their local event, the *New York Times* and *Sun Sentinel* reported that the girls had been planning to symbolically share their coming-of-age ceremonies with refusenik pen pals in Russia. Goldsmith was to read from the Torah on behalf of Muscovite Dahlia Brailovsky, whose father had spent three years in a prison camp for publishing Zionist literature. Dorn was to read in the name of Luba Gorbunov, who had been waiting ten years in Leningrad for permission to emigrate.[1]

Thousands of American Jewish middle schoolers, since the late 1970s, had been using their bar and bat mitzvahs to raise awareness about the oppression of Soviet Jews. In synagogues with large religious school enrollments, the proxy ceremonies—known as "twinnings"—were sometimes even weekly affairs. The Soviet Jewry movement's two national umbrella agencies, the "establishment" National Conference on Soviet Jewry (NCSJ) and the "grassroots" Union of Councils for Soviet Jews (UCSJ), each coordinated their own nationwide programs matching Jewish thirteen-year-olds with similarly aged refuseniks. With addresses and case histories in hand, young Americans spent the months prior to their bar and bat mitzvah celebrations writing letters to their "twins" and petitioning Congress on their behalf. During the services, they delivered sermons to raise awareness among their captive audience of friends and family. Twinning positioned the young people as voices of conscience—teaching their elders about the importance of speaking out. The twinned ceremonies also built on the bar and bat mitzvah rite's inherent theatricality. "The proxy ceremony *dramatizes* the contrast between the freedom in which American youth can fulfill its obligation to Judaism, and the oppression under which young refuseniks are denied this opportunity," wrote one twinning handbook.[2] The staging sought to make the Soviet Jewish absence palpable. Synagogues cordoned off seats for the Soviet twins and their families who would not arrive to fill the gaps in the pews. Rabbis called out Russian names, summoning refuseniks to come read from the Torah. Then they let the silence echo. Eventually, the American b'nai mitzvah (i.e., bar mitzvah boys and bat mitzvah girls) would chant the biblical readings in their place.

Newspaper coverage of Goldsmith's and Dorn's twinnings was not remarkable in itself. Twinning coordinators encouraged families to seek press. Local media obliged. Jewish weeklies and city newspaper religion sections featured dozens of articles in the 1980s with headlines like "Empty Chairs at Temple Judea: B'nai Mitzvot Paired with Refuseniks' Children" and "Proxy Bar Mitzvah for Soviet Youth."[3] Like the ceremonies, the news stories also revolved around the absence of the Soviet twin. But the 1987 bat mitzvahs broke with that formula. That made them newsworthy. "For the South Florida Jewish community," the *Sun Sentinel* reported, "it was an historic event. For the first time, a bar mitzvah [sic] twin actually was present at the ceremony instead of being represented symbolically by an empty chair." In June, the Dorns learned that the Gorbunovs had obtained exit visas and would soon be arriving in the United States. The proxy twinning became a joint bat mitzvah. Dawn and Luba ascended the Kol Ami pulpit together.[4]

The story out of Westchester County unfolded similarly: "On Labor Day weekend . . . Jill said to her mother, 'Wouldn't it be a miracle if Dahlia could actually be at my bas mitzvah.' That night, the Goldsmiths heard on television that the Brailovskys had just been released." The family moved to Israel. Three months later, Dahlia and her mother took a flight from Tel Aviv to attend the Washington rally, stopping in New York for the bat mitzvah: "Jill was called to the bima, or pulpit; so was Dahlia. Jill recited prayers in Hebrew, so did Dahlia. When it was all over, Jill presented Dahlia with a bas mitzvah gift: a gold charm in the shape of identical silhouettes, joined at the hands, inscribed 'Jill and Dahlia, Bat Mitzvah, Dec. 5, 1987.'"[5]

The end of December brought the number of Jews leaving the Soviet Union that year to eight thousand, nearly a tenfold increase from 1986. Emigration rose to just under twenty thousand in 1988, seventy thousand in 1989, and about two hundred thousand per year in 1990 and 1991.[6] As the emigration became an exodus, newspapers featured more stories like Jill's and Dahlia's, Dawn's and Luba's:

Ceremony Includes Refusenik: Zionsville Girl Shares Bat Mitzvah With Soviet
—*Morning Call*, Allentown, Pennsylvania, June 1988

Bat Mitzvah Turns Into Joyous "Twinning": Refusenik Family Arrives in Time for Daughter to Join in Jewish Rite
—*Boston Globe*, November 1988

U.S., Soviet Pals Have Bar Mitzvahs Together
—*Saint Louis Post-Dispatch*, April 1989[7]

The stories made for great press.[8] Here was a sign that for Soviet Jews, the gates were opening. But they were also a signal that for American Jews, a chapter was closing. Bar and bat mitzvah twinnings had become regular features of synagogue life in the 1980s, part of the weekly rhythm of Sabbath worship and a normal way to mark the life-cycle transition. But actually having the Soviet teens present undercut the logic of twinning. The point, after all, was to highlight absence, to "dramatize" the restrictions that kept Soviet Jews from their own synagogues as well as from joining fellow Jews in the West. The historical changes that made Dawn's and Luba's stories possible also threw twinning programs into disarray. There were "only a handful of Bar and Bat Mitzvah age refuseniks remaining," an October 1989 NCSJ report declared, but "hundreds, possibly thousands, of American Jewish teenagers seeking Soviet Jewish twins." Twinning coordinators had always been pairing refuseniks with multiple American twins, but even so, demand was outstripping supply. "This situation presents a dilemma," the NCSJ conceded. Organizations continued trying to match twins, but so quickly were exit visas being granted that pairings collapsed before the ceremonies could take place. In October 1990, Boston's Action for Soviet Jewry sent a "Dear 'Twin'" letter to the girls it had paired with Anna Shifrin of Kaunas, in the Lithuanian SSR. The Shifrins had succeeded in leaving for Israel, so the organization offered a plan B: "Because your Bat Mitzvah is still to come, we thought you would like to link with another 'Twin.' Therefore, we are enclosing the case of Yulia Gurvitch, a new refusenik family from Moscow."[9] A month later, Philadelphia's Soviet Jewry Council, which helped pioneer twinnings in the 1970s, bowed to the inevitable and disbanded its twinning program.[10]

MOBILIZING AMERICAN JEWRY'S SIGNATURE RITUAL

In the efforts to weave the fight for Soviet Jewry into the fabric of American Jewish communal life, bar and bat mitzvah twinning could be viewed as a culminating synthesis. Activists had honed their expertise in mass mobilization tactics piecemeal. They knew how to stage ritualized protests. They had mastered the intricacies of youth outreach. They understood how to cultivate feelings of personal connection with refuseniks, up close through tourism and at a distance by phone and mail. Toward the end of the 1970s, in a process of tactical innovation messier than those examined here so far, they drew these forms of expertise together and aimed them squarely at the core work of synagogues across the United States.

Proxy bar and bat mitzvah ceremonies began cropping up in 1975, the first two in Philadelphia and then a dozen more over the next few years in cities in the US, Canada, England, and Israel.[11] Seeing the potential to transform the practice into a tactic for mobilizing youth en masse, Soviet Jewry councils in Washington, DC, and Long Island instituted the first coordinated twinning programs in 1979. The practice quickly spread. In 1982, activists in Chicago reported one thousand paired ceremonies; New York, the same.[12] From Boston, Action for Soviet Jewry recorded 259 twinnings in Massachusetts that year, spread over forty-six municipalities.[13] Reports on twinnings from twenty states with Jewish populations large (California, Florida, Michigan, Pennsylvania) and small (Oklahoma, Kansas, Tennessee) filtered into NCSJ offices, indicating that by 1983, the practice had taken root in every region of the continental United States.[14] More communities added twinning programs in the following years. Overall, we can estimate that somewhere between ten thousand and thirty thousand Jewish teenagers twinned their bar and bat mitzvahs in the 1980s out of a total eligible population of about five hundred thousand.[15] Because Jewish seventh and eighth graders spent many weekends during those school years traveling the bar and bat mitzvah circuit, even those who did not adopt a refusenik pen pal stood a good chance of attending one or more twinnings of friends who did. It was a standard part of coming-of-age Jewishly in Generation X.[16]

Twinning also reached beyond youth, raising awareness among guests at ratios of fifty or a hundred to one or more.[17] Regular synagogue-goers sat through dozens of twinnings as they became part of the landscape of Sabbath worship. Again, records from 1982 give a sense of the scope. Temple Sinai in Miami, Florida, staged twenty-five twinning ceremonies that year, about one every other Sabbath. Old York Road Temple Beth Am outside Philadelphia conducted forty-one, at least one each month, with streaks of six Sabbaths in a row in the fall and seven consecutive Sabbaths in the spring. (Most Beth Am twinnings paired two Americans with one Soviet.)[18] As these patterns repeated themselves nationwide, it is likely that a Soviet Jewry movement bar or bat mitzvah twinning was taking place every Sabbath somewhere in America for the better part of a decade. Factoring in general statistics from that era on synagogue attendance, an estimated minimum of hundreds of thousands and possibly millions of Jewish Americans experienced a twinning at some point in the 1980s.[19] Those masses were not simply spectators. Twinnings implicated them too. Because these were coming-of-age rituals, they were saying something about what it meant to enter Jewish adulthood—namely, that it demanded acts of solidarity with oppressed Jews. This made moral claims on all adults in attendance.

To appreciate the chutzpah of trying to co-opt bar and bat mitzvahs and to grasp what an accomplishment it was to succeed at the scale that activists achieved, one needs to understand the significance of the bar and bat mitzvah in American Jewish culture. In the words of social historian Jenna Weissman Joselit, the bar mitzvah in eighteenth- and nineteenth-century Eastern Europe had been "traditionally more of a 'punctuation mark' than a watershed." The modest ritual simply attested that a child who had been responsible for obligations associated with religious boyhood was now responsible for obligations associated with religious manhood. But in the twentieth century, American Jews transformed the comma into an exclamation point, making it "one of the few Jewish ritual practices to grow rather than diminish in popularity." Reconfigured as a lavish celebration of American adolescence and individuality, it became an occasion for portrait photography, first dress suits, engraved invitations, and catered receptions with seven-piece orchestras and boys' names festooned in balloon letters. Influenced by the country's egalitarian norms, American Jews invented an equivalent ceremony for girls, the bat mitzvah, first introduced in New York in 1922.[20] With the baby boom, synagogues restructured their business models, worship services, and even physical plants to serve families' bar and bat mitzvah needs. As the main providers of Jewish education, synagogues oriented the curriculum to bar and bat mitzvah training. Parents who wanted the ritual for their children had to pay membership dues and enroll the youngsters in congregational schools for years prior to the event. Sabbath morning services were often given over to the ritual, the pews filled mainly by the celebrant's family and friends, leaving the congregations to struggle with "balanc[ing] communal needs for a regular public Shabbat service with the private elements of a family life-cycle event."[21] After the ceremony, worshippers could retire to reception halls adjacent to the sanctuaries, an innovation in synagogue design that responded to parents' enthusiasm for postceremony parties and to competition from commercial catering halls.[22] Considering the importance of bar and bat mitzvahs in American Jewish life, the fact that social movement organizations outside the synagogue successfully commandeered them and turned them to movement ends is no mean feat.

This chapter's analysis of bar and bat mitzvah twinning traces the origins of the tactic and analyzes the cultural meanings that it communicated. Twinning emerged as activists adapted and combined elements from earlier tactics. The process of tactical innovation proceeded along multiple paths simultaneously. First, we trace these. Then we examine the organizational work that activists undertook to systematize twinning for mass mobilization. Then we shift our attention from movement leaders to the twinning ceremonies themselves and to the children, parents, and rabbis who actually brought them to life. What did twinning look and sound like in practice? How did the thirteen-year-olds interpret them in their own words?[23] And what did it mean for American Jews to have bar and bat mitzvahs transformed into celebrations of Cold War–era youth activism?

PATHS TO TWINNING

As with tourism and ritualized holiday protests, bar and bat mitzvah twinning did not spring up fully formed. Activists in Washington, DC, and Long Island launched the first coordinated twinning programs in 1979. The four years prior saw about a dozen instances of symbolic bar and bat mitzvahs for Soviet Jews in absentia, sometimes connected to an American child's ceremony, sometimes not. Tactical development moved from the ad hoc to the systematized through a loose logic of combinations. Most of twinning's key elements—ritualized protest, youth mobilizations, pen-pals, adoption, and behind-the-scenes refusenik database management—were already present but operating separately. Activists drew them together, building something new. At first, the process unfolded piecemeal. Some early twinnings came about by extending refusenik adoptions to involve children. Others grew out of direct connections forged in tourist encounters. Some resulted from activist parents trying to engage their own children or treating their own family celebrations as opportunities to raise awareness. Once activists had a few examples they could keep in mind, and after enough common elements were in place, the reflexive character of the mobilizing gaze kicked in. Activists, seeing what they had done, began to systematize the tactic for mass engagement.

PATHS FROM ADOPTION AND YOUTH MOBILIZATION

Twinning was built around the idea of pairing American and Soviet youth and asking the Americans to write to, raise awareness about, and advocate for their Soviet match. It was a variation on the theme of prisoner and refusenik "adoption." The Soviet Jewry movement did not invent prisoner adoption; Amnesty International had introduced the practice and the term in 1963.[24] It entered Soviet Jewry movement parlance in the early 1970s through the Union of Councils in the context of its "People-to-People" strategy to build direct ties with Soviet activists. In 1971, UCSJ president Louis Rosenblum produced the movement's first instruction kit for sending letters and parcels to prisoners of conscience.[25] Betty Miller, who helped lead the UCSJ-affiliated Washington Committee for Soviet Jewry (WCSJ), created an organizational structure that same year to systematize an "Adopt-a-Prisoner" program for DC-area churches and synagogues.[26] Soon, Soviet Jewry groups were using "adoption," and calling it such, to support not only prisoners but refuseniks generally. The Minnesota Action Committee and South Florida Conference on Soviet Jewry each launched "Adopt-a-Family" programs in 1972.[27] In August 1973, the National Conference on Soviet Jewry introduced "Adopt-a-Family" to its network through Project Yachad (Heb., "together"), its equivalent to the UCSJ's "People-to-People" framework for coordinating tourism, adoption, phone calls, and other direct support.[28] Around the same time, possibly earlier, adoption came to Philadelphia as a synagogue-sponsored program. The sisterhood at Har Zion Temple in Wynnefield adopted the family of Ilya and Lydia Korenfeld—parents of the same Natasha Korenfeld who inspired the Washington Committee's children's handbook, *Natasha's Dream*, published a year later.[29]

It took three years from the creation of the first adoption programs before activists thought to combine adoption with their youth mobilization work. In February 1974, Rosenblum circulated a call to action entitled "Children of the Otkazniki" (the term's English translation, "refuseniks," had not yet taken hold in the US):[30] "We sometimes forget that the heroes have children who struggle along with their parents." Urging Jewish educators to have students "correspond with fellow Jews," Rosenblum presented the names and addresses of forty Soviet Jewish youth between the ages of five and eighteen. Each entry was labeled M or F, anticipating the gender matching of bar and bat mitzvah twins.[31] A few months later, the Washington Committee took up Rosenblum's call and made writing to pen-pals the central charge in *Natasha's Dream*, the movement's first guide to children's activism.[32]

On the path from adoption to twinning, the WCSJ played a key role. After introducing the movement's first Adopt-a-Prisoner program in 1971 and using the knowledge gained from that to publish the first children's guide for writing to pen-pals in 1974, it systematized youth adoption by launching the movement's first bar and bat mitzvah twinning program in 1979. With *Natasha's Dream*, the WCSJ had simply presented a list of names and told children to choose their own pen pal. For the twinning program, the group took on the work of assigning the matches, as it had done for churches and synagogues in its Adopt-a-Prisoner project.

But even before the Washington Committee instituted a formal twinning program, *Natasha's Dream* and a refusenik adoption had already inspired one of the earliest twinnings. In December 1975, newspapers in Philadelphia reported that Cindee Ivker celebrated an "unusual dual bat mitzvah" with none other than Natasha Korenfeld. "The idea of a joint celebration originated with Cindee when she read a coloring book on Soviet Jewry drawn by Natasha," the *Jewish Exponent* wrote.[33] Cindee had received her copy of *Natasha's Dream* from Philadelphia's Soviet Jewry Council (SJC), but she had also learned about the Korenfelds from her grandmother, Dorothy Rabinowitz. When Cindee celebrated the dual bat mitzvah at her synagogue in New Jersey, her grandmother's congregation, Philadelphia's Har Zion Temple, which had adopted the Korenfelds, also "held a special Shabbat dinner and service" to coincide with the celebration. Cindee and Natasha managed to contact each other. The SJC arranged for tourists from Chicago to transport tape recordings of bat mitzvah blessings, which the girls had recorded to exchange. Cindee conducted her ritual at her synagogue in Cherry Hill. A chair stood empty on the pulpit, reserved for Natasha. As part of the ceremony, Cindee recited Natasha's "Poem of My Land," the paean to emigration that opened *Natasha's Dream*.[34]

In contrast to Cindee, who marked her coming-of-age "in the traditional way," Natasha celebrated her bat mitzvah in a private ceremony in her Moscow apartment. The *Philadelphia Bulletin* presented this as evidence of state suppression of Judaism: "Natasha was not able to celebrate in public. She had to stay at home, with only a few loved ones, and hope she would not be discovered."[35] The article did not mention that Natasha could not have had a public bat mitzvah service even if Brezhnev had paid for the caterer himself. Soviet synagogues followed the Orthodox rite. Women and girls were forbidden from leading synagogue prayers. Bar mitzvahs were for boys only. Five decades of bat mitzvahs in the United States had so enshrined the new ritual that Americans failed to realize that this was an American Jewish tradition, not a universal one.

PATHS FROM TOURISM

When Philadelphia's Soviet Jewry Council helped Ivker and Korenfeld exchange cassette tapes, the idea of linking up the SJC's tourism program with some type of effort around bar and bat mitzvahs had already been broached. A few months earlier, in July 1975, SJC cochair Joseph Smukler visited Russia for meetings with leaders of the Jewish emigration movement. He brought along an invitation to Philadelphian Gidon Caine's August bar mitzvah. Caine's parents had made a similar trip the previous year and had met some of the people Smukler was visiting. In Leningrad, Smukler delivered the invitation to refuseniks Ilya and Ella Ginsburg as "a symbolic gesture."[36] Their daughter, Bella, was turning thirteen. The Ginsburgs translated the invitation, substituted Bella's name, and "distributed copies of both invitations to Leningrad Jewish activists as a protest." When Smukler informed the Caines of what had happened, they decided to have Gidon's ceremony also "mark Bella's bat mitzvah—in absentia." The SJC promoted the story with a press release that was picked up by Philadelphia's *Jewish Exponent*.[37] It also alerted the media a few months later when it helped Ivker and Korenfeld link their bat mitzvahs in Cherry Hill and Moscow.[38] Press coverage of one-offs like these appeared sporadically in newspapers from Miami to Montreal prior to the creation of formal twinning programs, helping seed the idea.[39]

Despite being aware that Soviet Jewish activists like the Korenfelds were finding ways to mark their children's bar and bat mitzvahs, American movement organizations highlighted the rarity of the practice among Soviet Jews overall and suggested that the government prevented Jewish children from becoming bar or bat mitzvah. That understanding was at the heart of an early synthesis of tourism, bar mitzvah, and ritual protest. In 1978, with the support of the Orthodox activist group Al Tidom, thirteen-year-old Maimon Kuhr traveled from his home in Upstate New York to perform his bar mitzvah at the main synagogue in Moscow. The intent, apparently, was to inspire Soviet Jews with a display of the ritual prowess that Jewish youth could attain in America. (Americans assumed, mostly correctly, that this was largely impossible for Jewish children in the USSR.) Landing in Leningrad, the Kuhrs called ahead to refuseniks in Moscow "to spread the word."[40] In New York, Al Tidom called the Jewish Telegraphic Agency, which gushed hyperbole in its report: "Worshippers at the synagogue were brought to tears of joy when the Bar Mitzvah boy read beautifully from the Torah and chanted the Maftir, an event unparalleled in the Soviet Union since the Communist Revolution over six decades ago. They expressed astonishment to see that the yeshiva student son of an observant American physician visiting the USSR to lecture for Soviet medical personnel could perform the Bar Mitzvah so flawlessly and beautifully."[41]

Kuhr's bar mitzvah travel to the USSR was exceptional. Most tourism connections worked the other way around, facilitating or raising awareness about the bar and bat mitzvah ceremonies of refusenik children.[42] In 1977, refuseniks Iosif Begun and Alla Drugova asked a visiting Long Island rabbi, Seymour Baumrind, to conduct a bar mitzvah ceremony for their child. He did, and he was expelled from the country. Invited by Drugova to return in 1979 to lead their younger son's ceremony, Baumrind declined, "fearing not only his own arrest but of those with whom he might meet." Instead, on the date that the boy was called to the Torah at the Marina Roscha synagogue (the smaller of Moscow's two synagogues), Baumrind organized a proxy bar mitzvah ceremony at his own congregation, enlisted 185 synagogues in Long Island and Queens to offer special prayers, and worked with the Long Island Committee for Soviet Jewry (LICSJ) to spread the word to other communities. (This also launched the LICSJ's twinning program.) Visiting Moscow a few weeks later, the editors of Philadelphia's *Jewish Exponent* met the Begun boy at the bar mitzvah of another refusenik and wrote a feature article on the spate of refusenik bar mitzvah celebrations in Russia.[43]

The Begun bar mitzvah was not the first to be marked with simultaneous proxy ceremonies. In March 1976, the Women's Campaign for Soviet Jewry (35s) staged protest bar mitzvahs for Sasha Roitburd, whose father, Lev, was a prisoner of conscience. In London, twenty boys performed the ritual on the street outside the Soviet Embassy. Similar proxy ceremonies were held across the United Kingdom.[44] A few months later, at the request of the National Jewish Community Relations Advisory Council's Abraham Bayer, visitors started soliciting refusenik leaders for lists of boys and girls of bar and bat mitzvah age. (There is no record that they received any.)[45] In March 1977, the 35s and the UCSJ organized proxy ceremonies across the UK, Canada, and the US to coincide with refusenik Misha Prestin's bar mitzvah, which he himself celebrated in Moscow's main synagogue.[46]

As noted, movement discourse tended to gloss over the fact that refusenik children like Prestin, Begun, and Korenfeld were able to celebrate their own bar and bat mitzvahs. This persisted even after twinning programs were well established. Activists continued to suggest that refuseniks did not have such opportunities. In instances when they clearly did, the rhetoric shifted to portray the refuseniks' ceremonies as inherently compromised by the oppressive circumstances under which they were conducted. Writing in April 1981 to a boy set to twin with Vladimir Fradkin, the head of Chicago Action for Soviet Jewry explained that Vladimir would be celebrating his bar mitzvah in Leningrad in two weeks' time: "However, they will not be able to have a regular Bar Mitzvah service and there is no Rabbi." The American boy's service, by implication, would be "regular," and it was this regularity that justified using it as a proxy ceremony for a Russian boy who was, in fact, able to mark his coming-of-age himself. From the American vantage point, refusenik bar mitzvahs—no matter how well intentioned—could not stand on their own. They needed American help to rectify their deficiencies. In the process, American Jews reinforced their convictions about the authenticity of their own tradition.[47]

PATHS FROM PERSONAL ACTIVISM

Another path to the creation of large-scale twinning programs originated in activists' own life-cycle events. This was an era when feminist activism was popularizing the phrase "the personal is political." For some, the idea to mobilize around bar and bat mitzvahs started at home, with family decisions to use their own celebrations to raise awareness. Most of the pioneers were adult women and teenage girls. They did not frame their activist interventions into the synagogue service as a gendered issue. (Mothers enlisted sons as well as daughters, bar mitzvahs as well as bat mitzvahs.) But it is possible that their readiness to assert a right to intervene in the service, and the congregations' and male rabbis' willingness to accede, was made easier by the fact that, in those very years, Jewish feminist activists were successfully battling for equal access in the religious spaces of Reform and Conservative Judaism.[48]

Likely the earliest use of a bar or bat mitzvah to raise awareness about Soviet Jewry came in September 1973 at the initiative of a bat mitzvah girl herself. Sharon Sobel was the daughter of the rabbi at a Reform temple in northern New Jersey. Inspired by the 1971 Cleveland Council on Soviet Anti-Semitism (CCSA) Freedom Caravan to Jewish summer camps (see chapter 6) and by the countercultural "do-it-yourself" Judaism associated with the recently published *Jewish Catalog*, Sobel crafted a "Creative Bat Mitzvah Service on the Plight of Soviet Jewry."[49] She compiled a twenty-one-page prayer booklet that wove together Sabbath liturgy, the Passover haggadah, Soviet Jewish poetry and song, quotations from Elie Wiesel's *The Jews of Silence*, and excerpts from tourist reports. She also drew the cover illustration by hand—a procession of ancient Israelites streaming out of an Egyptian pyramid topped by a Russian Orthodox onion dome emblazoned with a hammer and sickle. The drawing was her rendition of the cover graphic on artist Mark Podwal's 1972 Soviet Jewry haggadah. Above this, Sobel added her own touch: a raised blue fist atop a tattooed forearm. The meaning of tattooed Jewish forearms was unmistakable. Sobel inverted the symbol of Jewish powerlessness. Instead of numbers marking the victimhood of Auschwitz survivors, the tattoo on this arm bore a demand, inscribed proudly in Hebrew letters before a bold exclamation point: *Shallaḥ et ami!* "Let my people go!" The arm was neither covered in shame nor held out for examination but held high, ending in a raised fist—the familiar symbol of militant movements of the day, from the Black Panthers to the Jewish Defense League. But was this a call for Jews to unite—for people power—or for divine action? Floating in a cloud at the center of the graphic, Sobel placed a quotation from the Torah portion being read at Sabbath services that week, Deuteronomy 26:8: "And the Lord brought us out of Egypt with a mighty hand and an outstretched arm."[50]

Sobel's 1973 ceremony anticipated the twinning services of the 1980s, especially the DIY aspects that saw b'nai mitzvah create their own Soviet Jewry–related liturgies, booklets, and artwork. But Sobel's bat mitzvah differed in that it was themed, not twinned. She did not symbolically share her ceremony with any refusenik child. After the notion of proxy matching was introduced in 1975 with the SJC-supported Caine and Ivker b'nai mitzvah, some movement leaders—mainly mothers—began pairing their own children. In October 1977, WCSJ leader Shonny Kugler

Figure 7.1. Sharon Sobel, "Let My People Go," Bat Mitzvah service prayer booklet, cover page, 1973. American Jewish Historical Society, RG I-487, box 12, folder 1.

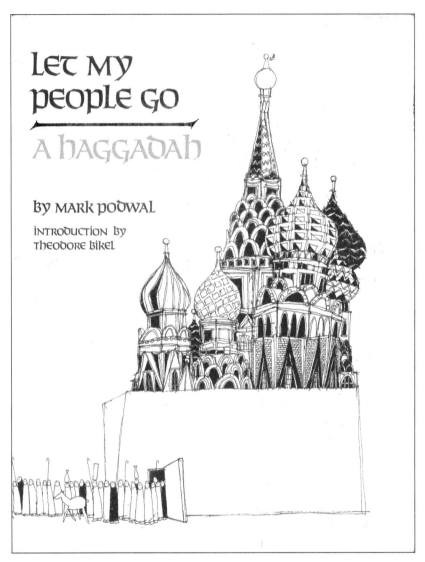

Figure 7.2. Mark Podwal, *Let My People Go: A Haggadah*. Mark Podwal, 1972.

matched her son, Danny, with Muscovite Mark Novikov, one of the pen pals in Rosenblum's memo and in *Natasha's Dream*.[51] In December, Carolyn Steinman, soon to head the Montreal Committee for Soviet Jewry, paired her son, Ned, with Felix Abramovich, also on the pen pal list.[52] Some adoption program coordinators helped their children initiate relationships that would later evolve into twinnings. Bobbie Morgenstern, cochair of Philadelphia's Adopt-a-Family program, paired her daughter, Andrea, with Dorina Paritsky in 1976, when they were eleven years old. Their twinned ceremony occurred in 1978. (Like Cindee Ivker, Andrea also recited Natasha Korenfeld's "Poem of My Land" during her sermon.) Adele Sandberg, founder of Miami's Adopt-a-Family program, and her husband, Joel, who chaired the South Florida Conference on Soviet Jewry, helped their nine-year-old daughter, Sheryl, start writing to Kira Volvovsky in 1978. Although Sheryl received only one response, she wrote regularly through the four years leading up to their twinned bat mitzvah in 1982.[53] WCSJ vice president Ruth Newman inaugurated the WCSJ's twinning program in August 1979 by twinning her own son.[54]

PATHS FROM RITUALIZED PROTEST

The movement's extensive development of ritualized holiday mobilizations seems the most obvious path to twinning, but this was less of an impetus than one would expect. A process of categorical reasoning had transformed isolated Passover campaigns into systematic deployments of the entire Jewish calendar. Once activists recognized that their Passover, Hanukkah, and Simchat Torah protests all fell under the general category of JEWISH HOLIDAYS, they set down the entire list of holidays and planned ways of using each. There was nothing preventing them from taking this a step further, thinking about JEWISH HOLIDAYS as a subset of the category SACRED JEWISH TIME and using this to arrive at other subsets, like JEWISH LIFE-CYCLE EVENTS, from which they could come to the elements {bar mitzvah, bat mitzvah}. But there is no hint that any categorical reasoning influenced the creation of the Caine, Ivker, Sobel, or other early Soviet Jewry–themed bar and bat mitzvah ceremonies. Later, after bar and bat mitzvah twinning programs were well established, their existence did prompt activists to make the conceptual leap to JEWISH LIFE-CYCLE EVENTS as a category. In 1983, the Minnesota-Dakotas Action Committee for Soviet Jewry was twinning American couples celebrating their anniversaries with refusenik couples "who did not have the opportunity to have a religious marriage ceremony." Synagogues marked the occasions with special ceremonies.[55] The years 1984 and 1985 also saw twinning ceremonies for a baby boy's *brit milah* circumcision in Palo Alto and for a religious school graduation in Columbus.[56] A brainstorming session at the Union of Councils' 1985 national convention generated a thirty-four-point list that suggested twinning circumcisions, consecrations, high school graduations, and weddings and naming newborns after Anatoly and Avital Shcharansky. The UCSJ, however, did not systematically implement these ideas.[57]

Although activists' prior experience with ritualized protest was not the proximate cause of bar and bat mitzvah twinning, it smoothed the way. Synagogues had been incorporating prayers for Soviet Jewry into their liturgies since at least 1964, when rabbinic associations around the world launched a Yom Kippur campaign to pray for the welfare of Soviet Jews.[58] By the time of the Sobel bat mitzvah in 1973 and the Caine and Ivker ceremonies in 1975, religious action for Soviet Jewry was a familiar part of movement culture. Synagogues were common venues for this. The paired b'nai mitzvah were novel and newsworthy but recognizably part of a larger context.

To see a direct line connecting earlier ritualized protests with the development of bar and bat mitzvah twinning, we have to look not at causation but at content. When Cindee Ivker, the Caine family, and the adult activists of the Washington Committee and Philadelphia SJC decided to pair bar and bat mitzvahs, they had to answer the question, What does a proxy ceremony look like? What actually happens? They solved this problem, in part, by repurposing existing elements of movement culture. We will see later how they adapted the Matzoh of Hope prayer. For now, consider the empty chair on the pulpit.

Worshippers entering a synagogue could know immediately that a bar or bat mitzvah twinning was taking place by looking at the pulpit, or *bimah*. They would see an empty chair cordoned off or set to the side to make its emptiness visible. The empty chair reserved for the absent Soviet twin was a ubiquitous feature of twinning ceremony stage design, its most recognizable symbol. It headlined the earliest coverage. "Altar Chair Empty for Russian Girl," proclaimed the *Philadelphia Bulletin* regarding the Ivker-Korenfeld pairing.[59] It was a staple recommendation in twinning guides, even rendered there as clip art.[60] And when the Soviet Union finally opened its gates, it offered reporters an irresistible hook that essentially wrote itself: "It was to have been a symbolic bat mitzvah at Temple Shir Tikva, where an empty chair was placed to commemorate the absence of one who was a half-world away, a virtual prisoner," the *Boston Globe* wrote in 1988. "But in March the Yurovitskys left Moscow . . . and what was to have been an empty chair was filled after all."[61]

The empty chair to symbolize the absent Soviet Jew was lifted from Passover campaigns. An activist group in Israel called Maʿoz ("Fortress") introduced the idea. In 1964, it asked Israelis to place an empty chair at the seder table. To mark the seat, they distributed placards bearing the words *Kes "Al-Domee."* This "'Be Not Silent' Chair" references Psalm 82, which appeals to God to not be silent. Below these words and also under the slogan *Shallaḥ et ami*, "Let my people go," the placards contained a color reproduction of Moshe Maimon's 1892 painting *Marranos: Secret Seder in Spain during the Times of Inquisition*. Maʿoz distributed the posters for free and sold them when they could, including in public schools (over the opposition of Israeli communists). From an initial print run of five thousand, the *Kes "Al-Domee"* campaign grew to sixteen thousand placards in 1965 and thirty-five thousand in 1966. Maʿoz also brought the idea to Jewish communities in Europe, Australia, South Africa, and the US. In 1965, New York's Park Avenue Synagogue implemented it at its congregational seder. The chief rabbi of Zurich called on his community to institute the "new custom."[62] In 1966, the Cleveland Council on Soviet Anti-Semitism's national newsletter informed readers that Maʿoz's empty chair ritual was becoming widespread.[63] The idea received its broadest publicity in 1972, when the National Conference on Soviet Jewry recommended the empty chair as part of its annual promotional campaign for the Matzoh of Hope. In a new twist, however, the NCSJ presented the ritual not as a remembrance of Soviet Jews at large but as a way specifically "to dramatize the plight of the more than 40 Jewish prisoners of conscience in the Soviet Union."[64]

This connection with prisoners had actually begun a few months before, at the end of 1971, when the Washington Committee for Soviet Jewry created its Adopt-a-Prisoner program for synagogues and churches. The WCSJ had circulated an eighteen-point checklist asking the congregations to indicate which actions they would undertake on behalf of their adoptees. Number one on the list was "Formal resolution by organization to adopt a prisoner." Number two was "EMPTY CHAIR on Bimah and/or organizational meetings."[65] With this, the WCSJ decoupled the empty chair ritual from the Passover holiday and started making it familiar in synagogue settings. It also focused the symbol so that it would represent specific individuals, not just broad categories. It was this prisoner connection that the NCSJ's 1972 Matzoh of Hope campaign imported back for Passover use. Philadelphia's Soviet Jewry Council picked up the NCSJ's suggestion and made it the centerpiece of a 1975 citywide Passover campaign that saw dozens of synagogues set aside empty chairs to commemorate prisoners Mark Nashpitz and Boris Tsitlionik at congregational seders.[66] A few months after this, with help from the same Philadelphia SJC, Cindee Ivker celebrated the movement's first paired bat mitzvah. On the bimah stood the empty chair specifically dedicated to Natasha Korenfeld.

COORDINATING THE TWINNINGS

When the Washington, DC, and Long Island Committees introduced the first bar and bat mitzvah twinning programs in 1979, not only did they transform the ad hoc celebrations into a standard template for large-scale youth mobilization, but they also introduced the word *twinning* into the movement's lexicon. Between 1975 and 1979, the scattered antecedents were referred to as dual, double, shared, or joint ceremonies; cosponsorings; proxy bar mitzvahs; bat mitzvahs in absentia; or symbolic honorings.[67] There was no agreed-upon term. Systematizing the practice also meant naming it. Like the word *adoption*, twinning suggested a family tie. But unlike adoption, which carried paternalistic or maternal overtones of a parent-child relationship, twinning suggested the parity of siblings and an intense family resemblance. To heighten this sense of similarity and foster feelings of identification, organizers typically matched twins by age and gender.

Activists developed a standard workflow to manage the twinning programs. They maintained lists of refusenik children, coordinated with synagogues to recruit American families, and provided instructions so that rabbis, parents, and children all understood their roles. The work was nonstop. The UCSJ's twinning coordinator, Fran Rapoport, of the Long Island Committee, circulated memos once or twice a month informing local councils of updates to the refusenik lists, such as who changed addresses or who emigrated and should no longer be twinned.[68]

It took a few years to get things running smoothly. The NCSJ's twinning coordinator, Kay Reiff, explained the problem in May 1983. Her lists of refuseniks born in 1969 had more names and more accurate information than the lists for those born later. But by 1983, the 1969 cohort was turning fourteen, a year past bar mitzvah age. "Parents do not seem to want them," she wrote. "I get protests when I send them out."[69] With demand increasing, Reiff found herself in a bind: "[I] wish I had names for 1970–1971—and 1972—I have to keep using the same names but although I have less to send out, at least they are still in Russia and we know that they are—too many people have been receiving names of people who left Russia long ago."[70]

Matching the twins involved at least three organizational layers. Closest to the families were synagogues, which often appointed a twinning chairperson.[71] Synagogues supplied the American youth. In the middle were citywide or regional groups, affiliates or appointees of the UCSJ or NCSJ. These coordinated downward with the synagogues and upward with the umbrella agencies. At the top, the UCSJ and NCSJ oversaw the operations, maintained master lists of refuseniks, and provided the names of Soviet twins. At the local level, volunteers, mostly women, handled the bulk of the work. After Soviet Jewry councils in Washington and Long Island had introduced twinning programs in 1979, a Jewish charitable organization, Women's American ORT, helped spread the practice.[72] A few chapters had begun sponsoring "proxy" bar and bat mitzvahs in 1980, seeing them not only as beneficial to Soviet Jewry but also as a means of "building our own ORT image in the community which will *result in the recruitment of new members*."[73] Their national umbrella agency adopted the project and even sought to claim exclusive rights to twinning: "The appeal of this simple idea is so enormous that other organizations are also seeking to promote it as their own. . . . In communities where our members have stepped in boldly and quickly, Twinning is clearly recognized as a Women's American ORT service program (i.e. Cleveland and New Jersey). On the other hand, where areas have not been fully active, a vacuum has been created which other organizations are moving in to fill."[74]

ORT's desire to take a high profile dovetailed with the NCSJ's need to unload some of the twinning work. In February 1982, Myrna Shinbaum, NCSJ's second-in-command, wrote the executive director, Jerry

Goodman. Her memo was reminiscent of her 1975 plea to create a volunteer tourist briefing committee. Then she had lamented that the flood of tourist inquiries was "getting too [big] to handle." Now Shinbaum talked of her small office "being inundated with requests for Bar/Bat Mitzvah Twinnings." She warned that unless they could "come up with some sort of mechanism very soon," the program—"a major success"—could "fall into chaos": "It is just enough for us to keep up with preparing profiles and securing photographs. It has been almost impossible to centrally coordinate who is twinned with whom and how many times one refusenik child has a Bar/Bat mitzvah in a city."[75] Shinbaum wrote the memo shortly after speaking with ORT's point person on twinning, Margery Kohrman, also a member of the NCSJ Executive Committee. The two solved the NCSJ's problem by outsourcing the twinning program to ORT.

Shinbaum's concern for knowing how many times each refusenik was being paired reflected the imbalance in the number of American and Soviet twins. While movement groups offered twinning to American Jewish children without restriction, they only presented children of refuseniks—a small and unrepresentative minority of Russia's Jewish population—as the pairing's Soviet half. In one case, the UCSJ decided to remove a name from the twinning list because the mother was intent on staying in the USSR even as the father applied to leave for Israel.[76] As a tactic for mobilizing American youth, twinning relied on creating a sense of personal connection. Few could fault the American b'nai mitzvah who thought that their twin was theirs and theirs alone. Activists tried to be honest that this was not so, but they recognized the potential for disappointment. The NCSJ's 1984 twinning handbook used an all-caps, underlined header and indented block text to emphasize its disclaimer:

> NOTE: Because of the limited number of refusenik children of Bar/Bat Mitzvah age, it is possible that the "twin" may have participated in absentia at other ceremonies. This should in no way diminish the symbolic significance of this shared experience.[77]

Not only was it possible; it was likely. Records in NCSJ files tracked 29 refuseniks born in 1970 who were matched between January 1982 and May 1984, when they would have been twelve to fourteen years old.

These 29 were paired with 260 American b'nai mitzvah. Although this averages to nine twinnings per refusenik, not all refuseniks were created equal. The popular German Abramova received 28 American twins; Dalia Gliksene, twenty-seven; and Yanna Grauer, twenty-two. Leonid Rabinovitch and Frida Mullakandova, in contrast, each got two. As for Aleksander Katz of Leningrad, this list shows him twinned only once, with a boy in South Plainfield. This might have been exciting news for the New Jersey boy had he been expecting a unique twin. For Aleksander, however, it meant that he would not have legions of American children advocating for him.[78] Twinning lists from other groups tell a similar story. Between August 1982 and May 1983, Boston's Action for Soviet Jewry (ASJ) twinned 65 refuseniks from the same 1970 cohort with 319 Americans. Half the twinnings went to just 13 refuseniks. Again, Dalia Gliksene and Yanna Grauer were among the most likely to be twinned.[79]

To encourage twinning and help those involved understand their roles, organizers created instruction kits. Like the curricula and tourist briefing packets, twinning handbooks were produced locally, circulated nationally, and cannibalized at every turn. After the Washington Committee for Soviet Jewry created the movement's first twinning guide in 1979, Boston's ASJ took scissors to its cover page, snipped the title words, and glued them onto the front of its own 1983 twinning handbook. ASJ did not, however, take the cover illustration—an Avrum Ashery graphic of a person raising a Torah scroll, the negative space forming a smaller person in an identical pose. Instead, it photocopied the onion-dome-and-ancient-Egyptian cover illustration from Podwal's *Let My People Go* haggadah, the same design Sharon Sobel had copied by hand for her DIY bat mitzvah booklet back in 1973.[80] As with the graphics, so with the text. To create its 1982 brochure, the Los Angeles Jewish Federation culled language written by ORT's Cleveland chapter and combined it with paragraphs lifted from Philadelphia's Soviet Jewry Council.[81] The SJC twinning guide served as a template for brochures nationwide, mainly because the National Conference copied much of it verbatim for its own widely circulated 1984 handbook. Although the booklets differed in some details, and although some addressed children and parents directly whereas others were directed to rabbis and local twinning coordinators, they spoke in a shared idiom and generally presented a uniform set of instructions.

Figure 7.3. *Bar and Bat Mitzvah Twinning with Soviet Jews*, cover page. Washington Committee for Soviet Jewry, 1979. Illustration by Avrum I. Ashery. Lillian and Albert Small Capital Jewish Museum, Voices of the Vigil, www.jhsgw.org.

ASJ's 1983 handbook, designed for use by Boston-area Jewish parents, opened with a boilerplate letter: "Thank you for your inquiry. . . . Your child's twin is: [blank]. A family biography is enclosed." It went on to provide instructions for writing to the twin. ("Don't include any political or anti-Soviet statements.") It also explained how and why to write to Congress. To encourage parents to "set the stage," it offered sample invitations from prior twinnings. ("Our son, Mark Allen, will become a Bar Mitzvah for himself and for Alex Hromchenko, son of Soviet Refuseniks Pavel and Maria Hromchenko, on Saturday, August twenty-first.") To encourage them to seek publicity, it provided press clippings. To commemorate the event, it suggested a calligraphed twinning certificate signed by the rabbi, available from ASJ, preprinted with space to write in the names, dates, and locations.[82] The handbook bullet-pointed the "many ways to make your twin part of the Shabbat service," from the sermon to the songs. It even offered a sample prayer:

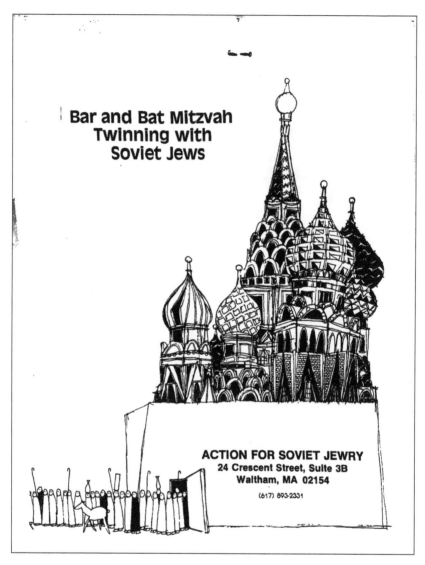

Figure 7.4. *Bar and Bat Mitzvah Twinning with Soviet Jews*, cover page. Action for Soviet Jewry (Boston), ca. 1983. Illustration by Mark Podwal, uncredited. American Jewish Historical Society, RG I-487, box 127, folder 3.

The Struggle of Soviet Jews
On this Shabbat, as we celebrate the Bar/Bat Mitzvah in absentia of _____, we are reaffirming our unity with three and one half million Jews in the Soviet Union.

We are pained by the knowledge that they are not free to learn of their Jewish past or to work for their Jewish future.

They are not free to learn the language of their fathers or to read the books of their heritage.

They are not free to join their families outside the Soviet Union or to share in the fellowship of co-religionists in other lands.[83]

If worshippers thought the text familiar, they would not have been wrong. It was the Matzoh of Hope prayer, adapted. Gone were the references to Passover and unleavened bread, replaced by mention of Shabbat and bar mitzvah twinning. The long single paragraph had been broken into alternating verses so that the congregation could recite it as a responsive reading. "The Struggle of Soviet Jews" appeared in other twinning guides across the country and was reprinted Sabbath after Sabbath in prayer book inserts at twinning services throughout the 1980s.[84] If the Matzoh of Hope itself could be said to have had a life course, its leap beyond the Passover seder to become a regular feature of weekly bar and bat mitzvah liturgies marked its own coming-of-age—a type of canonization.

The circulation of twinning handbooks through the national network standardized the practice of bar and bat mitzvah twinnings no matter where or when they were taking place. Activists established the template early on and stuck with it until the end. The details sometimes differed but the basic components—letter writing, an empty chair, the Torah service with the calling of the twin's name, a sermon—remained the same. This consistency forged a shared culture of Soviet Jewry activism nationwide, making an already large social movement feel even larger.

STAGING THE TWINNINGS

Many producers collaborated to stage twinnings. Activist groups set the template and articulated the rationales. (The Philadelphia SJC's handbook listed four: "The shared Bar/Bat Mitzvah links one part of the

Jewish people to another, increases American awareness of the plight of Soviet Jewry, stresses the importance of the acceptance of responsibility of one Jew for another, and provides support and a feeling of solidarity to young Refuseniks and their families.")[85] Teachers and rabbis recruited children and prepared the synagogues. Parents mainly built on what they were already doing to prepare for the joyous events: When pestering their children to practice their Torah reading, they reminded them to write their twins. When drafting invitations, they added Russian names. A few did more, writing to local newspapers or elected officials (jobs that were supposed to have been done by the teenagers).[86] Once the ceremony began, the bar mitzvah boys and bat mitzvah girls took center stage. For all the behind-the-scenes work trying to contact Soviet pen pals, the point of the twinnings, ultimately, was to perform them in front of an audience. On this, handbooks were explicit: "The Twinning Ceremony is one way to *dramatize* the absence of religious and cultural freedoms for Jews in the USSR."[87]

Dramatic they were. At the holiest moment in the Sabbath service, during the Torah ceremony, the rabbi would call the Soviet twin's name and leave it to echo in the silence. Eventually, the American bar mitzvah boy or bat mitzvah girl would ascend to chant from the scroll in their place. Since the act of blessing the Torah was restricted to Jewish adults, this was the key moment in the rite of passage when the child actually entered into ritual adulthood. Activists commandeered precisely this moment to stage the twinning's theater of the oppressed. But a secondary moment of dramatic focus still lay in store. After the Torah service, the newly minted adult would deliver a sermon. Twinnings co-opted this too. The sermon communicated concern for Soviet Jews through prose rather than pageantry. The thirteen-year-old would explain the problem, affirm his or her own commitment to act, and exhort the congregation to do the same. Not that the sermonizing was devoid of symbolic dimensions. Placing a middle schooler on the dais as a spokesperson dramatized the readiness of youth to speak out for Soviet Jewry.

To prepare audiences to witness these performances, twinnings made liberal use of the trappings of theater. Stages were designed and set, playbills distributed, and musical selections cued. Although each local performance was a unique production, and although rabbis, parents, and children exercised creative control, the stagings quickly came to resemble one another. By the 1980s, no one was creating entirely from scratch. Not only were people referring back to the same handbooks; they were also drawing from the same stock of texts, images, music, symbols, and practices that the Soviet Jewry movement had amassed over two decades. Families and their clergy mixed and matched these in new combinations. This was creativity under constraint, thousands of collages made with art supplies from the same kit.[88] We have seen this already, even from before the start of twinning programs, when bat mitzvah girls were reciting the "Poem of My Land" from *Natasha's Dream* and quoting Elie Wiesel's *The Jews of Silence*.[89] All this recycling made the internal coherence of Soviet Jewry movement culture even thicker. As its symbols continually occurred with each other, each new use recalled others, with the same elements of movement culture jumping between synagogues, seders, schools, and streets.

The ubiquitous centerpiece of twinning set design, the empty chair, represented twinning culture at its most standardized. Guidance came from the top down. Twinning handbooks recommended the staging. The realizations differed only in details. Some synagogues marked the chair with a ribbon or name placard or placed a photograph nearby. Some set it at a distance from the seats that people actually filled. Some congregations made the absence visible by cordoning off a row of pews to acknowledge the twin's family.[90]

Twinnings not only surrounded worshippers with visual symbols of absent refuseniks; they also placed printed materials into their hands. Prayer book inserts explaining the twinnings functioned like playbills. In contrast to the standardized empty chair, the inserts varied widely. Some were ready-made, others custom-designed. Pamphlets tucked between the pages of prayer books were regular features of Sabbath services in Conservative and Reform congregations, even in weeks when there were no b'nai mitzvah. They listed page numbers for the week's Torah readings, advertised upcoming events, and so forth. Bar and bat mitzvah ceremonies brought special pamphlets naming the relatives being called forth for honors and explaining the Jewish rite to guests who were not assumed to be familiar with it. Twinning added additional elements—explanations of what twinning was and why the family was choosing to do it, details about the Soviet twin's troubles, and special liturgies. Handbooks from the activist groups provided language, texts, and images that users could incorporate, as well as sample inserts from twinnings past, but there was no movement-wide template. Some synagogues prepared standardized materials for use in their own congregations in which only the names and dates would change. Temple Beth Am in Framingham, Massachusetts, took this approach. It printed a one-page prayer book insert that unfolded to the responsive reading, "The Struggle of Soviet Jews"—the repurposed Matzoh of Hope prayer taken from a twinning handbook. On the back cover was the chorus from "Leaving Mother Russia," one of the two main anthems of the American movement to free Soviet Jews, written and recorded in 1978 by the Boston-based band Safam. "We are leaving Mother Russia / We have waited far too long / We are leaving Mother Russia / When they come for us we'll be gone." (Temple Beth Am was one of many synagogues that brought the song out of the protest rallies and into the sanctuary. As liturgy, it was sung both by cantorial soloists and by congregations in communal prayer.)[91]

Four miles away, at Framingham's Temple Beth Shalom, families took more creative control over the program booklets. For their son Ethan's May 1986 twinning with Kirill Shapiro, Arlene and Michael Sobol printed a one-page pamphlet on high-quality card stock. On the back they included the familiar "Struggle of Soviet Jews" prayer. But the pamphlet unfolded to a unique collage. On the left, offset and angled, was a photocopy of bar mitzvah greetings on US Senate letterhead, addressed to Ethan and Kirill, signed by Senator John Kerry. Opposite that were images from a photo exhibition documenting Soviet Jewish life, taken by a photographer whom Boston's ASJ had sent to the USSR. The pamphlet credited the photographer as Richard Sobol. To Ethan, he was Uncle Richard.[92]

Some families followed the route that Sharon Sobel (no relation) had taken in 1973, creating homemade booklets with fully customized worship services. In May 1980, Lisa Muskat's fourteen-page DIY prayer book packet—stapled at the top right to open like a Hebrew text—celebrated her twinning through music, drawings, clip art, calligraphy, prayer, and prose. For the cover, she used the bat mitzvah certificate presented by her Manchester, New Hampshire, synagogue, signed by the rabbi and listing Olga Terlistksaya's name alongside Lisa's in calligraphic almost Cyrillic (an English *R* slipped in by accident). Inside, sandwiched between "Ani

Ma'amin" and "Eli Eli," and framed by those songs' associations with the Holocaust,[93] a typewritten page introduced Olga and her family's travails. Its five paragraphs also explained the twinning and asked guests to mail Olga postcards that Lisa was providing to them. Later in the service, a traditional prayer for redemption with no textual reference to Soviet Jewry was made to allude to the issue by placing it alongside a sketch of a chained man under the word *Svoboda* ("freedom") calligraphed in Russian. Toward the service's conclusion, under the title "The Voice of Soviet Jewry," came the song "Kachol va-Lavan" ("Blue and White"). Muskat had cut it out of a Jewish songster along with the description that said it had been "transmitted by a Jewish ham-radio operator somewhere in Russia, and recorded in Israel." Next to the transliterated and translated lyrics, Muskat pasted in the onion-dome cover image from the Podwal haggadah.[94]

As those who have attended bar or bat mitzvah celebrations in the United States know, the rite of passage into American adolescence often unfolds in two acts, beginning in a sanctuary and ending at a reception hall.[95] Like the synagogue services, the parties have also evolved their own rituals. In the 1980s, this commonly included some combination of blessing the bread, dancing the hora, dancing to Kool and the Gang's "Celebration," playing games like limbo and "Coke and Pepsi," and—relevant here—conducting a "candle-lighting ceremony."[96] Invented by caterers in or before the 1940s, this folk ritual saw the child honor loved ones by calling them up to the bandstand to light a candle on a birthday cake.[97] Usually, the summons came in doggerel, of the "Playing rummy with you is so much fun; Bubbie Sylvia, please light candle number one" type. Activists were not oblivious to this. Some twinning handbooks recommended lighting a candle in honor of the Soviet twin. There is scant evidence that people took up the suggestion, however. A candle lit by Roni Liebowitz of Scarsdale at her daughter Karen's November 1987 bat mitzvah reception probably represents the exception, not the rule:

> As you heard tell in Temple today
> We also celebrate for a girl who lives far away
> But we celebrate in freedom, in the glow of the light
> While she must be sure that the shades are drawn tight.[98]

The fact that twinning rituals did not spill over much into the parties hints at how American Jews understood them. Although twinnings were folk religion, newly invented by lay activists, they were associated with normative Judaism—solemn rites, endorsed and encouraged by rabbis, properly placed not at the party but in the sacred sanctuary of the synagogue.

BECOMING A JEWISH ADULT

If one might invoke the Roman pantheon to describe a Judaic ritual, bar and bat mitzvahs are notably Janus-faced. As coming-of-age ceremonies, they look not only to the individual at the center of the rite but also to the community of adults the adolescent is joining. The ritual makes assertions about both. In order to affirm the child's passage into adult status, the ceremony has to present some conception of what Jewish adulthood means. Since the ritual takes place in a synagogue, one might be forgiven for assuming that it conceptualizes this in terms of a particular relationship or standing before God. This may be the case in some communities. Twinning ceremonies, however, had little to say on such matters. Their version of the rite of passage framed American Jewish adulthood in terms of a certain type of relationship, not with God, but with a timeless, global Jewish collective:

> April 15, 1981
>
> Dear Mark:
> All of us at Chicago Action for Soviet Jewry would like to congratulate you on your approaching Bar Mitzvah. It is a very significant moment in your life for *you will be taking your place in the community of the People of Israel and as such, will be linking yourself to the history and the destiny of our people.* Therefore, it is very fitting that you have chosen to link symbolically your Bar Mitzvah with a young person in Russia....
> Pamela Cohen
> Co-Chairman[99]

What the Chicago group gently described here as a fitting choice, the National Conference on Soviet Jewry more openly pronounced as a moral obligation. Twinning, it explained in the opening paragraphs of its 1984 handbook, "is a personal way of activating the bond that exists between World Jewry and Soviet Jewry. . . . [It] *underscores the importance of accepting responsibility for fellow Jews*, thus creating a feeling of solidarity with the young refuseniks and their families."[100]

"Community," "People," "World Jewry," "history," "destiny," "taking your place," "activating the bond," "feeling solidarity," "accepting responsibility": twinning ceremonies were more than just isolated moments of advocacy. They gave ritual expression to the American Jewish ethos of "sacred survival" that was being expressed not only through the Soviet Jewry movement but also through the efforts to raise political and philanthropic support for Israel and to commemorate the Holocaust. Twinning took the rite of passage into traditional God-focused rabbinic Judaism and refashioned it to initiate teenagers into the religiously inflected American Jewish identity politics of the era—what sociologists were calling "Civil Judaism."[101] American bar and bat mitzvah twins stood at the pulpit to proclaim their membership in a strong but vulnerable global Jewish collective and to demonstrate their readiness to fulfill their adult duty to defend the rights of oppressed Jews. That this duty was sacred was made clear by the context, a religious rite in a synagogue sanctuary. That it was in fact a duty, obligatory, was indicated by the name of the ritual that the movement co-opted. *Bar mitzvah* refers to the person entering adulthood and is most faithfully translated as "one who is obligated to obey the sacred commandments."[102] That the imperative was political becomes clear if we contemplate roads not taken. Even as twinnings were becoming ubiquitous, Jewish American social welfare agencies were providing vocational training, English lessons, financial aid, and other support to hundreds of thousands of Soviet Jewish immigrants who had already arrived in the United States.[103] It is not hard to imagine a version of twinning that would have enlisted teenagers as volunteers in local resettlement efforts, matching them with newly arrived Russian-speaking teens. But this did not happen. Twinning's version of solidarity did not require providing social services quietly and confidentially. It demanded public activism. That is why handbooks instructed b'nai mitzvah to write not only to their twins but also to their senators and local newspapers. That is why they instructed teens to take the pulpit, speak out, and urge their elders to follow their example.

As rituals, twinnings were symbolic performances that represented values, affirmed community norms of behavior and feeling, and situated all this in the context of the sacred. Each twinning offered a Jewish world in microcosm. The Soviet twin, the American celebrant, the congregation—all stood as representatives of something larger. The Soviet twin represented all refuseniks. One learned about the general plight through the particular case. To advocate for one was to advocate for all. So, too, the American b'nai mitzvah were stand-ins for their entire generation of American Jewish youth. That was part of the reason that activists placed thirteen-year-olds out in front of congregations in the first place—to show that the next generation understood and accepted that it was duty bound to be politically active in defense of oppressed Jews. And because this duty was presented as a sacred obligation, a *mitzvah* incumbent on adult members of the community, the affirmation was witnessed by the congregation assembled. This cut two ways, because the ritual positioned the adults in the sanctuary both as objects of the teenagers' exhortations and also as their witnesses. As audiences on the receiving end of sermons preaching activism to aid Soviet Jews, congregants observing the rite of passage were treated as if they were potentially lapsed Jews. Twinnings reminded them of their own obligations as adults. What the b'nai mitzvah were responsible for, they were too. On the other hand, their role as witnesses assumed that such reminders were unnecessary, that the older generations knew how Jews should properly think, act, and feel. Their role was to say "Amen." And it was also to *kvell*, to look on the proceedings with pride and satisfaction, knowing that they as a community had successfully passed along their values to their children and grandchildren. In the moment when the b'nai mitzvah "link[ed themselves] to the history and the destiny of [their] people" and "accept[ed] responsibility for fellow Jews," the elders witnessed this not just on their own behalf but as symbolic representatives of the entire Jewish collective—past, present, and future.

A COLD WAR COMING-OF-AGE

Jewish education in the US has never only been about raising good Jews. It has almost always been about raising good Americans, too, and teaching that Jewishness and Americanness go hand in hand.[104] Twinning continued this tradition. Not only a Jewish ritual of sacred survival, it was also an American—or Western—ritual of Cold War liberalism. In its layered contrasts between Soviet absence and American presence, Soviet silence and American voice, Soviet need and American assistance, those partaking in the ritual displayed their self-confidence as Jews in an America that was a force for good. The service represented this in abstractions, through symbolic action. During the sermon, however, the teenagers explicitly articulated the Cold War themes.

American bar and bat mitzvah ceremonies typically include sermons. Twinnings co-opted this part of the ritual too. In addition to interpreting the weekly Torah portion and offering thanks to "all those who helped me reach this day," the b'nai mitzvah would also say something about the twinning itself. They informed, describing the travails faced by their Soviet pen pal. They interpreted, framing the cause in a moral context that compelled a responsibility to act. They professed, proclaiming their own readiness to answer the call to action. They exhorted, urging congregants to do the same. And they encouraged, expressing hope that their efforts would ultimately succeed.

As a Jewish rite of passage, traditional bar and bat mitzvah sermons typically affirm that for moral instruction, one looks to Judaism. At twinned ceremonies, however, the teenagers also spoke about looking to America. With the Soviet Union in mind as the counterexample, the b'nai mitzvah waxed poetic on the importance of "freedom." They invariably presented freedom as an American value. They often spoke of it as a Jewish one as well. The two were not separate. The Reagan-era thirteen-year-olds interpreted their Jewish texts through American lenses and reframed the American experience through Jewish narratives.[105] A May 1983 twinning sermon offers a case in point. That year, Boston's ASJ had matched Yanna Grauer, from Chernovtsy, in the Ukrainian SSR, with fourteen girls in the US, among them one Faith Lowy.[106] Speaking from the pulpit of Vassar Temple in Poughkeepsie, New York, Lowy began her meditation on freedom with biblical commentary: "When Moses and the Israelites were camping in the desert, manna fell from the sky. . . . After a while the people grew tired of the manna and complained to Moses. They desired the meat and vegetables they had eaten as slaves in Egypt. . . . They had forgotten that their freedom was more important than the fancy food they craved."[107]

Lowy quickly left the book of Exodus and segued from "they" to "we," directly addressing her Jewish American audience: "Sometimes, like the Israelites, we do not value our freedom in America. We complain about unimportant things, and forget the reason we are still living here. Jews, as well as many other persecuted groups, came to America because it offered them the independence that is essential for a rewarding life."

The notion of American freedoms taken for granted was a recurring theme in movement writings, also appearing frequently in travelers' trip reports. Here, too, it was prompted by thinking of the Soviet Union as a foil. The paragraph continued, "In nations like the Soviet Union, many people do not have freedom of religion, nor the freedom to leave the country." All this set up Faith Lowy's oration on the tribulations of Yanna Grauer: "I have been writing to a Soviet refusenik family; the Grauers.... Yanna's parents have been applying for exit visas for almost a decade. They are constantly denied the visas. They wish to leave because they wish to live and worship as Jews, which they are not allowed to do."

In her talk of freedoms denied, Lowy framed the issue primarily as a matter of *religious* freedom. Bar and bat mitzvah sermons often did this—no surprise, considering the synagogue context. But this was not the only reason. The twinning guides themselves used this language, priming the speakers. And of course, at the heart of twinning was the notion that government pressure prevented Soviet Jews from performing the religious bar mitzvah rites or drove them underground. There were also deeper cultural assumptions at work. First Amendment language loomed large in American Jewish discourse. Israelis tended to speak of Jewishness as a nationality, but American Jews filed Jewishness under "religion."[108] Lowy did not demand the Grauers' right to national repatriation in the Jewish homeland (the Israeli argument for emigration). Instead, she focused on freedom of religious education, which she suggested could best be found in the US: "I hope that one day Yanna will be able to come to America, so she will have the opportunity to study Judaism, which then guarantees her the freedom to be a Jew."

With this hope, the bat mitzvah girl moved to her conclusion, calling on the assembled to commit to the work of ensuring freedom at home and abroad, not just as a particular matter for Jews, but as a universal concern for all Americans. And learning from Lowy's example, they too would recognize that their American freedoms were not to be taken for granted: "We must work to ensure the freedom of all groups and individuals in America, now, and in the future. . . . Now that I know someone without it, I have realized that freedom is an important part of my life. Amen."[109]

This reassuring message that national heritage and religious tradition both preached the importance of freedom is as classically American Jewish as one gets. "In American Jewish history," writes historian Beth Wenger, "no theme resounds as loudly or as consistently as the perceived symbiosis between Judaism and American democracy"—emphasis on "perceived." This was a matter of faith, not an objective truth—a "cult of synthesis," in the words of another historian, Jonathan Sarna. He had observed that the Vietnam War had shaken this faith by introducing skepticism about such an idealized view of America. But as Lowy's sermon and others like it suggest, the Cold War politics of Ronald Reagan's America had relegated such concerns to a past that thirteen-year-olds had no memory of. With twinnings, the critical gaze was redirected abroad, the Soviet foil presented America in virtuous relief, and the cult of synthesis found its way back onto the pulpit.[110]

There were other pathways to this Jewish American symbiosis. Whereas Lowy had started from the Jewish texts, Jenny Ledewitz started from history. "Freedom. The history of the United States is the history of freedom-seekers," the young Floridian declared from the pulpit of Ormond Beach's Temple Beth El in December 1986.[111] Moving deftly from the Pilgrims, Quakers, and the First Amendment to her grandmother's flight from pogroms in czarist Russia, to 1986's centennial celebrations for the Statue of Liberty, the bat mitzvah girl wove American history, Jewish history, and family history into a cohesive story of freedom sought and achieved. Then she pivoted: "[But] what can people our age from Russia know of freedom?" Presenting the Soviet Union as the counterpoint to all she said before, Ledewitz introduced her bat mitzvah twin, Yulia Murash, from Odessa: "If Yulia were allowed to practice her religion," not only would she be "having her Bat Mitzvah about now. She would also be celebrating Chanukah, our festival of freedom." The holiday's four-word tagline is significant, and not only because of its first-person plural. Rabbinic tradition refers to Passover—not Chanukah—as *zman ḥeruteinu*, "the season of our freedom." But Ledewitz's gloss on the winter festival summed up her underlying message: Judaism, like

America, celebrates freedom; the Soviet Union, alas, does not. Having arrived at the same understanding as Lowy, Ledewitz concluded similarly, declaring that the bat mitzvah twinning helped her better appreciate what she had previously taken for granted: "Learning about Yulia has made me realize how lucky I am. Here in the United States we have the freedom to say what we want. We also have the freedom to pray and live as Jews. On this, my Bat Mitzvah, I promise to be aware . . . to be faithful, loyal, caring and sensitive; not only to my Jewish brothers and sisters, but to people of all religions."[112]

Ledewitz and Lowy both expanded the universe of moral responsibility beyond the ethnic community. They did this at their own initiative, diverging from the narrower framing suggested by twinning handbooks. But it was yet another way that twinning emerged as an American rite of passage as well as a Jewish one. Such words, publicly delivered, were a fitting seal to the work that the teenagers had done to prepare for the ceremony, work that the authors of any seventh-grade civics curriculum could have respected. A week before taking the pulpit, Faith Lowy handwrote a letter to her congressional representative, Hamilton Fish (R-NY). As in her sermon, she invoked "freedom" when asking Fish to act: "The family I am writing have lost their jobs just because they desire freedom. . . . I hope that you will give some thought to this and possibly write to the Soviet government. . . . Remember, the fate of Soviet Jews depends on the support they get from the West."[113]

Fish replied, commending the thirteen-year-old for her efforts. "Continue to write," he urged. "It helps." Fish enclosed a letter he had sent to Ronald Reagan three days after Lowy had written him, calling on the president to "use the issue of Soviet Jewry as a bargaining point during any future negotiations with the Soviet Union regarding the grain embargo." Lowy's efforts won further affirmation two weeks later when the *Poughkeepsie Journal* published an article about her twinning, along with a photo of the ceremony where she stood center stage, beaming.[114]

Not all who twinned got their pictures in the newspaper or received letters of praise from their mayors, governors, and senators or copies of correspondence between Capitol Hill and the White House. But neither were such occurrences rare.[115] Twinning handbooks reprinted newspaper clippings as exemplars of success. Even those who did the bare minimum for their twinnings could learn from them. For the teens who took on the full gamut of work, this crash course in civic engagement taught them about Jewish Americans' unqualified enfranchisement in American democracy, with nary a hint of the post-Holocaust trauma about powerlessness that other aspects of movement culture brought to the fore. Twinning helped a generation of Jewish American thirteen-year-olds discover their own self-efficacy in the political realm. Like Faith Lowy, they learned that they could take on a major issue of international human rights, challenge Soviet oppression, make direct contact with peers behind the Iron Curtain, see themselves and their stories in the newspapers, and appeal to their representatives for support and receive praise and a resounding "Yes!" in response. Twinning taught Jewish youth of the Reagan era that the struggle to extend freedom to the Jews of the Soviet Union was as much an American cause as a Jewish one, endorsed as enthusiastically by their political leaders as by their rabbis.

A GENERATIONAL EXPERIENCE

By 1988, American twins were receiving letters whose envelopes bore return addresses in Brooklyn: "Dear Lynne, At last come true my dream—I am in America! . . . Earlier I couldn't get your letters, but now we can be friends and you can to know about me. We are twins!"[116] Letters bearing Soviet postmarks also flooded in. They contained signs that twinning might soon be obsolete. "I hate Soviet Union," declared Olga Malievskaya of Tallinn in a 1990 letter to one of her sixty-one twins. Twinning was premised on the notion that Soviet Jews lacked the freedoms that American Jews enjoyed. Yet thirteen-year-old Olga felt safe enough to send explicit denunciations of her country through the Soviet post: "People here hate and killed Jewish people, the country is poor. There are not fruits and vegetables." Small hearts adorned her intricate handwritten script.[117] Yury Shinsky of Kiev expressed his feelings in art. In a letter to his twin, Jonathan Steinberg, he drew a daisy with a smiley face in the center, "my mother—refusenik." Its stem was bowed and the blossom hovered precariously between the jaws of a jagged-toothed alligator, which he labeled "our goverment" [sic].[118] Like Olga, no fear of censors deterred him from sending this. Perhaps the most telling indication of the changed situation came from an Odessan, Mikhail Marguilis. He wrote to one of his Long Island twins in 1989,

> On August 20, we took the ship "Feodor Shalyapin" and had voyage by the Black Sea. . . . We were in Yalta, Sochi, Batumi. We saw very many interesting things. On August 17, I had my birthday but we decided to celebrate it on that ship. On August 26, my American friend Ari Rabinovitch from N.Y. had his Bar Mitzvah. As a demonstration of solidarity with him I had my "Bar Mitzvah" on that day as well. It was not real Bar Mitzvah. We ordered a small restaurant in Sochi where was staying our ship and invited our friends from Vilnius and Armenia who were with us on the ship. It was great! The band played only Hebrew melodies and one of our friends who knows Hebrew proposed [toasted] my health. I liked it much.[119]

Twinning had begun as a way for "free" American youth to demonstrate solidarity with "oppressed" Soviet Jews. By 1989, a young refusenik could perceive his own Black Sea bar mitzvah vacation cruise as a "demonstration of solidarity" with a friend in New York whom he wanted to support. Was this a misunderstanding of the English phrase's nuanced directionality? The privileged are supposed to stand in solidarity with the weak. Not the other way around. Or did it reflect an intuition that the twinnings mattered a lot to American Jews? That even as they were ostensibly about supporting refuseniks, on a deeper level they gave voice to American Jews' own sense of who they were and what they valued?

Bar and bat mitzvah twinning helped define the texture of American Jewish synagogue life in the 1980s. Week after week, synagogues refashioned Judaism's primary rite of passage, the centerpiece of their Sabbath services, into a Jewish American civics lesson. A ritual originally intended to mark entry into religious adulthood became a primer on the contrast between Soviet oppression and American freedoms and a reminder of the responsibilities that Jewish heritage and American citizenship, in their imagined symbiosis, jointly imposed. This was not an intentional act of cultural engineering. Drawing on their expertise in ritualized protest and their experience with refusenik "adoption" and youth pen-pal programs, Soviet Jewry activists simply sought a way to turn American Jewry's favorite life-cycle ritual into a mass mobilization opportunity. Their goals were movement specific. They wanted to enlist youth into the campaign, build their commitment, and position them as spokespeople who could inspire adults by their example and broaden awareness of the Soviet Jewish cause.

All this they did—and at a greater scale than they might initially have imagined. Activists succeeded in engaging Jewish American youth in a new type of ritual behavior. Because they did this en masse, they ended up shaping a generation's experience of coming-of-age Jewishly. The Generation X teenagers at the center of the twinning ceremonies entered Jewish adulthood via a decade-specific Cold War ritual that spotlighted the American part of their Jewish American identities. Their older siblings bar mitzvahed before 1979 had not come of age in this manner, although they would watch many such twinnings sitting in the pews as high school and college students. So, too, their younger siblings bat mitzvahed after 1991. They had seen the ceremony as elementary schoolers but would not perform it themselves. As for the American twins' baby boomer parents and Gen-Z children, neither grew up with anything like it. Twinning burst on the American synagogue scene, was ubiquitous for a decade, and vanished when the statues of Lenin in Soviet Russia came tumbling down.

CONCLUSION

VOICES OF THE VIGIL

At 12:30 on January 27, 1991, a hundred Washingtonians gathered in front of the International Brotherhood of Electrical Workers' Philip Murray building on Sixteenth Street NW, across from the Soviet Embassy. They, or others like them, had been there before—7,353 times before, to be precise. Every day for twenty years. Ever since members of the Jewish Community Council of Greater Washington (JCCGW) had inaugurated its vigil for Soviet Jewry on December 10, 1970—International Human Rights Day. The daily vigil usually lasted only fifteen minutes. Protesters usually stood silently. When Jews were unable to attend due to Shabbat and religious holidays, Rev. John Steinbruck and members of his Luther Place Memorial Church ensured that the vigil went on.[1]

This day, however, the vigil was different. About two hundred thousand Jews had left the USSR in 1990. Almost every Soviet Jew who wanted an exit visa could get one. Freedom of emigration had become a reality. And for those who wanted to stay, Western-backed Jewish cultural institutions were opening to serve them.[2] "Let them live as Jews or let them leave" went the old movement slogan. By January 1991, eleven months before the dissolution of the USSR, Soviet Jews were free to do both. To continue protesting after having realized the goals of the protest would have been superfluous, indeed gratuitous. And so Washington's Jewish community decided to bring its twenty-year vigil to an end. ("Suspended," the organizers said, still wary of Soviet backsliding.) But first, there would be one last gathering. Not for protest, but for celebration. And this time, instead of facing off against one another, vigil-goers and Soviet officials would stand together. Press attaché Georgi Organov stepped out of the embassy to join the vigil. Then he invited the Washingtonians in.[3]

For the Americans, it was hard not to feel a sense of triumph. And why not? "This is a joyful day for me," the District of Columbia's congressional delegate, Eleanor Holmes Norton, said. "It's seldom that we see the goals of a human rights movement realized."[4] Activist Samuel "Buddy" Sislen, a JCCGW staffer throughout the vigil's twenty years, put it more succinctly:

> SISLEN: One of my programs was bringing the Soviets across the street on the last day of the vigil.
> INTERVIEWER: What did that feel like?
> SISLEN: Victory![5]

VICTORY AND LOSS

Soviet Jews' mass emigration in the final years of the Cold War ended a three-decade-long global campaign on their behalf. Political advocacy gave way to social service work. The Hebrew Immigrant Aid Society, New York Association of New Americans, and hundreds of local Jewish Family Service agencies stepped to the fore, resettling immigrants across the United States.[6] To assist similar work in Israel, Jewish American fundraising federations launched an emergency campaign that raised $58 million in its first hour. Donations to "Operation Exodus" eventually topped $882 million.[7] Advocacy groups that headed the political mobilization followed a different trajectory. By the year 2000, almost all the local councils and committees had shut down. The two national umbrella groups, the National Conference on Soviet Jewry and Union of Councils for Soviet Jews, changed their names, redefined their missions, and exited the spotlight. As the National Coalition Supporting Eurasian Jewry and the Union of Councils for Jews in the Former Soviet Union, they, along with Boston's Action for *Post*-Soviet Jewry, shifted to quietly providing cultural and social welfare support to the small Jewish communities remaining in former Soviet republics.

Demobilization did not just conclude a political struggle. Activists had achieved the political goal of mass mobilization by creating the campaign for Soviet Jewry as a Jewish American cultural movement in the broadest sense. Ending the one ended the other. True, Jewish groups adapted some of the old mobilization tactics for new purposes. Synagogues in the 1990s replaced bar and bat mitzvah twinnings with "mitzvah projects" that saw thirteen-year-olds take on charitable service work of their own choosing.[8] In the 2000s, Holocaust educators began encouraging bar and bat mitzvah celebrants to memorialize children murdered by the Nazis, reviving the term *twinning* to name the practice.[9] Every year, to the present day, American Passovers see the dissemination of Matzoh of Hope–style seder inserts promoting twenty-first-century causes like gun safety and prison reform. But these echoes of the Soviet Jewry movement are features of a newer Jewish culture from a later era. They are not the Soviet Jewry movement. That culture no longer exists. Jewish Americans ceased conjuring it the moment they closed down the campaign.

When the Soviet Jewry movement ended, Jewish Americans took brief victory laps but then found themselves confronting a void. A sustaining culture had suddenly disappeared. As they pondered "What next?" their fears rushed in quicker than their hopes. The undercurrent of doubt as to whether American freedoms were an unbridled good for Jewish life—those small moments of self-critique voiced in travelogues and bat mitzvah speeches—erupted into a moral panic that assimilation would soon spell the end of Judaism in the United States. A community that in 1987 celebrated its strength by quickly turning out a quarter million people to rally at the Capitol with top leaders of both political parties in attendance was, just four years later, lamenting its own imminent demise. American Jewry's so-called continuity crisis of the 1990s was ostensibly triggered by the release—just a few months before the Soviet Union's collapse—of a Jewish American demographic survey showing rising rates of interfaith marriage and declining rates of communal affiliation.[10] The topics of the continuity crisis conversation centered on issues of gender, sexuality, and the family—who should Jewish Americans marry, how many babies should they have, and in what religion should they raise their children?[11] The space for that conversation, however, was created by the sudden disappearance of the largest sustained mass mobilization in Jewish American history.[12] This did more than just clear the communal agenda. For three decades, a collective enterprise had been infusing Jewish American public culture with a sense of self-evident purpose. Then in an instant, it was not. This sudden loss of orienting meaning and structure—what sociologists call *anomie*—allowed alarmist readings of a demographic study to erupt into a full-blown crisis of collective self-confidence.

In their attempts to restore structure and create new meaning, participants in the continuity crisis conversation spoke in terms set by the movement to save Soviet Jewry. Historians used analogies to frame the problem: "Where for three decades the attention of the community had been focused on the dangers faced by Jews in the Middle East and Eastern Europe, and on the question of whether 'they' would survive, today attention is being paid to the dangers [of assimilation that American] Jews face within their own communities, and the wonder is whether 'we' will survive."[13] Sociologists used Soviet Jewry movement tropes to frame the solution, prescribing action to "save" American Jewry.[14] Having spent decades building a religious politics around Jewish survivalism and the rescue of Jews in distress, Jewish Americans found it disorienting to live in a world without Jews in need of saving. They quickly found new Jews to save.

COMMEMORATION AND LAMENT

The struggle to free Soviet Jews lives on today, but only in Jewish collective memory. Driven by former activists—and with the participation of Jewish communal workers, journalists, museum professionals, educators, and academics—memorialization work has become the primary theme of the movement's afterlife. In 2007, in Tel Aviv, the Beth Hatefusoth Museum of the Jewish Diaspora staged *Jews of Struggle: The Jewish National Movement in the U.S.S.R.* The exhibition opened with an academic conference and ended with a richly illustrated coffee table book. In 2017, in Philadelphia, the National Museum of American Jewish History introduced *Power of Protest: The Movement to Free Soviet Jews.* That exhibition's eleven panels subsequently toured more than a dozen cities across the US. In 2013, Washington's Jewish Historical Society commemorated local activism with *Voices of the Vigil*—a museum installation, oral history project, and website.[15]

Commemoration is not confined to museums. In 2012, under the banner "Freedom 25," Jewish American organizations marked the twenty-fifth anniversary of their 250,000-person Washington, DC, Freedom

Rally for Soviet Jews. The commemoration included a virtual march, Facebook group, and YouTube channel, along with in-person events nationwide.[16] In 2019, led by the daughter of two former Soviet Jewish prisoners of conscience, Bar Ilan University's Refusenik Project began developing educational resources about the movement for use in Jewish schools worldwide. American activists provided financial backing. So did Nativ.[17] Other commemorative projects have included documentary films, academic conferences and edited volumes, activist autobiographies, and any number of independently posted commemorative websites.[18]

A standard feature of the numerous commemorations are accompanying laments that Jewish Americans have failed to remember the Soviet Jewry movement, failed to retell its "story," failed to teach its "lessons" diligently to their children. Why is it, one of New York's main Jewish weeklies chided in 2017, that "this extraordinary episode has not been widely heralded and taught as part of our communal curriculum?"—especially as this "grassroots movement led to one of the great achievements of the American Jewish community."[19] When Freedom 25 launched in 2012, a CNN headline labeled the campaign to free Soviet Jewry "A Forgotten Movement."[20] One can take the network at its word. Ten years later, Freedom 25's highest-ranking video has still received only 6,100 views.[21] Or one can challenge CNN's claim, pointing out that in 2012, it was running a story about the Soviet Jewry movement—a campaign that had ended back in the twentieth century.[22] Not all episodes in Jewish Americans' rich and varied history receive such treatment—not from news networks, not from Jewish museums, not from Jewish educators. Why is the Soviet Jewry movement different? Of all the episodes available for memorialization, why do Jews in the US and Israel elevate this one for commemoration while fretting that it is not being commemorated enough?

Success has much to do with it. The movement achieved its aims against substantial odds and a powerful adversary. For those who had contributed to the effort, this is a source of pride. It's not often that citizens take on a superpower and win. Those pushing for greater public memory of the campaign encourage people to celebrate a victory. At a minimum, their commemorations celebrate the campaign's success in gaining for Soviet Jews the right to leave—first, when the Kremlin made concessions at the beginning of the 1970s, letting out tens of thousands per year, and later, when the government lifted all emigration restrictions at the end of the 1980s and hundreds of thousands rushed out.[23] Some argue that the success was even greater. "The liberation of Soviet Jewry, it must be recognized, tore a gaping hole in the Iron Curtain," former prisoner of conscience Natan Sharansky wrote in his introduction to Beth Hatefusoth's *Jews of Struggle* exhibition, "one that eventually spelled the end of the Soviet empire."[24] Cold War historians might not make so bold a claim, but commemorations speak to the imperatives of memory, not history.[25]

But more is at stake than just celebration for its own sake. Those urging remembrance—and simultaneously lamenting that it is not happening enough—also argue that commemoration can inspire and inform activism today. Which lessons the Soviet Jewry movement offers depends on who is teaching. Israel's Beth Hatefusoth celebrates the movement as an exemplar of sound Jewish politics, a framing that fits well with the museum's mission "to strengthen a sense of Jewish pride, to forge worldwide Jewish solidarity, and to reinforce the connections between Israel and the Jews of the world."[26] In contrast, Philadelphia's National Museum of American Jewish History, situated in clear view of the Liberty Bell and Independence Hall, speaks the language of the First Amendment. It presents the movement as a worthy civics lesson to those visiting the birthplace of American democracy: "The movement to free Soviet Jews provides a fascinating example of how American activists have played, and continue to play, significant roles in promoting religious liberty at home and abroad. . . . The exhibition will serve as a reminder of the unique promise of religious freedom in America and our continuing responsibility to preserve and protect that freedom."[27]

Such calls to celebrate and learn from the Soviet Jewry movement could be read as self-congratulatory. But that would be a mistake, at least in the American context. Continually accompanied by laments that the movement has been forgotten, no exuberant confidence undergirds the push to memorialize but rather a gnawing sense of loss. "We have lost our sense of community as a Jewish people," proclaimed a former activist in Virginia amid the quarter-century commemorations of the 1987 rally. "Twenty-five years ago, we were galvanized around a cause—to free Soviet Jews from oppression. We need to rally around something that brings us together."[28] The thirtieth anniversary commemorations brought the same refrain: "Are we still capable of functioning as one people, on any issue?"[29] These are elegies for a bygone era. Through commemoration, Jewish Americans try to resurrect the spirit of the past. By lamenting that forgetfulness nevertheless reigns, they express their fears that commemoration will not be up to the task—or perhaps their awareness that it cannot be.[30]

It is telling that Jewish American nostalgia centers not on what the campaign for Soviet Jewish emigration accomplished for Soviet Jews but on what taking up the struggle meant to American Jews—how it inspired them, united them in shared purpose, synthesized their Jewish and American identities, infused their political action with timeless religious significance, helped them feel empowered and effective on the timeliest Cold War stage, and enabled them to turn Holocaust trauma into redemptive action, thereby allowing them, partially, to heal.

For a generation, this social movement shaped Jewish Americans' civic and religious culture. (For the children raised in the 1970s and '80s, who had never known a Jewishness without Soviet Jewry activism, it shaped their basic definitions of Judaism itself.) The culture of the Soviet Jewry movement filtered into the daily life of Jewish Americans' synagogues, schools, nonprofit institutions, political bodies, social service agencies, and philanthropies. It also found its way into Jewish Americans' homes—when doing Hebrew school homework, when hosting seders, when planning vacations, when arranging life-cycle events. The Soviet Jewry movement succeeded in creating a total mobilization of America's Jewish community. Is it any surprise that when Jewish Americans reminisce about the movement, or commemorate it, they focus not only and not even primarily on the oppression of refuseniks but rather on their own efforts to help—wearing bracelets, twinning bar and bat mitzvahs, smuggling blue jeans into the USSR?[31] To recapture that lost sense of meaning, solidarity, purpose, and efficacy, Jewish Americans and their institutions recall the mass mobilization tactics that engaged them—body, heart, and soul.

These ways of enacting Jewishness no longer exist. They disappeared when the movement ended. They did not exist before activists created them. They certainly were not, as the two dominant models in the sociology of American Jews would propose, the product of demographic change or the aggregate of individual identities. For a brief historical moment, about the span of one generation, a social movement invented new ways of practicing and experiencing Jewishness in America. The Soviet Jewry movement's American Judaism was an engaged, optimistic, activist religious politics forged in the imperial center of the Cold War's Western alliance, one generation after Auschwitz, as post–civil rights movement multiculturalism was rebalancing notions of *pluribus* and *unum* and celebrating the Americanness of hyphenated identities. This Judaism synthesized post-Holocaust trauma with American ethnic identity politics, presenting vocal protest in defense of Jewish rights as a religious imperative and as a chance to redeem American Jewry's "failure" to save European Jewry from Hitler. It was a Jewish American culture steeped in Cold War liberalism. Indeed, this helps account for its staying power from the Johnson era through the Reagan-Bush years. It partook in the Cold War liberal faith that the United States, despite its flaws, was a force for good, committed to fighting oppression abroad, working to overcome the legacy of oppression at home, and capable of succeeding at both. Dispensing with Judaism's traditional notion that Jews everywhere were in exile—and oblivious to critiques that Jewish Americans were building vicarious identities centered primarily on Israel—the Soviet Jewry movement's culture celebrated the good fortune of being existentially at home in America. It conceived of the United States as fundamentally worthy of celebration. Presenting the Soviet Union as a foil, it represented America as a country whose domestic order guaranteed Jews' physical safety, guarded their religious freedom, enabled their socioeconomic advancement, and encouraged their cultural flourishing. The only caveat, prompted by encounters with Soviet Jews, was that an overabundance of freedom might breed Jewish complacency. As for America's foreign policy, it valued this for protecting the welfare of Jews abroad—defeating the Nazis, challenging the Soviets, and securing the State of Israel. Informed by all this, the Soviet Jewry movement's American Judaism demanded political engagement from men, women, and children equally. It taught Jewish Americans that—as citizens of the superpower leading the "Free World," free and empowered themselves just decades after the Holocaust, descendants of Russian Jews who had the good fortune or good sense to flee the czar and spare their children the ravages of Hitler and Stalin—they had an obligation to use their uniquely privileged position to aid their brothers and sisters who remained behind. And it filled them with confidence to assert American Jewry's presence as an actor on the global stage—making demands of superpowers, charting its own course independent of Israeli wishes, and seizing for Jewish Americans what Israel had claimed as its special province, the power to make Jewish history.

Such an American Judaism was rooted in its historical moment—in the America of its day and in the Jewish world of its day. That historical moment has passed. The Jewish culture of that era has passed too. Jewish Americans' nostalgia for the Soviet Jewry movement—all the commemorations, laments, and elegies that have become a staple of their twenty-first-century discourse—should make this clear. This book has shown that before the culture of the Soviet Jewry movement had an end, it had a beginning, and in the beginning were the activists. And the activists created.

INVENTING TACTICS, CREATING CULTURE

Creating a culture is no small feat. How did activists in the Soviet Jewry movement accomplish something so substantial? The answer, in two words, is *mass mobilization*—the invention of tactics to engage large numbers of people in tangible actions in support of a cause.

In the Soviet Jewry movement, activists and their organizations were continually inventing, testing, expanding, discarding, refining, and systematizing practices that gave Jewish Americans concrete behaviors to express support for Soviet Jews and aid them directly. Activists cast their mobilizing gaze widely. This meant they were always looking at the world with an eye toward figuring out how they could make what and who they saw useful for the Soviet Jewish cause. Getting dressed in the morning? Going for a jog? Shopping in the supermarket? Celebrating a holiday? Planning a vacation? You can do something for Soviet Jews at the same time. Are you a doctor? A lawyer? A teacher? Here is how you can contribute your professional expertise. Are you a homemaker? A parent? A student? You are not exempt from responsibility. You can and must help too.

Activists not only appealed directly to people. They also mobilized institutions—synagogues, community centers, schools, summer camps, volunteer associations, philanthropies, social service agencies—enlisting as many as they could in order to make their campaign a total mobilization of the Jewish American community. This also meant inventing different modes of engagement for different organizations—twinnings for synagogues, "Escape from Russia" simulations for summer camps. To spread their mobilization tactics, activists solicited press coverage, circulated newsletters, hosted conferences, and traveled the speakers' circuit. Most importantly, they channeled ideas through organizational networks. National umbrella agencies served as clearinghouses, gathering new mobilization tactics from local communities and then disseminating the ideas, reports, scripts, curricula, templates, graphics, and program materials nationwide.

A coherent system of interconnected cultural products and practices thereby evolved. Each tactic for engaging people borrowed from other tactics and shared elements with them. Activists transferred the empty chair and the Matzoh of Hope from Passover seders to bar mitzvah pulpits. They added Elie Wiesel's travelogue to school curricula and recited its passages when protesting and when praying. They incorporated the Pepsi boycott into their Freedom Runs, wearing Hebrew Coca-Cola T-shirts at Pepsi-sponsored races. They brought Shlomo Carlebach's "Am Yisroel Chai" and Safam's "Leaving Mother Russia" with them to the streets, to dance rallies, to concerts, and to synagogue services—giving the movement a unifying soundtrack.[32]

Contemporary activists scouring this book for lessons today might rephrase these findings into imperatives. How can social movements create sustainable mobilizations? Following the Soviet Jewry movement's approach, the answer might be this: Turn your political movement into a cultural movement that is far bigger than any particular issue or policy goal of the day. Do that by casting a mobilizing gaze on everything, to mobilize as many institutions as possible in their own tailored ways, as many people as possible in all their identities and roles, and as many cultural practices, cultural objects, and cultural scripts as possible, from the most timeless to the most timely, the most esteemed to the most mundane. Almost anything and anyone can be enlisted to serve a cause if one looks at them with mobilization in mind. And remember that the mobilized are also mobilizers. So encourage the grassroots to invent new ways of mobilizing themselves from the bottom up. Share their strategies widely so that people can mix and match them to suit their own needs.

And allow the tactics to take on lives of their own. One never knows which evolutionary variant will become the movement's next great mobilization success.

But such claims go beyond the historical sociologist's brief. Activists will decide for themselves what lessons, if any, the Soviet Jewry movement offers to them and their contemporary concerns. This account simply surveys how one successful human rights campaign approached mass mobilization, analyzes the processes of cultural production that this campaign used to invent its tactics, and traces how these efforts to engage people unexpectedly produced broad cultural outcomes.

Activists in the movement to free Soviet Jews did not set out to reinvent American Judaism. They were trying to change policies in the USSR. They rallied Jewish Americans as the foundation of their strategy of enlisting Washington to pressure Moscow. As activists developed their mass mobilization tactics, they worked piecemeal, responding to immediate needs and aiming for targeted goals. They were not thinking intentionally or systemically about creating a coherent movement culture, but they inadvertently achieved precisely that.

Only in retrospect, when we excavate the pathways and processes activists used to invent their mass mobilization tactics, do we see how movement culture evolved to become a holistic system—how the materials, practices, symbols, and discourses from any given tactic also became raw materials for the production of even newer ways to engage people. But to see this, we have to recognize that tactical innovation in the Soviet Jewry movement was never simply a matter of choosing among ready-made options in a preexisting repertoire. Tactical innovation was creative work, the invention of something new—in sociological terms, cultural production.

As with cultural production generally, activists' creation of mass mobilization tactics did not unfold at random. We observed consistent patterns in the Soviet Jewry movement's processes of tactical innovation. Since they are probably generalizable to other movements as well, let us phrase them here as rules.

First, the organizational contexts of production shape the resulting products. When a semiclandestine government agency mobilized tourism, it built a system for carefully selecting and vetting its travelers. When a coordinating agency serving Jewish American communities mobilized tourism, it responded to consumer demand and wrote a guide to Jewish heritage travel.

Second, the materials and media that activists choose to create with shape the resulting creations. When activists wrote the first version of the Matzoh of Hope ritual, they thought it impolitic to call for unfettered emigration. But Passover has its own logic. The ritual's authors, having used the seder as their medium for mobilizing, ultimately found it impossible not to demand, "Let my people go." Likewise, when movement organizations introduced $2.00 medallions as a mass mobilization tactic, they inadvertently introduced institutional logics native to the jewelry trade. Soon, they were offering high-fashion designer-label versions in 18K gold, tiered price points, and custom engraving. They also found themselves encouraging people to purchase the pendants as gifts.

Third, path dependencies structure tactical innovation. The initial choice to embrace particular tactics sets activists down paths that make new types of tactics possible. Prisoner adoption programs opened the way to family adoptions and children's pen pal programs, which in turn—with some help from the movement's tourist work—led to the invention of bar and bat mitzvah twinning.

Fourth, and related, new mobilization tactics emerge through mixing and matching elements from existing tactics. Tactics are not singular entities but composites. Their elements can be separated out and recombined to create something new.[33] The more that new tactics are mash-ups of existing tactics, the more a movement's full set of tactics will bear family resemblances. These resemblances create movement-wide cultural coherence.

Fifth, the awareness that each tactic can be thought of as but one element in larger sets of possible tactics encourages experimentation with other elements in the sets. This channels innovation and expands it. Initial uses of Passover and Hanukkah burgeoned into mobilizations of the full Jewish holiday calendar. Twinning began with bar and bat mitzvahs, then spread to other life-cycle moments like circumcisions and wedding anniversaries.

We could continue drawing examples of structuring factors from the previous chapters, but these five suffice to make the point. In the Soviet Jewry movement, mass mobilization tactics were not "chosen"; they were created, and the creation process had a discernible structure.

CONCLUSION

In none of this is the movement to free Soviet Jewry exceptional. Rather, it is typical of how social movements operate. By their nature, social movements produce new forms of culture in an attempt to engage large numbers of people. Regardless of whether they succeed or fail in attaining their policy aims, they intervene in the public square simply by these efforts to mobilize the masses. Some interventions ripple larger than others. Youth mobilizations shape children's basic understandings of what is normal in the world. But whether the movements succeed or fail, whether they are large are small, whether they target children or adults, a basic fact persists: social movements are engines of cultural innovation. They have to be if they are to have any chance of success. The first order of business for any social movement is enlisting supporters. That means creating tactics to mobilize people. But attention is a scarce commodity, old tactics get stale, and circumstances rapidly change. To engage people and keep them engaged, activists must continually create their mobilization tactics anew. For those whom the mass mobilization tactics successfully reach, their participation in movement-generated behaviors becomes part of their lived experience. Movements that succeed in engaging millions, as the Soviet Jewry movement did, not only touch individual lives but shape the public culture of their eras.

* * *

Somewhere in Babylonia in the middle to late years of the first millennium, the rabbis of the Talmud and the Midrash pondered an odd turn of phrase. In Exodus 24:7, Moses reads the book of the Law to the Israelites at Sinai, and the Israelites respond, "All that the Lord has spoken, *na'aseh v'nishma.*" The Hebrew has been translated variously as "we will do, and we will hear'" or "we will obey and we will understand.'" The word order strikes the rabbis as odd. How can the Israelites obey the Law if they do not first understand it? Should not the text read, "*Nishma v'na'aseh,* we will hear and then we will do?" For more than a thousand years, generations of rabbis have wrestled with the question. Because they presume that the text is divine, their answers must always assert that the order is not backward but teaches some profound truth. The most sociological answers present a rabbinic notion of praxis: *na'aseh v'nishma*—we will do and we will come to understand by realizing meaning through the doing itself. Do not think that the *nishma,* the meaning, precedes the *na'aseh*, the action, or that the one exists independently of the other. As this Talmudic take on the social construction of reality suggests, meaning constitutes itself through action. Action produces meaning. The two are inseparable. They emerge together when people act. They disappear together when people don't.[34]

For thirty years, activists in the campaign to free Soviet Jews sparked and sustained a total mobilization of America's Jewish community—thousands of institutions, millions of individuals. The mass mobilization tactics that they invented to engage Jewish Americans were the Soviet Jewry movement's *na'aseh*, its "we will do." Engaging Jews at work and at worship, at learning and at leisure, at home and abroad, these behaviors created their own *nishma*, shaping what a generation heard and understood about the meanings, opportunities, and obligations of being Jewish and American in the aftermath of the Holocaust, on the heels of the civil rights movement, and in the midst of the Cold War.

And then it all stopped.

ACKNOWLEDGMENTS

Were I lying, I would say that this book is my atonement for missing the December 1987 Freedom Rally on the National Mall, even though I lived just blocks away in the freshman dorms at the George Washington University. (Girlfriend's birthday. Boston University.) The truth is, it is the unintended consequence of a decision to take advantage of the City University of New York's consortium arrangement with Columbia. My graduate school mentor, Charles Kadushin a"h, recommended I study with Gillian Lindt. Her religious protest movements course required a research paper. I was already trekking uptown on the 1 and 9 trains, so I stayed on a few extra stops and dove into the Student Struggle for Soviet Jewry archives at Yeshiva University. I fell in love with the topic and kept working on it as a side project for years. In 2015, with a grant from the National Endowment for the Humanities and generous hospitality from my friends, Jeff Feig and Michelle Feig, I returned to New York City to spend two months working in the American Jewish Historical Society's Archive of the American Soviet Jewry Movement. I have been immersed in this project ever since.

A Cold War Exodus is about people who dedicated themselves to helping others. I am humbled by the support given to me by so many. At Vanderbilt, Dan Cornfield has been a wonderful mentor and compadre through it all. David Price's friendship and encouragement kept me going every day, and his generous and careful readings of draft chapters have made this a better work. Mariano Sana always helped me keep my writing on track. When Richard Lloyd read my early treatments, he encouraged me to aim higher and reminded me how world-historically big the big picture actually is. Holly McCammon paved my (re)entry into social movement studies by welcoming me into her graduate seminar. She, Dan,

Larry Isaac, David Hess, Zdravka Tzankova, and Joe Bandy helped me hone my sociological thinking about social movements. Across campus, Allison Schachter, Phil Lieberman, Julia Philips Cohen, Ari Joskowicz, Adam Meyer, Lenn Goodman, Markus Krah, and Katie David helped me develop my thinking on matters Jewish, American, Russian, and Soviet. Frank Wcislo opened the door to Slavic studies. Sam Lorber enriched my understanding of music in social movements. My students in undergraduate courses on the Soviet Jewry movement and on Jewish social movements taught me how to translate bygone days for the present moment. Those in my fall 2020 Soviet Jewry class made COVID time the best teaching experience of my career. My department chairs—the aforementioned Allison, Larry, Holly, and Ari and also Michael Bess, Lutz Koepnik, and Meike Werner—supported me throughout. I am grateful to the departments of Sociology, Jewish Studies, and German, Russian, and East European Studies and to the College of Arts and Science for supporting publication costs. Thank you also to the Lippman Kanfer Foundation for Living Torah for a generous subvention grant.

One of the things I have loved about this research has been the opportunity to learn a new language. For opening the world of Russian to me, I am grateful to Albina Khabibulina, Denis Zhernokleyev, Bradley Gorski, Sasha Spektor, Kostya Kustanovich, and most of all my teacher every year since *Golosa* chapter 1—David Johnson. *Bol'shoye spasibo* also to my classmates and especially Ilya (Ethan) Beaty, Nadia Matin, Simona (Simone) Stoyen, Yanna (Fan-Ching, Jasmine) Ding, and Olga (Lauren) Pratte. Thank you also to my conversation partners, Yuri Livshitz and Armen Safarian; to Faina Tsulia, wherever she may be; and to Seth Thomas for Russian textbooks. *Todah*, *a dank*, and *merci* to my other teachers, Yael Moses, Max Ticktin a"h, and Jean D'Addario, for giving me the ability to work in Hebrew, Yiddish, and French. Thanks to Sarah Benor for helping me give myself permission to write in American Jewish English vernacular and use "bat mitzvahed" as a verb. If the English is readable, you can join me in thanking Ilene Kalish and her team at New York University Press.

I workshopped ideas in the book through fellowships, conferences, and edited volumes. I am grateful to colleagues at the University of Michigan's spring 2016 Frankel Institute for Advanced Judaic Studies and at the Vanderbilt University Robert Penn Warren Center for the

Humanities' 2017–18 faculty fellowship on storytelling and 2019–20 East Europe Critical Encounters seminar. Special thanks to Jeff Veidlinger and Scott Spector at Michigan and Laura Carpenter, Catherine Molineux, Emily Greble, and Mona Frederick at Vanderbilt; to Marc Caplan, Miriamne Krummel, Letizia Modena, Stan Link, Jonathan Rattner, and Ellen Armour; and to artist Britt Stadig for helping me see my project in a new light. (You can see it too: https://tellingstoriesstoriesthattell.com.) My thanks to my dear friend Riv-Ellen Prell and to Ari Kelman and Tony Michels, whose Stanford Taube Center conference on the "Jewish 1968" steered my focus beyond student activism; to Sean Martin and John Grabowski, whose project on Cleveland's Jewish history offered an opportunity to study America's first Soviet Jewry organization; to Jon Levisohn, who helped sharpen my thinking about how activism creates its cultural consequences; and to Jacob Labendz and Rebekah Klein-Pejšová, whose conference on Jewish Cold War contacts helped me deepen my exploration of activism in Orthodox communities. Thank you to Adam Ferizger and Miri Freud-Kandel, whose invitation to the 2016 Oxford Summer Institute on Modern and Contemporary Judaism enabled me to expand this research to consider activism in the UK. Three conferences in Europe tore down academic Berlin Walls and helped me think beyond the confines of Jewish studies, sociology, and the American academy. Many thanks to Sune Bechmann Pedersen and Christian Noack for welcoming me to a pair of conferences on Cold War tourism at the University of Amsterdam and the Center for European Research at the University of Gothenburg (CERGU). Thanks also to Sune and CERGU for helping me get to Moscow. Sincere *remerciements* to Andreas Nijenhuis-Bescher and his fellow organizers of the conference on religion and travel writing at the Université Savoie Mont-Blanc, Chambéry, and the Université Grenoble Alpes. I am full of gratitude for my *chaver*, conversation partner, and cheerleader, Jeff Feig, who along with so much else also gave me opportunities to test out ideas with engaged Jewish audiences each year at the Manhattan JCC's Paul Feig z"l Memorial Tikkun Leyl Shavuot.

Many other colleagues have also helped me think through different aspects of this project. I wish to thank Deborah Lipstadt, Zvi Gitelman, Anna Shternshis, Sasha Senderovich, Shaul Magid, Mark Dollinger, Pam Nadell, Noam Pianko, Josh Tapper, Rebecca Kobrin, Lila Corwin

Berman, Jonathan Dekel-Chen, Maya Balakirsky-Katz, Emily Baran, Jonathan Krasner, and Ted Sasson. In a conversation he may not remember—but I do—Jeffrey Shandler was the first to encourage me to take this up as a book project.

I have been fortunate to be part of the Wexner Graduate Fellowship community for half my life. I would have quit graduate school in the first year had it not been for the WGF support network, and so my thanks again to the Wexner Foundation. Special thanks to Andy Koren for getting me onstage to perform "Leaving Mother Russia" and to Yossi Abramovitz and Jenny Bayer for teaching me the history. While writing, I was doubly blessed with the opportunity, as WGF selection committee chair, to build relationships with colleagues and with a younger generation of fellows. For the past decade of engagement and encouragement, I am grateful to them all. My gratitude especially to Or Mars, Stefanie Zelkind, Elka Abrahamson, Cindy Chazan, J. J. Schacter, Angie Atkins, and Ruthie Warshenbrot. For particular leads, ideas, connections, and contributions, I thank Menachem Kaiser, Matt Williams, Mijal Bitton, Ilana Horwitz, Gilah Kletenik, Yehuda Bernstein, Jeni Friedman, and Alina Gomulina Akselrod.

Steven Tepper and Simon Bronner wrote letters of reference to help me secure grant funding. Many others have also provided materials, information, referrals, or other support. I thank all the activists who took the time to speak with me. I thank my research assistants—Adam Schoenbachler, Andréa Becker, Liz Dultz, Roxana Maria Araş, Ben Tyndall, Katherine Pullen, Ethan Gibbons, and Isaac Stovall. When COVID shut down interlibrary loans, Sarah Benor sent me materials from Hebrew Union College's library. Morey Schapira, Enid Wurtman, and Jacob Birnbaum a"h shared generously from their collections. Long after our formal interviews, activists Glenn Richter, Zev Yaroslavsky, Pam Cohen, Bob Gordon, Zeesy Schnur, Margy-Ruth Davis, Joel and Adele Sandberg, Jerry Goodman, Jonathan Porath, Miriam Rosenblum, and others continued to share generously from their knowledge. Lou Rosenblum a"h hosted me for a memorable dinner with a surprise mutual friend. Ellen Bayer and Rivy Poupko Kletenik provided access to family papers. Marc Brettler and Josh Kanter shared trip reports. Frank and Elaine Parker a"h shared Soviet-era maps, tour books, and stories to help me prepare for my Moscow trip. Mark Kaplan, Irma Kaplan, and Alan Graber took the stage with me in Nashville to share stories from their Soviet travels. Lauren Turek shared files from her research on Soviet-era evangelical activism. Steven Cohen ran demographic data to help me think through contexts. Dovid Margolin supplied me with a steady stream of material on activism in Chabad. Saul Strosberg made shidduchim with Safam and reconnected me with Avi Weiss. Eileen and Jonathan Ruchman saved me from my worst draft titles. Eric and Anne Kiesewetter gave me a writing sanctuary on the Jersey shore. Expert colleagues on H-Judaic and Wexnet answered whatever queries I threw at them. For administrative support, I am especially grateful to Sandy Cherry, Pam Tichenor, and Anne Wall (of beloved memory). For grant-writing assistance, I thank Marion Pratt and Sarazen Kokodynsky. I am indebted to all the archivists and librarians who helped me, especially Valerie Hotchkiss, Pam Morgan, Sue Widmer, Susan Malbin, Melanie Meyers, Kevin Schlottman, Zachary Loeb, Sara Belasco, Adina Anflick, Shulamith Berger, Shuli Boxer Rieser, Kate Dietrick, Suzan Hallgren, Yochai Ben-Ghedalia, and Raquel Ukeles.

Since 2016, I have worn a vintage Anatoly Shcharansky refusenik bracelet as a reminder of what was at stake and as a daily cue to myself to stay focused and write. I thank Lorna Graff for that gift.

My heartfelt thanks to friends who have taken an interest in this project over these many years, among them David and Ruth Abusch-Magder, Daniella Pressner, Ur Barzel and Rachel Goodrich, Ilana Trachtman, Alyse and Mark Lefkowitz, Scott Lasensky, Warren Bass, Tal Daniel, David Umansky, Josh Barton, Sophie Rapoport, and Batsheva Capek. My archival travels were made easier and more fun thanks to the hospitality of friends and family. I am so glad for the time spent with Alyssa Dolman and Bill Anello, Paul Kelner, Nicki and Natan Tiefenbrun, and Ian Brecher and Angela Spera. I thank Bethamie Horowitz, Noam Neusner, Moshe Horn, and Shoshana Kelner (as well as others already mentioned) for sage feedback on drafts. I wish that Aaron Panken a"h, Rami Wernik a"h, Josh Mitnick a"h, and John Janusek a"h were here to receive my gratitude. May their memories bring blessing.

One family has played a special role in this project for a long time. When I headed to the University of Michigan to begin writing in 2016, Emma Rudy Srebnik, then in middle school, emailed me at least once a week to encourage me. Now in 2022, I am writing these words of gratitude at the home of Lynne and Kenny Srebnik on Lake Tansi, to which I have retreated to finish the book. To the three of them, *arigato gozaimashita*.

And to my own family. Thanks first to my mother, Rhoda Schulman, to whom I am grateful beyond words, for so much. Writing about twinning reminded me often of my twinned bar mitzvah in 1982 and the photo of my father, Barry Kelner a"h, kvelling as we raised a toast. Appropriately, he was drinking a White Russian. His love for the Jewish people infuses this work. My enduring thanks to Jared Kelner for sage career guidance; to David and Susan Richman for introducing me to great Russian Jewish writers, Soviet and American; to Rachel Kanter for artistic consulting; to her and to Andrew Ely for conversations that helped me keep this relevant to the Jewish present; to Debbie Kelner for hospitality; to Joan Ely for giving me an entry point to study scientists' activism; and to Avery Kelner for inspiring me to write about the Philadelphia Flyers, who crushed not only the Soviets but, more importantly, the Boston Bruins.

Had I been a faster writer, two men whom I dearly wanted to share this book with would have been alive to receive it. My father-in-law, Gerry Ely a"h, devoured mystery and spy novels, over a thousand of them. He introduced me to John le Carré. I wrote a substantial chunk of this book sitting in the leather chair in his Long Beach Island library. My stepfather, Mort Schulman a"h, was a Jewish educator during the years that the Soviet Jewry movement was active and one for whom the lessons of Jewish solidarity never faded.

To Boaz and Shoshana, I dedicate this book to you as a gift of thanks for your love and confidence and with the wish that it inspires you to keep choosing hope over cynicism and to continue carrying your people's legacy forward with pride.

To Pam, who has put up with so much borscht, Soviet World War II music, and Russian Netflix as this project dragged on: While I indulged in living in the Cold War era, you have been working nonstop to do real good in people's lives here and now, every day. How lucky am I, writing a book about heroes, to actually be living with one. Love of my life, I am glad I flew up to Boston for your birthday.

Lake Tansi
Crossville, Tennessee
July 2022

APPENDIX

SOVIET JEWISH EMIGRATION STATISTICS

TABLE A.1. Jewish emigration from the USSR and former Soviet Union, 1954–2018

Year	Number of emigrants	Year	Number of emigrants	Year	Number of emigrants
1954	53	1976	14,300	1998	71,200
1955	105	1977	16,800	1999	91,300
1956	454	1978	28,900	2000	73,200
1957	149	1979	51,400	2001	54,400
1958	12	1980	21,500	2002	40,300
1959	3	1981	9,500	2003	29,400
1960	60	1982	2,700	2004	22,400
1961	202	1983	1,300	2005	16,300
1962	184	1984	850	2006	9,200
1963	305	1985	1,150	2007	9,300
1964	537	1986	900	2008	7,200
1965	891	1987	8,200	2009	8,100
1966	2,047	1988	19,000	2010	8,200
1967	1,162	1989	69,500	2011	8,300
1968	379	1990	200,200	2012	7,800
1969	2,902	1991	191,000	2013	7,700
1970	1,000	1992	115,000	2014	12,000
1971	13,050	1993	118,600	2015	15,100
1972	31,650	1994	109,800	2016	15,200
1973	34,800	1995	101,700	2017	17,100
1974	20,600	1996	94,500	2018	19,800
1975	13,200	1997	88,500	Total	1,932,500

The 1959 Soviet census counted 2.3 million Jews. Numbers here reflect direct immigration to the West. They do not include the 1955–59 repatriation of Polish Jews who moved to the Soviet Union when the USSR annexed Eastern Poland during World War II. Of these, 18,743 repatriated to Poland, approximately 15,000 of whom used that as an exit route to the West, primarily to Israel.

Estraikh, "Escape through Poland," 311; Plocker, *Expulsion of Jews*, 29–33. *Data sources, 1954–69*: Peretz, *Le combat*, 361, table 2; *1970–2018*: Tolts, "Half Century," 2, table 1. Rounded.

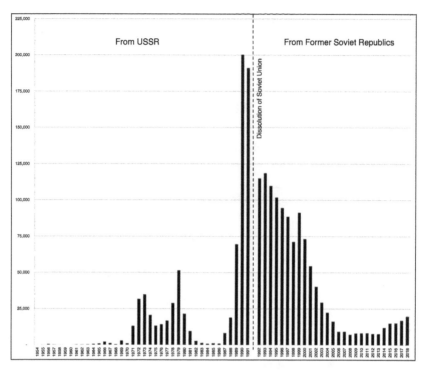

Figure A.1. Jewish emigration from the USSR and former Soviet Union, 1954–2018. *Data sources, 1954–69:* Peretz, *Le combat*, 361, table 2; *1970–2018:* Tolts, "Half Century," 2, table 1. Rounded.

NOTES

Introduction

1. Sharansky, *Fear No Evil*, 170.
2. Martin Luther King Jr., "Addressing Twelve American Jewish Communities by Telephone Hookup from Atlanta, Georgia," audio recording, 1 December 1966, NCSJ b.369 f.M10, https://archives.cjh.org.
3. "5000 Jews."
4. Beckerman, *When They Come*, 55–60.
5. Herbert S. Caron to Dear Friend, 31 March 1964, CCSA b.3 f.70; CCSA, "American Conference on Soviet Jewry, Washington April 5–6," memorandum, March 1964, CCSA b.3 f.70; "Washington Conference"; "Proposed Additional Key Resolution for Conference Follow-Up," April 1964, CCSA b.3 f.70; Orbach, *American Movement*, 25–26; Rosenblum and Rosenblum, "Involvement"; Beckerman, *When They Come*, 69–71.
6. Halevi, "Jacob Birnbaum," 33.
7. "Soviet U.N. Mission."
8. Frey, "Challenging," 40–41, 70, 76–77; Feingold, *"Silent No More,"* 88–89.
9. Dudziak, *Cold War Civil Rights*; Krenn, "Token Diplomacy."
10. SSSJ, *Save Soviet Jewry*, 7, 26–27.
11. Morse, *While Six Million Died*; Wyman, *Abandonment of the Jews*.
12. On a 1951 American Jewish Committee report, see N. Cohen, *Not Free to Desist*, 498–99. On 1956 Rabbinical Council of America and New York Board of Rabbis delegations, see chapter 3.
13. Beckerman, *When They Come*, 64–68.
14. On Israel's reasons for not acting sooner, see Bialer, *Israeli Foreign Policy*, 177.
15. Scholars debate the degree to which the Western campaign was a state-mobilized movement. Peretz emphasizes Nativ's guiding hand, speaking of "une campagne américaine guidée par Israël" (*Le combat*, 77–111). Kochavi, "Idealpolitik in Disguise," takes a similar position. Hägel and Peretz refer to diaspora Jewish movement organizations as "State *Influenced* Non-Governmental Organizations" rather than state *controlled* ("States and Transnational Actors"; emphasis mine). Cooper, *British Campaign*, documents Nativ's role in prompting British activism. In contrast, Lazin, *Struggle for Soviet Jewry*, shows Jewish American conflict with Nativ against Israeli wishes to steer emigrants to Israel. Kurz, *Jewish Internationalism*, presents Israel as losing control of a movement it had created and funded. Activists have engaged the debate as

partisans. Nativ's former director, Nehemiah Levanon, in his memoirs, *Haqod: Nativ*, presents American Jewish organizations as implementing ideas devised by Nativ. The UCSJ's Louis Rosenblum argues that although Nativ tried to control the movement, grassroots activists charted an independent course, provoking Nativ's ire (Rosenblum, "Control of Soviet Jewry Movement"). On state-mobilized movements generally, see Ekiert, Perry, and Yan, *Ruling by Other Means*. On global Jewish politics as essentially anarchic, see Waxman and Lasensky, "Jewish Foreign Policy."

16 Orbach, *American Movement*, 20–22. At SSSJ's founding meeting, Birnbaum set out a four-pillared strategy, described by Halevi as (1) "rouse a dormant American Jewry, working at the grassroots level, while simultaneously pressuring the establishment to transform the Conference on Soviet Jewry into an effective organization"; (2) "humiliate the Soviet Union"; (3) "pressure Washington into becoming the active protector and defender of Soviet Jews"; and (4) "boost" Soviet Jews' morale ("Jacob Birnbaum," 33–34). According to Freda Birnbaum, Jacob's wife and fellow activist, rousing American Jewry became an end in itself: "Part of the purpose was to galvanize Jews around something Jewish" (Fedeski, *Culture Is Not Apolitical*, audio excerpt #1, 1:28).

17 The attempt to use US trade preferences as a lever for changing Soviet policy was initiated by Senator Henry Jackson and his staff. The UCSJ embraced the idea enthusiastically, the NCSJ reluctantly. Beckerman, *When They Come*, 276–310.

18 Levin, "Before Soviet Jewry's Happy Ending"; Dekel-Chen, "Faith Meets Politics," 222–26.

19 Orbach, *American Movement*, 158–61.

20 On interfaith coalition building, see Lazin, *American Christians*.

21 While he was in Russia, Anatoly Shcharansky was known in the West by his Russian name. After he emigrated to Israel, Western press referred to him by his Hebrew name, Natan Sharansky. Here, I primarily use the refuseniks' Russian names, as that is how the public campaigns to secure their freedom referred to them at the time.

22 NCSJ, *Freedom Rally*; "More Than 200,000 Rally."

23 Peretz, *Le combat*, 361–62. For annual emigration figures, see the appendix.

24 Kochavi, "Insights Abandoned"; Lazin, *Struggle*; Schwartz, *Henry Kissinger*, 275–82. Jackson initiated the amendment; Jewish American activism gave it wings.

25 For Schultz's telling of Gorbachev's frustration with his embrace of the issue, see Bialis, *Refusenik*, 1:35:57.

26 Politburo transcripts record Soviet premier Leonid Brezhnev and KGB chief Yuri Andropov discussing token concessions to preempt Jackson-Vanik's passage (see minutes of 20 March 1973 meeting, in Morozov, *Documents*, 170–76). Debate over Jackson-Vanik's efficacy figures heavily in movement historiography. J. Goldberg, *Jewish Power*, 163–76; Korey, "Jackson-Vanik"; Goldman, "Jackson-Vanik"; Nathans, "Murray Friedman"; Dekel-Chen, "Faith Meets Politics," 222–26; Levin, "Before Soviet Jewry's Happy Ending."

27 Tolts, "Half Century"; Ro'i, "Achievements," 107.

28 Over 50 percent of all emigrants in 1990 and 1991 were Jews and their family members. Data compiled from Heitman, *Soviet Emigration in 1990*; and Zayanchovskaya, "*Razvitie vneshnikh migratsionnykh sviazeĭ Rossii*"; Tolts, "Half Century." Sadowski-Smith, *New Immigrant Whiteness*, compares and contrasts Jewish and non-Jewish FSU (former Soviet Union) emigrants' postmigration experiences in the US.

29 There were approximately 1,480,000 Jews in the USSR in 1989, half that in its successor states by 1994, and approximately 248,000 in 2019, one-sixth of the 1989 figure. Tolts, "Half Century," 14, 21; Schmelz and DellaPergola, "World Jewish Population, 1994," 453.

30 Tolts, "Half Century"; Tolts, "Demography"; Ro'i, "Achievements," 107; J. Gross, "Over 15,000 Have Immigrated." The post-Soviet era has also seen return migration as well as dual residencies. About 12 percent of the post-1989 Soviet emigrants to Israel had left the country by 2017, half to states of the former Soviet Union. Khanin, *From Russia to Israel–and Back?* During the Soviet era, the number of those returning was much smaller. A study of remigration to Soviet Moldavia found several hundred applications from Soviet Jews in Israel, almost all of them rejected. Nicorici, "Becoming a Soviet Citizen."

31 Shneer, "Saving Soviet Jews"; Remennick, *Russian Jews*; Remennick, "Professional Identities in Transit," 159; Gold, *From the Workers' State*; Zeltzer-Zubida and Kasinitz, "Next Generation"; Kobrin and Oppenheim, "Long Silent Revolution"; Tapper, "'This Is Who I Would Become'"; DellaPergola, "World Jewish Population, 2019"; Galili, *Other Tribe*; Tabarovsky, "Russian-Speaking Israelis."

32 Veidlinger, *In the Midst*; Finkelman, "Ghetto, Gulag, *Geulah*"; Brym, "*Perestroyka*, Public Opinion, and *Pamyat*."

33 None of the thaws resulted in a blanket liberalization of Soviet emigration policy. During the 1970s détente, only Jews (approx. 250,000 between 1971 and 1980), ethnic Germans (approx. 64,000), and Armenians (approx. 34,000) were allowed out. Almost no other Soviets enjoyed the option to leave. With glasnost, Mikhail Gorbachev restarted the emigration of Jews, Germans, and Armenians and expanded permission to approximately eighteen thousand Evangelical Christians and Pentecostals. The latter may have been a gesture to activism by Ronald Reagan's political base, the American Christian Right, which had taken up the cause of persecuted Christians. (Christian efforts focused less on emigration than on religious freedoms. Their theological imperative was evangelizing, not exodus; bringing Christ's word into the Soviet Union, not Christ's faithful out of it. Evangelical emigration came amid a religious liberalization that extended even to especially persecuted Jehovah's Witnesses.) Turek, *To Bring the Good News*; Baran, *Dissent on the Margins*.

34 The "Soviet Jew" of American Jewish imagination is an overgeneralization based on the mistaken assumption that refusenik leaders were representative of the Soviet Jewish population. They were not. They were an activist vanguard. The gap between the imagined "Soviet Jew" of American and Israeli discourse and the self-understandings of actual Jewish people from the Soviet Union is an enduring theme in research. Remennick, *Russian Jews*, sees the gap as responsible for a "crisis of mutual failed expectations" when the communities encountered each other in person after the mass emigration. The crisis was probably inevitable, as Western activism was premised on building solidarity through imagined relationships. Encounters among real people revealed the limits of imagination and changed the nature of the relationships (Polletta, *Inventing*). Jewish American social service literature treated the issue as a challenge facing resettlement efforts. Showstack, "Perspectives on the Resettlement." Writing on Soviet-born Jewish American novelists, Senderovich critiques the term *Soviet Jew*, arguing that it inherently represented Jewish people from the USSR as deficient and in need of Western beneficence ("Scenes"). Awareness

that Western discourse about "Soviet Jewry" typically overshadows Soviet Jews' own accounts of themselves informs other émigré studies (Sadowski-Smith, *New Immigrant Whiteness*) as well as oral histories of Jewish life in the former Soviet Union (Veidlinger, *In the Shadow*; Shternshis, *When Sonia Met Boris*).

35 This is common in successful social movements: activists secure collective benefits not only for themselves but for others uninvolved in the movement. Amenta et al., "Political Consequences," 290.

36 Article 13.2 of the Universal Declaration of Human Rights reads, "Everyone has the right to leave any country, including his own, and to return to his country."

37 A complete analysis of the movement's political outcomes has yet to be written. Of the four possible outcomes of social movement activism identified in Gamson's *Strategy of Social Protest—full response, preemption, co-optation*, and *collapse*—the Soviet Jewry movement ended with *full response*, acceptance of the challenger by its antagonists and receipt by movement beneficiaries of the advantages sought for them. My overview has tried to take account of Amenta, *When Movements Matter*, which presents three questions for assessing a social movement's contribution to policy outcomes: "What is the meaning of success?" "What else matters?" and "How can you tell?" To the first, I have offered a multidimensional approach against reductionist claims that hinge on Jackson-Vanik, which was but one strategy at one moment in a decades-long campaign. To the second, I have emphasized that the main external factors—strategic uses of the Jewish emigration issue by political leaders in the US and Soviet governments—were themselves *consequences* of activists having made Jewish emigration a Cold War issue in the first place. To the third, I have pointed to both longitudinal and comparative evidence showing a hundredfold increase in Jewish emigration from the 1960s to the 1970s with no corresponding leap in emigration for Soviet citizens generally.

38 In the pages ahead, I will use the term "Soviet *Jewry* activists" in its colloquial sense to refer to American and other Western activists in the campaign to free Soviet Jews. I reserve the term "Soviet *Jewish* activists" for refusenik leaders in the USSR itself. On activism by Jews in the USSR, see Ro'i, *Struggle*; Ro'i, *Jewish Movement*; Ro'i and Beker, *Jewish Culture*; and Morozova, *Anatomiia Otkaza*. For first-person testimonies from Soviet Jewish activists, see the memoirs analyzed in Hoffman, "Voices from the Inside." (Some refusenik memoirs are also covered in Nathans, "Talking Fish.") For an alternative view of first-person testimonies that argues against seeing Soviet Jews' Jewish engagements through the lens of political activism, see Shayduk-Immerman, "Feeling Alive." Zisserman-Brodsky, "'Jews of Silence'—the 'Jews of Hope'—the 'Jews of Triumph,'" explains the competing "Zionist" and Sovietological "totalitarian" paradigms in the historiography of the movement in the USSR itself. On Israel's role, see Levanon, *Haqod*; Levanon, "Israel's Role"; Peretz, *Le combat*; and Pinkus, "Israeli Activity." For the US campaign, see Orbach, *American Movement*; Feingold, *"Silent No More"*; and Lazin, *Struggle*. The most comprehensive integrated history is Beckerman, *When They Come*. The movement was also active in other Western countries. On Canada, see Eisen, *Count Us In*; and Avrich-Skapinker, "Canadian Jewish Involvement." On Australia, see Lipski and Rutland, *Let My People Go*. On the UK, see Cooper, *British Campaign*; Gerlis, *Those Wonderful Women*; Orbach, "British Soviet Jewry Movement"; and Rich, "Activist Challenge."

39 Beckerman, *When They Come*.

40 Peretz, *Le combat*; Lazin, *Struggle*; Feingold, "Silent No More"; Kochavi, "Insights Abandoned."
41 This book participates in the "cultural turn" in Cold War studies, which seeks to "de-centre the focus of attention . . . away from government and diplomacy, towards society and culture . . . and to establish the Cold War 'home front' as a sub-field in its own right." Major and Mitter, *Across the Blocs*, 2.
42 Researchers in social movement studies use the unfortunate term *micromobilization* to refer to tactics designed to engage supporters. This jargon says exactly the opposite of what it means. Activists sought to mobilize millions. There is nothing "micro" about that. I therefore stick with the more accurate colloquialism "mass mobilization."
43 On movements as agents of cultural production, see Van Dyke and Taylor, "Cultural Outcomes"; Isaac, "Movement of Movements"; Eyerman and Jamison, *Social Movements*; and Reed, *Art of Protest*. On the notion of cultural production generally, see Peterson and Anand, "Production of Culture Perspective."
44 Label A. Katz, "AJCSJ Inaugural Address," 5 April 1964, NCSJ b.1 f.1, 8–11. The statistics were most likely provided by Israel's Nativ.
45 During the Cold War, Western observers had a tendency to project post–World War II state-sponsored antisemitism back to the first decades of the USSR. The issue is complicated. Veidlinger, *Moscow State Yiddish Theater*, sets forth the debates over dating, intentionalism, the extent and limits of totalitarian control, Lenin's and Stalin's stances, and whether to characterize denationalized Soviet Jewish culture as Jewish. He notes the paradox: "In tandem with . . . anti-religious and anti-nationalist campaigns, a flourishing of secular Jewish cultural life emerged in the Soviet Union that has largely been ignored by foreign observers" (5). To appreciate the extent of this cultural life, consider David Shneer's observation: "In the 1920s, the Soviet Union was the only country in the world to have state-sponsored Yiddish language publishing houses, writers' groups, courts, city councils, and a school system." "Having It Both Ways," 377.
46 Katz, "Address," 10.
47 Slezkine, *Jewish Century*, 299. Similar processes unfolded across the Soviet bloc on slightly different timelines and with variations by country. On the Czechoslovakian experience, see Labendz, "Lectures, Murder, and a Phony Terrorist." On Poland, see Plocker, *Expulsion of Jews*.
48 Slezkine, *Jewish Century*, 299.
49 In his 1961 poem "Babi Yar," the Russian poet Yevgeny Yevtushenko famously criticized his country's erasure of Jewish victimhood—the government's refusal to acknowledge that Jews were targeted because they were Jews.
50 Slezkine, *Jewish Century*, 300.
51 Pinkus, "Soviet Campaigns.'"
52 Ro'i, *Struggle*, 45–53.
53 Although the Bolsheviks rejected the idea of nation as reactionary, they adopted a "nationalist in form, socialist in content" policy as a pragmatic accommodation to disseminate revolutionary values in a multinational empire.
54 Slezkine, *Jewish Century*, 298; Estraikh, "Life, Death, and Afterlife"; Saivetz and Woods, *Night of the Murdered Poets*; Colorado Committee of Concern for Soviet Jewry, "Memorial to the Murdered Writers and Poets," n.d. (ca. 1980), CASJ b.25 f.10.

55 Brandenberger, "Stalin's Last Crime?"
56 Fainberg, *Les discriminés*.
57 Rouvier, "Documents," 137.
58 Gitelman, *Jewish Nationality*. On the persistence of rural Jewish life in the USSR, see Veidlinger, *In the Shadow*.
59 Fainberg, *Les discriminés*.
60 Ro'i, "Move from Russia," 144, 51. For first-person accounts of occupational consequences of Jewishness, for better and worse, see Shternshis, *When Sonia Met Boris*, 93–187.
61 Katz, "Address," 6; Korey, *Soviet Cage*, 44–45. The ratio is for Russia, Ukraine, and the Baltics, where most Soviet Jews lived.
62 Katz, "Address," 11.
63 Shinbaum, "Mobilizing America," 176.
64 On emigration versus cultural rights, see Kurz, *Jewish Internationalism*, 140–43. On Jackson-Vanik and the "Freedom of Choice" debate, see Lazin, *Struggle*; and Rutland, "Conflicting Visions."
65 For dueling "establishment" and "grassroots" perspectives, contrast Chernin, "Making Soviet Jewry an Issue," with Naftalin, "Activist Movement."
66 On the convergence of practice across organizations in an institutional field, see DiMaggio and Powell, "Iron Cage Revisited."
67 On the notion that movements are carried by social movement organizations (SMOs), see McCarthy and Zald, "Resource Mobilization."
68 Some tellings reduce the divide to a generational conflict. This fails to explain why the married-with-children suburbanites running the grassroots councils were locked in the same conflict with the establishment Conference as were the student activists of SSSJ.
69 Nativ personnel sometimes attended Conference meetings. Contrast this with Rosenblum's curt dismissal of Nativ officer Yoram Dinstein's threats: "Yoram, shut up." Lazin, *Struggle*, 182; Beckerman, *When They Come*, 223–24.
70 Others, including Nativ and the theologian Abraham Joshua Heschel, also pressed organizational leaders to act.
71 Orbach, *American Movement*, 47–48, 61–65; Beckerman, *When They Come*, 219, 278. The Israeli government also pushed the AJCSJ's reorganization. Kochavi, "Idealpolitik in Disguise," 554–55; Jerry Goodman, interviewed by Shaul Kelner, 5 September 2019.
72 Gerlis, *Those Wonderful Women*; Eisen, *Count Us In*; Spiegel, *Triumph*, 69, 316–18; David Selikowitz, interviewed by Shaul Kelner, 26 July 2019; Beckerman, *When They Come*, 220–21.
73 Magid, *Meir Kahane*; Dollinger, *Black Power*.
74 Wolf, *Dyedushka*; Astor and Neustadt, *Underground*; Blau, *Learn Torah*.
75 On the term *Soviet Jewry* as a discursive formation, see Senderovich, "Scenes."
76 Kelner, "People-to-People."
77 Staub, *Torn*; Dollinger, *Quest*; Dollinger, *Black Power*; Lederhendler, *New York Jews*, 186–96; Orenstein, "'Let My People Go!'"; Kranson, *Ambivalent Embrace*, 143–45; Halevi, "Jacob Birnbaum"; Magid, *Meir Kahane*; Kelner, "Ritualized Protest." Caveats are offered by Fedeski, "Symbolism and Strategy," esp. 27–32, and Kelner, "'Uneventful' 1968." On movements influencing each other, see, e.g., Freeman and Johnson,

Waves of Protest; McAdam, "Initiator and Spin-Off Movements"; McAdam, Tarrow, and Tilly, *Dynamics*; Tarrow, *Democracy and Disorder*; Tarrow, "Cycles of Collective Action"; Meyer and Whittier, "Social Movement Spillover"; and Whittier, "Consequences of Social Movements."

78 SSSJ, *Save Soviet Jewry*, 5, quoted in Orenstein, "'Let My People Go!,'" 73.
79 Halevi, "Jacob Birnbaum"; Orenstein, "'Let My People Go!'"; Ferziger, "Outside the Shul"; Ferziger, *Beyond Sectarianism*; Kelner, "Ritualized Protest"; Kelner, "'Uneventful' 1968"; Lederhendler, *New York Jews*, 186–96; Staub, *Torn*; Staub, *Jewish 1960s*; Dollinger, *Quest*; Dollinger, *Black Power*; Magid, *Meir Kahane*; Kranson, *Ambivalent Embrace*, 143–45; Barnett, *Star and the Stripes*.
80 Feingold, "Silent No More"; Dekel-Chen, "Faith Meets Politics"; Golden, *O Powerful Western Star!*
81 Beckerman, *When They Come*, 48–49, 99–113, 150–51, 250.
82 Beckerman, 13–16, 39–41; Spiegel, *Triumph*; Feingold, "Silent No More"; Altshuler, *From Exodus*; Halevi, *Memoirs*; A. Weiss, *Open Up*, 37–39. On emotions as motivators of activism, see Kemper, "Structural Approach."
83 Magid, *Meir Kahane*, connects Kahane's Soviet Jewry activism to his broader anticommunism. Kelner, "'Uneventful' 1968," highlights the movement's grounding in Cold War liberalism.
84 Lazin, *Struggle*; Kochavi, "Insights Abandoned"; J. Goldberg, *Jewish Power*, 163–76; Korey, "Jackson-Vanik"; Goldman, "Jackson-Vanik"; Dekel-Chen, "Faith Meets Politics," 222–26; Levin, "Before Soviet Jewry's Happy Ending."
85 On the movement as a Cold War human rights campaign, see Loeffler, *Rooted Cosmopolitans*; and Galchinsky, *Jews and Human Rights*. Against classifying it as a human rights campaign, see Kurz, *Jewish Internationalism*, 138–63. As a movement entangled with but distinct from human rights activism, see Nathans, "Refuseniks"; and Nathans, "Talking Fish," 583n11. I believe the opposition presents a false dichotomy.
86 Ro'i, *Jewish Movement*; Levanon, *Haqod*; Kosharovsky, *We Are Jews Again*.
87 Israelis called this "dropout," Americans, "freedom of choice." Lazin, *Struggle*.
88 Essays in Friedman and Chernin, *Second Exodus*, offer competing perspectives from the American "establishment" and "grassroots" factions, as well as from Israel's Nativ. Altshuler, *From Exodus*, revisits movement debates from a grassroots vantage point.
89 E.g., Halevi, "Jacob Birnbaum"; Orenstein, "'Let My People Go!'"
90 E.g., Magid, *Meir Kahane*; Barnett, *Star and the Stripes*, 172–94.
91 Staub, *Torn*, 194–231.
92 On the way that multidimensional contexts constrain and enable strategic action, see Jasper and Polletta, "Cultural Context."
93 This problem may be endemic to research on social movements. Reviewing research on LGBTQ+ activism, Coley finds similar neglect of demographic diversity in favor of studying politicized youth. Coley, *Gay on God's Campus*, 64–66, 145–46.
94 Sharansky, *Fear No Evil*, 218.
95 Liner notes to Theodore Bikel's album of "Jewish Underground Songs from Soviet Russia" typify the rhetorical positioning: "Those who would use Soviet Jewry as yet another stick in general anti-Communist crusades should go elsewhere in their quest. For the objective of all responsible action in this area is not to oppose

Soviet foreign policies or gather debating points in East-West confrontations but solely to support the aspirations of Soviet Jewry in their quest for freedom." Bikel, *Silent No More*. Kahane's radical flank organization was an outlier, explicitly framing JDL action as part of a broader anticommunism. Magid, *Meir Kahane*. The avoidance of anticommunism in the 1970s contrasted with Jewish American organizations' embrace of anticommunism during the 1950s Red Scare prior to the Soviet Jewry movement. N. Cohen, *Not Free to Desist*, 498–99; Frey, "Challenging," 8–14. Concerned that anticommunists would coopt the fight against Soviet antisemitism, opponents of capitalism in the Jewish New Left formulated critiques that equated American and Soviet Jews as victims of their economic systems: "Those of us who believe that here in America *we* are free are deceived more brutally than our Sisters and Brothers in the Soviet Union." Quoted in Kranson, *Ambivalent Embrace*, 144.

96 The notion that Jews were leaving only for Israel was a convenient fiction. After émigrés arrived at transit stations in Vienna and Rome, most opted to change their final destination to America. Permitting the direct exit of hundreds of thousands of Soviet citizens to the United States would have been politically problematic for the Kremlin. It allowed emigration only under the pretense of family reunification in Israel. Nativ organized fake invitations from nonexistent family members, which the Soviets knowingly accepted. Levanon, *Haqod*, 390; Rozner, *Bintiv*, 54–55.

97 In demanding that the Soviet government respect its own laws, Western Soviet Jewry activists echoed calls by dissidents in the Soviet movement for democratic reform. Keys and Burke, "Human Rights," 493.

98 Irene Manekofsky, "Soviet Jewish Emigration, the Dissident Movement, and American Jewish Organizations," attachment circulated with UCSJ *Alert* newsletter, 13 December 1977, WCSJ b.14 f.2, 2.

99 The reluctance was informed both by strategic considerations and by the memory of Ukrainian and Lithuanian nationalist collaboration with the Nazis.

100 This points to a gap between the Western campaign and the movement in the USSR. In the Soviet Union, Jewish activists were enmeshed in the broader dissident, nationalist, and religious revivalist social movement fields. Ro'i and Rubenstein, "Human Rights"; Fürst, "Born under the Same Star"; Finkelman, "Ghetto, Gulag, Geulah." On Nativ's distancing from the democratic dissidents, including Shcharansky, see Peretz, *Le combat*, 267; and Beckerman, *When They Come*, 391.

101 May, *Homeward Bound*. More recently, intellectual historians have also taken it up. Menand, *Free World*.

102 May, *Homeward Bound*; Whitfield, *Culture of the Cold War*; Herzog, *Spiritual-Industrial Complex*.

103 Dudziak, *Cold War Civil Rights*.

104 Brinkley, "Illusion of Unity."

105 Filene, "'Cold War Culture,'" 157.

106 Others have argued for the plural to expand the concept to Europe and the Soviet Union. Major and Mitter, *Across the Blocs*; Vowinckel, Payk, and Lindenberger, *Cold War Cultures*.

107 They also saw it as endangering Israeli Jews. The Soviet government framed its domestic campaigns against Jewish culture as a fight against "Zionism." Persecution

of Jews at home was accompanied, in foreign policy, by patronage of military and diplomatic offensives against Israel.

108 Rottenberg, "To Russia with Levis"; Wiesel, *Jews of Silence*; Safam, "Leaving Mother Russia."

1. Illuminate the Past and Present

1 "Editorial Note"; Korey, "Right to Leave."
2 Kelner, "Commentary"; Martin, "William Korey"; Golden, *O Powerful Western Star!*, 179–80; Korey, *Soviet Cage*.
3 Beckerman, *When They Come*, 52–55; Peretz, *Le combat*, 81–84.
4 Decter, "Status of the Jews"; Beckerman, *When They Come*, 49, 55–60.
5 For the committee's sponsors, see Academic Committee on Soviet Jewry, "National Academic Conference," conference packet, 11–12 May 1968, MDP b.1 f.1. On Nativ's role in creating the committee, see Levanon, *Haqod*, 200–201; Rosenblum, "Control of Soviet Jewry Movement," 2, 9.
6 Fuchs, *Political Behavior*; Sklare, *Jews*; Sklare and Greenblum, *Jewish Identity*.
7 Woocher, *Sacred Survival*. Works of the era devoting chapters to Israel but only providing scant mentions of Soviet Jewry include Liebman, *Ambivalent American Jew*; S. Cohen, *American Modernity*; Fein, *Where Are We?*; Neusner, *Stranger at Home*; and Neusner, *Israel in America*. Support for Israel was a greater source of Jewish unity in that era than in the twenty-first century. Waxman, *Trouble in the Tribe*; Sasson, *New American Zionism*.
8 Horowitz, "Reframing the Study"; D. Kaufman, "Place of Judaism." Exemplary of the survey demographic approach are the National Jewish Population Studies of 1990 and 2001 and the Pew Research Center's 2013 and 2020 portraits of Jewish Americans. See Kosmin et al., *Highlights of the CJF 1990 NJPS*; and Pew Research Center, *Portrait of Jewish Americans*. Exemplary of the interview-identity approach is Kelman et al., "Social Self." Combining the two approaches are Horowitz, *Connections and Journeys*; and Cohen and Eisen, *Jew Within*.
9 In offering this corrective, I am not ignoring ethnographic research that explains Jewish culture as the product of social interaction. (I even wrote one: Kelner, *Tours That Bind*.) Nor am I ignoring social histories, as the bibliography shows. I am arguing that in the sociology of American Jews, the field's animating debate since the 1990s has been structured around a macro-micro dichotomy, and this binary is inadequate for an understanding of the major trends and dynamics in Jewish American life. Meso-level analyses are required. For an example of meso-level research as an effective intervention into an ongoing debate that had been framed as a matter of demographics and identity (this one over Jewish American attachments to Israel), see Sasson, *New American Zionism*. Not coincidentally, Sasson emphasizes mass mobilization to explain the creation of a public culture. See also Sasson, "Mass Mobilization."
10 On tactics as performance, see Juris, "Embodying Protest." As generative of emotion, see Van Ness and Summers-Effler, "Emotions in Social Movements."
11 For examples, see Balin, "Modern Transformation"; and Shternshis, *Soviet and Kosher*, 27–34.
12 McAdam, "Tactical Innovation"; McCammon, "'Out of the Parlors'"; McCammon, *U.S. Women's Jury Movements*; Meyer, "Protest and Political Opportunities"; Meyer

and Staggenborg, "Movements, Countermovements"; O'Hearn, "Repression and Solidary Cultures"; Walker, Martin, and McCarthy, "Confronting the State."
13 Jasper, *Art of Moral Protest*, 229–50; Polletta, *It Was like a Fever*, 53–81. This literature is reviewed in Polletta and Jasper, "Collective Identity"; Snow, "Collective Identity"; and Einwohner, Reger, and Myers, "Identity Work."
14 Rev. John Steinbruck, a leader in the interfaith coalition for Soviet Jews, did organize an Easter Sunday freedom walk and church adoptions of Soviet Jewish prisoners for Lent. Lazin, *American Christians*, 77.
15 Jasper, *Art of Moral Protest*, 240–48; Zald and McCarthy, "Social Movement Industries."
16 On congregations as resources, see C. Smith, *Disruptive Religion*; and Zald and McCarthy, "Religious Groups as Crucibles." On the Black church as an institutional base for civil rights activism, see McAdam, *Political Process*, 98–100, 25–41; and Morris, *Origins*.
17 Magid, *Meir Kahane*; A. Weiss, *Open Up*.
18 Tilly, *From Mobilization to Revolution*; Tilly, "Contentious Repertoires." Tilly was pushing against the once-prevalent notion that social movements were irrational. He introduced the concept of repertoire to show that "far from the image we sometimes hold of mindless crowds, people tend to act within known limits." Tilly, *Contentious French*, 390.
19 *Oxford English Dictionary Online*, s.v. "Repertoire, n.," www.oed.com.
20 On the power of metaphors to constrain thinking, the classic statement is Lakoff and Johnson, *Metaphors We Live By*.
21 Reviews of the literature make this clear. The authors of a 2004 *Companion to Social Movements* frame the question as "What factors influence a social movement's *selection* of tactics?" (Taylor and Van Dyke, "'Get Up, Stand Up'"). The authors of the *Companion*'s 2018 version pose the problem as "how best to explain the *decisions* over tactics and strategy that social movements make." One of their answers: "Actors *choose* tactical forms on the basis that they already know how to perform them" (Doherty and Hayes, "Tactics and Strategic Action"). Even critiques of repertoire analysis remain locked in the implication that tactics are chosen, not invented. "Why do protestors *choose* the tactical courses they do? . . . Explaining how protestors *choose* from among available tactics is often reduced to explaining the range of tactics available in the repertoire" (Jasper, *Art of Moral Protest*, 234–36; all emphases added).
22 On the field's relative silence on questions of how innovation happens, see Crossley, *Making Sense of Social Movements*, 129; Della Porta, "Repertoires of Contention"; and Polletta, *It Was like a Fever*, 55. Repertoire literature that has taken up the question of invention has mostly concerned itself with identifying contexts that lead to innovation, not unpacking the process of innovation itself. Researchers have found that new tactical innovation typically occurs at the beginning of protest cycles and then settles into a routine with only minor adaptations at the "perimeter" of major tactical forms (Tilly, "Contentious Repertoires"; McAdam, "Initiator and Spin-Off Movements"; Tarrow, "Cycles of Collective Action"; McAdam, Tarrow, and Tilly, *Dynamics*, 48–50, 138). Losses spur new innovations as part of the chess match with targets (McAdam, "Tactical Innovation"; McCammon, "Out of the Parlors"). Internal features that foster or constrain innovation include the degree of formal organization (Piven and Cloward, *Poor People's Movements*) and the amount of

internal debate among movement groups (McCammon, *U.S. Women's Jury Movements*). Wang and Soule, in "Tactical Innovation," identify features of protest events that encourage new tactics or novel recombinations of existing tactics.

23 For the contribution of human rights activism to the collapse of the Soviet bloc, see Thomas, *Helsinki Effect*; and Snyder, *Human Rights Activism*.

24 Full-text searches in the journals turn up zero hits. Other disciplines have treated it, so sociology's blind spot is hard to explain. One might expect scholars to have seized on it as a theoretically rich case, given that it queers many categories—simultaneously of the left *and* of the right, nationalist *and* human rights oriented, citizen based *and* state supported, and so on. Or maybe this is why it has been ignored—as it is easier to declare it a case of the opposite category from the one researchers are interested in rather than open the can of worms and rethink the categories. If so, this breaks with the discipline's origins. Marx, Weber, Durkheim, and others treated Jewish cases as useful tools to think with precisely because of "the way that Jews have straddled, confounded, or evaded the prevailing divisions of the social world" (C. Goldberg, *Modernity and the Jews*, 106). On the flip side, humanities-based Jewish studies' treatments of this and other Jewish social movements have rarely drawn on the knowledge amassed by social movement studies. For an exception, see Levine, "Problematics of Jewish Collective Action."

25 Becker is as unsparing in his critique of the problem as he is innovative in his solutions. See his *Tricks of the Trade*, 90–112, 120–28.

26 Peterson, "Production of Culture"; Peterson, "Why 1955?"; Peterson and Anand, "Production of Culture Perspective." Others have demonstrated the utility of Peterson's framework for analyzing social movements as agents of cultural production. See Isaac, "Movements, Aesthetics, and Markets."

27 Writing this at Vanderbilt University, where Peterson did his field-defining work, I am acutely aware that my approach draws more heavily from other streams in the sociology of culture. If Pete is looking down, I hope he will forgive me.

28 Foucault, *Birth of the Clinic*, ix–xiv, 89–90, 109; Foucault, *Discipline and Punish*, 27–28. See also Urry and Larsen, *Tourist Gaze 3.0*, 1–2. Foucault's notion of the gaze has been adopted in feminist and postcolonial theory, typically with a negative connotation (i.e., the "male gaze," the "colonial gaze"). It has entered tourism theory with a neutral, perhaps even positive, valence (the "tourist gaze"). I intend no value connotation when using the term *gaze* and proffer it here for its analytic power. In the present case, the mobilizing gaze served as a force for empowerment and liberation, but one can imagine instances in which it might not.

29 If we exchange Foucault for another French theorist, Pierre Bourdieu, we could also call this an *activist habitus*. Bourdieu, *Outline of a Theory of Practice*.

30 For more elaboration on the mobilizing gaze, see Kelner, "Bureaucratization of Ritual Innovation"; and Kelner, "Where Is the Next Soviet Jewry Movement?," 195–98.

31 On endogenous versus exogenous explanation, see J. Kaufman, "Endogenous Explanation"; and Lieberson, *Matter of Taste*.

32 Davis, *How Artifacts Afford*, 6. For an earlier treatment of affordances in the sociology of American Jews (specifically the affordances of tourism as a mode of engagement with Israel), see Kelner, *Tours That Bind*.

33 On path dependencies in tactical development, see Blee, *Democracy in the Making*, 32–41.

34 Davis, *How Artifacts Afford*.
35 Galili, *Other Tribe*; Tabarovsky, "Russian-Speaking Israelis."
36 Van Dyke and Taylor, "Cultural Outcomes."
37 Attempts to address cultural consequences that reverberate after mobilizations end have focused on collective memory (Isaac, "Movement of Movements") and long-term biographical consequences (McAdam, *Freedom Summer*; McAdam, "Biographical Consequences"; Cornfield et al., "Occupational Activism"). I am convinced by Eyerman and Jamison's argument in *Social Movements* that movements are, by definition, temporary moments. Accordingly, I consider the Soviet Jewry movement's post-1991 legacies to be *after*effects distinct from the mobilization itself.
38 The three-decade-plus trajectory of the concept can be traced through Snow et al., "Frame Alignment Processes" (1986); Benford and Snow, "Framing Processes" (2000; esp. pp. 623–25 on framing's explicitly discursive and strategic character); and Snow et al., "Emergence, Development, and Future" (2014).
39 Eyerman and Jamison, *Social Movements*, 55. Eyerman and Jamison speak specifically of *cognitive* praxis, which is too restrictive. Haluza-DeLay, in "A Theory of Practice for Social Movements," offers a critique. My treatment expands beyond the *cognitive* to view movements as constituted by additional forms of praxis—*emotional* and *embodied*. Social movements create new ways of feeling and acting as well as knowing.
40 Eyerman and Jamison narrowed this further, emphasizing a smaller group of "movement intellectuals" as creators of movement culture. Eyerman and Jamison, *Social Movements*, 94–119.
41 Social movements scholar T. V. Reed writes, "In my view, the best cultural studies work has attended to three interrelated levels of analysis: cultural production, the texts produced, and audience reception of those texts." *Art of Protest*, xvii. See also Childress, *Under the Cover*. I would add that analyses should attend to ways that production and reception are not distinct categories. Mobilized "audiences" create, refine, and reinvent the tactics by taking part in them. If we follow Griswold and model cultural dynamics as an interactional diamond connecting producers (activists), receivers (the mobilized masses), cultural objects (mobilization tactics), and social contexts, then this is an instance where creation through participation blurs the distinction between production and consumption and producer and consumer. See Griswold, *Cultures and Societies*, esp. pp. 153–54.

2. This Is the Matzoh of Hope

1 "Symbolic Passover Seder of Redemption for Soviet Jewry Climaxes Hagadah March to Soviet Mission," press release, 30 March 1969, SSSJ b.5 f.1.; SSSJ, "Passover Seder in Front of Soviet UN Mission Is Culmination of Redemption Hagadah March from Carnegie Hall," press release, 26 March 1969, SSSJ b.5 f.1; "1,000 Young People Protest"; "Seder Ceremony in Street." For a sociological overview of holiday protest, see Polletta, "Can You Celebrate Dissent?"
2 I treat Rabbi Arthur Waskow's similarly named 1969 New Left Freedom seder later in this chapter. Staub, *Torn*, 163–67; Dollinger, *Black Power*, 126; Magid, *Meir Kahane*, 60–62.
3 SSSJ Freedom Seder, assorted files, 1974–90, SSSJ b.11–b.36.
4 SSSJ, "Theory and Practice," D1a–D1b.

5 E.g., Turpie, "Freedom Seder."
6 Activists' "tastes in tactics" often outweigh rational calculations of efficacy. Jasper, *Art of Moral Protest*. This is especially true when movement organizations do not have early debates over tactics. McCammon, *U.S. Women's Jury Movements*. SSSJ falls into this category.
7 SSSJ, "Russian 'Nyet' to Passover Food at 'Freedom Seder,'" press release, 27 March 1988, SSSJ b.33 f.23.
8 Social historian Adam Ferziger has referred to this change in religious understanding as "the rise of Solidarity Orthodoxy." Ferziger, "Outside the Shul"; Ferziger, *Beyond Sectarianism*, 58–82.
9 SSSJ, "Story of 'Operation Jericho,'" 26–27. The ram's horn is not a Passover symbol.
10 Rosh Hashanah, in September, is the Jewish New Year. Simchat Torah, "Rejoicing in the Torah," celebrated with song and dance in October, marks the end and restarting of the annual cycle of Bible reading in the synagogue. Tu BiShvat, in January/February, is the "New Year for Trees." Shavuot, in May/June, commemorates the giving of the Law on Sinai.
11 C. Smith, *Disruptive Religion*, 9–22.
12 Here "Conservative," with a capital C, is an American Jewish denomination, not a political orientation. It represented a centrist movement between traditionalist Orthodoxy and change-oriented Reform. In the years of the Soviet Jewry movement, Conservative Judaism was America's largest Jewish denomination.
13 On the divide within American Orthodoxy, see Ferziger, *Beyond Sectarianism*, 70–74. A. Weiss, *Open Up*, 57–63, offers a view from the trenches. Tisha B'Av, the "Fast of the Ninth of Av," is a summertime day of mourning commemorating the destruction of the ancient temple in Jerusalem.
14 In SSSJ, the move into ritualized protest was led by Jacob Birnbaum, Glenn Richter, Rabbi Arthur Green, Rabbi Shlomo Riskin, and others. Rabbi Israel Miller, Rabbi Henry Siegman, Albert D. Chernin, and Abraham Bayer led the move in the AJCSJ. Most were Modern Orthodox. (Green was ordained Conservative.) On SSSJ's Modern Orthodox core, see Ferziger, "Outside the Shul," 91–94. On the synthesis, see Ferziger, *Beyond Sectarianism*, 76–82.
15 Moore, "Reconsidering the Rosenbergs"; Glenn, "Jewish Cold War"; Diner, *Jews of the United States*, 276–80; Frey, "Challenging," 8–14. On Jewish American socialism, see Michels, *Fire in Their Hearts*; and Howe, *World of Our Fathers*.
16 Sarna, *American Judaism*, 274–93. Lederhendler, *American Jewry*, 253.
17 Herberg, *Protestant—Catholic—Jew*, 46; Berman, *Speaking of Jews*, 110–11, 169–70; Herzog, *Spiritual-Industrial Complex*; Herzog, "From Sermon to Strategy"; Henry, "'And I Don't Care'"; Loeffler, "Problem with the 'Judeo-Christian' Tradition." The Cold War continued a pattern from the two World Wars, broadening American pluralism to better include Jews. Cooperman, *Making Judaism Safe*; Moore, *GI Jews*.
18 Fedeski, "Symbolism and Strategy," 14.
19 SSSJ, *Save Soviet Jewry*, 7, 16; Fedeski, "Symbolism and Strategy," 41–50. Accusations of Jewish American passivity during the Holocaust were polemical. For more balanced historical assessments, see Lipstadt, "Playing the Blame Game"; and Norwood, *Prologue to Annihilation*. Leaders who objected to public protest against the Soviet Union saw their stance not as quiescence but as smart politics. The World

Jewish Congress's Nahum Goldmann—arguably the most powerful diaspora Jewish community leader of his era—held that a "quiet, diplomatic approach" would prove more effective than public shaming. Goldmann became a lightning rod for opposition to the politics of *"shtadlanus"*—negotiations with gentile authorities undertaken by community elite. Rutland, "Soviet Jewry."

20 Empirical research confirms that timing protest to holidays increases the likelihood of press coverage. Oliver and Maney, "Political Processes"; Polletta, "Can You Celebrate Dissent?," 163–64. On the staging of protest rituals for media coverage, see Grimes et al., *Ritual, Media, and Conflict*.

21 "Soviet U.N. Mission." Readers familiar with the Passover seder will note the irony that the Russian boy's question is precisely the one asked by the third child in the Four Children section of the haggadah.

22 "Jewish Student Groups Use May Day."

23 Fedeski, "Symbolism and Strategy," 29.

24 Glenn Richter, interviewed by Yuli Kosharovsky, 18 May 2004, http://kosharovsky.com. Accounts of the demonstration and its planning can be found in Beckerman, *When They Come*, 79–81; Halevi, "Jacob Birnbaum," 34; and Orenstein, "'Let My People Go!,'" 53–55.

25 "Soviet U.N. Mission." See also Adler, "No Raisins, No Almonds."

26 Carlebach, "Am Yisroel Chai"; Jacob Birnbaum, "'Am Yisroel Chai': Shlomo Carlebach's Version and Earlier Versions," listserv post to jewish-music@shamash.org, 18 May 2003, personal papers, JBP; Yitzchak Dorfman to Reb-shlomo@shamash.org listserv, "Reb Shlomo's Version: The 'Am Yisrael Chai' Story," 2 July 2003, JBP, also reposted with additions at http://heichalhanegina.blogspot.com. On the role of music and song in social movements, see Eyerman and Jamison, *Music and Social Movements*; Reed, *Art of Protest*, 13–39; and Lorber, "*Tsum folk vel ikh fun keyver zingen*."

27 Glenn Richter, interviewed by Shaul Kelner, 27 July 2006.

28 Jacob Birnbaum, "Appeal to the Conscience of the World / Prayer Service for Soviet Jewry," 25 August 1964, SSSJ b.1 f.4.

29 Democratic Party, "1964 Platform."

30 Birnbaum, "Appeal / Prayer."

31 Birnbaum later referred to SSSJ's first years as its "Shofar period." The symbol was picked up by the AJCSJ, which used it at the 1965 Eternal Light Vigil, and by the CCSA, which emblazoned it on a lapel pin. Of the symbol's spread, Birnbaum reflected, "Later on [it] became cliché. I didn't like it. Everyone was using it." Jacob Birnbaum, interviewed by Shaul Kelner, 11 December 2003. Such disavowals are common in the art and music worlds. I take it as further evidence that tactical innovation is (and should therefore be analyzed as) creative cultural production. On the artistic avant-gardes bemoaning "aesthetic dilution" and mainstream appropriation of their cultural innovations, see Lena and Peterson, "Classification as Culture," 707–9.

32 Birnbaum, "Appeal / Prayer."

33 This is consistent with research on African American activism, which has detailed ways that Black church culture provides cultural scripts to activists. Pattillo-McCoy, "Church Culture."

34 As an observant Jew, Birnbaum would have heard the shofar daily during the month of penitential *selichot* prayers preceding Rosh Hashanah. His script, however, neither mentioned *selichot* nor framed the rally as a *selichot* observance.

35 Dramatization also addressed the challenge of making an invisible problem visible. In the absence of photographs and televised images of Soviet Jewish oppression, activists created their own visuals.
36 Birnbaum, "Appeal / Prayer" (italics added; text in small caps is emphasized in original). In performance, they may have skipped over this introduction to the shofar blasts. A line strikes the paragraph in a marked-up copy of the script.
37 Birnbaum, "'Am Yisroel Chai'"; Spiegel, "3,000 Here Protest"; SSSJ, "Story of 'Operation Jericho'"; Rubin, "Student Struggle"; Jacob Birnbaum to Youth Directors, "Outline: Leil Shimurim All Night Vigil, Geulah March and Rally," 28 March 1966, SSSJ b.2 f.3. Joshua 6:2–20 tells of the Israelites marching around Jericho for seven days, led by seven priests blowing shofar blasts. On the seventh day, they march around the city seven times. The walls collapse and the Israelites take the city.
38 There is one connection between Passover and the book of Joshua. The synagogue liturgy for Passover's first morning includes one selection from Prophets—Joshua 3:5–7, 5:2–6:1, 6:27. This reading (haftarah) places Joshua at Jericho but skips the battle itself (6:2–6:20).
39 Raspberry, "Demonstrators Protest"; Henry Siegman, "Report on the National Eternal Light Vigil in Washington, D.C.," 4 October 1965, NCSJ b.1 f.2; Henry Siegman to AJCSJ, "National Eternal Light Vigil," 1 June 1965, NJCRAC b.86 f.8.
40 New York Metropolitan Region of United Synagogue of America, "Demonstration to Save Russian Jewry," memo, 20 April 1965, SSSJ b.1 f.8.
41 SSSJ Rockaway Beach rally, assorted files, 1965, SSSJ, b. 1 f. 13. The Ninth of Av day of mourning is commemorated by fasting and reading the book of Lamentations.
42 "Thousands See Protest March"; "Menorah March during Hanukkah."
43 Celebrated in October, Sukkot, the Festival of Booths, commemorates Israelite wanderings in the Sinai Desert.
44 Fedeski, "Symbolism and Strategy," 18.
45 SSSJ, "Happy Fathers Day—Let My People Go," press release, 15 June 1975, SSSJ b.13 f.14.
46 Moshe Stern and Theodore Comet to North American Jewish Youth Conference Sub-Committee on Soviet Jewry, 14 January 1966, SSSJ b.2 f.3.
47 Also among the coalition members was United Synagogue Youth, which had staged the Passover "Festival of Freedom March" in 1965.
48 The coalition kept changing names until 1971, when the Greater New York Conference on Soviet Jewry was established as an independent agency.
49 NYYCSJ, "Minutes of Youth Directors' and Youth Representatives' Meetings," 8 March 1966, SSSJ b.2 f.3; Glenn Richter, "Geulah March for Soviet Jewry," *Queens College Hillel Newsletter*, March 1966, SSSJ b.2 f.3; Birnbaum to Youth Directors, "Outline: Leil Shimurim"; Spiegel, "Students Rally Here."
50 Albert D. Chernin to Israel Miller, "Summary of Conference Activity," 2 April 1968, NCSJ b.1 f.4; Glenn Richter to Fred Greenfield, 18 April 1967, SSSJ b.2 f.15; Glenn Richter, "Chicago Jewish Students to Stage Passover March to Protest Soviet Anti-Semitism," press release draft template, 30 April 1967, SSSJ b.2 f.15.
51 NYCCSJ, "Passover Vigil for Soviet Jewry," poster, 1967, SSSJ b.2 f.16.
52 NYCCSJ, "'We, the Organized Jewish Community,'" press release, 30 April 1967, SSSJ b.2 f.16. (Years later, a 1976 SSSJ benefit concert paired the Hasidic singer Rabbi Shlomo Carlebach with comedian Rodney Dangerfield. Playing on the comedian's signature phrase, the advertisement claimed, "The Kremlin doesn't give Jews any

respect.") SSSJ, "Soviet Jewry Benefit Concert at Carnegie Hall," press release, 6 November 1976, SSSJ b.15 f.10.
53 Alvin Boretz, "A Special Seder for Soviet Jewry" (NYCCSJ), 1968, SSSJ b.3 f.14, 3; Spiegel, "Passover Seder Is Held"; "Seder Ceremony in Street."
54 Mahla, "Between Socialism and Jewish Tradition"; Shapira, "Religious Motifs."
55 Shternshis, *Soviet and Kosher*, 27–34. Before Passover, any remaining leaven is burned to purge the house clean. On the purge of Yevsektsia leaders, see Gitelman, *Jewish Nationality*, 513–23.
56 Gereboff, "One Nation"; Balin, "Modern Transformation," 193.
57 Staub, *Torn*, 163–72.
58 Zylberberg, "Transforming Rituals." See also Ochs, *Inventing Jewish Ritual*; and Prell, *Women Remaking*.
59 On intermovement relations, movement fields, and crossover of tactics, see Meyer and Whittier, "Social Movement Spillover"; Isaac and Christiansen, "How the Civil Rights Movement Revitalized"; and Isaac, McDonald, and Lukasik, "Takin' It from the Streets."
60 For Soviet Jewry movement uses of the term *Freedom Seder*, see, for example, SSSJ, *Letter-Writing*, 14; BACSJ, "Freedom Seder 5745–1985," 1985, ASJ b.125 f.2; and BACSJ, "Freedom Seder for Soviet Jews in Front of the Soviet Consulate in San Francisco," video recording, 15 April 1986, BACSJ b.101 f.VHS Tape BACSJ 079, https://digipres.cjh.org.
61 In the Soviet Jewry movement, the JDL later adopted protest seders from the NYCCSJ and SSSJ. (Its claim to have initiated this tactic was self-aggrandizing.) Magid, *Meir Kahane*, 60–61. Although the specific use of a seder for guerrilla protest was novel in the Jewish political tradition, the general form has analogs in other social movements, such as same-sex wedding ceremony protests in the gay rights movement (1987–2004). On "rituals and practices typically used to create moral attachment to the social order . . . instead, mobilized in the interest of protest," see Taylor et al., "Culture and Mobilization," 868.
62 In ritual performances, gaps among the elements—actors, audiences, symbols, and scripts—make performances less convincing. Their fusion creates an aura of naturalness. Alexander, "Cultural Pragmatics." In the present case, hewing close to the traditional seder fused more elements more seamlessly than the previous ritual hodgepodge or Boretz-style text, whose constructedness was left evident.
63 Walzer, *Exodus and Revolution*, 4–6.
64 In Jewish tradition, the First Commandment begins at Exodus 20:2, "I the LORD am your God *who brought you out of the land of Egypt, the house of bondage*" (Jewish Publication Society translation, 1985; emphasis added). Christian traditions differ.
65 Massarik, *Jewish Identity*, 11; Joselit, *Wonders*, 227–28.
66 NCSJ-UKI, "Symbolic Seder Service for Soviet Refuseniks," 1981, NCSJ-UK f.825, 2–3.
67 SSSJ, "SSSJ Freedom Seder, 1982/5742," haggadah script, 1982, SSSJ b.24 f.12, 2.
68 The traditional Four Questions read as follows: "*Mah nishtanah halayla hazeh mikol haleilot?* Why is this night different from all other nights? For on all other nights, we eat leavened (*hametz*) and unleavened bread (*matzoh*). Why on this night only matzoh? On all other nights, we eat all types of vegetables. Why on this night bitter herbs (*maror*)? On all other nights, we do not dip our food even once. Why on this night, twice? On all other nights, we eat either sitting or reclining. Why on this night do we all recline?"

69 Boretz, "Special Seder," 3.
70 Queens Council for Soviet Jewry, "Passover 1975," haggadah, 30 March 1975, GNYCSJ b.1 f.13.
71 NCSJ-UKI, "A Seder for Soviet Jewry," 1981, NCSJ-UK f.825, 1.
72 BACSJ, "Freedom Seder 5745–1985."
73 For instance, the seder presents unleavened matzoh as "the bread of affliction," which symbolizes both slavery and the hasty flight to freedom. Bitter herbs traditionally symbolize the bitterness of slavery. Salt water symbolizes tears. The *charosis* fruit-nut-wine paste symbolizes bricks and mortar that slaves used to build Pharaoh's cities.
74 SSSJ, "Freedom Seder," press release, 27 March 1981, SSSJ b.23 f.19.
75 BACSJ, "Freedom Seder 5745–1985," 2.
76 Spiegel, "Students Rally Here"; Spiegel, "3,000 Here Mark Simhath Torah."
77 SSSJ, "Freedom Seder for Soviet Jews," press release, 11 April 1979, SSSJ b.22 f.4. "'Freedom Seder' for Soviet Jews," press release, 11 April 1979, b.22. f.4, SSSJ. BACSJ, "Freedom Seder," video recording, 36:17.
78 Waskow's New Left Freedom Seder did not do this. It remained ensconced in a friendly congregational space.
79 Henry Margolis to Louis Rosenblum, "Hebrew Academy Pesach Assembly 1966–5726," 15 April 1966, CCSA b.3 f.80.
80 Eisen, *Count Us In*, 65–66; SJC, "Action Program on Soviet Jewry for Jewish Organizations," 1971, personal papers, AJB; AJCSJ, "Programmatic Recommendations Adopted by the Biennial," 7–8 April 1968, NCSJ b.1 f.4, 2; assorted BACSJ Freedom Seder files b.29 f.21–25.
81 "World Jewry Prays."
82 "'Kisei' 'Al Domi'"; "Kisei' panu'i." On Ma'oz and the empty chair, see chapter 7.
83 Israel Miller to Member Organizations of AJCSJ, "Matzoh of Hope," 15 March 1967, NCSJ b.1 f.2; Israel Miller to Constituent Organizations of the AJCSJ, "Project Re 'Matzoh of Oppression,'" 18 February 1966, NJCRAC b.86 f.8.
84 Albert D. Chernin to NCRAC Membership, "Reprint of Statement on 'Matzoh of Oppression,'" 1 March 1966, NJCRAC b.86 f.8.
85 Miller to AJCSJ, "Matzoh of Hope." Chernin's authorship is attested in Miller to AJCSJ, "Project Re 'Matzoh of Oppression.'" Contributing consultants included Nathan Saperstein and Ephraim Sturm of the National Council of Young Israel, Joseph Edelman of the Labor Zionist Movement, Albert Vorspan of the Union of American Hebrew Congregations, and AJCSJ chair Israel Miller of the Rabbinical Council of America.
86 In April 1963, the organizations that would a year later establish the AJCSJ asked American Jews to add a special seder prayer: "When we recite in the Haggadah the age-hallowed 'Ho lachmo anyo—This is the bread of affliction which our fathers ate in the Land of Egypt,' let us be mindful of our fellow Jews in Soviet Russia who truly eat the bread of affliction." This was a one-time plea that did not add or designate a particular piece of matzoh. "U.S. Jews Observe Passover."
87 Bayer, "American Response," 215.
88 Orbach, *American Movement*, 84.
89 Miller to AJCSJ, "Matzoh of Hope"; Bayer, "American Response," 215; "Massive Rally for Solidarity"; Podwal, *Let My People Go*; AJCSJ, "That the Jews of the Soviet Union

May Know"; "Thousand Miracles"; Shapiro, "Jewish Passover Festival"; "Light of Freedom"; "Markets to Carry Passover Prayer"; Goldman, "Jews Debate Appropriateness"; Ginsberg, "Documenting the Struggle."

90 Albert D. Chernin to NCRAC Membership, "Edward G. Robinson Tape on 'Matzoh of Oppression,'" 10 March 1966, NJCRAC b.86 f.8.
91 Miller to AJCSJ, "Matzoh of Hope."
92 AJCSJ, "In the Name of Humanity"; Peretz, Le combat, 118, 137; Appelbaum, "Soviet Jewry Movement," 618; Moshe Decter, interviewed by Perry Haber, 22 February 1990, 1–15, American Jewish Oral History Collection, NYPL, b.294 f.2, https://digitalcollections.nypl.org.
93 NJCRAC, "Distribution of 1973 Issue of Matzah of Hope Statement for Passover Use," memo, with enclosures, 1973, NJCRAC b.87 f.3.
94 "'Matzah of Hope'"; Korey, Soviet Cage, 200–275.
95 Kolatch, Family Seder. Kolatch retained the text in the 1991 edition.
96 Kolatch.
97 Levy, On Wings of Freedom, 24–25.
98 Ethnographic descriptions of American Jewish celebrations of Simchat Torah can be found in Heilman, Synagogue Life; and Prell, Prayer and Community.
99 Ro'i, Struggle, 52, 296, 318–19; Grose, "Moscow Jews Dance."
100 Wiesel, Jews of Silence, 50. Wiesel visited in 1965. The New York Times put the number at "tens of thousands." Grose, "Moscow Jews Dance."
101 "Moscow Jews Dance"; Astrachan, "Jews Celebrate"; "10,000 Soviet Jews"; Kaiser, "Soviets Restrict Jewish Celebration"; Speed, "Parade Here to Celebrate"; Wintrob, "Support for Soviet Jews"; Goltsin, "Remembering Simchat Torah."
102 Jacobs, "Reflections on Temple Judea's Trip," trip report, October 1976, 15 (emphasis in original).
103 Chernin to Miller, "Summary of Conference Activity"; AJCSJ, "Programmatic Recommendations on Soviet Jewry for Youth and Campus," 3–5 September 1968, NCSJ b.1 f.3; Israel Miller to Member Organizations of AJCSJ, "Nationwide 'Demonstrations of Solidarity with Soviet Youth'—Sunday, October 13, 1968," 14 August 1968, NCSJ b.1 f.3; AJCSJ, "Simchat Torah 1969," brochure with press clippings, 1969, NCSJ b.1 f.6, 2, 10; NJCRAC, "Major Activities," 3.
104 Miller to AJCSJ, "Nationwide 'Demonstrations'" (emphasis in original).
105 The Hebrew and Arabic terms are from Israeli folk dancing, popular then in American Jewish youth culture. AJCSJ, "Program Suggestions for Youth Involvement in Simchat Torah Demonstrations," 13 October 1968, NCSJ b.1 f.3 (emphasis in original).
106 AJCSJ, "Program Suggestions for Youth" (emphasis in original).
107 On this custom, see Joselit, Wonders, 247–52.
108 Lawrence M. Lewin to CCSA, 25 June 1968, CCSA b.1 f.19.
109 JCRC of Minnesota, "'Rabbi Jerome Herzog . . .'" press release, 28 March 1969, MRA b.1 f.16.
110 Louis H. Weinstein to Harold Light, 11 August 1969, BACSJ b.3 f.29.
111 Weinstein to Light, 11 August 1969; "San Francisco Launches Campaign"; BACSJ, "'Alexei Kosygin Premier . . .'" press release, n.d. (ca. Summer) 1969, BACSJ b.33 f.12; BACSJ, "Holy Day Greetings Urged to Cheer Soviet Jews," promotional flyer, July 1969, BACSJ b.33 f.12; BACSJ, "Over 50,000 Cards!," newsletter, October 1969, BACSJ b.33 f.12.

112 Rosenblum and Rosenblum, "Involvement," 66–69; Dart, "Aid Soviet Jews." Soviet Jews began publicizing petitions in 1968. As Western activists learned the names of their Soviet Jewish counterparts, they reoriented their efforts to support and collaborate with them directly. See Kelner, "'Uneventful' 1968," 18–20; and Kelner, "People-to-People."
113 UCSJ, "Greeting Cards for Soviet Jews" (UCSJ), advertising flyer, 1970, attachment to Herschel Schacter to Conference Membership, "Sending Greeting Cards to Soviet Synagogues," 21 August 1970, NCSJ b.1 f.6.
114 Schacter to Conference Membership, "Sending Greeting Cards."
115 CCSA, "Order Form," 10 November 1972, CCSA b.8 f.219; Rosenblum and Rosenblum, "Involvement," 66–69; UCSJ, Rosh Hashanah greeting cards, assorted, 1970–73, CCSA b.8 f.252; UCSJ, "Greeting Cards." American Greetings' chairman, Irving Stone, served as an officer of the Jewish Community Federation of Cleveland. The federation's executive director connected Rosenblum with him.
116 Western artists contributing designs included Avrum Ashery and Betsy Platkin Teutch in the US and Josef Herman in the UK. Artists whose works were reproduced included Dan Rubinstein, Shmuel Katz, Reuven Rubin, and Shraga Weil. Refuseniks contributing designs included Lev Korenblitt and Carmela Raiz. "Soviet Jews to Get 'Greetings'"; GNYCSJ, *Sound the Great Shofar for Freedom: High Holiday Program Resource Guide*, 1976, GNYCSJ b.1 f.13, 39; Betsy Platkin Teutsch, "Reunite Our Scattered Dispersed among the Nations," greeting card, 1988, JCRCGP b.65 f.33; NCSJ-UKI, Rosh Hashanah greeting cards, assorted, 1976, NCSJ-UK f.317; "Banned Worshiper."
117 NCSJ-UKI, "International Card Competition," press release, 2 June 1981, NCSJ-UK f.317.
118 The greeting card campaigns are interesting for the diverse ways they were produced. Corporate graphics departments, professional artists, and amateur schoolchildren all contributed. On "aesthetic activism," see Isaac, "Movements, Aesthetics, and Markets."
119 Avrum Ashery, interviewed by Shaul Kelner, 13 August 2019.
120 Ashery, interview; "Banned Worshiper." Tefillin, or phylacteries, are small leather boxes worn on the forehead and arm during prayer.
121 The UCSJ reported 250,000 Passover cards sold in 1971. Local press reports usually put community-level figures in the thousands (e.g., Philadelphia, 7,000 cards in 1973; Lehigh Valley, Allentown, Pennsylvania, 2,000 in 1987). Dart, "Aid Soviet Jews"; Rosenblum and Rosenblum, "Involvement," 69; "JCRC Offers New 'Action Kits'"; Cleaveland, "Unity of Dissent."
122 Gendler, "Characters from Sesame Street."
123 "Area Jews Mark Rosh Hashanah."
124 Dart, "Aid Soviet Jews."
125 Ashery, interview; "Banned Worshiper."
126 AJCSJ, "Programmatic Recommendations Adopted," 1–3 (emphasis added). The Hanukkah recommendation did not conceive of the holiday on its own but tied it to Sabbath observances for Human Rights Day—the United Nations holiday commemorating the December 10, 1948, ratification of the Universal Declaration of Human Rights.
127 SSSJ, *Letter-Writing*, 7.

128 NJCRAC, "Joint Program Plan for Jewish Community Relations 1971–72," 10 November 1971, personal papers, AJB. The recommendations were taken up. For an example of a local planning calendar, see MACSJ, "1976–1977 Calendar: Dates to Remember and Programs to Plan," 1976, BHP b.2 f.2. On the general phenomenon of commemorating "anniversaries of injustices against [a] movement or its constituency," see Polletta, "Can You Celebrate Dissent?," 165.
129 SJC, "Action Program."
130 Weber, *Economy and Society*.
131 NCSJ, "Calendar," 1984, JCRCGP b.65 f.29.
132 JCCGW, *Soviet Jewry Kit*, 1.
133 Marise Zerobnick to All Councils, 18 September 1984, ASJ b.125 f.2; SJC, "Action Program"; SSSJ, "The Megillah of Anatoly Sharansky," purimshpiel script, 1981, SSSJ b.23 f.17. Independently, refuseniks began creating purimshpiels for themselves in the mid-1970s. Genzeleva, "Moskovskie i Leningradskie purimshpili."
134 "Israelis Hold Silent Protest."
135 Cf. J. Kaufman, "Endogenous Explanation."
136 This was messy. SSSJ had recognized Soviet holidays as mobilization opportunities from the outset, even before it had begun using Jewish holidays. It marched on May Day in 1964 and demonstrated in 1967 to mark the Bolshevik Revolution's fiftieth anniversary. As with its Jewish holiday mobilizations of the 1960s, these, too, were ad hoc. After the Conference began promoting the idea of systematically mobilizing around Jewish holidays, SSSJ issued a similar call in 1971 and was the first to list a Soviet holiday alongside Jewish holidays. But there was a gap between concept and practice. The Conference, not SSSJ, ended up listing out a calendar of Soviet holidays. But SSSJ, not the Conference, actually organized demonstrations around the holidays. SSSJ did not expand beyond May Day and the anniversary of the revolution, however. Interestingly, the movement never mobilized around the USSR's most popular holiday, Novy God (New Year's). SSSJ, *Letter-Writing*, 7.
137 Murphy, *Big Book of Concepts*.
138 JCCGW, *Teaching* (1st ed.), 11–12.
139 "Exodus March." On shared time frames and "temporal symmetry," see Zerubavel, *Hidden Rhythms*, 67–68, 73–74. The Soviet Jewry movement's successes at temporal coordination should not be underestimated. To appreciate the difficulties, contrast with Wagner-Pacifici and Ruggero, "Temporal Blindspots."
140 NJCRAC, "Joint Program Plan"; SJC, "Action Program" (emphasis added).
141 C. Smith, *Disruptive Religion*, 9–11.
142 Contrast the absence of outcry against Soviet Jewry seders with the accusations of profanation leveled by conservative opponents of Waskow's 1969 New Left Freedom Seder (Staub, *Torn*, 172–75, 192). Chabad, which avoided public protest in favor of direct aid to Soviet Jews, argued that new protest rituals would be better directed at encouraging greater American Jewish religious observance but did not speak of them as desecrations. Referring to the practice of adding an empty chair at the seder, Chabad's spiritual leader, Rabbi Menachem Mendel Schneerson, is reported to have said, "'You want to do something to help Soviet Jewry? Add another chair to your seder, but don't leave it empty! Instead invite someone to your seder who would otherwise not be taking part in one!'" (Margolin, "Today, a Moscow with More Synagogues").

143 Avraham (Avi) Weiss, interviewed by Shaul Kelner, 28 April 2006.
144 Trilling, *Sincerity and Authenticity*.
145 Wood, "Religious Culture and Political Action," finds religious protest movements more likely to succeed when they provide religious resources for compromise as well as for contestation.
146 In New York, a strategic, rather than religious, objection to ritualized protest was raised by ultra-Orthodox leadership. Rabbi Moshe Feinstein reportedly asked that the GNYCSJ not use Torah scrolls and prayer shawls at Solidarity Sundays on the grounds that maintaining the apolitical character of ritual objects was crucial for Soviet Jews' ability to use these objects in worship. Turning them into symbols of political protest risked giving the Soviet government a pretext for banning all uses of these objects. Malcolm Hoenlein, interviewed by Shaul Kelner, 30 May 2023.
147 In spite of the Union of Councils' factional affinity for the Student Struggle, its approach to ritualization more closely resembled the Conference's. Chabad staked out a third pole, opposed to public protest and dismissive of new rituals to express it, yet framing its own educational and aid missions to Chabad communities in Russia as religious action. Margolin, "Today, a Moscow with More Synagogues"; Wolf, *Dyedushka*.
148 Hindsight shows that they miscalculated. The Soviet government proved more willing to let Jews leave than to grant them their constitutionally mandated cultural rights.
149 AJCSJ, "In the Name of Humanity."
150 Glenn Richter to Michael D. Zimet, 4 March 1966, SSSJ b.2 f.3; NYYCSJ, "Passover Youth Protest for Soviet Jewry to Include Encirclement of Soviet U.N. Mission," press release, 17 March 1966, SSSJ b.2 f.3; NYYCSJ, "Minutes"; Richter, "Geulah March for Soviet Jewry"; Birnbaum to Youth Directors, "Outline: Leil Shimurim"; Spiegel, "Students Rally Here"; Jacob Birnbaum to Judith Herschlag, 6 March 1966, SSSJ b.2 f.3.
151 Spiegel, "Soviet Is Assailed." Assorted files, SSSJ b.6 f. 4–6. A 1971 reprise drew one to two thousand. "'Freedom Flag' Raised"; "2,000 Persons Participate."
152 The successor to the New York Coordinating Committee, the GNYCSJ was housed in the same offices as the NCSJ. It was run by three Modern Orthodox Jews: Malcolm Hoenlein, Margy-Ruth Davis, and Zeesy Schnur.
153 Police estimated the crowd in New York at 45,000. The GNYCSJ said 155,000. Cleveland saw 8,000, Dallas and Detroit 4,000 each, and Chicago 2,500. Theodore R. Mann to NJCRAC Member Agencies, "Minutes of Commission Meeting of November 22, 1971," 21 January 1972, GNYCSJ b.1 f.2; "Nationwide Preparations in High Gear"; "Hundreds of Thousands March"; Dugan, "Huge Crowd Here"; GNYCSJ, "New York, You've Really Done It!," *NYT*, 5 May 1972.
154 Goldman, "Protesters for Soviet Jewry"; Herman, "Marchers in Manhattan"; Spiegel, "100,000 March"; Goldman, "Rally for Soviet Jewry." Suspended in 1988 as a gesture of goodwill in response to the permission of mass emigration, Solidarity Sunday was revived in 1990 for one year amid concerns over antisemitism in the Russian nationalist movement. NJCRAC, "Report to the Workshop on Public Action and Demonstrations on Major Activities in Communities in the U.S," 17–19 February 1976, SSSJ b.16 f.3; Goldman, "Protesters for Soviet Jewry"; Zeesy Schnur and Margy-Ruth Davis, interviewed by Shaul Kelner, 24 September 2019; Hoenlein, interview, 30 May 2023.

155 Woocher, *Sacred Survival*; Herman, *Jewish Identity*; Fein, *Where Are We?*; Neusner, *Stranger at Home*; Neusner, *Israel in America*; Hertzberg, *Being Jewish in America*; Liebman and Cohen, *Two Worlds of Judaism*, 84, 179n8; Gans, "Symbolic Ethnicity"; Gans, "Symbolic Ethnicity and Symbolic Religiosity." For present-day analyses of that era's discourse, see Magid, "American Jewish Holocaust 'Myth'"; and Kelner, "Veneration and Critique."

156 Woocher, *Sacred Survival*, 67–89; SSSJ, "We Are One!," concert program, 24 June 1974, SSSJ b.12 f.2; CCSA, "Order Form"; Spiegel, "100,000 March."

157 Liebman, *Ambivalent American Jew*, criticized the sale of Israel Bonds from synagogue pulpits on Yom Kippur (102). Elazar, *Community and Polity*, called it "Israelolatry" (83).

158 Zerubavel identifies "mnemonic pasting" techniques that establish an illusion of contiguity between past and present. These include imitating the past, synchronizing the calendar, and using a language of discursive continuity. He shows how, when speaking of historical time, these techniques *analogize* present to past. Here, I would add that when mnemonic pasting techniques are applied to mythic, cosmological time, they move beyond *analogy* to establish *identity*—participation in a recurring cyclical time. Zerubavel, *Time Maps*, 37–54.

159 Berger and Thomas, *Social Construction of Reality*; Berger, *Rumor of Angels*. Anthropologists debate how much performances indicate actual beliefs versus proper attitudes, but they agree that performances embody societal norms and values. Bell, *Ritual*, xi; Tambiah, "Performative Approach," 499–500. As performance, Soviet Jewry rituals made public assertions about the religious character of the movement irrespective of the personal beliefs of those performing them.

3. How to Find and Meet Russian Jews

1 NCSJ, "The National Conference on Soviet Jewry Brings Suit against Intourist," press release, 25 June 1986, NCSJ b.337 f.6.

2 On the tensions between political and commercial imperatives in Soviet tourism policy, see Hazanov, "Porous Empire." On Soviet fear of tourists as agents of ideological subversion, see Bagdasaryan et al., *Sovetskoe zazerkal'e*.

3 Siris, "Encounter with Soviet Jewish Activists," trip report, July 1973, 3–4; Sternberg and Sternberg, "Encounter with Soviet Jewry," draft trip report, January 1975, 6; Weissman, "Report on Visit to Soviet Union," 28 February 1975; Leisch and Leisch, trip report, 13–20 March 1976, 6; Finkelstein, trip report, 24 June–8 July 1976, 14; Rosenfeld and Rosenfeld, trip report, 28 September–20 October 1976, 17, 26; Kuhr, "Debriefing Narrative / Russian Journey," trip report, 14–28 August 1978, 7; Silverstein, trip report, 6–13 March 1983; Stern, "Canadian Parliamentary Visit to the USSR," trip report, 18–24 January 1984, 4, 8, 23; Landis, trip report, 23 February–4 March 1987, 6.

4 Addressing what tourists should expect when passing through customs, a 1987 briefer's kit estimated that "between 10%–20% of travelers are harassed" (Simon S. Kaminetsky, "Briefing Checklist for Visitors to the Soviet Union" [United Jewish Federation of Metrowest, New Jersey], March 1987, NCSJ b.91 f.3, 10). Not including harassment at customs, about one hundred travelers on forty-five different trips recorded in AJHS archives (2 percent) reported being detained, arrested, interrogated,

or expelled. Examples of denunciations are found in Barsov, "*Sionskie bliznetsy*"; Nilov, "*Oplata . . . galetami*"; and Dimov, "Zionist Traveling Salesmen."
5   Barry and Sager, *Soviet Harassment*, appendices B, G, H, I; Diamant and Okunieff, trip report, 12 April–30 April 1981, 7, 9–10. Other attacks in 1982 are reported in Burns, "Whip Cracks"; and Belousovitch and Davis, *Chronology of Soviet Dissidence*, 72.
6   "Soviet Expels 2 U.S. Tourists"; "Soviet Expels 2 Britons"; "Soviet Travel Agency"; Schmemann, "Soviet Press." Although the three expelled pairs had been traveling on behalf of Israel's Nativ, Soviet news reports did not mention this, linking the tourists with British and American groups instead. "Inciters"; Taylor et al., trip report, 27 February–5 March 1984; Rozner, *Bintiv*, 90–93; Rakeffet-Rothkoff, *From Washington Avenue*, chap. 10, loc. 4940 of 6976, Kindle.
7   American tourists considered the gifts economic support and morale boosters for refuseniks. They knew, for instance, that Uris's *Exodus* was popular among refuseniks. (They may not have known that refuseniks had been reading samizdat versions—i.e., self-published underground translations—since the 1960s. Multiple translations circulated.) They did not fully understand what the gifts meant to the recipients because they were not privy to the deeper cultural meanings that blue jeans and rock albums held in Soviet society. On Uris's *Exodus*, see Hoffman, "Jewish Samizdat," 90–92; and Komaromi, "Jewish Samizdat," 276–78. On blue jeans, rock albums, and the "Imaginary West," see Yurchak, *Everything Was Forever*, 181–237.
8   For standard lists of items to bring, see, for example, Lorel Pollack to Joel Sandberg, 3 April 1975, NCSJ b.91 f.3; and Irene Manekofsky, "Guidelines for Briefers," memo, n.d. (ca. 1978), WCSJ b.9 f.6.
9   Graber, "Trip to a Closed World," trip report, 7–16 November 1987.
10 Fishbane, "Confidential Report," trip report, 18–28 May 1979, 2.
11 Champagne, "Report on Meetings with Soviet Jews," trip report, 12 October 1975, 9; Herbert N. Beller, "Reflections of the Soviet Jewry Movement" (Lillian and Albert Small Capital Jewish Museum), oral history, 25 March 2009, 7, www.jhsgw.org.
12 E.g., Borden, "Physicians Mission to the Soviet Union," trip report, November 1987.
13 E.g., Hertzog et al., trip report, 16–19 March 1977.
14 E.g., Tessler and Tessler, trip report, 3–16 December 1987.
15 E.g., Callen and Rallston, trip report, 6–10 February 1981.
16 Myrna Shinbaum to Merle Singer, 16 April 1986, NCSJ b.89 f.4. Mendy Goldberg was one of the principals in Agudath Israel's tourism effort, the Vaad L'Hatzolas Nidchei Yisroel. Founded in 1981 by Perfect Travel's co-owner Rabbi Mordechai Neustadt, the Vaad sent over two hundred Orthodox rabbis to teach Torah in the USSR. Astor and Neustadt, *Underground*.
17 These 4,700 or so individual travelers represent about 2,500 trips (i.e., couples or groups who traveled together as a unit). The precise number of trips depends on how one counts ambiguous situations (e.g., people who fly in with one group and leave with another, group tours that split up along the way). Archival records include trip reports or debriefing materials for just over 90 percent of the trips. The other 10 percent only have planning notes, itineraries, and other pretrip information.
18 Rozner, *Bintiv*, 78.

19 Wolf, *Dyedushka*; Astor and Neustadt, *Underground*; Landau, "To Russia with Love"; Ner Le'elef, *Story of Former Soviet Jewry*.

20 Much scholarship on gender and travel writing has portrayed nineteenth- and early twentieth-century travel as (temporarily) liberating women from traditional gender roles and norms of domesticity. In contrast, Jewish studies scholarship has emphasized Jewish women of these eras holding public roles and traveling as activists for political and social causes. The travelogues here situate Jewish American women of the 1970s and '80s in the tradition of their activist foremothers. Bird, *Travelling in Different Skins*; Klapper, "Great Adventure of 1929"; Klapper, "American Jewish Women"; McCune, *Whole Wide World*; Reinharz and Raider, *American Jewish Women*; Geerlings, *I Lay This Body Down*.

21 The figures are my best approximation based on available data from the archives, supplemented by web searches to fill in blanks. On recruitment of lawmakers, see Zeesy Schnur and Margy-Ruth Davis, interviewed by Shaul Kelner, 24 September 2019.

22 Place names are spelled using their conventional Cold War–era romanizations (e.g., Kiev, not Kyiv). Bear in mind that the thousands of travelers' reports in the AJHS exclude the vast majority of reports filed by those traveling for Nativ and for Western European groups. The 85 percent figure for Leningrad is probably low, as European activists typically used weekend excursions to Leningrad from Scandinavian departure points. Rozner, *Bintiv*, 62–63, 78.

23 Hinda Cantor, "Enclosed Travel Reports," memo, 26 April 1986, BACSJ b.39 f.58.

24 Donna Arzt to Neil Afran, 15 August 1985, ASJ b.115 f.5. On "cause-lawyering" and social movements' uses of litigation to pursue aims, see McCammon et al., "Supreme Court."

25 Arzt to Afran, 15 August 1985.

26 Bernard Dishler to Jerry Goodman, 8 July 1986, NCSJ b.337 f.5.

27 Travel as the turning point from marginal involvement to intensive commitment is a recurring theme in activists' autobiographical narratives. Enid Wurtman, interviewed by Shaul Kelner, 7 August 2019; Herbert N. Beller, interviewed by Shaul Kelner, 2 July 2019; Hillel Levine, interviewed by Shaul Kelner, 5 September 2018; Joel Sprayregen, interviewed by Shaul Kelner, 30 August 2019; Porath, *Here We Are All Jews*, 10; Yaroslavsky, *Zev's Los Angeles*, 55–57; Harrison, *Passover Revisited*, 53–54, 125–26.

28 On the history of tourism in the Cold War era, see Gorsuch, *All This Is Your World*; Gorsuch and Koenker, *Turizm*; Endy, *Cold War Holidays*; and Bechmann Pedersen and Noack, *Tourism and Travel*. On the history of tourism to the Soviet Union, the Soviet tourism industry, and the politics of Western travel to the USSR, see Salmon, "To the Land of the Future"; Hazanov, "Porous Empire"; and Jacobson, "American Studies." Transatlantic commercial jet travel began in 1958. Aeroflot and Pan Am inaugurated direct New York–Moscow flights in 1968. On this and for 1964–75 tourism statistics, see Kelner, "Foreign Tourists," 100. In addressing technological roots of tactical innovation, I follow Peterson's approach to analyzing cultural production. Peterson, "Production of Culture"; Peterson, "Why 1955?"; Peterson and Anand, "Production of Culture Perspective."

29 Barghoorn, *Soviet Cultural Offensive*, 74. The Soviet government created Intourist in 1929. The US Commerce Department estimated American tourist expenditures

of $2 million in the USSR in 1929 and $10 million in 1931 (as against $137 million in France). American Express estimated 10,210 travelers on its Russian and Baltic cruise line in summer 1934. Foreign tourism peaked in 1936, plummeted with the Great Terror in 1937 and '38, and dried up during the war. Salmon, "To the Land of the Future," 30–40, 103; Kravitz, "Business of Selling the Soviet Union," 52–53.

30 Barghoorn, *Soviet Cultural Offensive*, 61. On Khrushchev's considerations, see also Salmon, "To the Land of the Future," 141–47.
31 McNulty and Gill, "Party Going"; Middleton, "U.S. Frees Travel."
32 Barghoorn, *Soviet Cultural Offensive*, 75; "Gabriel Reiner."
33 On American opera singer Jan Peerce's performances of Yiddish songs before Soviet Jewish audiences at the same moment the rabbis were on their fact-finding mission, see Loeffler, "American Jewish Opera Star."
34 Hollander and Klaperman, "U.S. Rabbis Tell."
35 Hollander and Klaperman. A second delegation representing the interdenominational New York Board of Rabbis also traveled that summer. Rackman traveled with both delegations. Salisbury, "U.S. Rabbis Fear."
36 Herzog, *Spiritual-Industrial Complex*, 5, 11, 105, 108.
37 Levanon, *Haqod*, 155; Medoff, *Rabbi of Buchenwald*, 176, 199–201.
38 For a detailed account of the RCA trip, see Medoff, *Rabbi of Buchenwald*, 171–215. For a perspective from Soviet archives, see Charnyi, "Vneshnie sviazi," 216–19.
39 Tobenkin, "Russia Shifts."
40 Tobenkin; "Five Rabbis Sail"; "Leningrad Jews Hail U.S. Rabbis"; Hollander and Klaperman, "U.S. Rabbis Tell"; "New York Rabbis Report."
41 Klaperman, trip report, 21 June–3 August 1956.
42 Herzog, *Spiritual-Industrial Complex*, 55, 105, 45; Hollander and Klaperman, "U.S. Rabbis Tell"; Adelman and Rackman, "U.S. Rabbis Fight"; Schacter, "Hebrew Rites Fading"; Hollander and Rackman, "Mission to Soviet Jewry."
43 M. M. Schneerson to M. Perlov, 28 Nisan 5716 [9 April 1956], cited in Wolf, *Dyedushka*, 407; Beis Moshiach Magazine, "Secret Missions"; "Crack in the Iron Curtain"; Zaltzman, *Samarkand*, 327–28, 710–23. The Tanya, published in 1796, is the foundational work of Chabad Hasidism.
44 The 1956 RCA delegation had consulted with Schneerson prior to departure. He told them that he might not have advised the trip had they asked him beforehand, but having already requested an entry permit from the Soviets, they could not back down. Medoff, *Rabbi of Buchenwald*, 178.
45 *Hearings on Anti-Semitism in the Soviet Union, before the House Committee on Un-American Activities*, 90th Cong. 2197–2234 (19 June 1968) (statements of Meir Kahane, Harry Bronstein); Bronstein, *Al Tidom*, 325–41; Blau, *Learn Torah*, 243–301; Rivka Blau, interviewed by Shaul Kelner, 28 May 2019; A. Weiss, *Open Up*, 59–60; Nilov, "Oplata . . . galetami."
46 Ro'i, *Struggle*, 48–67, 115, 236.
47 A planned return in 1969 was scuttled when the Soviets withheld his visa, likely in response to his publications and to a sermon he preached in Russian in a Moscow synagogue on the eve of the Six-Day War, praising Israel's Independence Day. Edelstein, "Rav doresh beMosqvah 'al 'atzma'ut Yisra'el." Poupko, *In shotn fun Kremlin*, 131–39; Poupko, "Visit to Russia"; Poupko, "Mission to Soviet Jewry"; "Critical Pittsburgh Rabbi Barred"; Ro'i, *Struggle*, 241; Bernard A. Poupko, oral history

interview (National Council of Jewish Women, Pittsburgh), 26 July 1976, University of Pittsburgh Library, AIS.1964.40, https://digital.library.pitt.edu.
48 Hayward, "Russian Anti-Semitism"; Singer, "State of Fear."
49 On Decter and Litvinoff, see Beckerman, *When They Come*, 52–55; and Peretz, *Le combat*, 81–84.
50 In social movement theory terms, they recognized the power of "aesthetic activism" and cultivated Wiesel as a "literary activist." Isaac, "Movements, Aesthetics, and Markets."
51 On the relationship between what social movement theorists call "diagnostic" and "motivational" framing, see Snow and Benford, "Ideology," 199–204.
52 Wiesel, *All Rivers*, 365–66; Spiegel, *Triumph*, 53.
53 Meyer and Rohlinger, "Big Books."
54 Wiesel, *All Rivers*, 370; Wiesel, *Les juifs du silence*; Wiesel, *Yehudei hadmamah*.
55 Bar-Nir, "*Yehudei hadmamah—Behabimah*"; Porath, *Russian Jewish Community*, JH8; Meister, *Lesson Plans*, iv–v, 60; Tallman and Kahn, *Let My People Go*, 69; Wiesel, *Jews of Silence*. For a catalog listing the translations, see www.worldcat.org.
56 Wiesel, *Jews of Silence*, 87; Bikel, *Silent No More*; Feingold, "Silent No More"; Gilbert, *Jews of Hope*; Schnold, *Jews of Struggle*. A Canadian anthem for Soviet Jewry, *Let My People Go!*, written by Batsheva Paul (Capek) and distributed by the Canadian Jewish Congress, referenced it in song: "Forget your age and manners / Your decorum and your poise / If they must be Jews of silence / Then we must be Jews of noise." (Paul later won a North American Jewish songwriting competition for a second Soviet Jewry protest song, "Smaller Crowds"; see "Toronto Singer and Teacher.")
57 Wiesel, *All Rivers*, 365–66. Levanon's memoir, published the same year as Wiesel's, is vague about Nativ's initiating role. Levanon, *Haqod*, 207.
58 Rozner, *Bintiv*, 17; Levanon, *Haqod*, 68–73, 155.
59 Levine, interview, 5 September 2018; Beckerman, *When They Come*, 143; Levanon, *Haqod*, 155.
60 The ad hoc approach continued immediately after the Six-Day War too. Nativ sent Burton Roberts and Carl Vergari, district and state attorneys from New York, to investigate the legal situation of Soviet Jews in the postwar environment. Taylor, *Courts of Terror*, 15; Levanon, *Haqod*, 231–32.
61 The effort was publicized in 1970 when a former B'nai B'rith senior official, Saul Joftes, as part of a libel suit contesting his dismissal, accused the organization of serving as an unregistered foreign agent. B'nai B'rith staffer William Korey testified that the program was abandoned before it started. Phelps, "Libel Suit in U.S."; Peretz, *Le combat*, 100; Kurz, *Jewish Internationalism*, 147.
62 Seth Jacobson, interviewed by Shaul Kelner, 3 January 2018.
63 Rozner, *Bintiv*, 25–34.
64 Rozner, 35–46.
65 Quoted in Rozner, 46.
66 This analysis follows Peterson's emphasis on organizational structure, industry structure, and occupational careers as forces channeling cultural production. Peterson, "Why 1955?"; Peterson and Anand, "Production of Culture Perspective."
67 Rozner, *Bintiv*, 36–46.
68 Precise numbers remain classified. Rozner, *Bintiv*, 78; Rakeffet-Rothkoff, *From Washington Avenue*, chap. 10, Kindle location: 4885.

69 Rozner, *Bintiv*, 80–81, 137; Rakeffet-Rothkoff, *From Washington Avenue*; Roskies, *Yiddishlands*, 177–84.
70 Rozner, *Bintiv*, 74–76, 83, 88–90, 96–100; Tirosh, "*Haish shehadar et masakh habarzel*"; Jacobson, interview.
71 Rozner, *Bintiv*, 80–83, 90, 96, 131.
72 Cables to and from field officers referred to refuseniks not by name but by their database number. Rozner, *Bintiv*, 85.
73 For example, Joel Sandberg, sent by Nativ in 1975, subsequently chaired the Tourist Briefing Committee for the South Florida Conference on Soviet Jewry and coordinated the UCSJ's tourist work nationally. Joel Sandberg and Adele Sandberg, interviewed by Shaul Kelner, 15 August 2018; Joel Levin et al. to Future Tourist, n.d. (ca. 1976), JSAS b.2 f.5; Joel Sandberg, "Summary Tourist Briefing," memo, Summer 1976, JSAS b.2 f.5; Joel Sandberg to All Briefers, 10 August 1984, UCSJ b.96 f.11. SSSJ recruited tourists sent by Nativ. Glenn Richter, interviewed by Yuli Kosharovsky, 18 May 2004, http://kosharovsky.com. Nativ representatives maintained communication, albeit conflictual, with tourism personnel in other organizations. Rozner, *Bintiv*, 86.
74 Rozner, *Bintiv*, 77; Rakeffet-Rothkoff, *From Washington Avenue*; Jacobson, interview.
75 Rozner, 142–43, 147.
76 Rozner, 129–30.
77 Rozner, 144–47.
78 Astor and Neustadt, *Underground*, 54, 344.
79 Rozner, *Bintiv*, 84. Not all tourists followed the order to abort missions when in danger. In one instance, two college students engaged in fisticuffs with KGB agents on the street and were expelled from the country for it. (A group of sailors had come to the women's defense and "pounced upon the agents.") In their debriefing, one of the women explained that she chose to follow not Nativ's instructions but her father's, a Holocaust survivor who fought as a partisan: "You should know that you cannot retreat from achieving the goals of your mission. All objectives must be accomplished to the maximum. You are an agent of the Jewish state." Quoted in Rakeffet-Rothkoff, *From Washington Avenue*, chap. 10, Kindle location: 4966; Tirosh, "*Haish shehadar et masakh habarzel*."
80 Rozner, *Bintiv*, 58–60, 72. These tested the strategic utility of trying to "pass" as non-Jewish. Jews have used "passing" as a strategy in other activist contexts. For a high-stakes instance when passing as non-Jewish meant the difference between life and death, see Einwohner's "Passing as Strategic Identity Work in the Warsaw Ghetto Uprising."
81 Rozner, *Bintiv*, 90.
82 Levanon, "Israel's Role," 71.
83 The largest online repository of trip reports can be found at the website of the American Jewish Historical Society: https://ajhs.org.
84 Such language is not a literary device here. It is the terminology used in Nativ sources. See Rozner, *Bintiv*; Levanon, *Haqod*; and Jacobson, interview.
85 Weissman, "Report," 28 February 1975. The charge of working on behalf of foreign interests could be applied to those traveling for the NCSJ and UCSJ as well. But because these groups were American voluntary organizations, they afforded a de facto level of security that Nativ tourists—traveling for a government agency from a country without diplomatic ties to the USSR—could not expect.

86 Hazanov details the extent and limits of Soviet tolerance. The country "opened itself to the outside world, if not quite in a feat of absentmindedness, then without any sustained discussion of the implications of this dramatic shift." Its tourism policy reflected an ongoing "series of compromises." Hazanov, "Porous Empire," 10, 345.
87 Rozner, *Bintiv*, 83.
88 McClish, "Mission Accomplished"; Myrna Shinbaum to [redacted in original], 8 November 1983, UCSJ b.79 f.16.
89 Manekofsky, "Guidelines for Briefers."
90 Conference on the Status of Soviet Jews, "'An Appeal of Conscience,'" press release, 12 October 1963, AJCong b.48 f.2; Lewis Feuer, "The Soviet Jews: Resistance to Planned Culturocide," speech to the Conference on the Status of Soviet Jews, 12 October 1963, AJCong b.48 f.2; Hazanov, "Porous Empire," 2–3; Ro'i, *Struggle*, 237; D. Weiss, "Travels of an American Scientist"; Spiegel, *Triumph*, 241–43.
91 On tourism and détente, see Kelner, "Foreign Tourists," 99–101; and Pedersen, "Peace through Tourism."
92 Joel Sprayregen to Judah Graubert, 7 August 1970, NCSJ b.74 f.16; Sprayregen, "Memorandum on Contacts with Jews in the Soviet Union," trip report, 13 May–2 June 1970; Sprayregen, interview, 30 August 2019.
93 Israel Meyerstein and Michael Meyerstein to Jacob Birnbaum, 2 July 1972, CCSA b.4 f.125.
94 Although the couple assumed that they were being sent by Israel, they did not know this for certain: "What struck me most was that we didn't know who was recruiting us. . . . We would meet our contact in a field near Logan Airport." Sherry Israel, interviewed by Shaul Kelner, 14 August 2017. See also Israel and Israel, "USSR Trip," trip report, 19 May–12 June 1974.
95 Jerry Goodman to Phil Baum, 10 January 1974, NCSJ b.14 f.1; Deborah Lipstadt to Jerry Goodman, 23 December 1974, NCSJ b.91 f.2; Lipstadt, *History on Trial*, 10–14; Rozner, *Bintiv*, 58, 133, 220.
96 Lipstadt, "Guide to the Soviet Union"; Kelman, "Reading a Book."
97 Sandberg and Sandberg, interview, 15 August 2018; Levin et al. to Future Tourist, n.d. (ca. 1976); Sandberg, "Summary Tourist Briefing"; Sandberg and Sandberg, "Trip to the U.S.S.R," trip report, May 1975, with 2009 addendum; Sandberg to All Briefers, 10 August 1984; Andreyev, "*Slugi bol'shoĭ lzhi.*"
98 Ferziger, "Outside the Shul"; Ferziger, *Beyond Sectarianism*; Medoff, *Rav Chesed*, 60; Haskel Lookstein, "Minutes of Meeting to Coordinate Jewish Visits to Russia," 18 December 1972, NCSJ b.89 f.4.
99 Manekofsky, "Information on Direct Aid," trip report, 14–26 November 1974; Irene Manekofsky to UCSJ Briefers, 30 April 1976, ASJ b.115 f.5; Unknown [Jerry Goodman? Myrna Shinbaum?], handwritten meeting notes, 26 April 1976, NCSJ b.91 f.3; NCSJ, GNYSJ, and NJCRAC, "Agenda: Seminar on Travel," program agenda, 13 September 1976, NCSJ b.91 f.3; NCSJ, "Travel Group Meeting," agenda and minutes, 7–8 June 1987, NCSJ b.50 f.4. On refuseniks' tendency to give the same information to as many tourists as possible, see Rukin, trip report, 20 June–5 July 1975, 8.
100 AJCSJ, Jewish Community Federation of Cleveland, and CCSA, "Midwest Regional Leadership Conference on Soviet Jewry," conference program, 28 February–1 March 1970, CCSA2 b.3 f.3; Rosenblum, *Hear the Cry*.
101 Rosenblum, *Hear the Cry*, 13.

102 Nativ's efforts to court Rosenblum had ended in mutual recrimination. Rosenblum was appalled at Nativ's presumption that American activists should accept Israeli discipline. Nativ's Nehemiah Levanon and Yoram Dinstein were infuriated at what they considered Rosenblum's audacity in rejecting an Israeli-led unified framework for activism. Rosenblum, "Control of Soviet Jewry Movement"; Levanon, *Haqod*, 430.

103 Beckerman, *When They Come*, 295; Spiegel, *Triumph*, 69–70; Rosenblum and Rosenblum, "Involvement," 84–85.

104 Kelner, "People-to-People."

105 Stephen Shemin to Louis Rosenblum, 3 February 1972, CCSA b.4 f.125; Allan Shall to Louis Rosenblum, 31 October 1972, CCSA b.4 f.125; CCSA, "Tourist Debriefings," audio recording collection, 1971–77, CCSA b.4 f.125–30.

106 CCSA, "Membership Newsletter," February 1972, CCSA b.3 f.97; Carol Mandel and Morris Mandel to UCSJ Members, "Re: Tourist Briefing Project," 13 December 1972, WCSJ b.9 f.11; Carol Mandel, interviewed by Shaul Kelner, 10 July 2018.

107 Douglas Kahn to Louis Rosenblum, 23 August 1972, CCSA b.48 f.243; Louis Rosenblum, "'From Jack Cohen,'" handwritten notes and transcript from telephone calls with Douglas Kahn and Paul Jacobson, 17 August 1972, CCSA b.8 f.243; Kahn, "Advocacy on the Community Level," 183–87.

108 Frumkin, trip report on SCCSJ letterhead, 28 April–4 May 1974; Rosenblum, trip report under Action Central header, 29 April–4 May 1974; Zev Yaroslavsky, interviewed by Shaul Kelner, 13 September 2018.

109 Benjamin and Rosenblum, "Trip Report: Kiev, Kharkov, Moscow and Leningrad," 8–21 July 1974.

110 For other examples of affordances and constraints in cultural mobilizations, see Kelner, *Tours That Bind*; and McDonnell, *Best Laid Plans*. On affordances generally, see Davis, *How Artifacts Afford*.

111 Zev Yaroslavsky to Louis Rosenblum, "Outline for Project Lifeline," 1 July 1974, CCSA b.9 f.259; Louis Rosenblum and Zev Yaroslavsky, "Project Lifeline," July 1974, CCSA b.9 f.259.

112 Samuel H. Sislen, interviewed by Shaul Kelner, 1 July 2019; "Council Activities: Travel Program," memo, 1978, WCSJ b.9 f.8.

113 Feuer, "Soviet Jews"; Weinstein, *Masa*, 254–61; Teplitz, "Russian Jewish Youth."

114 Theodore R. Mann to NJCRAC Member Agencies, "Minutes of Commission Meeting of November 22, 1971," 21 January 1972, GNYCSJ b.1 f.2; Levanon, *Haqod*, 227.

115 Burg, trip report, 10–18 March 1975.

116 Mann to NJCRAC Agencies, "Minutes of November 22, 1971"; Porath, *Here We Are All Jews*, 29–99; Jonathan Porath, interviewed by Shaul Kelner, 29 August 2016.

117 The effort was led by Telford Taylor, chief US prosecutor at the Nuremberg war crimes tribunals. Taylor, *Courts of Terror*, 15–26.

118 NJCRAC, the national umbrella organization for local Jewish American community relations councils, was a member of the NCSJ and its closest partner. It previously had housed and staffed the AJCSJ.

119 In February 1970, AJCSJ coordinator Abraham Bayer and the CCSA's Louis Rosenblum collaborated to organize a conference in which Rosenblum led a workshop on tourist briefings. AJCSJ, Jewish Community Federation of Cleveland, and CCSA, "Midwest Regional."

120 Mann to NJCRAC Agencies, "Minutes of November 22, 1971"; Porath, *Here We Are All Jews*; Porath, interview, 29 August 2016.
121 Mann to NJCRAC Agencies, "Minutes of November 22, 1971"; Hester Beckman to AJCongress Chapter and Division Presidents, "Briefing Kits for Tourists to Russia," 22 January 1972, AJCong b.48 f.6.
122 Baum and Furst, *How to Find*, 1, 2, 6; Zev Furst, interviewed by Shaul Kelner, 19 July 2018; Rozner, *Bintiv*, 58, 133, 220.
123 Baum and Furst, *How to Find*, 7, 8, 11, 12, 16, 18–27.
124 Beckman to AJCongress Chapter and Division Presidents, "Briefing Kits."
125 Baum and Furst, *How to Find*, i.
126 Baum and Furst, i (emphasis in original).
127 Nilov, "*Oplata . . . galetami.*"
128 Furst, interview, 19 July 2018.
129 Contrast this with Union of Councils briefing kits, which had section headers labeled "post-trip expectations." BACSJ, "BACSJ Objectives for Travel to USSR," n.d., BACSJ b.33 f.45; Seattle Action for Soviet Jewry, "SASJ Objectives for Travel to USSR" (Seattle), n.d., SASJ b.9 f.4.
130 Jerry Goodman to Phil Baum, 5 December 1972, NCSJ b.14 f.1; "Meeting Russian Jews."
131 Jerry Goodman, interviewed by Shaul Kelner, 5 September 2019.
132 Freilich and Freilich, trip report, 3–17 June 1973; Lippert, trip report, 27 July–1 August 1973.
133 E.g., Rothschild, trip report, 16–22 April 1974; Hirschfield, trip report, 21–28 October 1974; Becker and Becker, trip report, 21 March–3 April 1975; Freeman, trip report, 23 May–11 June 1975. Shinbaum herself traveled to the USSR in 1974, 1977, and 1979 and then was denied permission to enter the country for the next ten years. Shinbaum, "Mobilizing America," 178.
134 Myrna Shinbaum to Jerry Goodman, August 1975, NCSJ b.61 f.30.
135 Dollinger, *Black Power*; Gans, "Symbolic Ethnicity"; E. Goldstein, *Price of Whiteness*; Fisher, "Place in History"; R. Gross, *Beyond the Synagogue*.
136 On uses of heritage tourism in Jewish American identity projects, see Kelner, *Tours That Bind*; and Diner, Shandler, and Wenger, *Remembering the Lower East Side*. On the imaginings of Eastern Europe in Jewish American identity projects, see Krah, *American Jewry*; and Zipperstein, *Imagining Russian Jewry*. The most well-known cultural artifact of Jewish American nostalgia for the Eastern European shtetl is the musical *Fiddler on the Roof*. Sure enough, when the film version premiered in November 1971, activists organized thematic protests around it. MACSJ, "The Fiddler's World Then and Now," pamphlet, 1971, BHP b.2 f.3.
137 Goodman to Baum, 10 January 1974; WCSJ, "Theater Group."
138 NCSJ, "Travel to the USSR: A Jewish Guide—Part 1," unpublished draft, 1 July 1974, NCSJ b.68 f.7, 1.
139 NCSJ, "Travel to the USSR," 1, 3–4, B1, B3, B8.
140 Postal and Abramson, *Landmarks of a People*, 237, 252–54 (second edition published as Postal and Abramson, *Traveler's Guide*, 305, 324, 327); Fodor, *Fodor's Europe*, 892, 894; Lipstadt, "Guide to the Soviet Union."
141 Louis Rosenblum to Jerry Goodman, 22 July 1974, NCSJ b.68 f.7; Goodman to Baum, 10 January 1974; Laurel Erazo to Jerry Goodman, "Re: 'Travel to the USSR—a Jewish Guide,'" 30 September 1974, NCSJ b.68 f.7.

142 In 1990, the Union of Councils began operating its own heritage tours as a way of raising funds. On profit margins and an analysis of competitors in the field, see David Waksberg to Pam Cohen, "Re: CJR Report," 23 March 1990, BACSJ b.1 f.1.
143 Manekofsky served as the UCSJ's national tourism coordinator during Weissman's term as president.
144 Noam Shudofsky to Joseph Feit et al., 21 November 1974, NCSJ b.91 f.3; Noam Shudofsky to Sandy Eisenstat et al., "Briefings and Debriefings," 23 January 1975, NCSJ b.91 f.3; "NCSJ Sets Up Bureau"; Goodman, interview, 5 September 2019.
145 For instance, leaders in both organizations were frustrated with the all-too-common situation of tourists seeking out separate briefings from each group, sometimes receiving contradictory instructions. (Briefers tended to be committed to the notion that the other group's briefings were rarely as good as their own.) Sislen, interview, 1 July 2019; Beller, interview, 2 July 2019; Ruth Newman, interviewed by Shaul Kelner, 8 August 2019; Irene Manekofsky to Dear Friend, 1 September 1974, WCSJ b.9 f.10; Samuel Sislen, "The Soviet Jewry Movement in the Greater Washington Community" (Lillian and Albert Small Capital Jewish Museum), October 2008, www.jhsgw.org; Beller, "Reflections."
146 At the time, other groups' tourism coordinators just kept the details in their heads. To explain Chicago Action for Soviet Jewry's practices to a briefer in another community, the lead activist could send no outline codifying their procedures. Instead, she wrote a letter reconstructing her practices from memory. Pollack to Sandberg, 3 April 1975.
147 The WCSJ's Irene Manekofsky became head of the Union of Councils' network of briefers in 1975. The JCCGW's Samuel "Buddy" Sislen became part of the NCSJ's informal team of tourism experts. Insiders Club materials are preserved not only in the archives of DC groups but also in the files of the National Conference, the Bay Area Council on Soviet Jewry, and other groups nationwide. Sheila Levin Woods to Jerry Goodman, 21 October 1974, NCSJ b.68 f.7; Jane Beller and Herb Beller to Briefers, 21 February 1975, NCSJ b.89 f.2; Samuel Sislen to Myrna Shinbaum, 18 December 1974, NCSJ b.68 f.13; Samuel Sislen, cover attachment to J. Berch debriefing questionnaire, forwarded to NCSJ, 1975, NCSJ b.55 f.12; Samuel Sislen to Myrna Shinbaum, 25 August 1976, NCSJ b.89 f.2; NCSJ, "Travel Group"; "Meeting and Helping Refusniks during Your Visit to the U.S.S.R.," draft guidebook, 1975, MSP b.99 f.1; Sislen, interview, 1 July 2019.
148 WCSJ, "Theater Group"; Goodman to Baum, 10 January 1974.
149 Insiders Club, *Guidebook*, 2, 6.
150 Insiders Club, 2–4. Untitled draft in Woods to Goodman, 21 October 1974.
151 Avrum Ashery, interviewed by Shaul Kelner, 13 August 2019; Insiders Club, *Guidebook*; Insiders Club to Area Rabbis, 29 December 1976, WCSJ b.9 f.10.
152 Beller and Beller to Briefers, 21 February 1975.
153 Beller and Beller to Briefers, 21 February 1975; Insiders Club, "Travellers Orientation Outline," 1975, WCSJ b.9 f.10.
154 Beller and Beller to Briefers, 21 February 1975; Insiders Club, "Travellers Orientation Outline."
155 Irene Manekofsky to All Union of Councils Briefers/Debriefers, 16 February 1975, MBSP b.3 f.5.
156 Weissman to All Councils, "Report on Visit," 28 February 1975.

157 Barsov, "*Sionskie bliznetsy*"; Michael Sherbourne, "'The Zionist Twins' by Oleg Barsov," translation from *Izvestia* Sunday Supplement, *Nedelya*, August 1975, NCSJ b.9 f.2. The present translation combines Sherbourne's and my own.
158 Soviet press attacks on meetings with Western activists and journalists were common, intended mainly to discredit Soviet activists. Walker, "Moscow Correspondents," 151–53.
159 Manekofsky to UCSJ Briefers, 30 April 1976.
160 Cantor, "Enclosed Travel Reports." Inequities in contact and in the material support that came with it contributed to tension among refuseniks. Morozova, *Anatomiia Otkaza*, 179. See also Walker, "Moscow Correspondents," 151.
161 Connie Smukler to Briefing Committee Members, "Guidelines," n.d., JCRCGP b.65 f.13.
162 Insiders Club, "Questionnaire," 1975, WCSJ b.9 f.10. (The penultimate draft was dated January 30. This version was in use by February.) Insiders Club Questionnaire, draft, Sislen, cover attachment to J. Berch debriefing questionnaire.
163 Insiders Club, "Questionnaire," 4.
164 Insiders Club Questionnaire, draft, Sislen, cover attachment to J. Berch debriefing questionnaire.
165 NCSJ, "USSR Refuseniks and Prisoners of Conscience Individual Files, Undated, 1971–1992, Subseries A: Individual Files on Soviet Refuseniks, Undated, 1971–1991," NCSJ b.92–115; UCSJ, "Prisoners of Conscience (POCs), Refuseniks and Persons Who Emigrated from the USSR, Undated, 1970, 1972–1996," case files, UCSJ b.32–42; NCSJ, "Jews Repeatedly Denied the Right to Leave the USSR," database list, 17 August 1973, CCSA b.9 f.263; Jerry Goodman, "Attached Is a List . . ." memo with attachment, 27 June 1973, CCSA b.9 f.263; Action Central, "Refusenik List," August 1975, CCSA b.8 f.224; Sanford and Sandberg, *Soviet Jews*; Sandberg and Sandberg, interview, 15 August 2018.
166 Irene Manekofsky to Briefers, 15 August 1977, ASJ b.91 f.1. The Union of Councils' newsletter, *Alert*, regularly shared updates from returning tourists. For a typical example, see the January 17, 1979, issue's "Traveler's Report."
167 Insiders Club, "Questionnaire."
168 Manekofsky to All Union of Councils Briefers/Debriefers, 16 February 1975. For an example of Philadelphia Soviet Jewish Council's first form, see Dishler and Dishler, trip report, 8–16 December 1975. For an NCSJ form, see Mervis, trip report, 12–20 March 1982. For Britain's National Council for Soviet Jewry, see Churney, trip report, 9–13 December 1987.
169 SJC, *Briefing Book for Travelers*; UCSJ, "Briefing Procedure," tourist briefer's kit, 1989, WCSJ b.9 f.11, 31–32; Comité des Quinze, "Practical Information for Your Own Security," n.d., PBC b.29 f.1, 1; CASJ, untitled briefers' notes, n.d., CASJ b.5 f.1, 10–12. The notion of innovation at the "perimeter" comes from Tilly, "Contentious Repertoires," 27–28.
170 Sometimes Soviet Jewry organizations mobilized professional identities to engage people who were not yet involved in the movement. Other times, the initiative came from "occupational activists" integrating their advocacy work and their professional lives. The GNYCSJ offers an example of the first approach. In or around 1978, it created four occupation-based groups to engage people in the legal, medical, mental health, and business sectors. GNYCSJ, *Soviet Jewry Catalog*, 21. (The GNYCSJ was connected to the New York Jewish Federation and was likely influenced by its practice of structuring fundraising along occupational lines for men and grouping

all women together in a Women's Division. The GNYCSJ's one nonindustry-based affinity group was the New York Women's Coalition for Soviet Jewry; Moore, *At Home in America*, 154–62.) Examples of the professional groups created by occupational activists include the Medical Mobilization for Soviet Jewry (Paul Appelbaum, Boston, 1973), the Soviet Jewry Legal Advocacy Center (Donna Arzt and Lawrence Lerner, Boston, 1977), and the Committee of Concerned Scientists (Fred Pollak, Jack S. Cohen, and Melvin Pomerantz, Washington, DC, and New York, 1972). Cash, "Mobilizing for Soviet Jewry"; Sandberg, "Our Other Patients"; Minker, *Scientific Freedom*, 7–8; SJLAC, "Materials on Formation of the Soviet Jewry Legal Advocacy Center," assorted, 1977–79, ASJ b.110 f.1. On occupational activism, see Cornfield et al., "Occupational Activism."

171 "Medical Mission Links Refuseniks"; NCSJ, "NCSJ Forms Medical Action Committee," press release, 18 March 1987, NCSJ b.156 f.2; Victor Borden, interviewed by Shaul Kelner, 8 January 2020.

172 Shudofsky to Feit et al., 21 November 1974; Shudofsky to Eisenstat et al., "Briefings," 23 January 1975; Caine, trip report, 2–10 October 1974; Frankel, trip report, 6–21 July 1974. Legal travel grew substantially after 1975 as part of the American legal community's larger mobilization to monitor compliance with the Helsinki Accords' human rights provisions. Thomas, *Helsinki Effect*; Snyder, *Human Rights Activism*; Cotler, "Soviet Jewry"; Gerjuoy, trip report, 26 July–9 August 1981, 14; Schnur and Ruth-Davis, interview, 24 September 2019.

173 Minker, *Scientific Freedom*, 79–90; Azbel, *Refusenik*, 418–19. On professional advocacy for dissident colleagues as a mode of scientific activism, see Hess et al., "Science, Technology, and Social Movements," 476–77.

174 Rakeffet-Rothkoff, *From Washington Avenue*; Wolf, *Dyedushka*; Astor and Neustadt, *Underground*; Landau, "To Russia with Love"; Hill, *Serving the Jewish People*, 109–55; Barbara Penzner, "Evaluation of Joint JCRC-RRC Sponsorship of Rabbinical Students Visiting Refuseniks," 6 August 1987, JCRCGP b.81 f.31; Henry Cohen to Harold Levine, 1 April 1986, JCRCGP b.81 f.31.

175 Applying to emigrate could result in being fired from work. Black market sales helped make up for lost incomes. Refuseniks preferred brand-new jeans; however, these shouted "black market" and might not make it through customs. Prewashing disguised them as the tourists' own clothes. Wurtman and Smuckler, "Simhat Torah Journey to the Soviet Union," trip report, 15–22 October 1976, 9. My mother, who washed jeans for travelers from our Manalapan, New Jersey, synagogue, recalled the heavy-duty settings to me. Personal communication, Rhoda Schulman, 26 February, 2020.

176 E.g., Gray, "My Soviet Odyssey"; Zwaik, "Lights Are Dim." Anita Gray was an ORT chapter member. Her husband, Alvin, was past president of Cleveland Men's ORT. Zwaik was the national commander of the Jewish War Veterans of the USA. The magazine's cover photo showed him smiling in front of the triumphal arch at the General Staff Building in Leningrad under the title "Our Man in Russia."

177 E.g., Richard Klein, "Yom Kippur 5750" (Main Line Reform Temple, Wynnewood, PA), sermon, 1989, NCSJ b.68 f.36.

178 For instance, Mary Travers—of the folk trio Peter, Paul and Mary—spoke at Congregation B'nai Jehoshua Beth Elohim. "Sabbath Evening Service" (Glenview, IL), prayer booklet, 20–21 April 1984, CASJ b.16 f.1.

179 Insiders Club, "Questionnaire"; CASJ, "Speakers' Bureau," brochure, n.d., CASJ b.5 f.2.

180 E.g., McEnroe, "Rabbi Used Soviet Tour"; Keegan, "U.S. Visitors Bring Hope"; McClish, "Mission Accomplished"; "Shenkers Visit Refuseniks."
181 CASJ, "Speakers Bureau Information," n.d., ASJ b.115 f.5, 2.

4. From Russia, with Angst

1 Shapiro, trip report, 20–28 March 1984, 2. On Cantor as Shapiro's briefer, see Howard Shapiro and Eileen Shapiro, interviewed by Shaul Kelner, 24 November 2019.
2 Tabachnikoff, trip report, 20–28 March 1984, 4 (all caps in original). The Cold War lenses that transformed an old street cleaner into a symbol of KGB surveillance were par for the course. Part of the appeal of Western travel to Soviet bloc nations was to "experience the thrill of the Cold War itself." Standley, "Experiencing Communism" 63. Desire was not, however, the sole impetus. Suspicions ran high among tourists and hosts alike, leading them to misinterpret mundane tourist problems as political in character. Stanoeva, "Exporting Holidays," 36–39.
3 Tabachnikoff, trip report, 1. Follett's spy novel is set in czarist Russia, just before the revolution.
4 Tabachnikoff, trip report, 16 (all caps in original).
5 Shapiro, trip report, 11.
6 Shapiro, trip report, 8.
7 Shapiro, trip report, 1.
8 Shapiro, trip report, 9.
9 Tabachnikoff, trip report, 10.
10 Shapiro, trip report, 3. On the complicated dynamics that gift giving sparked, see Walker, "Moscow Correspondents."
11 Shapiro, trip report, 4.
12 Tabachnikoff, trip report, 9.
13 Shapiro, trip report, 7.
14 Shapiro, trip report, 3.
15 Tabachnikoff, trip report, 5.
16 Tabachnikoff, trip report, 10.
17 Chirico, "Travel Narrative," 39. The outer parts of the definition are Chirico's; the inner part is cited from Chirico's citation of Borm, "Defining Travel," 17.
18 Thompson suggests the tripartite formulation—reporting the world, representing the Other, revealing the Self—to structure the analysis of travel writing. Thompson, *Travel Writing*.
19 For an examination of how Soviet Jewry movement travelers cast the tourist gaze on off-the-beaten-path Soviet spaces, particularly the insides of apartments, see Kelner, "Foreign Tourists." For a counterpoint—a Soviet Jewish émigré traveler's gaze on Western European spaces—see Veksler, "'We Left Forever,'" 169–201.
20 SJC, *Briefing Book for Travelers*, 53.
21 Soffin, "Mission to Moscow," trip report, 4–17 April 1987; Rose, "Our Russian Adventure," trip report, 20–22 July 1973; Mansheim and Mansheim, "Dr. M. Goes to the USSR," trip report, 15–30 September 1984; Hellman, "From Russia, with Angst," trip report, November 1987; Dubin, "They Are Surely Heroes," trip report, [ca. June?] 1988; Bodoff, "We Can All Be Heroes," trip report, 19 July 1988; Stern and Gropper, "How We Spent Our Christmas Vacation," trip report, January 1986.

22 The longest travelogues in the American Jewish Historical Society archives are over one hundred pages. The average ones range from seven to twenty-four pages (interquartile range), with the median at twelve.
23 By getting people to articulate the autobiographical consequences of their activism, travel writing not only described changes in self-understanding but helped generate these changes. On activism's power to alter life trajectories, see McAdam, "Biographical Consequences." On the mechanisms by which travelers' testimonials about the life-changing nature of tourism generate the attested life changes, see Kelner, *Tours That Bind*, 185–90.
24 Activists' use of narrative writing (journaling) to develop and articulate their own understandings of the Soviet Jewry movement and their participation in it is another form of social movement storytelling beyond those identified in Polletta, *It Was like a Fever*. The trope of "unreality" (including the question "Is this really happening?") is prominent in Neiter, "Reflections on Temple Judea's Trip to the Soviet Union," trip report, 15–30 October 1976, 9, 10, 15. On being part of history, see "Briefer's Checklist," September 1986, NCSJ b.91 f.3.
25 As with other Jewish cultural practices, such as Passover seders and bar mitzvah celebrations, non-Jews were invited to participate. Christian allies—mainly politicians, lawyers, and clergy—visited refuseniks at the behest of movement organizations.
26 The history of Jewish travel writing spans millennia. For analyses from antiquity to the present day, see Hezser, *Jewish Travel in Antiquity*; and Levinson and Bashkin, *Jews and Journeys*.
27 Trip reports can be accessed at the American Jewish History Society website: www.ajhs.org. For excerpts from reports submitted to Nativ, see Rozner, *Bintiv*.
28 *Methodological note:* The AJHS has scanned almost all the trip reports in its possession. The archivists provided me with digital copies, which I converted to readable text using optical character recognition in Adobe Acrobat. I acquired several dozen additional reports from other archives. I built a relational database in Microsoft Access and hired a team of assistants to enter details from all these trip reports. This enabled me to sort the corpus by date of travel. I then read every report written from 1956 to 1977 in chronological order—(209 in all, over 2,800 pages) and a selection of reports from each year thereafter, 1978 through 1991 (another 60 reports). To systematize my analysis, I conducted grounded analysis using the ATLAS.ti qualitative data analysis software package. To identify themes and patterns, I coded 80 reports: 22 fully and 58 for selected themes. A research assistant coded another 20. On the use of travel writing as a "privileged source for analyzing cultural identities," see Rubiés, "Cultural History of Travel."
29 Thompson, *Travel Writing*, 9.
30 Kobrin, "Long Silent Revolution."
31 Lewis, trip report, December 1973, 1.
32 Irene Manekofsky, "Debriefing Report: Barbara Cuban and Marcia Mazur," 30 March 1975, NCSJ b.58 f.2, 1.
33 Neiter, "Reflections," 5 (emphasis in original).
34 CASJ, "Speakers Bureau Information," n.d., ASJ b.115 f.5, 2.
35 Axelrad and Showstack, "Refusenik!," trip report, 21–29 September 1978, 4.
36 Comité des Quinze, "Practical Information for Your Own Security," n.d., PBC b.29 f.1, 7.

37 Weintraub and Yudenfriend, trip report, 17–25 August 1979, 1.
38 Myrna Shinbaum to [redacted in original], 8 November 1983, UCSJ b.79 f.16.
39 Abramson, Appel, and Schneider, trip report, 9–24 September 1978, 5.
40 Hinda Cantor and Marillyn Tallman to All Briefers, UCSJ tourist briefing guide, 21 March 1991, CASJ b.5 f.1.
41 Goodman and Margolis, trip report, 8–16 May 1978.
42 Kuznick and Gilbert, *Rethinking Cold War Culture*, 2.
43 Glajar, Lewis, and Petrescu, *Cold War Spy Stories*; Manning, *John le Carré*; Kackman, *Citizen Spy*; E. Horn, *Secret War*.
44 In reading folk writings as literary works and attending to their authors' choice to tell "personal history through the narrative idioms of fiction," I follow Kirshenblatt-Gimblett, Moseley, and Stanislawski's approach to reading Polish Jewish youth autobiographies from the 1930s. Introduction to Shandler, *Awakening Lives*, xxvi–xxxvii.
45 For examples that treat smuggling documents, see Neiter, "Reflections," 12. On invisible ink, see Arzt and Arzt, trip report, 29 July–2 August 1976, 2, 3. On film confiscations, see Irene Manekofsky, "Debriefing Report: Dennis Gannon," 24 May 1976, NCSJ b.60 f.15. On stashing film in others' luggage, see Sussman, trip report, 5–20 July 1975, 10. On brush passes, see Kameny, "Our Soviet Journey," trip report, 1–9 March 1974, 6. On whisperings and vanishings, see Klaperman, trip report, 21 June–3 August 1956, 2; and Sprayregen, "Memorandum on Contacts with Jews in the Soviet Union," trip report, 13 May–2 June 1970, 35. On shuttering windows, see Freilich and Freilich, trip report, 3–17 June 1973, 5. On telephoto surveillance, see Reznick, trip report, 2–16 September 1976, 15–16; and Kuhr, "Debriefing Narrative / Russian Journey," trip report, 14–28 August 1978, 7.
46 This failure to control the meaning of the tactic is par for the course. For an analysis of how activists inevitably lose control over their vehicles of public messaging, see McDonnell, *Best Laid Plans*.
47 On the constraining power of cultural ideas, see Swidler, "Cultural Power."
48 This simplicity serves a rhetorical purpose, suggesting to the reader that this is a true firsthand account. The style, "naïve empiricism," came into common use in travelogues with the rise of scientific travel in the eighteenth century. Thompson, *Travel Writing*, 78–79. On the text's invitation to be read as fictional imitation or as direct representation, see Frow, *Genre*, 16.
49 Bay, "Our Visits with Jews in the USSR," trip report, 15–29 May 1976, 5; Kuhr, "Debriefing Narrative," 10 (day 13); Morris and Morris, trip report, 22 May–6 June 1987, 4.
50 Rose, "Our Russian Adventure," 3.
51 After the 1985 trip, Borden joined the executive board of the NCSJ's Medical Action Committee and led medical missions to Russia for the UCSJ's International Physicians' Commission for the Protection of Prisoners. Victor Borden, interviewed by Shaul Kelner, 8 January 2020; Borden, "Physicians Mission to the Soviet Union," trip report, November 1987.
52 Borden, trip report, 4–13 July 1985, 1, 2.
53 Shapiro, trip report, 8 (emphasis added).
54 Kuhr, "Debriefing Narrative," 7 (emphasis added).
55 Neiter, "Reflections," 6.
56 Gerut, trip report, 20–29 May 1985, 5 (emphasis added).
57 Wellins, "Back from the USSR," trip report, 1986, 2 (emphasis added).

58 Kameny, "Our Soviet Journey," 6 (emphasis added).
59 Pfeffer, "Notes on Trip to Soviet Union to Photograph Refuseniks," trip report, 11 September–4 October 1985, 10, 18 (emphasis added).
60 Breslow, trip report, 26 October–3 November 1983, 16 (emphasis added).
61 Burg, trip report, 10–18 March 1975, 3; Stern, "Canadian Parliamentary Visit to the USSR," trip report, 18–24 January 1984, 19.
62 As anthropologist Jack Kugelmass has written, "Unprocessed experience generally lacks a dramatic structure to make it meaningful." Kugelmass, "Rites of the Tribe," 418.
63 Schmid, *Secrets*, lecture 30, 27:38–28:54.
64 Contrast this with spy novels that aspire to be, and are treated as, art. Powell, "Redemption for the Protagonist"; Campbell, "Dialectical Discourses."
65 Author unknown, "Debriefing Check List," in Action for Soviet Jewry (Boston) files, n.d., ASJ b.115 f.5.
66 When this passage was composed, the route from Russia to Israel passed through Austria. Soviet Jews departed by train, were housed in the Schoenau Castle transit center south of Vienna, and flew from there to Israel's Lydda airport. Other transit routes went through Ladispoli, Rome. On emigrants' experience in the transit points, see Shrayer, *Waiting for America*; Veksler, "'We Left Forever'"; Zborovsky, "'Venetian Waltz'"; and Fedeski, "From Refusenik to Refugee."
67 Siris, "Encounter with Soviet Jewish Activists," trip report, July 1973. All ellipses are Siris's in the original. On Siris's leadership in the United Jewish Appeal, see her autobiography, Winik, *Still Looking Forward*.
68 Leisch and Leisch, trip report, 13–20 March 1976.
69 On the place of Holocaust memory in Jewish American discourse about the USSR and Soviet Jews, see Diner, *We Remember*, 278–86. Among the ways Jews avoided overstating the comparison was to invoke Holocaust analogies "more in the form of questions than as statements of fact" (283).
70 Wiesel, *Jews of Silence*, 5.
71 On the charge of American Jewish passivity in responding to the Nazis, see Lipstadt, "Playing the Blame Game."
72 Brettler and Turner, trip report, 14 May–1 June 1981, 25; Epstein and Starr, trip report, May 1985, 5; Klatzker and Levine, trip report, 20–31 January 1985, 10.
73 On the political mainstreaming of Holocaust minimization, see Lipstadt, *Denying the Holocaust*, 2–15, 209–16. In the specific context of Socialist nation-building in Soviet bloc countries, see Zubrzycki, *Crosses of Auschwitz*, 103–8. On Jewish American concerns about the erasure of Jewish victimization, see Diner, *We Remember*, 282.
74 Finkelstein, trip report, 24 June–8 July 1976, 7, 14.
75 Sprayregen, "Memorandum on Contacts," 41 (handwriting represented here as small caps).
76 It is hard to overstate how important imaginings of Eastern Europe were to American Jewish identity and communal life in the twentieth century. For thorough treatments, see Krah, *American Jewry*; and Zipperstein, *Imagining Russian Jewry*.
77 Borden, trip report, 26.
78 For other examples of how travelers interpreted Soviet synagogues, see Kelner, "À la rencontre des Juifs."
79 Slezkine, *Jewish Century*. The term "tourist gaze" is Urry's, from *Tourist Gaze*. Jewish American tourists' contemplation of the gaps between present and past, US and

USSR, showed greater complexity in the 1920s and '30s, when visitors to the USSR could imagine the country leading Russian Jews into a promising Soviet Jewish future. Soyer, "Back to the Future." By the 1970s, the realities of "actually existing socialism" had closed down that option.

80 Cf. Kugelmass, "Green Bagels." Arnold Eisen argues that the "commanding power of nostalgia" has been core to modern Jewish religious sentiment throughout the nineteenth and twentieth centuries. Eisen, "Nostalgia as Modern Jewish Mitzvah." See also Kelner, "Boomers, Millennials"; and R. Gross, *Beyond the Synagogue*.
81 On Jews' use of Eastern European heritage travel to imagine alternative selves and alternative histories, see Lehrer, *Jewish Poland Revisited*.
82 Neiter, "Reflections," 5 (emphasis in original).
83 Gilbert, handwritten trip report, 17 May–7 June 1976, 5 ("Leningrad").
84 Feldman, *Above the Death Pits*; Kugelmass, "Rites of the Tribe," 431. See also Ferziger, *Beyond Sectarianism*, 85–113; and Sheramy, "From Auschwitz to Jerusalem."
85 Banana Republic, *Soviet Safari*, catalog no. 27 (Spring 1986). Another line of analysis could examine corporate support of the Soviet Jewry movement. The Zieglers were not the only business owners to volunteer company resources. Irving Stone had his American Greetings Corporation design and produce holiday greeting cards for the Cleveland Council on Soviet Anti-Semitism. Rosenblum and Rosenblum, "Involvement," 66–67. At the initiative of founding partner Alan Pesky, the New York advertising agency Scali, McCabe, Sloves did pro bono work promoting Solidarity Sunday rallies. Zeesy Schnur and Margy-Ruth Davis, interviewed by Shaul Kelner, 24 September 2019. The list is long.
86 Baum and Furst, *How to Find*.
87 Based on a string search of all travelogues scanned by the AJHS. Optical character recognition was performed using Adobe Acrobat on the author's computer. Two travelogues mentioned wearing or delivering safari slacks or suits.
88 Steif, "Refuseniks of Kiev," 21.
89 Senderovich, "Scenes," 98–132; Pratt, *Imperial Eyes*.
90 Jacobson, "American Studies," 10–11, 118, 287; Fodor and Fisher, *Fodor's Soviet Union*, 7.
91 Keller, "Soviet Aide Admits."
92 Rosenfeld and Rosenfeld, trip report, 28 September–20 October 1976, 39; Kling, trip report, August 1978, 49; Michelson, trip report, 29 September–1 October 1984, 12–13.
93 This trope persisted in later years. On an unsuccessful attempt, see Stern, "Canadian Parliamentary Visit," 20.
94 Sprayregen, "Memorandum on Contacts," 18–19.
95 Shapiro, trip report, 2.
96 Sprayregen, "Memorandum on Contacts," 29.
97 Rukin, trip report, 20 June–5 July 1975, 17.
98 Sprayregen, "Memorandum on Contacts," 20.
99 "Take close-ups of the refuseniks. . . . Don't take all pictures of the refuseniks with you or your friend/spouse. Those snaps are great for your scrapbook, useless to us." UCSJ, "Briefing Procedure," tourist briefer's kit, 1989, WCSJ b.9 f.11, VI:5.
100 If tourists did take other types of photos, they generally did not include them in their trip reports. They are largely absent from the archive of organizational files. Representative examples of travelogue photographs can be found in Wellish, trip report,

10–24 October 1978; Bair and Silberstein, trip report, May 1984; and Abella et al., trip report, 11–21 April 1988.
101 P. Cohen, *Hidden Heroes*, 22. Database construction to support package delivery preceded the mass mobilization. In the 1950s, Nativ and the American Jewish Joint Distribution Committee jointly initiated a package delivery program to needy Jews (mainly the elderly and the Orthodox) in Eastern bloc countries, including the USSR. To avoid Soviet backlash, they neither publicized it nor used it to engage popular participation. Nativ began compiling the first database of Soviet Jewish names and addresses to support this effort. By 1963, it had twenty-five thousand names. Beizer, "'I Don't Know Whom to Thank,'" 120–22.
102 Pomerantz, trip report, 15–30 August 1976, 7.
103 Leisch and Leisch, trip report, appendix H.
104 Tabachnikoff, trip report, 6.
105 Barnett, trip report, 26 October–3 November 1983, 9–10.
106 Hochstadter, trip report, November 1987, 5.
107 Stern, "Canadian Parliamentary Visit," 24. On building relationships and cultivating a sense of moral responsibility to strangers, see Polletta, *Inventing*, 117–42.
108 Trachtenburg, trip report, 4–14 September 1985, 11.
109 In oral history interviews, by contrast, activist leaders commonly described relationships with Soviet Jewish activists evolving into lifelong friendships, with mutual care and support at times of celebration and illness alike. Bobbie Morgenstern, interviewed by Shaul Kelner, 25 June 2020; Ruth Newman, interviewed by Shaul Kelner, 8 August 2019; Joel Sandberg and Adele Sandberg, interviewed by Shaul Kelner, 15 August 2018.
110 On scientific travel writing—naturalist and ethnographic—see Pratt, *Imperial Eyes*, 15–66; Rubiés, "Travel Writing."
111 On diaspora-building, see Kelner, *Tours That Bind*, 201–6.
112 The concept is Foucault's, from *Birth of Biopolitics*. For other examples of diaspora Jewish biopolitics, see Kravel-Tovi, "Wet Numbers."
113 Pianko, *Jewish Peoplehood*. At the same time, Nativ was undertaking identical work on behalf of the State of Israel.
114 To say that communities are "imagined" is not to say that they are not real, only that the bonds are grounded in abstract ideas of commonality rather than direct face-to-face relationships. No American knows every single other American, yet they can all imagine themselves being part of the same collective. Anderson, *Imagined Communities*; West and Zimmerman, "Doing Gender."
115 Salkin and Agler, trip report, 28 May–5 June 1983, 3 (ellipsis in original). The prayer giving thanks for the cock's crowing is part of the morning liturgy.
116 Thompson, *Travel Writing*, 96–129.
117 Levinstone and Levinstone, trip report, March 1974, 5.
118 See, for instance, Tallman and Opper, trip report, 4–12 November 1988; Cohen and Naftalin, trip report, 29 May–7 June 1988.
119 Jewish ambivalence about the price of American success is an enduring theme. Ambivalence and critique span the Jewish religious and political spectra. See Liebman, *Ambivalent American Jew*; Kranson, *Ambivalent Embrace*.
120 Rose, "Our Russian Adventure," 1, 10. The text is ambiguous, but Rose appears to be referring to his delivery of mezuzah amulet necklaces to Soviet Jews.

121 Gutin and Kanter, "Mission to the Soviet Union," trip report 3–13 June 1990, 26.
122 Trachtenburg, trip report, 11–12.
123 Whether such tropes were actually prominent in colonial travel writing or were more a feature of secondary literature on travel writing is a matter of debate. For a critique of the academic discourse, see Ellingson, *Myth of the Noble Savage*.
124 Beger, "Artek Camp"; Margulies, *Pilgrimage to Russia*; Hollander, *Political Pilgrims*.
125 Kelner, "Foreign Tourists," 100. On tourists' equation of "off the beaten path" with "authenticity," see MacCannell, "Staged Authenticity"; and MacCannell, *Tourist*. Standley, "Experiencing Communism," also found tourism reinforcing Westerners' negative images of the Soviet bloc.

5. We've Said No to PepsiCo

1 "Jewish Groups Threaten Boycott."
2 Yaroslavsky, *Zev's Los Angeles*, 57–61.
3 "Jewish Groups Threaten Boycott"; Lissner, "Jewish Defense League"; "Commerce Secretary Meets with JDL'ers"; Zev Yaroslavsky, personal communication, 31 May 2021; Boyarsky, "Handshakes Seal Pact." A ProQuest historical newspaper archive search on *Chavez, grape*, and *boycott* between December 1965 and August 1970 found 170 *Los Angeles Times* articles, more than in any other newspaper.
4 "Jewish Groups Threaten Boycott"; Theodore R. Mann to NJCRAC Member Agencies, "Minutes of Commission Meeting of November 22, 1971," 21 January 1972, GNYCSJ b.1 f.2.
5 "Jewish Youths Picket"; Yaroslavsky, interviewed by Shaul Kelner, 13 September 2018.
6 Zev Yaroslavsky and Si Frumkin to Signal Companies, 13 September 1971, WCSJ b.12 f.3; "Activists Seek Nixon's Veto," 1, 6; Harold Light to Len Shuster, audiotaped telephone conversation, August 1971, BACSJ b.99 f.10; "Mack Trucks Drops Plans."
7 Yaroslavsky, personal communication, 31 May 2021.
8 Holsendolph, "Russians to Get Pepsi-Cola."
9 Cioletti, "Back in the (Former) USSR."
10 Holsendolph, "Russians to Get Pepsi-Cola"; Bralove, "PepsiCo Will Sell."
11 SCCSJ and CSSJ, "Soviet Jewry Organizations to Boycott PepsiCola," press release, 11 November 1972, CCSA b.9 f.254.
12 Korey, *Soviet Cage*, 315–20; Feingold, *"Silent No More,"* 84–86, 115–18.
13 UCSJ, "Pepsi Boycott for Soviet Jews," press release, 6 December 1972, WCSJ b.12 f.3.
14 Meyer Greenberg to Moshe Brodetzky, 26 January 1973, WCSJ b.12 f.3; "Cedar Center Demonstration"; Morris Mandel to Dear [CCSA] Member, "Re: Pepsi Boycott," 14 February 1973, CCSA b.1 f.13; SSSJ, "Students Dump Pepsi-Cola from Bridge in 'Pepsi Party' to Protest Company's Trade with USSR," press release, 4 January 1972, SSSJ b.9 f.25; SCCSJ, "'Some Terrible People . . .'" flyer with photo clippings, n.d., SSSJ b.46 f.41; "Jewish Youths Assail Pepsico Stand"; SSSJ, "The Pepsi Generation Reacts," press release, 7 May 1975, SSSJ b.13 f.11; Orenstein, "'Let My People Go!,'" 175–78; Mervin Weinberg to Arthur Alintuck, 2 January 1973, CCSA b.9 f.254; Breskin, "Food Service to Terminate"; "JDL Diplomacy at Columbia U"; "Pepsi Strikes Back."
15 Stanley Rabinowitz to Moshe Brodetzky, 8 January 1973, WCSJ b.12 f.3.

16 Jerry Goodman to Owen Rachleff, "Re: No Boycott against Pepsico!," 3 April 1973, CCSA b.9 f.254.
17 Bert Silver to Morris Laub, 19 February 1973, WCSJ b.12 f.3.
18 Jews Against the Arab Boycott, "Baltimore Community Council"; Jews Against the Arab Boycott, "Why an 8-Page Supplement?"; "Critics of 'Establishment.'"
19 WCSJ, "Is Pepsi-Cola Suitable?" (emphasis in original).
20 Community Council of Jewish Organizations (Chicago), "An Account of a Meeting with Pepsi Cola Officials," 2 March 1973, WCSJ b.12 f.3; SSSJ, "Pepsi Generation"; Goodman to Rachleff, "Re: No Boycott," 3 April 1973; "Committee Will Honor Pepsi Chief."
21 H. Smith, "Donald Kendall"; MacKaye, "Jewish Group Cancels"; "Committee Cancels Award"; Polakoff, "Drive Underway."
22 Community Council of Jewish Organizations (Chicago), "Account of a Meeting"; Fisch, "JDL Spokesman."
23 "Some UNrefreshing Facts about Pepsi," multiple publishers, including Chicago Community Council of Jewish Organizations, SCCSJ, and SSSJ, n.d., SSSJ b.45 f.8, https://digital.library.yu.edu; "Denver Rabbi Urging Boycott"; "Critics of 'Establishment.'"
24 Goodman to Rachleff, "Re: No Boycott," 3 April 1973; Yaroslavsky, personal communication, 31 May 2021.
25 McDowell, "Shoot-Out in Soda Pop."
26 Louis Rosenblum to UCSJ and Action Central, "Few Americans Buy Mack Trucks," 18 November 1971, CCSA b.9 f.254; handwritten note appended to copy of Holsendolph, "Russians to Get Pepsi-Cola." Rosenblum's translation of *traif* understates the word's rhetorical force. In Jewish American colloquial usage, the word designates food that is not and cannot be kosher. To call Pepsi *traif* was to liken it to pork.
27 Westchester Students for Soviet Jewry, "PepsiCo Says: Profits before Human Rights," protest leaflet, [ca. May] 1975, SSSJ b.13 f.11.
28 Louis and Yazijian, *Cola Wars*; Pitts, "80s Singers"; Joel, "We Didn't Start the Fire."
29 On the classical treatments (or nontreatments), see Warde, "Introduction to the Sociology of Consumption"; Warde, "Sociology of Consumption," 119; and Campbell, "Sociology of Consumption," 100–102.
30 Warde refers to this as the "demise of economism." Warde, "Sociology of Consumption," 120.
31 Gottdiener, *Theming of America*.
32 Campbell, "Sociology of Consumption," 97; Joselit, *Perfect Fit*; Bowlby, *Carried Away*.
33 Social movement scholars call this "occupational activism." Cornfield et al., "Occupational Activism."
34 Fodor and Fisher, *Fodor's Soviet Union*; Insiders Club, *Guidebook*.
35 Yangzom, "Clothing and Social Movements."
36 Gerlis, *Those Wonderful Women*, iv, 226; Orbach, "British Soviet Jewry Movement," 22; Doreen Gainsford, interviewed by Shaul Kelner, 29 June 2021. Gerlis credits Golda Meir for the phrase "ladies in black."
37 Gerlis, *Those Wonderful Women*, 64, 225.
38 Schnold, *Jews of Struggle*, 36; Hudson, "Remembering Historic March"; Hoffman, "How We Freed Soviet Jewry"; M. Goldstein, "Bridges We Cross"; Woda, "If Not Now, When?"

39 SSSJ, "Story of 'Operation Jericho,'" 26–27.
40 Order form, *Spotlight* (Cleveland, OH), April–May 1966, 5.
41 Ghert-Zand, "Once Heroes of US Jewry."
42 "Conscience Medallion Draws Attention."
43 Zev Yaroslavsky, interviewed by Shaul Kelner, 17 June 2021.
44 "Conscience Medallion Draws Attention"; Yaroslavsky, interview, 17 June 2021; Allen, *Until the Last Man*, 57–60.
45 One might instead credit the Israeli government's Coins and Medals Corporation. In fall 1971, it minted a special-edition "Let My People Go" ten-lira silver coin "dedicated to Soviet Jewry in their struggle for freedom." For the $8 price, or $40 for a gold version, those purchasing the coin also received a lapel pin replica to wear "in token of your identification." Advertisements in Jewish newspapers such as Los Angeles's *B'nai B'rith Messenger* focused on the coin, only briefly mentioning the pin as a bonus. There was never any campaign to put the pin on people's lapels. As for the coin itself, the Jewish press ignored it, save for a searing indictment in London's *Jewish Chronicle*: "The genius who thought up this particular medallion deserves a medal of his own for the ultimate in sordid commercialism. Can we have no cause free from the importunities of the hucksters?" There is no evidence Frumkin was aware of the coin lapel pin, and Yaroslavsky had no recollection of it. Israel Government Coins and Medals Corporation, "Let My People Go"; Azai, "Personal Opinion"; Yaroslavsky, interview, 17 June 2021.
46 Mauss, *Gift*.
47 "'Prisoners of Conscience' Month."
48 On American consumer culture's positioning of jewelry as something to give as a gift, see Joselit, *Perfect Fit*, 172–76.
49 Other members of the Union of Councils later adopted this logo too.
50 Yaroslavsky, interview, 17 June 2021.
51 Kelner, "People-to-People"; Rosenblum and Rosenblum, "Involvement," 68–78.
52 Yaroslavsky, interview, 17 June 2021; UCSJ, "Anatoly Altman Prisoner of Conscience Kit," n.d., National Museum of American Jewish History, 1991.51.8.2, in Weitzman National Museum of American Jewish History, "Are We Responsible for Others?"
53 "Soviet Prisoners."
54 National Conference of Synagogue Youth, "The POWs Are Coming Home. The POCs Are Still in Chains," advertising flyer and order form, 1973, in Abraham J. Bayer to Soviet Jewry Chairmen, 30 March 1973, NJCRAC b.87 f.3. The advertising slogan refers to the prisoner releases connected with the Vietnam War's 1973 Paris Peace Accords.
55 "Soviet Jewry Bracelets Available"; Associated Press, "Horrors of War."
56 NCSJ, "Soviet Jews Will Never Forget. Will You?," advertising flyer, NCSJ b.69 f.14; SJC, "These Russians Committed the Same Horrendous Crime"; "JCRC Prepares Purim Greeting Postcards"; "Seeking Aid for Jews."
57 Gainsford purchased the original medallion. "Ingrid Bergman"; Lerner, "Young Housewives"; Grant, *Andrew Grima*; Foulkes, "Glam Rocks"; Joseph, "Original King of Bling"; Gainsford, interview, 29 June 2021.
58 Zalmanson was part of a group of refuseniks who, in 1970, purchased all the tickets on a twelve-seat aircraft, planning to steal the plane and fly themselves to freedom in Sweden. The KGB foiled the plan. Death sentences sparked an international outcry

and were quickly commuted. For first-person accounts, see Zalmanson-Kuznetsov, *Operation Wedding*; Kuznetsov, *Prison Diaries*; Mendelevich, *Unbroken Spirit*; and Butman, *From Leningrad*.
59 Women's Campaign for Soviet Jewry–35s, "Sylva Zalmanson Pendant / Keyring," order form, 1973, NLI P363-13.
60 Chronicler, "Medallions"; "Dora Eats a Prison Lunch"; "Labour Conference Petitioned"; "Miriam Karlin Helps 35s"; "Prisoners' Month Launched"; Schnold, *Jews of Struggle*, 57.
61 Chronicler, "Bring Out the Medallions."
62 SJC, *Adopt-a-Family*; GNYCSJ, *Soviet Jewry Catalog*.
63 Kanin, *Political History*, 115. Anticipating preemptive detentions, many activists left Moscow before the games. Kosharovsky, *We Are Jews Again*, 233.
64 "Slepak Sentenced"; "Trial of Anatoli Shcharansky"; Chronicle of Current Events, "Trial of Ida Nudel," "Trial of Slepak," and "Trial of Begun."
65 "Press Advisory"; 124 Cong. Rec. H32946–47, 51 (daily ed., 2 October 1978) (statement of Rep. Robert K. Dornan, R-CA, "Missing in Action in South-East Asia"); Allen, *Until the Last Man*, 57–60; Brown, "History of the POW/MIA Bracelet."
66 124 Cong. Rec. H32946–47, 51 (Dornan, "Missing in Action"); Polakoff, "Mrs. Shcharansky Clashes"; "Press Advisory." Dornan also discussed the bracelets with Shcharansky's mother and brother during a September trip to Moscow.
67 He probably meant ABC's *Good Morning America*, which had replaced *AM America* in 1975. 124 Cong. Rec. H32946–47, 51 (Dornan, "Missing in Action").
68 Søndergaard, *Reagan, Congress, and Human Rights*, 118; 132 Cong. Rec. H10443 (daily ed., 13 May 1986) (statement of Rep. Robert K. Dornan, R-CA, "'Old Glory' Respected around the World").
69 On museums, see Katz, "Collecting the Exile." For bracelets and blue jeans in reminiscences, see, e.g., Zlatoposly, "Remembering Our Local Heroes."
70 American Jewish Congress, "Freedom Run for Soviet Jewry" (San Francisco), registration brochure, 1981, JGA b.1 f.14; Joel D. Brooks to Joel Ackerman, 17 May 1981, JGA b.1 f.14; "Runners Calendar"; Swats, "Over 1,000 Take Part"; Schlegel, "Freedom Run."
71 Leavy and Okie, "Runner"; New York Road Runners, "NYC Marathon 1970," https://results.nyrr.org; New York Road Runners, "NYC Marathon 1980," https://results.nyrr.org; Gambaccini et al., "Unforgettable."
72 Wellins, "Back from the USSR," trip report, 1986, 5.
73 Ro'i, "Strategy," 67–68; Gerlis, *Those Wonderful Women*, 23, 30; A. Weiss, *Open Up*, 113–22.
74 Christian Aid and OXFAM introduced sponsored walk fundraisers in Britain and Canada in the 1960s. Organized by high schoolers, they drew tens of thousands of marchers, including prime ministers, and raised millions. Protestant and Catholic groups brought the idea to the US in 1969 with the Christian Rural Overseas Program (CROP) Hunger Walk. Bocking-Welch, "British Public," 171–74, 249; Myers, "Blistered and Bleeding"; Myers, "Local Action"; Church World Service, "History of the CROP Hunger Walk"; Church World Service, "CWS and CROP Hunger Walks."
75 "Third Annual Walkathon"; "250 March."
76 SSSJ, *Letter-Writing*, 10.
77 SSSJ, "Ancient Israelites' Passover Exodus Reinterpreted as Political and Civic Notables to Lead 10-Mile Walkathon for Soviet Jews," press release, 26 March 1975, SSSJ

b.13 f.2; Brooklyn SSSJ, "Walkathon for Soviet Jewry," publicity brochure, 1974, SSSJ b.11 f.11.
78 SSSJ, "Twelve-Mile Soviet Jewry Bike-a-Thon Brings Applause," press release, 31 October 1976, SSSJ b.17 f.6.
79 "Canton Jewish Center"; "Local Runners Win"; "Freedom Relays Sunday."
80 SSSJ, *Letter-Writing*, 11.
81 MACSJ, "The First Year," 1972, JCRCMD b.86 f.3, 6.
82 Dishler, trip report, 1–8 March 1977; Bernard Dishler and Lana Dishler, interviewed by Shaul Kelner, 5 July 2020. Kosharovsky was again arrested while jogging in 1980. Kosharovsky, *We Are Jews Again*, 235.
83 Joel Sandberg, personal communication, 14 December 2020.
84 Dishler and Dishler, interview; Joel Sandberg and Adele Sandberg, interviewed by Shaul Kelner, 15 August 2018; Bernard Dishler to Joel Sandberg, 27 November 1978, JSAS b.1 f.9; "Local Doctor Will Run"; SFCSJ, "Soviet Jewry Refusenik Entered in Jewish Community Center Chanukah Run," press release, 17 December 1978, JSAS b.1 f.9; UCSJ, conference agenda, 23–25 September 1978, BMP b. 1 f. 29.
85 Joel Sandberg to Groups All Action, "Re: Project for Yuli Kosharovsky," January 1979, JSAS b.1 f.9.
86 "Jewish Groups Sponsor"; Los Angeles Jewish Federation Council Commission on Soviet Jewry (LAJFC-CSJ), "Run for Soviet Jewry," publicity flyer, 2 December 1979, in NJCRAC, *Soviet Jewry Advocacy*, 1983, 76e&f (author's personal collection).
87 Sylvester and Dirkin, "Pursuit."
88 SSSJ, "Runners Challenge Pepsi on Human Rights," press release, 6 July 1981, SSSJ b.23 f.26; "Pepsi Challenged," captioned press photograph, 16 July 1981, SSSJ b.23 f.26.
89 LAJFC-CSJ, "Run for Soviet Jewry"; "Jewish Groups Sponsor"; Larsen, "1,700 in L.A."; W. B., "Postscripts."
90 Baker, "2,000 Join Westside Run"; "Fonda, Hayden to Join"; Kirschner, "Metro State Star Wins"; "On the Run"; "Upcoming Events"; SJC, "Freedom Run & Rally for Soviet Jewry," publicity flyer, 1986, BMP b.1 f.71; "Babbitt and Yuli Run"; Scheindlin, "Israelis Also Run"; NJCRAC, *Soviet Jewry Advocacy*, 73–77.
91 American Jewish Congress, "Freedom Run"; Tucson Jewish Community Council Soviet Jewry Commission (Tucson JCC-SJC), "Freedom Run for Soviet Jewry," publicity flyer, 14 December 1980, in NJCRAC, *Soviet Jewry Advocacy*, 1983, 76c&d (author's personal collection); SJC, "Freedom Run & Rally."
92 Kirschner, "Metro State Star Wins."
93 "Midland Run Just the Start"; "Rally, Race Set Sunday"; SJC, "Freedom Run & Rally"; "Unity Is Theme."
94 "Fonda, Hayden to Join."
95 Tucson JCC-SJC, "Freedom Run."
96 NJCRAC, *Soviet Jewry Advocacy*, 74.
97 "Unity Is Theme"; Dishler and Dishler, interview (emphasis added).
98 Ron Colman to Laurel Pollack et al., 1 December 1974, SSSJ b.12 f.13.
99 Caute, *Dancer Defects*, 5.
100 Peace rhetoric notwithstanding, Soviet officials believed that the US saw cultural exchange as a way of "eroding" the Soviet social system. State Department cultural exchange officer Yale Richmond argued that they were correct in this assessment but that

NOTES

"official Washington" nevertheless undervalued the exchanges. Richmond, *Cultural Exchange*, 17–18.
101   SSSJ, "Greetings," faux concert brochure, 22 January 1972, SSSJ b.9 f.7 (emphasis in original).
102   Beckerman, *When They Come*, 237–41; Halevi, *Memoirs*, 120, 67–72; "7 Held at Concert"; Olster, "Police Investigating"; Robinson, *Last Impresario*, 427–35.
103   Eisen, *Count Us In*, 67–68.
104   Colman to Pollack et al., 1 December 1974.
105   "Establishment" groups initially resisted the tactic. When Yaroslavsky launched California Students for Soviet Jews in 1969 by picketing University of Southern California dormitories housing a visiting Soviet track team, Los Angeles's Jewish Federation urged him to cancel the protest. The federation called it "counter-productive." Yaroslavsky called their objection "absurd." Yaroslavsky, *Zev's Los Angeles*, 57. On cultural protest in the UK, see Gerlis, *Those Wonderful Women*; and Cooper, *British Campaign*, 98–133. On Canada, see Eisen, *Count Us In*.
106   Assorted SSSJ files, 1970–90, SSSJ, e.g., b.7 f.3, b.9 f.23, b.10 f.11, b.11 f.17, b.12 f.1, and b.36 f.12. Activists also worked with New York's Jewish Museum and San Francisco's Magnes Museum to stage their own exhibitions of works by "unofficial" Soviet Jewish artists. Katz, "Staging Protest."
107   Rita Eker, quoted in Gerlis, *Those Wonderful Women*, 78.
108   Eisen, *Count Us In*, unnumbered photo insert, fifth page between pp. 78–79.
109   Joseph Smukler and Stuart Wurtman to Community Leadership, "Re: Demonstration to Greet the Soviet Ice Hockey Team," 2 January 1976, JCRCGP b.80 f.14; SJC, "You Can Take a Soviet Jew out of the Penalty Box Today," flyer, JCRCGP b.80 f.14; SJC, "The Puck Stops Here: Save Soviet Jews," protest sign, 11 January 1976, JCRCGP b.80 f.14; J. Porter, "Russians Told to Take a Flyer"; Herman, "Russians Stage Walkout"; "Flyers Fans Urged."
110   SSSJ, "'Greeting' Russian Festival at Lincoln Center," photograph, 28 June 1976, SSSJ b.16 f.16.
111   Cited in Gerlis, *Those Wonderful Women*, 129.
112   SSSJ, "Anti-Semitism: A Different Type of Soviet 'Art,'" leaflet, 16 September 1975, SSSJ b.14 f.1.
113   SSSJ, "Moscow State Symphony Orchestra," faux playbill, 19 November 1975, SSSJ b.15 f.5.
114   SSSJ, "Soviet Circus (Moscow Circus)," faux playbill, 21 December 1975, SSSJ b.15 f.7 (all caps and italics in original).
115   Kaiser, "Preview for 1980"; NCSJ, "Jewish Group Seeks to Bar Moscow as Olympic Site," press release, 22 August 1973, NCSJ b.156 f.4; 119 Cong. Rec. H30619 (daily ed. 20 September 1973) (statement of Rep. Mendel Jackson Davis, D-SC, "Scandalous Treatment of Soviet Jewish Sports Fans"); June Rogul to Jerry Goodman, 16 October 1974, NCSJ b.54 f.1; SCCSJ, "Remember the Headlines on the Reverse Side of This Page?," September 1974, NCSJ b.54 f.1; Ted Gorman to B'nai B'rith Lodge Presidents, "Re: Olympic Games," 14 September 1973, WCSJ b.12 f.1.
116   Joel Sandberg to All Action Groups, 27 April 1978, JSAS b.1 f.1.
117   Michele Sofios to Irene Manekofsky et al., "Olympics," 9 May 1978, WCSJ b.12 f.1; Irene Manekofsky to Warner Wolf, 29 May 1978, WCSJ b.12 f.1; IMC80, "Press Advisory"; P. Cohen, *Hidden Heroes*, 94.

118 Manekofsky, "Petition Campaign Begins"; Irene Manekofsky to Clergy, Organizational Chairmen, and Community Leaders, "Re: 1980 Olympics," 28 July 1978, WCSJ b.12 f.1; "Olympics," *Alert*, 22 November 1978; Morey Schapira to Shari Grossman, 22 June 1979, ASJ b.125 f.5.
119 Robert F. Drinan to Jimmy Carter, published in UCSJ, *Alert*, 12(16), 16 January 1980, WCSJ b.14 f.9.
120 NCSJ, "NCSJ Forms Committee on 1980 Moscow Olympics," press release, 30 June 1978, ASJ b.125 f.5; Jacqueline K. Levine to NJCRAC and CJFWF Member Agencies, "Re: 1980 Olympics in Moscow," 21 August 1978, WCSJ b.12 f.1.
121 Jewish Community Relations Council of [Unknown], "The Moscow Olympics" (city unknown), position paper, 27 July 1978, WCSJ b.12 f.1. The Soviets allowed over fifty thousand Jews to emigrate in 1979, the most up to that point.
122 Levine to NJCRAC and CJFWF Member Agencies, "Re: 1980 Olympics," 21 August 1978.
123 NCSJ, "Question and Answer Fact Sheet: The 1980 Moscow Olympics," 30 October 1978, NCSJ b.54 f.1, 1; Rutland, *Lone Voice*, 263–65; Levanon, *Haqod*, 456–57.
124 NCSJ, "Question and Answer Fact Sheet." On using the Olympics for leverage, see Rutland, *Lone Voice*, 244–305. When the Australian Olympic Federation named Jetset Tours as its travel agent, the company's owner, Isi Liebler, a leader of Australia's Jewish community, used the opportunity to aid the Soviet Jewish cause, shuttling among meetings with refuseniks, Soviet officials, Australian leaders, Nativ officers, and Soviet Jewry activists on four continents.
125 Wood, "NBC's Moscow Olympics"; Miller, "Networks' Ad Sales"; Rosenberg, "1980 Olympics."
126 Sofios to Manekofsky et al., "Olympics," 9 May 1978. On deliberately creating radical or moderate flank groups to create room to maneuver, see Downey and Rohlinger, "Linking Strategic Choice"; and Ellefsen, "Deepening the Explanation."
127 Glenn Richter to 1980 Committee on Human Rights, 29 September 1978, SSSJ b.44 f.9; "Carey Endorses '80"; 1980 Committee on Human Rights, "Great Sellout"; 1980 Committee on Human Rights, "Moscow's TV Con Job."
128 1980 Committee on Human Rights, "Moscow's TV Con Job."
129 Klehr, *Millionaire Was a Soviet Mole*, 80–82; Glenn M. Reisman to Leo Henzel, 24 August 1978, SSSJ b.44 f.8.
130 "Carey, Solarz Not Backing Group"; "Olympics," *Alert*, 10 October 1978.
131 Abraham Bayer, quoted in "Carey, Solarz Not Backing Group."
132 Sofios to Manekofsky et al., "Olympics," 17 April 1978, WCSJ b.12 f.1; Sofios to Manekofsky et al., "Olympics," 9 May 1978; "Olympics," *Alert*, 22 November 1978; GNYCSJ, "Ad Hoc Committee on Moscow Olympics Recommendation," 5 October 1978, ASJ b.125 f.5; Sandberg to All Action Groups, 27 April 1978.
133 Don Miller to Glenn Richter, 22 May 1978, WCSJ b.12 f.1; Michele Sofios to Don Miller, 28 August 1978, WCSJ b.12 f.1; P. Cohen, *Hidden Heroes*, 95.
134 "Olympics-Da"; Holden, "Boycott Old Issue"; SSSJ, "We Dare Not Forget," order form, n.d. (ca. 1978–79), ASJ b.125 f.3; "Olympic Stamps."
135 SSSJ, *SSSJ Handbook*, E-1d.
136 Sandberg to All Action Groups, 27 April 1978; Sol Goldstein to NCSJ Board of Governors, January 1979, NCSJ b.54 f.1.

137 Sofios to Manekofsky et al., "Olympics," 9 May 1978; NJCRAC, "Task Force Proposal," December 1978, ASJ b.125 f.5; IMC80, "KGB Olympics: Action Sheet," n.d., ASJ b.125 f.6; Goldstein to Governors, January 1979; NCSJ, "Question and Answer Fact Sheet"; Rosenberg, "1980 Olympics"; Hester Beckman, Lillian Elkin, and Phil Baum to AJCongress Governing Council, "1980 Moscow Olympics," 31 August 1978, ASJ b.125 f.5; GNYCSJ, "Ad Hoc Committee"; Schapira to Grossman, 22 June 1979. The last North American travelers before the Olympics to file a trip report with NCSJ and UCSJ, from June 1980, described being detained, interrogated, and deported back to Canada immediately upon landing in Moscow. Rotenberg, trip report, 20 June 1980; A. Daniel Rotenberg and Steven Shnider, transcript of debriefing interview, 20 June 1980, NCSJ b.71 f.26. The last European travelers to file a report, Comité des Quinze tourists from July 1980, reported that refuseniks they had hoped to meet had already left Moscow for the Olympics period. F. and T., trip report (authors identified only by first initials), June–July 1980, 30, 33. AJHS archives contain no trip reports from the time of the Olympics themselves.

138 Schapira to Grossman, 22 June 1979.

139 Irene Manekofsky to Rita Eker et al., "Re: Olympics," 22 June 1978, WCSJ b.12 f.1; Manekofsky, "Beginning of the Olympic Cleanup."

140 Appelbaum, "Soviet Jewry Movement," 630. Soviet Jewish affairs are entirely absent from the primary diplomatic history of the 1980 boycott: Sarantakes, *Dropping the Torch*.

141 "GOP Loses in Convention Ratings"; "NBC First in TV Ratings"; "ABC Takes Ratings Race."

142 "Freedom Olympics"; SSSJ, "Freedom Olympics: Program," 22 June 1980, SSSJ b.23 f.1.

143 Rosen, "'Freedom Run.'"

144 "Rally for Freedom."

145 Arkush and Rosen, "Competing for Freedom"; "Students Fight for Refuseniks"; "Games for Freedom"; "'Freedom Games' Marred"; "Freedom Campaign Gains Momentum"; "River Revels."

146 "Hurry, Hurry"; "Cartoon Wins a Trip."

6. Natasha's Dream

1 Manon and Manekofsky, *Natasha's Dream*, inside cover.
2 Tutnauer, "Poem of My Land"; "Former 'Refusnik' Tells."
3 Tutnauer, "Poem of My Land"; "Former 'Refusnik' Tells."
4 Tutnauer, "Poem of My Land"; Ann Gillen and National Interreligious Task Force on Soviet Jewry, "Operation Write-On" (BJE of Greater New York and GNYCSJ), action guide, 1974, GNYCSJ b.1 f.3–4; Lazin, *American Christians*, 61. Manon and Manekofsky, *Natasha's Dream*, 6–11.
5 Action Central, "Children of the Otkazniki" (CCSA, Cleveland, OH), action guide, 14 February 1974, CCSA b.8 f.224. Rosenblum used the Russian *otkazniki*, as its English translation, *refusenik*, had not yet entered American movement parlance.
6 Gillen and National Interreligious Task Force on Soviet Jewry, "Operation Write-On"; Manon and Manekofsky, *Natasha's Dream*, 6–11.
7 Manon and Manekofsky, *Natasha's Dream*, 8–10, 12–14; Manon and Manekofsky, *Natasha's Dream* (rev. ed.), 7; Avrum Ashery, interviewed by Shaul Kelner, 13 August 2019.

8   Manekofsky and Manekofsky, "Twelve Days with the Refuseniks," trip report, 14–26 November 1974, 2; Manon and Manekofsky, *Natasha's Dream* (rev. ed.); Litwack, *School Kit*, lesson 3:J; Andrea Morgenstern, "Bat Mitzvah of Andrea Morgenstern," sermon, 4 November 1978, ASJ b.127 f.12, 3.

9   Explicit treatments of youth-qua-youth in social movements studies are Earl, Maher, and Elliott, "Youth, Activism, and Social Movements"; Sherrod, *Youth Activism*; and two ethnographies of teenage activism, mainly girls': Gordon, *We Fight to Win*; and Taft, *Rebel Girls*. None focus on young children. Literature on civic engagement and political socialization is more likely to treat younger children. See, e.g., Astuto and Ruck, "Early Childhood." Scholarship on teen activism emphasizes youth agency and the struggle against adultist efforts to control their work, themes also highlighted in Gordon and Taft, "Rethinking Youth Political Socialization"; and Kettrey, "Activism without Activists." In contrast, Rodgers notes that the field of children's studies "has begun to question the overenthusiastic embrace of children's agency" and reemphasize constraints on children's autonomy. Rodgers, *Children in Social Movements*, 117. My treatment focuses attention on the role that adults play in mobilizing children, not out of disregard for children's agency (which operates here in adult-created contexts), but because of my main focus on activists' uses of a mobilizing gaze to target and enlist supporters.

10 Rodgers, "Children as Social Movement Participants"; Rodgers, *Children in Social Movements*, 3.

11 The Katz and Tiemkin cases were controversial at the time, but the later record confirms activists' claims. After "Baby Jessica" arrived in the US in good health, activists were accused of misrepresenting the severity of Katz's medical condition. The infant's condition had improved, however, thanks in part or in whole to activists sending over tourists with baby formula prior to her emigration. Cash, "Mobilizing for Soviet Jewry"; Knight, "Jewish Groups Deny They Misled." Most activists stopped advocating for Tiemkin after losing faith in the accuracy of the information they were receiving and learning that she was rejecting any communication with Jews or Israel. SSSJ continued pressing her case. In 2017, Tiemkin, in Israel, affirmed that the reports had been accurate, that she had been taken against her will, and that she had cut contact because of KGB threats. Tutnauer, "Poem of My Land"; Manekofsky, "Information on Direct Aid," trip report, 14–26 November 1974, 4; SSSJ, "Nationwide Campaign for Soviet Jewish Teenager Launched," press release, 13 December 1974, SSSJ b.12 f.14; Davidovsky, "Kidnapped as a Teenager."

12 McCarthy and Zald's distinction between movement beneficiaries and conscience constituencies lets us refine Rodgers's typology. Phrased as a hypothesis, the strategic use of children as symbols will emphasize innocent victimhood when children are beneficiaries and active agency when children are members of the conscience constituency. McCarthy and Zald, "Resource Mobilization."

13 Rodgers, "Children as Social Movement Participants"; Rodgers, *Children in Social Movements*.

14 Lisa Perlbinder, "Sylvia Zalmanson: A Russian-Jewish Heroine Near Death," school project, n.d., GPP b.1 f.8. Zalmanson had been sentenced to ten years in a labor camp for her role in the Leningrad hijacking affair.

15 ASJ, *Bar and Bat Mitzvah Twinning*.

16 Cornfield et al., "Occupational Activism."
17 Sharansky, *Fear No Evil*, 170.
18 Harrison, *Passover Revisited*, 78.
19 Krasner, *Benderly Boys*; Ingall, *Women Who Reconstructed*; Sarna, "Crucial Decade"; Fox, "'Is This What You Call Being Free?'"; Prell, "Summer Camp."
20 Gans, "Park Forest"; Gans, "Progress"; Glazer, "Jewish Revival"; Prell, *Prayer and Community*.
21 Benor, Krasner, and Avni, *Hebrew Infusion*; Prell, "Jewish Summer Camping"; Prell, "Summer Camp"; Fox, *Jews of Summer*; Rothenberg, *Serious Fun*, 79–99; Intrator and Rosov, "Sustaining the Work of Creation."
22 Abraham J. Bayer, "Re: Additional Passover Program Material," memo, 4 March 1969, BACSJ b.3 f.29, 4.
23 Beckerman, *When They Come*, 79.
24 Orenstein, "'Let My People Go!,'" 67–71.
25 Halevi, *Memoirs*, 65–67.
26 Henry Margolis to Louis Rosenblum, "Hebrew Academy Pesach Assembly 1966–5726," 15 April 1966, CCSA b.3 f.80. The word *haggadah* is typed in Hebrew.
27 AJCSJ, "Programmatic Recommendations Adopted by the Biennial," 7–8 April 1968, NCSJ b.1 f.4, 2–3.
28 Lynda Kranzberg to Jacob Birnbaum, 6 September 1964, SSSJ b.46 f.12; Danny Margolis to Glenn Richter, n.d. (ca. 1967–68), SSSJ b.46 f.12; Kehillath Israel United Synagogue Youth, "Sample Russian Jewry Program: Action Day for Soviet Jewry" (Brookline, MA), 11 November 1964, SSSJ b.46 f.12.
29 Orenstein, "'Let My People Go!,'" 67–71.
30 Bernstein and Bernstein, *Dmitry*; Meir and Rozen, *Alina*.
31 CCSA, "'To Eastern and Midwestern Jewish Camps,'" press release, 23 July 1971, CCSA b.1 f.13; Leonard Katkowitz to Louis Rosenblum, 29 July 1971, www.clevelandjewishhistory.net; Rosenblum, "Freedom Caravan"; Louis Rosenblum, interviewed by Shaul Kelner, 15 August 2015.
32 Porath, *Here We Are All Jews*; Porath, *Russian Jewish Community*; Porath, *Jews in Russia*; Jonathan Porath, interviewed by Shaul Kelner, 29 August 2016; Jonathan D. Porath, personal communication, 6 August 2020.
33 Noskowitz et al., *Resource Teaching Unit*; "Resource Teaching Unit on Soviet Jewry," curriculum, reprint (BJE identifiers removed in original), 1968, CCSA b.1 f.19, 6.
34 SFCSJ, meeting minutes, 14 December 1967, CCSA b.1 f.19; Louis Schwartzman and BJE of Miami to School Directors, "Teaching of the Jews of Russia," n.d., CCSA b.1 f.19; BJE of Miami, "Petition," 14 December 1968, CCSA b.1 f.19; BJE of Miami, "Essay Art Contest," poster and entry form, 1968, CCSA b.1 f.19.
35 Rosenblum, *Hear the Cry*.
36 Itzkowitz, *Stifled Exodus*.
37 Litwack, *School Kit*; Eisen, *Count Us In*, 105–6, 290n2.
38 Tallman and Kahn, *Let My People Go*.
39 JCCGW, *Teaching* (1st ed.), 11–12; JCCGW, *Teaching* (2nd ed.); Samuel Sislen, "The Soviet Jewry Movement in the Greater Washington Community" (Lillian and Albert Small Capital Jewish Museum), October 2008, 5, www.jhsgw.org; Litov, "History of Jewish Education," 19.

40 Weinberg, *Introduction*; Meister, *Lesson Plans*.
41 The mobilizations of tourism, art, and education all converged here. Family and institutional networks did too. In 1981, photographer Bill Aron traveled to Russia to take the pictures, accompanied by the director of the Los Angeles Jewish Federation's Commission on Soviet Jewry. Jewish educator Isa Aron directed the MUSE project at the HUC Skirball Museum, which created the exhibition and housed it before its national tour. The Arons were husband and wife. Scheindlin and Aron, trip report, 5–23 October 1981; Dorph, *By Spirit Alone*; Gail Dorph, interviewed by Shaul Kelner, 7 August 2020; Hebrew Union College–Jewish Institute of Religion, "HUC-JIR/Los Angeles Historical Timeline"; JCRC-ADL of Minnesota and the Dakotas, "Women's Plea for Soviet Jewry / National Photo Exhibit," press release, n.d. (ca. January) 1984, JCRCMD b.86 f.44.
42 CAJE, "Task Force on Soviet Jewish Education," agenda, 23–28 August 1979, CASJ b.7 f.4., 2; Bronstein, *Making Gates*, 1.
43 Pinar et al., *Understanding Curriculum*.
44 In social movement theory terms, curricula explicitly and methodically undertook "diagnostic," "prognostic," and "motivational" framing. Snow and Benford, "Ideology," 199–204.
45 JCCGW, *Teaching* (2nd ed.), 2.
46 For instance, an outline for "Soviet Jewry School Assemblies" was "based on an assembly held at the Jewish Day School of Greater Washington, December 1978." JCCGW, *Teaching* (2nd ed.), 9.
47 JCCGW, *Teaching* (2nd ed.), 2; personal communication, Judith Mars Kupchan, 1 September 2020.
48 JCCGW, *Teaching* (2nd ed.), 3, 7, 10. Hebrew language learning was an important part of the Jewish cultural revival in the USSR in the 1970s and '80s. Activists ran underground Hebrew classes. Kosharovsky, *We Are Jews Again*, 118–27, 232–36; Volvovsky, "Teaching and Study of Hebrew."
49 JCCGW, *Teaching* (2nd ed.), 3. Spanish Jewry is celebrated for producing philosophers and poets like Judah Halevi. By "narrowly averted destruction," the curriculum is referring to the biblical Purim story (for which there is no historical evidence) and the fifteenth-century expulsion of Jews from the Iberian peninsula (a destruction that was not "narrowly averted" but carried out). Neither ancient Persia nor medieval Spain were "totalitarian."
50 On the history/memory distinction, see Yerushalmi, *Zakhor*.
51 Another educational resource expressed the theme as follows: "*The Soviet Jewry Experience as a Microcosm of a Repetitive Jewish Historical Situation*: The Soviet Jewry experience is not new or unique. It represents a pattern that Jews have experienced in every generation, beginning with the Exodus from Egypt." Blaser, *Exodus*, 33.
52 JCCGW, *Teaching* (2nd ed.), 11–15. Shavuot, observed in late May or early June, commemorates the giving of the Law on Sinai.
53 Rabbinic texts offer two variants, *zeh bazeh* and *zeh lazeh*. *Lazeh* implies mutual responsibility. *Bazeh* implies shared fate. Soviet Jewry movement writings usually adopted *bazeh* in Hebrew but the mutual responsibility translation in English. Rudman, "Kol Yisrael Areivim Zeh Ba-Zeh."
54 These were listed as "Useful Themes for Studying Soviet Jewry" in JCCGW, *Teaching* (2nd ed.), 10.

55 JCCGW, *Teaching* (1st ed.), 11, 14.
56 JCCGW, *Teaching* (1st ed.), 11, 15. On Jewish education's treatment of Thanksgiving and other American holidays, see Wenger, *History Lessons*, 67–74.
57 JCCGW, *Teaching* (1st ed.), 12, 20. Lag Ba'Omer, a springtime holiday, commemorates resistance to Roman-era persecutions, among other meanings.
58 The author of CAJE's *Making Gates* curriculum explained, "I tried to create a combination of intellectual/cognitive lessons and 'see yourself in their shoes' activities to get American Jewish children to care about this cause emotionally." Les Bronstein, personal communication, 3 September 2020.
59 "M.U.S.E.—Museum Utilization for Student Education," National Endowment for the Humanities, grant no. ES-*0458–77, 1 July 1977–30 June 1981 ($267,574); Dorph, interview.
60 Dorph, *By Spirit Alone*, 1–3.
61 Dorph, interview.
62 Meister, *Lesson Plans*; Tallman and Kahn, *Let My People Go*; "Suggested Course on Soviet Jewry for 12–16 Year Olds" (London), curriculum, unbound in *Soviet Jewry Pack*, n.d. (ca. 1981), USUK b.16 f.1; Blaser, *Exodus*; National Board Institute '72, "Underground," 1; Dana Anesi, personal communication, 21 June 2021. The workshop was known as the National Board Institute.
63 The Dutch embassy represented Israeli interests in Moscow after the Soviets cut diplomatic ties in 1967. Buwalda, *They Did Not Dwell Alone*. American simulations had trouble keeping the small Western European nationalities straight. One sent participants to the Swiss embassy, another to the Finnish. Blaser, *Exodus*, 3; Meister, *Lesson Plans*, 82.
64 Blaser, *Exodus*, 1.
65 Blaser, 12.
66 Blaser, front cover text.
67 National Board Institute '72, "Underground," 1.
68 "Suggested Course on Soviet Jewry for 12–16 Year Olds," session 4. Lesson plans did not raise concerns about the simulations having negative psychological effects on children. The historian of Jewish education Jonathan Krasner suggested to me that this may reflect general tendencies of 1970s DIY curriculum design.
69 National Board Institute '72, "Underground," 7.
70 Blaser, *Exodus*, 1.
71 National Board Institute '72, "Underground," 7.
72 JCCGW, *Teaching* (2nd ed.), 21. See also Rothenberg, *Serious Fun*, 71. Before the USSR and Israel established direct flights, most emigrants first went to transit camps in Vienna and Rome.
73 Blaser, *Exodus*, Discussion Guide 1–2.
74 Blaser, Discussion Guide 11.
75 National Board Institute '72, "Underground," 8. When I have run the simulation in twenty-first-century college courses on Soviet Jewry activism, some students have chosen to play their Soviet officials as Boris Badenov and Natasha Fatale.
76 Simulations were a popular mode of Jewish American experiential education, also used to teach about Israel, anti-Black racism, and Jewish tragedies from the destruction of the ancient Jerusalem Temple to the Holocaust. Lainer-Vos, "Israel in the Poconos"; Benor, Krasner, and Avni, *Hebrew Infusion*, 40, 73–76; Prell, "Jewish

Summer Camping"; Prell, "Summer Camp"; Fox, "Tisha B'av.'" On social movements as sites of learning, see Haluza-DeLay, "Theory of Practice."
77 For European critiques of the role of simulation in American culture, see Eco, *Travels in Hyperreality*, 1–58; and Baudrillard, *Simulacra and Simulation*, 12–14. For an American riposte, see Bruner, "Abraham Lincoln."
78 GNYCSJ, *Purim Puzzler*.
79 Ramm, *Route to Freedom*; Connie Smukler, interviewed by Shaul Kelner, 23 July 2020.
80 SSSJ, "'Brezhnev Birthday Party' for Soviet Jews at Russian Performance," press release, 19 December 1976, SSSJ b.17 f.10.
81 *Brit milah* is the circumcision ceremony. The *mohel* performs it. Schapira was neither a mohel nor a caterer. Joel Sandberg to All Councils, "Program Suggestions for Local Groups Made at the Brainstorming Session at the UCSJ Annual Meeting," 25 October 1985, JSAS b.1 f.1.
82 Harris and Rabinovich, *Jokes of Oppression*, 48.
83 Freud, *Jokes*; Ben-Amos, "'Myth' of Jewish Humor." A 2013 survey found that 75 percent of American Jews said having a sense of humor was important or essential to their Jewish identity. Pew Research Center, *Portrait of Jewish Americans*, 168.
84 JCCGW, *Teaching* (2nd ed.), 10.
85 The Hebrew from 1 Samuel 15:29 translates literally as "The Eternal of Israel does not lie." Rabbinic interpretation understands this figuratively to refer to God's commitment to the eternity of the Jewish people. JCCGW, *Teaching* (2nd ed.), 10.
86 Leviticus 19:16, quoted in JCCGW, *Teaching* (2nd ed.), 10.
87 Dayenu is a fifteen-stanza litany tracing the stages of the exodus, praising God for each, and asserting that each alone would have been sufficient (e.g., "If God had split the sea for us but had not led us through on dry land, *dayenu*, it would have been enough for us"). JCCGW, *Teaching* (2nd ed.), 18.
88 Warshawsky, *Creative Puppetry*, 173–76.
89 SSSJ, "Soviet Jewry 'Guerilla Theater': 'Let Me Out'—the Trial of Boris Kochubiyevsky," script, n.d. (ca. 1970), CCSA b.3 f.80; Alvin Boretz, "A Symbolic Seder for Soviet Jewry" (AJCSJ, New York), 1970 [1968], NCSJ b.1 f.6.
90 Warshawsky, *Creative Puppetry*, 173.
91 Essay contests represent the mobilizing gaze at its most transformative. In the original sense intended by Montaigne, who coined the term *essai*, this form of composition was an *assay*, an *attempt* to use writing to clarify and express one's own thoughts. Essay contests co-opted this individualistic genre, directing writers to express themselves in ways constrained by the sponsors' interests. A. Porter, "Distributed Agency"; Cruce, "History of Progressive-Era."
92 Matt Penn, Allan Eisen, and Jacob Birnbaum, "From: Sub-Committee on Soviet Jewry," 22 December 1965, SSSJ b.2 f.3, 2; Metropolitan New York Jewish Youth Directors, meeting minutes, 26 January 1966, SSSJ b.2 f.3, 2.
93 BACSJ, "Community Wide Projects Completed in 1967–68 Season," June 1968, BACSJ b.10 f.35, 1; AJCSJ, "Programmatic Recommendations Adopted," 3.
94 On social movements' uses of graphic arts to raise awareness and build solidarity, see Reed, *Art of Protest*, 103–28, 179–217.
95 NCSJ-UKI, "International Card Competition," press release, 2 June 1981, NCSJ-UK f.317.

96 "Cartoon Wins a Trip"; NCSJ-UKI, "'Competing for Freedom' Poster Exhibition," contest entry form, 1980, NCSJ-UK f.317; NCSJ-UKI, "List of Submissions: 'Competing for Freedom' Poster Exhibition," 13 July 1980, NCSJ-UK f.317; NCSJ-UKI, "Competing for Freedom Poster Competition," press release, 7 July 1980, NCSJ-UK f.317.
97 Litwack, *School Kit*, cover, 51.
98 Harriet Wulfstadt to Sharon Silverman, 4 November 1983, CASJ b.27 f.2; Harriet Wulfstadt, Pamela Braun Cohen, and Marillyn Tallman to Director of Education, November 1983, CASJ b.27 f.2; CASJ, "Young Russian Immigrant Wins City-Wide Poster Contest," press release, 25 April 1984, CASJ b.27 f.2; "Soviet Jewry Poster."

7. My Soviet Twin

1 Ames, "'Twin' Bas Mitzvahs"; Curry, "South Florida Jews."
2 SJC, *Bar/Bat Mitzvah Twinning*, 1 (emphasis added).
3 Headlines from press clipping collage, NCSJ, *Bar/Bat Mitzvah Twinning*, 12.
4 Curry, "South Florida Jews."
5 Ames, "'Twin' Bas Mitzvahs."
6 Tolts, "Half Century," 2.
7 Wlazelek, "Ceremony Includes Refusenik"; Ferson, "Bat Mitzvah"; "U.S., Soviet Pals."
8 They still do. On his campaign webpage, Pennsylvania governor Josh Shapiro (elected 2022) featured a 1986 newspaper clipping of himself and his Soviet twin, Avi Goldstein, sharing their joint bar mitzvah in person. Shapiro, "Josh's Record"; Lieber, "2 Boys Share."
9 Action for Soviet Jewry to Dear "Twin," 10 October 1990, ASJ b.127 f.9.
10 Harrison, *Passover Revisited*, 81, 233n.
11 "For Gidon Here"; Golden, "Altar Chair Empty"; Kokesch, "Ned Shares Bar-Mitzvah"; Honig, "Activist Bar Mitzva."
12 Tennison, "Young Soviet Jews"; GNYCSJ, "1982 Annual Report," March 1983, ASJ b.125 f.1, 6.
13 Action for Soviet Jewry, "Summary of Twinnings: August 1, 1982–May 26, 1983" (Waltham, MA), 1983, ASJ b.127 f.12.
14 "German Abramova, Born 1970, Bar 1983," twinning list, 1970 birth cohort, January 1982 to May 1984 ceremonies, 1984, NCSJ b.35 f.5.
15 Not all of the eligible population (Jews by religion who turned thirteen in the 1980s) celebrated a bar or bat mitzvah. Kosmin et al., *Highlights of the CJF 1990 NJPS*, 7; S. Goldstein, "Profile of American Jewry," 143, 59.
16 Twinning testimonials in contemporary writings by Generation X Jewish Americans include Beckerman, *When They Come*, 1–4; Feldstein, "My Struggle"; and Martin, "My Russian Twin." Josh Shapiro highlighted his twinning in his Pennsylvania gubernatorial campaign biography. Shapiro, "Josh's Record." Dara Horn, of the same generation, offers a fictionalized account of twinning in her novel *The World to Come*.
17 Four hundred attended future Pennsylvania governor Josh Shapiro's twinning. Lieber, "2 Boys Share."
18 SJC, *Bar/Bat Mitzvah Twinning*, 18–19.
19 The 1990 National Jewish Population Study estimated 2.7 million core Jewish households (entirely Jewish or mixed), 40 percent of which—1.1 million—attended

synagogue at least a few times in the year prior to the survey. Multiply that across the decade when twinning programs were operating for the total Jewish American population eligible for exposure to a twinning service. (Another 30 percent who attended only on Rosh Hashanah and Yom Kippur would not have encountered twinnings, as bar and bat mitzvahs are not conducted on the High Holidays.) Lazerwitz et al., *Jewish Choices*, 161, 78; Kosmin et al., *Highlights of the CJF 1990 NJPS*, 17.
20 Joselit, *Wonders*, 89–133, esp. 90.
21 Munro, *Coming of Age*, 10.
22 Joselit, *Wonders*, 94–96.
23 We follow Klapper, who urges that studies of youth engage with texts created by youth, not just texts written by adults about youth. Klapper, *Jewish Girls*, 4–5.
24 Amnesty International, "1961–1976"; Loeffler, *Rooted Cosmopolitans*, 218–20.
25 UCSJ, *Soviet Prisoners of Conscience*, 19 November 1971, CCSA b.9 f.255.
26 WCSJ, "Adopt-a-Prisoner Action Sheet," December 1971, WCSJ b.10 f.12; Betty Miller to Adopt-a-Prisoner Project Members, 10 May 1972, CCSA b.9 f.256; Miller, "Oral History Transcription," 3.
27 Jeff Levy and Judy Silverman to Dear Friend, 17 April 1972, MBSP b.3 f.12; MACSJ, "About 'Adopt a Family,'" 15 May 1972, JCRCMD b.86 f.37; Adele Sandberg, "Adopt-a-Family Program: Annual Report" (SFCSJ), September 1974, JSAS b.1 f.2; Spiegel, *Triumph*, 267; Joel Sandberg and Adele Sandberg, interviewed by Shaul Kelner, 15 August 2018. By 1974, adoption programs had spread to around twenty cities. The Minnesota Action Committee established a National Adopt-a-Family Data Bank to help the UCSJ coordinate adoptions. "Minutes—MACSJ Steering Committee Meeting," October/November 1973, JCRCMD b.86 f.5; Janet Frisch to Stuart Wurtman, 12 May 1977, MBSP b.3 f.48.
28 GNYCSJ, "Enclosed Is a Project Yachad Kit," August 1973, JCRCGP b.64 f.20.
29 "Har Zion Temple 'Adopts'"; Harrison, *Passover Revisited*, 76.
30 The term *refusenik* was coined in 1971 by British activist Michael Sherbourne. It did not become settled language in the US until 1975. Before then, Americans who translated *otkazniki* also wrote of "rejectniks" and "refusniks" (without the *e*). Nelson, "Cataloguing"; Hurst, *British Human Rights*, 105.
31 Action Central, "Children of the Otkazniki."
32 Manon and Manekofsky, *Natasha's Dream*.
33 This mischaracterized *Natasha's Dream*. It was an activist handbook, not a coloring book, illustrated not by Natasha Korenfeld but by the niece and nephew of its graphic designer, Avrum Ashery.
34 "Joint Bat Mitzvah Celebrated"; Golden, "Altar Chair Empty."
35 Golden, "Altar Chair Empty."
36 "For Gidon Here."
37 William Epstein to Edgar Williams, 7 August 1975, JCRCGP b.65 f.26; "For Gidon Here."
38 "Joint Bat Mitzvah Celebrated"; Golden, "Altar Chair Empty."
39 Blanchard, "To Russia with Love"; Kokesch, "Ned Shares Bar-Mitzvah"; "Shared Bar Mitzvah."
40 Kuhr, "Debriefing Narrative / Russian Journey," trip report, 14–28 August 1978, 1.
41 "Bar Mitzvah in Moscow."
42 Bar and bat mitzvah travel to the USSR was rare. I know of only two instances in the 1980s, both involving twinnings. In 1984, the president of Reconstructionist

Rabbinical College took his son to the Soviet Union "to arrange [his] bar mitzvah twinning." Silverman, trip report, 15–24 March 1984. Later that year, a New York bat mitzvah girl, Alisa Jancu, went to Tashkent to meet her twin, Dina Altman. Jancu, "Two Youthful Sorts of Mitzvot."

43 McQuiston, "Bar Mitzvah by Proxy"; "Proxy Bar Mitzvah Tomorrow"; Oestreich, "Ritual Recalls Refuseniks"; Erlick and Gross, "Bar Mitzvah and Home." In November 1978, between the two Begun boys' 1977 and 1979 ceremonies, Australian Jewish community leader Isi Liebler paired his son's bar mitzvah with one of them. Rutland, *Lone Voice*, 255.
44 Gerlis, *Those Wonderful Women*, 91–92.
45 Robiner, trip report, 22 May 1976, 7; Sussman, "Group Trip to Moscow and Leningrad," 2–9 October 1977, 9.
46 Eisen, *Count Us In*, 96; Blanchard, "To Russia with Love."
47 Pamela Braun Cohen to Mark Williams, 15 April 1981, CASJ b.37 f.9.
48 Prell, *Women Remaking*; Fishman, *Breath of Life*; Nadell, *Women Who Would Be Rabbis*; Nadell, *America's Jewish Women*, 244–49. Congregations have often provided platforms for American women's activism. Einwohner, Leamaster, and Pratt, "Push, Pull, and Fusion." With twinning, synagogues empowered not just adult women's activism but preteen and teenage girls'.
49 Siegel, Strassfeld, and Strassfeld, *First Jewish Catalog*; Kelman, "Reading a Book."
50 Sharon L. Sobel, "Let My People Go! A Creative Bat Mitzvah Service on the Plight of Soviet Jewry" (Succasunna, NJ), prayer service booklet, 15 September 1973, ASJ b.127 f.12; Podwal, *Let My People Go*.
51 Novikov was symbolically bar mitzvahed without a local twin in many DC-area synagogues that weekend. "Shared Bar Mitzvah."
52 Kokesch, "Ned Shares Bar-Mitzvah"; Eisen, *Count Us In*, 98, 289n27–28.
53 "Shared Bar Mitzvah"; Andrea Morgenstern, "Bat Mitzvah of Andrea Morgenstern," sermon, 4 November 1978, ASJ b.127 f.12; Harrison, *Passover Revisited*, 78; Lieberstein, "Simchat Torah March"; Nadell, *America's Jewish Women*, 259; Sandberg, *Lean In*, 54–55; Ruth Newman, interviewed by Shaul Kelner, 8 August 2019; Bobbie Morgenstern, interviewed by Shaul Kelner, 25 June 2020; Sandberg and Sandberg, interview, 15 August 2018.
54 Newman, interview; Mansfield, "Bar Mitzvah 'Twinned.'"
55 Soviet Jewry Commission of the [Minnesota-Dakotas] JCRC-ADL, "Soviet Jewry Budget," 1983, JCRCMD b.86 f.4, 2; Marshall Levin and Rachel Levin (Minneapolis), anniversary service invitation, 15 June 1984, ASJ b.125 f.2.
56 Donovan, "Covenant of Brit Milah"; "Beth Shalom to Hold Dual Graduation."
57 It also suggested a "Mock funeral of the Helsinki Accords." In 1976, the 35s staged a proxy funeral for Colonel Yefim Davidovich, who died of a heart attack while waiting for an exit visa. Joel Sandberg to All Councils, "Program Suggestions for Local Groups Made at the Brainstorming Session at the UCSJ Annual Meeting," 25 October 1985, JSAS b.1 f.1; Gerlis, *Those Wonderful Women*, 176.
58 "World Jewry Prays."
59 Golden, "Altar Chair Empty."
60 SJC, *Bar/Bat Mitzvah Twinning*; GNYCSJ, *Writing to Your Twin*, 7; ASJ, *Bar and Bat Mitzvah Twinning*.
61 Ferson, "Bat Mitzvah."

62 Ma`oz, "Kes `al-domi leYehudei Rusiyah" ["Do Not Be Silent" Chair for Russian Jews] (Israel), poster, n.d., NLI digital library, *Masa Bazman* online exhibition, https://web.nli.org.il; "'Kisei' `Al Domi'"; "'Let My People Go' Campaign"; "*Hasatah anti-Soviyetit mita`am Ma`oz*"; "Kisei' panu'i"; "'Empty Chair' at Seder"; Chizhik, *MAOZ*. Jews symbolically reserve a chair for the biblical prophet Elijah at circumcision ceremonies and a cup of wine for Elijah at Passover seders. (Some communities may have left an empty chair and full place setting for Elijah at seders.) I found no evidence that these informed Ma`oz's creation of the Kes 'Al-Domee. Nor was the empty chair for Soviet Jews influenced by the American Legion's empty chair ritual for Vietnam War POW/MIAs, which the Legion introduced in 1985. American Legion, "POW/MIA Empty Chair," Res. 288, adopted 23–28 August 1985, https://archive.legion.org.

63 "Pesach 5726." Ma`oz was founded in December 1958 and led by Shabbetai Bet-Zvi (Baskin), who fled the USSR at the end of World War II. Chizhik, *MAOZ*; Ro'i, *Struggle*, 231–32; Pinkus, "Israeli Activity," 391.

64 "'Matzah of Hope.'"

65 WCSJ, "Adopt-a-Prisoner Action Sheet" (all caps in original).

66 SJC, "Activities of Soviet Jewry Council of JCRC—11/1/75 to 11/1/75," 1975, JCSP b.2 f.41.

67 "Joint Bat Mitzvah Celebrated"; "Special Bar Mitzva"; Blanchard, "To Russia with Love"; "Shared Bar Mitzvah"; Larry Marks to Abraham J. Bayer, 22 June 1978, JGA b.1 f.16; McQuiston, "Bar Mitzvah by Proxy"; Kanter, "Thousands Join."

68 Fran Rapoport to All Councils, assorted dates, ASJ b.127 f.9.

69 Kay Reiff to Bobbie Morgenstern, 5 February 1983, NCSJ b.35 f.5.

70 Reiff to Morgenstern, 5 February 1983. When researching this book, I discovered that my bar mitzvah twin, Leonid Barras, had been living in Israel for ten months when I stood at the pulpit demanding his freedom in October 1982. Kelner, "Bar and Bat Mitzvah Twinning."

71 Morgenstern, interview, 25 June 2020.

72 ORT was established in Russia in 1880 to support vocational education for the Jewish poor. Its letters were originally a Russian acronym. In the twentieth century, its work expanded worldwide. In the US, chapters to support the agency became popular vehicles for Jewish women's civic and philanthropic engagement. On civic organizations as channels for Jewish women's activism, see Nadell, *America's Jewish Women*, 186–92; Rogow, *Gone to Another Meeting*; Reinharz and Raider, *American Jewish Women*; and Klapper, *Ballots, Babies, and Banners*.

73 Women's American ORT District III to Chapter Presidents, "Revised Information and Procedures for Proxy Bar/Bat Mitzvah," January 1982, NCSJ b.35 f.3 (emphasis in original).

74 Margery Kohrman to District Community Relations Chairmen, "Bar Mitzvah Twinning Material and Promotion," 23 February 1983, NCSJ b.35 f.3. ORT was not alone in claiming ownership of twinning. The National Conference, Long Island Committee, and Washington Committee each claimed to have invented it. NCSJ, "NCSJ Announces Program to Involve Youth; Distributes Twinning Guide," press release, 18 May 1982, NCSJ b.36 f.5; Oestreich, "Ritual Recalls Refuseniks"; Mansfield, "Bar Mitzvah 'Twinned.'"

75 Myrna Shinbaum to Jerry Goodman, "Bar/Bat Mitzbah [sic] Twinning," 18 February 1982, NCSJ b.36 f.3.

76 Fran Rapoport to Kira Rapoport, 29 January 1990, ASJ b.127 f.9.

77 NCSJ, *Bar/Bat Mitzvah Twinning*, 4.
78 "German Abramova, Born 1970, Bar 1983."
79 Action for Soviet Jewry, "Summary of Twinnings."
80 WCSJ, "Bar and Bat Mitzvah Twinning with Soviet Jews," cover graphic, 1979, www.jhsgw.org; ASJ, *Bar and Bat Mitzvah Twinning*. The ASJ's photocopier left a shadow at the seam where the clipping met the page.
81 Women's American ORT District VII, "ORT Targets: Proxy Bar Mitzvah" (Cleveland, OH), 1980, NCSJ b.36 f.5; Women's American ORT District III, "Proxy Bar Mitzvah Bat Mitzvah for Soviet Jews" (East Orange, NJ), pamphlet, 1982, NCSJ b.35 f.3; SJC, *Bar/Bat Mitzvah Twinning*; Jewish Federation Council of Greater Los Angeles, *Bar/Bat Mitzvah Twinning*.
82 ASJ, *Bar and Bat Mitzvah Twinning*, 1–3, 5.
83 ASJ, 7.
84 Detroit Soviet Jewry Committee, *Make a Connection!*, 8; GNYCSJ, *Writing to Your Twin*, 8; Lisa Beth Muskat (Manchester, NH), prayer service booklet, Bat Mitzvah twinning of Lisa Muskat and Olga Terlitskaya, 17 May 1980, ASJ b.127 f.12; Arlene Sobol and Michael Sobol (Framingham, MA), prayer service booklet, Bar Mitzvah twinning of Ethan Daniel Sobol and Kirill Shapiro, 10 May 1986, ASJ b.128 f.4.
85 SJC, *Bar/Bat Mitzvah Twinning*, 1.
86 For examples of parental involvement, see materials from Andrew Levy's 27 November 1982 twinning with Alexander Magazinik (ASJ b.127 f.12) and Karen Liebowitz's 21 November 1987 twinning with Masha Meitina, (ASJ b.128 f.4).
87 NCSJ, *Bar/Bat Mitzvah Twinning*, 1 (emphasis added).
88 The assemblages could be compared to collage or pastiche, but technically they were neither. Unlike collage, which juxtaposes unrelated objects to create new meaning, the materials here were already related to each other. Unlike pastiche, there was no mimicry or caricature. Kjellman-Chapin, "Traces, Layers and Palimpsests."
89 Sobel, "Let My People Go!"; Morgenstern, "Bat Mitzvah."
90 Kelner, "Bar and Bat Mitzvah Twinning," 38; Jewish Federation Council of Greater Los Angeles, *Bar/Bat Mitzvah Twinning*, 2.
91 Temple Beth Am, "Twinning Service" (Framingham, MA), prayerbook insert, 27 May 1985, ASJ b.128 f.4; Temple Beth Am, "B'nai Mitzvah Twinning Service" (Framingham, MA), prayerbook insert, 12 October 1985, ASJ b.128 f.4; ASJ, *Bar and Bat Mitzvah Twinning*; Robbie Solomon, interviewed by Shaul Kelner, 24 February 2006. Lyrics from Robbie Solomon's "Leaving Mother Russia" provide the title for Beckerman's *When They Come for Us, We'll Be Gone*. Other Safam songs about Soviet Jewry include "Amnesty" (written by Joel Sussman, 1983): "Let 'em out! Let 'em out! Let 'em out tonight! / Let the Lord's word humble them / Watch the Kremlin tumble in," and "Just Another Foreigner" (written by Joel Sussman and Robbie Solomon, 1984). The latter also found its way into twinning services. To explain the situation of bat mitzvah twin Yulia Murash—an Odessan, five years in refusal, with a mother out of work—a Florida bat mitzvah girl quoted a verse: "A woman returns from the streets of Odessa / From looking for a job in the cold Russian wind / It's been five hungry years while she waits for a visa / She still lights the candles as Shabbes begins." It "seemed to have been written about Yulia," she said. Jennifer R. Ledewitz (Framingham, MA), bat mitzvah sermon, 27 December 1986, ASJ b.128 f.4; Joel Sussman interviewed by Shaul Kelner, 13 March 2006.

92 Sobol and Sobol, prayer service booklet; Bob Gordon, personal communication, 6 January 2021; Richard Sobol, personal communication, 7 January 2021.
93 "Ani Ma'amin," a statement of faith in the messiah's coming, is said to have been sung by Warsaw Jews headed to their deaths in the camps. Adler, "No Raisins, No Almonds," 55. "Eli Eli" was written by a soldier-poet who left Palestine to parachute behind Nazi lines, where she was killed. Neither song explicitly references the genocide. Both are staples of Holocaust memorial programs.
94 Muskat, prayer service booklet, 2, 7, 12. Blue and white refer to the colors of the Israeli flag.
95 For rabbinic critique of the folk customs, see Salkin, *Putting God on the Guest List*.
96 For hipster celebration of the folk customs, see Bennett, Shell, and Kroll, *Bar Mitzvah Disco*.
97 Joselit, *Wonders*, 100.
98 Roni Leibowitz, "Candlelighting Ceremony," poem, 21 November 1987, ASJ b.128 f.4. (Karen twinned with Masha Meitina.)
99 Cohen to Williams, 15 April 1981 (emphasis added).
100 NCSJ, *Bar/Bat Mitzvah Twinning* (emphasis added).
101 Woocher, *Sacred Survival*.
102 Other translations, such as "good deed" for *mitzvah* and "son" or "daughter" for *bar* and *bat*, fail to capture the Hebrew's imposing weight. *Mitzvah* means "sacred commandment." When *bar* and *bat* prefix a noun, they can mean "subject to" or "one who is subject to."
103 Kelner, "People-to-People"; Rubin, "Soviet Refugee"; Feldman, "Social Absorption."
104 Krasner, *Benderly Boys*; Wenger, *History Lessons*; Klapper, *Jewish Girls*.
105 For antecedents in Jewish American education, see Klapper, *Jewish Girls*, 143, 146–48, 161–63, 182–84.
106 Action for Soviet Jewry, "Summary of Twinnings," 2.
107 Faith Lowy, "Bat Mitzvah Sermon," 21 May 1983, enclosure in Faith Lowy to Hamilton Fish, 13 May 1983, ASJ b.128 f.4.
108 Consider Hanukkah. Jewish Americans speak of it as a celebration of religious freedom, as if it were a victory for the First Amendment. Israelis frame it as an ancient Independence Day, as if the Maccabean revolt was a proto-Zionist Jewish national liberation movement. Zion and Spectre, *Different Light*.
109 Lowy, "Bat Mitzvah Sermon."
110 Wenger, *History Lessons*, 2–3; Sarna, "Cult of Synthesis."
111 Ledewitz, bat mitzvah sermon.
112 Ledewitz, bat mitzvah sermon.
113 Lowy to Fish, 13 May 1983.
114 Hamilton Fish to Faith Lowy, 26 May 1983, ASJ b.128 f.4; Hamilton Fish to Ronald Reagan, 16 May 1983, ASJ b.128 f.4; Flore, "Bat Mitzvah Unites."
115 E.g., John Kerry to Ethan Sobol and Kirill Shapiro, 11 April 1986, ASJ b.128 f.4, reprinted in Sobol and Sobol, prayer service booklet; Nicholas Mavroules to Andrew Levy, 27 November 1982, ASJ b.127 f.12.
116 Diana Altman to Lynne (unknown bat mitzvah twin), n.d., circulated in Fran Rapoport to All Councils, "Twinning Updates," 16 November 1988, ASJ b.127 f.9 (strikethrough in the original).

NOTES

117 Olga Malievskaya to unnamed twin, 1990, circulated in Fran Rapoport to All Councils, "Twinning Updates," 16 July 1990, ASJ b.127 f.9.
118 Yury Shinsky to Jonathan Steinberg, 1990, circulated in Rapoport, "Twinning Updates," 16 July 1990.
119 Quoted in Rapoport, "Twinning Updates," 16 July 1990.

Conclusion

1 May, "Vigil Gives Way"; Brodetzky, "Transcript of Oral History"; Sislen, "Soviet Jewry Movement"; Lazin, *American Christians*, 32; Luther Place Memorial Church, "History of Free Soviet Jewry"; JCCGW, "Soviet Jewry Calendar 1977–1978," 1977, NCSJ b.84 f.3, 2.
2 Margolin, "Camp Gan Israel Russia"; "First Yeshiva in 60 Years"; "Five Jewish Schools Open."
3 May, "Vigil Gives Way."
4 May.
5 Samuel H. Sislen, interviewed by Shaul Kelner, 1 July 2019.
6 Gold, "Soviet Jews"; Kelner, "People-to-People," 211–19.
7 Nagel, *Operation Exodus*.
8 Google Ngram Viewer shows the term "mitzvah project" near zero in the 1980s and beginning its upward trajectory in 1995.
9 Yad Vashem, "Bar/Bat Mitzvah Twinning."
10 Kosmin, et al., *Highlights of the CJF 1990 NJPS*; Kravel-Tovi, "Wet Numbers," 147–51.
11 Berman, Rosenblatt, and Stahl, "Continuity Crisis"; Mehta and Krutzsch, "Changing Jewish Family."
12 Another way the end of the Cold War created space for the continuity panic to erupt was by destabilizing the Jewish American community's relationship with Israel. This relationship had been premised on defending an isolated and embattled Jewish state. The rush of formerly communist countries and nonaligned states to recognize Israel coupled with the hopes for a speedy peace inspired by the Oslo peace process (itself a product of post–Cold War geopolitics) struck at both these premises and set the Israel-diaspora relationship adrift.
13 Sarna, "Secret of Jewish Continuity."
14 Wertheimer, Liebman, and Cohen, "How to Save American Jews."
15 Schnold, *Jews of Struggle*; Weitzman National Museum of American Jewish History, *Power of Protest*; Zelaya, "20-Year Vigil"; Lillian and Albert Small Capital Jewish Museum, "Voices of the Vigil."
16 Freedom 25, "About"; Freedom 25, "FreedomTwentyFive," www.youtube.com; "Freedom Sunday"; Shroyer, "25 Years Later."
17 Lookstein Center for Jewish Education, Bar Ilan University, "Refusenik Project." The project's founder, Anat Zalmanson-Kuznetsov, is the daughter of political prisoners Sylva Zalmanson and Eduard Kuznetsov, arrested in the 1970 Leningrad hijacking affair. Her documentary film, *Operation Wedding*, recounts her parents' experience.
18 E.g., Bialis, *Refusenik*; Zalmanson-Kuznetsov, *Operation Wedding*; Friedman and Chernin, *Second Exodus*; Ro'i, *Jewish Movement*; A. Weiss, *Open Up*; Kedmi, *Hopeless Wars*; P. Cohen, *Hidden Heroes*; Kosharovsky, "Yuli Kosharovsky"; Kholmyansky, "Jewish Freedom"; Luntz, "Lighting the Flames"; and Association "Remember and Save," "Soviet Jews Exodus."

19 Rosenblatt, "30 Years Later."
20 Ravitz, "Defying the KGB."
21 Freedom 25, "Remembering the Passion," www.youtube.com.
22 Further evidence of the success of commemorative efforts comes from the presence of dissents to the politics of nostalgia. See, e.g. Benjamin, "Soviet Jewry Movement Revisited."
23 Lest one imagine that free emigration was simply a result of the USSR's dissolution, note that emigration restrictions were removed while the Soviet Union was still in existence. The leaders who made those policy decisions did not know what the future held in store. Morozov, *Documents*, 249–55.
24 Sharansky, Foreword, 154.
25 Cold War historians are circumspect about ascribing the USSR's dissolution to any single cause. They debate the relative weight to assign human rights activism versus other factors (economic, military, etc.). Gaddis, *Cold War*; Guyatt, "End of the Cold War"; Prados, *How the Cold War Ended*; Zubok, *Failed Empire*. The argument that human rights activism contributed to the system's collapse contends that the government maintained control through repression and that conceding to pressures to liberalize (including on emigration) increased pressure to liberalize further, "open[ing] a Pandora's Box of nationalist tensions that could not be reversed." Ro'i and Rubenstein, "Human Rights," esp. 223; Thomas, *Helsinki Effect*; Snyder, *Human Rights Activism*. With Ro'i and Rubenstein, one can also view refuseniks' Jewish activism as part of the rise in ethnic nationalisms that eroded citizens' identification with the Soviet state.
26 Israeli, Preface, 156.
27 Weitzman National Museum of American Jewish History, *Power of Protest*, 3.
28 Shroyer, "25 Years Later."
29 Yossi Klein Halevi, quoted in Rosenblatt, "30 Years Later."
30 Commemoration involves different behaviors from those that constituted Soviet Jewry movement activism itself. It therefore generates different meanings—mainly nostalgia.
31 Museum of Jewish Heritage, "'Prisoner of Conscience' Bracelet"; Weitzman National Museum of American Jewish History, "Are We Responsible for Others?"
32 Spiegel, "Soviet Is Assailed"; Theodore Mann to NJCRAC and CJFWF Member Agencies, "Program Kit for Simchat Torah Solidarity Observances," 25 August 1971, JCRCMD b.90 f.15; SSSJ, "Simchat Torah Festival of Redemption for Russian Jewry," program, 18 October 1970, SSSJ b.7 f.11; Bentley College Hillel, "Benefit Concert for Prisoner of Conscience Anatoly Shcharansky," publicity flyer, 1982, CASJ b.25 f.10; Sharlene Garfield to Pamela Braun Cohen and Marillyn Tallman, 26 September 1983, CASJ b.37 f.3.
33 This differs from Tarrow. His "modularity" refers to a single tactic being repeatedly employed by different actors in different settings for different purposes. "Modular Collective Action," 77.
34 *Babylonian Talmud*, Shabbat 88a:7–8; Epstein and Melamed, *Mekhilta De-Rabbi Shimon Bar Yohai* 24:7, 221.

INTERVIEWS

Ashery, Avrum — August 13, 2019
Atkins, Angie — August 21, 2019
Bayer, Jennifer — February 27, 2006
Beller, Herbert N. — July 2, 2019
Benjamin, Sheldon — October 29, 2020
Birnbaum, Jacob — December 11, 2003
Blau, Rivka — May 28, 2019
Borden, Victor — January 8, 2020
Caron, Herb — April 1, 2016
Cohen, Pamela Braun — August 5, 2020
Davis, Margy-Ruth — September 24, 2019
Dishler, Bernard — July 5, 2020
Dishler, Lana — July 5, 2020
Dorph, Gail — August 7, 2020
Furst, Zev — July 19, 2018
Gainsford, Doreen — June 29, 2021
Goodman, Jerry — September 5, 2019
Gordon, Robert (Bob) — January 6, 2021
Hoenlein, Malcolm — May 30, 2023
Israel, Sherry — August 14, 2017
Jacobson, Seth — January 3, 2018
Levine, Hillel — September 5, 2018
Mandel, Carol — July 10, 2018
Morgenstern, Bobbie — June 25, 2020
Newman, Ruth — August 8, 2019
Patkin, Judy — July 30, 2019
Porath, Jonathan — August 29, 2016

Richter, Glenn	July 27, 2006; July 23, 2019
Rosenblum, Louis	August 15, 2015
Rosenblum, Miriam	October 29, 2020
Sandberg, Adele	August 15, 2018
Sandberg, Joel	August 15, 2018
Schapira, Morey	January 10, 2020
Schnur, Zeesy	September 24, 2019
Selikowitz, David	July 26, 2019
Shapiro, Eileen	November 24, 2019
Shapiro, Howard	November 24, 2019
Sharansky, Natan	January 4, 2018
Sislen, Samuel H.	July 1, 2019
Smukler, Connie	July 23, 2020
Solomon, Robbie	February 24, 2006
Sprayregen, Joel	August 30, 2019
Sussman, Joel	Summer 2006
Waksberg, David	July 6, 2021
Weiss, Avi	April 28, 2006
Wurtman, Enid	August 7, 2019
Yaroslavsky, Zev	September 13, 2018; June 17, 2021

BIBLIOGRAPHY

Archives Consulted

- AJA American Jewish Archives, Hebrew Union College–Jewish Institute of Religion, Cincinnati
- AJHS American Jewish Historical Society, Center for Jewish History, New York
- LMA London Metropolitan Archives, London
- NLI National Library of Israel, Jerusalem
- NYPL New York Public Library
- TUL Temple University Library, Philadelphia
- UMJA Nathan and Theresa Berman Upper Midwest Jewish Archives, University of Minnesota, Minneapolis
- WRHS Western Reserve Historical Society, Cleveland
- YUA Yeshiva University Archives, Mendel Gottesman Library, New York

Unpublished Primary Sources

- AJB Abraham J. Bayer Papers. Personal files of Ellen Bayer.
- AJCONG American Jewish Congress Records. RG I-77. AJHS.
- ASJ Action for Soviet Jewry (Boston) Records. RG I-487. AJHS.
- BACSJ Bay Area Council for Soviet Jews Records. RG I-505/505A. AJHS.
- BAPP Rabbi Bernard A. Poupko Papers. Personal Files of Rivy Poupko Kletenik.
- BHP Bonnie Heller Papers. RG umja0156. UJMA.
- BMP Bobbie Morgenstern Papers on Soviet Jewry. SCRC 403. TUL.

CASJ Chicago Action for Soviet Jewry Records. RG I-530. AJHS.
CCSA Cleveland Council on Soviet Anti-Semitism Records. MS 4011. WRHS.
CCSA2 Cleveland Council on Soviet Anti-Semitism Records, Series II. MS 5110. WRHS.
GNYCSJ Greater New York Conference on Soviet Jewry Collection. RG I-362. AJHS.
GPP Grayce Perlbinder Papers. RG P-942. AJHS.
HAF Rabbi Herbert A. Friedman Collection. MS-763. AJA.
JBP Jacob Birnbaum Papers. Personal Files of Jacob Birnbaum.
JCRCGP Jewish Community Relations Council of Greater Philadelphia Records. SCRC 230. TUL.
JCRCMD Jewish Community Relations Council (Minnesota-Dakotas) Records. RG umja0013. UMJA.
JCSP Joseph and Connie Smukler Papers on Soviet Jewry. SCRC 414. TUL.
JGA Joel G. Ackerman Soviet Jewry collection. RG P-787. AJHS.
JSAS Joel Sandberg and Adele Sandberg Papers. RG P-872. AJHS.
LRP Louis Rosenblum Papers. MS 4926. WRHS.
MBSP Rabbi Moses B. Sachs papers. RG umja0046. UJMA.
MDP Moshe Decter Papers. RG P-899. AJHS.
MRA Minnesota Rabbinical Association Records, RG umja0032. UJMA.
MSP Morey Schapira Papers. RG P-906. AJHS.
NCSJ National Conference on Soviet Jewry Records. AJHS RG I-181/181A. AJHS.
NCSJ-UK National Council for Soviet Jewry (United Kingdom and Ireland) Records. ACC 3087. LMA.
NJCRAC National Jewish Community Relations Advisory Council Records. RG I-172. AJHS.
PBC Pamela B. Cohen Papers. RG P-897. AJHS.
RAC Religious Action Center for Reform Judaism Soviet Jewry Collection. RG I-538. AJHS.

- SASJ   Seattle Action for Soviet Jewry Records. RG I-507. AJHS.
- SSSJ   Student Struggle for Soviet Jewry Records. Call No. 1993.099. YUA.
- UCSJ   Union of Councils for Soviet Jews Records. RG I-410/410A. AJHS.
- USUK   United Synagogue (United Kingdom) Records. ACC 2712. LMA.
- WCSJ   Washington Committee for Soviet Jewry Records. RG I-540. AJHS.

News Sources

Abbreviations of Most Commonly Cited News Sources

- JC   *Jewish Chronicle* (London)
- JEX   *Jewish Exponent* (Philadelphia)
- JTA   Jewish Telegraphic Agency
- LAT   *Los Angeles Times*
- NYJW *Jewish Week* (New York)
- NYT   *New York Times*
- WJW   *Jewish Week* (Washington)
- WP   *Washington Post*

Repositories of News Sources Cited

Most newspapers cited here were accessed via ProQuest Historical Newspapers.

All Israeli newspapers and Los Angeles's *B'nai B'rith Messenger* were accessed via the National Library of Israel Newspaper Collection, www.nli.org.il.

London's *Jewish Chronicle* was accessed via https://archive.thejc.com.

Izvestia and *Nedelya* were accessed via microfilm.

Trip Reports

Abella, Irving, John Erb, Robert Fulford, Wendy Litwack, and John Oostrom. 11–21 April 1988. NCSJ b.54 f.2.

Abramson, Carole, Rudy Appel, and Sharyn Schneider. 9–24 September 1978. ASJ b.91 f.4.

Arzt, Lois, and Alvin Arzt. 29 July–2 August 1976. NCSJ b.76 f.22.

Axelrad, Albert S., and Gerald Showstack. "Refusenik! An Odyssey through the Land of Spiritual Resistance." 21–29 September 1978. ASJ b.91 f.6.

Bair, Stuart, and Stephen Silberstein. May 1984. BACSJ b.38 f.105.

Barnett, Harvey J. 26 October–3 November 1983. CASJ b.160 f.8.
Bay, Max W. "Our Visits with Jews in the USSR." 15–29 May 1976. NCSJ b.55 f.3.
Becker, Lucy, and Irwin Becker. 21 March–3 April 1975. NCSJ b.55 f.4.
Benjamin, Sheldon, and Miriam Rosenblum. "Trip Report: Kiev, Kharkov, Moscow and Leningrad." 8–21 July 1974. CCSA b.8 f.224.
Bodoff, Lippman. "We Can All Be Heroes." 19 July 1988. NCSJ b.56 f.6.
Borden, Victor. 4–13 July 1985. NCSJ b.56 f.10.
———. "Physicians Mission to the Soviet Union." November 1987. NCSJ b.62 f.11/12.
Breslow, Jeffrey. 26 October–3 November 1983. CASJ b.160 f.8.
Brettler, Marc, and Helene Turner. 14 May–1 June 1981. MSP b.100 f.2.
Burg, Richard B. 10–18 March 1975. NCSJ b.57 f.4.
Caine, Burton. 2–10 October 1974. NCSJ b.57 f.7.
Callen, Earl, and Anthony Rallston. 6–10 February 1981. BACSJ b.18 f.14.
Champagne, Margot. "Report on Meetings with Soviet Jews." 12 October 1975. NCSJ b.57 f.14.
Churney, Michael D. 9–13 December 1987. BACSJ b.70 f.6.
Cohen, Pamela Braun, and Micah H. Naftalin. 29 May–7 June 1988. SASJ b.10 f.1.
Diamant, Betsy, and Polly Okunieff. 12 April–30 April 1981. MSP b.100 f.2.
Dishler, Bernard. 1–8 March 1977. NCSJ b.58 f.19.
Dishler, Lana, and Bernard Dishler. 8–16 December 1975. NCSJ b.58 f.19.
Dubin, David. "They Are Surely Heroes." [ca. June?] 1988. NCSJ b.58 f.25.
Epstein, Julie, and David Starr. May 1985. NCSJ b.85 f.3.
F. and T. June–July 1980. MSP b.100 f.1.
Finkelstein, Nisson. 24 June–8 July 1976. NCSJ b.59 f.18.
Fishbane, Michael. "Confidential Report on Trip to the Soviet Union." 18–28 May 1979. ASJ b.92 f.7.
Frankel, Marvin. 6–21 July 1974. NCSJ b.59 f.30.
Freeman, Herb. 23 May–11 June 1975. NCSJ b.60 f.3.
Freilich, Estelle, and Dennis Freilich. 3–17 June 1973. NCSJ b.60 f.4.
Frumkin, Si. 28 April–4 May 1974. CCSA b.8 f.224.
Gerjuoy, Edward. 26 July–9 August 1981. BACSJ b.18 f.18.
Gerut, Rosalie W. 20–29 May 1985. BACSJ b.69 f.27.
Gilbert, Patsy. 17 May–7 June 1976. NCSJ b.60 f.29.
Goodman, Dean, and Allan Margolis. 8–16 May 1978. MSP b.99 f.4.
Graber, Alan L. "Trip to a Closed World." 7–16 November 1987. BACSJ b.156 f.1.
Gutin, Jules, and Joshua Kanter. "Mission to the Soviet Union." 3–13 June 1990. Personal papers of Joshua P. Kanter.
Hellman, Mark. "From Russia, with Angst: A Jewish Doctor's Week in the USSR." November 1987. NCSJ b.63 f.6.
Hertzog, Mitchell, Carole Burstein, Miriam Waltzer, Jerome Winsberg, Ronda Hertzog, and Isabel Winsberg. 16–19 March 1977. NCSJ b.63 f.12.
Hirschfield, Jay. 21–28 October 1974. NCSJ b.63 f.20.
Hochstadter, Bruce. November 1987. BACSJ b.18 f.20.
Israel, Richard J., and Sherry R. Israel. "USSR Trip." 19 May–12 June 1974. NCSJ b.63 f.31.
Jacobs, Ginger. "Reflections on Temple Judea's Trip to the Soviet Union." October 1976. NCSJ b.75 f.16.
Kameny, Nat. "Our Soviet Journey." 1–9 March 1974. NCSJ b.64 f.16.

Klaperman, Gilbert. 21 June–3 August 1956. HAF b.49 f.5.
Klatzker, David, and Murray Levine. 20–31 January 1985. ASJ b.108 f.8.
Kling, Elana. August 1978. ASJ b.90 f.3.
Kuhr, Murray D. "Debriefing Narrative / Russian Journey." 14–28 August 1978. NCSJ b.66 f.5.
Landis, Marc. 23 February–4 March 1987. NCSJ b.82 f.3.
Leisch, Nancy, and Greg Leisch. 13–20 March 1976. NCSJ b.66 f.24.
Levinstone, Millie, and Bert Levinstone. March 1974. NCSJ b.67 f.11.
Lewis, Jerry. December 1973. NCSJ b.67 f.15.
Lippert, Jules. 27 July–1 August 1973. NCSJ b.67 f.23.
Manekofsky, Irene. "Debriefing Report: Barbara Cuban and Marcia Mazur." 30 March 1975, NCSJ b.58 f.2.
———. "Debriefing Report: Dennis Gannon." 24 May 1976, NCSJ b.60 f.15.
———. "Information on Direct Aid and Miscellaneous Items for Concerned Individuals." 14–26 November 1974. NCSJ b.68 f.13.
Manekofsky, Irene, and Sydney Manekofsky. "Twelve Days with the Refuseniks." 14–26 November 1974. NCSJ b.68 f.13.
Mansheim, Paul A., and Renee Mansheim. "Dr. M. Goes to the USSR." 15–30 September 1984. NCSJ b.68 f.17.
Mervis, Michael. 12–20 March 1982. NCSJ b.68 f.29.
Michelson, William. 29 September–1 October 1984. NCSJ b.85 f.3.
Morris, Judy, and Les Morris. 22 May–6 June 1987. NCSJ b.81 f.7.
Neiter, Lois. "Reflections on Temple Judea's Trip to the Soviet Union." 15–30 October 1976. NCSJ b.75 f.16.
Pfeffer, Barbara. "Notes on Trip to Soviet Union to Photograph Refuseniks." 11 September–4 October 1985. NCSJ b.69 f.33.
Pomerantz, Bernard. 15–30 August 1976. NCSJ b.70 f.2.
Reznick, Janice. 2–16 September 1976. NCSJ b.70 f.18.
Robiner, Donald M. 22 May 1976. NCSJ b. 70 f.25.
Rose, Al. "Our Russian Adventure." 20–22 July 1973. MSP b.102 f.4.
Rosenblum, Louis. 29 April–4 May 1974. CCSA b.8 f.224.
Rosenfeld, Melodie, and Sherman Rosenfeld. 28 September–20 October 1976. BACSJ b.6 f.18.
Rotenberg, A. Daniel. 20 June 1980. NCSJ b.100 f.1.
Rotenberg, A. Daniel, and Steven Shnider. Transcript of debriefing interview, 20 June 1980, NCSJ b.71 f.26.
Rothschild, Jay. 16–22 April 1974. NCSJ b.71 f.5.
Rukin, Michael. 20 June–5 July 1975. ASJ b.90 f.8.
Salkin, Jeffrey K., and Richard D. Agler. 28 May–5 June 1983. UCSJ b.79 f.16.
Sandberg, Adele, and Joel Sandberg. "Trip to the U.S.S.R." May 1975. JSAS b.2 f.6.
Scheindlin, Ahavia, and Bill Aron. 5–23 October 1981. NCSJ b.71 f.23.
Shapiro, Howard. 20–28 March 1984. UCSJ b.96 f.11.
Silverman, Ira. 15–24 March 1984. NCSJ b.35 f.6.
Silverstein, Abraham. 6–13 March 1983. NCSJ b.78 f.1.
Siris, Elaine K. "Encounter with Soviet Jewish Activists: A Journey to the U.S.S.R." July 1973. NCSJ b.73 f.27.
Soffin, Joel E. "Mission to Moscow." 4–17 April 1987. NCSJ b.73 f.39.
Sprayregen, Joel. "Memorandum on Contacts with Jews in the Soviet Union." 13 May–2 June 1970. NCSJ b.74 f.16.

Stern, Barbara. "Canadian Parliamentary Visit to the USSR." 18–24 January 1984. BACSJ b.22 f.256.
Stern, Elise, and Bernard Gropper. "How We Spent Our Christmas Vacation." January 1986. NCSJ b.74 f.32.
Sternberg, Donna, and Hans J. Sternberg. "Encounter with Soviet Jewry." January 1975. NCSJ b.74 f.24.
Sussman, Eileen K. 5–20 July 1975. NCSJ b.75 f.3.
———. "Group Trip to Moscow and Leningrad." 2–9 October 1977. NCSJ b.75 f.4.
Tabachnikoff, Barry. 20–28 March 1984. UCSJ b.96 f.11.
Tallman, Marilynn, and Linda Opper. 4–12 November 1988. SASJ b.10 f.1.
Taylor, Terry, Mike Freeman, Mike Stevens, and Carl Evans. 27 February–5 March 1984. MSP b.101 f.1.
Tessler, Joel, and Aviva Tessler. 3–16 December 1987. NCSJ b.75 f.17.
Trachtenburg, Ellen. 4–14 September 1985. BACSJ b.6 f.41.
Weintraub, Sharon, and Vicki Yudenfriend. 17–25 August 1979. UCSJ b.100 f.2.
Weissman, Inez. "Report on Visit to Soviet Union." 28 February 1975. MSP b.99 f.1.
Wellins, Judy. "Back from the USSR." 1986. NCSJ b.76 f.20.
Wellish, Joan. 10–24 October 1978. BACSJ b.18 f.9.
Wurtman, Enid, and Connie Smuckler. "Simhat Torah Journey to the Soviet Union." 15–22 October 1976. ASJ b.90 f.14.

Published Primary and Secondary Sources

"7 Held at Concert after Disruption." *NYT*, 27 January 1972, 30.
"250 March to Aid Soviet Jews." *LAT*, 6 December 1971, E7.
"1,000 Young People Protest the Plight of Soviet Jews." *NYT*, 31 March 1969, 3.
1980 Committee on Human Rights. "The Great Sellout." Advertisement. *Jewish Week-American Examiner* (New York), 13 August 1978, 5. WCSJ b.12 f.2.
———. "Moscow's TV Con Job." Advertisement. *WP*, 22 August 1978, A9. SSSJ b.44 f.9.
"2,000 Persons Participate in Freedom Rally for Soviet Jewry." *JTA*, 5 April 1971, 1.
"5000 Jews at Simchat Torah Rally Say, 'Let My (Soviet) People Go.'" *JEx* (Philadelphia), 23 October 1970, 1.
"10,000 Soviet Jews Jam Street for Celebration." *Hartford Courant* (Connecticut), 12 October 1971, 10.
"ABC Takes Ratings Race with Reruns." *Indiana Gazette*, 6 August 1980, 15.
"Activists Seek Nixon's Veto on Truck Factory for Russia." *B'nai B'rith Messenger* (Los Angeles), 10 September 1971, 1, 6.
Adelman, Samuel, and Emanuel Rackman. "U.S. Rabbis Fight Red Religion Curb." *New York Journal-American*, 8 August 1956, 1.
Adler, Eliyana R. "No Raisins, No Almonds: Singing as Spiritual Resistance to the Holocaust." *Shofar* 24, no. 4 (2006): 50–66.
AJCSJ. "In the Name of Humanity." Advertisement. *NYT*, 17 April 1970, 26.
———. "That the Jews of the Soviet Union May Know That They Have Not Been Forgotten." Advertisement. *NYT*, 2 April 1969, 35.
Alexander, Jeffrey C. "Cultural Pragmatics: Social Performance between Ritual and Strategy." *Sociological Theory* 22, no. 4 (2004): 527–73.

Allen, Michael J. *Until the Last Man Comes Home: POWs, MIAs, and the Unending Vietnam War*. Chapel Hill: University of North Carolina Press, 2009.

Altshuler, Stuart. *From Exodus to Freedom: A History of the Soviet Jewry Movement*. Lanham, MD: Rowman & Littlefield, 2005.

Amenta, Edwin. *When Movements Matter: The Townsend Plan and the Rise of Social Security*. Princeton, NJ: Princeton University Press, 2006.

Amenta, Edwin, Neal Caren, Elizabeth Chiarello, and S. U. Yang. "The Political Consequences of Social Movements." *Annual Review of Sociology* 36, no. 1 (2010): 287–307.

Ames, Lynne. "'Twin' Bas Mitzvahs." *NYT*, 13 December 1987, WC3.

Amnesty International. "1961–1976: A Chronology." Amnesty International Publications, London, May 1976. www.amnesty.org.

Anderson, Benedict. *Imagined Communities*. London: Verso, 1991.

Andreyev, E. "*Slugi bol'shoĭ lzhi*" [Servants of the big lie]. *Sovetskaiā Moldaviiā* (Kishinev), 11 September 1975, with English translation. JSAS b.2 f.4.

Appelbaum, Paul S. "The Soviet Jewry Movement in the United States." In *Jewish American Voluntary Organizations*, edited by Michael N. Dobkowski, 613–38. Westport, CT: Greenwood Press, 1986.

"Area Jews Mark Rosh Hashanah." *Hartford Courant* (Connecticut), 24 September 1976, 20.

Arkush, Jonathan, and Howard Rosen. "Competing for Freedom." Letter to the editor. *JC* (London), 25 July 1980, 19.

ASJ. *Bar and Bat Mitzvah Twinning with Soviet Jews*. Waltham, MA, n.d. (ca. 1983). ASJ b.127 f.3.

Associated Press. "Horrors of War for McG Audience." *San Francisco Examiner*, 13 October 1972, 11.

Association "Remember and Save." "Soviet Jews Exodus." Accessed 13 July 2022. www.soviet-jews-exodus.com.

Astor, Yaakov, and Mordechai Neustadt. *The Underground*. Brooklyn: Judaica Press, 2015.

Astrachan, Anthony. "Jews Celebrate in Moscow Synagogue: Thousands Dance and Sing on Festival Night." *WP*, 5 October 1969, 19.

Astuto, Jennifer, and Martin D. Ruck. "Early Childhood as a Foundation for Civic Engagement." In *Handbook of Research on Civic Engagement in Youth*, edited by Lonnie R. Sherrod, Judith Torney-Purta, and Constance A. Flanagan, 249–75. Hoboken, NJ: John Wiley & Sons, 2010.

Avrich-Skapinker, Mindy B. "Canadian Jewish Involvement with Soviet Jewry, 1970–1990: The Toronto Case Study." PhD diss., University of Toronto, 1994. ProQuest (AAT NN82870).

Azai, Ben. "Personal Opinion." *JC* (London), 8 October 1971, 20.

Azbel, Mark Ya. *Refusenik: Trapped in the Soviet Union*. New York: Paragon House, 1981.

"Babbitt and Yuli Run for Freedom." *Arizona Post*, 1980, 6. Undated press clipping in NJCRAC, *Soviet Jewry Advocacy*, 1983, 76a. Author's personal collection.

Bagdasaryan, Vardan, Igor Orlov, Iosif Schneider, Alexander Fedulin, and Konstantin Mazin. *Sovetskoe zazerkal'e: Inostrannyĭ turizm v SSSR v 1930–1980-e gody* [Behind the Soviet looking glass: Foreign tourism in the USSR 1930–1980s]. Moscow: Forum, 2007.

Baker, Bob. "2,000 Join Westside Run for Soviet Jews." *LAT*, 27 November 1980, WS10.

Balin, Carole B. "The Modern Transformation of the Ancient Passover Haggadah." In *Passover and Easter: Origin and History to Modern Times*, edited by Paul F. Bradshaw and Lawrence A. Hoffman, 189–212. Notre Dame, IN: University of Notre Dame Press, 1999.

"The Banned Worshiper." *WJW*, 28 September–4 October 1978, 32.

Baran, Emily B. *Dissent on the Margins: How Soviet Jehovah's Witnesses Defied Communism and Lived to Preach about It*. Oxford: Oxford University Press, 2014.

Barghoorn, Frederick Charles. *The Soviet Cultural Offensive: The Role of Cultural Diplomacy in Soviet Foreign Policy*. Princeton, NJ: Princeton University Press, 1960.

"Bar Mitzvah in Moscow." *JTA*, 22 August 1978.

Barnett, Michael N. *The Star and the Stripes*. Princeton, NJ: Princeton University Press, 2016.

Bar-Nir, Dov. "*Yehudei hadmamah—Behabimah*" [*The Jews of Silence*, at Habimah Theater]. `*Al hamishmar* (Tel Aviv), 27 November 1970, 2.

Barry, Hugh, and Anthony P. Sager. *Soviet Harassment of Foreign Tourists Violates the Helsinki Final Act*. Boston: SJLAC, 1982. PBC b.29 f.2, appendices B, G, H, I.

Barsov, Oleg. "*Sionskie bliznetsy*" [The Zion twins]. *Nedelya* (Moscow), 7–13 July 1975, 11.

Baudrillard, Jean. *Simulacra and Simulation*. Translated by Sheila Faria Glaser. Ann Arbor, MI: University of Michigan Press, 1994.

Baum, Phil, and Zev Furst. *How to Find and Meet Russian Jews: Briefing Kit for Travelers to the U.S.S.R.* New York: American Jewish Congress, 1972. NCSJ b.91 f.2.

Bayer, Abraham J. "American Response to Soviet Anti-Jewish Policies." *American Jewish Year Book* 74 (1973): 210–25.

Bechmann Pedersen, Sune, and Christian Noack. *Tourism and Travel during the Cold War: Negotiating Tourist Experiences across the Iron Curtain*. London: Routledge, 2020.

Becker, Howard S. *Tricks of the Trade: How to Think about Your Research While You're Doing It*. Chicago: University of Chicago Press, 2008.

Beckerman, Gal. *When They Come for Us, We'll Be Gone: The Epic Struggle to Save Soviet Jewry*. Boston: Houghton Mifflin Harcourt, 2010.

Beger, Kathleen. "The Artek Camp for Young Pioneers and the Many Faces of Socialist Internationalism." In Bechmann Pedersen and Noack, 79–97.

Beis Moshiach Magazine. "Secret Missions." *Beis Moshiach Magazine* (blog), 2014. www.beismoshiachmagazine.org.

Beizer, Michael. "'I Don't Know Whom to Thank': The American Jewish Joint Distribution Committee's Secret Aid to Soviet Jewry." *Jewish Social Studies* 15, no. 2 (2009): 111–36.

Bell, Catherine. *Ritual: Perspectives and Dimensions*. New York: Oxford University Press, 1997.

Beller, Herbert N. "Reflections of the Soviet Jewry Movement." Voices of the Vigil. Oral history, Lillian and Albert Small Capital Jewish Museum, 25 March 2009. www.jhsgw.org.

Belousovitch, Igor, and Toby Davis. *Chronology of Soviet Dissidence: January 1970 through December 1982*. Washington, DC: Bureau of Intelligence and Research, Department of State, 1983.

Ben-Amos, Dan. "The 'Myth' of Jewish Humor." *Western Folklore* 32, no. 2 (1973): 112–31.

Benford, Robert D., and David A. Snow. "Framing Processes and Social Movements: An Overview and Assessment." *Annual Review of Sociology* 26 (2000): 611–39.

Benjamin, Tova. "The Soviet Jewry Movement Revisited." *Jewish Currents*, Winter/Spring 2022, 88–95.

Bennett, Roger, Jules Shell, and Nick Kroll. *Bar Mitzvah Disco: The Music May Have Stopped, but the Party's Never Over*. New York: Crown, 2005.

Benor, Sarah Bunin, Jonathan B. Krasner, and Sharon Avni. *Hebrew Infusion: Language and Community in American Jewish Summer Camps*. New Brunswick, NJ: Rutgers University Press, 2020.

Berger, Peter L. *A Rumor of Angels: Modern Society and the Rediscovery of the Supernatural*. New York: Anchor, 1990.

Berger, Peter L., and Luckmann Thomas. *The Social Construction of Reality: A Treatise in the Sociology of Knowledge*. New York: Anchor, 1967.

Berman, Lila Corwin. *Speaking of Jews: Rabbis, Intellectuals, and the Creation of an American Public Identity*. Berkeley: University of California Press, 2009.

Berman, Lila Corwin, Kate Rosenblatt, and Ronit Y. Stahl. "Continuity Crisis: The History and Sexual Politics of an American Jewish Communal Project." *American Jewish History* 104, no. 2 (2020): 167–94.

Bernstein, Joanne E., and Michael J. Bernstein. *Dmitry: A Young Soviet Immigrant*. New York: Clarion Books, 1981.

"Beth Shalom to Hold Dual Graduation for Religious School, Soviet Children." *Ohio Jewish Chronicle* (Columbus), 30 May 1985, 1.

Bialer, Uri. *Israeli Foreign Policy: A People Shall Not Dwell Alone*. Bloomington: Indiana University Press, 2020.

Bialis, Laura, dir. *Refusenik*, documentary film. USA: Foundation for Documentary Projects, 2007.

Bikel, Theodore. *Silent No More*. Star Record Co., 1971, LP record album.

Bird, Dúnlaith. *Travelling in Different Skins: Gender Identity in European Women's Oriental Travelogues, 1850–1950*. Oxford: Oxford University Press, 2012.

Blanchard, Louise. "To Russia with Love, Happy Bar Mitzvah." *Miami News*, 17 March 1977, 7B.

Blaser, Elissa. *Exodus: The Russian Jewry Simulation Game*. New York: Behrman House, 1974.

Blau, Rivkah Teitz. *Learn Torah, Love Torah, Live Torah: Harav Mordechai Pinchas Teitz, the Quintessential Rabbi*. Hoboken, NJ: Ktav, 2001.

Blee, Kathleen M. *Democracy in the Making: How Activist Groups Form*. New York: Oxford University Press, 2012.

Bocking-Welch, Anna. "The British Public in a Shrinking World: Civic Engagement with the Declining Empire, 1960–1970." PhD diss., University of York, 2012. ProQuest (AAT U603859).

Borm, Jan. "Defining Travel: On the Travel Book, Travel Writing and Terminology." In *Perspectives on Travel Writing*, edited by Glenn Hooper and Tim Youngs, 13–26. Aldershot, UK: Ashgate, 2004.

Bourdieu, Pierre. *Outline of a Theory of Practice*. Translated by Richard Nice. Cambridge: Cambridge University Press, 1977.

Bowlby, Rachel. *Carried Away: The Invention of Modern Shopping*. New York: Columbia University Press, 2002.

Boyarsky, Bill. "Handshakes Seal Pact Ending Grape Boycott." *LAT*, 30 July 1970, 3.

Bralove, Mary. "PepsiCo Will Sell Its Cola in Russia, Buy Soviet Liquor." *Wall Street Journal*, 17 November 1972, 3.

Brandenberger, David. "Stalin's Last Crime? Recent Scholarship on Postwar Soviet Antisemitism and the Doctor's Plot." *Kritika: Explorations in Russian and Eurasian History* 6, no. 1 (2005): 187–204.

Breskin, Ira. "Food Service to Terminate Supply Contract with Pepsi." *Columbia Spectator*, 2 April 1974. SSSJ b.46 f.1.
Brinkley, Alan. "The Illusion of Unity in Cold War Culture." In Kuznick and Gilbert, *Rethinking Cold War Culture*, 61–73.
Brodetzky, Moshe. "Transcript of Oral History." Voices of the Vigil. Lillian and Albert Small Capital Jewish Museum, 17 November 2008. www.jhsgw.org.
Bronstein, Les. *Making Gates: The New Soviet Jewish Crisis*. New York: Coalition for Alternatives in Jewish Education, 1984. RAC b.2 f.6.
Bronstein, Tzvi. *Al Tidom: Peraqim mimasekhet pe`ilut rabat-shanim lema`an hahatsalah haruḥanit shel "Yehadut Hadmamah"* [Dare not be silent: Chapters from a tractate about activity of many years for the spiritual salvation of the "Jews of Silence"]. Brooklyn: Mutzal Me'esh Institute and Al Tidom Association, 2000.
Brown, Carol Bates. "History of the POW/MIA Bracelet." Accessed 28 June 2021. www.thewall-usa.com.
Bruner, Edward M. "Abraham Lincoln as Authentic Reproduction: A Critique of Postmodernism." *American Anthropologist* 96, no. 2 (1994): 397–415.
Brym, Robert J. "*Perestroyka*, Public Opinion, and *Pamyat*." *Soviet Jewish Affairs* 19, no. 3 (1989): 23–32.
Burns, John. "The Whip Cracks." *Globe and Mail* (Toronto), 25 October 1982.
Butman, Hillel. *From Leningrad to Jerusalem*. Berkeley, CA: Benmir Books, 1990.
Buwalda, Petrus. *They Did Not Dwell Alone: Jewish Emigration from the Soviet Union, 1967–1990*. Washington, DC: Woodrow Wilson Center Press and Johns Hopkins University Press, 1997.
Campbell, Anthony. "Dialectical Discourses: A Study of John le Carré." Master's thesis, University of Alberta, 1991. ProQuest (AAT MM66640).
Campbell, Colin. "The Sociology of Consumption." In *Acknowledging Consumption*, edited by Daniel Miller, 95–123. London: Routledge, 1995.
"Canton Jewish Center to Hold Freedom Relays." *Daily Reporter* (Dover, OH), 4 October 1971, 17.
"Carey Endorses '80 Human Rights Move on Russia." *NYJW*, 28 October 1978, 14.
"Carey, Solarz Not Backing Group Flaying NBC Sponsors." *Indiana Jewish Post and Opinion*, 5 January 1979, 5.
Carlebach, Shlomo. "Am Yisroel Chai." In *Save Soviet Jewry: Call to Action; Summer 1965 Handbook*, edited by SSSJ, 22b. New York: SSSJ, 1965. SSSJ b.244 f.18.
"Cartoon Wins a Trip." *Times and Post Newspapers* (Hendon and Finchley, London), 7 August 1980. NCSJ-UK f.317.
Cash, Debra. "Mobilizing for Soviet Jewry: An M.D. Activist and His Organization Battle Medical Oppression." *New Physician*, February 1980. Reprinted in UCSJ, *Alert* 4, no. 22, 2 May 1980. WCSJ b.14 f.9.
Caute, David. *The Dancer Defects: The Struggle for Cultural Supremacy during the Cold War*. Oxford: Oxford University Press, 2003.
"Cedar Center Demonstration Spearheads Pepsi Boycott." *Cleveland Jewish News*, 23 March 1973. CCSA b.9 f.254.
Charnyi, Semen. "Vneshnie sviazi evreĭskikh religioznykh obshchin v period Ottepeli" [Foreign relations of Jewish religious communities during the period of the post-Stalin thaw]. *Judaica Rossica* 2 (2002): 212–23.

Chernin, Albert D. "Making Soviet Jewry an Issue: A History." In Friedman and Chernin, *Second Exodus*, 15–69.
Childress, Clayton. *Under the Cover: The Creation, Production, and Reception of a Novel.* Princeton, NJ: Princeton University Press, 2017.
Chirico, David. "The Travel Narrative as a (Literary) Genre." In *Under Eastern Eyes: A Comparative Introduction to East European Travel Writing on Europe, 1550–2000*, edited by Wendy Bracewell and Alex Drace-Francis, 27–59. Budapest: Central European University Press, 2008.
Chizhik, S. N. *MAOZ: Obshchestvo pomoshchi evreĭstvu SSSR* [MAOZ: Society for Aid to Soviet Jews]. Jerusalem: Tsur Ot, 2001.
Chronicle of Current Events. "The Trial of Begun, 28 June 1978." *A Chronicle of Current Events for Human Rights and Freedom of Expression in the USSR* 50, no. 8-5 (November 1978). https://chronicle-of-current-events.com.
———. "The Trial of Ida Nudel, June 1978." *A Chronicle of Current Events for Human Rights and Freedom of Expression in the USSR* 50, no. 8-2 (November 1978). https://chronicle-of-current-events.com.
———. "The Trial of Slepak, June 1978." *A Chronicle of Current Events for Human Rights and Freedom of Expression in the USSR* 50, no. 8-3 (November 1978). https://chronicle-of-current-events.com.
Chronicler. "Bring Out the Medallions." *JC* (London), 27 April 1979, 21.
———. "Medallions." *JC* (London), 23 February 1973, 27.
Church World Service. "CWS and CROP Hunger Walks." Accessed 16 June 2022. https://events.crophungerwalk.org.
———. "The History of the CROP Hunger Walk." Accessed 16 June 2022. https://resources.crophungerwalk.org.
Cioletti, Jeff. "Back in the (Former) USSR." *Beverage World*, 15 August 2009, 20–25.
Cleaveland, Carol. "A Unity of Dissent Trapped in a Climate of Fear, Soviet Jew Refuseniks Are Finding Support from Their American Friends." *Morning Call* (Allentown, PA), 24 September 1987, D01.
Cohen, Naomi W. *Not Free to Desist: The American Jewish Committee, 1906–1966.* Philadelphia: Jewish Publication Society, 1972.
Cohen, Pamela Braun. *Hidden Heroes: One Woman's Story of Resistance and Rescue in the Soviet Union.* Jerusalem: Gefen, 2021.
Cohen, Steven M. *American Modernity and Jewish Identity.* New York: Tavistock, 1983.
Cohen, Steven M., and Arnold M. Eisen. *The Jew Within: Self, Family and Community in America.* Bloomington: Indiana University Press, 2000.
Coley, Jonathan S. *Gay on God's Campus: Mobilizing for LGBT Equality at Christian Colleges and Universities.* Chapel Hill: University of North Carolina Press, 2018.
"Commerce Secretary Meets with JDL'ers Protesting Trade with the Soviet Union." *JTA*, 14 April 1971.
"Committee Cancels Award to PepsiCo Chief." *JEx* (Philadelphia), 28 September 1973, 3.
"Committee Will Honor Pepsi Chief." *JEx* (Philadelphia), 7 September 1973, 3.
"Conscience Medallion Draws Attention to Russ Prisoners." *B'nai B'rith Messenger* (Los Angeles), 21 July 1972, 3.
Cooper, John. *The British Campaign for Soviet Jewry 1966–1991: Human Rights and Exit Permits.* Manchester, UK: i2i Publishing, 2023.

Cooperman, Jessica. *Making Judaism Safe for America: World War I and the Origins of Religious Pluralism*. New York: New York University Press, 2018.

Cornfield, Daniel, Jonathan Coley, Larry Isaac, and Dennis Dickerson. "Occupational Activism and Racial Desegregation at Work: Activist Careers after the Nonviolent Nashville Civil Rights Movement." In *Race, Identity, and Work*, edited by Ethel L. Mickey and Adia Harvey Wingfield, 217–48. Research in the Sociology of Work 32. Bingley, UK: Emerald, 2018.

Cotler, Irwin. "Soviet Jewry, Human Rights, and the Rule of Law: A Pre- and Post-Glasnost Case-Study." *Touro Journal of Transnational Law* 2 (1991): 107–51.

"A Crack in the Iron Curtain." *A Chassidisher Derher* (Vaad Talmidei Hatmimim Haolomi), February–March 2015, 13. https://crownheights.info.

"Critical Pittsburgh Rabbi Barred by Soviet Union." *JEx* (Philadelphia), 21 February 1969, 1.

"Critics of 'Establishment' Buy 8-Page Ad to Demand More Vigorous Leadership." *NYJW*, 24 June 1979, 40.

Crossley, Nick. *Making Sense of Social Movements*. Buckingham: Open University Press, 2002.

Cruce, Ashley. "A History of Progressive-Era School Savings Banking, 1870–1930." Working Paper 01-3. St. Louis, MO: Center for Social Development, Washington University, 2001.

Curry, Pat. "South Florida Jews Share Celebration." *Sun Sentinel* (Fort Lauderdale, FL), 11 December 1987, 7e.

Dart, John. "Aid Soviet Jews: Holiday Cards like Passports." *LAT*, 7 March 1971, AA.

Davidovsky, Marina Tiemkin. "Kidnapped as a Teenager by the KGB." Translated by David Stahl, *Jewish Press*, 1 September 2017. www.jewishpress.com.

Davis, Jenny L. *How Artifacts Afford: The Power and Politics of Everyday Things*. Cambridge, MA: MIT Press, 2020.

Decter, Moshe. "The Status of the Jews in the Soviet Union." *Foreign Affairs* 41, no. 2 (January 1963): 420–30.

Dekel-Chen, Jonathan. "Faith Meets Politics and Resources: Reassessing Modern Transnational Jewish Activism." In *Purchasing Power: The Economics of Modern Jewish History*, edited by Rebecca A. Kobrin and Adam Teller, 216–37. New Brunswick, NJ: Rutgers University Press, 2015.

DellaPergola, Sergio. "World Jewish Population, 2019." In *American Jewish Year Book 2019*, edited by Arnold Dashefsky and Ira Sheskin, 263–353. Cham, Switzerland: Springer, 2019.

Della Porta, Donatella. "Repertoires of Contention." In *The Wiley-Blackwell Encyclopedia of Social and Political Movements*, edited by David Snow, Donatella Della Porta, Bert Klandermans, and Doug McAdam. Hoboken, NJ: John Wiley & Sons, 2013. https://onlinelibrary.wiley.com.

Democratic Party. "1964 Platform." American Presidency Project, University of California Santa Barbara. Accessed 17 July 2022. www.presidency.ucsb.edu.

"Denver Rabbi Urging Boycott of Pepsico." *Fort Collins Coloradan*, 24 March 1975.

Detroit Soviet Jewry Committee. *Make a Connection! Share Your Bar or Bat Mitzvah with a Russian Twin*. Detroit: Jewish Community Council of Metropolitan Detroit, 1982. AJHS BM707 .D28.

DiMaggio, Paul J., and Walter W. Powell. "The Iron Cage Revisited: Institutional Isomorphism and Collective Rationality in Organizational Fields." *American Sociological Review* 48, no. 2 (1983): 147–60.

Dimov, V. "Zionist Traveling Salesmen." *Sovetskai͡a Rossii͡a* (Moscow), 8 April 1983, with English translation. NCSJ b.88 f.6.

Diner, Hasia R. *The Jews of the United States, 1654 to 2000.* Berkeley: University of California Press, 2004.

———. *We Remember with Reverence and Love: American Jews and the Myth of Silence after the Holocaust, 1945–1962.* New York: New York University Press, 2009.

Diner, Hasia R., Jeffrey Shandler, and Beth S. Wenger. *Remembering the Lower East Side: American Jewish Reflections.* Bloomington: Indiana University Press, 2000.

Doherty, Brian, and Graeme Hayes. "Tactics and Strategic Action." In *The Blackwell Companion to Social Movements*, edited by David A. Snow, Sarah A. Soule, and Hanspeter Kriesi, 269–88. Hoboken, NJ: John Wiley & Sons, 2018.

Dollinger, Marc. *Black Power, Jewish Politics: Reinventing the Alliance in the 1960s.* Waltham, MA: Brandeis University Press, 2018.

———. *Quest for Inclusion: Jews and Liberalism in Modern America.* Princeton, NJ: Princeton University Press, 2000.

Donovan, Jennifer. "The Covenant of Brit Milah." Reprinted under UCSJ letterhead. *San Francisco Chronicle*, 30 May 1985, 23. ASJ b.125 f.2.

"Dora Eats a Prison Lunch." *JC* (London), 20 July 1973, 10.

Dorph, Gail. *By Spirit Alone: Jewish Life in the Soviet Union Today.* Cleveland, OH: BJE of Cleveland, n.d. (ca. 1983). JCRCGP b.80 f.27.

Downey, Dennis J., and Deana A. Rohlinger. "Linking Strategic Choice with Macro-organizational Dynamics: Strategy and Social Movement Articulation." *Research in Social Movements, Conflicts and Change* 28 (2008): 3–38.

Dudziak, Mary L. *Cold War Civil Rights.* Princeton, NJ: Princeton University Press, 2011.

Dugan, George. "A Huge Crowd Here Protests Soviet Imprisonment and Treatment of Jews." *NYT*, 1 May 1972, 3.

Earl, Jennifer, Thomas V. Maher, and Thomas Elliott. "Youth, Activism, and Social Movements." *Sociology Compass* 11, no. 4 (2017): e12465.

Eco, Umberto. *Travels in Hyperreality.* San Diego, CA: Harcourt Brace Jovanovich, 1986.

Edelstein, Yaakov. "*Rav doresh beMosqvah 'al 'atzma'ut Yisra'el*" [In Moscow a rabbi delivers a sermon on Israel's independence]. In *In shotn fun Kremlin: Dray bazukhn in Sovet-Rusland*, by Bernard A. Poupko, 208–12. New York: Aynikayt, 1968.

"Editorial Note." *Soviet Jewish Affairs* 1, no. 1 (1971): 1.

Einwohner, Rachel L. "Passing as Strategic Identity Work in the Warsaw Ghetto Uprising." In *Identity Work in Social Movements*, edited by Jo Reger, Daniel J. Myers, and Rachel L. Einwohner, 121–39. Minneapolis: University of Minnesota Press, 2008.

Einwohner, Rachel L., Reid J. Leamaster, and Benjamin Pratt. "Push, Pull, and Fusion: Women's Activism and Religious Institutions." In *The Oxford Handbook of US Women's Social Movement Activism*, edited by Holly J. McCammon, Verta Taylor, Jo Reger, and Rachel L. Einwohner, 561–81. Oxford: Oxford University Press, 2017.

Einwohner, Rachel L., Jo Reger, and Daniel J. Myers. "Identity Work, Sameness, and Difference in Social Movements." In *Identity Work in Social Movements*, edited by Jo Reger, Daniel J. Myers, and Rachel L. Einwohner, 1–17. Minneapolis: University of Minnesota Press, 2008.

Eisen, Arnold M. "Nostalgia as Modern Jewish Mitzvah." In *Rethinking Modern Judaism: Ritual, Commandment, Community*, 156–87. Chicago: University of Chicago Press, 1998.

Eisen, Wendy. *Count Us In: The Struggle to Free Soviet Jews, a Canadian Perspective.* Toronto: Burgher Books, 1995.

Ekiert, Grzegorz, Elizabeth J. Perry, and Xiaojun Yan, eds. *Ruling by Other Means: State-Mobilized Movements.* Cambridge: Cambridge University Press, 2020.

Elazar, Daniel J. *Community and Polity: The Organizational Dynamics of American Jewry.* Philadelphia: Jewish Publication Society, 1976.

Ellefsen, Rune. "Deepening the Explanation of Radical Flank Effects: Tracing Contingent Outcomes of Destructive Capacity." *Qualitative Sociology* 41, no. 1 (2018): 111–33.

Ellingson, Terry Jay. *The Myth of the Noble Savage.* Berkeley: University of California Press, 2001.

"'Empty Chair' at Seder to Note Plight of Jews in Soviet Union." *JTA*, 8 April 1965.

Endy, Christopher. *Cold War Holidays: American Tourism in France.* Chapel Hill: University of North Carolina Press, 2004.

Epstein, Jacob Nahum, and Ezra Zion Melamed. *Mekhilta De-Rabbi Shimon Bar Yohai.* Jerusalem: Yeshivat Shaarei Rahamim, Beit Hillel, 1955.

Erlick, Al, and David Gross. "Bar Mitzvah and Home." *JEx* (Philadelphia), 6 April 1979, 3.

Estraikh, Gennady. "Escape through Poland: Soviet Jewish Emigration in the 1950s." *Jewish History* 31, no. 3 (2018): 291–317.

———. "The Life, Death, and Afterlife of the Jewish Anti-Fascist Committee." *East European Jewish Affairs* 48, no. 2 (2018): 139–48.

"Exodus March to Dramatize Plight of Soviet Jewry Expected to Attract Thousands." *JTA*, 24 April 1970.

Eyerman, Ron, and Andrew Jamison. *Music and Social Movements: Mobilizing Traditions in the Twentieth Century.* Cambridge: Cambridge University Press, 1998.

———. *Social Movements: A Cognitive Approach.* University Park: Pennsylvania State University Press, 1991.

Fainberg, Sarah. *Les discriminés: L'antisémitisme soviétique après Staline.* Paris: Fayard, 2014.

Fedeski, Amy. *Culture Is Not Apolitical: The Art of Soviet Jewry Activism* (online multimedia), 14 April 2020. https://storymaps.arcgis.com.

———. "From Refusenik to Refugee: Jewish Americans Meet Soviet Jewish Migrants, 1965–1989." Paper presented at the Contact Symposium: Meetings and Movement of Jewish People and Artifacts across Cold War Boundaries, Youngstown State University and Purdue University, Youngstown, OH, 23 May 2022.

———. "Symbolism and Strategy of the Student Struggle for Soviet Jewry, 1964–1974." Master's thesis, University of Cambridge, 2018.

Fein, Leonard. *Where Are We? The Inner Life of America's Jews.* New York: Harper and Row, 1988.

Feingold, Henry L. *"Silent No More": Saving the Jews of Russia, the American Jewish Effort, 1967–1989.* Syracuse, NY: Syracuse University Press, 2007.

Feldman, Jackie. *Above the Death Pits, beneath the Flag: Youth Voyages to Poland and the Construction of Israeli National Identity.* New York: Berghahn, 2008.

Feldman, William. "Social Absorption of Soviet Immigrants: Integration or Isolation." *Journal of Jewish Communal Service* 54, no. 1 (September 1977): 62–68.

Feldstein, Jonathan. "My Struggle for Soviet Jewry, and Kate Shtein." *Tablet*, 1 May 2017. www.tabletmag.com.

Ferson, Joe. "Bat Mitzvah Turns into Joyous 'Twinning': Refusenik Family Arrives in Time for Daughter to Join in Jewish Rite." *Boston Globe*, 13 November 1988, 46.

Ferziger, Adam S. *Beyond Sectarianism: The Realignment of American Orthodox Judaism.* Detroit: Wayne State University Press, 2015.

———. "'Outside the Shul': The American Soviet Jewry Movement and the Rise of Solidarity Orthodoxy, 1964–1986." *Religion and American Culture* 22, no. 1 (2012): 83–130.

Filene, Peter. "'Cold War Culture' Doesn't Say It All." In Kuznick and Gilbert, *Rethinking Cold War Culture*, 156–74.

Finkelman, Samuel. "Ghetto, Gulag, *Geulah*: The Soviet Jewish Movement's Russian and Ukrainian Encounters, 1953–1985." PhD diss., University of Pennsylvania, 2023.

"First Yeshiva in 60 Years Opens in the Soviet Union." *JTA*, 24 February 1989.

Fisch, David. "JDL Spokesman Explains Pepsi-Cola Boycott Drive." *Jewish Journal* (New York), 30 March 1973. SSSJ b.46 f.1.

Fisher, Rachel Eskin. "A Place in History: Genealogy, Jewish Identity, Modernity." PhD diss., University of California, Santa Barbara, 1999. ProQuest (AAT 9956153).

Fishman, Sylvia Barack. *A Breath of Life: Feminism in the American Jewish Community.* New York: Free Press, 1993.

"Five Jewish Schools Open in Soviet Union and Hungary." *JTA*, 7 September 1990.

"Five Rabbis Sail June 18 for Russia." *Washington Post and Times-Herald*, 6 June 1956, 21.

Flore, Pamela Raye. "Bat Mitzvah Unites U.S. and Soviet Teens." *Poughkeepsie Journal* (New York), 6 June 1983. ASJ b.128 f.4.

"Flyers Fans Urged to Aid Soviet Jews." *JEx* (Philadelphia), 9 January 1976, 3.

Fodor, Eugene, ed. *Fodor's Europe.* New York: David McKay, 1973.

Fodor, Eugene, and Robert C. Fisher. *Fodor's Soviet Union.* New York: David McKay, 1974.

"Fonda, Hayden to Join in Run for Soviet Jewry." *LAT*, 18 October 1981, E11.

"For Gidon Here, Bella There—Mitzvot." *JEx* (Philadelphia), 15 August 1975, 3.

"Former 'Refusnik' Tells How Natasha's Dream Came True." *Omaha Jewish Press* (Nebraska), 29 October 1976, 10.

Foucault, Michel. *The Birth of Biopolitics: Lectures at the Collège de France, 1978–1979.* Translated by Graham Burchell. Edited by Michel Senellart and Arnold I. Davidson. New York: Palgrave Macmillan, 2008.

———. *The Birth of the Clinic: An Archaeology of Medical Perception.* London: Tavistock, 1973.

———. *Discipline and Punish: The Birth of the Prison.* Translated by Alan Sheridan. New York: Vintage, 1979.

Foulkes, Nicholas. "Glam Rocks." *Financial Times* (London), 3 November 2018, 5.

Fox, Sandra. "'Is This What You Call Being Free?' Intergenerational Negotiation, Democratic Education, and Camper Culture in Postwar American Jewish Summer Camps." *Journal of the History of Childhood and Youth* 13, no. 1 (2020): 19–37.

———. *The Jews of Summer.* Redwood City, CA: Stanford University Press, 2023.

———. "Tisha B'av, 'Ghetto Day,' and Producing 'Authentic' Jews at Postwar Jewish Summer Camps." *Journal of Modern Jewish Studies* 17, no. 2 (2018): 156–72.

"Freedom Campaign Gains Momentum." *JC* (London), 14 March 1980, 8.

"'Freedom Flag' Raised Here at Protest for Soviet Jews." *NYT*, 5 April 1971, 16.

"'Freedom Games' Marred by Ban." *JC* (London), 16 May 1980, 9.

"Freedom Olympics." *NYJW*, 6 July 1980, 4.

"Freedom Relays Sunday." *Massilon Evening Independent* (Ohio), 1 December 1976, 22.

"Freedom Sunday: 25 Years Later." eJewishPhilanthropy, 27 November 2012. https://ejewishphilanthropy.com.

Freedom 25. "About." Internet Archive Wayback Machine capture of 8 May 2013 version of http://freedom25.net. Accessed 12 July 2022 (site discontinued). http://web.archive.org.

Freeman, Jo, and Victoria Johnson. *Waves of Protest: Social Movements since the Sixties.* Lanham, MD: Rowman & Littlefield, 1999.

Freud, Sigmund. *Jokes and Their Relation to the Unconscious.* Translated by James Strachey. New York: W. W. Norton, 1960 [1905].

Frey, Marc E. "Challenging the World's Conscience: The Soviet Jewry Movement, American Political Culture, and United States Foreign Policy, 1952–1967." PhD diss., Temple University, 2002. ProQuest (AAT 3079115).

Friedman, Murray, and Albert D. Chernin, eds. *A Second Exodus: The American Movement to Free Soviet Jews.* Hanover, NH: Brandeis University Press, 1999.

Frow, John. *Genre.* London: Routledge, 2005.

Fuchs, Lawrence H. *The Political Behavior of American Jews.* Glencoe, IL: Free Press, 1956.

Fürst, Juliane. "Born under the Same Star: Refuseniks, Dissidents, and Late Socialist Society." In Ro'i, *Jewish Movement in the Soviet Union*, 137–63.

"Gabriel Reiner, Cut Travel Bars." Obituary. *NYT*, 12 March 1969, 47.

Gaddis, John Lewis. *The Cold War: A New History.* New York: Penguin, 2006.

Galchinsky, Michael. *Jews and Human Rights: Dancing at Three Weddings.* Lanham, MD: Rowman & Littlefield, 2007.

Galili, Lily. *The Other Tribe: Israel's Russian-Speaking Community and How It Is Changing the Country.* Washington, DC: Brookings, 2020.

Gambaccini, Peter, Kelly Bastone, Bob Cooper, Adam Buckley Cohen, and Marc Bloom. "Unforgettable: The 40 Most Influential People and Moments of the Past Four Decades." *Runner's World*, 13 October 2006. www.runnersworld.com.

"Games for Freedom." *JC* (London), 28 March 1980, 132.

Gamson, William A. *The Strategy of Social Protest.* Homewood, IL: Dorsey Press, 1975.

Gans, Herbert J. "Park Forest: Birth of Jewish Community." *Commentary*, April 1951, 330–39.

———. "Progress of a Suburban Jewish Community." *Commentary*, February 1957, 113–22.

———. "Symbolic Ethnicity and Symbolic Religiosity: Towards a Comparison of Ethnic and Religious Acculturation." *Ethnic and Racial Studies* 17, no. 4 (1994): 577–92.

———. "Symbolic Ethnicity: The Future of Ethnic Groups and Cultures in America." *Ethnic and Racial Studies* 2, no. 1 (1979): 1–20.

Geerlings, Lonneke. *I Lay This Body Down: The Transatlantic Life of Rosey E. Pool.* Athens: University of Georgia Press, 2022.

Gendler, Neal. "Characters from Sesame Street Tell Jewish Holidays Tale." *Star Tribune* (Minneapolis), 19 September 1978, 20A.

Genzeleva, Rita. "Moskovskie i Leningradskie purimshpili 1970–1980-kh godov: Problema mezhkul'turnykh sviazeĭ" [Moscow and Leningrad purimshpiels of the 1970s and 1980s: The problem of intercultural relations]. *Paralleli* 6–7 (2005): 137–53.

Gereboff, Joel. "One Nation, with Liberty and Haggadahs for All." In *Key Texts in American Jewish Culture*, edited by Jack Kugelmass, 275–92. New Brunswick, NJ: Rutgers University Press, 2003.

Gerlis, Daphne. *Those Wonderful Women in Black: The Story of the Women's Campaign for Soviet Jewry.* London: Minerva Press, 1996.

Ghert-Zand, Renee. "Once Heroes of US Jewry, Soviet Refuseniks Are Largely Forgotten. Not for Long." *Times of Israel*, 22 April 2019. www.timesofisrael.com.

Gilbert, Martin. *The Jews of Hope*. 1st American ed. New York: Viking, 1985.
Ginsberg, Johanna R. "Documenting the Struggle for Soviet Jews." *New Jersey Jewish News* (Whippany, NJ), 14 December 2016. https://njjewishnews.timesofisrael.com.
Gitelman, Zvi Y. *Jewish Nationality and Soviet Politics: The Jewish Sections of the C.P.S.U., 1917–1930*. Princeton, NJ: Princeton University Press, 1972.
Glajar, Valentina, Alison Lewis, and Corina L. Petrescu, eds. *Cold War Spy Stories from Eastern Europe*. Lincoln: University of Nebraska Press, 2019.
Glazer, Nathan. "The Jewish Revival in America: I." *Commentary*, December 1955, 493–99.
Glenn, Susan A. "The Jewish Cold War: Anxiety and Identity in the Aftermath of the Holocaust." *David W. Belin Lecture in American Jewish Affairs* 24 (2014).
GNYCSJ. "New York, You've Really Done It!" *NYT*, 5 May 1972, advertisement, 46.
———. *Soviet Jewry Catalog: A Do-It-Yourself Kit for Planning Demonstrations and Events*. New York: GNYCSJ, 1978. GNYCSJ b.1 f.13.
———. *Soviet Jewry Purim Puzzler*. New York: GNYCSJ, March 1983. GNYCSJ b.1 f.14.
———. *Writing to Your Twin: Questions and Answers*. New York: GNYCSJ, 1984. JCRCGP b.82 f.29.
Goffman, Erving. *Frame Analysis: An Essay on the Organization of Experience*. Boston: Northeastern University Press, 1986 [1974].
Gold, Steven J. *From the Workers' State to the Golden State: Jews from the Former Soviet Union in California*. Boston: Allyn and Bacon, 1995.
———. "Soviet Jews in the United States." *American Jewish Year Book* 94 (1994): 3–57.
Goldberg, Chad Alan. *Modernity and the Jews in Western Social Thought*. Chicago: University of Chicago Press, 2017.
Goldberg, J. J. *Jewish Power: Inside the American Jewish Establishment*. Reading, MA: Addison-Wesley, 1996.
Golden, Jeff. "Altar Chair Empty for Russian Girl." *Philadelphia Bulletin*, 8 December 1975, 17. JCSP b.2 f.9.
Golden, Peter. *O Powerful Western Star! American Jews, Russian Jews, and the Final Battle of the Cold War*. Jerusalem: Gefen, 2012.
Goldman, Ari L. "Jews Debate Appropriateness of Updating Seders." *NYT*, 16 April 1984, B4.
———. "Protesters for Soviet Jewry Urge Direct Flights to Israel." *NYT*, 2 April 1990, B3.
———. "Rally for Soviet Jewry: Large Crowd Rallies at U.N. in Support of Jews in Soviet Speakers." *NYT*, 28 April 1980, B1.
Goldman, Milton. "Jackson-Vanik: A Dissent." In Friedman and Chernin, *Second Exodus*, 115–23.
Goldstein, Eric L. *The Price of Whiteness: Jews, Race, and American Identity*. Princeton, NJ: Princeton University Press, 2006.
Goldstein, Mark L. "The Bridges We Cross." *HaKol Lehigh Valley*, 23 February 2016. www.jewishlehighvalley.org.
Goldstein, Sidney. "Profile of American Jewry: Insights from the 1990 National Jewish Population Survey." *American Jewish Year Book* 92 (1992): 77–173.
Goltsin, Raisa. "Remembering Simchat Torah in Moscow." *Jewish Advocate* (Boston), 11 October 1990, 8.
"GOP Loses in Convention Ratings." *Indiana Gazette*, 23 July 1980, 33.
Gordon, Hava Rachel. *We Fight to Win: Inequality and the Politics of Youth Activism*. New Brunswick, NJ: Rutgers University Press, 2009.

Gordon, Hava R., and Jessica K. Taft. "Rethinking Youth Political Socialization: Teenage Activists Talk Back." *Youth & Society* 43, no. 4 (2011): 1499–527.

Gorsuch, Anne E. *All This Is Your World: Soviet Tourism at Home and Abroad after Stalin.* Oxford: Oxford University Press, 2011.

Gorsuch, Anne E., and Diane Koenker. *Turizm: The Russian and East European Tourist under Capitalism and Socialism.* Ithaca, NY: Cornell University Press, 2006.

Gottdiener, Mark. *The Theming of America: American Dreams, Media Fantasies, and Themed Environments.* 2nd ed. Boulder, CO: Westview, 2001.

Grant, William. *Andrew Grima: The Father of Modern Jewellery.* Woodbridge, UK: ACC ART Books, 2020.

Gray, Anita. "My Soviet Odyssey." *District Seven in the Seventies* (ORT District VII, Cleveland, OH), Spring 1978. ASJ b.115 f.7.

Grimes, Ronald L., Ute Husken, Udo Simon, and Eric Venbrux. *Ritual, Media, and Conflict.* Oxford: Oxford University Press, 2011.

Griswold, Wendy. *Cultures and Societies in a Changing World.* 4th ed. Thousand Oaks, CA: SAGE, 2013.

Grose, Peter. "Moscow Jews Dance and Sing Outside Crowded Synagogue." *NYT*, 19 October 1965, 15.

Gross, Judah Ari. "Over 15,000 Have Immigrated to Israel since Russia Invaded Ukraine." *Times of Israel*, 25 April 2022. www.timesofisrael.com.

Gross, Rachel B. *Beyond the Synagogue: Jewish Nostalgia as Religious Practice.* New York: New York University Press, 2021.

Guyatt, Nicholas. "The End of the Cold War." In *Oxford Handbook of the Cold War*, edited by Richard H. Immerman and Petra Goedde, 605–22. Oxford: Oxford University Press, 2012.

Hägel, Peter, and Pauline Peretz. "States and Transnational Actors: Who's Influencing Whom? A Case Study in Jewish Diaspora Politics during the Cold War." *European Journal of International Relations* 11, no. 4 (2005): 474–93.

Halevi, Yossi Klein. "Jacob Birnbaum and the Struggle for Soviet Jewry." *Azure*, no. 17 (Spring 2004): 27–57.

———. *Memoirs of a Jewish Extremist: An American Story.* Boston: Little Brown & Company, 1995.

Haluza-DeLay, Randolph. "A Theory of Practice for Social Movements: Environmentalism and Ecological Habitus." *Mobilization* 13, no. 2 (2008): 205–18.

Harris, David A., and Izrail Rabinovich. *The Jokes of Oppression: The Humor of Soviet Jews.* Northvale, NJ: Jason Aronson, 1988.

Harrison, Andrew. *Passover Revisited: Philadelphia's Efforts to Aid Soviet Jews 1963–1998.* Madison, NJ: Fairleigh Dickinson University Press, 2001.

"Har Zion Temple 'Adopts' Two Soviet Jewish Families." *JEx* (Philadelphia), 23 November 1973, 37.

"*Hasatah anti-Soviyetit mita ʿam Maʿoz bein kotlei beit hasefer hamamlakhtiyim*" [Anti-Soviet incitement by Maʿoz inside the public school walls]. *Qol haʿam* (Tel Aviv), 25 March 1965, 4.

Hayward, Max. "Russian Anti-Semitism." Review of *The Jews of Silence*, by Elie Wiesel. *Commentary*, 8 January 1967.

Hazanov, Alex. "Porous Empire: Foreign Visitors and the Post-Stalin Soviet State." PhD diss., University of Pennsylvania, 2016. ProQuest (AAT 10241549).

Hebrew Union College–Jewish Institute of Religion. "HUC-JIR/Los Angeles Historical Timeline." *The Chronicle* 60, 2002. Accessed 27 October 2020. http://huc.edu.

Heilman, Samuel C. *Synagogue Life: A Study in Symbolic Interaction.* Chicago: University of Chicago Press, 1976.

Heitman, Sidney. *Soviet Emigration in 1990.* Cologne: Bundesinstitut für ostwissenschaftliche und International Studien, 1991.

Henry, Patrick. "'And I Don't Care What It Is': The Tradition-History of a Civil Religion Proof-Text." *Journal of the American Academy of Religion* 49, no. 1 (1981): 35–49.

Herberg, Will. *Protestant—Catholic—Jew: An Essay in Religious Sociology.* Chicago: University of Chicago Press, 1983 [1955].

Herman, Robin. "Marchers in Manhattan Show Their Support for Soviet Jews." *NYT*, 3 May 1982, B7.

———. "Russians Stage Walkout during 4–1 Hockey Loss to Philadelphia." *NYT*, 12 January 1976, 1.

Herman, Simon N. *Jewish Identity: A Social Psychological Perspective.* Beverly Hills: SAGE, 1977.

Hertzberg, Arthur. *Being Jewish in America: The Modern Experience.* New York: Schocken, 1979.

Herzog, Jonathan P. "From Sermon to Strategy: Religious Influence on the Formation and Implementation of US Foreign Policy in the Early Cold War." In *Religion and the Cold War: A Global Perspective*, edited by Philip E. Muehlenbeck, 44–64. Nashville, TN: Vanderbilt University Press, 2012.

———. *The Spiritual-Industrial Complex: America's Religious Battle against Communism in the Early Cold War.* Oxford: Oxford University Press, 2011.

Hess, David J., Steve Breyman, Nancy Campbell, and Brian Martin. "Science, Technology, and Social Movements." In *Handbook of Science and Technology Studies*, edited by Edward Hackett, Olga Amsterdamska, Michael E. Lynch, and Judy Wajcman, 473–98. Cambridge, MA: MIT Press, 2008.

Hezser, Catherine. *Jewish Travel in Antiquity.* Tübingen, Germany: Mohr Siebeck, 2011.

Hill, David H. *Serving the Jewish People: My Message to the Generations.* Lexington, KY: CreateSpace Independent Publishing Platform, 2012.

Hoffman, Allison. "How We Freed Soviet Jewry." *Tablet*, 6 December 2012. www.tabletmag.com.

Hoffman, Stefani. "Jewish Samizdat and the Rise of Jewish National Consciousness." In Ro'i and Beker, *Jewish Culture and Identity in the Soviet Union*, 88–111. New York: New York University Press, 1991.

———. "Voices from the Inside: Jewish Activists' Memoirs, 1967–1989." In Ro'i, *Jewish Movement in the Soviet Union*, 227–49.

Holden, Tom. "Boycott Old Issue for Activist." *Cincinnati Enquirer*, 29 January 1980, D1. ASJ b.125 f.6.

Hollander, David, and Gilbert Klaperman. "U.S. Rabbis Tell How Jews Exist under Red Rule." *New York Journal-American*, 5 August 1956, 1.

Hollander, David, and Emanuel Rackman. "Mission to Soviet Jewry Success, U.S. Rabbis Feel." *New York Journal-American*, 14 August 1956, 19.

Hollander, Paul. *Political Pilgrims: Travels of Western Intellectuals to the Soviet Union, China, and Cuba.* New York: Oxford University Press, 1981.

Holsendolph, Ernest. "Russians to Get Pepsi-Cola." *NYT*, 17 November 1972, 1.

Honig, Sarah. "Activist Bar Mitzva." *Jerusalem Post*, 31 January 1979, 5.
Horn, Dara. *The World to Come*. New York: W. W. Norton, 2006.
Horn, Eva. *The Secret War: Treason, Espionage, and Modern Fiction*. Translated by Geoffrey Winthrop-Young. Evanston, IL: Northwestern University Press, 2013.
Horowitz, Bethamie. *Connections and Journeys: Assessing Critical Opportunities for Enhancing Jewish Identity*. New York: UJA-Federation of New York, 2000.
———. "Reframing the Study of Contemporary American Jewish Identity." *Contemporary Jewry* 23, no. 1 (2002): 14–34.
Howe, Irving. *World of Our Fathers*. New York: New York University Press, 2005 [1976].
Hudson, Repps. "Remembering Historic March in Washington for Soviet Jews." *Jewish Light*, 5 December 2012. https://stljewishlight.org.
"Hundreds of Thousands March in 100 Cities to Proclaim Solidarity with Soviet Jews: Demand 'Let My People Go.'" *JTA*, 2 May 1972, 2.
"Hurry, Hurry." *JC* (London), 13 June 1980, 30.
Hurst, Mark. *British Human Rights Organizations and Soviet Dissent, 1965–1985*. London: Bloomsbury, 2016.
IMC80. "Press Advisory, July 3." *Alert* (UCSJ), 14 August 1978. WCSJ b.14 f.4.
"Inciters." *Leningradskaya Pravda*, 3 March 1984, translation of Soviet press article. PBC b.29 f.2.
Ingall, Carol K., ed. *The Women Who Reconstructed American Jewish Education, 1910–1965*. Hanover, NH: Brandeis University Press, 2010.
"Ingrid Bergman." Photograph. *JC* (London), 30 March 1973, 1.
Insiders Club. *A Guidebook for Contacting Jews in the Soviet Union*. Washington, DC: WCSJ, JCCGW, October 1974. NCSJ b.91 f.2.
Intrator, Sam M., and Wendy Rosov. "Sustaining the Work of Creation: An Exploration of Jewish Environmental Education." *Journal of Jewish Education* 64, nos. 1–2 (1998): 102–14.
Isaac, Larry. "Movement of Movements: Culture Moves in the Long Civil Rights Struggle." *Social Forces* 87, no. 1 (2008): 33–63.
———. "Movements, Aesthetics, and Markets in Literary Change: Making the American Labor Problem Novel." *American Sociological Review* 74, no. 6 (2009): 938–65.
Isaac, Larry, and Lars Christiansen. "How the Civil Rights Movement Revitalized Labor Militancy." *American Sociological Review* 67, no. 5 (2002): 722–46.
Isaac, Larry, Steve McDonald, and Greg Lukasik. "Takin' It from the Streets: How the Sixties Mass Movement Revitalized Unionization." *American Journal of Sociology* 112, no. 1 (2006): 46–96.
Israel Government Coins and Medals Corporation. "Let My People Go." Advertisement. *B'nai B'rith Messenger* (Los Angeles), 15 October 1971, 3.
Israeli, Hasia. Preface to *Jews of Struggle: The Jewish National Movement in the U.S.S.R., 1967–1989*, edited by Rachel Schnold, 156. Tel Aviv: Beth Hatefusoth, 2007.
"Israelis Hold Silent Protest." *The Times* (London), 30 December 1970, 5.
Itzkowitz, Gary S. *The Stifled Exodus: A Curriculum for Religious Schools on the Trials and Tribulations of the Soviet Jews*. Garden Grove, CA: Jewish Community Council of Orange County, 1971. CCSA b.3 f.80.
Jacobson, Ken. "The Free Soviet Jewry March: A Moment of Unity for American Jews." Anti-Defamation League, 6 December 2017. www.adl.org.

Jacobson, Zachary Jonathan. "American Studies, the Soviet Union: A Cultural History of US-Soviet Encounters through the Cold War." PhD diss., Northwestern University, 2014. ProQuest (AAT 3669260).

Jancu, Alisa. "Two Youthful Sorts of Mitzvot; Bat Mitzvah Girl Meets 'Twin' in Soviet Asia." *NYJW*, 5 October 1984, 4.

Jasper, James M. *The Art of Moral Protest*. Chicago: University of Chicago Press, 2008.

Jasper, James M., and Francesca Polletta. "The Cultural Context of Social Movements." In *The Blackwell Companion to Social Movements*, edited by David A. Snow, Sarah A. Soule, and Hanspeter Kriesi, 63–78. Hoboken, NJ: John Wiley & Sons, 2018.

JCCGW. *A Soviet Jewry Kit for Congregations and Organizations*. Washington, DC: JCCGW, 1979. NCSJ b.84 f.3.

———. *Teaching Soviet Jewry*. 1st ed. Washington, DC: JCCGW, August 1979. RAC b.2 f.8.

———. *Teaching Soviet Jewry*. 2nd ed. Washington, DC: JCCGW, 1984. WCSJ b.12 f.11.

"JCRC Offers New 'Action Kits' for High Holy Days." *JEx* (Philadelphia), 6 September 1974, 3.

"JCRC Prepares Purim Greeting Postcards for Riga Jews." *JEx* (Philadelphia), 28 March 1973, 3.

"JDL Diplomacy at Columbia U Displaces Pepsi." *NYJW*, 4 May 1974, 14.

Jewish Federation Council of Greater Los Angeles. *Bar/Bat Mitzvah Twinning: A Cultural Lifeline to Soviet Jews*. Los Angeles: Jewish Federation Council, 1982. JGA b.1 f.16.

"Jewish Groups Sponsor a 'Run for Soviet Jewry.'" *LAT*, 25 October 1979, WS5.

"Jewish Groups Threaten Boycott of Operators over U.S.S.R. Sales." *The Travel Agent*, 1 March 1971. WCSJ b.12 f.3.

"Jewish Student Groups Use May Day to Demand Amnesty for Soviet Jewry." *JTA*, 3 May 1971, 3.

"Jewish Youths Assail Pepsico Stand." *JTA*, 9 May 1975.

"Jewish Youths Picket Department Store to Protest Sale of Soviet Goods." *JTA*, 10 April 1980.

Jews Against the Arab Boycott. "Why an 8-Page Supplement for Simple Story?" *NYJW*, 24 June 1979, 24.

———. "Why Did Baltimore Community Council Spread Its Distortion of Pepsi Issue?" *NYJW*, 24 June 1979, 30.

Joel, Billy. "We Didn't Start the Fire." Track 2 on *Storm Front*. Columbia Records, 1989. LP record album.

"Joint Bat Mitzvah Celebrated." *JEx* (Philadelphia), 12 December 1975, 47.

Joselit, Jenna Weissman. *A Perfect Fit: Clothes, Character, and the Promise of America*. New York: Metropolitan Books, 2001.

———. *The Wonders of America: Reinventing Jewish Culture, 1880–1950*. New York: Hill and Wang, 1994.

Joseph, Claudia. "The Original King of Bling." *Daily Mail* (London), 30 January 2021, 38.

Juris, Jeffrey S. "Embodying Protest: Culture and Performance within Social Movements." In *Conceptualizing Culture in Social Movement Research*, edited by Britta Baumgarten, Priska Daphi, and Peter Ullrich, 227–47. New York: Palgrave Macmillan, 2015.

Kackman, Michael. *Citizen Spy: Television, Espionage, and Cold War Culture*. Minneapolis: University of Minnesota Press, 2005.

Kahn, Douglas. "Advocacy on the Community Level: A Personal Perspective." In Friedman and Chernin, *Second Exodus*, 181–99.

Kaiser, Robert G. "Preview for 1980: Games Put Soviet Readiness in Doubt." *WP*, 26 August 1973, D1.
———. "Soviets Restrict Jewish Celebration." *WP*, 2 October 1972, A20.
Kanin, David B. *A Political History of the Olympic Games*. Boulder, CO: Westview, 1981.
Kanter, Nat. "Thousands Join in Bar Mitzvah." *Daily News* (New York), 2 February 1979, 8XQ.
Katz, Maya Balakirsky. "Collecting the Exile: Shaping Collections of the Russian Jewish Immigration." *Images* 3, no. 1 (2009): 119–28.
———. "Staging Protest: The New York Jewish Museum and the Soviet Jewry Movement." *American Jewish History* 96, no. 1 (2010): 61–78.
Kaufman, Debra Renee. "The Place of Judaism in American Jewish Identity." In *The Cambridge Companion to American Judaism*, edited by Dana Evan Kaplan, 169–86. Cambridge: Cambridge University Press, 2005.
Kaufman, Jason. "Endogenous Explanation in the Sociology of Culture." *Annual Review of Sociology* 30 (2004): 335–57.
Kedmi, Yakov (Yasha). *Hopeless Wars*. Tel Aviv: Contento Now, 2015.
Keegan, Anne. "U.S. Visitors Bring Hope to 'Refuseniks.'" *Chicago Tribune*, 7 September 1981, 3.
Keller, Bill. "Soviet Aide Admits Maps Were Faked for 50 Years." *NYT*, 3 September 1988, 1.
Kelman, Ari Y. "Reading a Book like an Object: The Case of 'the Jewish Catalog.'" In *Thinking Jewish Culture in America*, edited by Ken Koltun-Fromm, 109–30. Lanham, MD: Rowman & Littlefield, 2014.
Kelman, Ari Y., Tobin Belzer, Ziva Hassenfeld, Ilana Horwitz, and Matthew Casey Williams. "The Social Self: Toward the Study of Jewish Lives in the Twenty-First Century." *Contemporary Jewry* 37 no. 1 (2017): 53–79.
Kelner, Shaul. "À la rencontre des Juifs de l'autre côté du rideau de fer: Récits de voyage de Juifs américains et représentation du judaïsme en Union soviétique." In *Frontières et altérité religieuse: La religion dans le récit de voyage*, edited by Andreas Nijenhuis-Bescher, Susanne Berthier-Fogler, Gilles Bertrand, and Frédéric Meyer, 253–73. Rennes: Presses Universitaires de Rennes, 2019.
———. "The American Soviet Jewry Movement's 'Uneventful' 1968: Cold War Liberalism, Human Interest, and the Politics of the Long Haul." *American Jewish History* 102, no. 1 (2018): 5–35.
———. "Bar and Bat Mitzvah Twinning in the American Soviet Jewry Movement." *Secularization and Sacralization*, Frankel Institute Annual 2015–16 (2016): 38–41.
———. "Boomers, Millennials—Gen Xers!—and Post-nostalgic American Judaism: A Response to Arnold Eisen's Sklare Address." *Contemporary Jewry* 39, no. 2 (2019): 351–57.
———. "The Bureaucratization of Ritual Innovation: The Festive Cycle of the American Soviet Jewry Movement." In *Revisioning Ritual: Jewish Traditions in Transition*, edited by Simon J. Bronner. Jewish Cultural Studies, 360–91. Oxford: Littman Library of Jewish Civilization, 2011.
———. "Commentary on William Korey's 'The "Right to Leave" for Soviet Jews: Legal and Moral Aspects.'" *East European Jewish Affairs* 50, no. 3 (2020): 284–86.
———. "Foreign Tourists, Domestic Encounters: Human Rights Travel to Soviet Jewish Homes." In Bechmann Pedersen and Noack, 98–122.

———. "People-to-People: Cleveland's Jewish Community and the Exodus of Soviet Jews." In *Cleveland Jews and the Making of a Midwestern Community*, edited by Sean Martin and John J. Grabowski, 203–22. New Brunswick, NJ: Rutgers University Press, 2020.

———. "Ritualized Protest and Redemptive Politics: Cultural Consequences of the American Mobilization to Free Soviet Jewry." *Jewish Social Studies* 14, no. 3 (2008): 1–37.

———. *Tours That Bind: Diaspora, Pilgrimage, and Israeli Birthright Tourism*. New York: New York University Press, 2010.

———. "Veneration and Critique: Israel, the Sociology of American Judaism and the Problematics of Sovereignty." *Jewish Studies Quarterly* 23, no. 3 (2016): 194–221.

———. "Where Is the Next Soviet Jewry Movement? How Identity Education Forgot the Lessons That Jewish Activism Taught." In *Beyond Jewish Identity: Rethinking Concepts and Imagining Alternatives*, edited by Jon Levisohn and Ari Y. Kelman, 193–215. Brighton, MA: Academic Studies Press, 2019.

Kemper, Theodore. "A Structural Approach to Social Movement Emotions." In *Passionate Politics: Emotions and Social Movements*, edited by Jeff Goodwin, James M. Jasper, and Francesca Polletta, 58–73. Chicago: University of Chicago Press, 2001.

Kettrey, Heather Hensman. "Activism without Activists: News Media Coverage of Youth as Illegitimate Political Agents in the Virginity-Pledge Movement and Gay-Straight Alliances." *Mobilization* 23, no. 3 (2018): 349–64.

Keys, Barbara, and Roland Burke. "Human Rights." In *Oxford Handbook of the Cold War*, edited by Richard H. Immerman and Petra Goedde, 486–502. Oxford: Oxford University Press, 2012.

Khanin, Vladimir Ze'ev. *From Russia to Israel—and Back? Contemporary Transnational Russian Israeli Diaspora*. Berlin: De Gruyter Oldenbourg, 2021.

Kholmyansky, Ephraim (Alexander). "Jewish Freedom." Accessed 13 July 2022. www.jewish-freedom.net.

Kirschner, Bruce. "Metro State Star Wins Jewry Tribute." *Rocky Mountain Running News* (Colorado), June 1983, 34. In NJCRAC, Soviet Jewry Advocacy, 1983, 76g. Author's personal collection.

Kirshenblatt-Gimblett, Barbara, Marcus Moseley, and Michael Stanislawski. Introduction to *Awakening Lives: Autobiographies of Jewish Youth in Poland before the Holocaust*, edited by Jeffrey Shandler, x–xliv. New Haven, CT: Yale University Press, 2002.

"'Kisei' 'Al Domi'—ke'ot hizdahut 'im Yehudei Rusiyah" ["Do not be silent chair" as a sign of identification with Russian Jews]. *Hatsofeh* (Tel Aviv), 17 March 1964, 4.

"Kisei' panu'i bevatei Yisrael bileil haseder lehityaḥadut 'im matzav Yehudei Rusiyah" [Empty chair in the houses of Israel on Seder Eve in solidarity with the plight of Russian Jews]. *Ḥerut* (Tel Aviv), 12 April 1965, 4.

Kjellman-Chapin, Monica. "Traces, Layers and Palimpsests: The Dialogics of Collage and Pastiche." *Konsthistorisk Tidskrift* 75, no. 2 (2006): 86–99.

Klapper, Melissa R. "American Jewish Women's International Travel and Activism at the Turn of the Twentieth Century." *Journal of Modern Jewish Studies* 21, no. 2 (2022): 172–89.

———. *Ballots, Babies, and Banners of Peace: American Jewish Women's Activism, 1890–1940*. New York: New York University Press, 2013.

———. "The Great Adventure of 1929: The Impact of Travel Abroad on American Jewish Women's Identity." *American Jewish History* 102, no. 1 (2018): 85–107.

———. *Jewish Girls Coming of Age in America, 1860–1920*. New York: New York University Press, 2005.

Klehr, Harvey. *The Millionaire Was a Soviet Mole: The Twisted Life of David Karr*. New York: Encounter, 2019.

Knight, Michael. "Jewish Groups Deny They Misled Press." *NYT*, 12 December 1978, A9.

Kobrin, Rebecca A. "The Long Silent Revolution: Narrating Russian Jewish Migration across the Long-Twentieth Century." Paper presented at the Simon-Dubnow-Institut für Geschichte und Kultur, Leipzig, Germany, 10 December 2020.

Kobrin, Rebecca A., and Jay Oppenheim. "The Long Silent Revolution: Capturing the Life Stories of Soviet-Jewish Migrants to the West, 1970–2010." *East European Jewish Affairs* 47, nos. 2–3 (2017): 275–91.

Kochavi, Noam. "Idealpolitik in Disguise: Israel, Jewish Emigration from the Soviet Union, and the Nixon Administration, 1969–1974." *International History Review* 29, no. 3 (2007): 550–72.

———. "Insights Abandoned, Flexibility Lost: Kissinger, Soviet Jewish Emigration, and the Demise of Détente." *Diplomatic History* 29, no. 3 (June 2005): 503–30.

Kokesch, Bill. "Ned Shares Bar-Mitzvah with 'Oppressed' Soviet." *Montreal Gazette*, 10 December 1977, 10.

Kolatch, Alfred J., ed. *The Family Seder: A Traditional Passover Haggadah for the Modern Home*. New York: Jonathan David, 1972 [1967].

Komaromi, Ann. "Jewish Samizdat: Dissident Texts and the Dynamics of the Jewish Revival in the Soviet Union." In Ro'i, *Jewish Movement in the Soviet Union*, 273–303.

Korey, William. "Jackson-Vanik: A 'Policy of Principle.'" In Friedman and Chernin, *Second Exodus*, 97–114.

———. *The Soviet Cage: Anti-Semitism in Russia*. New York: Viking, 1973.

———. "The 'Right to Leave' for Soviet Jews: Legal and Moral Aspects." *Soviet Jewish Affairs* 1, no. 1 (1971): 5–12.

Kosharovsky, Yuli. *We Are Jews Again: Jewish Activism in the Soviet Union*. Translated by Stefani Hoffman. Edited by Ann Komaromi. Syracuse, NY: Syracuse University Press, 2012.

———. "Yuli Kosharovsky." Accessed 13 July 2022. http://kosharovsky.com.

Kosmin, Barry A., Sidney Goldstein, Joseph Waksberg, Nava Lerer, Ariela Keysar, and Jeffrey Scheckner. *Highlights of the CJF 1990 National Jewish Population Survey*. New York: Council of Jewish Federations, 1991.

Krah, Markus. *American Jewry and the Re-invention of the East European Jewish Past*. Berlin: De Gruyter, 2017.

Kranson, Rachel. *Ambivalent Embrace: Jewish Upward Mobility in Postwar America*. Chapel Hill: University of North Carolina Press, 2017.

Krasner, Jonathan B. *The Benderly Boys and American Jewish Education*. Hanover, NH: Brandeis University Press, 2012.

Kravel-Tovi, Michal. "Wet Numbers: The Language of Continuity Crisis and the Work of Care among the Organized American Jewish Community." In *Taking Stock: Cultures of Enumeration in Contemporary Jewish Life*, edited by Michal Kravel-Tovi and Deborah Dash Moore, 141–63. Bloomington: Indiana University Press, 2016.

Kravitz, Samantha A. "The Business of Selling the Soviet Union: Intourist and the Wooing of American Travelers, 1929–1939." PhD diss., Concordia University, 2006. ProQuest (AAT MR20671).

Krenn, Michael L. "Token Diplomacy: The United States, Race, and the Cold War." In *Race, Ethnicity, and the Cold War: A Global Perspective*, edited by Philip E. Muehlenbeck, 3–32. Nashville, TN: Vanderbilt University Press, 2012.

Kugelmass, Jack. "Green Bagels: An Essay on Food, Nostalgia, and the Carnivalesque." *YIVO Annual* 19 (1990): 57–80.

———. "The Rites of the Tribe: The Meaning of Poland for American Jewish Tourists." *YIVO Annual* 21 (1993): 395–453.

Kurz, Nathan A. *Jewish Internationalism and Human Rights after the Holocaust*. Cambridge: Cambridge University Press, 2020.

Kuznetsov, Eduard. *Prison Diaries*. New York: Stein and Day, 1975.

Kuznick, Peter J., and James Burkhart Gilbert. *Rethinking Cold War Culture*. Washington, DC: Smithsonian Institution Press, 2001.

Labendz, Jacob Ari. "Lectures, Murder, and a Phony Terrorist: Managing 'Jewish Power and Danger' in 1960s Communist Czechoslovakia." *East European Jewish Affairs* 44, no. 1 (2014): 84–108.

"Labour Conference Petitioned by 35s." *JC* (London), 5 October 1973, 10.

Lainer-Vos, Dan. "Israel in the Poconos: Simulating the Nation in a Zionist Summer Camp." *Theory and Society* 43, no. 1 (2014): 91–116.

Lakoff, George, and Mark Johnson. *Metaphors We Live By*. Chicago: University of Chicago Press, 1980.

Landau, Aviva. "To Russia with Love . . . and Mesiras Nefesh." *Hamaor* (Federation of Synagogues, London), September 2017, 6.

Larsen, David. "1,700 in L.A. Run as One, and One More in Moscow." *LAT*, 3 December 1979, D1.

Lazerwitz, Bernard, J. Alan Winter, Arnold Dashefsky, and Ephraim Tabory. *Jewish Choices: American Jewish Denominationalism*. Albany: State University of New York Press, 1998.

Lazin, Fred A. *American Christians and the National Interreligious Task Force on Soviet Jewry: A Call to Conscience*. Lanham, MD: Rowman & Littlefield, 2019.

———. *The Struggle for Soviet Jewry in American Politics: Israel versus the American Jewish Establishment*. Lanham, MD: Lexington Books, 2005.

Leavy, Jane, and Susan Okie. "The Runner: Phenomenon of the '70s." *WP*, 30 September 1979, D1.

Lederhendler, Eli. *American Jewry: A New History*. Cambridge: Cambridge University Press, 2017.

———. *New York Jews and the Decline of Urban Ethnicity: 1950–1970*. Syracuse, NY: Syracuse University Press, 2001.

Lehrer, Erica T. *Jewish Poland Revisited: Heritage Tourism in Unquiet Places*. Bloomington: Indiana University Press, 2013.

Lena, Jennifer C., and Richard A. Peterson. "Classification as Culture: Types and Trajectories of Music Genres." *American Sociological Review* 73, no. 5 (2008): 697–718.

"Leningrad Jews Hail U.S. Rabbis." *NYT*, 9 July 1956, 2.

Lerner, Diana. "Young Housewives with a Mission." *Jerusalem Post*, 16 August 1974, 7.

"'Let My People Go' Campaign." *Jerusalem Post*, 22 March 1966, 4.

Levanon, Nehemiah. *Haqod: Nativ* [Code name: Nativ]. Tel Aviv: ʿAm ʿOved, 1995.

———. "Israel's Role in the Campaign." In Friedman and Chernin, *Second Exodus*, 70–83.

Levin, Geoffrey P. "Before Soviet Jewry's Happy Ending: The Cold War and America's Long Debate over Jackson-Vanik, 1976–1989." *Shofar* 33, no. 3 (2015): 63–85.

Levine, Eric. "The Problematics of Jewish Collective Action: Community and Conflict and Change." In *Contention, Controversy, and Change*, edited by Eric Levine and Simcha Fishbane, 3–57. New York: Academic Studies Press, 2016.

Levinson, Joshua, and Orit Bashkin, eds. *Jews and Journeys: Travel and the Performance of Jewish Identity*. Philadelphia: University of Pennsylvania Press, 2021.

Levy, Richard N., ed. *On Wings of Freedom: The Hillel Haggadah for the Nights of Passover*. Hoboken, NJ: Ktav, 1989.

Lieber, David. "2 Boys Share Special Rite of Passage." *Philadelphia Inquirer*, 27 May 1986.

Lieberson, Stanley. *A Matter of Taste: How Names, Fashions, and Culture Change*. New Haven, CT: Yale University Press, 2000.

Lieberstein, Marilyn S. "Simchat Torah March, Rally to Bring Refusenik Plight to Next Generation." *JEx* (Philadelphia), 30 September 1988, 6.

Liebman, Charles S. *The Ambivalent American Jew*. Philadelphia: Jewish Publication Society, 1973.

Liebman, Charles S., and Steven M. Cohen. *Two Worlds of Judaism: The Israeli and the American Experiences*. Cambridge, MA: Harvard University Press, 1990.

"Light of Freedom." *Atlanta Constitution*, 23 April 1973, 4A.

Lillian and Albert Small Capital Jewish Museum. Voices of the Vigil. Accessed 18 May 2022. www.jhsgw.org.

Lipski, Sam, and Suzanne D. Rutland. *Let My People Go: The Untold Story of Australia and the Soviet Jews 1959–89*. Jerusalem: Gefen, 2015.

Lipstadt, Deborah E. *Denying the Holocaust: The Growing Assault on Truth and Memory*. New York: Free Press, 1993.

———. "Guide to the Soviet Union." In *The First Jewish Catalog*, edited by Richard Siegel, Michael Strassfeld, and Sharon Strassfeld, 82–87. Philadelphia: Jewish Publication Society, 1973.

———. *History on Trial*. New York: Harper Perennial, 2005.

———. "Playing the Blame Game: American Jews Look Back at the Holocaust." *David W. Belin Lecture in American Jewish Affairs* 18 (2011).

Lissner, Will. "Jewish Defense League to Boycott Products of Concerns Dealing with Soviet." *NYT*, 21 January 1971, 9.

Litov, Samuel. "The History of Jewish Education in Washington, DC: 1852–1970." Master's thesis, Dropsie College, 1973.

Litwack, Wendy. *School Kit: A Course in Five Lessons*. Montreal: Montreal Committee for Soviet Jewry, 1978. WCSJ b.12 f.7.

"Local Doctor Will Run for Russian 'Refusenik.'" *Sun Reporter Midweek* (Florida), 13 December 1978, 39. JSAS b.1 f.9.

"Local Runners Win at Canton." *Daily Reporter* (Dover, OH), 9 December 1974, 21.

Loeffler, James. "How an American Jewish Opera Star Accidentally Launched the Soviet Jewish Movement." *Tablet*, 9 June 2016. www.tabletmag.com.

———. "The Problem with the 'Judeo-Christian' Tradition." *Atlantic*, 1 August 2020. www.theatlantic.com.

———. *Rooted Cosmopolitans: Jews and Human Rights in the Twentieth Century*. New Haven, CT: Yale University Press, 2018.

Lookstein Center for Jewish Education, Bar Ilan University. "The Refusenik Project." Accessed 12 July 2022. https://refusenikproject.org.

Lorber, John Samuel. "*Tsum folk vel ikh fun keyver zingen*, I Will Sing to the People from the Grave: The Emotions of Protest in the Songs of Dovid Edelshtat." Master's thesis, Vanderbilt University, 2014.

Louis, J. C., and Harvey Yazijian. *The Cola Wars*. New York: Everest House, 1980.

Luntz, Alan. "Lighting the Flames of Freedom: The American Movement to Save Soviet Jewry." Soviet Jewry Movement. Accessed 13 July 2022. www.sovietjewrymovement.org.

Luther Place Memorial Church. "History of Free Soviet Jewry." Accessed 3 July 2022. https://lutherplace.org.

MacCannell, Dean. "Staged Authenticity: Arrangements of Social Space in Tourist Settings." *American Journal of Sociology* 79, no. 3 (1973): 589–603.

———. *The Tourist: A New Theory of the Leisure Class*. New York: Schocken Books, 1989 [1976].

MacKaye, William R. "Jewish Group Cancels PepsiCo Chief's Award." Obituary. *WP*, 20 September 1973, A3.

"Mack Trucks Drops Plans to Build a Russian Plant." *NYT*, 16 September 1971, 61.

Magid, Shaul. "The American Jewish Holocaust 'Myth' and 'Negative Judaism': Jacob Neusner's Contribution to American Judaism." In *A Legacy of Learning: Essays in Honor of Jacob Neusner*, edited by Alan J. Avery-Peck, Bruce Chilton, William Scott Green, and Gary G. Porton, 319–37. Leiden: Brill, 2014.

———. *Meir Kahane: The Public Life and Political Thought of an American Jewish Radical*. Princeton, NJ: Princeton University Press, 2021.

Mahla, Daniel. "Between Socialism and Jewish Tradition: Bundist Holiday Culture in Interwar Poland." *Studies in Contemporary Jewry* 24 (2010): 177–85.

Major, Patrick, and Rana Mitter. *Across the Blocs: Exploring Comparative Cold War Cultural and Social History*. London: Frank Cass, 2004.

Manekofsky, Irene. "The Beginning of the Olympic Cleanup." *Alert* (UCSJ), 26 June 1978. WCSJ b.14 f.4.

———. "Petition Campaign Begins by International Monitoring Committee for the 1980 Olympics." *Alert* (UCSJ), 31 July 1978. WCSJ b.14 f.4.

Manning, Toby. *John le Carré and the Cold War*. London: Bloomsbury, 2017.

Manon, Davida, and Irene Manekofsky. *Natasha's Dream: Children's Handbook on Russian Jews*. Arlington, VA: WCSJ, 1974. WCSJ b.11 f.7.

———. *Natasha's Dream: Children's Handbook on Russian Jews*. Rev. ed. Arlington, VA: WCSJ, 1976. WCSJ b.11 f.7.

Mansfield, Virginia. "Bar Mitzvah 'Twinned' to Youths in Soviet Union." *WP*, 1 September 1984, C8.

Margolin, Dovid. "Today, a Moscow with More Synagogues Than Ever." Chabad.org, 31 March 2016. www.chabad.org.

———. "Camp Gan Israel Russia: 25 Years of Historic Transformation." Chabad.org, 9 July 2015. www.chabad.org.

Margulies, Sylvia R. *The Pilgrimage to Russia: The Soviet Union and the Treatment of Foreigners, 1924–1937*. Madison: University of Wisconsin Press, 1968.

"Markets to Carry Passover Prayer." *JEx* (Philadelphia), 22 March 1974, 61.

Martin, Douglas. "William Korey, B'nai B'rith Lobbyist, Dies at 87." Obituary. *NYT*, 3 September 2009, B9.

Martin, Ross. "My Russian Twin: I Will Find You, Bolislav Vainman." *Something Burning* (blog), 2009. http://somethingburning.com.

Massarik, Fred. *Jewish Identity: Facts for Planning.* New York: CJFWF, 1974.
"Massive Rally for Solidarity Coming May 21." *NYJW*, 23 April 1978, 31.
"'Matzah of Hope' for Soviet Jewry." *JTA*, 22 March 1972.
Mauss, Marcel. *The Gift: The Form and Reason for Exchange in Archaic Societies.* London: Routledge Classics, 2002 [1925].
May, Elaine Tyler. *Homeward Bound: American Families in the Cold War Era.* New York: Basic Books, 1988.
May, Eric Charles. "Vigil Gives Way to a Better Day: Gatherings for Soviet Jews Suspended after 20 Years." *WP*, 28 January 1991, D1.
McAdam, Doug. "The Biographical Consequences of Activism." *American Sociological Review* 54, no. 5 (1989): 744–60.
———. *Freedom Summer.* New York: Oxford University Press, 1988.
———. "Initiator and Spin-Off Movements." In *The Wiley-Blackwell Encyclopedia of Social and Political Movements*, edited by David Snow, Donatella Della Porta, Bert Klandermans, and Doug McAdam. Hoboken, NJ: John Wiley & Sons, 2013.
———. *Political Process and the Development of Black Insurgency, 1930–1970.* Chicago: University of Chicago Press, 1999.
———. "Tactical Innovation and the Pace of Insurgency." *American Sociological Review* 48, no. 6 (1983): 735–54.
McAdam, Doug, Sidney Tarrow, and Charles Tilly. *Dynamics of Contention.* Cambridge: Cambridge University Press, 2001.
McCammon, Holly J. "'Out of the Parlors and into the Streets': The Changing Tactical Repertoire of the US Women's Suffrage Movements." *Social Forces* 81, no. 3 (2003): 787–818.
———. *The U.S. Women's Jury Movements and Strategic Adaptation: A More Just Verdict.* Cambridge: Cambridge University Press, 2012.
McCammon, Holly J., Minyoung Moon, Brittany N. Hearne, and Megan Robinson. "The Supreme Court as an Arena for Activism: Feminist Cause Lawyering's Influence on Judicial Decision Making." *Mobilization* 25, no. 2 (2020): 221–44.
McCarthy, John D., and Mayer N. Zald. "Resource Mobilization and Social Movements: A Partial Theory." *American Journal of Sociology* 82, no. 6 (1977): 1212–41.
McClish, Loraine. "Mission Accomplished: There's a Bit of James Bond in Trip to Russia." *Farmington Observer* (Detroit), 31 October 1983. UCSJ b.79 f.16.
McCune, Mary. *The Whole Wide World, without Limits: International Relief, Gender Politics, and American Jewish Women, 1893–1930.* Detroit: Wayne State University Press, 2005.
McDonnell, Terence E. *Best Laid Plans: Cultural Entropy and the Unraveling of AIDS Media Campaigns.* Chicago: University of Chicago Press, 2016.
McDowell, Edwin. "The Shoot-Out in Soda Pop." *NYT*, 19 October 1980, F1.
McEnroe, Colin. "Rabbi Used Soviet Tour to See Dissidents, Teach Theology." *Hartford Courant* (Connecticut), 12 November 1978, 8.
McNulty, Faith, and Brendan Gill. "Party Going." *New Yorker*, 19 November 1955, 44–45.
McQuiston, John T. "Bar Mitzvah by Proxy Held on L.I. for a Soviet Boy." *NYT*, 28 January 1979, 32.
"Medical Mission Links Refuseniks to Bergen County." *Jewish Voice* (New York), n.d. 1987, 7. NCSJ b.56 f.11.
Medoff, Rafael. *The Rabbi of Buchenwald: The Life and Times of Herschel Schacter.* Brooklyn: Ktav, 2021.

———. *Rav Chesed: The Life and Times of Rabbi Haskel Lookstein.* Jersey City, NJ: Ktav, 2008.
"Meeting Russian Jews Is Theme of Booklet." *WP,* 1 December 1972, B21.
Mehta, Samira K., and Brett Krutzsch. "The Changing Jewish Family: Jewish Communal Responses to Interfaith and Same-Sex Marriage." *American Jewish History* 104, no. 4 (2020): 553–77.
Meir, Mira, and Yair Rozen. *Alina: A Russian Girl Comes to Israel.* Translated by Zeva Shapiro. Philadelphia: Jewish Publication Society, 1982.
Meister, David. *Lesson Plans and Programming on Soviet Jewry.* Baltimore, MD: Baltimore Board of Jewish Education, 1976. NCSJ-UK f.443.
Menand, Louis. *The Free World: Art and Thought in the Cold War.* New York: Farrar, Straus and Giroux, 2021.
Mendelevich, Yosef. *Unbroken Spirit: A Heroic Story of Faith, Courage and Survival.* Translated by Benjamin Balint. Jerusalem: Gefen, 2012.
"Menorah March during Hanukkah Sets Off New Campaign in Soviet Struggle." *Commentator* (Yeshiva University, New York), 18 January 1966, 1. Personal papers, JBP.
Meyer, David S. "Protest and Political Opportunities." *Annual Review of Sociology* 30 (2004): 125–45.
Meyer, David S, and Deana A. Rohlinger. "Big Books and Social Movements: A Myth of Ideas and Social Change." *Social Problems* 59, no. 1 (2012): 136–53.
Meyer, David S., and Suzanne Staggenborg. "Movements, Countermovements, and the Structure of Political Opportunity." *American Journal of Sociology* 101, no. 6 (1996): 1628–60.
Meyer, David S., and Nancy Whittier. "Social Movement Spillover." *Social Problems* 41, no. 2 (1994): 277–98.
Michels, Tony. *A Fire in Their Hearts: Yiddish Socialists in New York.* Cambridge, MA: Harvard University Press, 2005.
Middleton, Drew. "U.S. Frees Travel to East Europe as Spur to Amity." *NYT,* 1 November 1955, 1.
"Midland Run Just the Start." *The Courier-News* (Somerville, NJ), 19 May 1984.
Miller, Betty. "Oral History Transcription." Voices of the Vigil. Lillian and Albert Small Capital Jewish Museum, 8–9 September 2008. www.jhsgw.org.
Miller, Gay Sands. "Networks' Ad Sales for Next Season Boom as Olympics and Election Bolster Prices." *Wall Street Journal,* 25 July 1979, 46.
Minker, Jack. *Scientific Freedom and Human Rights: Scientists of Conscience during the Cold War.* Piscataway, NJ: IEEE Computer Society Press, 2012.
"Miriam Karlin Helps 35s." *JC* (London), 11 May 1973, 14.
Moore, Deborah Dash. *At Home in America: Second Generation New York Jews.* New York: Columbia University Press, 1981.
———. *GI Jews: How World War II Changed a Generation.* Cambridge, MA: Harvard University Press, 2004.
———. "Reconsidering the Rosenbergs: Symbol and Substance in Second Generation American Jewish Consciousness." *Journal of American Ethnic History* 8, no. 1 (Fall 1988): 21–37.
"More Than 200,000 Rally on Behalf of Soviet Jewry in Massive D.C. Gathering." *JTA,* 7 December 1987.
Morozov, Boris. *Documents on Soviet Jewish Emigration.* Portland, OR: Frank Cass, 1999.

Morozova, Marina A. *Anatomiia Otkaza* [Anatomy of refusal]. Moscow: RGGU, 2011.

Morris, Aldon D. *The Origins of the Civil Rights Movement: Black Communities Organizing for Change*. New York: Free Press, 1984.

Morse, Arthur D. *While Six Million Died: A Chronicle of American Apathy*. New York: Random House, 1968.

"Moscow Jews Dance the Hora in Street on Holiday." *NYT*, 15 October 1968, 12.

Munro, Patricia Keer. *Coming of Age in Jewish America: Bar and Bat Mitzvah Reinterpreted*. New Brunswick, NJ: Rutgers University Press, 2016.

Murphy, Gregory. *The Big Book of Concepts*. Cambridge, MA: MIT Press, 2004.

Museum of Jewish Heritage. "'Prisoner of Conscience' Bracelet." Living Museum. Accessed 13 July 2022. www.living-museum.org.

Myers, Tamara. "Blistered and Bleeding, Tired and Determined: Visual Representations of Children and Youth in the Miles for Millions Walkathon." *Journal of the Canadian Historical Association* 22, no. 1 (2011): 245–75.

———. "Local Action and Global Imagining: Youth, International Development, and the Walkathon Phenomenon in Sixties' and Seventies' Canada." *Diplomatic History* 38, no. 2 (2014): 282–93.

Nadell, Pamela S. *America's Jewish Women: A History from Colonial Times to Today*. New York: W. W. Norton, 2019.

———. *Women Who Would Be Rabbis: A History of Women's Ordination, 1889–1985*. Boston: Beacon Press, 1998.

Naftalin, Micah H. "The Activist Movement." In Friedman and Chernin, *Second Exodus*, 224–41.

Nagel, Gerald S. *Operation Exodus: The Inside Story of American Jews in the Greatest Rescues of Our Time*. New York: Contemporary History Press, 2006.

Nathans, Benjamin. "Murray Friedman Memorial Lecture." Paper presented at the Soviet Jewry Activists and Civic Engagement Symposium, Temple University and National Museum of American Jewish History, Philadelphia, 6 March 2014. https://vimeo.com/144019809.

———. "Refuseniks and Rights Defenders: Jews and the Soviet Dissident Movement." In *From Europe's East to the Middle East: Israel's Russian and Polish Lineages*, edited by Kenneth B. Moss, Benjamin Nathans, and Taro Tsurumi, 362–76. Philadelphia: University of Pennsylvania Press, 2021.

———. "Talking Fish: On Soviet Dissident Memoirs." *Journal of Modern History* 87, no. 3 (2015): 579–614.

National Board Institute '72. "Underground: A Simulation of the Path of Soviet Jews from Oppression to Freedom." *How about This* (Kutz Camp-Institute, Warwick, NY), November 1972. CASJ b.24 f.14.

"Nationwide Preparations in High Gear for Solidarity Day for Soviet Jewry." *JTA*, 24 April 1972.

"NBC First in TV Ratings." *Santa Cruz Sentinel* (California), 30 July 1980, 11.

NCSJ. *Bar/Bat Mitzvah Twinning*. New York: NCSJ, 1984. NCSJ b.35 f.3.

———. *Freedom Rally for Soviet Jews*. Aired 6 December 1987, on C-SPAN. www.c-span.org.

"NCSJ Sets Up Bureau to Monitor Soviet Emigration Practices." *JTA*, 10 January 1975.

Nelson, Lara. "Cataloguing the Papers of Michael Sherbourne." *University of Southampton Special Collections* (blog), 8 February 2019. https://specialcollectionsuniversityofsouthampton.wordpress.com.

Ner Le'elef. *The Story of Former Soviet Jewry and Their Rebirth.* Jerusalem: Ner Le'elef, 2007.
Neusner, Jacob. *Israel in America: A Too-Comfortable Exile?* Boston: Beacon Press, 1985.
———. *Stranger at Home: "The Holocaust," Zionism and American Judaism.* Chicago: University of Chicago Press, 1981.
"New York Rabbis Report on U.S.S.R." *Christian Science Monitor* (New York), 13 July 1956, 7.
Nicorici, Irina. "Becoming a Soviet Citizen: Migration, Citizenship, and the Politics of Belonging in the USSR, 1960–1990." PhD diss., Rutgers, 2021. ProQuest (AAT 28771356).
Nilov, V. "*Oplata . . . galetami*" [Payment with biscuits]. *Izvestia* (Moscow), 8–9 August 1976, with accompanying English translation. PBC b.29 f.2.
NJCRAC. "Major Activities in Communities in the US." Paper presented at the Workshop on Public Actions and Demonstrations, 2nd World Conference on Soviet Jewry, Brussels, 17–19 February 1976.
———, ed. *Soviet Jewry Advocacy: A Guide to Community Action.* New York: NJCRAC, 1983. Author's personal collection.
Norwood, Stephen H. *Prologue to Annihilation: Ordinary American and British Jews Challenge the Third Reich.* Bloomington: Indiana University Press, 2021.
Noskowitz, Jack, George Ende, Philip Jaffe, Benjamin Miller, Elias Shulman, and Israel S. Weisberger. *Resource Teaching Unit on Soviet Jewry.* New York: Jewish Education Committee, n.d. [ca. 1968]. CCSA b.3 f.80.
Ochs, Vanessa L. *Inventing Jewish Ritual.* Philadelphia: Jewish Publication Society, 2007.
Oestreich, Judith R. "Ritual Recalls Refuseniks Plight." *NYT,* 23 January 1983, WC10.
O'Hearn, Denis. "Repression and Solidary Cultures of Resistance: Irish Political Prisoners on Protest." *American Journal of Sociology* 115, no. 2 (2009): 491–526.
Oliver, Pamela E., and Gregory M. Maney. "Political Processes and Local Newspaper Coverage of Protest Events: From Selection Bias to Triadic Interactions." *American Journal of Sociology* 106, no. 2 (2000): 463–505.
Olster, Margie. "Police Investigating Tear Gas Bombing Which Disrupted Soviet Dance Troupe and Injured 21 People." *JTA,* 4 September 1986.
"Olympics." *Alert* (UCSJ), 10 October 1978. WCSJ b.14 f.5.
"Olympics." *Alert* (UCSJ), 22 November 1978. WCSJ b.14 f.5.
"Olympics-Da, Moscow-Nyet T-Shirts." *Alert* (UCSJ), 4 October 1978. WCSJ b.14 f.5.
"Olympic Stamps." *Alert* (UCSJ), 13 December 1978. WCSJ b.14 f.5.
"On the Run." *Chicago Tribune,* 27 September 1982, ND17.
Orbach, William W. *The American Movement to Aid Soviet Jews.* Amherst, MA: University of Massachusetts Press, 1979.
———. "The British Soviet Jewry Movement." *Forum* 32–33 (Fall 1978): 21–27.
Orenstein, Amaryah. "'Let My People Go!' The Student Struggle for Soviet Jewry and the Rise of American Jewish Identity Politics." PhD diss., Brandeis University, 2014. ProQuest (AAT 3611652).
Pattillo-McCoy, Mary. "Church Culture as a Strategy of Action in the Black Community." *American Sociological Review* 63, no. 6 (1998): 767–84.
Paul, Batsheva. "Let My People Go!" Canadian Jewish Congress, 1977, 45 rpm vinyl single.
Pedersen, Sune Bechmann. "Peace through Tourism: A Brief History of a Popular Catchphrase." In *Cultural Borders and European Integration,* edited by M. Andrén, 29–37. Gothenburg: Center for European Studies, University of Gothenburg, 2017.

"Pepsi Strikes Back." *Jewish Press* (Omaha, Nebraska), 26 January 1973, 2.

Peretz, Pauline. *Le combat pour les juifs soviétiques: Washington—Moscou—Jérusalem, 1953-1989.* Paris: Armand Colin, 2006.

"Pesach 5726." *Spotlight* (Cleveland, OH), April–May 1966, 5. CCSA b.4 f.123.

Peterson, Richard A. "The Production of Culture: A Prolegomenon." *American Behavioral Scientist* 19, no. 6 (1976): 669–84.

———. "Why 1955? Explaining the Advent of Rock Music." *Popular Music* 9, no. 1 (1990): 97–116.

Peterson, Richard A., and Narasimhan Anand. "The Production of Culture Perspective." *Annual Review of Sociology* 30 (2004): 311–34.

Pew Research Center. "Topline Survey Results." Appendix B in *A Portrait of Jewish Americans.* Washington, DC: Pew Research Center, 2013. www.pewresearch.org.

Phelps, Robert H. "Libel Suit in U.S. to Test Charges on B'nai B'rith." *NYT*, 19 June 1970, 36.

Pianko, Noam. *Jewish Peoplehood: An American Innovation.* New Brunswick, NJ: Rutgers University Press, 2015.

Pinar, William F., William M. Reynolds, Patrick Slattery, and Peter M. Taubman. *Understanding Curriculum.* New York: Peter Lang, 1995.

Pinkus, Benjamin. "Israeli Activity on Behalf of Soviet Jewry." In *Organizing Rescue: National Jewish Solidarity in the Modern Period*, edited by S. Ilan Troen and Benjamin Pinkus, 373–402. London: Frank Cass, 1992.

———. "Soviet Campaigns against 'Jewish Nationalism' and 'Cosmopolitanism,' 1946–1953." *Soviet Jewish Affairs* 4, no. 2 (1974): 53–72.

Pitts, Rachel. "80s Singers That Did Coke and Pepsi Jingle Commercials." *Q105*, 13 September 2019. https://myq105.com.

Piven, Frances Fox, and Richard Cloward. *Poor People's Movements: Why They Succeed, How They Fail.* New York: Vintage, 1979.

Plocker, Anat. *The Expulsion of Jews from Communist Poland: Memory Wars and Homeland Anxieties.* Bloomington: Indiana University Press, 2022.

Podwal, Mark. *Let My People Go: A Haggadah.* New York: Darien House, 1972.

Polakoff, Joseph. "Drive Underway to Change U.S. Law on Soviet Trade." *JTA*, 24 February 1975, 4.

———. "Mrs. Shcharansky Clashes with Professor on Issue of 'Private Diplomacy' to Help Dissidents." *JTA*, 1 July 1978, 1.

Polletta, Francesca. "Can You Celebrate Dissent? Holidays and Social Protest." In *We Are What We Celebrate: Understanding Holidays and Rituals*, edited by Amitai Etzioni, 151–77. New York: New York University Press, 2004.

———. *Inventing the Ties That Bind: Imagined Relationships in Moral and Political Life.* Chicago: University of Chicago Press, 2020.

———. *It Was like a Fever: Storytelling in Protest and Politics.* Chicago: University of Chicago Press, 2009.

Polletta, Francesca, and James M. Jasper. "Collective Identity and Social Movements." *Annual Review of Sociology* 27, no. 1 (2001): 283–305.

Porath, Jonathan. *Here We Are All Jews: 175 Russian-Jewish Journeys.* Jerusalem: Gefen, 2022.

Porath, Jonathan [Yonaton]. *Jews in Russia: The Last Four Centuries, a Documentary History.* New York: United Synagogue Commission on Jewish Education, 1973.

———. *The Russian Jewish Community: Past, Present and Future*. Great Neck, NY: Temple Israel, 1967. CCSA b.3 f.80.
Porter, Anne E. "Distributed Agency and the Rhetorical Work of Essay Contests." PhD diss., University of Michigan, 2014.
Porter, Jill. "Russians Told to Take a Flyer." *Philadelphia Daily News*, 12 January 1976, 3.
Postal, Bernard, and Samuel H. Abramson. *The Landmarks of a People: A Guide to Jewish Sites in Europe*. New York: Hill and Wang, 1962.
———. *The Traveler's Guide to Jewish Landmarks of Europe*. New York: Fleet Press, 1971.
Poupko, Bernard A. *In shotn fun Kremlin: Dray bazukhn in Sovet-Rusland* [In the shadow of the Kremlin: Three visits to Soviet Russia]. New York: Aynikayt, 1968.
———. "Mission to Soviet Jewry." *Jewish Life* (Union of Orthodox Jewish Congregations of America) 33, no. 1, September–October 1965, 8–25.
———. "Visit to Russia." *JEx* (Philadelphia), 19 June 1964, 17. Personal papers, RBPP.
Powell, Cheryl C. "Redemption for the Protagonist in Three Novels by John le Carré." PhD diss., Florida State University, 1991. ProQuest (AAT 9124633).
Prados, John. *How the Cold War Ended: Debating and Doing History*. Washington, DC: Potomac Books, 2011.
Pratt, Mary Louise. *Imperial Eyes: Travel Writing and Transculturation*. London: Routledge, 1992.
Prell, Riv-Ellen. "Jewish Summer Camping and Civil Rights: How Summer Camps Launched a Transformation in American Jewish Culture." *David W. Belin Lecture in American Jewish Affairs* 13 (2006).
———. *Prayer and Community: The Havurah in American Judaism*. Detroit: Wayne State University Press, 1989.
———. "Summer Camp, Post-war American Jewish Youth and the Redemption of Judaism." In *The Jewish Role in America: An Annual Review*, edited by Bruce Zuckerman and Jeremy Schoenberg, 5:77–106. West Lafayette, IN: Purdue University Press, 2007.
———, ed. *Women Remaking American Judaism*. Detroit: Wayne State University Press, 2007.
"Prisoners' Month Launched." *JC* (London), 29 November 1974, 8.
"'Prisoners of Conscience' Month Is Set for December." *B'nai B'rith Messenger* (Los Angeles), 7 December 1973, 10.
"Proxy Bar Mitzvah Tomorrow." *Evening Press* (Binghamton, NY), 26 January 1979, 2A.
Rakeffet-Rothkoff, Aaron. *From Washington Avenue to Washington Street*. Jerusalem: Gefen, 2011.
"Rally for Freedom." *NYJW*, 27 July 1980, 1. SSSJ b.45 f.3.
"Rally, Race Set Sunday." *JEx* (Philadelphia), 25 October 1985, 5.
Ramm, Shoshana. *Route to Freedom: A Game of Escape from the Soviet Union*. New York: BJE of Greater New York and GNYCSJ, March 1976. GNYCSJ b.OS1 f.1.
Raspberry, William J. "Demonstrators Protest Treatment of Jews." *WP*, 20 September 1965, A1.
Ravitz, Jessica. "Defying the KGB: How a Forgotten Movement Freed a People." CNN, 30 December 2012. www.cnn.com.
Reed, T. V. *The Art of Protest: Culture and Activism from the Civil Rights Movement to the Present*. Minneapolis: University of Minnesota Press, 2005.
Reinharz, Shulamit, and Mark A. Raider. *American Jewish Women and the Zionist Enterprise*. Hanover, NH: Brandeis University Press, 2005.

Remennick, Larissa I. "Professional Identities in Transit: Factors Shaping Immigrant Labour Market Success." *International Migration* 51, no. 1 (2013): 152–68.

———. *Russian Jews on Three Continents: Identity, Integration, and Conflict*. New Brunswick, NJ: Transaction, 2007.

Rich, Dave. "The Activist Challenge: Women, Students, and the Board of Deputies of British Jews in the British Campaign for Soviet Jewry." *Jewish History* 29, no. 2 (2015): 163–85.

Richmond, Yale. *Cultural Exchange and the Cold War*. University Park: Pennsylvania State University Press, 2003.

Richter, Glenn. Interviewed by Yuli Kosharovsky. 18 May 2004. http://kosharovsky.com.

"River Revels." *JC* (London), 6 June 1980, 13.

Ro'i, Yaacov. "The Achievements of the Jewish Movement." In Ro'i, *Jewish Movement in the Soviet Union*, 96–116.

———, ed. *The Jewish Movement in the Soviet Union*. Washington, DC: Woodrow Wilson Center Press, 2012.

———. "The Move from Russia/the Soviet Union to Israel: A Transformation of Jewish Culture and Identity?" In *The New Jewish Diaspora*, edited by Zvi Y. Gitelman, 139–55. New Brunswick, NJ: Rutgers University Press, 2016.

———. "Strategy and Tactics." In Ro'i, *Jewish Movement in the Soviet Union*, 46–95.

———. *The Struggle for Soviet Jewish Emigration 1948–1967*. Cambridge: Cambridge University Press, 1991.

Ro'i, Yaacov, and Avi Beker. *Jewish Culture and Identity in the Soviet Union*. New York: New York University Press, 1991.

Ro'i, Yaacov, and Joshua Rubenstein. "Human Rights and National Rights: The Interaction of the Jewish Movement with Other Dissident Groups." In Ro'i, *Jewish Movement in the Soviet Union*, 198–224.

Robinson, Harlow. *The Last Impresario: The Life, Times, and Legacy of Sol Hurok*. New York: Viking, 1994.

Rodgers, Diane M. "Children as Social Movement Participants." In *Sociological Studies of Children and Youth*, edited by David A. Kinney and Katherine Brown Rosier, 11:139–259. Amsterdam: Elsevier, 2005.

———. *Children in Social Movements: Rethinking Agency, Mobilization and Rights*. New York: Routledge, 2020.

Rogow, Faith. *Gone to Another Meeting: The National Council of Jewish Women, 1893–1993*. Tuscaloosa: University of Alabama Press, 1993.

Rosen, Michael J. "'Freedom Run' Spotlights Prisoners of Conscience." *JEx* (Philadelphia), 18 July 1980, 5.

Rosenberg, Howard. "1980 Olympics: Is It NBC vs Moscow?" *LAT*, 6 July 1979, F1.

Rosenblatt, Gary. "30 Years Later, 'The Big Rally' Is Little Remembered." *NYJW*, 15 November 2017. https://jewishweek.timesofisrael.com.

Rosenblum, Louis. "Control of Soviet Jewry Movement by Israeli Government." Interview by Hillel Levine, 27 December 1987. LRP b.1 f.24.

———. "The Freedom Caravan." Cleveland and the Freeing of Soviet Jewry. Cleveland Jewish History, 2008. www.clevelandjewishhistory.net.

———. *Hear the Cry of the Oppressed: A Handbook on Soviet Anti-Semitism*. Cleveland, OH: CCSA, 1970. CCSA b.1 f.7.

Rosenblum, Louis, and Daniel Rosenblum. "Involvement in the Soviet Jewry Movement: A Personal Account, 1961–1978." Cleveland Jewish History, 13 August 1996. https://clevelandjewishhistory.net.

Roskies, David G. *Yiddishlands: A Memoir*. Detroit: Wayne State University Press, 2008.

Rothenberg, Celia E. *Serious Fun at a Jewish Community Summer Camp: Family, Judaism, and Israel*. Lanham, MD: Lexington Books, 2016.

Rottenberg, Dan. "To Russia with Levis." *Philadelphia Inquirer: Today*, 9 January 1977, 10. JCRCGP b.65 f.13.

Rouvier, Henry. "Documents." Appendix in *Les juifs du silence*, by Elie Wiesel, 111–42. Paris: Editions du Seuil, 1966.

Rozner, Shelomoh. *Bintiv hadmamah: Hape'ilut haḥashai'it lema'an Yehudei Brit Hamo'atsot* [The silent route: The clandestine support for Soviet Jews]. Edited by Eli Somer and Tzemach Jacobson. Jerusalem: Zalman Shazar Center, 2012.

Rubiés, Joan-Pau. "Travel Writing and Ethnography." In *The Cambridge Companion to Travel Writing*, edited by Peter Hulme and Tim Youngs, 242–60. Cambridge: Cambridge University Press, 2002.

———. "Why Do We Need a Cultural History of Travel—and What Do Jews Have to Do with It?" In *Jews and Journeys: Travel and the Performance of Jewish Identity*, edited by Joshua Levinson and Orit Bashkin, 10–19. Philadelphia: University of Pennsylvania Press, 2021.

Rubin, Burton S. "The Soviet Refugee: Challenge to the American Jewish Community Resettlement System." *Journal of Jewish Communal Service* 52, no. 2 (December 1975): 195–201.

Rubin, Ronald. "Student Struggle for Soviet Jewry." *Hadassah Magazine*, December 1966, 7, 34–35. Personal papers, JBP.

Rudman, Reuben M. "Kol Yisrael Areivim Zeh Ba-Zeh." *Tradition: A Journal of Orthodox Jewish Thought* 42, no. 2 (2009): 35–49.

"Runners Calendar." *San Francisco Examiner*, 14 October 1981, F6.

Rutland, Suzanne D. "Conflicting Visions: Debates Relating to Soviet Jewish Emigration in the Global Arena." *East European Jewish Affairs* 47, nos. 2–3 (2017): 222–41.

———. *Lone Voice: The Wars of Isi Leibler*. Jerusalem: Gefen, 2021.

———. "Soviet Jewry: Debates and Controversies." In *The World Jewish Congress 1936–2016*, edited by Menachem Z. Rosensaft, 145–59. New York: World Jewish Congress, 2017.

Sadowski-Smith, Claudia. *The New Immigrant Whiteness: Race, Neoliberalism, and Post-Soviet Migration to the United States*. New York: New York University Press, 2018.

Safam. "Amnesty." Track 9 on *Bittersweet*. Safam Records, 1983. LP record album.

———. "Just Another Foreigner." Track 2 on *Bittersweet*. Safam Records, 1983. LP record album.

———. "Leaving Mother Russia." Track 5 on *Encore*. Safam Records, 1978. LP record album.

Sahlins, Marshall. *Islands of History*. Chicago: University of Chicago Press, 2013.

Saivetz, Carol R., and Sheila Levin Woods, eds. *The Night of the Murdered Poets*. New York: NCSJ, 1973. BACSJ b.58 f.17.

Salisbury, Harrison E. "U.S. Rabbis Fear Soviet Jews Face Extinction of Religious Life." *NYT*, 13 July 1956, 2.

Salkin, Jeffrey K. *Putting God on the Guest List: How to Reclaim the Spiritual Meaning of Your Child's Bar or Bat Mitzvah*. Woodstock, VT: Jewish Lights, 1992.

Salmon, Shawn Connelly. "To the Land of the Future: A History of Intourist and Travel to the Soviet Union, 1929–1991." PhD diss., University of California, Berkeley, 2008. ProQuest (AAT 3353153).

Sandberg, Joel. "Our Other Patients: Behind the Red Curtain." *Miami Medicine* (Miami, FL), January 1980, 18–20. JSAS b.1 f.7.

Sandberg, Sheryl. *Lean In: Women, Work and the Will to Lead*. New York: Knopf, 2013.

Sanford, Margery, and Adele Sandberg. *Soviet Jews: Hostages All*. Case Histories of the Refuseniks 12. Miami: South Florida Conference on Soviet Jewry, 1985.

"San Francisco Launches Campaign to Send Rosh Hashanah Greetings to Soviet Jews." *JTA*, 5 August 1969.

Sarantakes, Nicholas Evan. *Dropping the Torch: Jimmy Carter, the Olympic Boycott, and the Cold War*. Cambridge: Cambridge University Press, 2010.

Sarna, Jonathan D. *American Judaism*. New Haven, CT: Yale University Press, 2004.

———. "The Crucial Decade in Jewish Camping." In *A Place of Our Own: The Rise of Reform Jewish Camping*, edited by Michael M. Lorge and Gary P. Zola, 27–51. Tuscaloosa: University of Alabama Press, 2006.

———. "The Cult of Synthesis in American Jewish Culture." *Jewish Social Studies* 5, no. 1/2 (1998): 52–79.

———. "The Secret of Jewish Continuity." *Commentary*, October 1994, 55–58.

Sasson, Theodore. "Mass Mobilization to Direct Engagement: American Jews' Changing Relationship to Israel." *Israel Studies* 15, no. 2 (2010): 173–95.

———. *The New American Zionism*. New York: New York University Press, 2013.

Schacter, Herschel. "Hebrew Rites Fading in Soviet, U.S. Rabbis Find." *New York Journal-American*, 10 August 1956, 13.

Scheindlin, Ahavia. "Israelis Also Run for Refuseniks." *JFC Bulletin* (New York), 15 December 1980, 4. In NJCRAC, *Soviet Jewry Advocacy*, 1983, 76b. Author's personal collection.

Schlegel, Chad C. "Freedom Run Likely to Draw Thousands." *Arizona Daily Star* (Tucson), 1 December 1993, 4C.

Schmelz, U. O., and Sergio DellaPergola. "World Jewish Population, 1994." *American Jewish Year Book* 96 (1996): 434–63.

Schmemann, Serge. "Soviet Press Tells of Spies, All American." *NYT*, 23 August 1984, A9.

Schmid, David. *The Secrets of Great Mystery and Suspense Fiction*. Chantilly, VA: Great Courses, the Teaching Company, 2016.

Schnold, Rachel, ed. *Jews of Struggle: The Jewish National Movement in the U.S.S.R., 1967–1989*. Tel Aviv: Beth Hatefusoth, 2007.

Schwartz, Thomas A. *Henry Kissinger and American Power: A Political Biography*. New York: Hill and Wang, 2020.

"Seder at Russian Mission Site Vows Relentless Freedom Fight." *Jewish Week–American Examiner* (New York), 20 April 1974. SSSJ b.11 f.13.

"Seder Ceremony in Street near Soviet Mission Asks Freedom for Russian Jews." *JTA*, 11 April 1968, 4.

"Seeking Aid for Jews in Soviet." *Daily News* (New York), 28 March 1973, Q7.

Senderovich, Sasha. "Scenes of Encounter: The 'Soviet Jew' in Fiction by Russian Jewish Writers in America." *Prooftexts* 35, no. 1 (2015): 98–132.

Shapira, Anita. "The Religious Motifs of the Labor Movement." In *Zionism and Religion*, edited by S. Almog, Jehuda Reinharz, and Anita Shapira, 251–72. Hanover, NH: University Press of New England, 1998.

Shapiro, Josh. "Josh's Record." Shapiro for Governor. Accessed 10 July 2023. https://joshshapiro.org.

Shapiro, Leo. "Jewish Passover Festival Opens Tonight." *Boston Globe*, 20 April 1970, 40.

Sharansky, Natan. *Fear No Evil*. Translated by Stefani Hoffman. New York: Random House, 1998.

———. Foreword to *Jews of Struggle: The Jewish National Movement in the U.S.S.R., 1967–1989*, edited by Rachel Schnold, 154–55. Tel Aviv: Beth Hatefusoth, 2007.

"A Shared Bar Mitzvah." *WJW*, 20–26 October 1977, 24. Reprinted in *Alert* (UCSJ) 2, no. 7, 24 October 1977. WCSJ b.14 f.4.

Shayduk-Immerman, Olesya. "Feeling Alive: Unofficial Jewish Practices in the USSR in the 1970s and 1980s." PhD diss., University of California, Berkeley, 2019. ProQuest (AAT 13886245).

"Shenkers Visit Refuseniks." *Portland Jewish Review* (Oregon), June 1984, 1. NCSJ b.72 f.20.

Sheramy, Rona. "From Auschwitz to Jerusalem: Re-enacting Jewish History on the March of the Living." In *Polin*, edited by Biskupski Mieczyslaw and Antony Polonsky, 19:307–26. Oxford: Littman Library of Jewish Civilization, 2007.

Sherrod, Lonnie R. *Youth Activism: An International Encyclopedia*. Vol. 2. Westport, CT: Greenwood, 2006.

Shinbaum, Myrna. "Mobilizing America: The National Conference on Soviet Jewry." In Friedman and Chernin, *Second Exodus*, 173–80.

Shneer, David. "Having It Both Ways: Jewish Nation Building and Jewish Assimilation in the Soviet Empire." *Ab Imperio* 2003, no. 4 (2003): 377–93.

———. "Saving Soviet Jews and the Future of the Global Jewish Diaspora." In *The Oxford Handbook of the Jewish Diaspora*, edited by Hasia R. Diner. Oxford: Oxford University Press, 2021. https://academic.oup.com.

Showstack, Gerald. "Perspectives on the Resettlement of Soviet Jews." *Journal of Jewish Communal Service* 67, no. 1 (1990): 66–72.

Shrayer, Maxim D. *Waiting for America: A Story of Emigration*. Syracuse, NY: Syracuse University Press, 2007.

Shroyer, Leslie. "25 Years Later: Soviet Jews and the Freedom 25 Movement." *Jewish News* (Tidewater, VA), 21 November 2012. www.jewishnewsva.org.

Shternshis, Anna. *Soviet and Kosher: Jewish Popular Culture in the Soviet Union, 1923–1939*. Bloomington: Indiana University Press, 2006.

———. *When Sonia Met Boris: An Oral History of Jewish Life under Stalin*. New York: Oxford University Press, 2017.

Siegel, Richard, Michael Strassfeld, and Sharon Strassfeld. *The First Jewish Catalog*. Philadelphia: Jewish Publication Society, 1973.

Singer, Isaac Bashevis. "A State of Fear." Review of *The Jews of Silence*, by Elie Wiesel. *NYT*, 8 January 1967, 290.

SJC. *Adopt-a-Family and Adopt-a-Prisoner Handbook*. Philadelphia: JCRC of Greater Philadelphia, 1977. JCRCGP b.64 f.20.

———. *Bar/Bat Mitzvah Twinning: A Guide for Synagogue Chairmen*. Philadelphia: JCRC of Greater Philadelphia, October 1982. BMP b.1 f.15.

———. *Briefing Book for Travelers to the USSR.* Philadelphia: JCRC of Greater Philadelphia, 1988. BMP b.1 f.18.

———. "These Russians Committed the Same Horrendous Crime: They Were All Born Jews!" Advertisement. *JEx* (Philadelphia), 19 January 1973, 60.

Sklare, Marshall, ed. *The Jews: Social Patterns of an American Group.* Glencoe, IL: Free Press, 1958.

Sklare, Marshall, and Joseph Greenblum. *Jewish Identity on the Suburban Frontier: A Study of Group Survival in the Open Society.* New York: Basic Books, 1967.

"Slepak Sentenced to 5 Years, Nudel 4 Years of Internal Exile." *JTA,* 22 June 1978.

Slezkine, Yuri. *The Jewish Century.* Princeton, NJ: Princeton University Press, 2004.

Smith, Christian, ed. *Disruptive Religion: The Force of Faith in Social Movement Activism.* New York: Routledge, 1996.

Smith, Harrison. "Donald Kendall, Who Built PepsiCo into a Soda and Snack-Food Giant, Dies at 99." Obituary. *WP,* 21 September 2020, n.p.

Snow, David A. "Collective Identity and Expressive Forms." In *International Encyclopedia of the Social and Behavioral Sciences* 4, edited by Neil J. Smelser and Paul B. Baltes, 4:2212–19. Amsterdam: Elsevier, 2001.

Snow, David A., and Robert D. Benford. "Ideology, Frame Resonance, and Participant Mobilization." *International Social Movement Research* 1, no. 1 (1988): 197–217.

———. "Master Frames and Cycles of Protest." In *Frontiers in Social Movement Theory,* edited by Aldon D. Morris and Carol McClurg Mueller, 133–55. New Haven, CT: Yale University Press, 1992.

Snow, David A., Robert D. Benford, Holly McCammon, Lyndi Hewitt, and Scott Fitzgerald. "The Emergence, Development, and Future of the Framing Perspective: 25+ Years since 'Frame Alignment.'" *Mobilization* 19, no. 1 (2014): 23–46.

Snow, David A., E. Burke Rochford Jr., Steven K. Worden, and Robert D. Benford. "Frame Alignment Processes, Micromobilization, and Movement Participation." *American Sociological Review* 51, no. 4 (1986): 464–81.

Snyder, Sarah B. *Human Rights Activism and the End of the Cold War: A Transnational History of the Helsinki Network.* New York: Cambridge University Press, 2011.

Søndergaard, Rasmus Sinding. *Reagan, Congress, and Human Rights: Contesting Morality in US Foreign Policy.* Cambridge: Cambridge University Press, 2020.

"Soviet Expels 2 Britons over Zionist Literature." *NYT,* 6 March 1984, A5.

"Soviet Expels 2 U.S. Tourists." *NYT,* 23 February 1984, A4.

"Soviet Jewry Bracelets Available." *American Jewish World* (Minneapolis), 3 November 1972, 9.

"Soviet Jewry Poster Contest Winners Named." Press clipping from unknown Pioneer Press newspaper (Illinois), 3 May 1984. CASJ b.27 f.2.

"Soviet Jews to Get 'Greetings': JCRC Sponsors 8,000 High Holiday Cards." *JEx* (Philadelphia), 14 September 1973, 2.

"Soviet Prisoners: 100,000th Medallion Sold by Activists." *B'nai B'rith Messenger* (Los Angeles), 26 January 1973, 37.

"Soviet Travel Agency Calls U.S. Warning 'Silly.'" *NYT,* 11 August 1984, 4.

"Soviet U.N. Mission Is Picketed by 700 over Anti-Semitism." *NYT,* 2 May 1964, p. 2.

Soyer, Daniel. "Back to the Future: American Jews Visit the Soviet Union in the 1920s and 1930s." *Jewish Social Studies* 6, no. 3 (2000): 124–59.

"Special Bar Mitzva at Beth Shalom Calls Attention to Soviet Jew Roitburd." Press clippings. *Detroit Jewish News,* 5 May 1976. JCRCGP b.82 f.30.

Speed, Billie Cheney. "Parade Here to Celebrate Simchat Torah." *Atlanta Constitution*, 13 October 1979, 8B.
Spiegel, Irving. "3,000 Here Mark Simhath Torah in Street near Soviet Mission; Observed in Moscow." *NYT*, 29 October 1967, 4.
———. "3,000 Here Protest Soviet Curb on Jews." *NYT*, 5 April 1965, 3.
———. "100,000 March Here in Support of Soviet Jewry." *NYT*, 14 April 1975, 49.
———. "Passover Seder Is Held Here for Jews of Soviet." *NYT*, 11 April 1968, 16.
———. "Soviet Is Assailed in 'Exodus March.'" *NYT*, 27 April 1970, 18.
———. "Students Rally Here to Protest Suppression of Jews in Soviet." *NYT*, 9 April 1966, 23.
Spiegel, Philip. *Triumph over Tyranny: The Heroic Campaign That Saved 2,000,000 Soviet Jews*. New York: Devora Press, 2008.
SSSJ. *Letter-Writing Campaigns / Action for Soviet Jewry*. New York: SSSJ, [ca. 1971]. WCSJ b.11 f.4.
———. *Save Soviet Jewry: Call to Action*. Handbook, Summer 1965. SSSJ b.244 f.18.
———. *SSSJ Handbook: A Source Book on Soviet Jewry Activism*. New York: SSSJ, August 1979. WCSJ b.12 f.11.
———. "The Story of 'Operation Jericho.'" In *Save Soviet Jewry: Call to Action; Summer 1965 Handbook*, 26–27. New York: SSSJ, 1965. SSSJ b.244 f.18.
———. "The Theory and Practice of Soviet Jewry Activism." In *SSSJ Handbook: A Source Book on Soviet Jewry Activism*, D1a–D1b. New York: SSSJ, 1979. WCSJ b.12 f.11.
Standley, Michelle. "Experiencing Communism, Bolstering Capitalism: Guided Bus Tours of 1970s East Berlin." In Bechmann Pedersen and Noack, *Tourism and Travel during the Cold War*, 61–76.
Stanoeva, Elitza. "Exporting Holidays: Bulgarian Tourism in the Scandinavian Market in the 1960s and 1970s." In Bechmann Pedersen and Noack, *Tourism and Travel during the Cold War*, 23–46.
Staub, Michael E., ed. *The Jewish 1960s: An American Sourcebook*. Edited by Jonathan D. Sarna. Lebanon, NH: Brandeis University Press / University Press of New England, 2004.
———. *Torn at the Roots: The Crisis of Jewish Liberalism in Postwar America*. New York: Columbia University Press, 2002.
Steif, William. "The Refuseniks of Kiev." *Saturday Review*, 17 September 1977. BACSJ b.6 f.19.
"Students Fight for Refuseniks." *JC* (London), 29 February 1980, 9.
Swats, Ric. "Over 1,000 Take Part in Freedom Run." *Arizona Daily Star* (Tucson), 9 December 1991, 1B.
Swidler, Ann. "Cultural Power and Social Movements." In *Social Movements and Culture*, edited by Hank Johnston and Bert Klandermans, 25–40. Minneapolis: University of Minnesota Press, 1995.
Sylvester, Ed, and Alan Dirkin. "The Pursuit of the Long-Distance Runner." *LAT*, 14 January 1979, B1.
Tabarovsky, Izabella. "Russian-Speaking Israelis Go to the Polls." *Russia File* (blog). Kennan Institute, 4 April 2019. www.wilsoncenter.org.
Taft, Jessica K. *Rebel Girls: Youth Activism and Social Change across the Americas*. New York: New York University Press, 2010.
Tallman, Marillyn, and Betty Kahn. *Let My People Go: A Curriculum for the Study of Jewish History in Russia and the Soviet Union*. Curriculum ed. Highland Park, IL: CASJ, 1984. WCSJ b.12 f.12.

Tambiah, Stanley J. "A Performative Approach to Ritual." In *Readings in Ritual Studies*, edited by Ronald L. Grimes, 495–511. Upper Saddle River, NJ: Prentice Hall, 1996 [1979].

Tapper, Joshua. "'This Is Who I Would Become': Russian Jewish Immigrants and Their Encounters with Chabad-Lubavitch in the Greater Toronto Area." *Canadian Jewish Studies* 29 (2020): 57–80.

Tarrow, Sidney. "Cycles of Collective Action: Between Moments of Madness and the Repertoire of Contention." *Social Science History* 17, no. 2 (1993): 281–307.

———. *Democracy and Disorder: Protest and Politics in Italy, 1965–1975*. Oxford: Oxford University Press, 1989.

———. "Modular Collective Action and the Rise of the Social Movement: Why the French Revolution Was Not Enough." *Politics & Society* 21, no. 1 (1993): 69–90.

Taylor, Telford. *Courts of Terror: Soviet Criminal Justice and Jewish Emigration*. New York: Vintage, 1976.

Taylor, Verta, Katrina Kimport, Nella Van Dyke, and Ellen Ann Andersen. "Culture and Mobilization: Tactical Repertoires, Same-Sex Weddings, and the Impact on Gay Activism." *American Sociological Review* 74, no. 6 (2009): 865–90.

Taylor, Verta, and Nella Van Dyke. "'Get Up, Stand Up': Tactical Repertoires of Social Movements." In *The Blackwell Companion to Social Movements*, edited by David A. Snow, Sarah A. Soule, and Hanspeter Kriesi, 262–93. Oxford: Blackwell, 2004.

Tennison, Patricia. "Young Soviet Jews Find a Place in Hearts and Minds of American 'Twins.'" *Chicago Tribune*, 17 December 1982, SD10.

Teplitz, Saul I. "Russian Jewish Youth Is Not Missing in Action." *Our Age: A Magazine for Jewish Youth* 10, no. 7 (January 1969): 1–2.

"The Third Annual Walkathon for Soviet Jewry." *Democrat and Chronicle* (Rochester, NY), 24 March 1972, 18.

Thomas, Daniel Charles. *The Helsinki Effect: International Norms, Human Rights, and the Demise of Communism*. Princeton, NJ: Princeton University Press, 2001.

Thompson, Carl. *Travel Writing*. 1st ed. New York: Routledge, 2011.

"A Thousand Miracles a Day." Advertisement. *LAT*, 28 March 1991, SBA22.

"Thousands See Protest March for Soviet Jews." *Jewish Press* (New York), 24 December 1965. JBP.

Tilly, Charles. *The Contentious French: Four Centuries of Popular Struggle*. Cambridge, MA: Harvard University Press, 1986.

———. "Contentious Repertoires in Great Britain, 1758–1834." In *Repertoires and Cycles of Collective Action*, edited by Mark Traugott, 15–42. Durham, NC: Duke University Press, 1995.

———. *From Mobilization to Revolution*. Reading, MA: Addison-Wesley, 1978.

Tirosh, Avraham. "Haish sheḥadar et masakh habarzel" [The man who penetrated the Iron Curtain]. *Ma`ariv* (Tel Aviv), 19 April 2000, 24–26, 39.

Tobenkin, Paul. "Russia Shifts, Opens Door to 5 U.S. Rabbis." *New York Herald Tribune*, 14 May 1956, 1.

Tolts, Mark. "Demography of the Contemporary Russian Speaking Jewish Diaspora." In *The New Jewish Diaspora: Russian-Speaking Immigrants in the United States, Israel, and Germany*, edited by Zvi Y. Gitelman, 23–40. New Brunswick, NJ: Rutgers University Press, 2016.

———. "A Half Century of Jewish Emigration from the Former Soviet Union: Demographic Aspects." Paper presented at the Project for Russian and Eurasian Jewry,

Davis Center for Russian and Eurasian Studies, Harvard University, Cambridge, MA, 20 November 2019.
"Toronto Singer and Teacher Wins 1st Prize in Second Annual Koomkoom Song Festival." *Canadian Jewish News*, 10 December 1981, 20.
"Traveler's Report from the Soviet Union." *Alert* (UCSJ), 17 January 1979. WCSJ b.14 f.7.
"The Trial of Anatoli Shcharansky." *Time*, 24 July 1978, cover. http://content.time.com/time/covers/0,16641,19780724,00.html.
Trilling, Lionel. *Sincerity and Authenticity*. New York: Harcourt Brace Jovanovich, 1972.
Turek, Lauren Frances. *To Bring the Good News to All Nations: Evangelical Influence on Human Rights and US Foreign Relations*. Ithaca, NY: Cornell University Press, 2020.
Turpie, Julie. "Freedom Seder for Soviet Jews: Mayor, City Council Members Attend Observance." *Jewish Herald-Voice* (Houston, TX), 25 April 1985. ASJ b.125 f.2.
Tutnauer, Moshe. "The Poem of My Land." *Jerusalem Post*, 8 February 1974, A13.
"Unity Is Theme for Israel 41." *JEx* (Philadelphia), 9 May 1989, 6.
"Upcoming Events: Running." *Detroit Free Press*, 19 September 1984, 5D.
Urry, John. *The Tourist Gaze*. London: SAGE, 1990.
Urry, John, and Jonas Larsen. *The Tourist Gaze 3.0*. London: SAGE, 2011.
"U.S. Jews Observe Passover with Special Seder Prayer for Soviet Jewry." *JTA*, 10 April 1963.
"U.S., Soviet Pals Have Bar Mitzvahs Together." *Saint Louis Post-Dispatch*, 29 April 1989, D6.
Van Dyke, Nella, and Verta Taylor. "The Cultural Outcomes of Social Movements." In *The Blackwell Companion to Social Movements*, edited by David A. Snow, Sarah A. Soule, and Hanspeter Kriesi, 482–98. Hoboken, NJ: John Wiley & Sons, 2018.
Van Ness, Justin, and Erika Summers-Effler. "Emotions in Social Movements." In *The Blackwell Companion to Social Movements*, edited by David A. Snow, Sarah A. Soule, Hanspeter Kriesi, and Holly J. McCammon, 411–28. Oxford: Blackwell, 2019.
Veidlinger, Jeffrey. *In the Midst of Civilized Europe: The Pogroms of 1918–1921 and the Onset of the Holocaust*. New York: Metropolitan Books, 2021.
———. *In the Shadow of the Shtetl: Small-Town Jewish Life in Soviet Ukraine*. Bloomington: Indiana University Press, 2013.
———. *The Moscow State Yiddish Theater: Jewish Culture on the Soviet Stage*. Bloomington: Indiana University Press, 2000.
Veksler, Inga P. "'We Left Forever and into the Unknown': Soviet Jewish Immigrants' Experiences of Transit Migration." PhD diss., Rutgers, 2014. ProQuest (AAT 3681645).
Volvovsky, Ari. "The Teaching and Study of Hebrew." In Ro'i, *Jewish Movement in the Soviet Union*, 334–55.
Vowinckel, Annette, Marcus M. Payk, and Thomas Lindenberger. *Cold War Cultures: Perspectives on Eastern and Western European Societies*. New York: Berghahn, 2012.
Wagner-Pacifici, Robin, and E. Colin Ruggero. "Temporal Blindspots in Occupy Philadelphia." *Social Movement Studies* 19, nos. 5–6 (2020): 675–96.
Walker, Barbara. "The Moscow Correspondents, Soviet Human Rights Activists, and the Problem of the Western Gift." In *Americans Experience Russia*, edited by Choi Chatterjee and Beth Holmgren, 151–70. New York: Routledge, 2013.
Walker, Edward T., Andrew W. Martin, and John D. McCarthy. "Confronting the State, the Corporation, and the Academy: The Influence of Institutional Targets on Social Movement Repertoires." *American Journal of Sociology* 114, no. 1 (2008): 35–76.
Walzer, Michael. *Exodus and Revolution*. New York: Basic Books, 1985.

Wang, Dan J., and Sarah A. Soule. "Tactical Innovation in Social Movements: The Effects of Peripheral and Multi-issue Protest." *American Sociological Review* 81, no. 3 (2016): 517–48.

Warde, Alan. "Introduction to the Sociology of Consumption." *Sociology* 24, no. 1 (February 1990): 1–4.

———. "The Sociology of Consumption: Its Recent Development." *Annual Review of Sociology* 41, no. 1 (2015): 117–34.

Warshawsky, Gale Solotar. *Creative Puppetry for Jewish Kids*. Denver: Alternatives in Religious Education, 1985.

"Washington Conference." Editorial. *Jewish Times* (Boston), 2 April 1964. CCSA b.3 f.70.

Waxman, Dov. *Trouble in the Tribe: The American Jewish Conflict over Israel*. Princeton, NJ: Princeton University Press, 2016.

Waxman, Dov, and Scott Lasensky. "Jewish Foreign Policy: Israel, World Jewry and the Defence of 'Jewish Interests.'" *Journal of Modern Jewish Studies* 12, no. 2 (2013): 232–52.

W. B. "Postscripts." *Jerusalem Post*, 21 December 1979, 16.

WCSJ. "Is Pepsi-Cola Suitable for Passover Use?" Advertisement. *WJW*, April 1974. WCSJ b.12 f.3.

———. "Theater Group Tells of Meetings." *WJW*, 24 October 1973. NCSJ b.14 f.1.

Weber, Max. *Economy and Society*. Berkeley: University of California Press, 1978.

Weinberg, Julius. *An Introduction to the History of Soviet Jewry*. Cleveland, OH: BJE of Cleveland, 1976. CCSA b.3 f.80.

Weinstein, Lewis H. *Masa: Odyssey of an American Jew*. Boston: Quinlan Press, 1989.

Weiss, Avi. *Open Up the Iron Door: Memoirs of a Soviet Jewry Activist*. London: Toby Press, 2015.

Weiss, David W. "Travels of an American Scientist in the U.S.S.R.: Report on Soviet Jewry." In *Handbook for Community Action on Soviet Anti-Semitism*, edited by Louis Rosenblum, 59–72. Cleveland, OH: Cleveland Bureau of Jewish Education, 1966. CCSA b.1 f.6.

Weitzman National Museum of American Jewish History. "Are We Responsible for Others?" Teacher's guide, *Open Book*, n.d. https://info.nmajh.org.

———. *Power of Protest: The Movement to Free Soviet Jews*. Exhibition publicity pamphlet, 2019. https://info.nmajh.org.

Wenger, Beth S. *History Lessons: The Creation of American Jewish Heritage*. Princeton, NJ: Princeton University Press, 2010.

Wertheimer, Jack, Charles S. Liebman, and Steven M. Cohen. "How to Save American Jews." *Commentary*, January 1996, 47–51.

West, Candace, and Don H. Zimmerman. "Doing Gender." *Gender & Society* 1, no. 2 (1987): 125–51.

Whitfield, Stephen J. *The Culture of the Cold War*. 2nd ed. Baltimore: Johns Hopkins University Press, 1996.

Whittier, Nancy. "The Consequences of Social Movements for Each Other." In *The Blackwell Companion to Social Movements*, edited by David A. Snow, Sarah A. Soule, and Hanspeter Kriesi, 531–52. Oxford: Blackwell, 2004.

Wiesel, Elie. *All Rivers Run to the Sea*. London: HarperCollins, 1995.

———. *The Jews of Silence: A Personal Report on Soviet Jewry*. Translated by Neal Kozodoy. New York: Schocken, 2011 [1966].

———. *Les juifs du silence: Témoignage*. Paris: Editions du Seuil, 1966.
———. *Yehudei hadmamah*. Translated by Haim Gouri. Tel Aviv: ʻAm ʻOved, 1967.
Winik, Elaine K. *Still Looking Forward*. Bethel, CT: Rutledge, 1996.
Wintrob, Suzanne. "Support for Soviet Jews Aim of Rally at City Hall." *Globe and Mail* (Toronto), 15 October 1984, M3.
Wlazelek, Ann. "Ceremony Includes Refusenik: Zionsville Girl Shares Bat Mitzvah with Soviet." *Morning Call* (Allentown, PA), 5 June 1988, B01.
Woda, Rachel Mersky. "If Not Now, When? NFTY's Role in Freeing Soviet Jews." Union for Reform Judaism, 4 November 2014. https://urj.org.
Wolf, Zusha, ed. *Dyedushka: haRebbe miLubavitch veYahadut Rusiyah*. Kfar Ḥabad: Yad Haḥamishah, 2006.
Woocher, Jonathan S. *Sacred Survival: The Civil Religion of American Jews*. Bloomington: Indiana University Press, 1986.
Wood, Peter. "NBC's Moscow Olympics—Money, Politics and Ballyhoo." *NYT*, 14 May 1978, D1.
Wood, Richard L. "Religious Culture and Political Action." *Sociological Theory* 17, no. 3 (1999): 307–32.
"World Jewry Prays for Jews in Russia on Yom Kippur during Services." *JTA*, 16 September 1964.
Wyman, David S. *The Abandonment of the Jews: America and the Holocaust, 1941–1945*. New York: Pantheon, 1984.
Yad Vashem. "Bar/Bat Mitzvah Twinning Program." Accessed 18 May 2023. www.yadvashem.org.
Yangzom, Dicky. "Clothing and Social Movements: Tibet and the Politics of Dress." *Social Movement Studies* 15, no. 6 (2016): 622–33.
Yaroslavsky, Zev. *Zev's Los Angeles: From Boyle Heights to the Halls of Power; A Political Memoir*. Boston: Cherry Orchard Books, 2023.
Yerushalmi, Yosef Hayim. *Zakhor: Jewish History and Jewish Memory*. Seattle: University of Washington Press, 1982.
Yurchak, Alexei. *Everything Was Forever, until It Was No More: The Last Soviet Generation*. Princeton, NJ: Princeton University Press, 2005.
Zald, Meyer N., and John D. McCarthy. "Religious Groups as Crucibles of Social Movements." In *Social Movements in an Organizational Society: Collected Essays*, edited by Meyer N. Zald and John D. McCarthy, 67–95. New Brunswick, NJ: Transaction, 1987.
———. "Social Movement Industries: Competition and Conflict among SMOs." In *Social Movements in an Organizational Society: Collected Essays*, edited by Meyer N. Zald and John D. McCarthy, 161–80. New Brunswick, NJ: Transaction, 1987.
Zalmanson-Kuznetsov, Anat, dir. *Operation Wedding*, documentary film. Israel, Latvia, 2016. www.operation-wedding-documentary.com.
Zaltzman, Hillel. *Samarkand: The Underground with a Far-Reaching Impact*. New York: Chamah and Yachad, 2019.
Zayanchovskaya, Zhanna Antonovna. "*Razvitie vneshnikh migrat͡sionnykh svi͡azeĭ Rossii*" [Development of Russian external migration relations]. *Sot͡siologicheskiĭ zhurnal*, no. 1 (1995): 29–44.
Zborovsky, Alexandra. "'Venetian Waltz, Roman Holiday, American Tragedy': Soviet Jewish Expectations and Encounters in Transit." Paper presented at the Association for Jewish Studies, 53rd Annual Conference, Chicago, 19 December 2021.

Zelaya, Ian. "The 20-Year Vigil." *WJW*, 4 December 2013. www.washingtonjewishweek.com.

Zeltzer-Zubida, Aviva, and Philip Kasinitz. "The Next Generation: Russian Jewish Young Adults in Contemporary New York." *Contemporary Jewry* 25, no. 1 (2005): 193–225.

Zerubavel, Eviatar. *Hidden Rhythms: Schedules and Calendars in Social Life*. Berkeley: University of California Press, 1985.

———. *Time Maps: Collective Memory and the Social Shape of the Past*. Chicago: University of Chicago Press, 2003.

Zion, Noam, and Barbara Spectre. *A Different Light: The Big Book of Hanukkah*. Jerusalem: Devora Press and Shalom Hartman Institute, 2000.

Zipperstein, Steven J. *Imagining Russian Jewry: Memory, History, Identity*. Seattle: University of Washington Press, 2013.

Zisserman-Brodsky, Dina. "The 'Jews of Silence'—the 'Jews of Hope'—the 'Jews of Triumph': Revisiting Methodological Approaches to the Study of the Jewish Movement in the USSR." *Nationalities Papers* 33, no. 1 (2005): 119–39.

Zlatoposly, Ashley. "Remembering Our Local Heroes: How Grassroots Efforts, Secret Trips and Rallies Paved the Way for Soviet Jewish Freedom." *Detroit Jewish News*, 15 September 2021. https://thejewishnews.com.

Zubok, Vladislav M. *A Failed Empire: The Soviet Union in the Cold War from Stalin to Gorbachev*. Chapel Hill: University of North Carolina Press, 2007.

Zubrzycki, Geneviève. *The Crosses of Auschwitz: Nationalism and Religion in Post-Communist Poland*. Chicago: University of Chicago Press, 2009.

Zwaik, Stanley N. "The Lights Are Dim for Our Brethren in Russia." *The Jewish War Veteran*, January/February/March 1983, 8–12. ASJ b.115 f.7.

Zylberberg, Sonia. "Transforming Rituals: Contemporary Jewish Women's Seders." PhD diss., Concordia University, 2006. ProQuest (AAT NR16280).

INDEX

Page numbers followed by *f* and *t* refer to figures and tables, respectively.

Abramova, German, 278
Academic Committee for Soviet Jewry, 28
Action Committee of Newcomers from the Soviet Union (Israel), 17
Action for Post-Soviet Jewry, 298
Action for Soviet Jewry (ASJ), 151, 260, 278, 279, 280*f*, 284, 289
activists: appeals of, 16, 305–6; contemporary, lessons for, 306–7; Soviet Jewish, 4, 6, 321–22n34; tactics, 10–12, 29; tourism as recruiting, 91; young urban, 18
Adelman, Samuel, 93
ADL. *See* Anti-Defamation League
Adopt-a-Family programs, 37, 91, 264, 272
Adopt-a-Prisoner programs, 37, 91, 195, 264, 274
affordances, 37
Afghanistan (Soviet invasion of), 216, 219–21
Age of Exploration tropes, 159, 160
Agler, Richard, 172–73
Agudath Israel, 17, 89, 94. *See also* Vaad L'Hatzolas Nidchei Yisroel
AJC. *See* American Jewish Committee
AJCongress. *See* American Jewish Congress
AJCSJ. *See* American Jewish Conference on Soviet Jewry
AJHS. *See* American Jewish Historical Society
Al Tidom ("Dare Not Remain Silent"), 94–95, 266
American Greetings Corporation, 72
American Jewish Committee (AJC), 3, 17, 28, 183
American Jewish Conference on Soviet Jewry (AJCSJ), 16–17, 46, 81–82; 1968 action plan, 76; creation of, 2, 12, 15, 61; grassroots efforts to reform, 320n16; reconstitution as NCSJ, 5, 324n71; ritualized protests, 51–53, 60–65, 68–69, 71–72, 331n14, 332n31, 338n136; tactics, 15–16; tourism and, 106, 112, 347n119; youth mobilizations, 233–34, 253
American Jewish Congress (AJCongress), 113–14, 117, 121, 122, 158, 201
American Jewish Historical Society (AJHS), 88, 89, 345n83
American Jewish Year Book, 27
Amnesty International, 263
"Am Yisroel Chai" (The Jewish people lives; Carlebach), 46, 48, 306
Andropov, Yuri, 320n26
anticommunism, 23–25, 94, 325n83, 325–26n95
Anti-Defamation League (ADL), 3, 27
antisemitism, Soviet, 12–15, 27–28, 59–60; Western misconceptions of, 323n45
Archive of the American Soviet Jewry Movement, 88
art: design contests, 222, 236, 253–56, 255*f*; as DIY grassroots expression, 229, 293; protests at Soviet art exhibitions, 214; by Soviet Jewish artists, 72, 363n106; in twinning service booklets, 273, 284. *See also* graphic design
Arzt, Donna, 90
Ashery, Avrum, 74, 123*f*, 124, 215, 216*f*, 225, 278, 279*f*, 337n116, 372n33; "The Prayer," 75*f*
ASJ. *See* Action for Soviet Jewry
Aviad, Yaacob, 116
Avigur, Shaul, 100

Babi Yar, 72, 153–54
"Babi Yar" (Yevtushenko), 323n49

baby boomers, 18, 20, 22, 231, 244, 262, 295
BACSJ. *See* Bay Area Council on Soviet Jewry
Ballet: Bolshoi, 32, 210, 211, 212; Kirov, 211
Banana Republic, 11, 157–58, 158*f*, 356n85
bar and bat mitzvahs, 261–62; of Soviet Jews in USSR, 265, 267, 268, 294; traditions, 285, 289; travel and, 372–73n42
bar and bat mitzvah twinning, 18, 25, 32, 35–36, 37, 91; adulthood and, 286–88; Americanness and, 288–93; as civic engagement, 279, 284, 292–93; coordination of, 275–81, 279*f*, 280*f*; as culminating synthesis of movement tactics, 260–63; development of, 260–61, 263–75; ending of, 259–60, 293–94; imbalance of American and Soviet twins, 277–78; process of, 257–58; sermons, 289–93; staging of, 281–86; statistics, 261, 277–78; tourism and, 308
Battle of Jericho, 21, 44, 50–51, 53, 55, 333n37
Baum, Phil, 113, 117
Baumrind, Seymour, 267
Bay Area Council on Soviet Jewry (BACSJ), 16, 71, 110, 216, 254
Bayer, Abraham, 267, 331n14, 347n119
Beckerman, Gal, 9, 371n16, 375n91
Begun, Iosif, 197, 199, 267
Beilina, Dina, 87
Bell, Daniel, 28
Beller, Herbert, 121, 125
Beller, Jane, 125
Ben-Gurion, David, 4, 100
Benjamin, Sheldon, 111, 219
Bergelson, Dovid, 13
Bergman, Ingrid, 195, 196*f*
Bettelheim, Bruno, 28
Bikel, Theodore, 325–26n95
Birnbaum, Freda, 320n16
Birnbaum, Jacob (Yaakov), 4, 16, 47–50, 53, 55, 82, 106, 189, 320n16, 331n14, 332n31; SSSJ founding, 47, 233, 320n16
BJEs. *See* Boards/Bureaus of Jewish Education
"Black Years" (1948–53), 12, 13
B'nai Akiva, 100, 102
B'nai B'rith, 3, 12, 27, 98, 112, 344n61
Boards/Bureaus of Jewish Education (BJEs), 227, 231; Baltimore, 237, 245; Cleveland, 237, 245; Miami, 234, 235, 254; New York, 249, 251*f*; Oakland, CA, 232; Washington, DC, 237
Bolshevik Revolution, anniversary as Soviet holiday, 77, 338n136

Bond, James Bond, 105, 133, 135, 142, 143, 144, 146, 151
Borden, Victor, 145–46, 155–56
Boretz, Alvin, 54
boycotts, 177, 185; Arab League boycott of Israel, 183; Olympic Games, 215; PepsiCo, 179–85, 181*f*, 184*f*; tourism to USSR, 112, 178
bracelets. *See* Prisoner of Conscience: bracelets
Brailovsky, Dahlia, 257–59
branding, 122, 124, 208
Brezhnev, Leonid, 83, 179, 212, 251, 320n26
briefing kits (tourist), 113–16, 115*f*, 121–28, 123*f*
Brochin, Jeff, 193–94
Bronstein, Harry (Herschel Tzvi), 94–95
Bush, George H. W., 5
By Spirit Alone curriculum, 237, 244

Caine, Gidon, 266, 269, 273
CAJE. *See* Coalition for Alternatives in Jewish Education
calendar, 37, 44, 51–52, 65, 69–70, 71, 72, 74–80. *See also* holiday mobilizations; holidays; ritualized protests
California Students for Soviet Jews (CSSJ), 16, 177, 178, 180, 363n105
camp (summer), 227, 231, 233, 234–35, 245
Canada, 17, 72, 202, 211, 212, 260, 267, 322n38, 344n56. *See also* Montreal
Canadian Jewish Congress, 234, 236
Cantor, Hinda, 134
Capek (Paul), Batsheva, 344n56
Carlebach, Shlomo, "Am Yisroel Chai," 48, 306
Caron, Herbert, 1, 2, 4
Carter, Jimmy, 7, 201, 216, 219
categorical induction, 79–80
CCSA. *See* Cleveland Council on Soviet Anti-Semitism
celebrities, 6, 54, 83, 133, 173, 194, 195, 205, 333–34n52
Chabad-Lubavitch, 17, 89, 94, 95, 338n142, 339n147
Chernin, Albert, 61–62, 331n14
Chicago, 106, 183, 205, 219, 260, 265, 339n153
Chicago Action for Soviet Jewry, 142, 236, 245, 254–55, 268, 286, 349n146
children: activism by, 224, 229, 264, 366n9; education, 22, 59–60, 227; empowerment of, 252–56; engagement of, 11, 35, 251–53; mobilization of, 227, 252–56; protests and,

59, 229f; seders and, 59–60, 233; social movements and, 228–30. *See also* youth
Christians, 14, 56, 74, 94, 186, 202, 361n74; allies in the movement, 6, 224, 297, 328n14, 353n25; Soviet persecution of, 321n33
civic engagement, 241, 293, 366n9
Civil Judaism, 84, 85, 287
Cleveland Council on Soviet Anti-Semitism (CCSA), 1–2, 16, 234, 274, 356n85; creation of, 15, 28; curricula, 236; handbooks, 105–6, 108, 236; jewelry, 190; tactics, 4, 15–16; tourism and, 105, 108–10
"cloak-and-dagger" language, 122, 144, 145. *See also* spy tropes
Coalition for Alternatives in Jewish Education (CAJE), 234, 237
Coca-Cola, 25, 180, 185
cognitive logics, 35, 37
cognitive praxis, 39, 330n39
Cohen, Pamela B., 286
Cola Wars, 11, 185
Cold War, 3, 7, 8, 12, 291; activists' rhetorical distancing from, 23; Jewish American experience of, 10, 11, 21, 24, 45–46; in scholarship on Soviet Jewry movement, 19, 23
Cold War culture, 23–25, 210, 323n41; Jews and, 46, 331n17; spy thriller genre, 144; tourism and, 124, 139–41; twinning and, 288–93
Cold War liberalism, 11, 21, 289, 304
Columbia University, 2, 27, 47, 180
Comité des Quinze, 17, 88–89, 104, 108, 215, 365n137
"Competing for Freedom" (Olympics campaign), 221–22; poster contest, 254–55, 255f
Conference on the Status of Soviet Jews (1963), 105–6
Conservative Judaism, 45, 112, 182, 331n12. *See also* United Synagogue Youth
consumer culture, 11, 21, 186–87
contests, 236; art, 40, 72–73, 222, 253–56; essay, 253–54, 370n91
continuity crisis, 299–300, 377n12
corporate sponsorship, 208, 215
creative expression, 40, 145, 256
CSSJ. *See* California Students for Soviet Jews
"cult of synthesis," 291
cultural consequences, 35, 38–39, 133, 330n37
cultural coproduction, 35, 38–41
cultural exchange, 92, 362n100; protests at events, 187, 209–14, 219, 221
cultural mobilization, 10–11, 36, 111, 298, 306

cultural production, 10, 33, 34, 235, 256, 305–9, 323n43, 332n31
cultural sociology, 33, 34–41

dance, 102–3, 306; outside Moscow synagogue for Simchat Torah, 52–53; protest of Soviet cultural exchange, 209, 211, 213; at Simchat Torah rallies in US and West, 68–70
Dangerfield, Rodney, 333n52
Davis, Margy-Ruth, 339n152
Day of Atonement. *See* Yom Kippur
Decter, Moshe, 28, 96, 106
demobilization, 298–99
denunciations (in Soviet press), 14, 87, 95, 107, 126–27, 340–41n4
desecration, 80–81, 338n142
détente, 15, 17, 19, 179, 321n33; cultural exchange and, 209; Soviet Jewry movement and, 7, 83, 177, 197; tourism and, 92, 106
Detroit, 205, 209f, 339n153
diaspora, 8, 100, 141–42, 160; diaspora-building, 171
Dishler, Bernard, 91, 203–4, 209, 221
Doctor's Plot, 13–14
Dorn, Dawn, 257–59
Dornan, Robert, 198–99, 209
Dorph, Gail, 244
Drinan, Robert, 216
Drugova, Alla, 267
Dymshits, Mark, 83

Easter, mobilization of, 328n14
emigration: as Cold War issue, 7, 8, 322n37; curtailed, 5; "dropout" / "freedom of choice" debate, 20, 277, 325n89; dual residency after, 321n30; evangelical, 321n33; monitoring of, 120; return migration and, 321n30; for Soviet Jews versus other Soviet citizens, 321n33, 322n37; statistics, 6, 7–8, 259, 317t, 318f, 320n28; success of activism for, 297–99; as symbol, for USSR, 7, 8, 326n96; tax, 180
empty chair, 338n142; in bar mitzvah twinnings, 258, 273, 283; origins of symbol, 61, 274; at Passover seders, 64, 65; on synagogue pulpits, 275, 306
endogenous explanation, 35, 36–37
establishment. *See* factionalism; National Conference on Soviet Jewry
eternal light (*ner tamid*), 51, 54, 155
Exodus: book of, 5, 22, 50; paradigm, 22, 56, 85; symbolism of, 56

Exodus (Uris), 87, 341n7
"Exodus March" (1970), 82
Exodus: The Russian Jewry Simulation Game (Blaser), 245–47, 248f
exploration tropes, 159, 160–62
Eyerman, Ronald, 39; *Social Movements*, 330n37, 330nn39–40

factionalism, 15–18
family heritage research, 243, 244
family reunification, 326n96
fashion, 37, 187–89, 191, 194–95, 308
fasting, 45, 49, 52, 53, 78
Father's Day, 52
Fefer, Itzik, 13
Feinstein, Moshe, 339n146
feminism, 55, 186, 232, 268, 329n28
Feuer, Lewis, 105
Fish, Hamilton, 88, 292
fitness culture, 201–9
Florida, 110, 134, 172, 180, 203–4, 235–36, 257–58, 261, 264. *See also* Sandberg, Adele; Sandberg, Joel; Shapiro, Howard; Tabachnikoff, Barry
Fodor's, 106, 119, 187
Fonda, Jane, 205, 206f
Foreign Affairs magazine, 2, 28
Foucault, Michel, 329n28
"Four Children" (seder tradition), 232, 332n21
"Four Questions" (seder tradition), 57–58, 334n68
four-step plan of activists, 4–5, 6–7
"fourth matzoh," 62. *See also* Matzoh of Hope
Fradkin, Vladimir, 168f, 268
framing (social movement theory), 38–40, 344n51
freedom: in American Cold War discourse, 25, 29, 152, 208, 227, 243, 258, 289–94, 302, 304; contributing to Jewish assimilation, 160, 173–74, 299, 304; taken for granted, 290
Freedom Caravan for Soviet Jews, 234–35, 269
Freedom Rally for Soviet Jews (1987), 5, 257, 258, 300–301
Freedom Runs, 200–209, 206f, 207f, 209f, 221
Freedom Seders. *See* seders
Freedom Shields, 194, 195. *See also* Prisoner of Conscience: medallions
Freedom 25, 300–301
Friedman, Milton, 28
Frumkin, Si, 110, 177–78, 179–80, 185; Prisoner of Conscience medallions and, 190–92

Fun. *See* play
Furst, Zev, 113

Gainsford, Doreen, 194
Gamson, William A., *The Strategy of Social Protest*, 322n37
generations, 21–22, 45, 186, 237–38, 293–95; conflict, 2, 18, 20, 46, 156, 324n68
Generation X, 22, 238, 261, 295, 371n16
Geulah (Redemption) March. *See* Passover Youth Protest
gifts: jewelry as, 192; from tourists, 87, 136
Gillen, Ann, 224
Ginzburg, Alexander, 199
glasnost, 88, 321n33
Glazer, Nathan, 28
Gliksene, Dalia, 278
GNYCSJ. *See* Greater New York Conference on Soviet Jewry
Goldberg, Arthur, 2
Goldberg, Mendy, 88, 103, 341n16
Goldmann, Nahum, 331–32n19
Goldsmith, Jill, 257–59
Goldstein, Norman, 121
Goodman, Jerry, 17, 91, 106, 117, 182, 183
Gorbachev, Mikhail, 5–6, 320n25, 321n33
Gorbunov, Luba, 257–59
graphic design, 11, 74, 124, 213, 215, 222, 226f, 254, 269, 278, 284, 337n118, 370n94. *See also* Ashery, Avrum; Podwal, Mark
grassroots activism, 6, 15–18, 35, 61, 70–74; Cold War culture and, 25; conflict with Nativ, 16, 319–20n15. *See also* Student Struggle for Soviet Jewry; Union of Councils for Soviet Jews; Women's Campaign for Soviet Jewry
Grauer, Yanna, 278, 289, 290
Greater New York Conference on Soviet Jewry (GNYCSJ), 63, 83, 107, 194, 195, 211, 219, 220, 249, 250f, 251f, 333n48, 339n146, 339n152
greeting cards, 44, 66, 70–74, 73f, 254, 337n118, 356n85
Grima, Andrew, 194, 196f
guerrilla theater, 45, 50, 213, 253; seders as, 55, 59, 334n61
Guidebook for Contacting Jews in the Soviet Union (Insiders Club), 121–24, 123f

Hadassah, 62
haggadahs, 54–55, 56–59; text in "Matzoh of Hope," 63

428

INDEX

Halevi, Yossi Klein, 233
Hanukkah, 76, 80, 192, 204; framings of, 376n108; ritualized protests, 51–52, 65, 78, 203, 337n126
Har Zion Temple, Philadelphia, 224, 264, 265
"Have Guts, Will Travel," 110
Hayden, Tom, 205
Hayward, Max, 96
Hebrew Academy of Cleveland, Ohio, 59–60
Hebrew Immigrant Aid Society, 298
Hebrew Union College (HUC), 237, 244
Helsinki Accords, 27, 106, 351n172, 373n57
Helsinki Watch Group, 197, 199
Henzel, Leo, 218
heritage travel, 37, 118–20, 155, 156, 163, 308
Heschel, Abraham Joshua, 4, 106, 324n70
Hillel (college student organization), 65, 180
Hirsch, Ernie (Yeshayahu), 89
Hoenlein, Malcolm, 339n152
holiday mobilizations, 65–70, 83–85; bar and bat mitzvah twinning and, 272; Christian holidays, 328n14; throughout entire Jewish year, 79–80. *See also* calendar; holidays; ritualized protests
holidays: as category, 79, 85; groupings of, 76, 79–80; mobilization of, 37, 73*f*; as scheduling hooks, 76; Soviet, 77, 79, 338n136; themed protests, 43–44, 76; in USSR, 67. *See also* calendar; holiday mobilizations; ritualized protests; *and individual holidays*
Hollander, David B., 93
Holocaust, 11; accusations of Jewish American passivity during, 331n19; American response to, 3; bar mitzvah twinning and, 299; devastation of Soviet Jewish life, 12; memorialization as Jewish identity politics, 29–30, 84, 287, 304, 376n93; memory, 6, 355n69; pilgrimages, 156–57; sites, 153–54; songs, 48, 284–85; Soviet Jewry movement as response to, 22, 46, 96–97, 159–60, 303; Soviet silence about, 13, 355n73; survivors, 22, 177; travelogues and, 151–57, 163, 172, 175. *See also* post-Holocaust trauma
Horowitz, Bethamie, 30
Horowitz Margareten, 63, 64
How to Find and Meet Russian Jews (American Jewish Congress), 113–16, 115*f*, 122, 158
HUC. *See* Hebrew Union College
human rights, 19–20, 27, 197, 215, 217, 298, 322n36, 325n85; American policy, 7, 11, 19, 34; contributions to end of Cold War, 34, 329n23, 378n25; failure of appeals to, 3, 178, 220. *See also* Helsinki Accords
Human Rights Day, 297, 337n126
humor, 251, 252, 370n75

identity politics, 83–85, 287, 304
IMC80. *See* International Monitoring Committee for the 1980 Olympics
Insiders Club, 121–31; debriefing questionnaire, 128–31, 129*f*; guidebook, 121–24, 123*f*; logo, 123*f*, 124; outline for briefers, 125–28
institutional logics, 35, 37
International Committee for the Rescue of Georgian Jews, 211
International Monitoring Committee for the 1980 Olympics (IMC80), 215–16, 216*f*, 217, 220
Intourist, 92, 178, 342–43n29; lawsuit against, 86, 90–92
Ioffe, Alexander, 128
Ioffe, Rosa, 128
Israel: American organizations and, 16, 17, 20, 82, 107, 109, 112, 116, 255, 324n71; Arab League boycott of, 183–85; creation of, 12, 19; in curricula, 240, 247, 254; demography, 8, 38; emigration and, 15, 20, 95, 225, 252, 258, 298, 326n96; holidays, 76, 78, 102; Jewish American independence from, 20, 160, 171, 290, 305; Jewish American support for, 29–30, 84, 152, 287, 302, 304; newspapers, 95, 97, 224; PepsiCo and, 183; relations with USSR, 98–99, 217; return migration from, 321n30; Soviet Jewish ties to, 12–13, 87, 97, 197, 215, 223; as symbol, 156–57; tourist gifts from, 87, 136. *See also* Ma`oz; Nativ
Israel, Sherry, 346n94
Ivker, Cindee, 265–66, 269, 272, 273, 275
Izvestia, 116, 126–27

Jackson, Henry, 320n17, 320n24
Jackson, Michael, 185
Jackson-Vanik Amendment to the Trade Act of 1974, 7, 11, 109, 120, 182, 183, 322n37; Nixon and, 15, 19; Soviet response to, 5, 7, 320n26
Jacobs, Ginger, 67–68
Jamison, Andrew, 39; *Social Movements*, 330n37, 330nn39–40
Javits, Jacob, 2
JCCGW. *See* Jewish Community Council of Greater Washington

INDEX

JDL. *See* Jewish Defense League
JEC. *See* Jewish Education Committee
Jericho Marches, 50. *See also* Battle of Jericho
Jerusalem Post, 205, 224
jewelry, 37, 189–200, 200f, 308, 360n45; as gifts, 192. *See also* Prisoner of Conscience: bracelets; Prisoner of Conscience: medallions
Jewish Americans: communal engagement, 29; as community, 3; heritage, 245; identity and, 11; intergenerational issues, 46; meanings of Soviet Jewry movement, 22–23, 303–5; meanings of USSR travel, 141–42; mobilization of, 4–5, 9, 16, 17; politics, 19, 84, 287; search for ethnic roots, 118–19; sociology of, 29, 30–31, 327n9; statistics, 3–4; synthesizing Americanness and Jewishness, 291
Jewish Anti-Fascist Committee (USSR), 13
Jewish Catalog, 107, 269
Jewish Community Council of Greater Washington (JCCGW), 73f, 121, 123f, 129f, 237, 241f, 297. *See also* Insiders Club; *Teaching Soviet Jewry*
Jewish Defense League (JDL), 18, 95, 114; as anticommunist, 325–26n95, 334n61; boycotts, 177, 180; violence and, 17, 32, 210
Jewish Education Committee, New York (JEC), 235–36
Jewish heritage travel. *See* heritage travel
Jewish memory, 155, 241; collective, 240; of Holocaust, 6, 29; of Soviet Jewry movement, 300–305
Jewish Minority Research bureau, 28
Jewish national movement, in USSR, 9, 20, 63, 67, 266, 300, 322n38; partnership with American activists, 4, 44, 108, 110, 126. *See also* refuseniks: as activist vanguard
Jewishness, 14, 19, 303; Americanness and, 288–89; performance of, 46; "vicarious," 29–30, 304
Jewish New Year. *See* Rosh Hashanah
Jewish organizations, 3, 236; joint actions, 53; tourism and, 105–20; women's, 55, 186; youth, 51, 53, 69, 112
Jewish Telegraphic Agency, 71, 267
Jewish Theological Seminary, 100, 102
"Jewish Underground Songs from Soviet Russia" (album; Bikel), 325–26n95
Jews for Urban Justice, 18
Jews of Silence, The (Wiesel), 6, 54, 67, 96–98, 153, 159; Nativ and, 97–98; uses of by activists, 69, 113, 269, 283, 344n56

Jews of Struggle: The Jewish National Movement in the U.S.S.R. (exhibit), 300
Jokes of Oppression, The (Harris and Rabinovich), 252
Joselit, Jenna Weissman, 261
Joshua, book of, 50–51, 333n37
"Judeo-Christian," 46, 56, 331n17

Kahane, Meir, 17, 18, 95, 177, 210, 325n83, 325–26n95
Katz, Jessica, 228, 366n11
Katz, Label, 12, 13, 14–15
Kemp, Jack, 6, 215
Kendall, Donald M., 178–79, 183
Kerry, John, 284
KGB (Komitet Gosudarstvennoy Bezopasnosti, Committee for State Security), 1, 57, 74, 107, 122, 125, 143, 144, 148, 149, 150, 211, 224, 228, 230, 246, 320n26, 345n79, 360n58
Khassin, Gennady, 128
Khassin, Natasha, 128
Khrushchev, Nikita, 14, 92, 93, 179
King, Martin Luther, Jr., 1, 54
Kissinger, Henry, 7, 19
Klaperman, Gilbert, 93
Kohrman, Margery, 277
Kolatch, Alfred, 64
Korenfeld, Natasha, 224–27, 228, 264–66, 273, 275; "Poem of My Land," 223, 224, 243, 272
Korey, William, 27–28, 344n61
Kosharovsky, Yuli, 88, 103, 203–5, 208–9, 221, 362n82
Kroll, Aryeh, 99–102, 106
Kugler, Shonny, 269, 271
Kuhr, Maimon, 266–67
Kuhr, Murray, 146–47
Kuznetsov, Eduard, 83, 377n17

Labor Zionist Movement, 61, 335n85
Landmarks of a People, The (Postal and Abramson), 119, 161, 163
Ledewitz, Jenny, 291–92, 375n91
legal affairs, 8, 28; professional mobilization of attorneys, 132, 187; tourism as vehicle for legal aid, 88, 112, 137, 169. *See also* Intourist: lawsuit against
leisure culture, 186–87
"Let My People Go" (bat mitzvah prayer booklet), 269, 270f
Let My People Go (Tallman and Kahn), 236, 238

Let My People Go: A Haggadah (Podwal), 269, 271*f*, 278, 280*f*, 285
Levanon, Nehemiah, 93, 319–20n15, 347n102
Lewis, John, 5–6
LICSJ. *See* Long Island Committee for Soviet Jewry
life-cycle events, 11, 35–36, 79, 268, 272–73, 308
Light, Harold (Hal), 71, 110
Lipset, Seymour Martin, 28
Lipstadt, Deborah, 107
Litt, Daniel, 1, 109
Litvinoff, Emmanuel, 28, 96
Long Island Committee for Soviet Jewry (LICSJ), 120, 229, 267, 275, 374n74
Lookstein, Haskell, 107
Los Angeles, 74, 110, 177–78, 180, 198, 218, 219; Run for Soviet Jewry, 201, 204–5, 206*f*, 208, 221
Los Angeles Jewish Federation Council, 204, 278
Lowy, Faith, 289–93

Mack Trucks, Inc., 178
Making Gates: The New Soviet Jewish Crisis (CAJE), 237, 369n58
Mandel, Carol, 110
Mandel, Morris, 110
Manekofsky, Irene, 23, 120, 126, 220, 224–25, 349n143, 349n147
Mann, Theodore, 112
Manon, Davida, 224
Ma`oz, 61, 64, 274, 374n63
maps: falsification of, 160; hand-drawn, 163–64, 164*f*, 165*f*
Markish, Peretz, 13
mass mobilization, 4–5, 6, 298–99, 303, 305–9; cessation of, 299, 310; continuity, 22; cultural consequences, 25, 133; protest turnout, 43; tactics, 9–12, 15, 17, 29, 31–41, 139, 204, 232, 260
mass tourism, 33, 92; cultural consequences, 139; systematic approach to, 98–105, 106, 131–32
matzoh, 59, 61–63, 335n73; restrictions on baking, 11, 51, 63
Matzoh of Hope, 53, 61–65; revisions, 63, 81–82, 273, 308; transformation for bar and bat mitzvah twinning, 281
May Day demonstrations, 2, 47–49, 338n136
medallions. *See* Prisoner of Conscience: medallions
media, 63, 94, 204, 212, 258–59, 265, 266, 292, 293; protest coverage, 47, 332n20; in USSR, 87

medical aid, 228; professional mobilization of doctors, 132, 187, 350–351n170; tourism as vehicle for, 137, 169, 231, 354n51
"Me generation," 21
memory: collective, 240, 330n37; erasure, 34, 323n49, 329n24; immigrant, 244; public, 301; traumatic, 29–30
Mendelevich, Yosef, 6
Merton, Robert, 28
Miami Bureau of Jewish Education, 235, 254
micromobilization. *See* mass mobilization
Mifal Hatzolas Yehudei Rusiah (MOHIR; Enterprise for the Rescue of the Jews of Russia), 17, 94–95
Mikhoels, Solomon, 13
Miller, Betty, 264
Miller, Israel, 61, 68–69
Minnesota Action Committee for Soviet Jewry (also Minnesota-Dakotas Action Committee), 264, 272, 372n27
Minnesota Rabbinical Association, 71
mnemonic pasting, 340n158
mobilization: agents, 36; of children, 230–34; education system and, 229; objects, 35–36; tactics, 20–21. *See also* mass mobilization
mobilizing gaze, 35–37, 49, 60–61, 81, 186, 240, 263, 305, 306, 329n28, 329n30, 366n9; education and, 233, 240, 370n91; institutional context channeling, 101, 103; tourism and, 92–105, 132
MOHIR. *See* Mifal Hatzolas Yehudei Rusiah
Montreal, Canada, 170, 211, 212, 236, 254, 266, 271
Morgenstern, Andrea, 272
Morgenstern, Bobbie, 272
Morgenthau, Hans, 28
Moshavi, Avi, 102–3
movement culture, 15, 18–19, 21, 53, 273, 293; artifacts of, 24; coherence of, 283, 307; production of, 35, 252
Murash, Yulia, 291–92, 375n91
MUSE. *See* Museum Utilization for Student Education
Museum Utilization for Student Education (MUSE), 237, 244
music, 11, 33, 40, 185, 234, 239, 325n95, 332n31, 343n33, 344n56, 375n91, 376n93; use in demonstrations, 48, 51, 53, 56, 213; use in twinnings, 269, 279, 284–85
Muskat, Lisa, 284–85

na'aseh v'nishma, 309–10
Nashpitz, Mark, 275
Natasha's Dream: Children's Handbook on Russian Jews and What We Can Do (Manon and Manekofsky), 224–27, 226f, 232, 234, 264–65
National Community Relations Advisory Council (NCRAC), 61–62. *See also* National Jewish Community Relations Advisory Council
National Conference of Synagogue Youth, 193
National Conference on Soviet Jewry (NCSJ), 5, 16–17, 27, 77–78, 83; "adoption" programs, 264; bar and bat mitzvah twinning and, 259, 260, 276–77; empty chair ritual and, 274–75; guidebook, 107, 114, 116–17, 118–20; Intourist lawsuit, 86, 90–91; Jackson-Vanik and, 320n17; jewelry, 195, 199; Nativ and, 119; Olympics and, 215–18; PepsiCo boycott and, 182–83; tourism and, 88, 108, 112–21, 127–28, 131–32, 140, 178, 345n85
National Council for Soviet Jewry of the United Kingdom and Ireland (NCSJ-UK), 58, 72, 221, 254
National Jewish Community Relations Advisory Council (NJCRAC), 77–77, 83, 112, 205, 208, 216, 217, 218–19, 347n118
Nativ, 4, 19, 20, 28, 217, 301, 319–20n15, 326n96, 357n101; AJCSJ/NCSJ and, 17, 112, 116, 119, 323n44; conflict with American organizations, 15, 16, 109, 116, 166, 319–20n15, 324n69; distancing from Soviet democratic dissidents, 23, 326n100; tourism and, 88, 93, 95–105, 106–7, 112, 116, 119, 341n6; Wiesel and, 95–98
Nazis, 3, 12; comparison and contrast with Soviets, 153
NBC, 217
NCRAC. *See* National Jewish Community Relations Advisory Council
NCSJ. *See* National Conference on Soviet Jewry
NCSJ-UK. *See* National Council for Soviet Jewry of the United Kingdom and Ireland
Neiter, Lois, 142, 148, 156, 353n24
ner tamid. See eternal light
Neustadt, Mordechai, 103, 341n16
New Left, 18, 55, 325–26n95, 338n142
Newman, Ruth, 272
New York Association of New Americans, 298
New York Coordinating Committee for Soviet Jewry (NYCCSJ), 53–54, 58, 339n152

New York Youth Conference for Soviet Jewry (NYYCSJ), 82
"Night of the Murdered Poets," 13
Nixon, Richard, 7, 15, 19, 83, 178–79
NJCRAC. *See* National Jewish Community Relations Advisory Council
nonviolence, 17, 32, 46, 55, 59, 81, 210, 211
Norton, Eleanor Holmes, 298
nostalgia, 195, 303, 348n136, 356n80, 378n22, 378n30
nuclear weapons, 1, 3, 210; arms reduction pact (1987), 5
Nudel, Ida, 6, 87, 197, 199
NYCCSJ. *See* New York Coordinating Committee for Soviet Jewry
NYYCSJ. *See* New York Youth Conference for Soviet Jewry

occupational activism. *See* professional mobilizations
Office of Visas and Registration. *See* Otdel Viz i Registratsii
Olympic Games, 195, 197, 215–22, 254, 364n124, 365n137; boycott of, 220–21
"Olympics Da, Moscow Nyet" logo, 215, 216f, 219
Operation Exodus, 298
Operation Write-On, 224, 225
Orlov, Yuri, 197, 199
ORT. *See* Women's American ORT
Orthodox Judaism, 17, 19, 45, 62, 88, 94, 107, 193, 266, 339n146; Modern Orthodoxy, 42, 331n14, 339n152; in USSR, 88, 103, 265, 351n101. *See also* Agudath Israel; Chabad-Lubavitch; Rabbinical Council of America
Otdel Viz i Registratsii (OVIR; Office of Visas and Registration), 6

pageantry, 47, 50
Park Avenue Synagogue, New York City, New York, 61, 274
Passover: as central holiday of rallies, 52–65; seders, 22, 31; symbolism, 43, 85
Passover protests, 37, 42, 52; NYCCSJ rally (1967), 53–54; NYCCSJ rally (1968), 54. *See also* seders: Soviet Jewry Freedom Seders
Passover Youth Protest (1966), 48, 53, 82
path dependencies, 37, 308
pen pals, 224, 225, 257; bar and bat mitzvah twinning and, 271–72, 282
peoplehood, 25, 357n113; data collection as a practice of, 170–71

"People-to-People" efforts, 17–18, 71–72, 109, 193, 264
PepsiCo, 306; boycott, 179–85, 181*f*, 184*f*, 205, 306; sponsor of running races, 205; USSR distribution, 178–79
Perlbinder, Grayce, 229
Perlbinder, Lisa, 229–30
Peterson, Richard, 34, 344n66
Philadelphia, 76–77, 91, 178, 224, 250, 264, 300, 302; bar and bat mitzvah twinning, 260, 261, 265–66; Freedom Runs, 203, 205, 207*f*, 208, 209, 221; tourism to USSR, 108, 112, 117, 121, 128, 131. *See also* Soviet Jewry Council of the JCRC of Greater Philadelphia
Philadelphia Flyers, 212, 213*f*
photography, 165–66, 237, 244
play: board games, 249–51, 251*f*; puzzle books, 249, 250*f*; role-playing simulations, 245–49
"plight of Soviet Jewry," 12, 64, 237, 282
POC. *See* Prisoner of Conscience
Podwal, Mark, 269, 271*f*, 278, 280*of*, 285
"Poem of My Land" (Korenfeld), 223, 224, 243, 272
Poland, 95, 156, 317*t*
political prisoners, 6, 11, 13, 14, 18, 83, 87, 112, 189, 263, 274–75. *See also* Adopt-a-Prisoner programs; Prisoner of Conscience
Porath, Jonathan, 113, 235
post-Holocaust trauma, 3, 11, 19, 21, 25, 29–30, 46, 118, 175, 293, 303, 304; travel and, 151–57
Potok, Chaim, 136, 159
Poupko, Baruch (Bernard), 95
Power of Protest: The Movement to Free Soviet Jews (exhibit), 300
POW-MIA bracelets, 191, 193, 198–99
Pratt, Yehoshua, 106, 107
praxis, 39–40, 330n39
"Prayer, The" (Ashery), 75*f*
Prestin, Misha, 268
Prisoner of Conscience (POC): bracelets, 197–200, 200*f*; medallions, 190–95, 190*of*, 191*f*, 196*f*, 308
professional mobilizations, 11, 22, 88, 89, 305, 350–351n170; in academia and science, 28, 132, 351n173; in the arts, 74, 337n118; in education, 230–32, 237; in law, 132, 187; in medicine, 132, 187. *See also* legal affairs; medical aid
Project Lifeline, 111–12
publicity, 60, 71, 76, 93, 105, 133, 188, 204, 212, 213, 258, 259, 266, 279, 292, 293
Purim, 53, 76, 78, 249, 338n133, 368n49

Queens Council for Soviet Jewry, 58

Rabbinical Council of America (RCA), 61, 335n85; delegation to USSR (1956), 92–93, 95, 96, 132, 343n44
Rackman, Emmanuel, 93, 343n35
Ramm, Shoshana, 250–51; *Route to Freedom* game, 251*f*
ram's horn. *See* shofar
Rapoport, Fran, 275
RCA. *See* Rabbinical Council of America
Reagan, Ronald, 5, 7, 292, 321n33
Reagan Revolution, 11, 21
Red Scare, 45, 325–26n95
Reform Judaism, 245. *See also* Union of American Hebrew Congregations
Refusenik Project, 301
refuseniks, 6, 351n175; as activist vanguard, 9, 175, 321–22n34; "adoption," 263; children, 226–27, 243, 250, 264, 277; databases, 166–69, 167*f*; origin of term, 372n30; overburdened by tourists, 127–28; prominence of, 197; tourism and, 111, 126–28, 130
Reiff, Kay, 276
Remennick, Larissa I., 321–22n34
research (in the Soviet Jewry campaign), 28
Ribicoff, Abraham, 2
Richter, Glenn, 48–49, 220, 233, 331n14
Riskin, Steven (Shlomo), 42, 331n14
ritualized protests, 40; development of, 46, 47–52, 75–78, 84–85; as realization of religious values, 78, 81; symbols and, 70. *See also* calendar; holiday mobilizations; holidays
rituals, 35–36; emotional power of, 76; losing sanctity through mobilization, 80–81
Rodgers, Diane, 228
Roitburd, Sasha, 267
Rosenberg trial, 45
Rosenblum, Louis, 1, 2, 4, 16; children's mobilizations and, 225, 264; conflict with Nativ, 319–20n15, 324n69, 347n102; creation of Cleveland Committee, 28; education and, 236; greeting cards and, 71–72; PepsiCo boycott and, 185; prisoner adoption and, 264; tourism and, 105–6, 108–12, 347n119
Rosenblum, Miriam, 111
Rosenne, Meir, 96, 98, 106
Rosh Hashanah, 44, 49–50, 65–66, 70–74, 254, 331n10, 332n34
Route to Freedom: A Game of Escape from the Soviet Union (Ramm), 249–51, 251*f*

433

Rubin, Jackie, 254, 255f
Run for Soviet Jewry. *See* fitness culture; Freedom Runs

SAC. *See* Student Action Committee for Soviet Jewry
"sacred survival," 29–30. *See also* Civil Judaism
Safam, 284, 306, 375n91
safari tropes, 113, 157–58
Sakharov, Andrei, 23, 197
Salkin, Jeffrey, 172–73
Sandberg, Adele, 107, 272
Sandberg, Joel, 107, 203–4, 272, 345n73
Sandberg, Sheryl, 272
San Francisco Jewish Community Relations Council, 63, 201
Sarna, Jonathan, 291
SCCSJ. *See* Southern California Council for Soviet Jews
Schacter, Herschel, 93
Schapira, Morey, 220, 229f, 251–52
Schneerson, Menachem Mendel, 94, 338n142, 343n44
Schnur, Zeesy, 339n152
Schultz, George, 7, 320n25
seders: home, 53; political, 31, 54–55; in schools, 59–60, 233–34; Soviet Jewry Freedom Seders, 56–60, 338n142; "Symbolic Seder of Redemption" (1969), 42–43; traditions, 57–58, 335n73; Waskow New Left Freedom seder, 55, 335n78, 338n142
Senderovich, Sasha, 159, 321–22n34
SFCSJ. *See* South Florida Conference on Soviet Jewry
Shapiro, Howard, 134–39, 144–45, 146, 162
Shapiro, Josh, 371n8, 371nn16–17
Shavuot, 44, 52, 76, 78, 241, 368n52
Shcharansky, Anatoly (Natan Sharansky), 6, 23, 58, 83, 195, 197, 198–99, 200f, 209, 216, 221, 230, 273, 302, 320n21
Shcharansky, Avital, 83, 198, 273
Shiffrin, Mark, 134–35
Shiffrin, Slava, 134–35
Shinbaum, Myrna, 15, 17, 105, 117, 276–77, 348n133
Shneer, David, 323n45
shofar, 49–50, 51, 53, 70, 211, 331n9, 332n31, 332n34
Simchat Torah, 331n10; dance rallies, 44, 68–70; ritualized protests, 52, 65–66; Soviet Jews and, 66, 67

simulations, 243, 245–49, 369n76
Siris (Winik), Elaine, 151–53
Sislen, Samuel H., 121, 298, 349n147
Six-Day War (1967), 11, 19, 99, 112
SJC. *See* Soviet Jewry Council of the JCRC of Greater Philadelphia
SJLAC. *See* Soviet Jewry Legal Advocacy Center
Slepak, Maria, 6, 128, 197
Slepak, Vladimir, 6, 111, 127–28, 143, 197, 199
Slezkine, Yuri, 13
Smith, Christian, 45
Smukler, Connie, 250
Smukler, Joseph, 266
Sobel, Sharon, 269, 270f, 278
Sobol, Ethan, 284
Sobol, Richard, 284
social movement studies, 31–41; children in, 228–30; cultural consequences, 35, 330n37; framing theory, 38–40, 344n51; movement outcomes, 322n37; silence on Soviet Jewry movement, 34; tactical choices, 31–34, 328–29nn21–22. *See also* tactical repertoires
Solidarity Sunday ("Solidarity Day for Soviet Jews"), 82–83, 339n154
Somers, Susan, 109–10
Southern California Council for Soviet Jews (SCCSJ), 16, 177, 178, 180, 192, 197
South Florida Conference on Soviet Jewry (SFCSJ), 107, 110, 134, 203, 235, 264. *See also* Sandberg, Adele; Sandberg, Joel
Soviet Cage, The (Korey), 27
Soviet Jewish Affairs, 27
Soviet Jewry Council of the JCRC of Greater Philadelphia (SJC), 195, 212, 275; bar and bat mitzvah twinning and, 260, 265, 266, 273, 278, 281–82; cultural exchange protests, 212, 213f; Freedom Runs and, 203, 207f, 221; tourism and, 131, 250, 265
Soviet Jewry Legal Advocacy Center (SJLAC), 90, 187, 350–51n17
Soviet Jewry movement: aftereffects, 330n37; characteristics of, 304–5; commemoration, 300–305; education and, 235–37; factional differences, 15–18, 81; historiographic approaches, 18–23; impact of end of, 298–300; lessons of, 302–5; meaning to American Jews, 303–5; operation of, 309; religious politics of, 84–85; strategy, 4–5, 6–7; success of, 7–9, 301–3
Soviet Jewry Purim Puzzler, 249, 250f

Soviet Jewry School Kit (Eisen), 236, 238, 254
Soviet Jews: activists, 326n100; in American Jewish imagination, 17, 171–72, 173–76, 321–22n34; bar and bat mitzvahs, 265, 267, 268, 294; demographics, 321n29; after fall of Soviet Union, 7–9, 321n30; literary representations of, 159; Simchat Torah and, 66, 67; treated as symbols, 17, 174–75; Western discourse about, 321–22n34
Soviet United Nations Mission, New York: protests at, 2, 42, 47, 50, 53–54, 55, 59, 82
sports, 180, 187. *See also* fitness culture; Freedom Runs; Olympic Games; Philadelphia Flyers
Sprayregen, Joel, 154, 163
spy thriller genre, 11, 135, 140, 143–44, 150. *See also* Bond, James Bond
spy tropes, 104–5, 142–51; disparaged as B-grade clichés, 148–51
SSSJ. *See* Student Struggle for Soviet Jewry
Stalin, Josef, 12–14, 92, 247, 248f
State Department. *See* United States Department of State
Steinbruck, John, 297, 328n14
Steinman, Carolyn, 271
Stern, Barbara, 170
Student Action Committee for Soviet Jewry, University of Minnesota (SAC), 193–94
Student Struggle for Soviet Jewry (SSSJ), 2, 4, 18, 83, 333n52; children and, 233, 366n11; costuming, 188f, 189; cultural exchange protests, 211–14; educational materials, 234; founding, 15, 47, 320n16, 332n31; generational politics and, 46, 324n68; jewelry and, 189–90; Olympics and, 217–21; PepsiCo boycott and, 180, 205; religious logic of, 81; ritualized protests, 42–44, 47–58, 60, 77, 81–82, 331n14, 338n136; tactics, 15–16, 210, 331n6; "thons" and runs, 202–3; tourism and, 106, 345n73
Sukkot, 52, 76, 78, 94, 242, 333n43
synagogues, 32, 46, 47, 51, 231; bar and bat mitzvah twinning and, 257–76, 282–87, 295–95, 299; education and, 227; holiday rituals in, 59, 66, 70; mobilization of, 11, 59, 63, 88, 133, 180, 191; in USSR, 14, 67–68, 71–72, 80, 87, 93, 94, 98, 113, 126, 155, 161

Tabachnikoff, Barry, 134–39, 144–45
tactical repertoires, 33–34, 36, 120, 132, 307, 328n18, 328–29nn21–22
tactics: in action, 25; evolution, 254; innovation, 36–37, 76, 79–80, 328–29n22, 332n31; invention, 32–34, 305–9; mixing and matching, 308
Tari, Ephraim, 96, 98
Taylor, Telford, 347n117
Teaching Soviet Jewry (JCCGW), 237, 238–43, 241f, 252–53
Teitz, Basya (Bess), 94
Teitz, Mordechai Pinchas, 17, 94–95
Tenth of Tevet, 78
theater, 33, 97, 253; closure of Soviet Jewish, 12; protests at performances, 210–13; ritualized protest as, 46, 48, 55; staging of twinnings, 281–85. *See also* guerrilla theater
themed protests, 188–89, 221, 269; at cultural exchange events, 212–14; holidays, 44, 47, 51, 52, 76, 78, 202
35s, the. *See* Women's Campaign for Soviet Jewry
Tiemkin, Marina, 214, 225, 228, 366n11
Tilly, Charles, 32–33, 328n18
Tisha B'Av, 78, 80, 331n13, 333n41; ritualized protests, 51, 52, 65
tourism, 33, 105–20, 178; activist recruitment and, 91; bar and bat mitzvah twinning and, 266; briefings, 108–9, 113–16, 115f, 134, 340n4; Cold War culture and, 124; debriefing, 116, 128–31; demographics, 89–90; gifts, 87, 341n7; heritage, 118–20; leisure, 111, 112, 114, 118, 124, 132, 187; mobilization of, 11, 116–17, 120, 131–32, 139, 307–8; photography, 165–66; publicity and, 95–98; by rabbinic elites, 92–95; spy tropes and, 142–51; statistics, 88, 89f, 90, 128, 342–43n29; theory of, 329n28; thrill of, 352n2
tourists, 37; categories of, 125–28, 130–31; connections to Soviet Jews, 155–57, 170, 243; debriefing, 140; education of, 114; as emissaries, 132; harassment of, 86–87; surveillance of, 101, 125, 127
travel guidebooks, 37, 114, 118–25, 123f
travelogues, 96–98, 105–6, 134–39, 155; spy tropes in, 142–51; themes in, 152–53, 159
travel writing, 139–51, 353nn23–24; archives, 170–71; authors of, 166–70, 175–76; as self-expression, 140; spy tropes in, 142–51; themes in, 172–74
Trilling, Lionel, 28
trip reports. *See* travelogues
Tsitlionik, Boris, 275
Tu BiShvat, 44, 76, 78, 331n10

435

INDEX

UCSJ. *See* Union of Councils for Soviet Jews
Underground: A Simulation of the Path of Soviet Jews from Oppression to Freedom (Kutz Camp), 245–47
Union of American Hebrew Congregations, 3, 62, 335n85
Union of Councils for Soviet Jews (UCSJ), 16–17, 22, 178, 203, 210, 224–25, 229f, 320n17; creation of, 71; Olympics and, 215, 218–19; "People-to-People" framework, 71–72, 264; PepsiCo boycott and, 180–85; Prisoner of Conscience jewelry, 192, 197–200; tourism and, 88, 90, 107, 108–12, 120–21, 126–31, 132; twinning and, 251, 257, 267, 273, 275–77
United Jewish Appeal, 3, 151
United Kingdom. *See* National Council for Soviet Jewry of the United Kingdom and Ireland; Women's Campaign for Soviet Jewry
United States Department of State, 3, 87, 92, 362n100
United Synagogue Youth (USY), 51, 112–13, 174, 235, 333n47
Universal Declaration of Human Rights, 27, 322n36, 337n126
USY. *See* United Synagogue Youth

Vaad L'Hatzolas Nidchei Yisroel (Organization to Rescue Dispersed Jews; also called Vaad Hahatzolah), 17, 89
VIVA (Victory in Vietnam Association; later, Voices in Vital America), 191, 198

walkathons, 202
Washington Committee for Soviet Jewry (WCSJ), 16, 71, 120, 121, 224; adoption and twinning programs, 264–65, 269, 272, 274–75, 278; Prisoner of Conscience bracelets, 197–99. *See also* Insiders Club; *Natasha's Dream*
Waskow, Arthur, 54–55, 335n78, 338n142

WCSJ. *See* Washington Committee for Soviet Jewry
Weiss, Avraham (Avi), 43, 331n13
Weiss, David, 106
Weissman, Inez, 120, 126–27
Wellins, Judy, 148
Wenger, Beth, 291
Wiesel, Elie, 6, 83; *The Jews of Silence*, 6, 54, 67–68, 69, 96–98, 113, 153, 159, 269, 283, 306; as literary activist, 96–98, 344n50; on Soviet Jewish traditions, 67
Wolf, Robert, 110
Women's American ORT, 276–77, 351n176, 374n72
Women's Campaign for Soviet Jewry (the 35s), 17, 88–89, 108, 186, 236, 254; actions by, 219, 267–68, 373n57; costuming, 187–89; cultural exchange protests, 211–14; Prisoner of Conscience medallions, 194–95, 196f
Woocher, Jonathan, 84
World Jewish Congress, 27, 331–32n19
Wurtman, Enid, 342n27, 351n175

Yaroslavsky, Zev, 177–78, 180, 185, 190–92, 360n45, 363n105; tourism and, 110, 111–12
Yeshiva University, 100, 102
Yevtushenko, Yevgeny ("Babi Yar"), 323n49
Yom Kippur, 52, 61, 70, 76, 100, 273
Youngman, Henny, 54
youth: activism by, 2, 21, 202–3, 228; engagement of, 53, 68–69, 72–73, 112, 113, 193, 224, 264. *See also* bar and bat mitzvah twinning; children; *Natasha's Dream*

Zalmanson, Sylva, 194–95, 196f, 229, 360–61n58, 377n17
Zalmanson-Kuznetsov, Anat, 377n17
Ziegler, Mel, 157–58
Ziegler, Patricia, 157–58
Zionism, 13, 326–27n107

ABOUT THE AUTHOR

SHAUL KELNER is Associate Professor of Jewish studies and sociology at Vanderbilt University. He is the author of the award-winning *Tours That Bind: Diaspora, Pilgrimage, and Israeli Birthright Tourism.*

Milton Keynes UK
Ingram Content Group UK Ltd.
UKHW032157261024
450101UK00003B/31/J